M000116622

Table of Contents

Chapter 3
Planning Business Messages 85

Chapter 4
Writing Business Messages 113

Chapter 5
Completing Business Messages 139

Chapter 6
Crafting Messages for Digital Channels 185

Chapter 7
Writing Routine and Positive Messages 221

Chapter 8
Writing Negative Messages 247

Chapter 9
Writing Persuasive Messages 285

Chapter 10
Understanding and Planning Reports and Proposals 315

Chapter 11
Writing and Completing Reports and Proposals 359

Chapter 12
Developing and Delivering Business Presentations 411

Introduction

No matter what profession you want to pursue, the ability to communicate will be an essential skill—and a skill that employers expect you to have when you enter the workforce.

This class introduces you to the fundamental principles of business communication and gives you the opportunity to develop your communication skills. You'll discover how business communication differs from personal and social communication, and you'll see how today's companies are using blogs, social networks, podcasts, virtual worlds, wikis, and other technologies. You'll learn a simple three-step writing process that works for all types of writing and speaking projects, both in school and on the job. Along the way, you'll gain valuable insights into ethics, etiquette, listening, teamwork, and nonverbal communication. You'll also learn effective strategies for the many types of communication challenges you'll face on the job, from writing routine messages about transactions to producing complex reports and websites.

Studying professional communication can benefit you:

In your other classes. The communication skills you learn in this class can help you in every other class you take. From simple homework assignments to complicated team projects to class presentations, you'll be able to communicate more effectively with less time and effort.

During your job search. You can reduce the stress of searching for a job and stand out from the competition. Every activity in the job-search process relies on communication. The better you can communicate, the more successful you'll be at landing interesting and rewarding work.

On the job. After you get that great job, the time and energy you have invested in this course will continue to yield benefits year after year. As you tackle each project and every new challenge, influential company leaders—the people who decide how quickly you'll get promoted and how much you'll earn—will be paying close attention to how well you communicate. They will observe your interactions with colleagues, customers, and business partners. They'll take note of how well you can collect data, find the essential ideas buried under mountains of information, and convey those points to other people. They'll observe your ability to adapt to different audiences and circumstances. They'll be watching when you encounter tough situations that require careful attention to ethics and etiquette. The good news: Every insight you gain and every skill you develop in this class will help you shine in your career.

How to Succeed in This Class

Although this class explores a wide range of message types and appears to cover quite a lot of territory, the underlying structure of the class is actually rather simple. You'll learn a few basic concepts, identify some key skills to use and procedures to follow—and then practice, practice, practice. Whether you're writing a blog posting in response to one of the real-company cases or drafting your own resume, you'll be practicing the same skills again and again. With feedback and reinforcement from your instructor and your classmates, your confidence will grow and the work will become easier and more enjoyable.

The following sections offer advice on approaching each assignment, using your textbook, and taking advantage of some other helpful resources.

Approaching Each Assignment

In the spirit of practice and improvement, you will have a number of writing (and possibly speaking) assignments throughout this class. These suggestions will help you produce better results with less effort:

First, don't panic! If the thought of writing a report or giving a speech sends a chill up your spine, you're not alone. Everybody feels that way when first learning business communication skills, and even experienced professionals can feel nervous about major projects. Keeping three points in mind will help. First, every project can be broken down into a series of small, manageable tasks. Don't let a big project overwhelm you; it's nothing more than a bunch of smaller tasks. Second, remind yourself that you have the skills you need to accomplish each task. As you move through the course, the assignments are carefully designed to match the skills you've developed up to that point. Third, if you feel panic creeping up on you, take a break and regain your perspective.

Focus on one task at a time. A common mistake writers make is trying to organize and express their ideas while simultaneously worrying about audience reactions, grammar, spelling, formatting, page design, and a dozen other factors. Fight the temptation to do everything at once; otherwise, your frustration will soar and your productivity will plummet. In particular, don't worry about grammar, spelling, and word choices during your first draft. Concentrate on the organization of your ideas first, then the way you express those ideas, and then the presentation and production of your messages. Following the three-step writing process is an ideal way to focus on one task at a time in a logical sequence.

Give yourself plenty of time. As with every other school project, putting things off to the last minute creates unnecessary stress. Writing and speaking projects in particular are much easier if you tackle them in small stages with breaks in between, rather than trying to get everything done in one frantic blast. Moreover, there will be instances when you simply get stuck on a project, and the best thing to do is walk away and give your mind a break. If you allow room for breaks in your schedule, you'll minimize the frustration and spend less time overall on your homework, too.

Step back and assess each project before you start. The writing and speaking projects you'll have in this course cover a wide range of communication scenarios, and it's essential that you adapt your approach to each new challenge. Resist the urge to dive in and start writing without a plan. Ponder the assignment for a while, consider the various approaches you might take, and think carefully about your objectives before you start writing. Nothing is more frustrating than getting stuck halfway through because you're not sure what you're trying to say or you've wandered off track. Spend a little time planning, and you'll spend a lot less time writing.

Use the three-step writing process. Those essential planning tasks are the first step in the three-step writing process, which you'll learn about in Chapter 3 and use throughout the course. This process has been developed and refined by professional writers with decades of experience and thousands of projects ranging from short blog posts to 500-page textbooks. It works, so take advantage of it.

Learn from the examples and model documents. This textbook offers dozens of realistic examples of business messages, many with notes along the sides that explain strong and weak points. Study these and any other examples that your instructor provides. Learn what works and what doesn't, then apply these lessons to your own writing.

Learn from experience. Finally, learn from the feedback you get from your instructor and from other students. Don't take the criticism personally; your instructor and your classmates are commenting about the work, not about you. View every bit of feedback as an opportunity to improve.

Using This Textbook

This book introduces you to the key concepts in business communication while helping you develop essential skills. As you read each chapter, start by studying the learning objectives. They will help you identify the most important concepts in the chapter and give you a feel for what you'll be learning. Each learning objective corresponds to one major heading within the chapter, so you can easily find the information it relates to.

As you work through each chapter, look for definitions of important terms in the margin. Some of these terms may be brand-new to you; others may be familiar words that are being used in different ways than you may have heard them before.

At the end of each chapter, a *Chapter Summary* section gives you the chance to quickly verify your grasp of important concepts. Following that, you'll see two sets of questions. Those in the *Test Your Knowledge* section relates to concepts discussed in the chapter. Those in the *Apply Your Knowledge* section challenges you to think critically about what you've learned, and in some cases to think about a scenario in which your newfound knowledge may apply.

Some chapters include a *Practice Your Skills* section, which provides activities in which you edit sentences or paragraphs to strengthen and improve them using the skills acquired from the chapter. The *Activities* section provides a series of simple exercises that can help increase your familiarity and comfort level with the skills taught in the chapter. Your instructor may assign one or more of these per chapter.

Each chapter concludes with an *Expand Your Skills* section, challenging you to go beyond the basics to tackle more challenging scenarios or research activities in realistic scenario-based activities.

Preview of Your Textbook

CHAPTER

1

Communicating Professionally in Today's Digital, Social, Mobile World

After studying this chapter, you will be able to:

- Define *communication* and explain the importance of effective business communication.
- Explain what it means to communicate as a professional in a business context.
- Describe the communication process model and explain how social media are changing the nature of business communication.
- Outline the challenges and opportunities of mobile communication in business.
- Define *ethics*, explain the difference between an ethical dilemma and an ethical lapse, and list six guidelines for making ethical communication choices.
- Explain how cultural diversity affects business communication and describe the steps you can take to communicate more effectively across cultural boundaries.
- List four general guidelines for using communication technology effectively.
- Demonstrate an understanding of careers in arts, audio/video technology, and communications.

Each chapter has numerous **objectives** that identify the key skills explained in the chapter.

2

Understanding Why Communication Matters

Communication: The process of transferring information and meaning using one or more media.

Communication is the process of transferring information and meaning between senders and receivers, using one or more print, oral, visual, or digital media. The essence of communication is sharing—providing data, information, insights, and inspiration in an exchange that benefits both you and the people with whom you are communicating. As Figure 1.1 indicates, this sharing can happen in a variety of ways. It can include a simple and successful transfer of information, a negotiation in which the sender and receiver arrive at an agreed-upon meaning, and a situation in which the receiver creates a different message than the one the sender intended to convey.

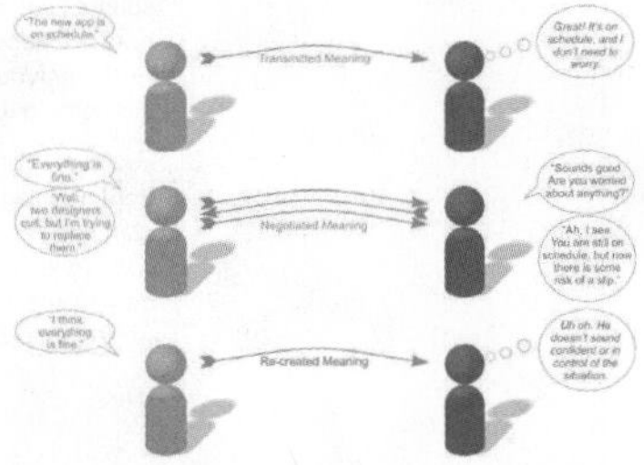

Figure 1.1
Sharing Information
These three exchanges between a software project manager (left) and his boss (right) illustrate the variety of ways in which information is shared between senders and receivers. In the top exchange, the sender's meaning is transmitted intact to the receiver, who accepts what the sender says at face value. In the middle exchange, the sender and receiver negotiate the meaning by discussing the situation. The negotiated meaning is that everything is fine *so far*, but the risk of a schedule slip is now higher than it was before. In the bottom exchange, the receiver has a negative emotional reaction to the word "think" and as a result creates her own meaning—that everything probably is *not* fine, in spite of what the sender says.

You will invest a lot of time and energy in this course developing your communication skills, so it's fair to ask whether it will be worthwhile. This section outlines the many ways in which good communication skills are critical for your career and for any company you join.

Communication and Society

To communicate effectively in a culture, whether it's with business colleagues or personal friends, it's important to understand society's communication customs and expectations.

As communication has become increasingly digital and immediate, societal expectations about communication have shifted into high gear. For example, fifty years ago, postal mail was the most common business communication method. It was not unusual for a business conversation to take weeks, with

Key vocabulary terms are called out in the margin for easy reference.

Numerous **illustrations**, **photos**, and **tables** help reinforce the concepts.

Chapter Summary section gives you the chance to quickly verify your grasp of important concepts.

Test Your Knowledge section relates to concepts discussed in the chapter.

Apply Your Knowledge section challenges you to think critically about what you've learned, and in some cases to think about a scenario in which your newfound knowledge may apply.

108

Organizing Your Message

Good organization helps your audience understand and accept your message with less time and effort. It also saves you time when preparing messages. With a clear path to follow when writing, you'll produce messages faster and spend less time revising. To organize any message, define your main idea, limit the scope for maximum impact, choose the direct or indirect approach to match the situation, and outline your information in a logical sequence.

Acquiring Information to Support Your Message

A web search using a search engine is often the best way to find information to support your message. Search engines such as Google enable you to use advanced syntax to narrow a search and to search for images or videos using the search keywords. If you are looking specifically for videos, a specialized site such as YouTube may be useful. To find royalty-free images to use in a document, use the Bing image search within Office 2016 applications, or use the image search tool at Bing.com or another search engine. Make sure you cite all sources to avoid plagiarism, and only use materials that you are legally entitled to use to avoid copyright violation.

Test Your Knowledge

1. What are the three major steps in the writing process?
2. What do you need to know to develop an audience profile?
3. What are the three attributes of quality information in a business message?
4. Why are in-person conversations considered a rich medium?
5. What is the difference between the topic of a message and its main idea?
6. List two ways find an informational video online for a specific topic.

Apply Your Knowledge

1. Some writers argue that planning messages wastes time because they inevitably change their plans as they go along. How would you respond to this argument? Briefly explain.
2. A day after sending an email to all 1,800 employees in your company regarding income tax implications of the company's retirement plan, you discover that one of the sources you relied on for your information plagiarized from other sources. You quickly double-check all the information in your message and confirm that it is accurate. However, you are concerned about using plagiarized information, even though you did nothing wrong. How you would handle this situation?
3. You are organizing an exploratory in-person meeting with engineering representatives from a dozen manufacturers around the world to discuss updates to a technical standard that all the companies' products must adhere to. The representatives have a wide range of firmly held opinions on the subject, because the changes could help some companies and hurt others. They can't even agree on what should be addressed first so you need to develop a minimum level of consensus on what should be on the agenda.

Completing Business Messages 181

Activities

1. **Making Ethical Choices** The time and energy required for careful revision can often benefit you or your company directly. For example, reader-friendly product descriptions will increase the probability that website visitors will buy your products. But what about situations in which the quality of your writing and revision work really doesn't stand to benefit you directly?
   Say you know that an upcoming construction project at your manufacturing plant will seriously impact the people who live nearby; it will disrupt traffic and create noise and air pollution. The more people know about the project schedule, the more they can adjust their lives to minimize its negative impact.
   These people are not potential customers, however; your company does not sell its products locally. You could update the neighbors with a website notice, but doing so will take time away from your other responsibilities. Do you have an ethical obligation to keep the local community informed with accurate, up-to-date information? Why or why not? In a post on your class blog, explain your position on this question.

2. **Revising for Readability** Use what you know about readability to improve this paragraph:

   > Although major league baseball remains popular, more people are attending minor league baseball games because they can spend less on admission, snacks, and parking and still enjoy the excitement of America's pastime. Connecticut, for example, has three AA minor league teams, including the New Haven Ravens, who are affiliated with the St. Louis Cardinals; the Norwich Navigators, who are affiliated with the New York Yankees; and the New Britain Rock Cats, who are affiliated with the Minnesota Twins. These teams play in relatively small stadiums, so fans are close enough to see and hear everything, from the swing of the bat connecting with the ball to the thud of the ball landing in the outfielder's glove. Best of all, the cost of a family outing to see rising stars play in a local minor league game is just a fraction of what the family would spend to attend a major league game in a much larger, more crowded stadium.

3. **Structuring a Business Letter** Figure 5.13 on the next page contains all the elements for creating a business letter, but they are in the wrong order. Retype these elements into a new Modified Block letter in the correct order, with correct spacing between them. Use alignment, leading, and white space as needed. Select an appropriate font and size for the text, and set appropriate margins. Save your work and submit it to your instructor.

4. **Designing for Readability** Compare the home pages of Bloomberg and MarketWatch, two websites that cover financial markets. What are your first impressions of these two sites? How do their overall designs compare in terms of information delivery and overall user experience? Choose three pieces of information that a visitor to these sites would be likely to look for, such as a current stock price, news from international markets, and commentary from market experts. Which site makes it easier to find this information? Why? Present your analysis in a post for your class blog.

The **Activities** section provides a series of simple exercises that can help increase your familiarity and comfort level with the skills taught in the chapter.

CHAPTER

1

Communicating Professionally in Today's Digital, Social, Mobile World

After studying this chapter, you will be able to:

- Define *communication* and explain the importance of effective business communication.
- Explain what it means to communicate as a professional in a business context.
- Describe the communication process model and explain how social media are changing the nature of business communication.
- Outline the challenges and opportunities of mobile communication in business.
- Define *ethics*, explain the difference between an ethical dilemma and an ethical lapse, and list six guidelines for making ethical communication choices.
- Explain how cultural diversity affects business communication and describe the steps you can take to communicate more effectively across cultural boundaries.
- List four general guidelines for using communication technology effectively.
- Demonstrate an understanding of careers in arts, audio/video technology, and communications.

Understanding Why Communication Matters

Communication:
The process of transferring information and meaning using one or more media.

Communication is the process of transferring information and meaning between senders and receivers, using one or more print, oral, visual, or digital media. The essence of communication is sharing—providing data, information, insights, and inspiration in an exchange that benefits both you and the people with whom you are communicating. As Figure 1.1 indicates, this sharing can happen in a variety of ways. It can include a simple and successful transfer of information, a negotiation in which the sender and receiver arrive at an agreed-upon meaning, and a situation in which the receiver creates a different message than the one the sender intended to convey.

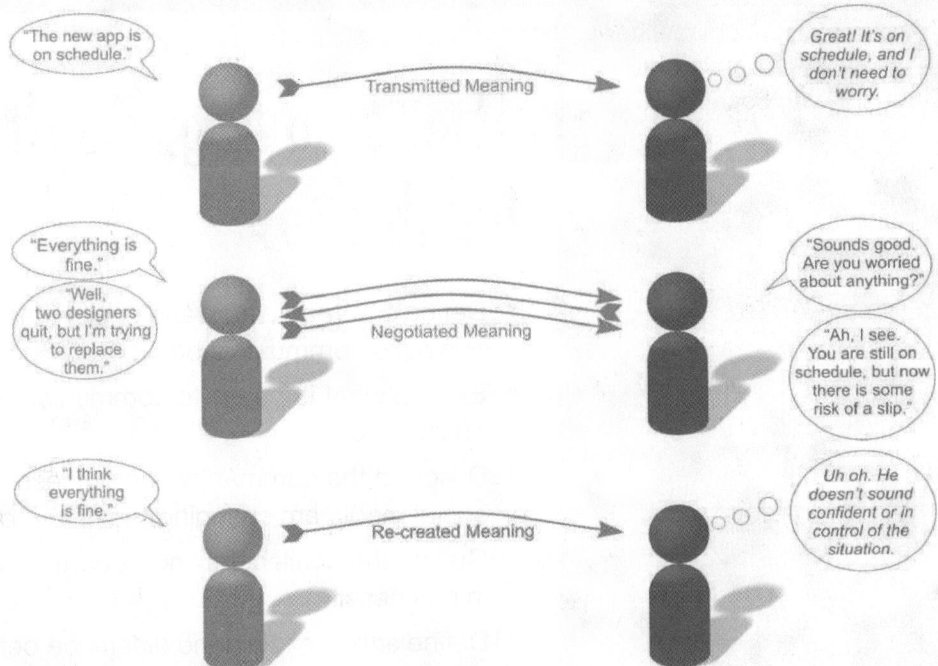

Figure 1.1
Sharing Information
These three exchanges between a software project manager (left) and his boss (right) illustrate the variety of ways in which information is shared between senders and receivers. In the top exchange, the sender's meaning is transmitted intact to the receiver, who accepts what the sender says at face value. In the middle exchange, the sender and receiver negotiate the meaning by discussing the situation. The negotiated meaning is that everything is fine *so far*, but the risk of a schedule slip is now higher than it was before. In the bottom exchange, the receiver has a negative emotional reaction to the word "think" and as a result creates her own meaning—that everything probably is *not* fine, in spite of what the sender says.

You will invest a lot of time and energy in this course developing your communication skills, so it's fair to ask whether it will be worthwhile. This section outlines the many ways in which good communication skills are critical for your career and for any company you join.

Communication and Society

To communicate effectively in a culture, whether it's with business colleagues or personal friends, it's important to understand society's communication customs and expectations.

As communication has become increasingly digital and immediate, societal expectations about communication have shifted into high gear. For example, fifty years ago, postal mail was the most common business communication method. It was not unusual for a business conversation to take weeks, with several days between sending a letter and receiving a reply. Twenty years ago, land-based telephone lines were the primary communication method for business. Important phone calls were commonly planned days in advance and coordinated with in-office availability. Today, however, many businesspeople rely on email or text messages, where replies within a few hours are the norm, and the cultural expectation for reply time has shifted. The changes in the dominant communication technologies in society have affected society itself.

Communication Is Important to Your Career

No matter what career path you pursue, communication skills will be essential to your success at every stage. You can have the greatest ideas in the world, but they're no good to your company or your career if you can't express them clearly and persuasively. Some jobs, such as sales and customer support, are primarily about communicating. In fields such as engineering or finance, you often need to share complex ideas with executives, customers, and colleagues. Your ability to connect with people outside your field can be as important as your technical expertise. If you have the entrepreneurial urge, you will need to communicate with a wide range of audiences, from investors, bankers, and government regulators to employees, customers, and business partners.

Figure 1.2
Communicating for Success
Communication skills are essential for success in the modern business world. Workers must know how to speak and write professionally and how to choose effective communication strategies and media.

The changing nature of employment is putting new pressure on communication skills, too. Many companies now supplement their permanent workforces with independent contractors who are brought on for a short period or even a single project. Chances are you will spend some of your career as one of these independent freelancers, working without the support network that an established company environment provides. You will have to "sell yourself" into each new contract, and communicate successfully in a wide range of work organization. You can expect communication to consume the majority of your time. Top executives spend most of their workdays communicating, and businesspeople who can't communicate well don't stand much chance of reaching the top.

In fact, improving your communication skills may be the single most important step you can take in your career. The world is full of good marketing strategists, good accountants, good engineers, and good attorneys—but it is not full of good communicators. View this as an opportunity to stand out from your competition in the job market.

Employers sometimes express frustration at the poor communication skills of many employees—particularly recent high school or college graduates who haven't learned how to adapt their communication styles to a professional business environment. If you learn to write well, speak well, listen well, and recognize the appropriate way to communicate in any situation, you'll gain a major advantage that will serve you throughout your career.

This course teaches you how to send and receive information more effectively. It helps you improve your communication skills through practice in an environment that provides honest, constructive criticism. You will discover how to collaborate in teams, listen effectively, master nonverbal communication skills, and participate in productive meetings. You'll learn about communicating across cultural boundaries. You'll learn a three-step process that will help you write effective business messages, and you'll get specific tips for crafting business messages using a wide range of media, from social networks to blogs to online presentations. Develop these skills, and you'll start your business career with a clear competitive advantage.

Communication Is Important to Your Company

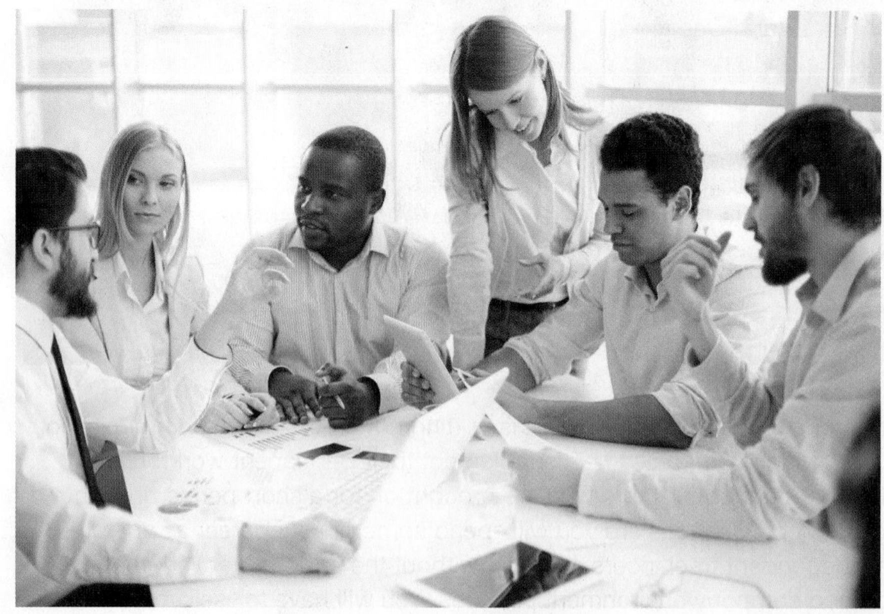

Figure 1.3
Collaboration is Key
Not all business communication takes place in a formal environment. It's important to understand the dynamics of informal discussions and brainstorming sessions as well as more structured events like interviews and sales meetings.

Aside from the personal benefits, communication should be important to you because it is important to your company. Effective communication helps businesses in numerous ways. It provides:

- Closer ties with important communities in the marketplace
- Opportunities to influence conversations, perceptions, and trends
- Increased productivity and faster problem solving
- Better financial results and higher return for investors
- Earlier warning of potential problems, from rising business costs to critical safety issues
- Stronger decision making based on timely, reliable information
- Clearer and more persuasive marketing messages
- Greater employee engagement with their work, leading to higher employee satisfaction and lower employee turnover

Communication Keeps People Safe

One hundred or so years ago, most countries did not have established laws or guidelines about safety. People learned to survive by trial and error, or by watching bad things happen to other people. They learned not to run with scissors because they fell down and stabbed themselves. They learned to wear protective clothes when beekeeping because they got stung. Of course, not everyone learned and survived. Many people died from preventable accidents simply because nobody communicated to them the information they needed to stay safe.

Today's societies are governed by laws and rules designed to make the world a safer place for everyone. You follow these rules every day, perhaps without thinking about it. For example, when you drive a car or ride a bike, you observe traffic rules like stopping for a red light or staying to the right (in the United States and Canada) or to the left (in most other places). These laws are communicated to us by the government in various ways, including traffic signs, drivers' education books, and police officers who stop motorists when they break the rules.

Businesses and schools also have their own safety procedures and guidelines. They communicate them to employees and students in various ways, such as in orientation handbooks, announcements, assemblies, company meetings, and formal training classes. For example, a business or school might have an evacuation procedure in the event of a fire or hurricane with yearly drills where everyone practices the procedure. Communicating the safety procedures to everyone in the organization and allowing people time to practice and reinforce them, can prevent injuries, limit the organization's legal liability for any injuries that do occur, and even save lives.

Stakeholders:
People or groups affected by a business decision.

What Makes Business Communication Effective?

Effective communication strengthens the connections between a company and all of its **stakeholders**, people or groups affected by the company's actions. Stakeholders can include customers, employees, shareholders, suppliers, neighbors, the community, the nation, and the world as a whole. To make your communication efforts as effective as possible, focus on making them practical, factual, concise, clear, and persuasive:

- **Provide practical information.** Give recipients useful information, whether it's to help them perform a desired action or understand a new company policy.
- **Give facts rather than vague impressions.** Use concrete language, specific detail, and information that is clear, convincing, accurate, and ethical. When an opinion is called for, present compelling evidence to support your conclusion.
- **Present information in a concise, efficient manner.** Concise messages show respect for people's time, and they increase the chances of a positive response.
- **Clarify expectations and responsibilities.** Craft messages to generate a specific response from a specific audience. When appropriate, clearly state what you expect from audience members or what you can do for them.
- **Offer compelling, persuasive arguments and recommendations.** Show your readers precisely how they will benefit by responding the way you want them to respond to your message.

Keep these five characteristics in mind as you read the poor and improved versions of the message in Figure 1.4.

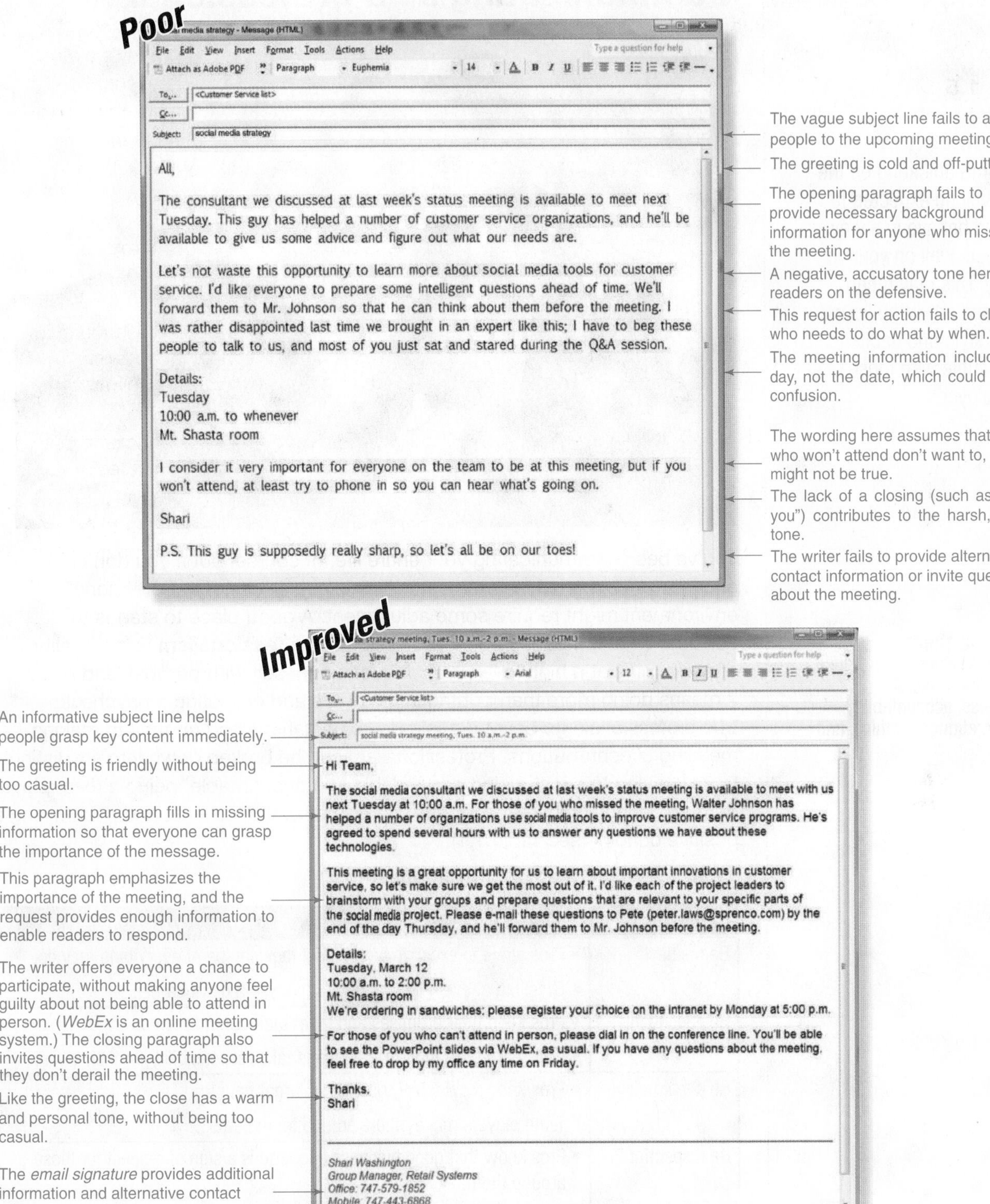

Figure 1.4 Effective Professional Communication

At first glance, the top email message looks like a reasonable attempt at communicating with the members of a project team. Review the blue annotations to see just how many problems the message *really* has.

Communicating as a Professional

Figure 1.5 Professional Communication When communicating on the job, you will be expected to speak and behave in a way that reflects well on your company. This may mean filtering and adjusting your personal style and habits to be compatible with those of your employer.

Professionalism: Excellence in work performance, displaying the traits of effectiveness, accountability, teamwork, etiquette, ethics, and positivity.

You've been communicating your entire life, of course, but if you don't have a lot of work experience yet, meeting the expectations of a professional environment might require some adjustment. A good place to start is to consider what it means to be a professional. **Professionalism** is the quality of performing at a high level and conducting oneself with purpose and pride. It means doing more than putting in the hours and collecting a paycheck; true professionals go beyond minimum expectations and commit to making meaningful contributions. Professionalism can be broken down into six distinct traits: striving to excel, being dependable and accountable, being a team player, demonstrating a sense of etiquette, making ethical decisions, and maintaining a positive outlook (see Table 1.1).

Table 1.1 Elements of Professionalism

Trait	What It Means
Be the best	• Pros strive to excel, to be the best they can be at everything they do. • Excelling at every level is how pros build a great career.
Be dependable	• Pros keep their promises and meet their commitments. • Pros learn from their mistakes and take responsibility for their errors.
Be a team player	• Pros know how to contribute to a larger cause. • Team players make others around them better.
Be respectful	• Pros know that good business etiquette is a sign of respect for those around them. • Respecting others is not only good etiquette—it's good for your career.
Be ethical	• Responsible professionals strive to avoid ethical lapses. • Pros weigh their options carefully when facing ethical dilemmas.
Be positive	• Successful people believe in what they're doing and in themselves. • Pros don't complain about problems; they find them and fix them.

A key message to glean from Table 1.1 is how much these elements of professionalism depend on effective communication. For example, to be a team player, you have to be able to collaborate, resolve conflicts, and interact with a wide variety of personalities. Without strong communication skills, you won't be able to perform to your potential—and others won't recognize you as the professional you'd like to be.

This section offers a brief look at the skills that employers will expect you to have, the nature of communication in an organizational environment, and the importance of adopting an audience-centered approach.

Understanding What Employers Expect from You

Given the importance of communication in business, employers expect a wide range of communication skills. Your employer will expect you to:

- Recognize information needs, use efficient search techniques to locate reliable sources of information, and use gathered information ethically; this collection of skills is often referred to as **digital information fluency**
- Organize ideas and information logically and completely
- Express ideas and information coherently and persuasively
- Listen actively to others
- Communicate effectively with people with diverse backgrounds and experiences
- Follow accepted standards of grammar, spelling, and other aspects of high-quality writing and speaking
- Communicate in a civilized manner that reflects contemporary expectations of business etiquette, even when dealing with indifferent or hostile audiences
- Communicate ethically, even when choices aren't crystal clear
- Manage your time wisely and use resources efficiently

Digital information fluency: Effectiveness in retrieving and understanding digital information and using it ethically.

You'll have the opportunity to practice these skills throughout this course, but don't stop there. Successful professionals continue to hone communication skills throughout their careers.

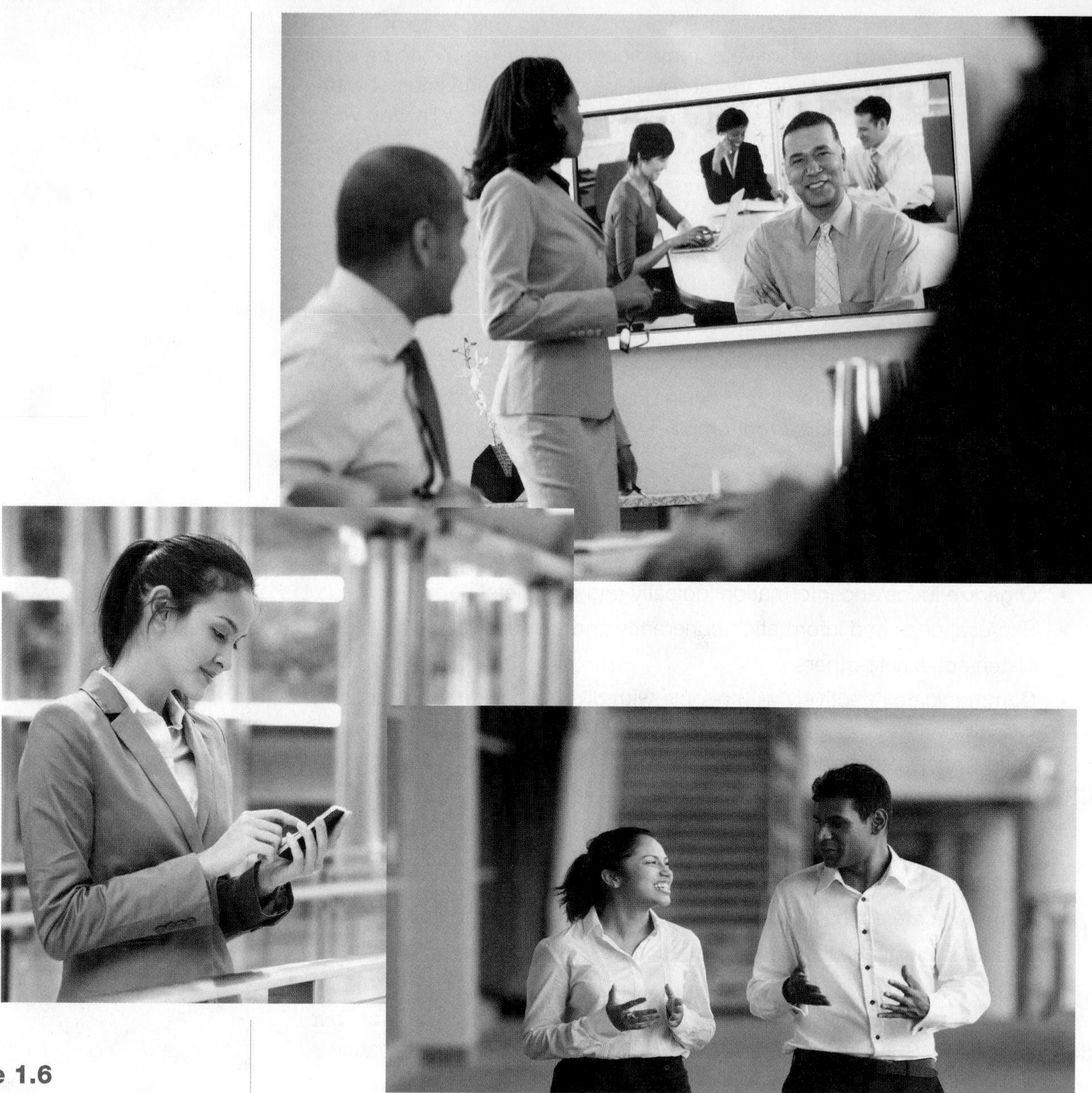

Figure 1.6
Many Faces of Business Communication
An effective employee is able to communicate using a wide range of methods and technologies, as appropriate for the situation.

Communicating in an Organizational Environment

You must not only have the proper skills, but you must learn how to *apply* those skills in the business environment, which can be quite different from social and scholastic environments. Every company has a unique communication system that connects people within the organization and connects the organization to the outside world. The "system" in this sense is a combination of communication channels (such as the Internet and department meetings), company policies, organizational structure, and personal relationships.

To succeed in a job, you must figure out how your company's system operates, how to use it to gather information you need, and how to share information you want others to have. For example, one company might rely heavily on instant messaging, social networks, and blogs used in an open, conversational way by everyone in the company. Another company might use a more rigid, formal approach in which information and instructions are passed down from top managers and employees follow the "chain of command" when seeking or distributing information.

Adopting an Audience-Centered Approach

Successful business professionals take an **audience-centered approach** to their communication: they focus on understanding and meeting the needs of their readers and listeners. Providing the information your audience needs is obviously an important part of this approach, but it also involves your ability to listen, your style of writing and speaking, and your ability to maintain positive working relationships. You'll have the chance to explore all these aspects throughout this course.

Audience-centered approach: An approach that makes the audience's needs a top priority.

An important element of audience-centered communication is **etiquette**, the expected norms of behavior in a particular situation. In today's hectic, competitive world, the notion of etiquette might seem outdated and unimportant. Some people might even consider such "rules" a threat to their individual freedom of expression. However, the way you conduct yourself can have a profound influence on your company's success and your career. When executives hire and promote you, they expect your behavior to protect the company's reputation. The more you understand this expectation, the better chance you have of avoiding career-damaging mistakes. The principles of etiquette discussed in Chapter 2 will help you communicate with an audience-centered approach in a variety of business settings.

Etiquette: Socially accepted behaviors in a specific environment or situation.

Figure 1.7 Communication Etiquette
It's important to understand the customs and rituals of business etiquette, such as what to wear, when to speak, and how much eye contact to make. You can read guides to these cues, but experience is often the best teacher of them.

Exploring the Communication Process

Even with the best intentions, communication efforts can fail. Fortunately, by understanding communication as a process with distinct steps, you can improve the odds that your messages will reach their intended audiences and produce their intended effects. This section explores the communication process in two stages. First, it follows a message from one sender to one receiver in the basic communication model. Then it expands on that approach, demonstrating multiple messages and participants in the social communication model.

The Basic Communication Model

Many variations of the communication process model exist, but these eight steps provide a practical overview (see Figure 1.8):

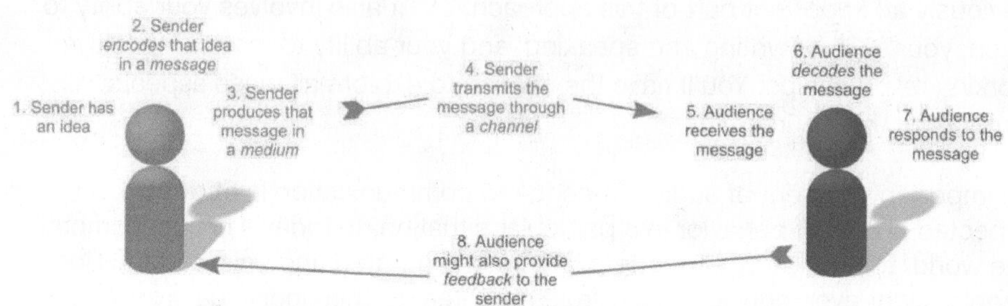

Figure 1.8
The Basic Communication Process
This eight-step model is a simplified view of how communication works in real life; understanding this basic model is vital to improving your communication skills.

1. **The sender has an idea.** Communication effectiveness starts here, and depends on the nature of the idea and the motivation for sending it. For example, if your motivation is to offer a solution to a problem, you have a better chance of crafting a meaningful message than if your motivation is merely to complain about a problem.
2. **The sender encodes the idea as a message.** When someone puts an idea into a **message**, he or she is **encoding** it, or expressing it in words or images. Much of the focus of this course is on developing the skills needed to successfully encode your ideas into effective messages.
3. **The sender produces the message in a transmittable medium.** With the appropriate message to express an idea, the sender now needs a **communication medium** to present that message to the intended audience. To update your boss on the status of a project, for instance, you might have a dozen or more media choices, from a phone call to an instant message to a slideshow presentation.
4. **The sender transmits the message through a channel.** Just as technology continues to increase the number of media options, it also continues to provide new **communication channels** senders can use to transmit their messages. The distinction between medium and channel can get a bit murky, so think of the medium as the *form* a message takes (such as a Twitter update) and the channel as the system used to *deliver* the message (such as a mobile phone).
5. **The audience receives the message.** If the channel functions properly, the message reaches its intended audience. However, mere arrival is not enough. For a message to truly be received, the recipient has to *sense* the presence of a message, *select* it from all the other messages clamoring for attention, and *perceive* it as an actual message (as opposed to random noise).
6. **The receiver decodes the message.** After a message is received, the

Message:
An idea expressed in words or images so another person can understand it.

Encoding:
To express an idea as a message to share with others.

Communication medium:
A means of transmitting a message, such as text message or email.

Communication channel:
A specific device or pathway used for sending a message, such as a mobile phone.

receiver needs to extract the idea from the message, a step known as **decoding**. Even well-crafted, well-intentioned communication efforts can fail at this stage because extracting meaning is a highly personal process: it is influenced by culture, experience, learning and thinking styles, hopes, fears, and even temporary moods. As you saw in Figure 1.1, receivers sometimes decode the meaning the recipient intended, but sometimes they can decode—or create—an entirely different meanings. Moreover, audiences tend to extract the meaning they expect to get from a message, even if it's the opposite of what the sender intended.

Decoding: The process of the message receiver extracting the idea from the received message.

7. **The receiver responds to the message.** In most instances, senders want to accomplish more than simply delivering information. They often want receivers to respond in a particular ways, whether it's to invest millions of dollars in a new business venture or to accept management's explanation why the company can't give employee bonuses this year. Whether a receiver responds as the sender hopes depends on the receiver remembering the message long enough to act on it, being able to act on it, and being motivated to respond.
8. **The receiver provides feedback.** If a mechanism is available for them to do so, a receivers can "close the loop" in the communication process by giving the sender **feedback.** Feedback helps the sender evaluate the effectiveness of the communication effort. Feedback can be verbal (using written or spoken words), nonverbal (using gestures, facial expressions, or other signals), or both. Just like the original message, however, feedback also needs to be decoded carefully. A smile, for example, can have many different meanings.

Feedback: Information the receiver provides to the sender about the effectiveness of the communication.

Considering the complexity of this process—and the barriers and distractions that often stand between sender and receiver—it should come as no surprise that communication efforts frequently fail to achieve the sender's objective. Fortunately, the better you understand the process, the more successful you'll be.

The Social Communication Model

The basic model presented in Figure 1.8 illustrates how a single idea moves from one sender to one receiver. In a larger sense, it also helps represent the traditional model of much business communication, which was primarily defined by a publishing or broadcasting mindset. Externally, a company issued carefully scripted messages to a mass audience that often had few options for responding to those messages or initiating messages of their own. Customers and other interested parties had few ways to connect with one another to ask questions, share information, or offer support. Internally, communication tended to follow the same "we talk, you listen" model, with upper managers issuing directives to lower-level supervisors and employees.

In recent years, a variety of technologies have enabled and inspired a new approach to business communication. In contrast to the publishing mindset, this **social communication model** is interactive, conversational, and usually open to all who wish to participate. Audience members are no longer passive recipients messages—they're active participants in a conversation. Social media have given customers and other stakeholders a voice they did not have in the past.

Social communication model: A communication model in which everyone may participate freely, such as using online social media tools like Facebook or Twitter.

And businesses are listening to that voice. In fact, one of the most common uses of social media among US businesses is monitoring online discussions about a company and its brands. Inside companies, social media make it easier for employees to voice concerns and frustrations, increasing the chances that managers will address problems that get in the way of people doing their jobs.

A sender in a social media environment initiates a conversation by sharing information. This information is often revised and reshaped by the web of participants as they share it and comment on it. People can add to it or take pieces from it, depending on their needs and interests.

Just as *Web 2.0* signified the second generation of web technologies (blogs, wikis, podcasts, and other social media tools), *Business Communication 2.0* is a convenient label for this approach to business communication. Figure 1.9 lists the significant differences between traditional and social models of business communication.

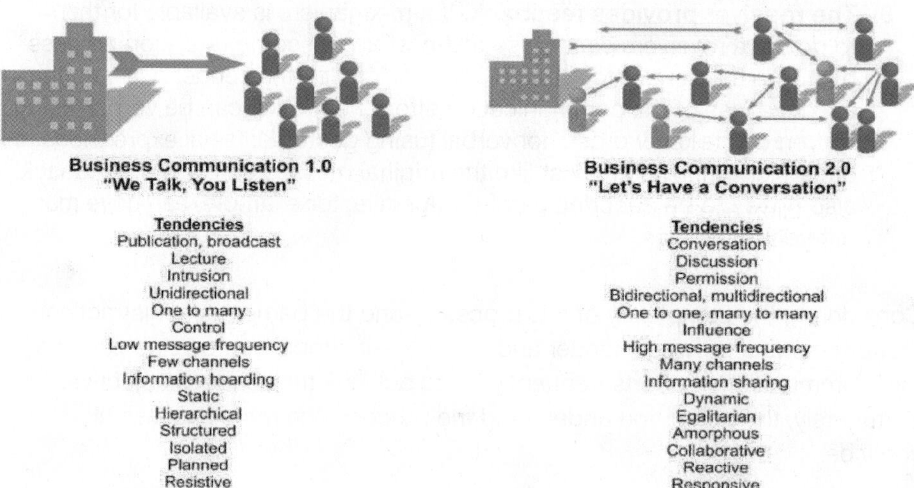

Figure 1.9 Business Communication: 1.0 Versus 2.0
Business Communication 2.0 differs from conventional communication strategies and practices in a number of significant ways. You're probably already an accomplished user of many new-media tools, and this experience will help you on the job.

The social communication model offers many advantages, but it has a number of disadvantages as well. Potential problems include information overload, fragmented attention, information security risks, distractions that hurt productivity, the need to monitor and respond to numerous conversational threads, and a blurring of the line between personal and professional lives, which can make it difficult for people to disconnect from work.

Of course, no company, no matter how enthusiastically it embraces the social communication model, is going to give everyone a say in every business matter. Instead, a hybrid approach is emerging in which some communications (such as strategic plans and policy documents) follow the traditional approach, while others (such as project management updates and customer support messages) follow the social model.

The Mobile Revolution

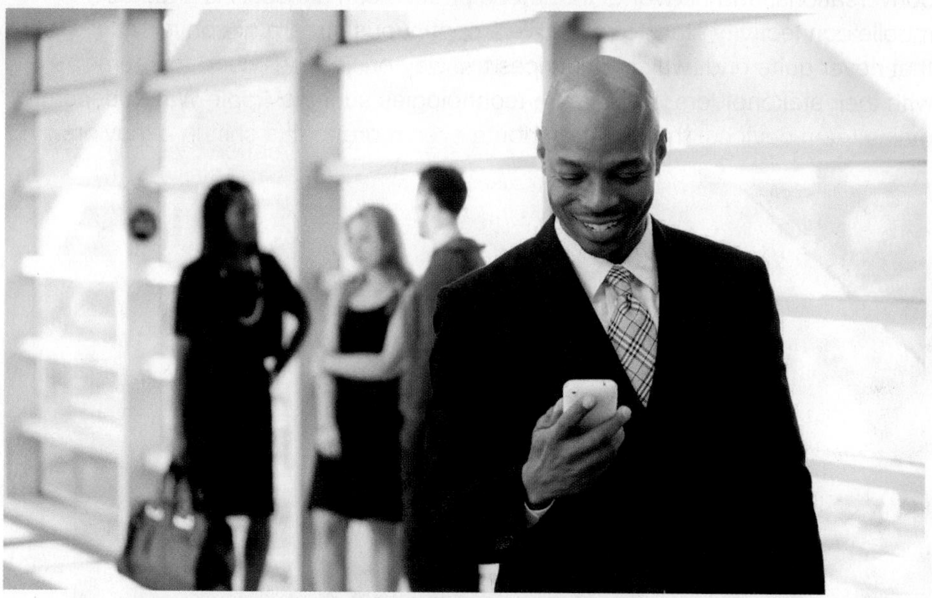

Figure 1.10 Mobile Communication Business professionals today are expected to be able to use mobile communication technologies such as smart phones and tablets. These devices help them stay available to handle business matters while they are on-the-go.

As much of a game-changer as social media have been, some experts predict that mobile communication will change the nature of business and business communication even more. This section offers a high-level view of the mobile revolution.

The Rise of Mobile as a Communication Platform

Whether it's emailing, social networking, watching video, or doing research, the percentage of communication and media consumption performed on mobile devices continues to grow. For millions of people around the world, a mobile device is their primary way, if not their only way, to access the Internet. Globally, roughly 80 percent of Internet users access the web at least some of the time with a mobile device.

Mobile has become the primary communication tool for many business professionals, including a majority of executives under age 40. Email and web browsing rank first and second in terms of the most common non-voice uses of smartphones, and more email messages are now opened on mobile devices than on computers. Roughly half of U.S. consumers use a mobile device exclusively for their online search needs, and many online activities that eventually migrate to a computer screen start out on a mobile screen. For many people, the fact that a smartphone can make phone calls is practically a secondary consideration; data traffic from mobile devices far outstrips voice traffic.

Moreover, mobile phones—particularly smartphones—have become intensely personal devices in ways that computers never were. For many users, the connection is so close they feel a sense of panic when they don't have frequent access to their phones. When people are connected to their phones, day and night, they are more closely connected to the all the information sources, conversations, and networks that those phones can access. As a result, mobile connectivity start to resemble a continuous stream of conversations that never quite end, which influences the way businesses need to interact with their stakeholders. If wearable technologies such as Apple Watch become mainstream devices, they will contribute even more to this shift in behaviors.

Figure 1.11
The Influence of Mobile Technology on Business Communication
When people are connected to information sources for most of their waking hours, either through a mobile device or wearable technology, the communication experience starts to resemble an endless conversation.

The parallels between social media and mobile communication are striking. Both change the nature of communication, alter the relationships between senders and receivers, create opportunities as well as challenges, and force business professionals to hone new skills. In fact, much of the rise in social communication can be attributed to the connectivity made possible by mobile devices. Companies that work to understand and embrace mobile, both internally and externally, stand the best chance of capitalizing on this monumental shift in the way people communicate.

How Mobile Technologies Are Changing Business Communication

The rise of mobile communication has some obvious implications, such as the need for websites to be mobile-friendly. If you've ever tried to browse a conventional website on a tiny screen or fill in complicated online forms using the keypad on your phone, you know how frustrating the experience can be. Increasingly, users expect websites to be mobile-friendly, and they're likely to avoid sites that aren't optimized for mobile. As mobile access overtakes computer-based access, some companies now take a **mobile-first** approach, in which websites are designed for optimum viewing on smartphones and tablets. Another successful approach is creating mobile apps that offer a more interactive and mobile-friendly experience than a conventional website can offer.

Mobile-first:
A design approach that plans for optimal viewing on small screens such as on smartphones or tablets.

However, device size and portability are only the most obvious changes. Just as with social media, the changes brought about by mobile go far deeper than the technology itself. Mobile changes the way people communicate, which has profound implications for virtually every aspect of business communication.

Social media pioneer Nicco Mele coined the term **radical connectivity** to describe "the breathtaking ability to send vast amounts of data instantly, constantly, and globally." Mobile plays a major and ever-expanding role in this phenomenon by keeping people connected 24/7, wherever they may be. People who've grown up with mobile communication technology expect to have immediate access to information and the ability to stay connected to their various social and business networks.

Radical connectivity: The ability to send vast amounts of data instantly, constantly, and globally.

Here are the most significant ways mobile technology is changing the practice of business communication:

- Constant connectivity is a mixed blessing. Like social media, mobile connectivity can blur the boundaries of personal and professional time and space, preventing people from fully disengaging from work during personal and family time. On the other hand, it can give employees more flexibility to meet their personal and professional obligations. Mobile plays an important role in efforts to reduce operating costs through telecommuting and other nontraditional work models.
- Mobile presents challenges for creating and consuming content, whether it's typing an email message or watching a video. As you'll read in Chapter 6, for example, email messages need to be written and formatted differently to make them easier to read on mobile devices.
- Mobile users are multitasking. Roughly half of mobile phone usage happens while people are walking, for instance, so they can't give full attention to the information on their screens. Moreover, mobile use often occurs in environments with multiple distractions and barriers to successful communication.

Figure 1.12
The Mobile Audience: Distracted and Multitasking
If the intended recipients of your business messages will view your messages on mobile devices, chances are you'll be fighting for their attention.

- Mobile communication, particularly text messaging, has put pressure on traditional standards of grammar, punctuation, and writing in general. Chapter 4 has more on this topic.
- Mobile devices can serve as sensory and cognitive extensions. They can help people experience more of their environment (such as augmented

Location-aware content: Online content that is customized depending onthe reported location of the device accessing it.

Bring Your Own Device (BYOD): The assumption that a communicator will have and prefer to use his or her own electronic device, such as a PC, tablet, or smartphone.

reality apps that superimpose information on a live camera view) and have instant access to information.The addition of **location-aware content**, such as facility maps and property information, enhances the mobile experience.

- Mobile devices create a host of security and privacy concerns, for end users and corporate technology managers alike. Companies are wrestling with the **bring your own device** or BYOD phenomenon, in which employees want to access company networks and files with their personal smartphones and tablets, both in the office and away from it. However, these devices don't always have the rigorous security controls that corporate networks need, and users don't always use them in secure ways.
- Mobile tools can enhance productivity and collaboration by making it easier for employees to stay connected and giving them access to information and work tasks during forced gaps in the workday or while traveling.
- Mobile apps can assist in a wide variety of business tasks, from research to presentations (see Figure 1.13).

Figure 1.13 Mobile Communication: Opportunities and Challenges
From 24/7 connectivity to business-oriented apps that let professionals perform work tasks on the go, mobile technology is revolutionizing business communication.

- Mobile connectivity can accelerate decision making and problem solving by putting the right information in the hands of the right people at the right time. For example, if the people in a decision-making meeting need more information, they can do the necessary research on the spot. Mobile communication also makes it easier to quickly tap into pockets of expertise within a company. Customer service can be improved by making sure technicians and other workers have the information they need always at hand. Companies can also respond and communicate faster during crises.
- With interactivity designed to take advantage of the capabilities of mobile devices (including cameras, accelerometers, compasses, and GPS), companies can create more engaging experiences for customers and other users.

The mobile revolution complicates business communication in some ways, but it can enhance communication in many ways if done thoughtfully. You'll read more about mobile in the chapters ahead.

Committing to Ethical Communication

Figure 1.14 Communication Ethics
An employer will expect you to act ethically in your communications, demonstrating values such as honesty and integrity.

Ethics are the accepted principles of conduct that govern behavior within a society. Ethical behavior is a companywide concern, but because communication efforts are the public face of a company, they are subject to scrutiny from regulators, legislators, investors, consumer groups, environmental groups, labor organizations, and anyone else affected by the business's activities. **Ethical communication** includes all relevant information, is true in every sense, and is not deceptive in any way. In contrast, unethical communication can distort the truth or manipulate audiences in a variety of ways.

Ethics: Accepted principles of conduct that govern behavior within a society.

Ethical communication: Communication that includes all relevant information, is true in every sense, and is not deceptive in any way.

Examples of unethical communication include:

- **Omitting essential information.** Information is essential if your audience needs it to make an intelligent, objective decision.
- **Selective misquoting.** Distorting or hiding the true intent of someone else's words is unethical.
- **Misrepresenting numbers.** Statistics and other data can be unethically manipulated by increasing or decreasing numbers, exaggerating, altering statistics, or omitting numeric data.
- **Distorting visuals.** Images can be manipulated in unethical ways, such as making a product seem bigger than it really is or changing the scale of graphs and charts to exaggerate or conceal differences.
- **Failing to respect privacy or information security needs.** Failing to respect the privacy of others or failing to adequately protect information entrusted to your care can also be considered unethical (and is sometimes illegal).

Plagiarism:
Presenting someone else's words or ideas as your own without attributing the source.

- **Plagiarism.** **Plagiarism** is presenting someone else's words or other creative product as your own without attributing the source.

Transparency:
Openness with the information needed to accurately process received messages.

Stealth marketing:
The practice of secretly embedding marketing content into non-marketing communications.

The widespread use of social media has brought increased attention to the issue of **transparency**, or openness, with all the information the participants in a conversation need to accurately process the messages they are receiving. In addition to the information itself, audiences deserve to know when they are being marketed to and who is behind the messages they read or hear. For example, with **stealth marketing**, companies recruit people to promote products to friends and other contacts in exchange for free samples or other rewards, without requiring them to disclose the true nature of the communication. Critics, including the U.S. Federal Trade Commission (FTC), assert that such techniques are deceptive because they don't give their targets the opportunity to raise their instinctive defenses against the persuasive powers of marketing messages. Aside from ethical and legal concerns, trying to fool the public is simply bad for business.

Distinguishing Ethical Dilemmas from Ethical Lapses

Ethical dilemma:
A decision among alternatives that each have ethical pros and cons.

Deciding what is ethical in complex business situations is not always easy. An **ethical dilemma** involves choosing among alternatives that aren't clear-cut. Perhaps two conflicting alternatives are both ethical and valid, or perhaps the alternatives lie somewhere in the gray area between clearly right and clearly wrong. Every company has responsibilities to multiple groups of people inside and outside the firm, and those various groups often have competing interests. For instance, employees generally want higher wages and more benefits, but investors who have risked their money in the company want management to keep costs low so that profits are strong enough to drive up the stock price. Both sides have a valid ethical position.

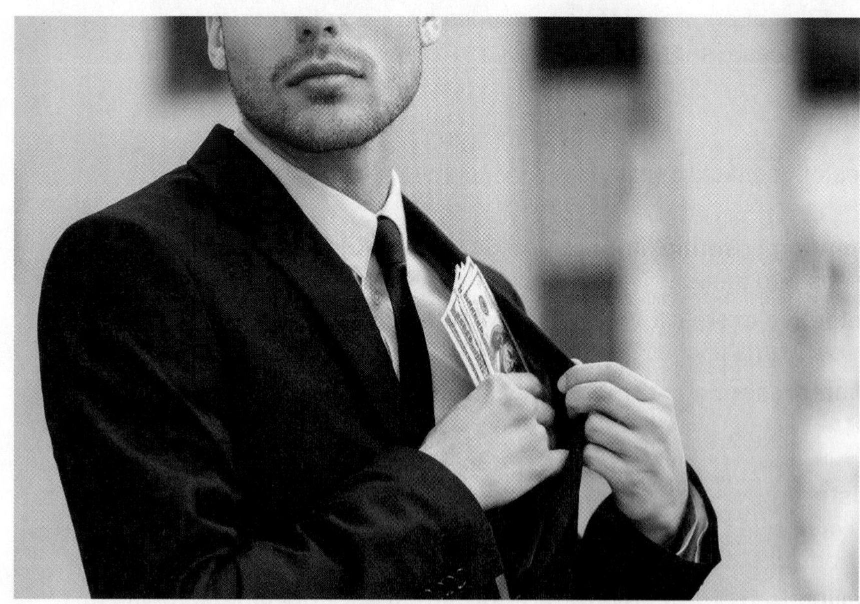

Figure 1.15
Ethical Lapses
Every day the news is filled with stories of people who have committed ethical lapses in business. These can include lying to employers, customers, or government regulators, stealing money, and violating safety.

Unlike a dilemma, an **ethical lapse** is a clearly unethical choice. With both internal and external communication efforts, the pressure to produce results or justify decisions can make unethical communication a tempting choice. Telling a potential customer you can complete a project by a certain date when you know you can't is simply dishonest, even if you need the contract to save your career or your company. There is no ethical dilemma here.

Ethical lapse: Making a clearly unethical choice or behaving dishonestly.

Making Ethical Choices

Ensuring ethical business communication requires three elements: ethical individuals, ethical company leadership, and policies and structures that support ethical decision making. Many companies establish a written **code of ethics** to help employees determine what is acceptable. Showing employees that the company is serious about ethical behavior is also vital.

Code of ethics: A policy that provides guidelines to decide what behavior is most ethical.

Even the best codes and policies can't address every unique situation. If you find yourself in a communication situation in which the law or a code of ethics can't guide you, answer the following questions:

- Have you defined the situation fairly and accurately?
- What is your intention in communicating this message?
- What impact will this message have on the people who receive it or who might be affected by it?
- Will the message achieve the greatest possible good while doing the least possible harm?
- Will the assumptions you've made change over time? That is, will a decision that seems ethical now seem unethical in the future?
- Are you comfortable with your decision? Would you be embarrassed if it were printed in tomorrow's newspaper or spread across the Internet? Think about a person you admire and ask yourself what he or she would think of your decision.

Distinguishing Ethical Issues from Legal Issues

Ethical issues are often matters of subjective opinion, and may vary based on the situation. Legal issues, on the other hand, involve fixed, objective standards set in place by the national, state, or local government. If what you are doing could land you in jail, or make you subject to a fine, it is probably illegal. If it would only embarrass you and your family or ruin your personal reputation, it is probably unethical but not illegal. For example, in some countries there are no environmental pollution regulations, so companies may dump as much waste into the waterways as they like. One could argue that doing so is unethical, although not illegal.

Conversely, not everything that is illegal is necessarily unethical. For example, people who participate in acts of civil disobedience, such as protesting a law that they consider to be unjust, may find themselves arrested and charged with a crime, even though they believe they've done nothing unethical.

Copyright, Fair Use, and Plagiarism

Works of communication such as books, speeches, magazine and newspaper articles, website content, and even emails don't just pop into being spontaneously; they are created by people and companies, and are their **intellectual property (IP)**. IP grants people the exclusive rights to the ownership of content that they have created. Intellectual property provides protection for the owner of the material.

Intellectual property:
The ownership rights to a communicated idea such as a book, speech, or song.

Copyright:
A legal protection that ensures the owner of an idea or creative work will retain ownership of it.

Copyright is a legal protection that usually gives the creator of a work—be it written or artistic—exclusive rights to its use and distribution for a limited time period. For example, when an author writes a book, he might choose to obtain the copyright for that book. Then, the author (and his descendants) will be entitled to royalties from the sale of the book until the copyright expires. In many countries, a work's copyright lasts for the duration of the creator's lifetime plus an additional 50 years after his death. The creator may assign the copyright to some other person or business, so it is not always the creator who owns a work. For example, if you write an article for your employer, your employer may own it, and authors of books may sell or transfer their ownership of the manuscript. Photos and drawings can also be copyrighted, as can any other creative work, like a play, video, sculpture, or speech.

When you visit a website, library, or other place where other people's copyrighted information appears, and "borrow" a picture or article from it without the owner's permission, you are essentially stealing it, which is both unethical and illegal. Doing so without permission is a copyright violation. Doing so without attributing the source (that is, trying to pass off the work as your own original work) is plagiarism. Plagiarism is a major problem in both academic classrooms and businesses today, partly because the Internet makes it so easy to find and copy other people's work. However, people caught plagiarizing can be subject to harsh penalties, ranging from failing a class to losing a job and professional credibility.

Fair use:
An exception to copyright law that permits people to use a limited portion of a creative work for commentary, satire, parody, news reporting, teaching, or archiving.

Fair use is an exception to copyright law that permits people to use a limited portion of a creative work for commentary, satire, parody, news reporting, teaching, or archiving. For example, if a political commentator wants to criticize a politician's speech, she can run a clip of that speech on her news show without permission from the speaker, and then state her opinion about it. Fair use originated in the US, but many other countries have similar laws.

Public domain:
A creative work for which the creator or owner has relinquished all rights of ownership, so that everyone may use and modify it freely without violating legal or ethical standards.

Some owners of copyrightable works choose to make their work freely reusable, so that you do not have to ask permission to use it. When examining a work to see what rights you might have to reuse it, look for fine print that indicates the permissions the author grants. Some works are released into the **public domain**, meaning that anyone may use them freely. When using public-domain works, make sure you cite the original author as its source; plagiarism of public domain work may not be illegal, but it is still unethical, and may violate the rules of your school or company.

Communicating in a Diverse World

Throughout your career, you will interact with people from a variety of cultures, people who differ in race, age, gender, sexual orientation, national and regional attitudes and beliefs, family structure, religion, native language, physical and cognitive abilities, life experience, and educational background. Although the concept is often narrowly framed in terms of ethnic background, a broader and more useful definition of **diversity** includes all the characteristics and experiences that define each of us as individuals including military experience, parental status, marital status, and thinking style. As you'll learn in this chapter, these characteristics and experiences can have a profound effect on the way businesspeople communicate.

Diversity:
All the characteristics and experiences that define us as individuals, including physical and mental characteristics, cultural background, and personal life.

This section looks at the advantages and challenges of a diverse workforce from a communication perspective, examines key differences among cultures, and offers advice for communicating across cultures.

Advantages and Challenges of a Diverse Workforce

Smart business leaders recognize the competitive advantages of a diverse workforce: it offers a broader spectrum of viewpoints and ideas, helps companies understand and identify with diverse markets, and enables companies to benefit from a wider range of employee talents.

For all their benefits, however, diverse workforces and markets do present some communication challenges, so understanding the effect of culture on communication is essential.

Culture is a shared system of symbols, beliefs, attitudes, values, expectations, and norms for behavior. You are a member of several cultures based on your national origin, religious beliefs, age, and other factors. Culture influences the way people perceive the world and respond to others, which affects the way they communicate as both senders and receivers. These influences operate on such a fundamental level that people often don't even recognize the influence of culture on their beliefs and behaviors. The first step to making sure cultural differences don't impede communication is to reconize key factors that distinguish one culture from another.

Culture:
A shared system of symbols, beliefs, attitudes, values, expectations, and norms for behavior.

Cultural competency is an appreciation for cultural differences that affect communication and the ability to adjust one's communication style to ensure that efforts to send and receive messages across cultural boundaries are successful. It requires a combination of attitude, knowledge, and skills.

Cultural competency:
The ability to adjust one's communication style to ensure that messages are successfully sent across cultural boundaries.

Figure 1.16 **Cultural Differences Matter**
When two people communicate, each one brings assumptions to the conversation based on his or her background and experiences.

Key Aspects of Cultural Diversity

You don't need to become an expert in the details of every culture with which you do business, but you do need to attain a basic level of cultural proficiency to ensure successful communication. You can start by recognizing and accommodating the differences described in the following sections. This is an overview, so some of what follows won't be accurate in every situation. Always consider the unique circumstances of each encounter when you make communication decisions.

Cultural Context

Cultural context:
The pattern of physical cues, environmental stimuli, and implicit understanding that convey meaning between two members of the same culture.

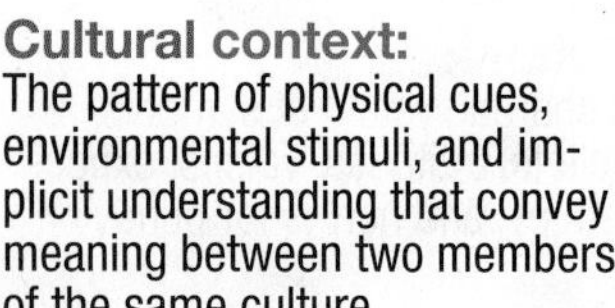

All communication occurs within a **cultural context**, the pattern of physical cues, environmental stimuli, and implicit understanding that convey meaning between members of the same culture. Cultures around the world vary widely in the role that context plays in communication.

High-context culture:
A culture in which nonverbal actions and environmental settings are more important than the actual words said in conveying meaning.

In a **high-context culture**, people rely less on verbal communication and more on the context of nonverbal actions and environmental setting to convey meaning. For instance, a Chinese speaker may expect the receiver to discover the essence of a message and uses indirectness and metaphor to provide a web of meaning. The indirect style can be a source of confusion during discussions with people from low-context cultures, who are more accustomed to receiving direct answers. Also, in high-context cultures, the rules of everyday life are rarely explicit; instead, as individuals grow up, they learn how to recognize situational cues (such as gestures and tone of voice) and how to respond as expected. The primary role of communication in high-context cultures is building relationships, not exchanging information.

Low-context culture:
A culture in which people rely heavily on verbal communication, rather than on circumstances and cues, to convey meaning.

In a **low-context culture**, such as the United States, people rely more on verbal communication and less on circumstances and cues to convey meaning. In such cultures, rules and expectations are usually spelled out through explicit statements such as "Please wait until I'm finished" or "You're welcome to browse." The primary task of communication in low-context cultures is exchanging information.

Contextual differences are apparent in the way businesspeople approach situations such as decision making, problem solving, negotiating, interaction among levels in the organizational hierarchy, and socializing outside the workplace. For instance, in low-context cultures, businesspeople tend to focus on the results of the decisions they face, a reflection of the cultural emphasis on logic and progress. In comparison, higher-context cultures emphasize the means or the method by which a decision will be made. Building or protecting relationships can be as important as the facts and information used in making the decisions. Consequently, negotiators working on business deals in such cultures may spend most of their time together building relationships rather than hammering out contractual details.

Figure 1.17
Cultural Context
Business communication in high-context cultures is indirect and subtle, involving nonverbal cues and metaphors. Such an environment can be confusing and frustrating to people from low-context cultures who don't understand the differences.

The distinctions between high and low context vary, of course, but they are important to keep in mind as guidelines. Communication tactics that work well in a high-context culture may backfire in a low-context culture and vice versa.

Legal and Ethical Differences

Cultural context influences legal and ethical behavior, which in turn can affect communication. For example, the meaning of business contracts can vary from culture to culture. A manager from a U.S. company would tend to view a signed contract as the end of the negotiating process, with all the details hammered out. His or her counterpart in many Asian cultures might view the signed contract as an agreement to do business—and only then begin to negotiate the details of the deal.

As you conduct business with colleagues and customers around the world, you'll find that legal systems and ethical standards differ from culture to culture. Making ethical choices across cultures can seem complicated, but you can keep your messages ethical by applying four basic principles:

- Actively seek mutual ground.
- Send and receive messages without judgment.

- Send messages that are honest.
- Show respect for cultural differences.

Social Customs

Social behavior is guided by numerous rules, some of them formal and specifically articulated (table manners are a good example) and others more informal and learned over time (such as the comfortable standing distance between two speakers in an office). The combination of formal and informal rules influences the overall behavior of everyone in a society in areas such as manners, attitudes toward time, individual versus community values, attitudes toward status and wealth, respect for authority, and degrees of openness and inclusiveness. Understanding the nuances of social customs takes time and effort, but most businesspeople are happy to explain the habits and expectations of their culture. They might even view your curiosity as a sign of respect.

Nonverbal Communication

Nonverbal communication (communicating without the use of words) is a vital part of the communication process. Factors ranging from facial expressions to style of dress can influence the way receivers decode messages, and the interpretation of nonverbal signals can vary widely from culture to culture. Gestures or clothing choices that you don't think twice about, for example, might seem inappropriate or even offensive to someone from another culture. You'll learn more about nonverbal communication in Chapter 2.

Age Differences

In some cultures, youth is associated with strength, energy, possibilities, and freedom, while age is often associated with declining powers and a loss of respect and authority. In contrast, in cultures that value age and seniority, longevity earns respect and increasing power and freedom.

Figure 1.18
Age Diversity
As a business professional you will be communicating with people of different generations. Remember that people much older or younger than you have had different cultural experiences, even if they grew up in the same city and socioeconomic class as you.

In addition to cultural values associated with various life stages, multiple generations in the workplace present another dimension of diversity. Each of these generations has been shaped by dramatically different world events, social trends, and technological advances, so it is not surprising that they often have different values, expectations, and communication habits. For instance, Generation Y workers (those born between 1981 and 1995) have a strong preference for communicating via short digital messages, but baby boomers (born between 1946 and 1964) and Generation X workers (1965 to 1980) sometimes find these brief messages abrupt and impersonal.

Each generation can bring particular strengths to the workplace. For instance, older workers can offer broader experience, the benefits of important business relationships nurtured over many years, and high degrees of *practical intelligence*—the ability to solve complex, poorly-defined problems. However, making the most of multiple generations in a workplace may require some accommodation on everyone's part because of differing habits and perspectives.

Gender Differences

Gender influences workplace communication in several important ways. First, the perception of men and women in business varies from culture to culture, and gender bias can range from overt discrimination to subtle and even unconscious biased assumptions.

Second, although the ratio of men and women in entry-level professional positions is roughly equal, the percentage of management roles held by men increases steadily the further one looks up the corporate ladder. This imbalance can significantly affect communication in such areas as **mentoring**, which is a vital development opportunity for lower and middle managers who want to move into senior positions. In one recent survey, for example, some men in executive positions expressed reluctance to mentor women, partly because they find it easier to bond with other men and partly out of concerns over developing relationships that might look inappropriate.

Mentoring: Working with someone knowledgeable and experienced in your field who is willing to teach you, advise you, and help you reach your goals.

Third, evidence suggests that men and women tend to have somewhat different communication styles. Broadly speaking, men emphasize content and outcomes in their communication efforts, whereas women place a higher premium on relationship maintenance. As one example, men are more likely than women to try to negotiate a pay raise. Moreover, according to research by Linda Babcock of Carnegie Mellon University, both men and women tend to accept this disparity, viewing the assertiveness as a positive quality in men but a negative quality in women. Changing these perceptions could go a long way toward improving communication and equity in the workplace.

Figure 1.19
Gender Diversity
It's important to be able to communicate professionally in a business environment with both men and women.

Religious Differences

As one of the most personal and influential aspects of life, religion brings potential for controversy and conflict in the workplace setting—as evidenced by a significant rise in the number of religious discrimination lawsuits in recent years. Many employees believe they should be able to follow and express the tenets of their faith in the workplace. However, companies may need to accommodate employee behaviors that conflict with each other or with the demands of operating the business. The situation is complicated, and no simple answers apply to every situation. As more companies work to establish inclusive workplaces, you'll see this issue being discussed more often in the coming years.

Ability Differences

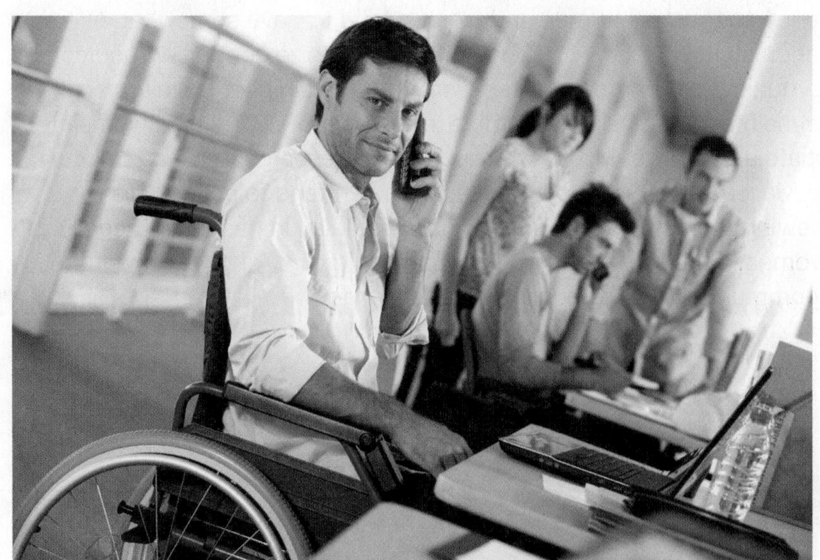

Figure 1.20
Ability Diversity
Keep in mind that not every person you interact with has the same abilities, and don't make assumptions.

People whose hearing, vision, cognitive ability, or physical ability to operate computers or other tools is impaired can be at a significant disadvantage in today's workplace. As with other elements of diversity, success starts with respect for individuals and sensitivity to differences. Employers can also invest in a variety of **assistive technologies** that help create a vital link for thousands of employees with disabilities, giving them opportunities to pursue a greater range of career paths and giving employers access to a broader base of talent.

Assistive technology: Technology that helps reduce the impact of handicap on a person's ability to participate fully in an activity or conversation.

Advice for Improving Intercultural Communication

In any cross-cultural situation, you can communicate more effectively if you heed the following tips:

Ethnocentrism: The tendency to judge all other groups according to the standards, behaviors, and customs of one's own group.

Stereotyping: Assigning a wide range of generalized and often inaccurate attributes to an individual on the basis of membership in a particular group.

- Avoid **ethnocentrism**, the tendency to judge all other groups according to the standards, behaviors, and customs of one's own group. When making such comparisons, people too often decide that their own group is superior.
- Similarly, avoid **stereotyping**, or assigning a wide range of generalized—and often inaccurate—attributes to an individual on the basis of membership in a particular group, without considering the individual's unique characteristics.
- Don't automatically assume that others think, believe, or behave as you do.
- Accept differences in others without judging them.
- Learn how to communicate respect in various cultures.
- Tolerate ambiguity and control your frustration.
- Don't be distracted by superficial factors such as personal appearance.
- Recognize your own cultural biases.
- Be flexible and be prepared to change your habits and attitudes.
- Observe and learn; the more you know, the more effective you'll be.

Travel guidebooks are a great source of information about norms and customs in other countries. Also, check to see whether your library has online access to the CultureGrams database.

Writing for Multilingual Audiences

Ideally, businesses can communicate with employees, customers, and other stakeholders in their native languages, and many companies invest a lot of time and money translating print and online communication to achieve this. However, translation isn't always cost effective or possible. To write effectively for people who may not be comfortable using your language, remember these tips:

- **Use plain language.** Use short, precise words that say exactly what you mean.
- **Avoid words with multiple meanings.** As much as possible, choose words that have only one obvious meaning in the context you're using them. For example, "assess" can mean to analyze a situation, but it can also mean to impose a penalty or a fee.

- **Be clear.** Rely on specific terms and concrete examples to explain your points.
- **Cite numbers carefully.** Use figures (such as 27) instead of spelling them out (twenty-seven).
- **Avoid slang and be careful with technical jargon and abbreviations.** Slang and other nonstandard usages can be difficult or impossible for your audience to translate.
- **Be brief.** Construct sentences that are short and simple.
- **Use short paragraphs.** Each paragraph should stick to one topic.
- **Use transitions generously.** Help readers follow your train of thought; you'll learn more about transitions in Chapter 4.

Speaking to Multilingual Audiences

When speaking to people whose native language is not your own, you may find these tips helpful:

- **Speak clearly, simply, and relatively slowly.** Pronounce words clearly, stop at distinct punctuation points, and make one point at a time.
- **Look for feedback, but interpret it carefully.** Nods and smiles don't necessarily indicate understanding.
- **Rephrase if necessary.** If someone doesn't seem to understand you, rephrase using simpler words.
- **Clarify your meaning with repetition and examples.** Use concrete and specific examples to illustrate difficult or vague ideas.
- **Don't talk down to the other person.** Don't blame the listener for not understanding. Say, "Am I going too fast?" rather than "Is this too difficult for you?"
- **Learn important phrases in your audience's language.** Learning common greetings and a few simple phrases simplifies initial contact and shows respect.
- **Listen carefully and respectfully.** If you do not understand a comment, ask the person to repeat it.
- **Adapt your conversation style to the other person's.** For instance, if the other person appears to be direct and straightforward, follow suit.
- **Check frequently for comprehension.** After you make each point, pause to gauge the other person's comprehension before moving on.
- **Clarify what will happen next.** At the end of a conversation, be sure that you and the other person agree on what has been said and decided.

Finally, remember that oral communication can be more difficult for audiences because it happens in real time and in the presence of other people. In some situations, written communication will be more successful because it gives the recipient the opportunity to translate in private and at his or her own pace.

Poor

Assessing the Office Merger: Bad, Bad, and Not Good

APRIL 22, 2015 BY CYNTHIA MARTIN LEAVE A COMMENT (EDIT)

When we folded the Broken Arrow office into the Tulsa headquarters last year, we anticipated some significant challenges during and after the consolidation. Closing a facility and combining two teams into one is never easy, but as I explained at the time, economic pressures—primarily the need to improve our all-important average profit per client metric—forced us to make a difficult decision.

I wish I could say that we hit this one out of the park. If one were to judge from the three most important indicators, we have not yet accomplished our goals. Our performance has actually declined in two of the three. The latest customer satisfaction survey shows a fifteen-percent increase in the number of customers who say they will consider other service providers when their current contracts expire. Employee satisfaction scores have also dropped since the offices were merged. Only seventy-two percent of employees rate their job satisfaction as "high" or "very high," compared to eighty-seven percent before the merger. The only measure of the three that has stayed steady is our average profit per client. While this might sound like good news in comparison to the other two, improving this variable was the primary reason for combining the offices in the first place.

I'll be blunt: This ain't gonna cut it, folks.

FILED UNDER: STRATEGIC PLANNING

The headline tries to be clever regarding the three factors discussed in the post, but the message is not clear.

"Folded" is an example of an English word with multiple meanings; these multiple possibilities make translation more difficult and can lead to confusion.

Complicated sentences are difficult to translate and force readers to follow multiple ideas at once.

The idiomatic phrase "hit one out of the park" might not make sense to readers who aren't familiar with baseball.

Spelling out numbers instead of using numerals creates more work for readers.

Long paragraphs are visually intimidating and more difficult to process.

Nonstandard language ("ain't") and the idiomatic phrase "cut it" will confuse some readers.

Improved

We Have Not Met Our Goals for the Office Merger

APRIL 22, 2015 BY CYNTHIA MARTIN LEAVE A COMMENT (EDIT)

When we merged the Broken Arrow office with the Tulsa headquarters last year, we knew the move would be challenging. Closing a facility and combining two teams is never easy, but economic pressures forced us to make a difficult decision.

Unfortunately, we have not met the three goals we had for the merger: improving customer satisfaction, improving employee satisfaction, and increasing the average profit per client. In fact, our performance has actually *declined* in two of the three areas:

- The latest customer satisfaction survey shows a 15-percent increase in the number of customers who say they will consider other service providers when their current contracts expire.
- Employee satisfaction has also dropped since the offices were merged. Only 72 percent of employees rate their job satisfaction as "high" or "very high," compared to 87 percent before the merger.
- The only indicator of the three that has remained steady is our average profit per client. While this might sound like good news in comparison to the other two, improving this variable was the primary reason for combining the offices.

Clearly, we need to take a closer look at this situation to see where we went wrong and where we can make improvements.

FILED UNDER: STRATEGIC PLANNING

The clear, direct headline leaves no question about the content of the message.

Simpler sentence structures are easier to translate and create fewer chances for misunderstanding.

Breaking the long paragraph into a brief introduction and three bullet points simplifies reading and makes it easy to find the key points.

Numerals are easier to read quickly than spelled-out quantities.

Standard English and plain language decrease the potential for confusion.

Pointers for Writing for Multilingual Audiences

- Use plain language.
- Be clear.
- Cite numbers carefully.
- Avoid slang and be careful with technical jargon and abbreviations.
- Be brief.
- Use short paragraphs.
- Use transitions generously.

Figure 1.21 Writing for Multilingual Audiences

When writing for multilingual audiences, it's important to be clear and brief and to avoid slang and idioms. Notice how the poor example fails, and how the improved one succeeds, in providing a clear message that anyone can understand.

Using Technology to Improve Business Communication

Today's businesses rely heavily on technology to facilitate the communication process. In fact, many of the technologies you might use in your personal life, from Facebook to Twitter to video games, are also used in business. The benefits of technology are not automatic, of course. To communicate effectively, you need to keep technology in perspective, use technological tools productively, guard against information overload, and disengage from the computer frequently to communicate in person.

Keep Technology in Perspective

Remember that technology is an aid to communication, not a replacement for it. Technology can't think for you, make up for a lack of essential skills, or ensure that communication really happens. For example, you might have a presence on every new social media platform that comes along, but if the messages you are sending are confusing or self-serving, none of that technology will help.

Use Tools Productively

You don't have to become an expert to use most communication technologies effectively, but to work efficiently you do need to be familiar with basic features and functions. Conversely, don't worry about learning advanced features unless you really need to use them. Many software packages contain dozens of obscure features that typical business communicators rarely need.

Guarding Against Information Overload

Figure 1.22 **Too Much Communication?** More information is not always better. Being able to summarize and filter information is as important a skill as being able to collect large quantities of raw data.

Information overload: A situation in which people receive more information than they can effectively process.

The overuse or misuse of communication technology can lead to **information overload**, in which people receive more information than they can effectively process. Information overload makes it difficult to discriminate between useful and useless information, inhibits the ability to think deeply about complex situations, lowers productivity, and amplifies employee stress both on the job and at home—even to the point of causing health and relationship problems.

As a sender, make sure every message you send is meaningful and important to your receivers. As a recipient, take steps to control the number and types of messages you receive. Use the filtering features of your communication systems to isolate high-priority messages that deserve your attention. Also, be wary of following too many blogs, Twitter accounts, social networking feeds, and other sources of recurring messages. Focus on the information you truly need to do your job.

Connect with People in Other Ways

Even the best technologies can hinder communication if they are overused. For instance, a common complaint among employees is that managers rely too heavily on email and don't communicate face-to-face often enough. Speaking with people over the phone or in person can take more time and effort, and can sometimes force you to confront unpleasant situations directly, but it is often essential for solving tough problems and maintaining productive relationships.

Moreover, even the best communication technologies can't show people who you really are. Remember to step out from behind the technology frequently to learn more about the people you work with—and to let them learn more about you.

Collaborating

Thanks to advances in mobile and distributed communication, the "office" is no longer what it used to be. Technology lets today's professionals work on the move while staying in close contact with colleagues, customers, and suppliers. These technologies are also redefining the very nature of some companies, as they replace traditional hierarchies with highly adaptable, virtual networks. The technologies highlighted below help businesses redefine the office, collaborate and share information, connect with stakeholders, and build communities of people with shared interests and needs.

Web-Based Meetings

Web-based meetings allow team members from all over the world to interact in real time. Meetings can also be recorded for later playback and review. Various systems support instant messaging, video, collaborative editing tools, and more.

Videoconferencing and Telepresence

Videoconferencing provides many of the benefits of in-person meetings at a fraction of the cost. Advanced systems feature telepresence, in which the video images of meeting participants are life-sized and extremely realistic.

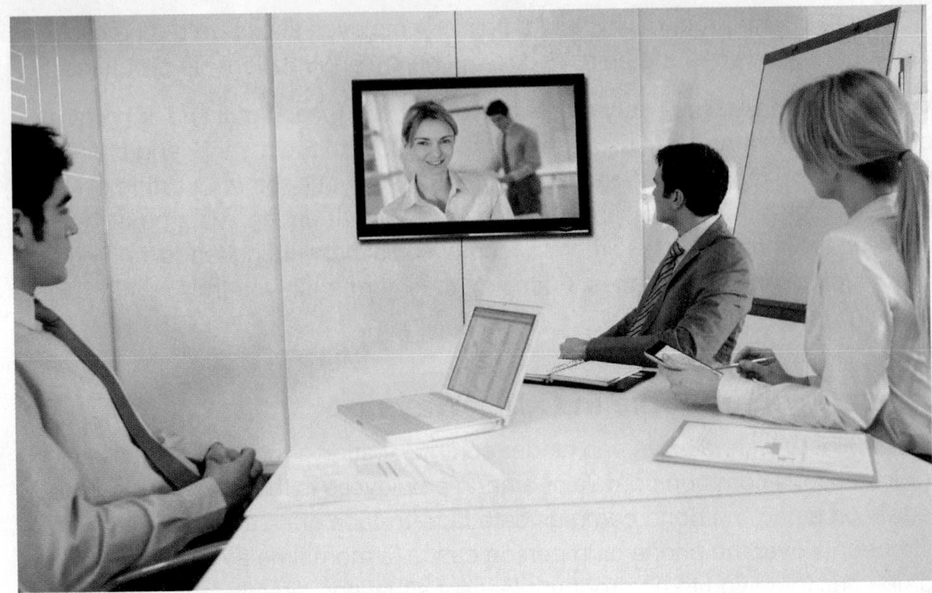

Figure 1.23 **Remote Communication** Videoconferencing can bring people together without them being physically in the same place, saving employees time and saving businesses money.

Wikis

Wikis promote collaboration by simplifying the process of creating and editing online content. Anyone with access (some wikis are private; some are public) can add and modify pages as new information becomes available.

Crowdsourcing and Collaboration Platforms

Crowdsourcing, inviting input from groups of people inside or outside the organization, can give companies access to a much wider range of ideas, solutions to problems, and insights into market trends.

Blogging

Blogs let companies connect with customers and other audiences in a fast and informal way. Commenting features let readers participate in the conversation, too.

Podcasting

With the portability and convenience of downloadable audio and video recordings, podcasts have become a popular means of delivering everything from college lectures to marketing messages. Podcasts are also used for internal communication, in place of conference calls, newsletters, and other media.

Social Networking

Businesses use a variety of social networks as specialized channels to engage customers, find new employees, attract investors, and share ideas and challenges with peers.

Remote Management Tools

Dispersed workforces also present a variety of supervision and management challenges. Mobile workforce management apps can solve many of these, from ensuring that workers show up on time at remote job sites to rescheduling customer appointments on the fly. Sales managers can give just-in-time coaching and encouragement to representatives who are about to call on potential customers. Some systems can even embed information on best practices from experienced workers and deliver virtual coaching to less-experienced workers in the field.

Work teams are often spread out over wide geographic ranges and frequently on the move, so mobile communication is an essential element of contemporary project management. Instant access to task status and other vital information helps project managers stay on top of rapidly moving projects and helps team members communicate efficiently.

Studies and Careers in Communications

While nearly every career requires basic communication skills, certain kinds of jobs require advanced or specialized communication training. If you enjoy your studies in this course, you might be interested in learning more about academic studies and careers in communications.

Communication Studies

Communication studies is the academic study of how people, groups, and societies create and interpret messages. Business communication, the subject of this textbook, is one branch of this very broad and diverse field of study.

Communication studies: The academic study of how people, groups, and societies create and interpret messages.

Communication as a formal field of academic study is very young; it did not exist until the middle of the 20th century. People certainly communicated and studied the art of doing so well before then. In classical Greece and Rome, philosophers such as Socrates and Plato taught students by challenging them with an oral tradition known as rhetoric. **Rhetoric** is the art of discourse; people study it to improve their capabilities to inform, persuade, and motivate audiences with oral speech or writing.

Rhetoric: The art of communicating to inform, persuade, and motivate audiences.

After World War II, communication began to be accepted as an academic discipline, and the Institute for Communications Research was founded at the University of Illinois. This was the first formal academic communication program to offer undergraduate and graduate degrees. Many other schools followed suit, and today thousands of universities offering degrees in Communications. Communication studies programs typically include courses in English, political science, psychology, and sociology. These are important because effective communication requires an understanding of the political climate, social climate, and individual psychologies of the speaker and the listener.

Starting in the 1950s, Communication studies programs began to recognize the effect of mass media on society, and studies such as journalism and radio communication appeared alongside classical rhetoric. Scholars also explored the intersections of social topics such as linguistics and language development. In the 1960s, business and technical communication became a focus.

Social and political unrest in the USA in the late 1960s contributed to the desire for better understanding of the changing role of communication in an increasingly diverse and media-saturated world. Television and radio became as popular as print communication, and Communication studies increasingly included these audio and video media studies.

As technology has advanced, the field of communication studies has expanded along with it. Today's Communications studies students create and interpret messages for media including speech, print, radio, television, television, and a rapidly-growing array of Internet-based applications. The communicative effects have been wide-reaching: new careers in the field have emerged as businesses seek to develop new ways to communicate with their customers, and those same customers are demanding better and faster ways to access information and entertainment.

Communication Businesses and Careers

Career cluster: A grouping of careers that require similar education and training.

A **career cluster** is a grouping of careers that require similar education and training. The Arts, Audio/Video Technology, and Communications career cluster includes many different jobs that all have one thing in common: they generate, enable, or facilitate communication between people or businesses. If you pursue a career in professional communications, you could end up working for just about any type of business or employer in any type of industry. The nature of a business is to provide goods or services, usually to earn money and make a profit. There are four major types of businesses:

- Manufacturer, which takes materials and builds goods that it can sell to others.
- Wholesaler, which buys goods in large quantities and resells them in smaller batches to retailers.
- Retailer, which guys goods, often from wholesalers, and sells them directly to consumers.
- Service, which provides services to customers for a fee.

A few decades ago, a career in "communications" meant that the person was involved in a traditional medium such as print, radio, or television. As communication media have become more computer-centric, this career cluster has also changed. It now includes new technologies such as digital audio, video, and Internet communications.

This career cluster includes the following pathways:

Audio and video technology and film. In this career pathway, workers make movies, videos, and other creative content. They create, repair, and use communications technology equipment, and present audiovisual (AV) content to others. When you see a laser light show at a theme park, or interact with a learning kiosk at a museum, a communications professional is responsible for creating, editing, and delivering that content. Technicians also install, use, and troubleshoot many types of AV equipment, such as projectors, teleconferencing systems, and video editing and duplication equipment.

Journalism and broadcasting. People working in this area research, write, and produce news stories and broadcasts, write and publish books and magazines, and install, operate, and repair equipment involved in transmitting radio and TV broadcasts. A technical writer might create a book like the one you are reading now and an editor might prepare it for publication. A journalist might interview the author of the book and write an online story about it, and a television reporter might interview the journalist on video for a TV station. Back at the TV station, an editor might prepare that video for broadcast, editing it to a certain time limit prescribed by the show's producer.

Figure 1.24
Broadcast Journalism
Being a broadcast journalist is an exciting, fast-paced job. It requires not only a polished appearance, but an assertive personal style, and a sharp mind for investigative reporting and interviewing.

Performing arts. There are many workers involved in performing arts besides the actors, singers, and dancers you see onstage. A host of behind-the-scenes communication professionals make each show possible.They include sound and lighting technicians, advertising and marketing staff, directors, producers, and even stage hands. All of these jobs share a common purpose of helping to enable the communication between the artists and the audiences.

Figure 1.25
Behind the Scenes
The person on the stage or in front of the camera might receive the most attention, but for every performer, there are dozens of people behind the scenes making it possible. Most of those people have specialized skills and training.

Printing technology. Although audio and video content is becoming more and more popular, print technology is far from obsolete. When this textbook was created, for example, it went through a pre-press process where a digital layout technician created the page layouts you see now. A press operator set up the print job on a printing press, and a binding technician trimmed and bound the pages into book form.

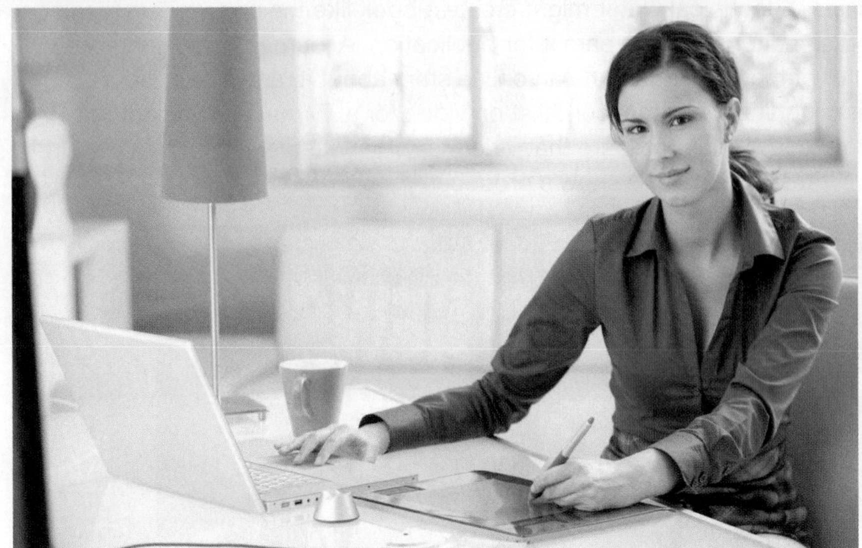

Figure 1.26
Digital Publishing
Most publications created today use computer technology to develop the content digitally. A career in printing and publishing may require graphic design, desktop publishing, and page layout skills.

Telecommunications. Originally a shortened form of *telephone communications*, telecommunications has since expanded to include many types of data transfer technologies, both analog and digital. In the telecommunications field, workers install and troubleshoot communication cables, connection hardware, and wireless technology devices, from simple phone systems in small businesses to wireless cell phone towers and antennas.

Visual arts. This pathway includes workers who create works of art in visual media such as painting, sculpting, fashion, and floral design. They may use a wide range of materials, including paint, plaster, clay, and textiles.

Each of these career pathways has evolved significantly due to technology advances in the last several decades. Prior to the 1990s, when computers became a standard part of many communication environments, communication was mostly accomplished in print and with analog recording and transmission equipment like videotape, cables, and non-digital TV broadcasts. Today, most communication jobs use computer equipment to digitally transmit, record, and play back communication messages. Technicians that set up and maintain communications systems, print and broadcast journalists, printing press operators, and many other communications professionals work with computer hardware and software.

Computers have also affected the way creative artists produce their artwork. From fashion design to screenplay writing, artists are now using computers to plan, design, and even create their works of artusing computer software.

Economic Factors that Influence Communications Studies and Careers

Economic base:
The careers and industries that contribute to wealth entering the community from outside it.

The **economic base** of a community is formed by the businesses and industries that contribute to wealth coming into the community from outside it. For example, in a town where most people are grain farmers, farming is the economic base because farming brings money into the community. Everyone understands the value of a job within the economic base because there is a direct correlation between the work being done and the wealth of the community.

If you look back over the careers in the Arts, Audio/Video Technology, and Communications career cluster you won't see many jobs that are part of the economic base of most communities. While these jobs serve important roles in making people more informed, more effective, and happier, most of the time they don't directly generate wealth. This can mean that jobs in these careers can be harder to find or may not pay as well as jobs more directly related to wealth and its creation, like engineering and accounting.

Communications departments and programs may also be more vulnerable in times of financial trouble. When administrators and executives are looking for ways to cut costs in organizations and businesses, communication-related departments are often hit the hardest because the impact of eliminating communications jobs isn't felt immediately. For example, a mining company might not immediately lose money by eliminating the position of Communications Director; the monetary losses to the company from less effective communications would occur over time, and although real, they'd be difficult to quantify.

While professionals who work in arts, audio/video technology, and communications may face some challenges, don't let this discourage you from pursuing a career that fits your interests and skills. A career as a communication professional might not be as financially rewarding as some others, but it can be more fun, interesting, and personally rewarding.

Chapter Summary

Understanding Why Communication Matters

Communication is the process of transferring information and meaning between senders and receivers, using one or more written, oral, visual, or digital media. The ability to communicate well will play a key role in your success as a business professional. Communication is essential to every function in business, and poor communication skills will limit your career prospects, no matter how ambitious or skilled you are in other areas. Communication skills also give you an important competitive advantage in the job market.

Employees with effective communication skills help companies in many ways. They build closer ties with important communities in the marketplace and influence conversations, perceptions, and trends. They increase productivity, solve problems in less time, and attain better financial results for investors. Effective communicators enable earlier warning of potential problems and make better decisions. They create more compelling promotional messages and they improve employee engagement.

To make your communication efforts as effective as possible, focus on making them practical, factual, concise, clear, and persuasive.

Communicating as a Professional

Communicating as a professional starts with being a professional, which embodies striving to excel, being dependable and accountable, being a team player, demonstrating a sense of etiquette, making ethical decisions, and maintaining a positive outlook.

As a professional, you will be expected to demonstrate a wide range of communication skills. You'll organize ideas and information, express yourself coherently and persuasively in a variety of media, and evaluate information critically. You'll listen actively to others, communicate effectively with diverse audiences, and use communication technologies while following accepted standards of grammar, spelling, and other aspects of high-quality writing and speaking. You will adapt your communication style as needed, demonstrate strong business etiquette, and communicate ethically, following applicable laws and regulations. You will also manage your time wisely and use resources efficiently.

Communicating in an organizational context involves adapting your skills to a professional environment and using your company's unique communication system to gather and distribute information. An audience-centered approach to communication means focusing on understanding and meeting the needs of all your audience members, rather than focusing on your own needs.

Exploring the Communication Process

Communication can be modeled as an eight-step process: 1) the sender has an idea; 2) the sender encodes that idea in a message; and 3) the sender produces the message in a transmittable medium. Next: 4) the sender transmits the message through a channel; 5) the audience receives the message; and 6) the audience decodes message. Finally: 7) the audience responds to the message; and 8) the audience provides feedback to the sender.

Social media has given customers and other stakeholders a voice they did not have in the past. Now, they have the tools to gather information from multiple sources, to respond to companies and other organizations, and to initiate conversations in the marketplace. Social media is also changing the nature of messages. A message initiated by one party is often revised and reshaped by the web of participants who share it and comment on it.

The Mobile Revolution

The challenges and opportunities of mobile communication include the mixed blessing of constant connectivity and the challenge of creating and consuming content on small screens and keyboard. Mobile messages compete for the attention of multitasking users and challenge the traditional expectations of grammar and spelling. Mobile devices can be sensory and cognitive extensions that improve our productivity, collaboration, decision making, and problem solving, but they come with security and privacy concerns. Supervisors can use business-focused apps for a variety of tasks, and businesses can use the unique properties of mobile devices to create more engaging experiences for customers.

Committing to Ethical Communication

Ethics are the accepted principles of conduct that govern behavior within a society; they define the boundary between right and wrong. Ethical communication includes all relevant information, is true in every sense, does not violate the rights of others, and is not deceptive in any way.

An ethical dilemma involves choosing among alternatives that aren't clear-cut; an ethical lapse is a choice that is clearly unethical—and frequently illegal. To ensure the decisions you make are ethical, follow these six guidelines: 1) make sure you have defined the situation fairly and accurately; 2) make sure your intentions are honest and fair; 3) understand the impact your messages will have on others; 4) ensure that your messages will achieve the greatest possible good while doing the least possible harm; 5) make sure your underlying assumptions won't change over time; and 6) make sure you are comfortable with your choices.

Legally, most intellectual property is protected by copyright laws. Limited exceptions are made through fair use, so that works can be partially reused for purposes such as news reporting and satire. Some copyright owners choose to give up their rights and release their work into the public domain. Reusing any creative work without citing the source, so that people mistakenly believe it is your own creation, is plagiarism. Plagiarism is always unethical, and may sometimes be illegal as well.

Communicating in a World of Diversity

Cultural diversity affects business communication because culture influences the way people create, send, and interpret messages. The influences of culture can be profound, and they often go unrecognized by the people involved. Major aspects of culture that affect communication include cultural context, legal and ethical differences, social customs, nonverbal communication, age differences, gender, religion, and ability.

To communicate effectively across cultures, avoid ethnocentrism and stereotyping. Don't make assumptions about others' beliefs and values, avoid judgment, and learn to communicate respect, and tolerate ambiguity. Don't be distracted by superficial elements, recognize your own cultural biases, be flexible, and learn about cultures in which you do business. Also, follow the advice for writing and speaking in multilanguage environments (pages 30–31).

Using Technology to Improve Business Communication

To help avoid the potential drawbacks of using communication technology, keep technology in perspective so that it doesn't overwhelm the communication process, and learn your tools so you can use them productively. Guard against information overload by sending only those messages of value to your audiences and by protecting yourself from low-value incoming messages. Finally, remember to disengage from the computer frequently to communicate in person.

Studies and Careers in Communications

Communication studies is a relatively new academic discipline, gaining popularity after World War II. The field has expanded since its inception to take into account the effects of political, social, and psychological factors on communication. As technology and mass media have changed and gained in prominence, communication programs of study have changed as well to prepare students to work in those areas.

The Arts, Audio/Video Technology, and Communications career cluster includes careers that generate, enable, or facilitate communication between people or businesses. It includes these career pathways: 1) Audio and video technology and film; 2) Journalism and broadcasting; 3) Performing arts; 4) Printing technology; 5) Telecommunications; and 6) Visual arts. Each of these career pathways requires a significant amount of technological understanding, including familiarity with computer hardware and software.

Careers in this cluster are not usually part of the economic base of a community, so workers in these careers may find it more difficult to find a job, and those jobs may be less stable than jobs that directly produce wealth. Communication professionals are essential to the success of a company in the long run and jobs in communications can be interesting, fun, and personally rewarding.

Test Your Knowledge

1. What are the six traits of professionalism?
2. What does BYOD refer to and what are the implications of this phenomenon?
3. Define ethics and explain ethical communication.
4. How does cultural context affect communication?
5. What kinds of careers are available in the areas of arts, audio/video technology, and communications?
6. Describe the nature of businesses and how their communication needs differ from your communication needs.
7. Describe the four different types of business, and how they differ from each other.

Apply Your Knowledge

1. Why do you think communication is vital to the success of every business organization? How can you use appropriate interpersonal communication strategies—including communication management skills—in a professional context? Explain briefly.
2. How does the presence of a reader comments feature on a corporate blog reflect audience-centered communication?
3. How does your understanding of the communication process help you conduct business more effectively?
4. What changes would you make to your email messages if you know your recipients are typically walking or riding on mass transit when they read your messages?
5. You're the CEO of a company whose sales are declining, and there is a 50–50 chance you will need to lay off some of your employees sometime in the next two to three months. You have to decide whether to tell them now so they can look for new jobs as soon as possible, even though you're not yet sure layoffs will be necessary, or wait until you are sure layoffs will occur. Explain why this is an ethical dilemma. Be sure to consider the effect the loss of valuable employees could have on the company's prospects.
6. Suppose you are writing a paper for a class and you find a web site that says exactly what you want to say in your paper. Explain how to ethically and legally use the information you find on that site without violating any copyright laws or committing plagiarism.
7. Recall one instance in which you were confused by a behavior, an attitude, or a belief you observed in another culture. (Don't limit yourself to ethnic or national definitions of culture; consider religion, age, and other factors as well.) What about this cultural difference confused you? Why do you think the culture exhibits this behavior, attitude, or belief? How might it impede communication?
8. Think about a concert or performance you have attended, and brainstorm a list of all of the various arts, audio/visual, and communications workers that were needed to make that performance happen.
9. Suppose a national news magazine is in financial trouble and needs to cut costs to stay in business. The top management decides to fire all the copy editors and proofreaders, since they are not directly a part of the magazine's economic base. Describe the economic impact of this decision on the magazine, both short term and long term.

Activities

1. **Microblogging** Write four messages of no more than 140 characters each (short enough to work as Twitter tweets, in other words) to persuade other college students to take the business communication course. Think of the first message as the "headline" of an advertisement that makes a bold promise regarding the value this course offers every aspiring business professional. The next three messages should be support points that provide evidence to back up the promise made in the first message.
2. **Communicating Safety Procedures in Writing** Suppose a new student has joined your class, and doesn't know the safety rules and guidelines for your classroom. Write a note to her explaining what she needs to know to be safe in your classroom and school. For example, what is the evacuation procedure in case of fire? What do you do if a storm warning siren sounds? Where is the nearest fire extinguisher? Submit your note using email, blog, or social network, as indicated by your instructor.
3. **Analyzing Communication Effectiveness** Identify a video clip (on YouTube or another online source) that you believe represents an example of effective communication. It can be in any context, business or otherwise, but make sure it is something appropriate to discuss in class. Why is this video clip an example of effective communication? Which was more effective—the oral language (verbal) communication or the nonverbal communication? Why? Post a link to the video on your class blog, along with a brief written summary of why you think this example shows effective communication—both verbal and nonverbal—in action.
4. **Assessing Audience Needs** Choose a business career that sounds interesting to you and imagine you are getting ready to apply for jobs in that field. Naturally, you want to create a compelling, audience-focused resume that answers the key questions a hiring manager is most likely to have. Identify three personal or professional qualities you have that would be important for someone in this career field. Write a brief statement (one or two sentences) regarding each quality, describing in audience-focused terms how you can contribute to a company in this respect. Submit your statements via email or class blog.
5. **Communicating with Sensitivity and Tact** Potential customers often visit your production facility before making purchase decisions. You and the people who report to you in the sales department have received extensive training in etiquette issues because you frequently deal with high-profile clients. However, the rest of the workforce has not received such training, and you worry that someone might inadvertently say or do something that would offend one of these potential customers. In a two-paragraph email, explain to the general manager why you think anyone who might come in contact with customers should receive basic etiquette training.
6. **Evaluating Communication Effectiveness** Use the eight phases of the communication process to analyze a miscommunication you've recently had with a coworker, supervisor, classmate, instructor, friend, or family member. What idea were you trying to share? How did you encode and transmit it? Did the receiver get the message? Did the receiver decode the message as you had intended? How do you know? Based on your analysis, what do you think prevented your successful communication in this instance? Summarize your conclusions in an email message to your instructor.
7. **Writing to Persuade** Social media use varies widely from company to company. Some firms enthusiastically embrace these new tools and new approaches. Others have taken a more cautious approach, either delaying the adoption of social media or restricting their use. You work for an "old school" manufacturing firm that prohibits employees from using social media during work hours. Company management believes that social

media offer little or no business value and distract employees from more important duties. In a brief email message to your boss, identify the ways that social media are changing the communication process and relationships between companies and their employees, customers, and communities. Provide at least one example of a real manufacturing company that uses social media.

8. **Analyzing Web Content for Mobile Accessibility** Using a mobile device, visit the websites of five companies that make products or provide services you buy or might buy in the future. Which of the websites is the most user-friendly? How does it differ from the other sites? Do any of the companies offer a mobile shopping app for your device?
9. **Distinguishing Ethical Dilemmas and Ethical Lapses** In a report of no more than one page, explain why you think each of the following is or is not ethical:
   - Deemphasizing negative test results in a report on your product idea
   - Taking an office computer home to finish a work-related assignment
   - Telling an associate and close friend that she should pay more attention to her work responsibilities or management will fire her
   - Recommending the purchase of excess equipment to use up your allocated funds before the end of the fiscal year so that your budget won't be cut next year
10. **Protecting Company Resources** Blogging is a popular way for employees to communicate with customers and other parties outside the company. In some cases, employee blogs have been quite beneficial for both companies and their customers, providing helpful information and "putting a human face" on otherwise formal and imposing corporations. However, in some cases, employees have been fired for posting information their employers said was inappropriate. One particular area of concern is criticism of the company or individual managers. Should employees be allowed to criticize their employers in a public forum such as a blog? In a brief email message, argue for or against company policies that prohibit any critical information in employee blogs.
11. **Providing Ethical Leadership** Visit Cisco's website and find the Code of Conduct. In a brief email message or post to a class blog, describe three specific examples of things you could do that would violate these provisions; then list at least three opportunities that Cisco provides its employees to report ethics violations or ask questions regarding ethical dilemmas.
12. **Resolving Ethical Dilemmas** Knowing that you have numerous friends throughout the company, your boss relies on you for feedback concerning employee morale and other issues affecting the staff. She recently approached you and asked you to start reporting any behavior that might violate company polices, from taking office supplies home to making personal long-distance calls. What are your social responsibilities as a communicator, to your company, to your boss, and to your coworkers? List the issues you'd like to discuss with her before you respond to her request.
13. **Writing for Multiple-Language Audiences** Your boss wants to send a brief email message to welcome employees recently transferred to your department from your Hong Kong branch. They all speak English to some degree, but your boss asks you to review her message for clarity. What would you suggest your boss change in the following email message—and why? Would you consider this message to be audience centered? Why or why not?

> I wanted to welcome you ASAP to our little family here in the states. It's high time we shook hands in person and not just across the sea. I'm pleased as punch about getting to know you all, and I for one will do my level best to sell you on America.

14. **Recognizing Cultural Variations in Language** Working with two other students, prepare a list of 10 examples of slang (in your own language) that would probably be misinterpreted or misunderstood during a business conversation with someone from another culture. Next to each example, suggest other words you might use to convey the same message. Do the alternatives mean exactly the same as the original slang or idiom? Summarize your findings in an email message or post for a class blog.

15. **Interviewing: Communicating with Diverse Individuals** Identify someone who is significantly different from you (such as age, cultural upbringing, nationality, native language spoken, or disability, for example) and spend at least 10 minutes interviewing them about communication. What is their preferred method of communicating with friends and family? With work colleagues? What communication methods do they dislike, and why? What challenges have they experienced in communicating with others different from themselves? Share your findings with the class in an oral or written report.

16. **Role-Playing: Communicating with Diverse Individuals** Differences in gender, age, and physical and cognitive abilities contribute to the diversity of today's workforce. Working with a classmate, role-play a conversation in which:

    - A woman is being interviewed for a job by a male human resources manager
    - An older person is being interviewed for a job by a younger human resources manager
    - A person using a wheelchair is being interviewed for a job by a person who can walk

    How did differences between the applicant and the interviewer shape the communication? What can you do to improve communication in such situations? Summarize your findings in an email message or post for a class blog.

17. **Identifying Online Communication Tools** Find a free online communication service that you have no experience using as a content creator or contributor. Services to consider include blogging (such as Blogger), microblogging (such as Twitter), community Q&A sites (such as Yahoo! Answers), and user-generated content sites (such as Flickr). Perform a basic task such as opening an account or setting up a blog. Was the task easy to perform? Were the instructions clear? Could you find help online if you needed it? Is there anything about the experience that could be improved? Summarize your conclusions in a brief email message to your instructor.

18. **Using Technology to Enhance Productivity** Identify a task that you perform in one of your classes, at home, or in an organization or club you belong to, and identify a communication technology that could increase your efficiency or effectiveness at that task. For example, you could locate a mobile phone or tablet app that could organize data that you collect and make it easy to retrieve when you need it.

19. **Finding a Path to a Career You'll Love** Identify a communications-related job that you would like to have in one of these fields: audio and video technology and film, journalism and broadcasting, performing arts, printing technology, telecommunications, and visual arts. Research online to find out what education and experience you would need to do that job.

20. **Preparing Future Generations of Professionals** Communication studies as an academic discipline has changed over the years to include classes in new technologies such as TV, radio, and the Internet. Using the Internet, research what classes are taught in a four-year degree program in Communications at several universities. Then propose two additional courses that the school could add to account for the latest advances in technology.

Expand Your Skills

1. **Evaluating Professional Communication.** Communication examples surround you, every day, from the web sites you visit to the educational materials you study. While not all of them may be effective, they all provide an opportunity for analysis using the information you learned in this chapter.

   Your task: Locate an example of professional communication from a reputable online source. It can reflect any aspect of business communication, from an advertisement or a press release to a company blog or website. Evaluate this communication effort in light of any aspect of this chapter that is relevant to the sample and interesting to you. For example, is the piece effective? Audience-centered? Ethical? Using whatever medium your instructor requests, write a brief analysis of the piece (no more than one page), citing specific elements from the piece and support from the chapter.

2. **Analyze and Summarize the Communication Field.** Many of the specific careers and fields of study you learned about in this chapter did not exist in their current form 100 or even 50 or 20 years ago. For example, nobody had even heard of the Internet 50 years ago, let alone envisioned a career as a social media specialist.

   Your task: Choose a specific field of study related to Communication studies that you learned about in this chapter. Summarize and analyze the history and evolution of that field of study in a brief report (1-2 pages). When did careers in this field become common, and how have they changed over time? When did universities start offering majors in this field?

3. **Determine the Needed Information and Appropriate Media.** Your boss calls you into her office to tell you that 25 workers in your department are going to be laid off. She asks you to inform the people who are to be laid off immediately, and provides you with a list of their names. However, she is in a hurry, and doesn't have time to provide more information right now.

   Your task: Make a list of the additional details you will need to gather from your boss before you can communicate the bad news to the employees. Then, decide what channel of communication you will use for this task (in-person meetings, email, letters, etc.) and write a paragraph justifying your decision.

CHAPTER

2

Collaboration, Interpersonal Communication, and Business Etiquette

After studying this chapter, you will be able to:

- List the advantages and disadvantages of working in teams and describe the characteristics of effective teams.
- Use critical thinking skills independently and in groups to solve problems.
- Offer guidelines for collaborative communication, identify major collaboration technologies, and explain how to give constructive feedback.
- List key steps needed to ensure productive team meetings and identify the most common meeting technologies.
- Describe the listening process and explain how good listeners overcome barriers to effective listening.
- Explain the importance of nonverbal communication and identify six types of nonverbal expression.
- Explain the importance of business etiquette and identify four key areas in which good etiquette is essential.
- Define digital citizenship and explain the role it plays in effective business communication.

Communicating Effectively in Teams

Collaboration—working together to meet complex challenges—has become a core job responsibility for roughly half the U.S. workforce. No matter what career path you pursue, it's highly likely that you will be expected to collaborate on at least some of your work activities. Your interpersonal skills, including communication, listening, problem-solving, and decision-making, will pay off handsomely in these interactions, because the productivity and quality of collaborative efforts depend heavily on application of these skills.

Collaboration:
People working together to accomplish a task.

Working Together

Almost all careers require working in professional groups—or **teams**—at least part of the time. Developing team building and collaboration skills will not only make you more valuable to your employer, but can position you for entry into management. In a professional setting, there are numerous types and functions of teams—or groups—that have different purposes, duration, and membership.

Team:
A unit of two or more people who share a mission and the responsibility for working together to achieve a goal.

A group or team is a unit of two or more people who share a mission and the responsibility for working to achieve their goal. You will participate in groups and teams throughout your career, so developing the skills to communicate successfully in team setting will give you an important advantage. Each team will require its members to assume different roles, such as leader or facilitator, implementer, worker, and investigator, but to be productive in any role, a team member should help other members when they need it, should not blame teammates for problems or mistakes, and should offer ideas and suggestions instead of criticism.

Businesses use a wide variety of groups and teams to accomplish differing goals. Here are some of the more common types of professional groups or teams that have different purposes, duration, and membership that you will likely serve on throughout your career.

Functional Teams: Functional Teams are one of the most common forms of teams in an organization. The members come from the same function within an organization—for example, all come from IT—and the manager of the unit usually leads the team. The manager's subordinates, or direct reports, are part of the team and carry out the activities set forth by the manager. The purpose of functional teams is to accomplish goals and business objectives specific to one function of the business. For example, a functional IT team would work together to address computing problems within the organization. These teams are normally permanent.

Cross Functional Teams: Cross Functional Teams are organized around a problem that needs to be solved, rather than ongoing operations. In a Cross Functional Team, members come from a variety of functions within the organization—such as Marketing, Sales, IT, Product Development—to solve a larger business problem. Members are usually at similar hierarchical levels, and the team leader is appointed by Senior Management. The role of the members is to bring their diverse expertise as it relates to the problem at hand.

Cross Functional Teams are normally temporary—they disband once the problem is either solved or recommendations have been provided to Senior Management.

Leadership Teams: Leadership Teams are similar to a Cross Functional Team in that they have membership from a variety of functions. However, the composition of the Leadership Team is made of Managers up to Executives, with members holding a similar hierarchical position. The role of the members of Leadership Teams are to work together to determine strategic direction of the organization and to solve larger, more complex issues. Leadership Teams are often permanent.

Virtual Teams: Virtual Teams are a growing trend, as more and more companies offer telecommuting and use communication tools—such as Google Hangout, JoinMe, and other Video Conferencing tools. Virtual Teams are very similar in purpose and membership roles to either a Functional Team or a Cross Functional Team. The defining feature of a Virtual Team is that team members meet virtually only.

Self-Directed Teams: Self-Directed Teams operate without a manager and without an authority figure on the team. This type of team started several decades ago in the Unites States, with the primary purpose of empowering team members to accomplish more without the constraints of managerial influence. The role of the members is to work collaboratively and proactively to develop creative solutions to organizational problems. This type of team works well when all members are motivated and participate equally.

Task Forces: A Task Force is a very temporary team, often short-lived, that focuses on a very specific issue. There is always a leader of the Task Force, and the members of the Task Force represent different functions from within the business whose expertise would be highly relevant to the immediate problem. A Task Force is very similar to a Cross Functional Team except that it is shorter in duration.

Committees: A Committee is a group that focuses on a broader topic, one that takes a longer time to complete, or one that is an ongoing issue. A Committee will elect a chair, and the other members will provide input and expertise to the particular topic. The Committee will make decisions by consensus, meaning that the majority of Committee members must agree before an action is taken. An example of a Committee would be a Communication Committee, one that is designed to help improve communication channels within an organization. Another example would be an Employee Morale Committee, one that is designed to help build the morale and spirits of the employees. Committees can last anywhere from six months to perpetuity.

Types of Group Discussions

Group discussions can take place in a variety of different formats including:

- Free discussions that are not structured or led by one individual.
- Moderated discussions where one individual controls the flow of the conversation. Usually this individual is more familiar with the topic being discussed.
- Presentation followed by a discussion.

- Scenarios or case studies presented followed by discussion. To ensure all members of the group get an opportunity to participate, it is often best to take turns giving feedback to the scenario or case study.

Benefits and Challenges of Working in Teams

When teams are successful, they can improve productivity, creativity, employee involvement, and even job security. Teams are often at the core of **participative management**, the effort to involve employees in the company's decision making.

Participative management: A style of management that encourages all employees to participate in making decisions.

Figure 2.1 Participative Management Including people in the decision-making process who will be responsible for implementing the final plan creates a sense of investment and ownership.

Benefits of successful teamwork include:

- **Increased information and knowledge.** By pooling the experience of its members, a team gains access to more information.
- **Increased diversity of views.** Access to a variety of perspectives can improve decision making—as long as these diverse viewpoints are guided by a shared goal.
- **Increased acceptance of a solution.** Those who participate in making a decision are more likely to support it and encourage others to accept it.
- **Higher performance levels.** Effective teams can be better than top-performing individuals at solving complex problems.

Although teamwork has many advantages, teams need to be aware of and work to overcome—and work to counter the following potential challenges:

- **Groupthink.** Like other social structures, business teams can generate tremendous pressures to conform. **Groupthink** occurs when peer pressure causes individual team members to withhold their opinions and go along with decisions they don't really believe in.
- **Hidden agendas.** Some team members may have a **hidden agenda**—a private, counterproductive motive, such as the desire to take control of the group, to undermine someone else on the team, or to pursue an incompatible goal.
- **Cost.** Aligning team members' schedules, arranging meetings, and coordinating individual parts of a project can eat up a lot of time and money.

Groupthink: A situation in which peer pressure causes individual team members to go along with decisions they don't really agree with.

Hidden agenda: A secret motivation that is unknown to the rest of the group, such as the desire to take control, undermine another person, or sabotage progress.

Characteristics of Effective Teams

Effective teams share a number of traits, including a clear objective, a shared sense of purpose, full participation from all team members, procedures for reaching decisions by consensus, and the right mix of creative and technical talents for the tasks at hand. Of these, the single most important factor is how well team members communicate.

In contrast, teams that lack one or more of these attributes can get bogged down in conflict or waste time and resources pursuing unclear goals. Two of the most common reasons cited for unsuccessful teamwork are a lack of trust and poor communication. A lack of trust can result when team members are suspicious of each other's motives or doubt others' ability to contribute. Poor communication can arise from basic differences in conversational style. Some people might expect conversation to follow an orderly pattern in which team members wait their turn to speak. Others might view conversation as more spontaneous prefer an overlapping, interactive style.

Many teams experience conflict in the course of work. Conflict can be constructive: it can force important issues into the open, increases the involvement of team members, and generate creative ideas for solving a problem. You will be more successful in resolving or minimizing conflict if you work with the other members of your team to effectively problem solve. Together you can identify the problem. You can then negotiate, or discuss options that will lead to an agreement that satisfies everyone. Finally, you can compromise and select and implement the best solution. Teams that experience conflict can excel if they have effective leadership and members who are committed to a positive outcome.

Leading a Team

Even when all members of a team have an equal say, it is important to have a team leader. An effective leader keeps the team on track and focused on achieving its goals. A team leader may be formally assigned or chosen, or a member with leadership abilities may step up to fill the role.

Teams take time to become effective. At first, the team members need to get to know one another, appoint a leader if necessary, and to clarify the purpose and duration of the team. Professional groups go through very predictable processes and stages of development, which will be outlined here. You will experience these stages of development whether you are on a team in a professional setting or in a school setting. Watch for these stages and once you learn them, you will be able to recognize them on teams to which you currently belong.

Forming: Forming is the beginning stage of a team. The team members introduce themselves to each other, each member settles into their role on the team—whether it is the leader, the expert, the "doer", etc.—and the team clarifies its purpose. This phase can last a little while, depending upon how outgoing or inclusive the team members are. Regardless, this is an important time as the members get to know each other and become confident in what the team is tasked to accomplish.

Storming: Storming is the stage when the team members begin pushing against the boundaries established during the Forming stage. Members become more comfortable and act more like their true selves. Conflicts can arise, and often there is a "jockeying" for power within the group.

Norming: Norming is the stage when the group team members have settled into their roles and have accepted the tasks the group has set out to accomplish. Often the Norming and Storming stages will overlap and smoothly and almost invisibly transition from one to the other.

Performing: Performing is the stage where the group gets to work and accomplishes the tasks set out for the group at the beginning. Here, leadership roles are established and respected, team members acknowledge each other's strengths and roles, and the work is accomplished.

Adjourning: Adjourning is the last stage of the group process, and this is when the group disbands because they have accomplished their goals. Often, the group will document what they accomplished and the work they did to get there. Once this is done, the group adjourns and is over.

In addition to the responsibilities shared by all members of the team, the best team leaders demonstrate the following communication management skills:

- **Encourage everyone to share ideas and give opinions.** Every team member deserves to be heard. A team leader pays attention during group discussions and encourages anyone who may be hanging back to jump in and make suggestions. The leader may also gently rein in members who dominate a conversation or are too assertive in stating opinions.
- **Help the team come to a consensus about goals and strategies.** A team leader facilitates discussion and listens to opinions from members, then suggests consensus-building statements to summarize. For example, if the team is choosing between two potential logos, the team leader might call for a vote, or say something like, "It seems like most of us prefer logo A."
- **Manage conflict.** Differences of opinion are inevitable on a team. The team leader listens to the concerns of everyone involved, tries to help the parties find common ground, and guides them toward a compromise that all can accept. The team leader also steers discussions away from personal conflicts, and back toward the business issues at hand.
- **Assign tasks to team members and ensuring a fair division of labor.** When there is work to be done as a team, the team leader divides the work into tasks. The leader makes sure that each person on the team receives a task assignment that is a good fit for their abilities and that represents a fair share of the overall workload.
- **Motivating team members and holding them accountable.** A team leader inspires and prompts team members to complete their assigned tasks. The team leader checks in to make sure members are on track for completing their work, and troubleshoots any problems that prevent task completion. For example, if a team member hasn't completed

Figure 2.2
Assigning Tasks
An effective team leader ensures that tasks within the team are assigned fairly and that each member's unique strengths are utilized.

their task, the leader might say, "You agreed to complete this by today. When do you think it will be done? What needs to happen in order for you to complete it?"

- **Communicating and reporting on behalf of the team.** When reporting the team's findings to management, the leader generally serves as the **spokesperson** for the team. He or she needs to be able to speak confidently and clearly about the team's mission and progress.

Spokesperson:
The person who speaks or writes as a representative of a group.

Leading a team can be challenging because you don't necessarily have authority over the people you lead. You must use your words and behavior to inspire them to follow your lead. You'll succeed if you remember to:

- **Display confidence.** Speak positively and confidently, both within the team and when presenting team findings to others.
- **Be attentive.** Observe the interactions and behaviors of team members so you can determine what tasks each person should take on.
- **Demonstrate fairness.** Don't play favorites among team members. Ensure that everyone is represented fairly and tasked equally.
- **Be unselfish.** Put the needs of the team before your own preferences. Sometimes you must take on the most difficult tasks that nobody else wants to do, and give credit more to other team members than to yourself.
- **Be professional.** Dress, speak, and behave in a manner that reflects well on the team and the company. The level of formality required may vary, but certain minimum standards are common across all businesses. Clean clothes that are in good repair, good grooming, the use of standard English speech, and an avoidance of profanity or slang are always expected.
- **Be tactful.** As a team leader, you don't have the luxury to say exactly what you think at all times. Even if you think a manager has made a terrible decision, it might not be in the best interest of the team to come out and say so directly. A good team leader is able to phrase comments and requests in a neutral, tactful way that doesn't stir up negative feelings.

Leadership and Professional Development Opportunities for Students

Figure 2.3
Student Leadership
Your everyday life as a student offers opportunities for leadership, such as leading and supporting sports teammates, starting and leading clubs, and running for offices in student government.

You don't have to wait to get into the business world to start developing your team leadership and professional development skills. There are many opportunities available for students to lead groups. They include:

- **Student government.** You can participate in student leadership at your school, such as running for class president or a seat on the student council.
- **Sports teams.** If you participate in team sports, you may take a leadership role, either formally or informally, with your teammates.
- **Clubs.** Most schools have a wide variety of clubs and organizations for students. You can run for an elected office in a club, or even start a club yourself.
- **Professional Development.** Even before you graduate, you can take local and online courses and participate in seminars designed to build certain professional skills, such as negotiating and team-building.

Solving Problems and Thinking Critically

A **problem** is a difficulty that you must resolve before you can make progress. Any barrier or obstacle between you and a goal is a problem. You can solve a problem either individually or as part of a collaborative team.

Problem:
A difficulty to be resolved in order to make progress toward a goal.

Problems pop up all the time. You can solve most of them without worrying why the problem exists or thinking too hard about a solution. Say your team is about to meet and there aren't enough chairs in the room. You have a problem: there are more people on your team than there are places for them to sit. Wondering why there aren't enough chairs doesn't help. To solve the problem, you might move to a room with more chairs, borrow chairs from the room next door, or ask team members who sit nearby to go get their desk chairs.

Some problems require more thought than that. Suppose your company's website sales are low. The *why* behind this problem is critical. You have to understand the **root cause**—the basic reason behind the problem—before you can figure out how to fix it. Is the site hard for customers to navigate? Are your prices too high? Do search engines not show the site on the first page of search results? You may need more information, like customer feedback or usability testing, to be able identify the root cause or causes of the problem. And you may need a team—including sales and marketing professionals, web designers, programmers, user experience experts, and more—find that root cause, design a solution, and implement the fix.

Root cause:
The basic reason behind a problem.

Six Steps to a Solution

When problems are difficult to identify, or difficult to solve, you might find this decision-making process helpful:

1. **Identify the root cause of the problem.** Be honest, acknowledge the problem, and determine what goal it is blocking.
2. **Consider all possible solutions.** There may be one obvious solution, or there may be many possible solutions. Write down as many as you can

think of. You will need to consider your values, standards, and resources, too. Some solutions might be harder implement, or take too long to be practical. One might cost money while another is free. Some might solve only part of the problem.

3. **Identify the consequences of each solution.** Like decisions, each solution will have consequences, and it is important to recognize how the consequences will affect you and others. Again, write them down.
4. **Select the best solution.** The best solution offers the best possible opportunity for you to continue your progress toward your goal.
5. **Make and implement a plan of action.** Recognizing and selecting a solution are only part of the process. You must take the necessary steps to make the solution real.
6. **Evaluate the solution, process, and outcome.** Did your solution work? Did you achieve your goal? Would you do anything differently if you had the same problem again?

Thinking Critically

Critical thinking can help you evaluate your options, not only when solving problems, but also when you make decisions and set goals. When you think critically, you are honest, rational, and open-minded about your options.

- Being honest means you acknowledge selfish feelings and preexisting opinions.
- Being rational means you rely on reason and thought instead of on emotion or impulse.
- Being open-minded means you are willing to evaluate all possible options—even those that are unpopular.

You can think critically about a lot of things—in fact, you probably already do. You don't have to believe everything you hear or read. You can question a news report, look deeper into the meaning of a magazine article, or investigate the truth behind a rumor.

When you think critically, you consider all possible options and other points of view. Start by looking at information objectively. **Objective** means fairly, without emotion or prejudice. Then use your values, standards, and ethics to interpret the information subjectively. **Subjective** means affected by opinions, feelings, or beliefs. Examining something both objectively and subjectively can help you make a choice that is right for you. For example, you can look at a candidate for class president objectively and see that she is smart, hard-working, and honest. Subjectively, you can disagree with everything she stands for, and vote for someone else.

Objective:
Fair, without emotion, bias, or prejudice.

Subjective:
Affected by existing opinions, feelings, and beliefs.

Figure 2.4
Emotions and Critical Thinking
It's hard to think objectively about a problem when strong emotions are involved, but taking a step back from your feelings is often necessary to make a wise decision as a professional.

Emotions can affect critical thinking. Be sure a short-term emotion doesn't push you to make a decision you'll regret in the long run. Leaving work early because your supervisor criticized your performance might feel good at the time, but the consequence might be getting in even more trouble, and maybe even losing your job. If you think critically, you acknowledge that you are angry and are honest about why. Then, you can let the anger go and assess your options with a clear head. Maybe it would be better to go to your supervisor and ask what you can do to improve. The consequences might be better job performance, an improved relationship with the supervisor, and—best of all—no more anger.

Collaborating on Communication Efforts

Figure 2.5
Team Communication
When a team collaborates on a communication effort, the result is often a stronger end product that reflects a variety of perspectives.

When a team collaborates on a report, website, presentation, or other communication project, the collective energy and expertise of the various members can produce a result that transcends what each individual could do alone. But collaborating on team messages requires special effort and planning.

Guidelines for Collaborative Writing

In any collaborative effort, team members from different backgrounds may have different priorities. A technical expert may focus on accuracy and scientific standards, for example. An editor may be more concerned about organization and coherence, and a manager may focus on schedule, cost, and corporate goals. In addition, team members differ in writing styles, work habits, and personality traits.

To collaborate effectively, everyone involved must be flexible, open to other opinions, and willing to focus on team objectives rather than on individual priorities. Most ideas can be expressed in many ways, so avoid the "my way is best" attitude when working with others. The following guidelines will help you collaborate successfully:

- **Select collaborators carefully.** Choose a combination of people who have the experience, information, and talent needed for each project.
- **Agree on project goals before you start.** Starting without a clear idea of what the team hopes to accomplish inevitably leads to frustration and wasted time.
- **Give your team time to bond before diving in.** If people haven't had the opportunity to work together before, they need time to get to know each other before their asked to collaborate.
- **Clarify individual responsibilities.** Members will depend on each other, so make sure individual responsibilities are clear.
- **Establish clear processes.** Make sure everyone knows how the work will progress from start to finish.
- **Avoid writing as a group.** The actual composition is the only part of developing team messages that does not usually benefit from group participation. Brainstorming the wording of short pieces of text, particularly headlines, slogans, and other high-visibility elements, can be an effective way to stimulate creative word choices. For longer projects, it is usually more efficient to plan, research, and outline together, then assign the writing to one person—or divide a larger project among multiple writers. If you divide the writing, try to have one person do the final revision to ensure a consistent style.
- **Make sure tools and techniques are ready and compatible across the team.** Even minor details such as different versions of software can delay the project.
- **Check to see how things are going along the way.** Don't assume that everything is working just because you don't hear anything negative.

Technologies for Collaborative Writing

A variety of tools are available to help writers collaborate on everything from short documents to entire websites. Software allows multiple users to comment on a document without changing the original text. Other features track the changes each user makes, but keep everyone's edits separate and reversible. The widely used Adobe Acrobat electronic document system (which creates PDF or Portable Document Format files) also has features for group review, shared commenting, and live collaboration

Collaboration and Content Sharing

At a very basic level, a team can share calendars and schedule meetings using **personal information management (PIM) applications** such as Microsoft Outlook. A team can maintain a master calendar on which all meetings appear, and then individual users can browse each other's calendars to see who is available when. Group to-do lists in PIM applications also allow users to share lists of goals or tasks to be accomplished.

Personal information management (PIM) application: Software that enabled individuals and groups to organize, track, and share information about schedules, meetings, contacts, tasks, and activities.

Technologies often referred to as **groupware** let people communicate, share files, review previous message threads, work on documents simultaneously, and connect using social networking tools. These systems help companies capture and share knowledge from multiple experts, putting greater insights to work on tough challenges. Microsoft SharePoint is an example of a groupware platform. Multiple users can sign into a common SharePoint server to work together in a secure and consistent environment.

Groupware: Software systems that enable people to communicate, share files, work on documents simultaneously, and connect using social networking tools.

Groupware collaboration systems often take advantage of **cloud computing,** in which applications and files are available via the Internet. Microsoft's OneDrive is one such cloud-based file storage system. It lets users with different devices—and different operating systems—access the same files and software applications.

Cloud computing: Computing activities that are based in an Internet environment, such as an application being run from a web browser rather than being installed on the individual computers.

A **shared workspace** is a virtual online office that gives a team access to the same set of tools, resources, and information. A company intranet is a shared workspace that only employees can access. (Extranets, by comparison, are available to employees and others invited to access it.) Intranets and extranets allow people to work together regardless of where they are.

Shared workspace: An online work area in which multiple team members or coworkers can collaboratively participate in accomplishing tasks.

With a **shared file storage system**, an administrator or "owner" can create an online folder, put documents into it, and invite others to access that folder. As the owner, you decide what level of access other users have. For example, you might allow a trusted user to view documents, edit them, add new ones, and invite new users to join the folder, but not delete any of what's inside. You might let another user view the files, but not make changes or invite others. Dropbox and Google Drive are two popular shared file storage systems.

Shared file storage system: File storage that can be accessed by multiple users from different computing devices.

Collaborating on website content often involves the use of a **content management system**, which organizes and controls changes to the site. When a collaborator makes an update to a site field, the CMS automatically converts the new content to the same font, size, and color used in the existing field.

Content Management system: An application that organizes, manages changes to, and controls access to a database or file storage system.

In contrast to the formal controls of a content management system, a **wiki** is a website that allows anyone with access to add new material and edit existing material. The word wiki comes from the Hawaiian word for *quick*. Public wikis, like Wikipedia, allow any registered user to edit pages; private wikis are accessible only with permission. Either way, a wiki user has the freedom to post new or revised material without approval or verification.

Wiki: A web-based collaborative database of information.

Collaboration via Mobile Devices

Today, mobile devices are another option for collaborative writing and other communication projects. Now, mobile systems can do virtually everything from writing on virtual whiteboards to sharing photos, videos, and other multimedia files. Mobility lets workers participate in online brainstorming sessions, seminars, and other events from anywhere. This flexibility can be particularly helpful during the review and production stages of major projects, when deadlines loom and decisions and revisions need to be made quickly.

Figure 2.6
Mobile Collaboration
Mobile devices make it easy for people to work together on electronic communication projects.

A growing aspect of mobile collaboration and communication in general is **unified communication**, which integrates such capabilities as voice and video conferencing, instant messaging, and real-time collaboration software in a single system. By minimizing the need to manage multiple communication systems and devices, unified communication promises to improve response times, productivity, and collaboration efforts.

Unified communication: A communication system that integrates multiple communication methods, such as voice and video conferencing, instant messaging, and real-time collaboration on electronic documents.

Giving and Receiving Constructive Feedback

Collaborative communication involves more than just processes and tools: it usually involves giving and receiving feedback about writing efforts. **Constructive feedback**, sometimes called constructive criticism, focuses on the process and outcomes of communication, not on the people involved (see Table 2.1). In contrast, **destructive feedback** delivers criticism without stimulating improvement. For example, "This proposal is a confusing mess, and you failed to convince me of anything" is destructive feedback. A more constructive review might say, "Your proposal could be more effective with a clearer description of the manufacturing process and a well-organized explanation of why the positives outweigh the negatives."

Constructive feedback: Feedback that provides helpful suggestions for improving the work and focuses on the processes and outcomes.

Destructive feedback: Feedback that delivers criticism with no effort to stimulate improvement.

Table 2.1 Giving Constructive Feedback

To be Constructive	How and Why to Do It
Think through your suggested changes carefully.	Because many business documents must illustrate complex relationships between ideas and other information, isolated and superficial edits can do more harm than good.
Discuss improvements rather than flaws.	Instead of saying "this is confusing," for instance, explain how the writing can be improved to make it clearer.
Focus on controllable behavior.	The writer may not have control over every variable that affected the quality of the message, so focus on those aspects the writer can control.
Be specific.	Comments such as "I don't get this" or "Make this clearer" don't give the writer much direction.
Keep feedback impersonal.	Focus on the message, not on the person who created it.
Verify understanding.	If in doubt, ask for confirmation from the recipient to make sure that the person understood your feedback.
Respond promptly.	Respond in a timely fashion so that the writer will have sufficient time to implement the changes you suggest.
Highlight any limitations your feedback may have.	If you didn't have time to give the document a thorough edit, or if you're not an expert in some aspect of the content, let the writer know so that he or she can handle your comments appropriately.

When you receive constructive feedback, resist the urge to defend your work or deny the validity of the feedback. Remaining open to criticism isn't easy when you've poured your heart and soul into a project, but good feedback provides a valuable opportunity for you to learn and to improve the quality of your work.

Making Your Meetings More Productive

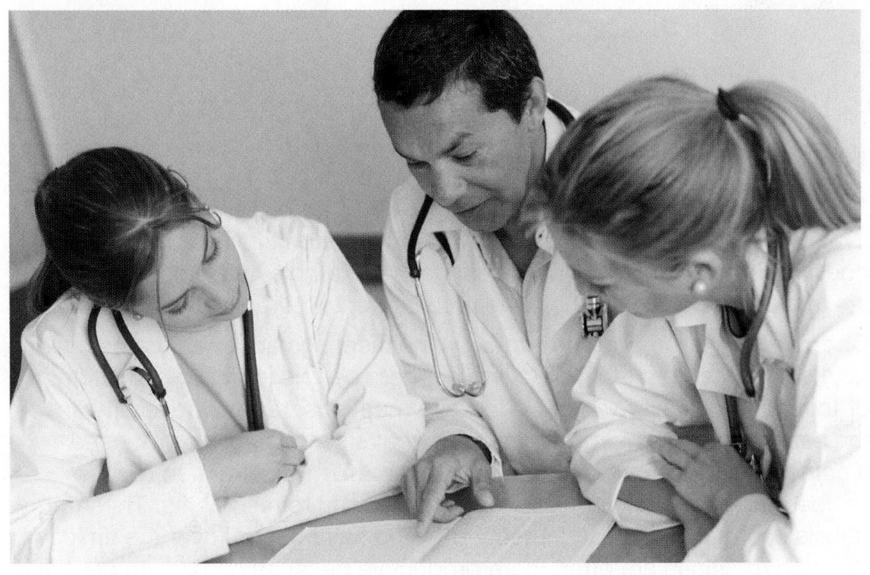

Figure 2.7 **Communication in Meetings**
In-person meetings are common in many businesses. Working together in person enables participants to read each other's nonverbal cues and to communicate without relying on technology.

Much of your workplace communication will occur during in-person or online meetings. To a large degree, your ability to contribute to the company—and to be recognized for your contributions—will depend on your meeting skills. Well-run meetings can help companies solve problems, develop ideas, and identify opportunities. Meetings can also be a great way to promote team building through social interaction.

Preparing for Meetings

The first step in preparing for a meeting is to make sure the meeting is really necessary. Meetings consume productive time and take people away from other work, so don't hold a meeting if some other form of communication can serve the purpose as effectively. If a meeting is truly necessary, proceed with these four planning tasks:

Informational meeting: A meeting that involves sharing information and coordinating action to implement a plan or goals that have already been set.

Decision-making meeting: A meeting that involves analysis, problem solving, and persuasive communication aimed at reaching a decision.

- **Clarify your purpose.** Most meetings are one of two types: **Informational meetings** involve sharing information, perhaps about plans or goals that have already been set. **Decision-making meetings** involve analysis, problem solving, and in many cases, persuasive communication. Whatever your purpose, make sure it is clear and specific—and clearly communicated to all participants.

Figure 2.8
Inviting Participants
One key to organizing a productive meeting is to ensure that the right people are invited to it, including people with knowledge that may affect the decision being made.

- **Select participants for the meeting.** The rule here is simple: Invite everyone who really needs to be involved, and don't invite anyone who doesn't. For decision-making meetings, for example, invite only those who are in a direct position to help the meeting reach its objective.
- **Choose the venue and the time.** Online meetings are often the best way (and sometimes to the only way) to connect people in multiple locations or to reach large audiences. For on-site meetings, review the facility and the seating arrangements. Are rows of chairs suitable, or do you need a conference table or some other arrangement? Pay attention to room temperature, lighting, ventilation, acoustics, and refreshments. These details can make or break a meeting. If you have control over the timing, morning meetings are often more productive because people are generally more alert and not yet engaged with the work of the day.

- **Set and share the agenda.** Before the meeting, people who will present information need to know what is expected of them, non-presenters need to know what will be presented so they can prepare questions. Everyone needs to know how long the meeting will last. During the meeting, the agenda helps the meeting run on time and stay on task (see Figure 2.11).

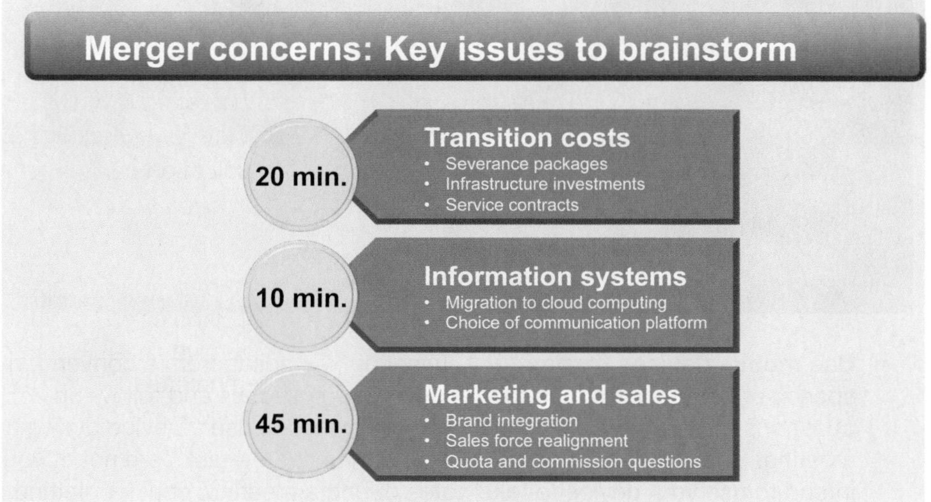

Figure 2.9
Typical Meeting Agenda
Agenda formats vary widely, depending on the complexity of the meeting and the presentation technologies that will be used. One good approach is to first distribute a detailed planning agenda so that presenters know what they need to prepare, then create a simpler display agenda such as this PowerPoint slide to guide the progress of the meeting. Note how the agenda includes the time limit for each topic.

Conducting and Contributing to Meetings

Everyone in a meeting shares the responsibility for keeping the meeting productive and making it successful. If you are the designated leader of a meeting, however, you have an extra degree of responsibility and accountability. To ensure productive meetings, be sure to do the following:

- **Keep the meeting on track.** A good meeting often draws out ideas and that are beyond the meeting's scope. Good leaders need to guide, mediate, summarize, and redirect discussions when they head off track.
- **Follow agreed-upon rules.** The larger the meeting, the more formal you'll need to be to maintain order. Formal meetings often use **parliamentary procedure**, a time-tested method for planning and running effective meetings. The best-known guide to this procedure is **Robert's Rules of Order.**
- **Encourage participation.** You may discover that some participants are too quiet and others are too talkative. Draw out nonparticipants by asking for their input. For the overly talkative, you can say that time is limited and others need to be heard.
- **Participate actively.** Try to contribute to the progress of the meeting and the smooth interaction of the participants. Use your listening skills and powers of observation to size up the interpersonal dynamics of the group, then adapt your behavior to help the group achieve its goals. Speak up if you have something useful to say, but don't talk or ask questions just to demonstrate how much you know about the subject at hand.

Parliamentary procedure: A formalized method of running a meeting in which a chairperson directs who may speak.

Robert's Rules of Order: A well-known set of specific rules for running a meeting in a formalized manner.

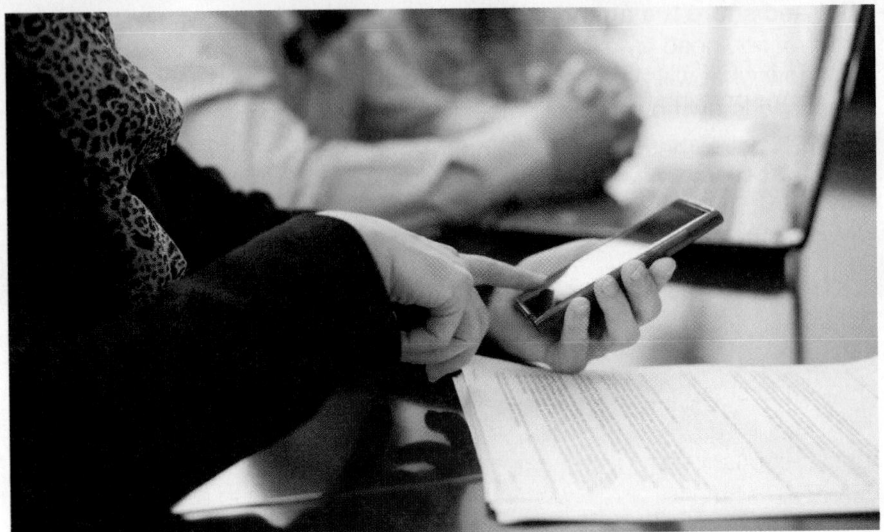

Figure 2.10
Mobile Devices in Meetings
It is usually acceptable to take notes during a meeting on a tablet or laptop. However, avoid activities that are not directly related to the meeting, like responding to email or checking social media.

- **Use mobile devices respectfully.** Tweeting key points from a convention speech or using your phone to jot down essential ideas and follow-up questions can be productive and respectful ways to use a device during a meeting. Checking Facebook or working on unrelated tasks are not. If you intend to use your device to take notes during a meeting, consider letting others know that's what you're doing.
- **Close effectively.** At the conclusion of a meeting, verify that the objectives have been met. If they have not, arrange for follow-up work as needed. Either summarize the decisions reached or list the actions to be taken. Make sure all participants understand and agree on the outcome.

Managing Conflicts

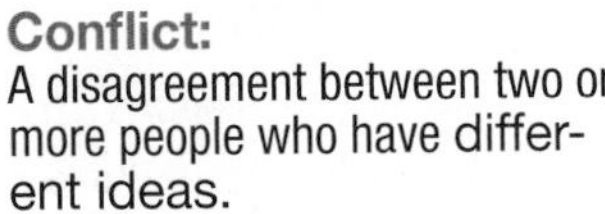

Conflict:
A disagreement between two or more people who have different ideas.

A **conflict** is a disagreement between two or more people who have different ideas. Conflicts occur in all relationships at one time or another, including between team members in a business setting. Managing conflict does not mean eliminating it completely. It means recognizing the cause of the conflict and working through it in honest and respectful ways.

Conflict is most often caused by:

- **Differences in values, standards, or priorities.** For example, one person might think the current website is fine, while someone thinks it needs an overhaul.
- **Personal qualities.** Sometimes stubbornness or ego get in the way of agreement. The person who created the website might be unwilling to accept that it needs improvement, for example.
- **Ineffective communication and misunderstanding.** For instance, two people might actually want the same thing, but they express it so differently that it doesn't seem the same.

There is a problem—something that blocks people from achieving a goal—at the root of every conflict. You can use problem-solving processes to find a solution. You can identify the root cause, and negotiate a compromise that works for everyone.

Following Up

In most cases, the value of a meeting doesn't end when the meeting ends. Problems or opportunities brought up during a meeting need to be addressed. Action items assigned during the meeting need follow up. Key decisions and announcements need to be shared with those who are affected but were unable to attend. Having a written, audio, or video record of a meeting also gives the participants a chance to verify their impressions and conclusions.

The conventional method of recording meetings is through written **minutes**, which summarize the important information presented and the decisions made (see Figure 2.13). One person is usually assigned to keep notes during the meeting and to share them afterward. The specific format of the minutes is less important than making sure you record all the key information, particularly regarding responsibilities that were assigned during the meeting. Typical minutes begin with a list of those present, those who were invited but didn't attend, and the time the meeting started and ended. Next is a summary of all major decisions reached at the meeting, all assignments of tasks to meeting participants, and all subjects that were deferred to a later meeting. In addition, the minutes objectively summarize important discussions, noting the names of those who contributed major points. Any handouts, electronic slides, or supporting documents can be attached to the minutes when they are distributed.

Minutes:
A written record of the proceedings of a meeting.

MINUTES: Planning Committee Meeting
Human Resources Employee Programs
Wednesday, May 15, 2017

Present: Tabitha Brown, Peter Crantz, Kathi Kazanopolis, Agatha Myers, Julie Owens, Bob Phelps, Judith Williams

Absent: Joseph Kingman, Maria Lopez

Meeting called to order by Agatha Myers at 9:30 a.m.

1. November program (speaker replacement)

Kathi Kazanopolis offered to give a presentation about continuing education in job skills, to include detailed information about available workshops, online courses, etc.

Julie Owens volunteered to help Kathi with preparation: handouts, possible topics for small group discussions, research, etc.

2. Future programs

Bob Phelps contacted Edie Orlofsky, who teaches business communication courses at UCLA Extension, about the possibility of a writing skills workshop. He expects to hear from her this week.

Tax program: Still targeted for January or February. Judith Williams will try to locate a tax attorney or tax accountant as speaker.

3. New-employee orientation

Tabitha Brown announced that the executive team has asked the HR department to explore ways to use more computer-based training in the new-employee orientation program. Tabitha will investigate and report back next month.

Figure 2.11
Typical Meeting Minutes
The specific format of meeting minutes is less important than making sure you record all the key information, particularly regarding responsibilities assigned during the meeting. Key elements of meeting minutes include a list of a list of participants, absentees, followed by decisions made, tasks assigned, and subjects that were deferred to a later meeting. Outlines, subheadings, and lists help organize the minutes; additional documentation is noted in the minutes and attached during distribution.

Depending on the meeting technologies at your disposal (see next section), you may have software specifically designed to record, distribute, and store meeting minutes. Some systems automatically forward action items to each employee, record audio discussions for future playback, and make all the relevant documents and files available in one convenient place.

Using Meeting Technologies

Virtual meeting: A meeting that uses technology to connect people in different physical locations

Virtual whiteboard: A whiteboard that people can access remotely to work collaboratively.

Today's companies use a number of technologies to enhance—or even replace—traditional in-person meetings. Replacing in-person meetings with **virtual meetings** can dramatically reduce costs and resource usage, reduce employee workload, and give teams access to a wider pool of expertise.

Instant messaging and teleconferencing are the simplest forms of virtual meetings. **Virtual whiteboards** let teams collaborate in real time. Advanced videoconferencing lets participants see and hear each other, demonstrate products, and transmit other visual information—almost as if they were in the same room. The ability to convey nonverbal subtleties such as facial expressions and hand gestures makes these systems particularly good for negotiations, collaborative problem solving, and other complex discussions.

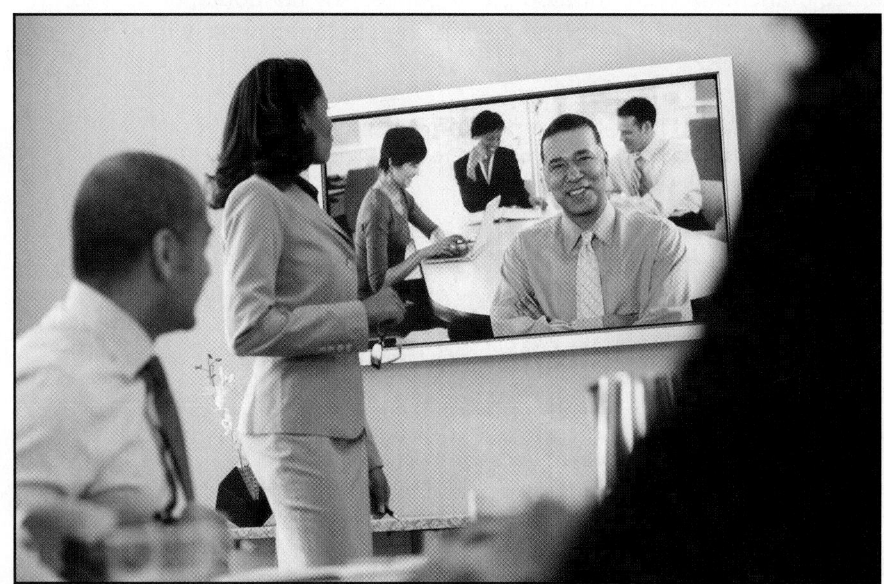

Figure 2.12 Virtual Meeting Technologies
Virtual meeting technologies connect people spread across the country or around the world.

Webinar: A web-based seminar.

Virtual meeting technologies are used for everything from spontaneous discussions among small groups to carefully planned formal events such as press conferences, training sessions, sales presentations, and **webinars** (web-based seminars). One virtual tools is online brainstorming, in which a company can conduct "idea campaigns" to generate new ideas from people across the organization.

Conducting a successful virtual meetings requires extra planning before the meeting and more diligence during the meeting. Recognizing the limitations of the virtual meeting format is a key to using it successfully. Because virtual meetings offer less visual contact and nonverbal communication than in-person meetings, leaders need to make sure everyone stays engaged and has the opportunity to contribute. Paying attention during online meetings takes greater effort as well. Participants need to stay committed to the meeting and resist the temptation to work on unrelated tasks.

Improving Your Listening Skills

Your long-term career prospects are closely tied to your ability to listen effectively. In fact, some 80 percent of top executives say that listening is the most important skill needed to get things done in the workplace.

Effective listening strengthens organizational relationships, alerts the organization to opportunities for innovation, and allows the organization to manage growing diversity both in the workforce and among the customers it serves. Companies whose employees and managers listen effectively are able to stay informed, up to date, and out of trouble. Conversely, poor listening skills can cost companies millions of dollars per through lost opportunities, legal mistakes, and other errors. Effective listening is also vital to the process of building trust between organizations and among individuals.

Figure 2.13
Listening Skills
Employ deliberative, critical, active, and/or empathetic listening as appropriate to the situation.

Types of Listening

Effective listeners adapt their listening approaches to different situations. The primary goal of **deliberative listening** is to understand and retain the information in the speaker's message. With this type of listening, you ask questions to clarify the material but don't argue or judge. Try to overlook the speaker's style and any limitations in the presentation; just focus on the information.

Deliberative listening: Listening with the primary goal of understanding and retaining the information in the speaker's message.

The goal of **critical listening** is to understand and evaluate the meaning of the speaker's message on several levels: the logic of the argument, the strength of the evidence, the validity of the conclusions, the implications of the message for you and your organization, the speaker's intentions and motives,

Critical listening: Listening with the intent to understand and evaluate the message on several levels, including logic, evidence, validity of conclusions, implications of the conclusion, and the speaker's motivations and intentions.

and the omission of any important or relevant points. Be on the lookout for bias that might color the way the information is presented, and be careful to separate opinions from facts. (Note that "critical listening" does not mean you are listening with the intent to criticize. Your purpose is to understand the full meaning and implications of the speaker's message.)

Empathetic listening: Listening to understand the speaker's feelings, wants, and needs so you can appreciate his or her point of view.

The goal of **empathic listening** is to understand the speaker's feelings, needs, and wants so that you can appreciate his or her point of view, regardless of whether you share that perspective. By listening in an empathic way, you help the individual release emotions that can prevent a calm, clear-headed approach to the subject. Don't jump in with advice unless the person asks for it, and don't judge the speaker's feelings. Instead, let the person know that you appreciate his or her feelings and understand the situation. After you establish that connection, you can then help the speaker search for a solution.

Active listening: Listening with a goal of fully understanding the message and encouraging the speaker. Active listening may involve asking questions, providing positive body language, and offering supportive feedback.

No matter what mode they are using at any given time, effective listeners try to engage in **active listening**, making a conscious effort to turn off their own filters and biases to truly hear and understand what the other party is saying. They ask questions or summarize the speaker's message to verify key points and encourage the speaker through positive body language and supportive feedback.

The Listening Process

Listening is a far more complex process than most people think—and most of us aren't very good at it. People typically listen at no better than a 25 percent efficiency rate, remember roughly half of what's said during a 10-minute conversation, and forget half of that within 48 hours. Furthermore, when questioned about material they've just heard, they are likely to get the facts mixed up.

Why is such a seemingly simple activity so difficult? The reason is that listening is not a simple process, by any means. Listening follows the same sequence as the basic communication process model you explored in Chapter 1 (page 12), with the added difficulty that it happens in real time. To listen effectively, you need to successfully complete five steps:

1. **Receiving.** Physically hear the message and recognize it as incoming information.
2. **Decoding.** Assign meaning to sounds, according to your own values, beliefs, ideas, expectations, roles, needs, and personal history.
3. **Remembering.** Store the information for future processing.
4. **Evaluating.** Analyze the quality of the information.
5. **Responding.** React based on the situation and the nature of the information.

If any one of these steps breaks down, the listening process becomes less effective—or fails entirely. As both a sender and a receiver, you can reduce the failure rate by recognizing and overcoming a variety of physical and mental barriers to effective listening.

Barriers to Effective Listening

Good listeners look for ways to overcome the many potential barriers to successful listening (see Table 2.2). Some factors may be beyond your control, such as conference room acoustics or poor phone reception. There are other factors you *can* control. Don't interrupt a speaker. Don't multitask when someone is talking to you. Don't create distractions that make it difficult for others to pay attention. And don't think that you're not interrupting just because you're not talking. Such actions as sighing or checking your watch can interrupt a speaker and lead to a communication breakdown.

Table 2.2 Effective Listening Behaviors

Effective Listeners	Ineffective Listeners
Listen actively	Listen passively
Take careful and complete notes, when applicable.	Take no notes or ineffective notes
Make frequent eye contact with the speaker (depends on culture to some extent)	Make little or no eye contact—or inappropriate eye contact
Stay focused on the speaker and the content	Allow their minds to wander, are easily distracted, work on unrelated tasks
Mentally paraphrase key points to maintain attention level and ensure comprehension	Fail to paraphrase
Adjust listening style to the situation	Listen with the same style, regardless of the situation
Give the speaker nonverbal cues (such as nodding to show agreement or raising eye-brows to show surprise or skepticism)	Fail to give the speaker nonverbal feedback
Save questions or points of disagreement until an appropriate time	Interrupt whenever they disagree or don't understand
Overlook stylistic differences and focus on the speaker's message	Are distracted by or unduly influenced by stylistic differences; are judgmental
Make distinctions between main points and supporting details	Unable to distinguish main points from details
Look for opportunities to learn	Assume they already know everything that's important to know

Selective listening is one of the most common barriers to effective listening. If your mind wanders, you may stay tuned out until you hear a word or phrase that gets your attention once more. But by that time, you may be unable to recall what the speaker actually said; instead, you're likely to remember what you think the speaker probably said.

Selective listening: Listening in which your mind wanders and you do not pay careful attention to the message.

One reason listeners' minds tend to wander is that people think faster than they speak. Most people speak at 120 to 150 words per minute, while listeners can process audio information at 500 words per minute or more. That leaves your brain with a lot of free time and the capacity to find a thousand other things to think about. Make a conscious effort to focus on the speaker, and use the extra mental energy to analyze and paraphrase what you hear or to take relevant notes.

Selective perception: Hearing a message incompletely by molding it to fit your own conceptual framework.

Defensive listening: Protecting your ego while listening by tuning out anything that doesn't confirm your belief or view of yourself.

Selective perception leads listeners to mold messages to fit the way they see the world. Listeners sometimes make up their minds before they fully hear a speaker's message. Others engage in **defensive listening**—protecting their egos by refusing to hear anything that doesn't fit their beliefs or their view of themselves. These listening behaviors can be especially hard to counteract because the listener doesn't realize what they're doing.

Even when your intentions are good, you can still misinterpret an incoming message if you and the speaker don't share enough language or experience. When listening to a speaker whose language, style, or life experience is different from yours, try to paraphrase that person's ideas. Give the speaker a chance to confirm what you think you heard or to correct any misinterpretation.

Improving Your Nonverbal Communication Skills

Nonverbal communication: The process of sending and receiving information in ways other than written or spoken language.

Nonverbal communication is the process of sending and receiving information, both intentionally and unintentionally, without using written or spoken language. Nonverbal signals play a vital role in communication because they can strengthen a verbal message (when the nonverbal signals match the spoken words), weaken a verbal message (when nonverbal signals don't match the words), or replace words entirely. For example, you might say to a client that a project is coming along nicely, while your forced smile and nervous glances will send an entirely different message.

You've been tuned in to nonverbal communication since your first contact with other human beings. Paying special attention to nonverbal signals in the workplace will go a long way toward enhancing your ability to communicate. As you work with a diverse range of people in the global marketplace, you'll also need to grasp the different meanings of common gestures, expressions, and other signals in various cultures. The following six types of signals are particularly important.

- **Facial expressions.** Your face expresses the majority of your emotions; it reveals both the type and the intensity of your feelings. Your eyes indicate attention and interest, influence others, and establishing dominance. Like other nonverbal expressions, facial signals can vary widely from culture to culture. For instance, maintaining eye contact is usually a sign of sincerity and openness in the United States, but it can be viewed as rude in Japan.

Figure 2.14
Interpreting Facial Expressions
What emotion does this person's facial expression suggest?

- **Gestures and postures.** Many gestures—a wave of the hand, for example—have a specific and intentional meaning. Other types of body movement are often unintentional and express more general messages. Slouching, leaning forward, fidgeting, and walking briskly are all unconscious signals that can reveal whether you feel confident or nervous, friendly or hostile, powerful or passive.

Figure 2.15
Interpreting Gestures
What does it usually mean when a person places a hand on his or her forehead like this?

- **Vocal characteristics.** Voice carries both intentional and unintentional messages. A speaker can intentionally control pitch, pace, and stress to convey a specific message. For instance, compare "What are you *doing*?" and "What are *you* doing?" Unintentional vocal characteristics can convey happiness, surprise, fear, and other emotions. For example, people often speak more quickly and at a higher pitch when they are nervous or afraid.
- **Personal appearance.** Some issues are beyond our control. But grooming, clothing, accessories, piercings, tattoos, hairstyle—you can control all of these. Many employers have guidelines concerning attire, body art, and other issues. Make sure you understand and follow them.
- **Touch.** Touch is an important way to convey warmth, comfort, and reassurance—as well as control. Touch is so powerful, in fact, that cultural customs establish who can touch whom and how in various circumstances. In the United States and Great Britain, for instance, people usually touch less frequently than people in France or Costa Rica do. Even within a culture's norms, individual attitudes toward touch vary widely. A manager might be comfortable using hugs to express support or congratulations, but his or her subordinates could interpret those hugs as a show of dominance or sexual interest. Touch is a complex subject. The best advice: when in doubt, don't touch.
- **Time and space.** Like touch, time and space can be used to assert authority, imply intimacy, and send other nonverbal messages. For instance, some people try to demonstrate their own importance or disregard for others by making people wait; others show respect by being on time. Similarly, taking care not to stand too close when talking is a way to show respect for others. Keep in mind that expectations regarding time and space vary by culture.

When you listen to others, be sure to pay attention to nonverbal clues. Do signals support the spoken words or contradict them? Is the speaker intentionally using nonverbal signals to send you a message that he or she can't put into words? Be observant, but don't assume that you can "read someone like a book." Nonverbal signals are powerful, but they aren't infallible. For example, when someone avoids eye contact and covers his face, it's not a reliable clue that he is lying. These behaviors may be influenced by culture or might just be ways of coping with a stressful situations.

Think carefully about the entire package of nonverbal signals you send to those around you. Are you talking like a serious business professional but dressing like you belong in a dance club or a basketball court? If your goal is to make a good impression, adopt the style of the people you want to impress. Whether or not you think it is fair to be judged on superficial matters, the truth is that you are judged this way. Don't let careless choices or disrespectful habits undermine all the great work you do on the job.

Developing Business Etiquette

You may have noticed a common thread running through the topics of successful teamwork, productive meetings, effective listening, and nonverbal communication. They all depend on mutual respect and consideration. Nobody wants to work with someone who is rude to colleagues or an embarrassment to the company. Moreover, shabby treatment of others can be a huge drain on morale and productivity. Poor etiquette can drive away customers, investors, and other critical audiences—and it can limit your career potential.

Figure 2.16
Etiquette Skills
Using expected business etiquette practices can help make a positive impression in the workplace.

This section addresses some key etiquette points to remember when you're in the workplace, out in public, and online. You don't have to memorize a long list of rules. You can get by in most every situation by remembering to be aware of your effect on others, treat everyone with respect, and keep in mind that the impressions you leave behind have a lasting effect on you and your company.

Etiquette in the Workplace

Workplace etiquette includes a variety of behaviors, habits, and aspects of nonverbal communication. Your personal appearance in the workplace sends a strong signal to managers, colleagues, and customers. Pay attention to the style of dress where you work and adjust your style to match. Observe others and don't be afraid to ask for advice. It's not a question of mindlessly conforming or surrendering your individuality; it's a question of showing respect for an organizational culture that is bigger than you. If you're not sure, dress modestly and simply—earn a reputation for what you do, not for what you wear.

Figure 2.17 **Showing Respect for Organizational Culture**
Being aware of expectations for personal appearance in a business setting is not only a sign of respect, but it will also keep you from making career-limiting mistakes.

Grooming is as important as attire. Pay close attention to cleanliness and avoid using products with powerful scents, such as perfumed soaps, colognes, shampoos, and after-shave lotions. Many people are bothered by these products, and some are allergic to them.

Etiquette on the Phone

Text-based tools have taken over many exchanges that used to take place over the phone, but phone skills are still essential. Because phone calls lack the visual richness of face-to-face conversations, you have to rely on your attitude and tone of voice to convey confidence and professionalism. Here are some important tips for using phones at work:

- **Be conscious of how your voice sounds.** Don't speak in a monotone; vary your pitch and inflections so people know you're interested. Slow down with people whose native language isn't the same as yours.
- **Be courteous when you call someone.** Identify yourself and your organization, briefly describe why you're calling, and verify that you've called at a good time. Minimize the noise level in your environment as much as possible. For important or complicated conversations, plan what you want to say before calling.

- **Convey a positive, professional attitude when you answer the phone.** Answer promptly in a welcoming tone. Identify yourself and your company, or follow your company's instructions for what to say when you answer. Ask, "How may I help you?" and if you know the caller's name, use it. If you can't answer the caller's questions, forward the call to a colleague who can, or suggest another way for the caller to find an answer. If you forward a call, put the caller on hold and call the next person to verify that he or she is available.
- **End calls with courtesy and clarity.** Double-check key information such as dates or meeting times, and close in a friendly, positive manner.
- **Use your own voicemail features to help callers.** When you will be away or unable to answer the phone for an extended period, record a temporary greeting that tells callers when you will respond. If you don't check your messages regularly or at all, disable your voicemail so callers won't be left waiting to hear from you and wondering if you received their messages. Letting voicemail messages pile up for days or weeks without answering them is extremely thoughtless.
- **Be considerate when leaving voicemail messages.** Retrieving voicemail messages can be a chore, so be thoughtful about leaving them. Unless voicemail is the best or only choice, consider leaving a message via text messaging or email. If you do leave a voicemail message, make it brief. Leave your name, number (don't assume the recipient has caller ID), reason for calling, and times you can be reached. State your name and telephone number slowly so the other person can easily write them down.

Business Etiquette in Social Settings

From business lunches to industry conferences, you may be asked to represent your company when you're out in public. Make sure your appearance and actions are appropriate to the situation. Get to know the customs of the culture when you meet new people. For example, in North America, a firm handshake is expected when two people meet. In Japan, a respectful bow is more appropriate. If you do shake hands, be aware that the passive "dead fish" handshake creates an extremely negative impression with most people. If you are physically able, always stand up to someone's hand.

When you introduce yourself, include a brief description of your role in the company. When introducing people to one another, speak their first and last names. Then, try to offer some information (perhaps a shared professional interest) to help the two people ease into a conversation. Generally speaking, the lower-ranking person is introduced *to* the senior-ranking person, without regard to gender.

Business is often conducted over meals, and knowing the basics of dining etiquette will make you more effective and comfortable in these situations. Start by choosing foods that are easy to eat. Avoid alcoholic beverages in most instances. Leave business documents under your chair until entrée plates have been removed; the business aspect of the meal doesn't usually begin until then.

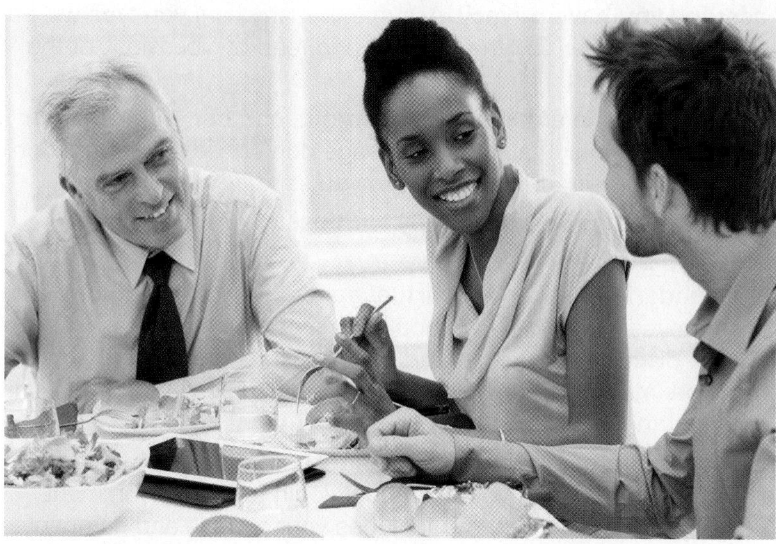

Figure 2.18
Business Etiquette in Social Settings
Some etiquette rules change when business associates meet in social situations, such as at meals or parties. Remember that even though the atmosphere may seem more informal, you are still responsible for representing your company professionally.

Remember that business meals are a forum for business, period. Don't discuss politics, religion, or any other topic that's likely to stir up emotions. Don't complain about work, and don't ask deeply personal questions. Avoid profanity, and be careful with humor—a joke that entertains some people could easily offend others.

Business Etiquette Online

Electronic media seem to be a breeding ground for poor etiquette. Learn the basics of professional online behavior to avoid mistakes that could hurt your company or your career. Here are some guidelines to follow whenever you represent your company on electronic media.

- **Avoid personal attacks.** The anonymous and instantaneous nature of online communication can cause even level-headed people to lose their tempers and go after others.
- **Stay focused on the original topic.** If you want to change the subject of an online conversation, start with a new message or thread.
- **Don't present opinions as facts; support facts with evidence.** This guideline applies to all communication, but online venues seem to tempt people to present their beliefs and opinions as unassailable truths.
- **Follow basic expectations of spelling, punctuation, and capitalization.** Sending careless, acronym-filled messages that look like you're texting your high school buddies makes you look like an amateur.
- **Use virus protection and keep it up to date.** Sending or posting a file that contains a computer virus puts others at risk.
- **Ask if this is a good time for an IM chat.** Don't assume that just because a person shows as "available" that he or she can chat at this moment.
- **Watch your language and keep your emotions under control.** A single indiscretion could haunt you forever.
- **Avoid multitasking while using IM or other tools.** You might think you're saving time by doing a dozen things at once, but you're probably making the other person wait while you bounce back and forth between tasks.

- **Never assume you have privacy.** Assume that anything you type will be stored forever, forwarded to other people, and read by your boss or the company's security staff.
- **Don't use "reply all" in email unless everyone can benefit from your reply.** If some recipients of an email message don't need the information in your reply, remove their addresses before you send.
- **Don't waste others' time with sloppy, confusing, or incomplete messages.** Doing so is disrespectful.
- **Respect boundaries of time and virtual space.** For instance, don't start using an employee's personal Facebook page for business messages unless you've discussed it beforehand. Don't assume people are available to discuss work matters around the clock, even if you do find them online in the middle of the night.
- **Be careful of online commenting mechanisms.** For example, many blogs and websites now use your Facebook login to let you comment on articles. If your Facebook profile includes your job title and company name, those could show up along with your comment.
- **Use systems responsibly.** Do not exploit limitations or security weaknesses that you may find. Do not use any online medium in ways that are illegal, unethical, or annoying or hurtful to others.

Business Etiquette and Mobile Devices

Like every other aspect of communication, your mobile device habits say a lot about how much respect you have for the people around you. If you're on your mobile in an open office or public place, keep your voice—and your ring tone volume—as low as possible. Move away from others to talk, avoid personal calls during work hours, and don't invade someone's privacy by using your phone's camera without permission. Don't take or make calls in restrooms or other inappropriate places, and don't text during a conversation, a meeting, or a meal. Mobile device use is a sensitive issue, especially with co-workers, managers, and customers who are older than you. Make sure your choices reflect positively on you and your company.

Figure 2.19
Digital Etiquette
When using a mobile device, remember that you are still representing your company. Although the medium lends itself to more informal communication, it is still important to express yourself professionally.

Virtual assistants, such as the Siri voice recognition system in Apple iPhones, raise another etiquette dilemma. These systems may be convenient for users, but they can create distractions and annoyances for other people. As with other public behaviors, think about the effect you have on others before using these technologies.

Expectations and policies regarding mobile device use vary widely from company to company. Venture capitalist Ben Horowitz fines his employees if they even look at a mobile device while an entrepreneur is making a business plan pitch. Make sure you understand the situation in your workplace.

Elements of Digital Citizenship

Because so much communication occurs electronically in business today, an effective business communicator must also be a digital citizen—responsible member of the online community. **Digital citizenship** includes online etiquette, but is more than that; it is being a knowledgeable, responsible adult who exercises good judgment online. This can include expressing yourself appropriately, protecting yourself and others from online threats to security and privacy, conducting online sales safely and ethically, and understanding the laws, rights, and responsibilities of the online community.

Digital citizen: A responsible member of the online community, participating in the community in knowledgeable, appropriate, and ethical ways.

According to digitalcitizenship.net, the nine elements of digital citizenship are:

1. **Digital access.** To be a citizen in the digital world, you must have access to it.
2. **Digital commerce.** A digital citizen understands the benefits and dangers of buying, selling, and and using credit cards online.
3. **Digital communication.** A digital citizen can identify and use the most appropriate online communication medium for a given message.
4. **Digital literacy.** A digital citizen is able to use various digital devices, such as computers, smartphones, peripheral devices like printers and scanners, and computer-enabled appliances.
5. **Digital etiquette.** A digital citizen knows and follows expectations regarding online etiquette, and understands that certain mediums require more formality than others.
6. **Digital law.** A responsible digital citizen understands what activities are illegal online and avoids participating in them.
7. **Digital rights and responsibilities.** A digital citizen understands his or her online rights, such as free speech and privacy, and uses those rights responsibly.
8. **Digital health.** A digital citizen knows and takes steps to avoid of the physical stresses that digital devices place on the body—including strain, headaches, and repetitive stress injuries.
9. **Digital security.** A digital citizen guards his personal safety online by with measures including virus protection, regular data backups, and strong passwords.

Figure 2.20
Digital Citizenship
Why is being a responsible member of the online community so important?

So far, we've focused mostly on digital access, communication, and etiquette. In upcoming chapters, you'll explore the responsible, professional use of digital communication channels including emails, texts, instant messages, blogs, and podcasts.

Chapter Summary

Communicating Effectively in Teams

The benefits of successful teamwork include improved productivity, creativity, and employee involvement. Additional benefits include increased information and knowledge, greater diversity of views, and increased acceptance of new solutions and ideas. Potential challenges of working in teams include groupthink (the tendency to let peer pressure overcome one's better judgment), the pursuit of hidden agendas, and the cost—in money and time—of planning and conducting team activities. The most effective teams have a clear objective, a shared sense of purpose, full engagement from all team members, procedures for reaching decisions by consensus, the right mix of creative and technical talents for the tasks at hand, and the ability to communicate well.

A team leader takes on additional responsibilities for the team's success beyond being a regular member. An effective team leader encourages participation, builds consensus, assigns tasks, holds members accountable, and communicates on the team's behalf. A good team leader exhibits confidence, attentiveness, fairness, unselfishness, professionalism, and tact.

Solving Problems and Thinking Critically

A problem is a difficulty that you must resolve before you can make progress. Any barrier or obstacle between you and a goal is a problem. You can solve a problem either individually or as part of a collaborative team. Use this six-step process to find a solution: 1) identify the problem; 2) consider all possible solutions; 3) identify the consequences of each solution; 4) select the best solution; 5) make and implement a plan of action; and 6) evaluate the solution, process, and outcome. Employ critical thinking to determine the best solution, evaluating the situation both objectively and subjectively, and being honest, rational, and open-minded.

Collaborating on Communication Efforts

To succeed with collaborative writing, 1) select team members carefully to balance talents and viewpoints; 2) agree on project goals; 3) make sure team members have time to get to know one another; 4) make sure that everyone clearly understands individual responsibilities, processes, and tools; 5) generally, avoid writing as a group (assign the writing phase to one person, or assign separate sections to individual writers and have one person edit them all); 6) make sure tools and techniques are compatible; and 7) check in with everyone periodically.

Collaboration technologies include reviewing and commenting features in document preparation software, wikis, content management systems, groupware, and shared workspaces.

When you are asked to give feedback on someone's writing, focus on how the writing can be improved. Avoid personal attacks and give the person clear and specific advice.

Making Meetings Productive

Productive meetings are an essential business activity. Ineffective meetings waste time and money. To make meetings more productive, prepare carefully, conduct meetings efficiently, and use meeting technologies wisely. Make sure every meeting is necessary, carefully planned, includes only the necessary participants, and follows a clear agenda.

A variety of meeting technologies are available to help teams and other groups communicate more successfully. Virtual meetings use these technologies to connect people in different locations. The tools range from simple instant messaging and teleconferencing to videoconferencing and web-based online collaboration systems.

Improving Your Listening Skills

The listening process involves five steps: receiving, decoding, remembering, evaluating, and responding. Barriers can disrupt any stage of the process. Good listeners practice active listening, avoid disrupting the speaker or other people, work to see past superficial differences and distractions, and keep selective perception from filtering out important information.

Improving Your Nonverbal Communication Skills

Nonverbal signals play a vital role in communication. They can strengthen a verbal message (when the nonverbal signals match the spoken words), weaken a verbal message (when nonverbal signals don't match the words), or replace words entirely. The six major categories of nonverbal expression are facial expressions, gestures and postures, vocal characteristics, personal appearance, touch, and use of time and personal space.

Developing Business Etiquette

Etiquette is an essential business skill because the impressions you make on others will be major contributors to your career success. Poor etiquette can hinder team efforts, drain morale and productivity, drive away customers and investors, and limit your career potential. Good business etiquette is key in the workplace, in social settings in which you represent your company, in online venues, and while using mobile devices.

Elements of Digital Citizenship

Being a digital citizen involves nine elements of behavior and competency: digital access, digital commerce, digital communication, digital literacy, digital etiquette, digital law, digital rights and responsibilities, digital health, and digital security. To be an effective business communicator, a person should be a full digital citizen, with particular emphasis on skills and abilities in the areas of digital communication and digital etiquette.

Test Your Knowledge

1. What are six characteristics of effective teams?
2. List three ways that teams can use technology to collaborate.
3. How does an agenda help make a meeting more successful?
4. How is selective listening a barrier to listening effectively?
5. What are the six main categories of nonverbal signals?
6. How do your mobile phone habits demonstrate your sensitivity to business etiquette?
7. Think of a topic that would best lend itself to each form of group discussion:
   Moderated discussion
   Presentation followed by discussion
   Scenario or Case Study discussion

Apply Your Knowledge

1. You are the manager for a manufacturer of high-performance motorcycles, and things are not going well at the moment. The design engineers and marketing strategists keep arguing about which should be a higher priority, performance or aesthetics. The accountants say both groups are driving the cost of the new model through the roof by adding too many new features. Everyone has valid points to make, but the team is getting bogged down in conflict. In order to meet the company's goals, identify the type of professional group or team you would form and identify the purpose of the professional group or team. For bonus points, explain how you would move the team through the processes of Forming, Storming, Norming, and Performing.
2. You have decided to run for Class President. What qualities do you think your classmates look for in a leader? Design a campaign strategy that explains to your classmates why you would be effective in that position.
3. Whenever your coworker asks for feedback, she gets angry at anyone who offers criticism, so people tend to agree with everything she says. You want to talk to her about it, but what should you say? List some of the points you want to make when you discuss this issue with your colleague.
4. Suppose that you are one of five students picked to participate in a student exchange weekend. It means traveling to a different state, staying with a host family, and participating in community activities. Your parents will approve, but you will need to come up with $75 to pay for the trip. You have $150 in savings, but you'd planned to spend that money on a new outfit for a school dance. Use critical thinking skills to decide whether you will spend $75 on the school trip or not, and explain how you reached your decision.
5. You are an editor at a book publishing company. Your team needs to share word processing documents and photos as you collaboratively edit content and choose photos that will abecome chapters of the book. Describe the qualities of the ideal collaboration software system that would facilitate this sharing.
6. Several members of your sales team are protesting the company's "business casual" dress code. They claim that dressing nicely makes them feel awkward and overly formal in front of customers. You have to admit that most of the company's customers dress like they've just walked in from a picnic or a bike ride, but that doesn't change the fact that you want your company to be seen as conscientious and professional. How will you explain the policy to these employees in a way that will help them understand and accept it?
7. Your company provides several mobile productivity apps that let employees access the company network while working from home, waiting for trains, and during other times when they are away from their desks. The apps work well, but some of your employees have begun using them to work on other things during meetings and presentations. You explained to several employees that this behavior can be considered rude to speakers and fellow team members, but your employees protested that they have mountain of work to do and meetings are sometimes a waste of time. Explain how you will respond to this dilemma.

Activities

1. **Working in Teams** In a team assigned by your instructor, prepare a 10-minute presentation on the potential advantages of using social media for business communication. When the presentation is ready, discuss how effective the team was in 1) having a clear objective and a shared sense of purpose; 2) communicating openly and honestly; 3) reaching decisions by consensus; 4) thinking creatively; and 5) knowing how to resolve conflict. Be prepared to discuss your findings with the rest of the class.

2. **Collaborating on Online Writing Projects** In this project, you will conduct research on your own and then merge your results with those of the rest of your team. Starting with your own social media accounts, search online for the subject of workplace safety. Compile at least five general safety tips that apply to any office setting, and then meet with your team to select the five best tips from all those the team has collected. Collaborate on a blog post that lists the team's top five tips.

3. **Giving and Receiving Feedback** Create a set of directions that an out-of-town visitor could use to reach a specific point on your school's campus, such as a gym or cafeteria. Then exchange directions with a partner and provide constructive feedback on their work. Switch papers again and talk about the feedback you received, how it made you feel, and whether you understood what your partner wanted you to do. Be prepared to share with the class what you learned about giving and receiving constructive feedback.

4. **Planning Meetings** Below are your project leader's notes for the quarterly budget meeting. Prepare an agenda by putting these items into a logical order and rewriting them, where necessary, to give phrases a more consistent sound. Present your agenda in a presentation slide.

    - Budget Committee meeting to be held on December 12 of the current year, at 9:30 a.m.
    - I will call the Meeting to order.
    - Site director's report: A closer look at cost overruns on Greentree site.
    - The group will review and approve the minutes from last quarter's meeting.
    - I will ask the finance director to report on actual vs. projected quarterly revenues and expenses.
    - I will distribute copies of the overall divisional budget and announce the date of the next budget meeting.
    - Discussion: How can we do a better job of anticipating and preventing cost overruns?
    - Meeting will take place in Conference Room 3.
    - What additional budget issues must be considered during this quarter?

5. **Participating in Meetings** With a classmate, attend a local community or campus meeting where you can observe group discussion. Take notes individually during the meeting and then work together to answer these questions. Email your answers to your instructor.

    - How effective was the meeting's leader? Consider whether he or she clearly stated and engaged members in meaningful discussion.
    - How well did the individual participants listen? How could you tell?
    - Compare the notes you took during the meeting with those of your classmate. What differences do you notice? How do you account for these differences?

6. **Leading Meetings** Every month, each employee in your department is expected to give a brief oral presentation on the status of his or her ongoing projects. Since last month, your department has recently hired an employee with a severe speech impediment that prevents people from understanding most of what he has to say. As assistant department manager, how will you resolve this dilemma? Explain your plan in an email message to your instructor.

7. **Listening Actively** For the next several days, take notes on your listening performance during at least a half-dozen situations in class, with friends or family, and at work, if applicable. Refer to the traits of effective listeners in Table 2.2, and rate yourself using always, frequently, occasionally, or never on positive listening habits. In a report no longer than one page, summarize your analysis and identify specific areas in which you can improve your listening skills.

8. **Listening to Empathize** Think back over conversations you have had with friends, family members, coworkers, or classmates in the past week. Select a conversation in which the other person wanted to talk about something that was troubling him or her—perhaps a bad situation at work, a scary exam on the horizon, difficulties with a teacher, or a health problem. Were you a good empathic listener? For example, did you find yourself being critical when the person really just needed someone to listen? Did you let the person know, by your words or actions, that you cared about his or her dilemma, even if you were not able to help in any other way? Analyze your listening performance in a brief email to your instructor. Be sure not to disclose any private information; you can change the names of the people involved or the circumstances as needed to maintain privacy.

9. **Analyzing Nonverbal Signals** Select a piece of mail that you received at work or at home. Analyze its appearance. What does the way the piece looks say about its content? About the person or company that sent it? Does the visual presentation enhance or distract from the written message? How? Summarize your findings in a post on your class blog or in an email message to your instructor.

10. **Analyzing Nonverbal Signals** Explain what the following gestures or postures could mean when they are exhibited by someone during a conversation. How do you know? How do such signals influence your interpretation of what the person says? Summarize your findings in a post on your class blog or in an email message to your instructor.

    a. Shifting one's body continuously while seated

    b. Twirling and playing with one's hair

    c. Sitting in a sprawled position

    d. Rolling one's eyes

    e. Extending a weak handshake

11. **Using Good Telephone Etiquette** Late on a Friday afternoon, you learn that the facilities department is going to move you—your computer, your desk, and all your files—to another office first thing Monday morning. You have an important client meeting scheduled in your office for Monday afternoon, and you need to finalize some contract details on Monday morning. You simply can't lose access to your office at that point, and you're more than a little annoyed that your boss didn't ask you before approving the move. He has already left for the day, but you know he usually checks his voicemail over the weekend. You decide to leave a voicemail message, asking him to cancel the move or at least call you at home as soon as possible. Plan your message. As directed by your instructor, submit either a written script of the message or a recording of the actual message.

12. **Applying Etiquette in the Workplace** As the regional manager of an international accounting firm, you place high priority on professional etiquette. It shows your clients you respect them, and it makes your staff confident that they can be professional in any situation. Earlier today, however, you took four new employees to lunch with an important client and it was a disaster. One of the new employees made three calls on his mobile phone during lunch without leaving the table. Another made a political joke that didn't go over well. And the fourth came straight from the gym without showering or changing clothes. You've called the client to apologize, and now you need to coach these employees on proper business etiquette. Draft a brief memo explaining why etiquette is so important to the company's success—and to their individual careers.
13. **Increasing Digital Citizenship** An elderly uncle just got his first computer, and has been on the Internet, all day, every day. Your family is concerned. Your uncle had used his credit card to buy things online without an awareness of the site's reputation and safety, and he has been playing poker for money at a site that may not be legal. He is also developing some neck and shoulder pain from sitting with his laptop for hours at a time. In which aspects of digital citizenship does he need education? What could you say to help him without wounding his pride? Choose an appropriate digital or non-digital medium, and create an outline of the topics you will cover.
14. **Providing Writing Feedback** Create the message that you planned in practice activity 13. Trade work with classmates and offer feedback: Does the message offer help in the needed areas? Is the tone of the message appropriate? Is it likely to be effective in changing your uncle's behavior?

Expand Your Skills

1. **Analyzing Celebrity Use of Social Media.** Celebrities can learn from successful businesses when it comes to managing their careers, but businesses can learn from successful celebrities, too—particularly when it comes to building communities online using social media.

   Your Task: Locate three celebrities who have a sizable fan bases on Facebook and analyze how they use the social network. Using whatever medium your instructor requests, write a one-page analysis of the lessons, positive or negative, that a business could learn from these celebrities. Be sure to cite specific elements from the Facebook pages you've chosen, and if you think any of the celebrities have made mistakes in their use of Facebook, describe those as well.

2. **Identifying Professional Development Opportunities.** Professional development need not be costly or difficult, and it is never too early to get started building your set of professional skills.

   Your task: Find several courses you could take locally or online for little or no expense that would help you develop professional business communication skills. For example, your local community college may offer continuing education courses that anyone may take, or an online school may offer free or low-cost courses. If you don't know where to start, check out Open Yale (http://oyc.yale.edu), where you can take courses for free online from Yale University professors.

CHAPTER

3

Planning Business Messages

After studying this chapter, you will be able to:

- List the three steps of the business message writing process.
- Explain what it means to analyze the situation when planning a message.
- Describe techniques for gathering information for simple messages and identify three attributes of quality information.
- Identify six basic combinations of media and channels and highlight the unique challenges of communication on mobile devices.
- Explain why good organization is important to both you and your audience and explain how to organize any business message.
- Use electronic technologies to acquire information in a variety of formats to support your message.

Understanding the Three-Step Writing Process

No matter what kind of information you need to convey, your goal is to craft a message that is *effective* (it meets your audience's needs and gets your points across) and *efficient* (it makes the best use of your time and your audience's time). Following a clear and proven three-step process (see Figure 3.1) will help you meet both goals:

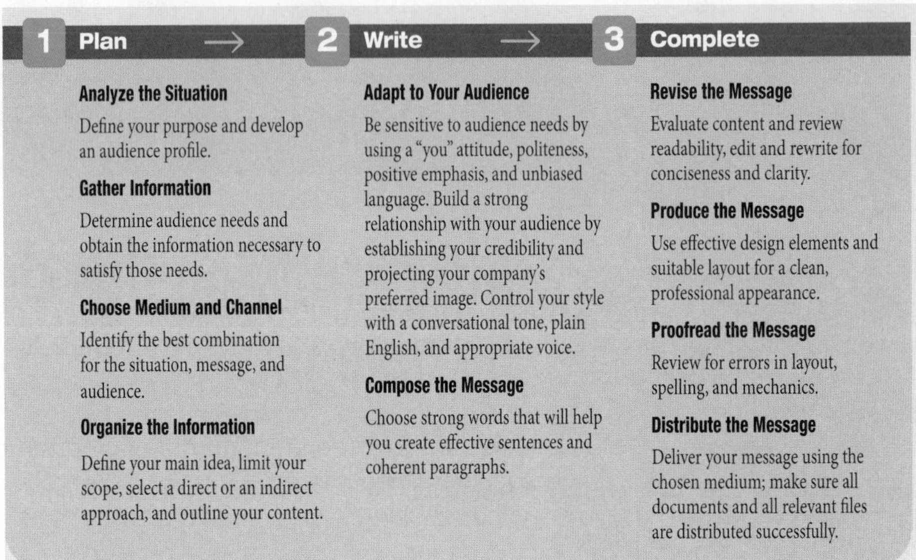

Figure 3.1
The Three-Step Writing Process
This three-step process will help you create more effective messages in any medium. As you get more practice with the process, it will become easier and more automatic.

- **STEP 1: Plan your message.** To plan any message, first analyze the situation by defining your purpose and developing a profile of your audience. When you're sure about what you need to accomplish, gather information that will meet your audience's needs. Next, select the right combination of medium and channels for producing and delivering your message. Then, organize the information by defining your main idea, limiting your scope, selecting a direct or indirect approach, and outlining your content. This chapter details this *planning* phase of the three-step writing process.
- **STEP 2: Write your message.** After you've planned your message, adapt your approach to your audience with sensitivity, relationship skills, and style. Then you're ready to compose your message by choosing strong words, creating effective sentences, and developing coherent paragraphs. In Chapter 4 focuses on the *writing* phase of the three-step process.
- **STEP 3: Complete your message.** After writing your first draft, revise your message to make sure it is clear, concise, and correct. Next, produce your message, giving it an attractive, professional appearance. Proofread the final product to ensure high quality and then distribute your message. Chapter 5 details the *completing* phase of writing business messages.

Throughout this book, you'll see the three steps in this process applied to a wide variety of business messages. The more you use the process, the easier and faster writing will become for you. You'll also get better at allocating your time for each step. As a general rule, for anything beyond short and simple messages, set aside roughly 50 percent of your available time for planning, 25 percent for writing, and 25 percent for completing. Using half your time for planning might seem excessive, but careful planning—particularly for lengthy or difficult writing projects—can save you lots of time and trouble in the long run and lead to better results.

Analyzing the Situation

Every communication effort takes place in a particular situation, meaning you have a specific message to send to a specific audience under a specific set of circumstances. Analyzing the situation gives you the insights necessary to meet your own needs as a communicator while also meeting the information needs of your recipients.

Define Your Purpose

A successful message starts with a clear purpose that connects the sender's needs with the audience's needs. All business messages have a **general purpose**: to inform, to persuade, to collaborate, or to initiate a conversation. This purpose helps define the overall approach you'll need to take, gathering information to organizing your message. Within the scope of that general purpose, each message also has a **specific purpose**, which identifies what you hope to accomplish with your message. The more precisely you can define your specific purpose, the better you'll be able to fine-tune your message to achieve your desired outcome. For example, "Get approval to hire three programmers by June 1 in order to meet our November 15 deadline" is more helpful as a planning device than "Get approval to hire more staff."

General purpose:
The broad goal of a message: to inform, persuade, collaborate, or initiate a conversation.

Specific purpose:
The specific thing you hope to accomplish with a message, such as a certain person agreeing to a request.

After you have defined your specific purpose, make sure it merits the time and effort required for you to prepare and send the message. Ask these four questions:

- Will anything change as a result of your message? Make sure you don't contribute to information overload by sending messages that won't change anything. Complaining about things you have no influence over is a good example of a message that probably shouldn't be sent.
- Is your purpose realistic? Recognizing whether a goal is realistic is an important part of having good business sense. For example, if you request a raise while the company is struggling, you might send the message that you're not tuned into the situation around you.
- Is the time right? People who are busy or distracted when they receive your message are less likely to pay attention to it.
- Is your purpose acceptable to your organization? Your company's business objectives and policies, and even laws that apply to your industry, may dictate whether a given purpose is acceptable.

When you are satisfied that you have a clear and meaningful purpose and that now is a smart time to proceed, your next step is to understand the members of your audience and their needs.

Figure 3.2 Analyzing a Communication Situation
Compare these three communication situations to see how in each case the general purpose, specific purpose, and key questions help determine whether the communication should occur.

Benefits Explanation

- General Purpose: To inform
- Specific Purpose: To inform hourly employees of new health plan options
- Will anything change as a result of your message?
  - Yes, employees will know their options.
- Is your purpose realistic?
  - Yes, employees should be able to understand after hearing the message
- Is the time right?
  - Yes, benefit enrollment is coming up soon.
- Is your purpose acceptable to the organization?
  - Yes, top management has asked employees to be informed

Asking for a Raise

- General Purpose: To persuade
- Specific Purpose: To persuade supervisor to approve a 15% raise for Bob Smith, effective January 1.
- Will anything change as a result of your message?
  - Uncertain
- Is your purpose realistic?
  - Yes, other employees at Bob Smith's level of responsibility are paid more
- Is the time right?
  - Uncertain, need to find out when payroll budget is approved for next year
- Is your purpose acceptable to the organization?
  - Uncertain, need to find out how the company is doing financially

Complaint about Rude Customer

- General Purpose: To initiate a conversation
- Specific Purpose: To relate a story to your supervisor about a customer being rude to you
- Will anything change as a result of your message?
  - No
- Is your purpose realistic?
  - No, a supervisor would not do anything to embarrass or anger a customer
- Is the time right?
  - No, your supervisor is busy with more important things
- Is your purpose acceptable to the organization?
  - No. The organization accepts that customers are sometimes rude.

Develop an Audience Profile

The more you know about your audience members, their needs, their expectations, and their preferences, the more effectively you'll be able to communicate with them.

Audience Analysis

This report will recommend that we close down the on-site exercise facility and subsidize private memberships at local health clubs.

Primary audience: Nicole Pelt, vice president of operations, and her supervisory team.

Size and geographic distribution: Nine managers total. Nicole and five of her staff are here on site; three other supervisors are based in Hong Kong.

Composition: All have experience in operations management, but several are new to the company.

Level of understanding: All will understand the financial considerations, but newer managers may not understand the importance of on-site exercise facilities to employees.

Expectations and preferences: They're expecting a firm recommendation, backed up with well-thought out financial rationale and suggestions for communicating the news to employees.

Probable reaction: Several managers are active users of the on-site facility and won't welcome the suggestion that we shut it down. Non-exercisers generally think it's a luxury the company can't afford. Audience reactions will range from highly positive to highly negative.

Figure 3.3
Using Audience Analysis to Plan a Message
For simple, routine messages, you usually don't need to analyze your audience in depth. For complex messages or messages for indifferent or hostile audiences, take the time to study their information needs and potential reactions to your message.

To develop an audience profile:

- **Identify your primary audience.** For some messages, certain audience members might be more important than others.
- **Determine audience size and geographic distribution.** A message aimed at 10,000 people spread around the globe will likely require a different approach than one aimed at a dozen people down the hall.
- **Determine audience composition.** Look for similarities and differences in culture, language, age, education, organizational rank and status, attitudes, experience, motivations, biases, beliefs, and any other factors that might affect the success of your message.
- **Gauge audience members' level of understanding.** If audience members share your general background, they'll probably understand your material without difficulty. If not, your message may need an element of education.
- **Understand audience expectations and preferences.** For example, will members of your audience expect complete details or just a summary of the main points? For internal communication, the higher up the organization your message goes, the fewer details people want to see.
- **Forecast probable audience reaction.** If you expect a favorable response, you can state conclusions and recommendations up front and offer minimal supporting evidence. If you expect skepticism or resistance, you can introduce conclusions gradually and with more proof.

Gathering Information

When you have a clear picture of your audience, your next step is to assemble the information you will include in your message. For simple messages, you may already have all the information at hand, but for more complex messages, you may need to do considerable research and analysis before you're ready to begin writing. Chapter 10 explores formal techniques for finding, evaluating, and processing information, but you can often use a variety of informal techniques to gather insights and guide your research efforts:

- **Consider the audience's perspective.** Put yourself in the audience's position. What are these people thinking, feeling, or planning? What information do they need in order to move forward? If you are initiating a conversation in a social media context, what information will stimulate discussion in your target communities?
- **Listen to the community.** For almost any subject related to business these days, chances are there is a community of customers, product enthusiasts, or other people linked through social media who engage in online discussions. Find them and listen to what they have to say.
- **Read reports and other company documents.** Annual reports, financial statements, news releases, blogs and microblogs by industry experts, marketing reports, and customer surveys are just a few of the many potential sources. Find out whether your company has a knowledge-management system, a centralized database that collects the experiences and insights of employees throughout the organization.

Figure 3.4
Read Internal Company Documents and Reports
Often the key information you need to understand a communication task more clearly can be found in the company's own internal documents, such as annual reports, internal memos, and white papers.

- **Talk with supervisors, colleagues, or customers.** Fellow workers and customers may have information you need, or they may have good insights into the needs of your target audience.
- **Ask your audience for input.** If you're unsure what audience members need from your message, ask them if at all possible. Admitting you don't know but want to meet their needs will impress an audience more than guessing and getting it wrong.

Uncovering Audience Needs

In many situations, your audience's information needs are readily apparent, such as when a consumer sends an email asking a specific question. In other situations, your audience might be unable to articulate exactly what they want, or you won't have the opportunity to communicate with audience members before you need to create a message.

In some cases, you may need to do some detective work to find out what information is needed. If you're asked to suggest steps a company can take to improve employee morale, for example, you'll need to investigate the underlying reasons for low morale. By including this information in your report—even though it wasn't specifically requested—you demonstrate to your audience that you've thoroughly investigated the problem.

Assess the Quality of Your Information

After you have defined your audience's information needs, your next step is to satisfy those needs completely. In addition to delivering the right quantity of information to your audience, you are responsible for verifying the quality of that information. Ask yourself these three questions:

- **Is the information accurate?** Inaccuracies can cause a host of problems, from embarrassment and lost productivity to serious safety and legal issues. Be sure to review any mathematical or financial calculations. Check all dates and schedules. Examine your own assumptions and conclusions to be certain they are valid.
- **Is the information ethical?** By working hard to ensure the accuracy of the information you gather, you'll also avoid many ethical problems in your messages. However, messages can also be unethical if important information is omitted or obscured.
- **Is the information pertinent?** Some points will be more important to your audience than others. By focusing on the information that concerns your audience the most, you increase your chances of sending an effective message.

Selecting the Best Combination of Media and Channels

With the necessary information in hand, your next decision involves the best combination of media and channels to reach your target audience. As you recall from Chapter 1, the medium is the *form* a message takes and the channel is the *system* used to deliver the message. The distinction between the two isn't always crystal clear, and some people use the terms in different ways, but these definitions are a good way to think about the possibilities for business communication.

Most media can be distributed through more than one channel, so whenever you have a choice, think through your options to select the optimum combination. For example, a brief written message could be distributed as a printed letter or memo, or it could be distributed through a variety of digital channels, from email to blogging to social networking.

Common Media and Channel Combinations

The simplest way to categorize media choices is to divide them into oral (spoken), written, and visual. Each of these media can be delivered through digital and non-digital channels, which creates six basic combinations discussed in the following sections.

Oral Medium, In-Person Channel

The oral medium, in-person combo involves talking with people who are in the same location, whether it's a one-on-one conversation over lunch or a more formal speech or presentation. Being in the same physical space is a key distinction, because it enables the nuances of nonverbal communication more than any other media-channel combo. As Chapter 2 points out, these nonverbal signals can carry as much weight in the conversation as the words being spoken.

By giving people the ability to see, hear, and react to each other, in-person communication encourages people to ask questions, make comments, and work together to reach a consensus or decision. Face-to-face interaction is particularly helpful in complex, emotionally charged situations in which establishing or fostering a business relationship is important. Managers who engage in frequent "walk-arounds," chatting with employees face-to-face, can get input, answer questions, and interpret important business events and trends.

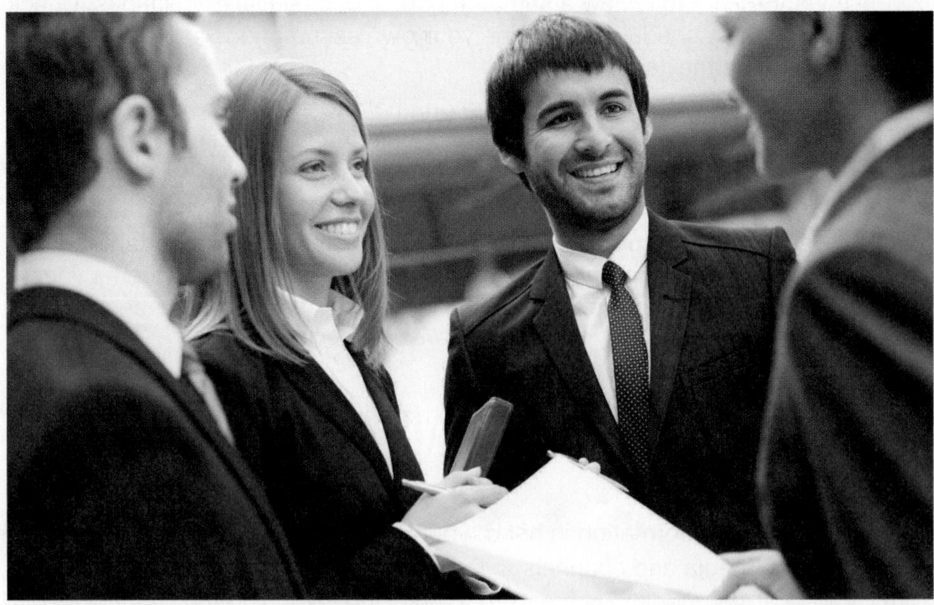

Figure 3.5 Face-to-Face Communication
Talking with people in person provides multiple types of informational cues visual, verbal, and vocal cues as well as immediate feedback.

Oral Medium, Digital Channel

Oral medium via digital channel includes any transmission of voice via electronic means, both live and recorded, including telephone calls, podcasts, and voicemail messages. Live phone conversations offer the give-and-take of in-person conversations and can be the best alternative to talking in person. However, without a video component, they can't provide the nuances of nonverbal communication. Podcasts can be a good way to share lectures, commentary, and other spoken content. You'll learn more about podcasting in Chapter 6.

Figure 3.6
Phone Conversations
Communicating by telephone is immediate and personal, and you can listen for feedback and indirect auditory cues like pauses and tone of voice.

Written Medium, Print Channel

Written, printed documents are the classic format of business communication. **Memos** are brief printed documents traditionally used for the routine, day-to-day exchange of information within an organization. **Letters** are brief written messages sent to customers and other recipients outside the organization. Reports and proposals are usually longer than memos and letters, although both can be created in memo or letter format. These documents come in a variety of lengths, ranging from a few pages to several hundred, and are usually fairly formal in tone. **Reports** are longer, multi-page informational documents, usually containing a substantial amount of technical detail and resource citation. **Newsletters** convey information informally to either internal or external audiences within a company or organization, and typically present less technical information in an attractive, often graphical layout.

Memo:
A brief printed document traditionally used for routine exchange of information within an organization.

Letter:
A brief printed document traditionally sent to customers and other recipients outside the organization.

Report:
A multi-page informational document, usually containing a substantial amount of technical detail and resource citation.

Newsletter:
A document that conveys information informally in an attractive, graphical layout.

While it's still a useful format, printed documents have been replaced by digital alternatives in many instances. However, here are several situations in which you should consider a printed message over electronic alternatives:

- When you want to make a formal impression, such as when presenting a proposal to a client
- When you are legally required to provide information in printed form
- When you want to stand out from the flood of electronic messages
- When you need a permanent, unchangeable, or secure record
- When you can't reach your audience electronically

Written Medium, Digital Channel

Most of your business communication efforts will involve this combination, with everything from 160-character tweets to website content to book-length reports distributed as PDF files. Business uses of written, digital messages evolve as companies look for ways to communicate more effectively. For example, email has been a primary business medium for the past decade or two, but it is being replaced in many cases by a variety of other digital formats.

Visual Medium, Print Channel

Photographs and diagrams can be effective communication tools for conveying emotional content, spatial relationships, technical processes, and other content than can be difficult to describe using words alone. You may occasionally create a visual, printed message as standalone items, but most will be used as supporting material in printed documents.

Visual Medium, Digital Channel

Business messages can really come alive when conveyed by visual media in digital channels. Infographics, interactive diagrams, animation, and digital video have the potential to engage audiences in ways that other formats can't, which is why the use of visual elements in business communication continues to grow.

Traditional business messages rely primarily on text, with occasional support from graphical elements such as charts, graphs, or diagrams to help illustrate points discussed in the text. However, many business communicators are discovering the power of messages in which the visual element is dominant and supported by small amounts of text. For the purposes of this discussion, you can think of visual media as formats in which one or more visual elements play a central role in conveying the message content.

Messages that combine powerful visuals with supporting text can be effective for a number of reasons. Today's audiences are pressed for time and bombarded with messages, so anything that communicates quickly is welcome. Visuals are also effective at describing complex ideas and processes because they can reduce the work required for an audience to identify the parts and relationships that make up the whole. Also, in a multilingual business world, diagrams, symbols, and other images can lower communication barriers by requiring less language processing. Finally, visual images can be easier to remember than purely textual descriptions or explanations.

Table 3.1 Medium-Channel Combinations: Advantages and Disadvantages

Medium, Channel	Advantages	Disadvantages
Oral, In-Person	• Provide opportunity for immediate feedback • Parties can resolve misunderstandings and negotiate meaning quickly • Involve rich nonverbal cues (both physical gesture and vocal inflection) • Allow you to express the emotion behind your message	• Restrict participation to those physically present • Unless recorded, provide no permanent, verifiable record of the communication • Live interaction reduces communicator's control over the message
Oral, Digital	• Live phone or online conversations can provide opportunity for immediate feedback • Not restricted to participants in the same location • Recorded messages (e.g., podcasts) allow time-shifted consumption	• Lack nonverbal cues other than voice inflections • Recorded messages can be tedious to listen to if not audience focused
Written, Printed	• Allow writers to plan and control their messages • Can reach geographically dispersed audiences • Offer a permanent, verifiable record • Minimize the distortion that can accompany oral messages • Can be used to avoid immediate interactions • Deemphasize emotional components • Give recipients time to process messages before responding (compared to oral communication)	• Offer limited opportunities for timely feedback • Lack the rich nonverbal cues provided by oral media • Often take more time and more resources to create and distribute • Can require special skills in preparation and production
Written, Digital	Generally, all the advantages of written printed documents plus: • Messages can be delivered quickly • Can reach geographically dispersed audiences • Flexibility of multiple formats and channels, from microblogs to wikis • Flexibility to structure messages in creative ways, such as writing a headline on Twitter and linking to the full message on a blog • Ability to link to related and more in-depth information • Can increase accessibility and openness in an organization through broader sharing • Enable audience interaction through social media features • Ease of integrating with other media types, such as embedded videos or photos	• Can be limited in terms of reach and capability (e.g., on Twitter you can reach only those people who follow you or search for you) • Require Internet or mobile phone connectivity • Vulnerable to security and privacy problems • Are easy to overuse (sending too many messages to too many recipients) • Create privacy risks and concerns (exposing confidential data; employer monitoring; accidental forwarding) • Entail security risks (viruses, spyware; network breaches) • Create productivity concerns (frequent interruptions; nonbusiness usage)
Visual, Printed	• Can convey complex ideas and relationships quickly • Often less intimidating than long blocks of text • Can reduce the burden on the audience to figure out how the pieces of a message or concept fit • Simple charts and graphs easy to create in spreadsheets and other software, then integrate with reports	• Can require artistic or technical skills to create • Can require more time to create than equivalent amount of text • Large, high-quality visuals can be expensive to print
Visual, Digital	Generally, all the advantages of visual printed documents and all the advantages of written digital formats plus: • Interactivity can personalize and enhance the experience for audience members • Offer the persuasive power of multimedia formats, particularly video	• Potential time, cost, and skills needed to create • Bandwidth requirements of video and high-resolution graphics

Unique Challenges of Communication on Mobile Devices

Mobile devices can be used to create and consume virtually every digital form of oral, written, and visual media. Thanks to the combination of portability and the flexibility enabled by a wide array of business-focused apps, mobile devices have become a primary tool in business communication. In addition to the factors discussed in Chapter 1, consider these issues whenever your messages are likely to be viewed on mobile devices:

- **Screen size and resolution.** The screen resolution of phones and tablets has improved considerably in recent years, but the limited size of these screens still presents a challenge simply because many messages are significantly larger than the screens they will be viewed on. The result is a dilemma that pits clarity again context. Readers can zoom in to make text readable and visuals understandable, but particularly on phone screens, the inability to see an entire document page or visual at once can limit a reader's ability to grasp its full meaning. This can be particularly troublesome if you are collaborating on writing or presentation projects and team members need to review documents or slides.
- **Input technologies.** Even for accomplished texters, typing on mobile keyboards can be a challenge. Voice recognition is one way around the keyboard limitation, but anyone using it in public areas or shared offices runs the risk of sharing private message content and annoying anyone within earshot. Even with a stylus, selecting items on a touchscreen can be more difficult than doing so on a computer screen using a mouse. If your website content or other messages and materials require a significant amount of input activity from recipients, try to make it as easy as possible for them. Simple steps such as increasing the size of buttons and text-entry fields can help.
- **Bandwidth, speed, and connectivity limitations.** The speed and quality of mobile connectivity varies widely by device, carrier, service plan, and geographic location. Even users with higher bandwidth service don't always enjoy the advertised transfer speeds they are paying for. Moreover, mobile users can lose connectivity while traveling, passing through network "dead spots," or during peak-demand hours or events (trade shows and conventions are notorious for this). Be aware that mobile recipients are unlikely to receive your messages with equal speed and reliability.
- **Data usage and operational costs.** Some mobile users have unlimited data usage plans; others don't. Even those who do may be subject to carrier restrictions that reduce connection speed. Given these factors, be careful about expecting or requiring mobile users to consume a lot of video or other data-intensive content.

Others Factors to Consider

You don't always get to choose which medium or channel to use for a particular message. For example, many companies have internal instant messaging (IM) or social networking systems that you are expected to use for certain types of communication, such as project updates. When you do have a choice, consider these factors:

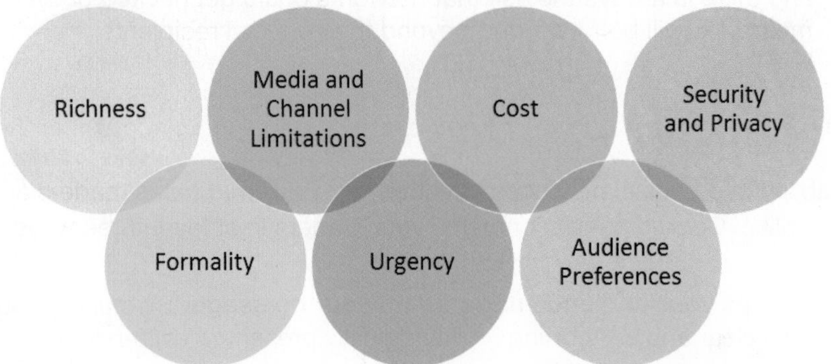

Figure 3.7
Factors Influencing the Choice of Medium
Consider these seven factors when choosing the medium to use for a particular communication.

- **Richness.** Richness is a medium's ability to 1) convey a message through more than one informational cue (visual, verbal, vocal), 2) facilitate feedback, and 3) establish personal focus. The richest medium is face-to-face communication; it's personal, it provides immediate feedback (verbal and nonverbal), and it conveys the emotion behind a message. At the other extreme are the leanest media, such as texting and IM—those that communicate in the simplest ways, provide no opportunity for audience feedback, and are the least personalized. (A text from one person looks very much like a text from anyone else.) In general, use richer media to send nonroutine or complex messages, to humanize your presence throughout the organization, to communicate caring to employees, and to gain employee commitment to company goals. Use leaner media to send routine messages or to transfer information that doesn't require significant explanation.
- **Formality.** Your media choice is a nonverbal signal that affects the style and tone of your message. For example, a printed memo or letter is likely to be perceived as a more formal gesture than an IM or email message.
- **Media and channel limitations.** Every medium-and-channel combination has limitations. For instance, IM is perfect for communicating simple, straightforward messages between two people, but it is less effective for complex messages or conversations that involve three or more people.
- **Urgency.** Some media establish a connection with the audience faster than others, so choose wisely if your message is urgent. However, be sure to respect audience members' time and workloads. If a message isn't urgent and doesn't require immediate feedback, choose a medium such as an email or blog that allows people to respond at their convenience.
- **Cost.** Cost is both a real financial factor and a perceived nonverbal signal. For example, depending on the context, extravagant (and expensive) video or multimedia presentation can send a nonverbal signal of sophistication and professionalism—or careless disregard for company budgets.
- **Audience preference.** If you know that your audience prefers a particular media and channel combination, use that format if it works well for the message and the situation. Otherwise you risk annoying the audience or having your message missed or ignored.
- **Security and privacy.** Your company may have restrictions on the media and channels that can be used for certain types of messages. Even if it doesn't, think carefully whenever your message includes sensitive information. Never assume that your email, IM, and other digital

communications are private. Many companies monitor these channels, and there is always the risk that networks could get hacked or that messages will be forwarded beyond their original recipients.

Organizing Your Message

The ability to organize messages effectively is a skill that helps readers and writers alike. Good organization helps your readers in at least three ways:

- **It helps your audience understand your message.** By making your main idea clear and supporting it with logically presented evidence, you help your audience grasp the essential elements of your message.
- **It helps your audience accept your message.** Careful organization also helps you select and arrange your points in a diplomatic way that can soften the blow of unwelcome news or persuade skeptical readers to see your point of view. In contrast, a poorly organized message can trigger negative emotions that prevent people from seeing the value of what you have to say.
- **It saves your audience time.** Readers don't have to wade through irrelevant information, seek out other sources to fill in missing information, or struggle to follow your train of thought.

In addition to saving time and energy for your readers, good organization saves you time and consumes less of your creative energy. Having a good organizational plan before you start writing helps the words flow because you can focus on how you want to say something, rather than struggling with what you want to say next. (In fact, whenever you struggle with "writer's block," step back and think about the organization of your message. Chances are what you're really facing is a thinking block, not a writing block.) A clear plan also helps you avoid composing material you don't need, and it minimizes the time you have to spend revising your first draft.

Good organizational skills are also good for your career. When you develop a reputation as a clear thinker who cares about your readers and listeners, people will be more inclined to pay attention to what you have to say.

That said, what exactly is good organization? You can think of it as structuring messages in a way that helps recipients get all the information they need while requiring the least amount of time and energy from everyone involved. Good organization starts with a clear definition of your main idea.

Define Your Main Idea

Topic:
The overall subject of a message

Main idea:
A specific statement about the topic.

The **topic** of your message is the overall subject, and your **main idea** is your specific statement about that topic. For example, if you believe that the current system of using paper forms for filing employee insurance claims is expensive and slow, you might craft a message in which the topic is employee insurance claims and the main idea is that a new web-based claim-filing system would reduce costs for the company and reimbursement delays for employees.

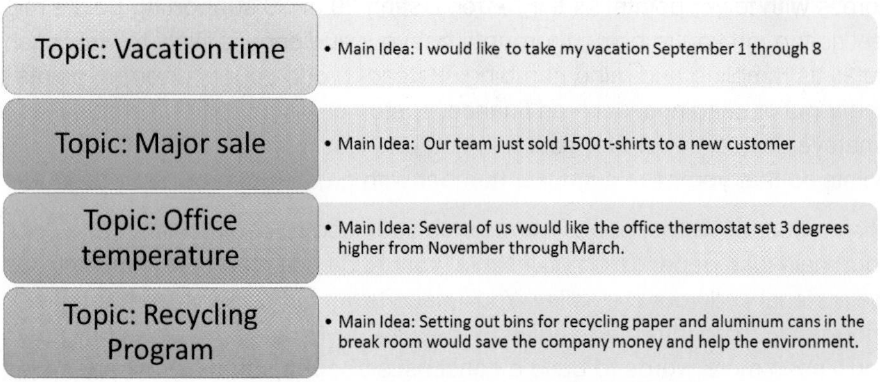

Topic	Main Idea
Topic: Vacation time	• Main Idea: I would like to take my vacation September 1 through 8
Topic: Major sale	• Main Idea: Our team just sold 1500 t-shirts to a new customer
Topic: Office temperature	• Main Idea: Several of us would like the office thermostat set 3 degrees higher from November through March.
Topic: Recycling Program	• Main Idea: Setting out bins for recycling paper and aluminum cans in the break room would save the company money and help the environment.

Figure 3.8
Topics and Main Ideas
These examples illustrate the difference between a topic and a main idea. A topic is typically just a noun phrase. The main idea contains a statement about the topic.

In longer documents and presentations, you may need to unify a mass of material with a main idea that encompasses all the individual points you want to make. Sometimes you won't even be sure what your main idea is until you sort through the information. For tough assignments like these, consider a variety of techniques to generate creative ideas:

- **Brainstorming.** Working alone or with others, generate as many ideas and questions as you can, without stopping to criticize or organize. After you capture all these pieces, look for patterns and connections to help identify the main idea and the groups of supporting ideas.
- **Journalistic approach.** The journalistic approach asks who, what, when, where, why, and how questions to focus unorganized information.
- **Question-and-answer chain.** Start with a key question the audience is likely to have, and work back toward your message. In cases, you'll find that each answer generates new questions, until you identify the information that needs to be in your message.
- **Talk it out.** Some writers find it helpful to talk through a communication challenge before trying to write about it. Tell another person what you want to communicate and get their feedback. Or record yourself as you describe what you intend to write. Then listen to the playback, identify ways to tighten and clarify the message, and repeat the process until you distill the main idea down to a single, concise message.
- **Mind mapping.** You can generate and organize ideas by using a graphic method called mind mapping. Start with a main idea and then branch out to connect every other related idea that comes to mind. You can find a number of mind-mapping tools online.

Limit Your Scope

The **scope** of your message is the range of information you present, the overall length, and the level of detail—all of which need to correspond to your main idea. The length of some business messages has a preset limit, whether from a boss's instructions, the technology you're using, or a time frame such as individual speaker slots during a seminar. However, even if you don't have a preset length, limit your scope to the minimum amount of information needed to convey your main idea.

Scope:
The range of information you present, the overall length, and the level of detail.

In addition to limiting the overall scope of your message, limit the number of major supporting points to a half dozen or so—and if you can get your idea across with fewer points, all the better. Listing 20 or 30 supporting points might feel as though you're being thorough, but your audience is likely to view such detail as rambling and mind numbing. Instead, group your supporting points under major headings, such as finance, customers, competitors, employees, or whatever is appropriate for your subject. Look for ways to distill your supporting points so that you have a smaller number with greater impact.

The number of words, pages, or minutes you need to communicate and support your main idea depends on your topic, your audience members' familiarity with the material and your credibility. You'll need fewer words to present routine information to an informed audience that already knows and respects you. You'll need more words to build a consensus about a complex and controversial subject, especially if the members of your audience are skeptical or hostile strangers.

Figure 3.9
Limiting the Scope
Trying to include too much in a single message can dilute your central point. As you plan your message, include only the facts that are relevant for the audience you will address.

	Direct Approach	Indirect Approach	
Audience Reaction	Eager/interested/ pleased/neutral	Displeased	Uninterested/unwillin
Opening Message	Start with the main idea, the request, or the good news.	Start with a neutral statement that acts as a transition to the reasons for the bad news.	Start with a statement question that capture attention.
Message Body	Provide necessary details.	Give reasons to justify a negative answer. State or imply the bad news, and make a positive suggestion.	Arouse the audience' interest in the subject Build the audience's de: to comply.
Message Close	Close with a cordial comment, a reference to the good news, or a statement about the specific action desired.	Close cordially.	Request action.

Choose Your Approach

After you've defined your main idea and scope, you're ready to decide on your approach, the sequence you will use to present your information. You have two basic options:

Direct approach:
A communication that starts with the main idea and follows up with supporting evidence.

Indirect approach:
A communication that starts with evidence first and follows up with a conclusion.

- **Direct approach.** When you know your audience will be receptive to your message, use the **direct approach**: start with your main idea (such as a recommendation, conclusion, or request) and follow that with your supporting evidence.
- **Indirect approach.** When your audience will be skeptical about or even resistant to your message, use the **indirect approach**: start with the evidence first and build your case before presenting the main idea. Note that taking the indirect approach does not mean avoiding tough issues or talking around in circles. It simply means building up to your main idea in a logical or sensitive way.

To choose between these two alternatives, analyze your audience's likely reaction to your purpose and message, as shown in Figure 3.10. Bear in mind, however, that this presents only general guidelines; always consider the unique circumstances of each message and audience situation. The type of message also influences the choice of the direct or indirect approach. In the coming chapters, you'll get specific advice on choosing the best approach for a variety of different communication challenges.

	Direct Approach	Indirect Approach	
Audience Reaction	Eager/interested/ pleased/neutral	Displeased	Uninterested/unwilling
Opening Message	Start with the main idea, the request, or the good news.	Start with a neutral statement that acts as a transition to the reasons for the bad news.	Start with a statement or question that captures attention.
Message Body	Provide necessary details.	Give reasons to justify a negative answer. State or imply the bad news, and make a positive suggestion.	Arouse the audience's interest in the subject. Build the audience's desire to comply.
Message Close	Close with a cordial comment, a reference to the good news, or a statement about the specific action desired.	Close cordially.	Request action.

Figure 3.10
Choosing Between a Direct or Indirect Approaches
Think about the way your audience is likely to respond before you choose your approach.

Outline Your Content

After you have chosen the direct or indirect approach, the next task is to figure out the most logical and effective way to present your major points and supporting details. Even if you've resisted creating outlines in your school assignments over the years, get into the habit of creating outlines when you're preparing most business messages. You'll save time, get better results, and do a better job of navigating through complicated situations.

You're no doubt familiar with basic outline formats that identify each point with a number or letter and indent certain points to show which ones are of equal status. A good outline divides a topic into at least two parts, restricts each subdivision to one category, and ensures that each subdivision is separate and distinct (see Figure 3.11).

Figure 3.11
Structuring an Outline
No matter what outlining format you use, think through your major points and the examples and evidence that support each point.

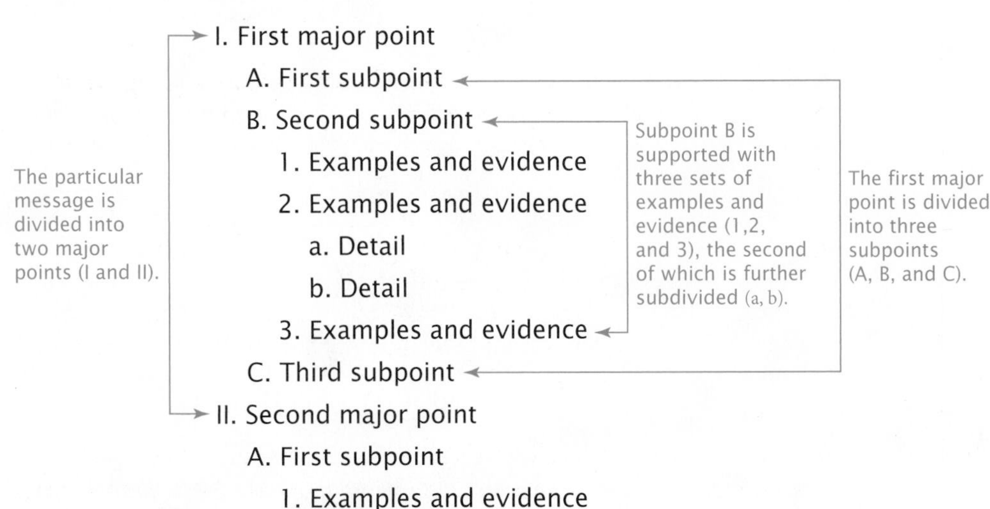

Whichever outlining or organizing scheme you use, start by stating your main idea. Then list your major supporting points and follow each with examples and evidence:

- **Start with the main idea.** The main idea helps you establish the goals and general strategy of the message, and it summarizes 1) what you want your audience members to do, think, or feel after receiving the message and 2) why it makes sense for them to do so. Everything in your message should either support the main idea or explain its implications. (Remember that if you choose the indirect approach, the main idea will appear toward the end of your message, *after* you've presented your major supporting points.)
- **State the major points.** Support your main idea with the major points that clarify and explain your ideas in more concrete terms. When you're describing a process, the major points are usually steps in the process. When you're describing an object, the major points often correspond to the parts of the object. When you're giving a historical account, major points represent events in the chronological chain of events. If your purpose is to persuade, select major points that develop a line of reasoning or a logical argument that proves your central message.
- **Provide examples and evidence.** After you've defined the main idea and identified major supporting points, you're ready to back up those points with examples and evidence that help audience members understand, accept, and remember your message. Choose your examples and evidence carefully. You want to be compelling and complete but also as concise as possible. One strong example or piece of evidence can be more effective than three or four weaker items.

Figure 3.12 illustrates several of the key themes about organizing a message: helping readers get the information they need quickly, defining and conveying the main idea, limiting the scope of the message, choosing the approach, and outlining your information.

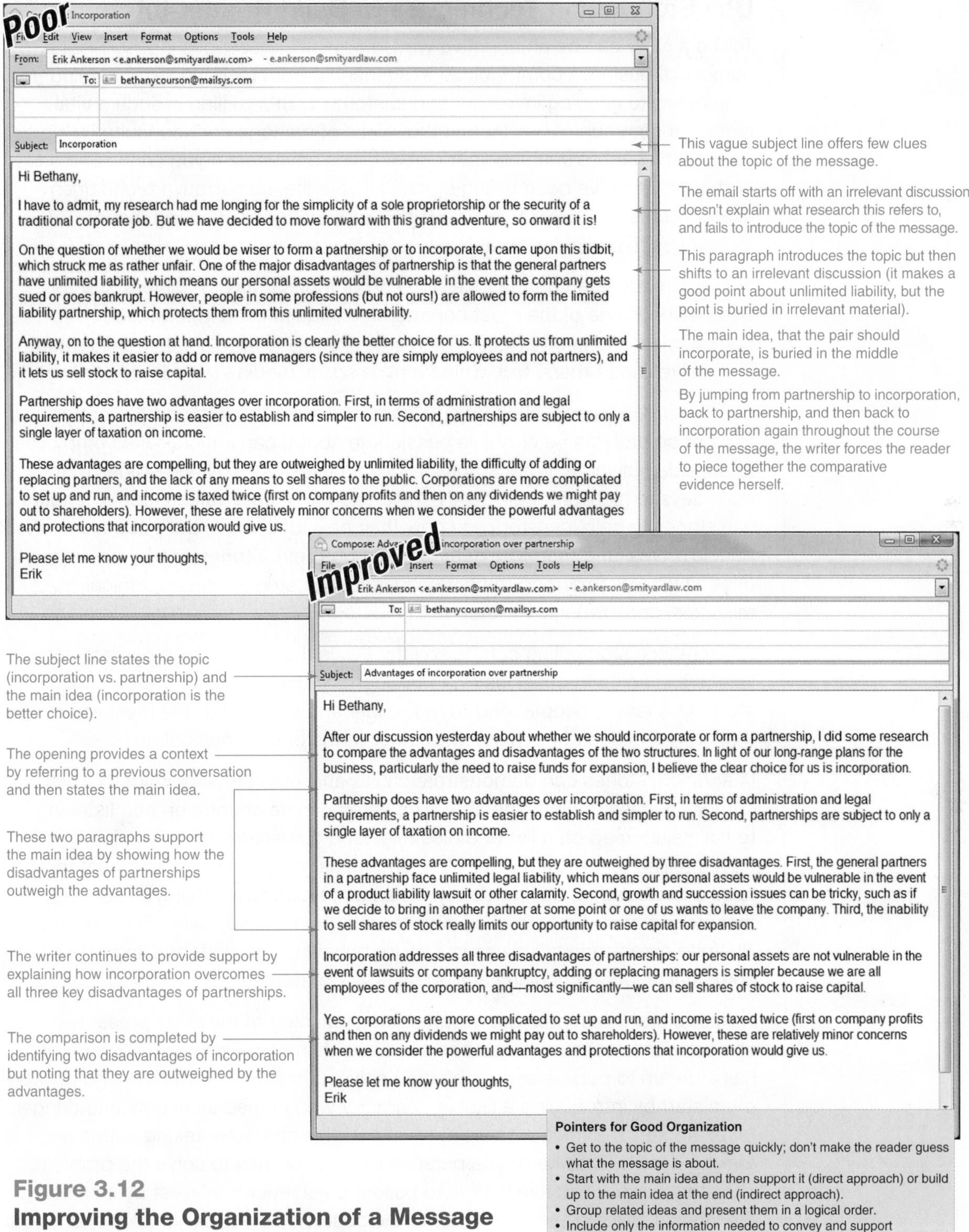

Figure 3.12
Improving the Organization of a Message
This writer is following up on a conversation from the previous day, in which he and the recipient discussed which of two forms of ownership, a partnership or a corporation, they should use for their new company.

Use Storytelling Techniques to Build Reader Interest

Telling a story can be an effective way to organize messages in a surprising number of business communication scenarios, from recruiting and training employees to enticing investors and customers. Storytelling is such a vital means of communicating that, in the words of management consultant Steve Tobak, "It's hard to imagine your career going anywhere if you can't tell a story." Fortunately, you've been telling stories all your life, so narrative techniques already come naturally to you; now it's just a matter of adapting those techniques to business situations.

You've already been on the receiving end of thousands of business stories. Storytelling is one of the most common techniques used in television commercials and in other advertisements. People love to share stories about themselves and others, too, which makes social media ideal for storytelling.

Career-related stories, such as how someone sought and found the opportunity to work on projects he or she is passionate about, can entice skilled employees to consider joining a firm. Established companies often tell the stories of their early days to highlight their depth of experience or core values. Entrepreneurs use stories to help investors see how their new ideas have the potential to affect people's lives (and therefore generate lots of sales). Stories can be cautionary tales as well, dramatizing the consequences of career blunders, ethical mistakes, and strategic missteps.

A key reason storytelling can be so effective is that stories help readers and listeners imagine themselves living through the experience of the person in the story. As a result, people tend to remember and respond to the message in ways that can be difficult to achieve with other forms of communication.

In addition, stories can demonstrate cause-and-effect relationships in a compelling fashion. Imagine attending an employee orientation and listening to the trainer read off a list of ethics rules and guidelines. Now imagine the trainer telling the real-life story of an ambitious new employee who bent the rules and wound up paying dearly. As an ambitious new employee yourself, that story is more likely to stick in your mind than a list of rules. This ability to illustrate organizational values is a major benefit of using storytelling in business communication, particularly across diverse workforces.

A classic story has three basic parts. The beginning of the story presents someone whom the audience can identify with in some way, and this person has a dream to pursue or a problem to solve. (Think of how movies and novels often start by introducing a likable character who immediately gets into danger, for example.) The middle of the story shows this character taking action and making decisions as he or she pursues the goal or tries to solve the problem. The storyteller's objective here is to build the audience's interest by increasing the tension: will the "hero" overcome the obstacles in his or her path and defeat whatever adversary is keeping him or her from away from her goal? The end of the story answers those questions. It usually also offers a lesson to be learned about the outcome.

In business, even though these are "stories," they must not be made-up tales. Telling stories that didn't happen about people who don't exist while presenting them as real-life events is a serious breach of ethics that damages a company's credibility.

Consider adding an element of storytelling whenever your main idea involves the opportunity to inspire, persuade, teach, or warn your audience about the potential outcomes of a particular course of action.

Acquiring Information to Support Your Message

As you begin planning your message, you may discover that supporting materials will help make the message more authoritative or effective. For example, you might need statistics that back up your assertion that a particular change is needed in a policy, or you might want some artwork that will liven up a dull presentation. You can use a variety of online research and multimedia sources to gather the needed materials.

Perform Web Searches

A web search can help you discover not only specific content such as a particular statistic, but also libraries and archives of content that you can explore. To do a web search, you start with a **search engine** such as Google, Yahoo!, or Bing. A search engine is a web content database that you access from a **web browser**, like Firefox, Google Chrome, or Safari.

Search engine:
A web content database that you access from a web browser.

Web browser:
Software that displays web pages.

To use a search engine at a basic level, you simply type keywords into the search box and press Enter. You can fine-tune the results of searches by using advanced **search syntax**. For example, suppose you are looking for information about safety statistics for infant car seats, but your search results are all about about cars, seats, and infants in general. If you enclose *infant car seats* in quotation marks when you search, the results will contain only websites where the words appear together in that order:

Search syntax:
Punctuation and codes that enable you to fine-tune a web search.

Table 3.2 provides some search syntax examples for Google.com, but the tips also work for many other search engines.

Table 3.2 Advanced search syntax for Google

To do this...	Use this syntax	Example
Find a multi-word phrase	"word1 word2"	"infant car seats"
Find pages that use at least one of two or more keywords	OR	child OR infant
Exclude a word	-word	-prices
Find social tags	@name	@johndoe
Find popular hashtags for trending topics	#word	#carseatreviews
Find results from only certain sites or domains	site:sitename	site:consumerreports.com

Acquire Multimedia Content

There are many ways to find online multimedia content including graphics, audio clips, and video clips. You can start with a web search, as in the preceding section, and narrow the results for a particular kind of content. For example, click Images at the top of a Google search results page to show images related to your keywords, or Videos to find videos.

Figure 3.13
Online Image Acquisition
The Internet is a rich source of multimedia content, and some of it is free. For professional quality stock photos and video, however, be prepared to pay for licensing.

You can also search specific sites for multimedia content. YouTube is a popular repository of videos, for example, on nearly every topic you can imagine. Videos cannot be downloaded, but you can link to them for playback through a document or presentation, or send a link to a video via email. For professional-quality stock photos, two popular sites are iStock.com and shutterstock.com. Both sell high-quality digital images for use in professional publishing/printing projects.

Another way to search for online artwork by keyword is by using the Bing image search tool that is built into Microsoft Office applications such as Microsoft Word, Excel, and PowerPoint. When you use the Insert Online Pictures command, you can type keywords in a Bing Image Search box, and then browse, select, and insert pictures into your document as you work, without having to open a separate browser window to perform the search. You can also do an image search from the Bing.com website, so you do not need to have an Office application to do this search.

Cite Your Sources

Make sure that you accurately cite your sources when you use multimedia content you find online, and get permission from the owner if needed, to avoid copyright violations. Acknowledging that the material came from some other source also helps you avoid plagiarism, which can result in a failing grade or a loss of credibility. Different citation methods are appropriate for different projects and resources. For example, you might cite an image's source in its figure caption, or you might include the information in a footnote, endnote, or bibliography entry. You will learn more about source citation in Chapter 10.

Chapter Summary

Understanding the Three-Step Writing Process

The three-step writing process is built around planning, writing, and completing business messages. Planning involves analyzing the situation, gathering the information you will need to meet audience needs, selecting the right medium or combination of media, and organizing your information. The writing step involves adapting to your audience and composing your message. Completing involves the four tasks of revising, proofreading, producing, and distributing the message. The three-step process helps you create more effective messages because it keeps you focused on what your audience needs to get from a message, and it saves you time by reducing the amount of reworking that can happen when someone starts you writing without clear goals or organization in mind.

Analyzing the Situation

Analyzing the situation gives you the insights necessary to meet your own needs as a communicator while also meeting the information needs of your recipients. You can accomplish this goal by looking at the communication process from both ends, by defining your purpose in sending the message, and creating a profile of your target audience. The general purpose of a message identifies your overall intent—to inform, to persuade, to collaborate, or to initiate a conversation. The specific purpose identifies what you hope to accomplish with the message. Without a clear purpose in mind, you are likely to spend more time and energy than you really need to, and chances are you won't create an effective message.

Understanding your audience is a vital aspect of planning because: the more you know about your audience members, their needs, and their expectations, the more effectively you'll be able to communicate with them. To create an audience profile, identify the primary audience, its size and geographic distribution, its composition (language, education, experience, and other factors that could affect message reception), its level of understanding, its expectations and preferences, and its probable reaction to your message.

Gathering Information

Simple messages usually don't require extensive information gathering, but to acquire useful insights, consider the audience's perspective; find and listen to online communities; read reports and other company documents; talk with supervisors, colleagues, or customers; and ask your audience for input, if possible. Judge the quality of any information you include by making sure it is accurate, ethical, and pertinent.

Selecting the Best Combination of Media and Channels

Media can be divided in to oral (spoken), written, and visual, and these three formats can be delivered through digital and non-digital channels. There are advantages and disadvantages to each media-and-channel combination.

Organizing Your Message

Good organization helps your audience understand and accept your message with less time and effort. It also saves you time when preparing messages. With a clear path to follow when writing, you'll produce messages faster and spend less time revising. To organize any message, define your main idea, limit the scope for maximum impact, choose the direct or indirect approach to match the situation, and outline your information in a logical sequence.

Acquiring Information to Support Your Message

A web search using a search engine is often the best way to find information to support your message. Search engines such as Google enable you to use advanced syntax to narrow a search and to search for images or videos using the search keywords. If you are looking specifically for videos, a specialized site such as YouTube may be useful. To find royalty-free images to use in a document, use the Bing image search within Office 2016 applications, or use the image search tool at Bing.com or another search engine. Make sure you cite all sources to avoid plagiarism, and only use materials that you are legally entitled to use to avoid copyright violation.

Test Your Knowledge

1. What are the three major steps in the writing process?
2. What do you need to know to develop an audience profile?
3. What are the three attributes of quality information in a business message?
4. Why are in-person conversations considered a rich medium?
5. What is the difference between the topic of a message and its main idea?
6. List two ways find an informational video online for a specific topic.

Apply Your Knowledge

1. Some writers argue that planning messages wastes time because they inevitably change their plans as they go along. How would you respond to this argument? What percentage of time should a writer spend on planning their message? Writing their message? Completing their message? Describe how proper planning is a good time management technique.
2. A day after sending an email to all 1,800 employees in your company regarding income tax implications of the company's retirement plan, you discover that one of the sources you relied on for your information plagiarized from other sources. You quickly double-check all the information in your message and confirm that it is accurate. However, you are concerned about using plagiarized information, even though you did nothing wrong. How you would handle this situation?
3. You are organizing an exploratory in-person meeting with engineering representatives from a dozen manufacturers around the world to discuss updates to a technical standard that all the companies' products must adhere to. The representatives have a

wide range of firmly held opinions on the subject, because the changes could help some companies and hurt others. They can't even agree on what should be addressed first so you need to develop a minimum level of consensus on what should be on the agenda. Which combination of media and channels would you use to move the conversation forward and finalize the agenda and why? Each company has one representative, and any discussions need to be kept confidential.

4. You have been invited to speak at an annual industry conference. After preparing the outline for your presentation, you see that you've identified 14 separate points to support your main idea. Should you move ahead with creating the slides for your presentation or move back and rethink your outline? Why?

Practice Your Skills

1. **Identifying a Specific Purpose** For each of the following communication tasks, state a specific purpose (if you have trouble, try beginning with "I want to . . ....").
   a. A report to your boss, the store manager, about the outdated items in the warehouse
   b. A blog posting to customers and the news media about your company's plans to acquire a competitor
   c. An email message to employees about the office's high water bills
   d. A phone call to a supplier to check on an overdue parts shipment
   e. A podcast to new users of the company's online content management system

2. **Profiling an Audience** For each communication task below, write brief answers to three questions: 1) Who is my audience? 2) What is my audience's general attitude toward my subject? 3) What does my audience need to know?
   a. A final-notice collection letter from an appliance manufacturer to an appliance dealer, sent 10 days before initiation of legal collection procedures
   b. An advertisement for peanut butter
   c. A letter to the property management company responsible for maintaining your office building, complaining about persistent problems with the heating and air conditioning
   d. A cover letter sent along with your resume to a potential employer
   e. A request (to the seller) for a price adjustment on a piano that incurred $150 in damage during delivery to a banquet room in the hotel you manage

3. **Analyzing Media and Purpose** List three messages you have read, viewed, or listened to lately (such as direct-mail promotions, letters, email or instant messages, phone solicitations, blog posts, social network pages, podcasts, or lectures). For each message, determine the general and the specific purpose, then answer the questions listed.
   a. What was the general purpose?
   b. What was the specific purpose?
   c. Was the message well timed?
   d. Did the sender choose an appropriate medium and channel for the message?
   e. Was the sender's purpose realistic?

4. **Choosing the Approach** Indicate whether the direct or the indirect approach would be best for each of the following:
   a. An email message to a car dealer, asking about the availability of a specific make and model of car
   b. A letter from a recent college graduate, requesting a letter of recommendation from a former instructor
   c. A letter turning down a job applicant
   d. An internal blog post explaining that because of high air-conditioning costs, the plant temperature will be held at 78 degrees during the summer
   e. A final request to settle a delinquent debt

5. **Drafting Persuasive Messages** For each of the following scenarios, give three examples of information you would use to support your request.
   a. You want your boss to approve your plan for hiring two new people.
   b. You want to be hired for a job.
   c. You want to be granted a business loan.
   d. You want to collect a small amount from a regular customer whose account is slightly past due.
   e. You want to collect a large amount from a customer whose account is seriously past due.

Activities

1. **Determining the Audience** Visit the PepsiCo website and locate the latest annual report. Read the annual report's letter to shareholders. Who is the audience for this message? What is the general purpose of the message? What do you think this audience wants to know from the chairman of PepsiCo? Summarize your answers in a one-page report or five-slide presentation, as your instructor directs.

2. **Creating an Audience Profile** With a team assigned by your instructor, compare the Facebook pages of three companies in the same industry. Analyze the content on all the available tabs. What can you surmise about the intended audience for each company? Which of the three does the best job of presenting the information its target audience is likely to need? Prepare a brief presentation, including slides that show samples of the Facebook content from each company.

3. **Assessing Audience Needs** Visit the website of any well-known company and review its About or About Us page. Identify three ways you would modify this page to meet the needs of readers accessing it with smartphones.

4. **Sharpening Media Skills** You are the head of public relations for a cruise line that operates out of Miami. You are shocked to read a letter in a local newspaper from a disgruntled passenger, complaining about the service and entertainment on a recent cruise. You need to respond to these publicized criticisms in some way. What audiences will you need to consider in your response? What medium or media and channels should you choose? If the letter had been published in a travel publication widely read by travel agents and cruise travelers, how might your course of action have differed? In an email message to your instructor, explain how you will respond.

5. **Limiting Your Scope** Suppose you are preparing to recommend that top management install a new heating system that uses the cogeneration heating process. The following information is in your files. Eliminate topics that aren't essential and then arrange the other topics so that your report will give top managers a clear understanding of the heating system and a balanced, concise justification for installing it. Submit a clear and concise outline to your instructor.
   - History of the development of the cogeneration heating process
   - Scientific credentials of the developers of the process
   - Risks assumed in using this process
   - Your plan for installing the equipment in the headquarters building
   - Stories about the successful use of cogeneration technology in comparable facilities
   - Specifications of the equipment that would be installed
   - Plans for disposing of the old heating equipment
   - Costs of installing and running the new equipment
   - Advantages and disadvantages of using the new process
   - Detailed 10-year cost projections
   - Estimates of the time needed to phase in the new system
   - Alternative systems that management might want to consider
6. **Using Storytelling Techniques** Research recent episodes of ethical lapses by a business professional or executive in any industry. Choose one example that has a clear story "arc" from beginning to end. Outline a cautionary tale that explains the context of the ethical lapse, the choice the person made, and the consequences of the ethical lapse. Script a podcast (aim for roughly 3 to 5 minutes) that tells the story. If your instructor directs, record your podcast and post to your class blog.
7. **Finding Research Data Online** What percentage of online game players are women, and what types of games do women play more than men do? Using web searches, gather some statistical data that answers these questions, along with at least one informational graphic that charts such data or shows it in a graphical way. Send a summary of the information you found to your instructor in a word processing document, citing your sources.

Expand Your Skills

Locate an example of professional communication in any medium-channel combo that you think would work equally well—or perhaps better—in another combination. Using the media and channel selection guidelines in this chapter and your understanding of the communication process, write a brief analysis (no more than one page) of the company's choice and explain why your choice would be at least as effective. Be sure to cite specific elements from the piece and support from the chapter.

CHAPTER

4

Writing Business Messages

After studying this chapter, you will be able to:

- Identify four aspects of being sensitive to audience needs when writing business messages.
- Explain how establishing your credibility and projecting your company's image are vital aspects of building a strong relationship with your audience.
- Explain how to achieve a tone that is conversational but businesslike, explain the value of using plain language, and define active and passive voice.
- Describe how to select words that are correct and effective.
- Define four types of sentences and explain how sentence style affects emphasis within a message.
- Define three key elements of a paragraph and list five ways to develop coherent paragraphs.
- List five techniques for writing effective messages for mobile devices.

"You" attitude:
Speaking and writing in terms of your audience's wishes, interests, hopes, and preferences.

Adapting Your Message to Your Audience

Successful communicators will tell you that audiences tend to greet incoming messages with a selfish question: "What's in this for me?" If your target readers or listeners don't think a message applies to them, or if they don't think you are being sensitive to their needs, they won't pay attention. You can improve your audience sensitivity by adopting the "you" attitude, maintaining good standards of etiquette, emphasizing the positive, and using bias-free language.

Adopting the "You" Attitude

You are already becoming familiar with the audience-centered approach, trying to see a subject through your audience's eyes. Now you want to project this approach in your messages by adopting the "you" attitude—by speaking and writing in terms of your audience's wishes, interests, hopes, and preferences.

On a simple level, you can adopt the **"you" attitude** by replacing terms that refer to yourself and your company with terms that refer to your audience. In other words, use *you* and *your* instead of *I*, *me*, *mine*, *we*, *us*, and *ours*:

Instead of This	Write This
Tuesday is the only day that we can promise quick response to purchase order requests; we are swamped the rest of the week.	If you need a quick response, please submit your purchase order requests on Tuesday.
We offer MP3 players with 50, 75, or 100 gigabytes of storage capacity.	You can choose an MP3 player with 50, 75, or 100 gigabytes of storage.

Of course, you will have occasions when it is entirely appropriate to write or speak from your perspective, such as when you are offering your opinions or reporting on something you have seen. However, even in those instances, make sure you focus on your readers' needs.

Also, be aware that the "you" attitude involves a lot more than just using particular pronouns. It's a matter of demonstrating genuine interest in your readers and concern for their needs. You can use *you* 25 times in a single page and still offend your audience or ignore readers' true concerns. If you're writing to a retailer, try to think like a retailer; if you're dealing with a production supervisor, put yourself in that position; if you're writing to a dissatisfied customer, imagine how you would feel at the other end of the transaction.

Figure 4.1
The "You" Attitude
Phrasing a message to emphasize the audience's needs and desires can make your message more positively received.

Keep in mind that on some occasions it's better to avoid using *you*, particularly if doing so will sound overly authoritative or accusing. For instance, instead of saying, "You failed to deliver the customer's order on time," you could avoid the confrontational tone by saying, "The customer didn't receive the order on time," or "Let's figure out a system that will ensure on-time deliveries."

Maintaining Standards of Etiquette

Good etiquette shows respect for your audience and helps foster a more successful environment for communication by minimizing negative emotional reaction. Here are a few examples:

Instead of This	Write This
Once again, you've managed to bring down the website through your incompetent programming.	Let's review the last website update to explore ways to improve the process.
You've been sitting on our order for two weeks, and we need it now!	Our production schedules depend on timely delivery of parts and supplies, but we have not yet received the order scheduled for delivery two weeks ago. Please respond today with a firm delivery commitment.

Some situations require more diplomacy than others. If you know your audience well, a less formal approach might be more appropriate. However, when you are communicating with people who outrank you or with people outside your organization, an added measure of courtesy is usually needed.

Written messages and most forms of digital communication generally require more tact than oral communication. When you're speaking to someone live, you can soften your words by your tone of voice and facial expressions and adjust your approach according to the feedback you get. However, if you inadvertently offend someone in writing or in a podcast, for example, you don't get the immediate feedback you would need in order to resolve the situation. In fact, you may never know that you offended your audience.

Emphasizing the Positive

Throughout your career, you will encounter situations in which you need to convey unwanted news. However, sensitive communicators understand the difference between delivering negative news and being negative. Never try to hide the negative news, but look for positive points that will foster a good relationship with your audience, as in these examples:

Instead of This	Write This
It is impossible to repair your laptop today.	We'll have your computer ready by Tuesday. Would you like a loaner until then?
We wasted $300,000 advertising in that magazine.	Our $300,000 advertising investment did not pay off; let's analyze the experience and apply the insights to future campaigns.

If you're trying to persuade audience members to perform a particular action, point out how doing so will benefit them, as in these examples:

Instead of This	Write This
We will notify all three credit reporting agencies if you do not pay your overdue bill within 10 days.	Pay your overdue bill within 10 days to avoid a negative entry on your credit record.
I am tired of seeing so many errors in the customer service blog.	Proofread your blog postings to avoid embarrassing mistakes that erode confidence in our brand.

Euphemism:
A synonym that conveys your meaning without negative connotations.

Look for appropriate opportunities to use **euphemisms**, synonyms which convey your meaning without a negative connotations. For example, when referring to people beyond a certain age, use "senior citizens" rather than "old people." *Senior* conveys respect in a way that *old* doesn't.

However, take care when using euphemisms. It's easy to push the idea too far and wind up sounding ridiculous—or worse yet, obscuring the truth. Speaking to your local community about the disposal of "manufacturing by-products" would be unethical if you're really talking about toxic waste. Even if it is unpleasant, people respond better to an honest message delivered with integrity than they do to a sugar-coated message that obscures the truth.

Bias-free language:
A language that avoids words and phrases that unfairly or unethically categorize or stigmatize people in ways related to gender, race, ethnicity, age, disability, or other personal characteristics.

Using Bias-Free Language

Bias-free language avoids words and phrases that unfairly or unethically categorize or stigmatize people in ways related to gender, race, ethnicity, age, disability, or other personal characteristics. Contrary to what some might think, biased language is not simply about "labels." To a significant degree, language reflects the way people think and what they believe, and biased language may well perpetuate the underlying stereotypes and prejudices that it represents. Moreover, because communication is largely about perception, it isn't enough that your beliefs are fair; that fairness must also come across in the way your express yourself. Good communicators make every effort to eliminate biased language (see Table 4.1), which can take a variety of forms.

Table 4.1 Overcoming Bias in Language

Gender Bias	Unacceptable	Preferable
Using words containing *man*	Man-made Mankind Manpower Businessman Salesman Foreman	Artificial, synthetic, manufactured, constructed, human-made Humanity, human beings, human race, people Workers, workforce Executive, manager, businessperson, professional Sales representative, salesperson Supervisor
Using female-gender words	Actress, stewardess	Actor, flight attendant
Using special designations	Woman doctor, male nurse	Doctor, nurse
Using he to refer to "everyone"	The average worker . . . he	The average worker . . . he or she OR Average workers . . . they
Identifying roles with gender	The typical executive spends four hours of his day in meetings. The consumer . . . she The nurse/teacher . . . she	Most executives spend four hours a day in meetings. Consumers . . . they Nurses/teachers . . . they
Identifying women by marital status	Mrs. Norm Lindstrom Norm Lindstrom and Ms. Drake	Maria Lindstrom OR Ms. Maria Lindstrom Norm Lindstrom and Maria Drake OR Mr. Lindstrom and Ms. Drake
Racial and Ethnic Bias	**Unacceptable**	**Preferable**
Assigning stereotypes	Not surprisingly, Shing-Tung Yau excels in mathematics.	Shing-Tung Yau excels in mathematics.
Identifying people by race or ethnicity	Mario M. Cuomo, Italian-American politician and ex-governor of New York	Mario M. Cuomo, politician and ex-governor of New York
Age Bias	**Unacceptable**	**Preferable**
Including age when irrelevant	Mary Kirazy, 58, has just joined our trust department.	Mary Kirazy has just joined our trust department.
Disability Bias	**Unacceptable**	**Preferable**
Putting the disability before the person	Disabled workers face many barriers on the job. An epileptic, Tracy has no trouble doing her job.	Workers with physical disabilities face many barriers on the job. Tracy's epilepsy has no effect on her job performance.

- **Gender bias.** Avoid sexist language by using the same labels for everyone, regardless of gender. Don't refer to a woman as *chairperson* and then to a man as *chairman*. Use chair, chairperson, or chairman consistently. (Note that it is not uncommon to use *chairman* when referring to a woman who heads a board of directors. Reword sentences to use *they* or to use no pronoun at all rather than refer to all individuals as *he*. Note that the preferred title for women in business is *Ms*. unless the individual asks to be addressed as *Miss* or *Mrs*. or has some other title, such as *Dr*.
- **Racial and ethnic bias.** Avoid identifying people by race or ethnic origin unless such identification is relevant to the matter at hand—and it rarely is.
- **Age bias.** Mention the age of a person only when it is relevant. Moreover, be careful of the context in which you use words that refer to age; such words carry a variety of positive and negative connotations. For example, *young* can imply youthfulness, inexperience, or even immaturity, depending on how it's used.
- **Disability bias.** Physical, cognitive, sensory, or emotional impairments should never be mentioned in business messages unless those conditions are directly relevant to the subject. If you must refer to someone's disability, put the person first and the disability second. For example, by saying "employees with physical disabilities," not "handicapped employees," you focus on the whole person, not their disabilities. Never use outdated terminology such as *crippled* or *retarded*.

Building a Relationship with Your Audience

Successful communication requires a positive relationship between sender and receiver. Establishing your credibility and projecting your company's image are two vital ways to create and build positive business relationships.

Establishing Your Credibility

Credibility:
A measure of believability based on reliability and evoking trust in others.

Audience responses to your messages depend heavily on your **credibility**, which is a measure of your believability and is based on how reliable you are and how much trust you evoke in others. With audiences who don't know you and trust you already, you need to establish credibility before they'll accept your messages. When you do establish credibility, communication is much easier because you no longer have to spend time and energy convincing people that you are a trustworthy source of information and ideas.

Figure 4.2
Building Credibility
Credibility as a professional can come not only from credentials and seniority, but from demonstrated competence and confidence.

To build, maintain, or repair your credibility, emphasize the following characteristics:

- **Honesty.** Demonstrating honesty and integrity will earn you the respect of your audiences, even if they don't always agree with or welcome your messages.
- **Objectivity.** Show that you can distance yourself from emotional situations and look at all sides of an issue.
- **Awareness of audience needs.** Directly or indirectly, let your audience members know that you understand what's important to them.
- **Credentials, knowledge, and expertise.** Audiences need to know that you have whatever it takes to back up your message, whether it's education, professional certification, special training, past successes, or simply the fact that you've done your research.
- **Endorsements.** An endorsement is a statement on your behalf by someone who is accepted by your audience as an expert.
- **Performance.** Demonstrating impressive communication skills is not enough; people need to know they can count on you to get the job done.
- **Confidence.** Audiences need to know that you believe in yourself and your message. If you are convinced that your message is sound, you can state your case confidently, without sounding boastful or arrogant.
- **Sincerity.** When you offer praise, don't use *hyperbole*, such as "You are the most fantastic employee I could ever imagine." Instead, point out specific qualities that warrant praise.

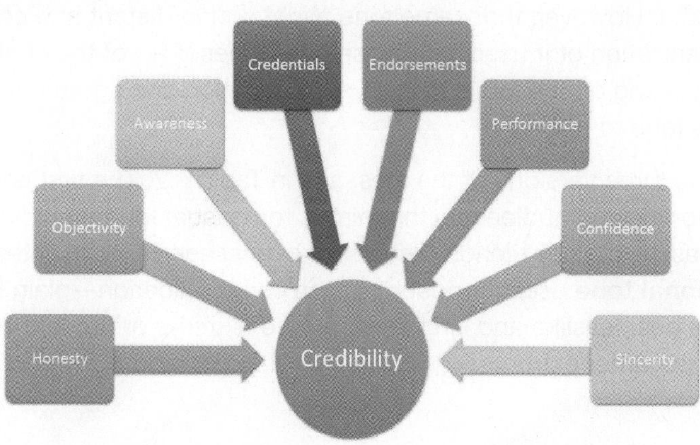

Figure 4.3
Factors Influencing Credibility

To appear credible in a business environment, make sure that your communication has the qualities shown here. Project confidence without being arrogant, and honesty without being overly blunt. Make sure your credentials are known, without bragging about them.

Be aware that credibility can take days, months, even years to establish—and it can be wiped out in an instant. An occasional mistake or letdown may be forgiven, but major lapses in honesty or integrity can destroy your reputation.

Projecting Your Company's Image

When you communicate with anyone outside your organization, it is more than a conversation between two individuals. You represent your company and therefore play a vital role in helping the company build and maintain positive relationships with all of its stakeholders. Most successful companies work hard to foster a specific public image, and your external communication efforts need to project that image. It is part of your responsibility to see that the company's interests and communication style take precedence over your own.

Many organizations have specific communication guidelines for everything from the correct use of the company name to preferred abbreviations and other grammatical details. Specifying a desired style of communication is more difficult, however. Observe more experienced colleagues to see how they communicate, and never hesitate to ask for help to make sure you're conveying the appropriate tone. For instance, with clients entrusting thousands or millions of dollars to it, an investment firm likely communicates in a style quite different from that of a clothing retailer. And a clothing retailer that specializes in high-quality business attire communicates in a different style than a store that carries the latest trends in casual wear.

Controlling Your Style and Tone

Communication style:
The choices you make to express yourself, including words, sentences, and paragraphs.

Tone:
The overall impression in your messages.

Your **communication style** involves the choices you make to express yourself: the words you select, the manner in which you use those words in sentences, and the way you build paragraphs from individual sentences. Your style creates a certain **tone**, or overall impression, in your messages. The right tone depends on the nature of your message and your relationship with its audience.

Creating a Conversational Tone

The tone of your business messages can range from informal to conversational to formal. If you're in a large organization and you're communicating with your superiors or with customers, the right tone will usually be more formal and respectful. However, that same tone might sound distant and cold in a small organization or if used with close colleagues. Part of the challenge of communicating on the job is to read each situation and figure out the appropriate tone to use.

Conversational tone:
Plain language that sounds professional without being stuffy or too informal.

Compare the three versions of the message in Table 4.2. The first is too formal and stuffy for today's audiences, the third is too casual for any audience other than close associates or friends. The second message demonstrates the **conversational tone** used in most business communication—plain language that sounds businesslike and isn't stuffy at one extreme or too laid-back and informal at the other extreme.

Table 4.2 Formal, Conversational, and Informal Tones

Tone	Examples
Stuffy: too formal for today's audiences	Dear Ms. Navarro: Enclosed please find the information that was requested during our telephone communication of May 14. As was mentioned at that time, Midville Hospital has significantly more doctors of exceptional quality than any other health facility in the state. As you were also informed, our organization has quite an impressive network of doctors and other health-care professionals with offices located throughout the state. In the event that you should need a specialist, our professionals will be able to make an appropriate recommendation. In the event that you have questions or would like additional information, you may certainly contact me during regular business hours. Most sincerely yours, Samuel G. Berenz
Conversational: just right for most business communication	Dear Ms. Navarro: Here's the information you requested during our phone conversation on Friday. As I mentioned, Midville Hospital has the highest-rated doctors and more of them than any other hospital in the state. In addition, we have a vast network of doctors and other health professionals with offices throughout the state. If you need a specialist, they can refer you to the right one. If you would like more information, please call any time between 9:00 and 5:00, Monday through Friday. Sincerely, Samuel G. Berenz
Unprofessional: too casual for business communication	Here's the 411 you requested. IMHO, we have more and better doctors than any other hospital in the state. FYI, we also have a large group of doctors and other health professionals w/offices close to U at work/home. If U need a specialist, they'll refer U to the right one Any? just ring or msg. L8R, S

You can achieve a tone that is conversational but still businesslike following these guidelines:

- **Understand the difference between texting and writing.** The casual, acronym-filled language friends often use in texts and on social media is not professional business writing. It is an efficient way for friends to communicate—particularly given the limitations of a phone keypad—but if you want to be taken seriously in business, you simply cannot write like this on the job.
- **Avoid obsolete and pompous language.** Most companies now shy away from such dated phrases as "attached please find" and "please be advised that." Similarly, avoid using obscure words, stale or clichéd expressions, and complicated sentences whose only intent is to impress others.
- **Don't preach or brag.** Don't insult your audience by talking down to them—or alienate them by going on about yourself or your accomplishments.

Figure 4.4
Nobody Likes a Know-It-All
Bragging or preaching to an audience is a sure way to turn them off and make them less receptive to your message. Address recipients respectfully, without assuming that they don't know or can't understand what you are saying.

- **Be careful with intimacy.** Business messages should generally avoid intimacy, such as sharing personal details or adopting a casual, unprofessional tone. However, when you have a close relationship with audience members, such as among the members of a close-knit team, a more intimate tone is sometimes appropriate and even expected.
- **Be careful with humor.** Humor can easily backfire and divert attention from your message. If you don't know your audience well or you're not skilled at using humor in a business setting, don't use it at all. Avoid humor in formal messages and when you're communicating across cultural boundaries.

Using Plain Language

An important aspect of creating a conversational tone is using plain language. Plain language presents information in a simple, straightforward style that your audience can easily understand. Using plain language supports the "you" attitude and shows respect for your audience. It can also make companies more productive and profitable because people spend less time trying to figure out messages that are confusing or aren't written to meet their needs.

Selecting Active or Passive Voice

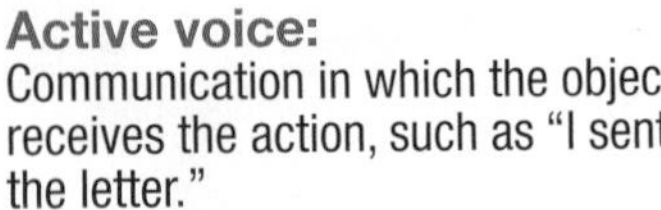

Active voice:
Communication in which the object receives the action, such as "I sent the letter."

Passive voice:
Communication in which the subject receives the action, such as "The letter was sent by me."

The choice of active or passive voice also affects the tone of your message. In a sentence written in the **active voice**, the subject performs the action and the object receives the action: "Jodi sent the email message." In a sentence written in the **passive voice**, the subject receives the action: "The email message was sent by Jodi."

Using the active voice often makes your writing more direct, more lively, and easier to understand (see Table 4.3). Passive voice is not wrong grammatically, but it can be cumbersome, lengthy, and vague. In most cases, the active voice is the better choice. Occasionally, however, the passive voice can soften the blow of a difficult message.

Use passive voice when:

- You want to be diplomatic about pointing out a problem or an error
- You want to point out what's being done without taking or attributing the credit or the blame
- You want to avoid personal pronouns (I and we) in order to create an objective tone

Table 4.3 Active vs. Passive Voice

In general, avoid passive voice to make your writing lively and direct.	
Dull and Indirect in Passive Voice	**Lively and Direct in Active Voice**
The new procedure was developed by the operations team.	The operations team developed the new procedure.
Legal problems are created by this contract.	This contract creates legal problems.
Reception preparations have been undertaken by our PR people for the new CEO's arrival.	Our PR people have begun planning a reception for the new CEO.
Use passive voice when you need to be diplomatic or want to focus attention on problems or solutions rather than on people.	
Accusatory or Self-Congratulatory in Active Voice	More Diplomatic in Passive Voice
You lost the shipment.	The shipment was lost.
I recruited seven engineers last month.	Seven engineers were recruited last month.
We are investigating the high rate of failures on the final assembly line.	The high rate of failures on the final assembly line is being investigated.

Choosing Strong Words

After you have decided how to adapt to your audience, you're ready to begin composing your message. As you write your first draft, let your creativity flow. Don't try to draft and edit at the same time, and don't worry about getting everything perfect. Don't get hung up on spelling or grammar at this point. Guess, draw pictures, or talk out loud—do whatever it takes to get the ideas out of your head and onto your paper or screen. If you've planned carefully, you'll have time to revise and refine the material before anyone else sees it. In fact, many writers find it helpful to establish a personal rule of never showing a first draft to anyone. By working in this "safe zone," away from the critical eyes of others, your mind will stay free to think clearly and creatively.

When it's time to assess your work-in-progress, look for three things: strong words, effective sentences, and coherent paragraphs. Succesful writers pay close attention to the correct use of words. If you make errors in grammar or usage, you lose credibility with your audience—even if your message is otherwise correct. Poor grammar suggests to readers that you lack professionalism, and they may choose not to trust you. Moreover, poor grammar may imply that you don't respect your audience enough to get things right.

The rules of grammar and usage are complex and some evolve over time. Even professional editors and grammarians occasionally have questions about correct usage, and they sometimes disagree about the answers.

With practice, you'll become more skilled at making correct choices over time. If you have doubts about what is correct, you have many ways to find the answer. Consult the many special reference books and resources available in libraries, in bookstores, and on the Internet.

In addition to using words *correctly*, successful writers and speakers take care to use the most *effective* words and phrases. Selecting and using words effectively is often more challenging than using words correctly because doing so is a matter of judgment and experience. Careful writers continue to work at their craft to find words that communicate with power.

Abstract vs. Concrete Words

Abstract word:
A word that expresses a concept, quality, or characteristic.

Concrete word:
A word that stands for something you can touch, see, or visualize.

An **abstract word** expresses a concept, quality, or characteristic. Abstractions are usually broad, encompass a category of ideas, and can be intellectual, academic, or philosophical. Love, honor, progress, tradition, and beauty are abstractions, as are such important business concepts as productivity, quality, and motivation. In contrast, a **concrete word** stands for something you can touch, see, or visualize. Most concrete terms are anchored in the tangible, material world. Chair, green, two, database, and website are concrete words; they are direct, clear, and exact.

Of the two types, abstractions tend to cause more trouble because they are often "fuzzy" and can be interpreted differently, depending on the audience and the circumstances. The best way to minimize such problems is to balance abstract terms with concrete ones. State the concept, and then pin it down with details expressed in more concrete terms. Save the abstractions for ideas that cannot be expressed any other way.

Weak vs. Strong Words

When you compose business messages, look for the most powerful words for each situation (see Table 4.4):

- **Choose strong, precise words.** Choose words that express your thoughts clearly, specifically, and strongly. If you find yourself using many adjectives and adverbs, chances are you're trying to compensate for weak nouns and verbs. Saying that *sales plummeted* is stronger and more efficient than saying sales *dropped dramatically* or *sales experienced a dramatic drop.*
- **Choose familiar words.** You'll communicate best with words that are familiar to both you and your readers. Moreover, trying to use unfamiliar words can lead to embarrassing mistakes.
- **Avoid clichés and use buzzwords carefully.** Although familiar words are generally the best choice, avoid cliches—terms and phrases so common that they have lost some of their power to communicate. Buzzwords, newly coined terms often associated with technology, business, or cultural changes, are more difficult to handle than **cliches** because in small doses and in the right situations, they can be useful. The careful use of a **buzzword** can signal that you're an insider, someone in the know. However, buzzwords quickly become cliches, and using them too late in their "life cycle" can mark you as an outsider desperately trying to look like an insider.

Cliche:
A term or phrase that is so commonly used that it has lost its effectiveness.

Buzzword:
A newly coined term that is temporarily popular, but may become cliche or outdated quickly.

- **Use jargon carefully. Jargon**, the specialized language of a particular profession or industry, has a bad reputation, but it's not always bad. Using jargon is usually an efficient way to communicate within the specific groups that understand these terms. After all, that's how jargon develops in the first place, as people with similar interests develop ways to communicate complex ideas quickly.

Jargon: Specialized language or terminology associated with a certain profession, industry, or field of study.

If you need help finding the right words, try some of the visual dictionaries and thesauruses available online.

Table 4.4 Selected Examples of Finding Powerful Words

Potentially Weak Words and Phrases	Stronger Alternatives (effective usage depends on the situation)
Increase (as a verb)	Accelerate, amplify, augment, enlarge, escalate, expand, extend, magnify, multiply, soar, swell
Decrease (as a verb)	Curb, cut back, depreciate, dwindle, shrink, slacken
Large, small	(use a specific number, such as $100 million)
Good	Admirable, beneficial, desirable, flawless, pleasant, sound, superior, worthy
Bad	Abysmal, corrupt, deficient, flawed, inadequate, inferior, poor, substandard, worthless
We are committed to providing . . .	We provide . . .
It is in our best interest to . . .	We should . . .
Ascertain	Find out, learn
Consummate	Close, bring about
Peruse	Read, study
Circumvent	Avoid
Unequivocal	Certain
An uphill battle	A challenge
Writing on the wall	Prediction
Call the shots	Lead
Take by storm	Attack
Costs an arm and a leg	Expensive
A new ballgame	Fresh start
Fall through the cracks	Be overlooked
Think outside the box	Be creative
Run it up the flagpole	Find out what people think about it
Mission-critical	Vital
Green light (as a verb)	Approve
Space (as in, "we compete in the XYZ space")	Market or industry
Human capital	People, employees, workforce
Low-hanging fruit	Tasks that are easy to complete or sales that are easy to close
Pushback	Resistance

Creating Effective Sentences

Arranging your carefully chosen words into effective sentences is the next step in creating successful messages. Start by selecting the best type of sentence to communicate each point you want to make.

The Four Types of Sentences

Sentences come in four basic varieties: simple, compound, complex, and compound-complex.

Simple sentence:
A sentence with one main clause.

A **simple sentence** has one main clause (a single subject and a single predicate), although it may be expanded by nouns and pronouns serving as objects of the action and by modifying phrases. Consider this example (with the subject underlined once and the predicate verb underlined twice):

> Profits increased 35 percent in the past year

Compound sentence:
A sentence with two main clauses that express two or more independent thoughts of equal importance.

A **compound sentence** has two or more main clauses that express two or more independent but related thoughts of equal importance, usually joined by *and*, *but*, or *or*. In effect, a compound sentence is a merger of two or more simple sentences (independent clauses) that are related. For example:

> Wages declined by 5 percent, and employee turnover has been higher than ever.

The independent clauses in a compound sentence are always separated by a comma or by a semicolon. If a semi-colon is used, the connecting word like *and* or *but* is omitted.

Complex sentence:
A sentence that expresses one main thought and one or more subordinate thoughts related to it, often separated by a comma.

A **complex sentence** expresses one main thought (the independent clause) and one or more subordinate thoughts (dependent clauses) related to it, often separated by a comma. The subordinate thought, which comes first in the following sentence, could not stand alone:

> Although you may question Gerald's conclusions, you must admit that his research is thorough.

Compound-complex sentence: A sentence with two main clauses, at least one of which contains a subordinate clause.

A **compound-complex sentence** has two main clauses, at least one of which contains a subordinate clause:

> Profits increased 35 percent in the past year, so although the company faces long-term challenges, I agree that its short-term prospects look quite positive.

Strive for variety and balance among all four sentence types. If you use too many simple sentences, you won't be able to properly express the relationships among your ideas, and your writing will sound choppy and abrupt. At the other extreme, a long series of compound, complex, or compound-complex sentences can be tiring to read.

Using Sentence Style to Emphasize Key Thoughts

In every message, some ideas are more important than others. You can emphasize key ideas through your sentence style. One obvious technique is to give important points the most space. When you want to call attention to a thought, use extra words to describe it. Consider this sentence:

> The chairperson called for a vote of the shareholders.

To emphasize the importance of the chairperson, you might describe her more fully:

> Having considerable experience in corporate takeover battles, the chairperson called for a vote of the shareholders.

You can increase the emphasis even more by adding a separate, short sentence to augment the first:

> The chairperson called for a vote of the shareholders. She has considerable experience in corporate takeover battles.

You can also call attention to a thought by making it the subject of the sentence. In the following example, the emphasis is on the person:

> I can write letters much more quickly using a computer.

However, when you change the subject, the computer takes center stage:

> The computer enables me to write letters much more quickly.

Another way to emphasize an idea is to place it either at the beginning or at the end of a sentence:

> **Less emphatic:** We are cutting the price to stimulate demand.
>
> **More emphatic:** To stimulate demand, we are cutting the price.

In complex sentences, the ideal placement of the dependent clause depends on the relationship between the ideas expressed. If you want to emphasize the idea expressed in the dependent clause, put that clause at the end of the sentence (the most emphatic position) or at the beginning (the second most emphatic position). If you want to downplay the idea, position the dependent clause within the sentence. How does emphasis change in three versions of the same complex sentence?

> **Most emphatic:** The electronic parts are manufactured in Mexico, which has lower wage rates than the United States.
>
> **Emphatic:** Because wage rates are lower in Mexico than in the United States, the electronic parts are manufactured there.
>
> **Least emphatic:** Mexico, which has lower wage rates than the United States, was selected as the production site for the electronic parts.

Techniques such as these give you a great deal of control over the way your audience will interpret what you have to say.

Crafting Coherent Paragraphs

Paragraphs organize sentences that are related to the same general topic. Readers expect every paragraph to be *unified*—focusing on a single topic—and *coherent*—presenting ideas in a logically connected way.

The Elements of a Paragraph

Paragraphs vary widely in length and form, but most contain three basic elements: a topic sentence, support sentences that develop the topic, and transitional words and phrases.

Topic Sentence

Topic sentence:
A sentence that introduces the topic of the paragraph.

Most effective paragraphs deal with a single topic, and the sentence that introduces that topic is called the **topic sentence**. This sentence, often the first one in the paragraph, gives readers a summary of the idea that will be covered in the rest of the paragraph. The following example shows how a topic sentence can introduce the subject and suggest the way the subject will be developed:

> Public relations problems have troubled the medical products division for many years.

Support Sentences

In most paragraphs, the topic sentence needs to be explained, justified, or extended with one or more support sentences. These sentences must be related to the topic and provide examples, evidence, and clarification:

> The medical products division has been troubled for many years by public relations problems. Since 2014, the local newspaper has published 15 articles that portray the division in a negative light. We have been accused of everything from mistreating laboratory animals to polluting the local groundwater. Our facility has been described as a health hazard. Our scientists are referred to as "Frankensteins," and our profits are considered "obscene."

Notice how these support sentences give examples that support the topic sentence. Each one provides another piece of evidence to demonstrate the general truth of the main thought. Also, each sentence is clearly related to the general idea being developed, which gives the paragraph its unity. A paragraph is well developed when it contains enough information to make the topic sentence convincing and interesting and doesn't contain any unneeded or unrelated sentences.

Transitions

Transitions connect ideas by showing how one thought is related to another. They also help alert the reader to what lies ahead so that shifts and changes don't cause confusion. In addition to helping readers understand the connections you're trying to make, transitions give your writing a smooth, even flow.

Transition:
A word or phrase that connects ideas by showing how one idea is related to another.

Depending on the specific need within a document, transitional elements can range in length from a single word to an entire paragraph or more. You can establish transitions in a variety of ways:

- **Use connecting words.** Use words such as *and, but, or, nevertheless, however,* and *in addition*.
- **Echo a word or phrase from a previous paragraph or sentence.** "We need to establish a system to monitor inventory levels. This system will provide . . ."
- **Use a pronoun that refers to a noun used previously.** "Ms. Arthur is the leading candidate for the president's position. She has excellent qualifications."
- **Use words that are frequently paired.** "The machine has a minimum output of. . . Its maximum output is . . ."

Some transitions serve as mood changers, alerting the reader to a change in mood from the previous material. Some transitions announce a total contrast with what's gone on before, some announce a cause-and-effect relationship, and some signal a change in time. Here is a list of common transitions:

- **Cause-and-effect relationship:** therefore, because, accordingly, thus, consequently, hence, as a result, so
- **Comparison:** similarly, here again, likewise, in comparison, still
- **Contrast:** yet, conversely, whereas, nevertheless, on the other hand, however, but, nonetheless
- **Condition:** although, if
- **Illustration:** for example, in particular, in this case, for instance
- **Time sequence:** formerly, after, when, meanwhile, sometimes
- **Intensification:** indeed, in fact, in any event
- **Summary:** in brief, in short, to sum up
- **Repetition:** that is, in other words, as I mentioned earlier
- **Additional detail:** moreover, furthermore, in addition, besides, first, second, third, finally

Consider using a transition whenever it might help the reader understand your ideas and follow you from point to point. You can use transitions inside paragraphs to tie together related points and between paragraphs to ease the shift from one distinct thought to another. In longer reports, a transition that links major sections or chapters is often a complete paragraph that serves as a summary of the ideas presented in the section just ending and/or as a mini-introduction to the next section.

Developing Paragraphs

You have a variety of options for developing paragraphs, each of which can convey a specific type of idea. Five of the most common approaches are illustration, comparison or contrast, cause and effect, classification, and problem and solution (see Table 4.5).

Table 4.5 Five Techniques for Developing Paragraphs

Technique	How it works	Example
Illustration	Gives examples that demonstrate the general idea	Some of our most popular products are available through local distributors. For example, Everett & Lemmings carries our frozen soups and entrees. The J. B. Green Company carries our complete line of seasonings, as well as the frozen soups. Wilmont Foods, also a major distributor, now carries our new line of frozen desserts.
Comparison or contrast	Uses similarities or differences to develop the topic	When the company was small, we could handle our recruiting informally. The need for new employees was limited, and each manager could comfortably screen and hire her or his own staff. However, our successful bid on the Owens contract means that we will be doubling our labor force over the next six months. To hire that many people without disrupting our ongoing activities, we will create a separate recruiting group within the human resources department.
Cause and effect	Focuses on the reasons for something	The heavy-duty fabric of your Wanderer tent probably broke down for one of two reasons: 1) a sharp object punctured the fabric, and without reinforcement, the hole was enlarged by the stress of pitching the tent daily for a week or 2) the fibers gradually rotted because the tent was folded and stored while still wet.
Classification	Shows how a general idea is broken into specific categories	Successful candidates for our supervisor trainee program generally come from one of several groups. The largest group by far consists of recent graduates of accredited business management programs. The next largest group comes from within our own company, as we try to promote promising workers to positions of greater responsibility. Finally, we occasionally accept candidates with outstanding supervisory experience in related industries.
Problem and solution	Presents a problem and discusses the solution	Selling handmade toys online is a challenge because consumers are accustomed to buying heavily advertised toys from major chain stores or well-known websites such as Amazon.com. However, if we develop an appealing website, we can compete on the basis of product novelty and quality. In addition, we can provide unusual crafts at a competitive price: a rocking horse of birch with a hand-knit tail and mane, a music box with the child's name painted on the top, and a real teepee made by Native American artisans.

Writing for Mobile Devices

One obvious adaptation to make for audiences using mobile devices is to modify the design and layout of your messages to fit smaller screen sizes and different user interface features. However, modifying your approach to writing is also an important step. Reading is more difficult on small screens; consequently the users' ability to comprehend what they read on mobile devices is lower than it is on larger screens. Use these five techniques to make your mobile messages more effective:

- **Use a linear organization.** In a printed document or on a larger screen, readers can easily take in multiple elements on a page, such as summary boxes, tables and other supporting visuals, and sidebars with related information. All these elements are in view at the same time, so readers can jump around the page to read various parts without feeling lost. However, with small mobile device screens, a complicated organization requires readers to zoom in and out and pan around to see all these elements at readable text sizes. This makes reading slower and raises the odds that readers will get disoriented and lose the thread of the message because they can't see the big picture. To simplify reading, organize with a linear flow from the top to the bottom of the message or article.
- **Prioritize information.** Small screens make it difficult for readers to scan the page to find the information they want most. Prioritize the information based on what you know about their needs and put that information first. Use the *inverted pyramid* style favored by journalists, in which you reveal the most important information briefly at first and then provide successive layers of detail that readers can consume if they want. Note that you may need to avoid using the indirect approach (see page 100) if your message is complicated, because it will be more difficult to readers to follow your chain of reasoning.
- **Write shorter and more-focused messages and documents.** Mobile users often lack the patience or time to read lengthy messages or documents, so keep it short. In some cases, this could require you to write two documents: a shorter *executive summary* for mobile use and a longer supporting document that readers who want more detail can optionally access.
- **Use shorter subject lines and headings.** Mobile devices, particularly phones, can't display as many characters in a single line of text as the typical computer screen can. Depending on the app or website, email subject lines and page headings will either be truncated or will wrap around to take up multiple lines. Both formats make reading more difficult. A good rule of thumb is to keep subject lines and headlines to around 25 characters. This doesn't give you much text to work with, so make every word count, and make sure you start with the key words so readers can instantly see what the subject line or heading is about.
- **Use shorter paragraphs.** Shorter paragraphs are less intimidating and let readers take frequent "micro rests" as they move through a document. Because far less text is displayed at once on a mobile screen, keep paragraphs as short as possible so readers don't have to swipe through screen after screen between paragraph breaks.

Compare the messages in Figure 4.5 to get a sense of how to write reader-friendly mobile content.

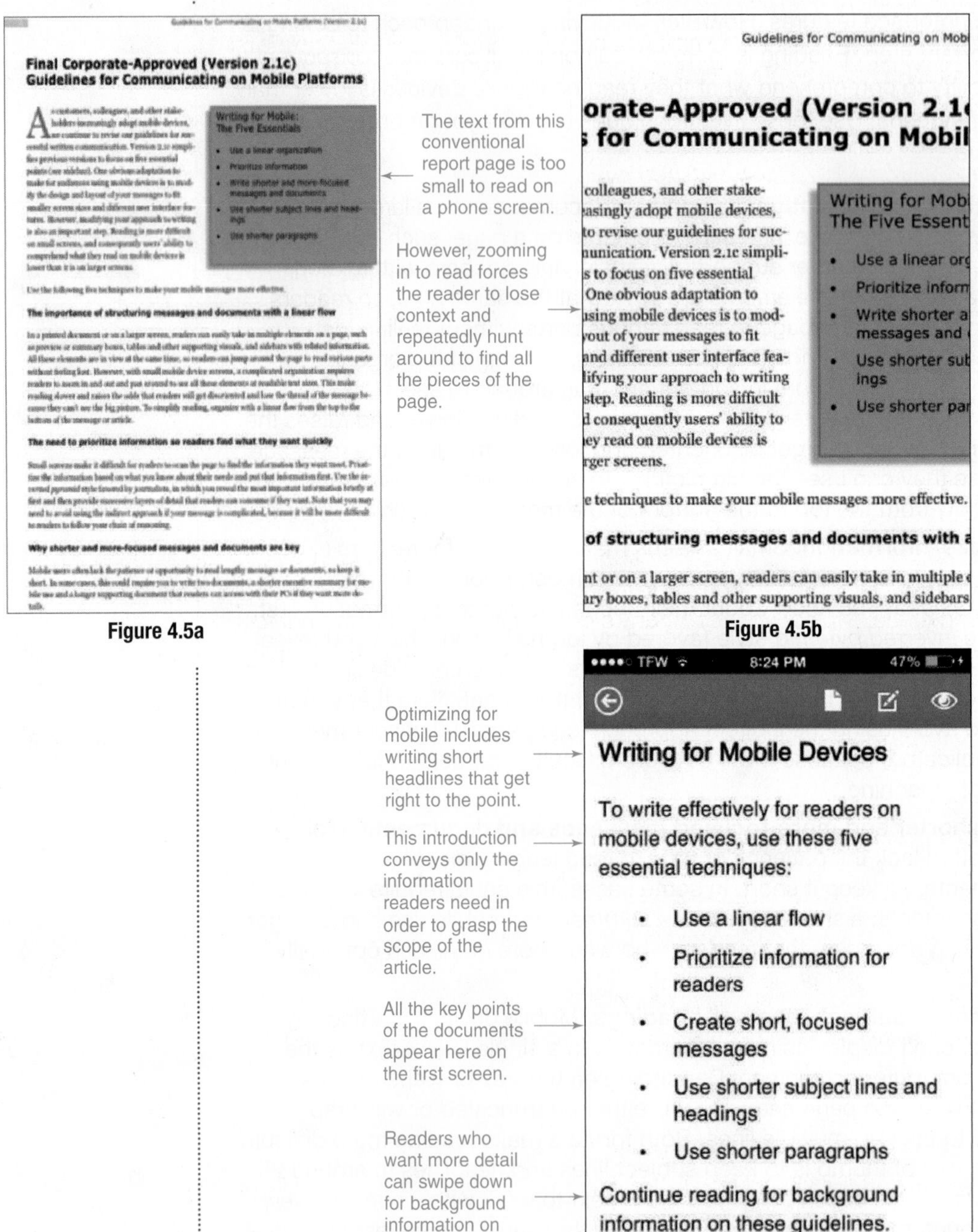

Figure 4.5a

Figure 4.5b

Figure 4.5c

Figure 4.5
Writing for Mobile Devices
Messages and documents created for printed pages and full-sized screen can be difficult and frustrating on mobile devices (Figures 4.5a and 4.5b). For mobile audiences, rewrite with short headlines and concise, linear content—notice how much easier Figure 4.5c is to read.

Chapter Summary

Adapting Your Message to Your Audience

The "you" attitude refers to speaking and writing in terms of your audience's wishes, interests, hopes, and preferences rather than your own. Writing with this attitude is essential to effective communication because it shows your audience that you have their needs in mind, not just your own. Good etiquette not only indicates respect for your audience, but also helps foster a more successful environment for communication by minimizing negative emotional reaction. Sensitive communicators understand the difference between delivering negative news and being negative. Without hiding the negative news, they look for ways to emphasize positive aspects. Being sensitive includes taking care to avoid biased language that unfairly and even unethically categorizes or stigmatizes people in ways related to gender, race, ethnicity, age, disability, or other personal characteristics.

Building a Relationship with Your Audience

Successful communication relies on a positive relationship between sender and receiver. The way audiences respond to your messages depends heavily on your credibility, which is a measure of your believability based on how reliable you are and how much trust you evoke in others. When you have established credibility with an audience, communication becomes much easier because you no longer have to spend time and energy convincing people that you are a trustworthy source of information and ideas. Project your company's desired image when communicating with external audiences. You represent your company and therefore play a vital role in helping the company build and maintain positive relationships with all stakeholders.

Controlling Your Style and Tone

To achieve a tone that is conversational but still businesslike, avoid obsolete and pompous language, avoid preaching and bragging, be careful with intimacy (sharing personal details or adopting an overly casual tone), and be careful with humor. Plain language is a way of presenting information in a simple, unadorned style so that your audience can easily grasp your meaning. By writing and speaking in plain terms, you demonstrate the "you" attitude and show respect for your audience. In the active voice, the subject performs the action and the object receives the action. In the passive voice, the subject receives the action. The passive voice combines the helping verb to be with a form of the verb that is usually in the past tense.

Choosing Strong Words

Selecting the correct and most effective words involves balancing abstract and concrete words, choosing powerful and familiar words, avoiding clichés, and using buzzwords and jargon carefully.

Creating Effective Sentences

The four types of sentences are simple (one main clause), compound (two main clauses that express independent but related ideas of equal importance), complex (one main clause and one subordinate clause of lesser importance), and compound-complex (two main clauses, at least one of which contains a subordinate clause). Sentence style affects emphasis by playing up or playing down specific parts of a sentence. To emphasize a certain point, you can place it at the end of the sentence or make it the subject of the sentence. To deemphasize a point, put it in the middle of the sentence.

Crafting Coherent Paragraphs

The three key elements of a paragraph are a topic sentence that identifies the subject of the paragraph, support sentences that develop the topic and provide examples and evidence, and transitional words and phrases that help readers connect one thought to the next. Five ways to develop coherent paragraphs are illustration, comparison or contrast, cause and effect, classification, and problem and solution.

Writing for Mobile Devices

Five techniques for writing effective messages for mobile readers are using a linear organization so readers don't have to jump around the screen to find important message elements; prioritizing information and delivering the most important information first; writing short, focused messages; using short subjects lines and headings; and using short paragraphs.

Test Your Knowledge

1. What is the "you" attitude?
2. In what situations should you consider using passive voice?
3. How does an abstract word differ from a concrete word?
4. How can you use sentence style to emphasize key thoughts?
5. What functions do transitions serve?

Apply Your Knowledge

1. When composing a business messages, how can you communicate with an authentic voice and project your company's image at the same time?
2. Should you bother using transitions if the logical sequence of your message is already obvious? Why or why not?
3. Why can it be difficult to use the indirect approach for a complex message that will be read on mobile devices?

Practice Your Skills

1. **Adopting the "You" Attitude** Rewrite the following sentences to reflect your audience's viewpoint.
   - **a.** We request that you use the order form supplied in the back of our catalog.
   - **b.** We insist that you always bring your credit card to the store.
   - **c.** We want to get rid of all our 25-inch monitors to make room in our warehouse for the 30-inch screens. Thus we are offering a 25 percent discount on all sales this week.
   - **d.** We are sending the refund for $25 as requested.

2. **Emphasizing the Positive** Revise these sentences to be positive rather than negative.
   a. To avoid damage to your credit rating, please remit payment within 10 days.
   b. We don't make refunds on returned merchandise that is soiled.
   c. You should have realized that waterbeds will freeze in unheated houses during winter. Therefore, our guarantee does not cover the valve damage and you must pay the $9.50 valve-replacement fee (plus postage).

3. **Emphasizing the Positive** Revise the following sentences to replace unflattering terms (in italics) with euphemisms.
   a. The new boss is (*stubborn*) when it comes to doing things by the book.
   b. When you say we've doubled our profit level, you are (*wrong*).
   c. Just be careful not to make any (*stupid*) choices this week.
   d. Jim Riley is (*incompetent*) for that kind of promotion.

4. **Communicating Courteously** Revise the following sentences to make them more respectful.
   a. You claim that you mailed your check last Thursday, but we have not received it.
   b. It is not our policy to exchange sale items, especially after you have worn them.
   c. You neglected to sign the enclosed contract.
   d. You failed to enclose your instructions for your new will.

5. **Using Bias-Free Language** Rewrite each of the following sentences to eliminate bias.
   a. A pilot must have the ability to stay calm under pressure, and then he must be trained to cope with any problem that arises.
   b. Candidate Renata Parsons, married and the mother of a teenager, will attend the debate.
   c. For as old as he is, Sam Nugent is still one of our most active sales reps.

6. **Replacing Vague Phrases** In the following sentences, replace vague phrases (underlined) with concrete phrases. Make up any details you might need.
   a. We will be opening our new facility sometime this spring.
   b. After the reception, we were surprised that such a large number attended.
   c. The new production line has been operating with increased efficiency on every run.
   d. Over the holiday, we hired a crew to expand the work area.

7. **Replacing Weak Terms** In the following sentences, replace weak terms (in italics) with words that are stronger.
   a. The two reporters (*ran after*) every lead enthusiastically.
   b. The (*bright*) colors in that ad are keeping customers from seeing what we have to sell.
   c. Health costs (*suddenly rise*) when management forgets to emphasize safety issues.
   d. Once we solved the zoning issue, new business construction (*moved forward*), and the district has been flourishing ever since.

8. **Replacing Cliches** Rewrite these sentences to replace the cliches with fresh, personal expressions.
   a. Being a jack-of-all-trades, Dave worked well in his new selling job.
   b. Moving Leslie into the accounting department, where she was literally a fish out of water, was like putting a square peg into a round hole, if you get my drift.
   c. It's a dog-eat-dog world out there in the rat race of the asphalt jungle.

9. **Replacing Complicated Words** In the following sentences, replace long, complicated words with short, simple ones.
   a. Management (*inaugurated*) the recycling policy six months ago.
   b. You can convey the same meaning without (*utilizing*) the same words.
   c. You'll never be promoted unless you (*endeavor*) to be more patient.
   d. I have to wait until payday to (*ascertain*) whether I got the raise.
   e. John will send you a copy once he's inserted all the (*alterations*) you've requested.

10. **Replacing Obsolete Phrases** Rewrite the following sentences, replacing obsolete phrases with up-to-date versions. Write none if you think there is no appropriate substitute.
    a. I have completed the form and returned it to my insurance company, as per your instructions.
    b. Attached herewith is a copy of our new contract for your records.
    c. Please be advised that your account with National Bank has been compromised, and we advise you to close it as soon as possible.

11. **Writing Active Sentences** Rewrite the following sentences so that they are active rather than passive.
    a. The raw data are submitted to the data processing division by the sales representative each Friday.
    b. High profits are publicized by management.
    c. Our computers are serviced by the Santee Company.
    d. The employees were represented by Janet Hogan.

12. **Using Transitions** Add transitions to the following sentences to improve the flow of ideas. (Note: You may need to eliminate or add some words to smooth out the sentences.)
    a. Facing some of the toughest competitors in the world, Harley-Davidson had to make some changes. The company introduced new products. Harley's management team set out to rebuild the company's production process. New products were coming to market and the company was turning a profit. Harley's quality standards were not on par with those of its foreign competitors. Harley's costs were still among the highest in the industry. Harley made a U-turn and restructured the company's organizational structure. Harley's efforts have paid off.

    b. Whether you're indulging in a doughnut in New York or California, Krispy Kreme wants you to enjoy the same delicious taste with every bite. The company maintains consistent product quality by carefully controlling every step of the production process. Krispy Kreme tests all raw ingredients against established quality standards. Every delivery of wheat flour is sampled and measured for its moisture content and protein levels. Krispy Kreme blends the ingredients. Krispy Kreme tests the doughnut mix for quality. Krispy Kreme delivers the mix to its stores. Krispy Kreme knows that it takes more than a quality mix to produce perfect doughnuts all the time. The company supplies its stores with everything they need to produce premium doughnuts—mix, icings, fillings, equipment—you name it.

Activities

1. **Creating a Businesslike Tone** Read the following email message and then analyze the strengths and weaknesses of each sentence, and revise the message so that it follows this chapter's guidelines. The message was written by the marketing manager of an online retailer of baby-related products in the hope of becoming a retail outlet for Inglesina strollers and high chairs. As a manufacturer of stylish, top-quality products, Inglesina (based in Italy) is extremely selective about the retail outlets through which it allows its products to be sold.

> Our e-tailing company, Best Baby Gear, specializes in only the very best products for parents of newborns, infants, and toddlers. We constantly scour the world looking for products that are good enough and well-built enough and classy enough—good enough that is to take their place alongside the hundreds of other carefully selected products that adorn the pages of our award-winning website, www.bestbabygear.com. We aim for the fences every time we select a product to join this portfolio; we don't want to waste our time with onesey-twosey products that might sell a half dozen units per annum—no, we want every product to be a top-drawer success, selling at least one hundred units per specific model per year in order to justify our expense and hassle factor in adding it to the abovementioned portfolio. After careful consideration, we thusly concluded that your Inglesina lines meet our needs and would therefore like to add it.

2. **Creating Effective Sentences** If you are interested in business, chances are you've had an idea or two for starting a company. If you haven't yet, go ahead and dream up an idea now. Make it something you are passionate about. Now write a four-sentence summary that could appear on the Info tab on a Facebook profile. Make sure the first sentence is a solid topic sentence, and make sure the next three sentences offer relevant evidence and examples. Feel free to make up any details you need. Email your summary to your instructor or post it on your class blog.

3. **Writing for Mobile Devices** Find an interesting website article on any business topic. Write a three-paragraph summary that would be easy to easy to read on a phone screen.

Expand Your Skills

Locate an example of professional communication from a reputable online source. Choose a paragraph with at least three sentences. Evaluate the effectiveness of this paragraph at three levels, starting with the paragraph structure. Is the paragraph unified and cohesive? Does it have a clear topic sentence and sufficient support to clarify and expand on that topic? Second, evaluate each sentence. Are the sentences easy to read and easy to understand? Did the writer vary the types and lengths of sentences used to produce a smooth flow and rhythm? Is the most important idea presented prominently in each sentence? Third, evaluate at least six word choices. Did the writer use these words correctly and effectively? Using whatever medium your instructor requests, write a brief analysis of the piece (no more than one page), citing specific elements from the piece and support from the chapter.

CHAPTER

5

Completing Business Messages

After studying this chapter, you will be able to:

- Discuss the value of careful revision and describe the tasks involved in evaluating a first draft.
- List tips to keep in mind as you evaluate the work of another writer.
- List four techniques you can use to improve the readability of your messages.
- Describe the steps you can take to improve the clarity of your writing and give four tips on making your writing more concise.
- List four principles of effective design and explain the role of design and typographical elements in document readability.
- Structure business letters, envelopes, and memos using commonly accepted layouts.
- Explain the importance of proofreading and give six tips for successful proofreading.
- Discuss the most important issues to consider when distributing your messages.

Revising Your First Draft

This chapter covers the tasks in the third step of the three-step writing process: revising your message to achieve optimum quality and then producing, proofreading, and distributing it. After you complete your first draft, you may be tempted to breathe a sigh of relief, send the message on its way, and move on to the next project. Resist that temptation. Successful communicators recognize that the first draft is rarely as tight, clear, and compelling as it needs to be. Careful revision improves the effectiveness of your messages and sends a strong signal to your readers that you respect their time and care about their opinions.

The scope of the revision task can vary somewhat, depending on the medium and the nature of your message. For informal messages to internal audiences, particularly when using short-message tools such as IM and email, the revision process is often as simple as quickly looking over your message to correct any mistakes before sending or posting it.

However, don't fall into the common trap of thinking you don't need to worry about grammar, spelling, clarity, and other fundamentals of good writing don't matter in when you use digital formats. These qualities can be *especially* important with digital, particularly if these messages are the only contact your audience has with you. First, poor-quality messages create an impression of poor-quality thinking, and even minor errors can cause confusion, frustration, and costly delays. Second, assume that anything you write for digital channels will be stored forever and could be distributed far beyond your original audience. Don't join the business professionals who have seen ill-considered or poorly written messages wind up in the news media or as evidence in lawsuits or criminal cases.

Particularly with longer or more complicated messages, try to plan your work schedule so that you can put your first draft aside for a day or two before you begin the revision process. Doing so will allow you to approach the material with a fresh perspective. Then start with the "big picture," making sure that the document accomplishes your overall goals, before moving to finer points such as readability, clarity, and conciseness. Compare the before and after versions of the letter in Figures 5.1 and 5.2 on the following pages for examples of how careful revision makes a message more effective and easier to read.

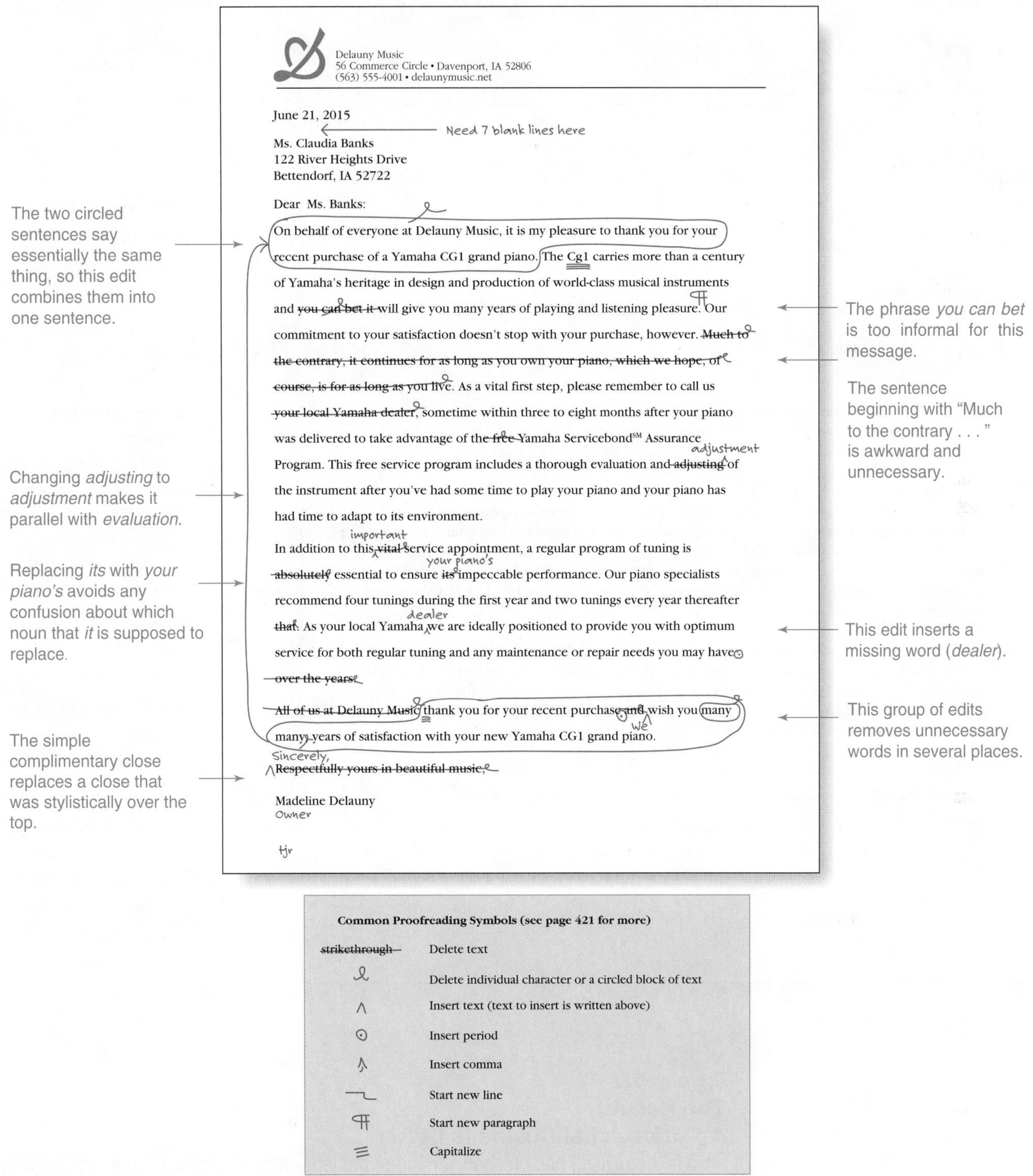

Delauny Music
56 Commerce Circle • Davenport, IA 52806
(563) 555-4001 • delaunymusic.net

June 21, 2015

Ms. Claudia Banks
122 River Heights Drive
Bettendorf, IA 52722

Dear Ms. Banks:

On behalf of everyone at Delauny Music, it is my pleasure to thank you for your recent purchase of a Yamaha CG1 grand piano. The Cg1 carries more than a century of Yamaha's heritage in design and production of world-class musical instruments and you can bet it will give you many years of playing and listening pleasure. Our commitment to your satisfaction doesn't stop with your purchase, however. Much to the contrary, it continues for as long as you own your piano, which we hope, of course, is for as long as you live. As a vital first step, please remember to call us your local Yamaha dealer, sometime within three to eight months after your piano was delivered to take advantage of the free Yamaha Servicebond[SM] Assurance Program. This free service program includes a thorough evaluation and adjusting of the instrument after you've had some time to play your piano and your piano has had time to adapt to its environment.

In addition to this vital service appointment, a regular program of tuning is absolutely essential to ensure its impeccable performance. Our piano specialists recommend four tunings during the first year and two tunings every year thereafter that. As your local Yamaha we are ideally positioned to provide you with optimum service for both regular tuning and any maintenance or repair needs you may have over the years.

All of us at Delauny Music thank you for your recent purchase and wish you many many years of satisfaction with your new Yamaha CG1 grand piano.

Respectfully yours in beautiful music,

Madeline Delauny

Common Proofreading Symbols (see page 421 for more)

Symbol	Meaning
~~strikethrough~~	Delete text
ℓ	Delete individual character or a circled block of text
∧	Insert text (text to insert is written above)
⊙	Insert period
∧ (comma)	Insert comma
⌐	Start new line
¶	Start new paragraph
≡	Capitalize

Figure 5.1
Improving a Customer Letter through Careful Revision

Careful revision makes this draft shorter, clearer, and more focused. The proofreading symbols you see here are still widely used whenever printed documents are edited and revised. Note that many business documents are now "marked up" using such technological tools as revision marks in Microsoft Word and comments in Adobe Acrobat. No matter what the medium, careful revision is key to a more effective message.

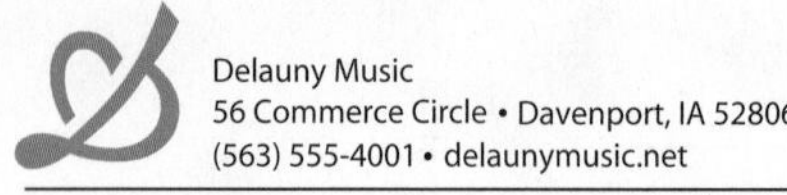

Delauny Music
56 Commerce Circle • Davenport, IA 52806
(563) 555-4001 • delaunymusic.net

June 21, 2016

Ms. Claudia Banks
122 River Heights Drive
Bettendorf, IA 52722

Dear Ms. Banks:

Thank you for your recent purchase. We wish you many years of satisfaction with your new Yamaha CG1 grand piano. The CG1 carries more than a century of Yamaha's heritage in design and production of world-class musical instruments and will give you many years of playing and listening pleasure.

Our commitment to your satisfaction doesn't stop with your purchase, however. As a vital first step, please remember to call us sometime within three to eight months after your piano was delivered to take advantage of the Yamaha Servicebond[SM] Assurance Program. This free service program includes a thorough evaluation and adjustment of the instrument after you've had some time to play your piano and your piano has had time to adapt to its environment.

In addition to this important service appointment, a regular program of tuning is essential to ensure your piano's impeccable performance. Our piano specialists recommend four tunings during the first year and two tunings every year thereafter. As your local Yamaha dealer, we are ideally positioned to provide you with optimum service for both regular tuning and any maintenance or repair needs you may have.

Sincerely,

Madeline Delauny

Madeline Delauny
Owner

tjr

The letter is now properly formatted.

The content is now organized in three coherent paragraphs, each with a distinct message.

The tone is friendly and engaging without being flowery.

Figure 5.2
The Result: A Professional Business Letter
Here is the revised and finished version of the letter from Figure 5.1. Note that the block format used here is just one of several layout options; other layouts are discussed later in this chapter.

Evaluating Your Content, Organization, and Tone

When you begin the revision process, focus on content, organization, and tone. Today's time-pressed readers want messages that convey important content clearly and quickly. To evaluate the content of your message, make sure it is accurate, relevant to the audience's needs, and complete.

When you are satisfied with the basic content of your message, review its organization by asking yourself these questions:

- Are all your points covered in the most logical and convincing order?
- Do the most important ideas receive the most space and greatest emphasis?
- Are any points repeated unnecessarily?
- Are details grouped together logically, or are some still scattered through the document?

Next, consider whether you have achieved the right tone for your audience. Is your writing formal enough to meet the audience's expectations without being too formal or academic? Is it too casual for a serious subject? Finally, spend a few extra moments on the beginning and end of your message; these sections usually have the greatest impact on the audience.

Evaluating the Work of Other Writers

At many points in your career, you will be asked to evaluate, edit, or revise the work of others. Before you dive into someone else's work, recognize the dual responsibility that you have. First, unless you've specifically been asked to rewrite something in your own style, keep in mind that your job is to help the other writer succeed at his or her task, not to impose your writing style. Second, make sure you understand the writer's intent before you begin suggesting or making changes. With those thoughts in mind, ask yourself the following questions as you evaluate someone else's writing:

- What is the purpose of this document or message?
- Who is the target audience?
- What information does the audience need?
- Are there any special circumstances or sensitive issues that the writer had to consider (or should have considered)?
- Does the document provide this information in a well-organized way?
- Does the writing demonstrate the "you" attitude toward the audience?
- Is the tone of the writing appropriate for the audience and the situation?
- Is the writing clear? If not, how can it be improved?
- Is the writing as concise as it could be?
- Does the page or screen design support the intended message?

You can read more about using these skills in the context of wiki writing in Chapter 6.

Revising to Improve Readability

After confirming the content, organization, and tone of your message, make a second pass to improve readability. Most professionals receive far more reading material than they can ever hope to consume; they'll appreciate your efforts to make your documents easier to read—and easier to skim for the highlights. You'll benefit from this effort, too. If you earn a reputation for creating well-crafted documents that respect the audience's time, people will pay more attention to your work.

Four powerful techniques for improving readability are varying sentence length, using shorter paragraphs, replacing narrative with lists, and adding effective headings and subheadings.

Vary Sentence Length

Varying sentence length maintains reader interest and controls the emphasis given to major and minor points. Look for ways to combine a mixture of sentences that are short (up to 15 words or so), medium (15–25 words), and long (more than 25 words). Each sentence length has advantages. Short sentences can be processed quickly and are easier for nonnative speakers to interpret. Medium-length sentences are useful for showing the relationships among ideas. Long sentences are often the best way to convey complex ideas, to list a number of related points, or to summarize or preview information.

Of course, each sentence length has disadvantages as well. Too many short sentences in a row can make your writing feel choppy and disconnected. Medium sentences can lack the punch of short sentences and the informative power of longer sentences. Long sentences are usually harder to understand than short sentences because they are packed with information; they are also harder to skim when readers are looking for key points in a hurry.

Keeping Paragraphs Short

Large blocks of text can be visually daunting, particularly on screen, so keep your paragraphs as short as possible. Unless you break up your thoughts somehow, you'll end up with lengthy paragraphs that will intimidate even the most dedicated reader. Short paragraphs, roughly 100 words or fewer, are easier to read than long ones and make your writing look inviting. Short, forceful paragraphs also serve to emphasize your ideas.

However, don't go overboard with short paragraphs at the expense of maintaining a smooth and clear flow of information. In particular, use one-sentence paragraphs only occasionally and only for emphasis. Also, if you need to divide a subject into several pieces in order to keep paragraphs short, use transitions to help your readers keep the ideas connected.

Using Lists and Bullets to Clarify and Emphasize

In some instances, a list can be more effective than conventional sentences and paragraphs. Lists can show the sequence of your ideas, heighten their impact visually, and increase the likelihood that readers will find your key points. In addition, lists help simplify complex subjects, highlight the main points, enable skimming, and give readers a visual break. Compare these two approaches to the same information:

Table 5.1 Using Lists and Bullets

Narrative	List
Owning your own business has many potential advantages. One is the opportunity to pursue your own personal passion. Another advantage is the satisfaction of working for yourself. As a sole proprietor, you also have the advantage of privacy because you do not have to reveal your financial information or plans to anyone.	Owning your own business has three advantages: • Opportunity to pursue personal passion • Satisfaction of working for yourself • Financial privacy

When creating a list, you can separate items with numbers, letters, or bullets. Bullets (graphical symbols that precede each item in a list) are generally preferred over numbers, unless the list is in some logical sequence or ranking or specific list items will be referred to later. Make your lists easy to read by making all the items parallel (see "Impose parallelism" on page 146) and keeping individual items as short as possible. Also, be sure to introduce a list clearly so that people know what they're about to read.

Adding Headings and Subheadings

A **heading** is a brief title that tells readers about the content of the section that follows. **Subheadings** indicate subsections within a major section; complex documents may have several levels of subheadings. Headings and subheadings help in three important ways: they show readers at a glance how the material is organized, they call attention to important points, and they highlight connections and transitions between ideas.

Descriptive headings, such as "Cost Considerations," simply identify a topic without suggesting anything more. **Informative headings**, such as "Redesigning Material Flow to Cut Production Costs," give the reader some context and may point toward any conclusions or recommendations that you offer in the section. Well-written, informative headings are self-contained, which means readers can skim just the headings and subheadings and understand them without reading the rest of the document. Whatever types of headings you choose, keep them brief and grammatically parallel.

Heading:
A brief title that tells readers about the content of the section that follows.

Subheading:
A subordinate heading indicating a subsection within a major section.

Descriptive heading:
A heading that identifies a topic without suggesting anything more.

Informative heading:
A heading that gives the reader context and may point toward a conclusion or recommendation.

Editing for Clarity and Conciseness

After you've reviewed and revised your message for readability, your next step is to make sure your message is as clear and as concise as possible.

Editing for Clarity

Make sure that every sentence conveys the meaning you intend and that readers can extract your intended meaning without reading the sentence more than once. To ensure clarity, look closely at your paragraph organization, sentence structure, and word choices. Can readers make sense of the related sentences in a paragraph? Is the meaning of each sentence easy to grasp? Is every word clear and unambiguous (meaning it doesn't have any risk of being interpreted in more than one way)? See Table 5.2 for examples of the following tips:

- **Break up overly long sentences.** If you find yourself stuck in a long sentence, you're probably trying to make the sentence do more than it can reasonably do, such as expressing two dissimilar thoughts or peppering the reader with too many pieces of supporting evidence at once.
- **Rewrite hedging sentences.** Hedging means pulling back from making an absolutely certain, definitive statement about a topic. Granted, sometimes you have to write *may* or *seems* to avoid stating a judgment as a fact. However, when you hedge too often or without good reason, you come across as being unsure of what you're saying.
- **Impose parallelism.** Making your writing parallel means expressing similar ideas using the same grammatical structure. Doing so helps your audience understand that the ideas are related, are of similar importance, and are on the same level of generality. Parallel patterns are also easier to read. You can impose parallelism by repeating a pattern in words, phrases, clauses, or entire sentences.
- **Correct dangling modifiers.** Sometimes a modifier is not just an adjective or an adverb but an entire phrase modifying a noun or a verb. Be careful not to leave this type of modifier dangling, with no connection to the subject of the sentence.
- **Reword long noun sequences.** When multiple nouns are strung together as modifiers, the resulting sentence can be hard to read. See if a single well-chosen word will do the job. If the nouns are all necessary, consider moving one or more to a modifying phrase, as shown in Table 5.2.
- **Replace camouflaged verbs.** Watch for words that end in *ion*, *tion*, *ing*, *ment*, *ant*, *ent*, *ence*, *ance*, and *ency*. These endings often change verbs into nouns and adjectives, which requires you to add a verb to get your point across.
- **Clarify sentence structure.** Keep the subject and predicate of a sentence as close together as possible. Similarly, adjectives, adverbs, and prepositional phrases usually make the most sense when they're placed as close as possible to the words they modify.
- **Clarify awkward references.** Try to avoid vague references such as the *above-mentioned, as mentioned above, the aforementioned, the former, the latter,* and *respectively*. Use a specific pointer such as "as described in the second paragraph on page 22."

Table 5.2 Revising for Clarity

Issues to Review	Ineffective	Effective
Overly Long Sentences Taking compound sentences too far	The magazine will be published January 1, and I'd better meet the deadline if I want my article included because we want the article to appear before the trade show.	The magazine will be published January 1. I'd better meet the deadline because we want the article to appear before the trade show.
Hedging Sentences Over-qualifying sentences	I believe that Mr. Johnson's employment record seems to show that he may be capable of handling the position.	Mr. Johnson's employment record shows that he is capable of handling the position.
Unparallel Sentences Using dissimilar construction for similar ideas	Mr. Simms had been drenched with rain, bombarded with telephone calls, and his boss shouted at him. To waste time and missing deadlines are bad habits.	Mr. Sims had been drenched with rain, bombarded with telephone calls, and shouted at by his boss. Wasting time and missing deadlines are bad habits.
Dangling Modifiers Placing modifiers close to the wrong nouns and verbs	Walking to the office, a red sports car passed her. [suggests that the car was walking to the office] Reduced by 25 percent, Europe had its lowest semiconductor output in a decade. [suggests that Europe shrank by 25 percent]	A red sports car passed her while she was walking to the office. Europe reduced semiconductor output by 25 percent, its lowest output in a decade.
Long Noun Sequences Stringing too many nouns together	The window sash installation company will give us an estimate on Friday.	The company that installs window sashes will give us an estimate on Friday.
Camouflaged Verbs Changing verbs into nouns	The manager undertook implementation of the rules. Verification of the shipments occurs weekly. reach a conclusion about give consideration to	The manager implemented the rules. We verify shipments weekly. conclude consider
Sentence Structure Separating subject and predicate Separating adjectives, adverbs, or prepositional phrases from the words they modify	A 10% decline in market share, which resulted from quality problems and an aggressive sales campaign by Armitage, the market leader in the Northeast, was the major problem in 2017. Our antique desk lends an air of strength and substance with thick legs and large drawers.	The major problem in 2017 was a 10% loss of market share, which resulted from quality problems and an aggressive sales campaign by Armitage, the market leader in the Northeast. With its thick legs and large drawers, our antique desk lends an air of strength and substance.
Awkward References	The Law Office and the Accounting Office distribute computer supplies for legal secretaries and beginning accountants, respectively.	The Law Office distributes computer supplies for legal secretaries; the Accounting Office distributes those for beginning accountants.

Editing for Conciseness

Many of the changes you make to improve clarity also shorten your message by removing unnecessary words. The next step is to examine the text with the specific goal of reducing the number of words you use. Readers appreciate conciseness and are more likely to read your documents if you have a reputation for efficient writing. See Table 5.3 for examples of the following tips:

- **Delete unnecessary words and phrases.** To test whether a word or phrase is essential, try the sentence without it. If the meaning doesn't change, leave it out.
- **Replace long words and phrases.** Short words and phrases are generally more vivid and easier to read than long ones.
- **Eliminate redundancies.** In some word combinations, the words say the same thing. For instance, "visible to the eye" is redundant because visible is enough without further clarification; "to the eye" adds nothing.
- **Recast "It is/There are" starters.** If you start a sentence with an indefinite pronoun such as *it* or *there*, odds are the sentence could be shorter and more active. For instance, "We believe . . ." is a stronger opening than "It is believed that . . ."

Table 5.3 Revising for Conciseness

Issues to Review	Ineffective	Effective
Unnecessary Words and Phrases		
Using wordy phrases	for the sum of in the event that prior to the start of in the near future at this point in time due to the fact that in view of the fact that until such time as with reference to	for if before soon now because because when about
Using too many relative pronouns	Cars that are sold after January will not have a six-month warranty. Employees who are driving to work should park in the underground garage.	Cars sold after January will not have a six-month warranty. Employees driving to work should park in the underground garage. Employees should park in the underground garage.
Using too few relative pronouns	The project manager told the engineers last week the specifications were changed.	The project manager told the engineers last week that the specifications were changed.

Issues to Review	Ineffective	Effective
Long Words and Phrases		
Using overly long words	During the preceding year, the company accelerated productive operations. The action was predicated on the assumption that the company was operating at a financial deficit	Last year the company sped up operations. The action was based on the belief that the company was losing money.
Using wordy phrases rather than infinitives	If you want success as a writer, you must work hard. He went to the library for the purpose of studying. The employer increased salaries so that she could improve morale.	To succeed as a writer, you must work hard. He went to the library to study. The employer increased salaries to improve morale.
Redundancies		
Repeating meanings	absolutely complete basic fundamentals follows after free and clear refer back repeat again collect together future plans return back important essentials end result actual truth final outcome uniquely unusual surrounded on all sides	complete fundamentals follows free refer repeat collect plans return essentials result truth outcome unique surrounded
Using double modifiers	modern, up-to-date equipment	modern equipment
It Is/There Are Starters		
Starting sentences with *It* or *There*	It would be appreciated if you would sign the lease today. There are five employees in this division who were late to work today.	Please sign the lease today. Five employees in this division were late to work today.

As you make all these improvements, concentrate on how each word contributes to an effective sentence and on how each sentence helps to develop a coherent paragraph.

Designing Business Documents

Now it's time to put your hard work on display. The production quality of your message—the total effect of page or screen design, graphical elements, typography, and so on—plays an important role in its effectiveness. A polished, inviting design not only makes your document easier to read but also conveys a sense of professionalism and importance.

Designing for Readability

Design affects readability in two important ways. First, depending on how they are used, design elements can increase or decrease the effectiveness of your message. Thoughtful, reader-focused design makes messages easier to read, whereas poorly chosen design elements can act as barriers that impede communication. Second, visual design sends a nonverbal message to your readers, influencing their perceptions of the communication before they read a single word.

Figure 5.3 Designing for Readability Whether it's a website, a presentation, or a printed report, readability plays an important role in helping the audience comprehend what you are saying.

To achieve an effective design, pay careful attention to the following design elements:

- **Consistency.** Throughout each message, be consistent in your use of margins, typeface, type size, spacing, color, lines, and position. In most cases, you'll want to be consistent from message to message as well; that way, audiences who receive multiple messages from you recognize your documents and know what to expect. Style sheets and themes can be a big help here.
- **Balance.** Balance is an important but sometimes subjective design issue. One document may have a formal, rigid design in which the various elements are placed in a grid pattern, another may have a less formal design in which elements flow more freely across the page. Both could

be in balance. Like the tone of your language, visual balance can be too formal, just right, or too informal for a given message.

- **Restraint.** Strive for simplicity. Don't clutter your message with too many design elements, colors, or decorative touches.
- **Detail.** Pay attention to details that affect your design—and your message. For instance, an extremely wide column of text can be difficult to read; in many cases a better solution is to split the text into two narrower columns.

Character and Paragraph Formatting

Even without special training in graphic design, you can make your printed messages more effective by understanding the use of some key design elements.

Typefaces

Typeface refers to the physical design of letters, numbers, and other text characters. (Font and typeface are often used interchangeably, although strictly speaking, a **font** is a set of characters in a given typeface.) Typeface influences the tone of your message, making it look authoritative or friendly, businesslike or casual, classic or modern, and so on (see Table 5.4). Be sure to choose fonts that are appropriate for your message; many of the fonts on your computer are not appropriate for business use.

Typeface:
The physical design of letters, numbers, and other text characters

Font:
A set of characters using a given typeface.

Table 5.4 Typeface Personalities: Serious to Casual to Playful

Serif Typefaces	Sans Serif Typefaces	Specialty Typefaces (rarely used for routine business communication
Baskerville	Arial	Bradley Hand
Century Schoolbook	Helvetica Neue LT Std	Chalkduster
Courier	Gil Sans	Comic Sans MS
Goudy	Lucida Grande	Marker Felt
Georgia	Tahoma	Noteworthy
Times New Roman	Verdana	Present LT Std

Serif typefaces have small crosslines (called serifs) at the ends of each letter stroke. **Sans serif typefaces**, in contrast, lack these serifs. For years, the conventional wisdom in typography was that serif faces were easier to read in long blocks of text, because the serifs made it easier for the eye to pick out individual letters. Accordingly, the standard advice was to use serif faces for the body of a document and sans serif for headings and subheadings.

Serif typeface:
A typeface with small crosslines at the ends of each letter stroke.

Sans serif typeface:
A typeface that lacks serifs (crosslines) at the ends of each letter stroke.

However, the research behind the conventional wisdom is not as conclusive as once thought. In fact, many sans serif typefaces work as well or better for body text than some serif typefaces. This seems to be particularly true on screens, which often have lower resolution than printed text. Many contemporary documents and webpages now use sans serif for body text.

For most documents, you shouldn't need more than one typeface, although if you want to make captions or other text elements stand out, you can use a second font. More than that can clutter a document and produce an amateurish look.

Type Styles

Type style:
Any modification that lends contrast or emphasis to type, such as boldface, italics, underlining, and color.

Type style refers to any modification that lends contrast or emphasis to type, including boldface, italic, underlining, and color. For example, you can boldface individual words or phrases to draw more attention to them. Italic type has specific uses as well, such as highlighting quotations and indicating foreign words, irony, humor, book and movie titles, and unconventional usage. Use any type style in moderation. For instance, underlining or using all-uppercase letters can interfere with the reader's ability to recognize the shapes of words, improperly placed boldface or italicized type can slow down your reader, and shadowed or outlined type can seriously hinder legibility.

Type Size

Point:
A measurement of type size. One point is 1/72 of an inch when printed.

Type size is measured in **points**; one point is 1/72 of an inch on the printed page. For most printed business messages, use a type size of 10 to 12 points for regular text and 12 to 18 points for headings and subheadings. Resist the temptation to reduce the type size to squeeze in text or to enlarge it to fill up space. Type that is too small is hard to read, whereas extra-large type often looks unprofessional.

Contrast

Contrast:
The difference in color or shade between the document's background and its text.

Contrast refers to the difference in color or shade between the document's background and its text. Business documents are almost always printed on white paper (or very occasionally light gray or cream-colored paper). For maximum contrast, text is nearly always black. A letter may have text in some other color as an accent, such as the company's mailing address or website address, but as a general rule, business communications should be printed in black because it provides the best contrast with the background.

When creating materials designed to be viewed online, such as in a presentation, colored backgrounds may be used, opening up the possibility of other font colors. For example, yellow text on a dark blue background contrasts very well, and is easy for an audience to read on a large screen or presentation slide.

Kerning

Kerning:
The process of adjusting the spacing between characters in a proportional font, usually to achieve a visually pleasing result.

With 10- or 12-point type, you probably never notice the size of the spaces between letters. With much larger type, like you might use on the title slide of a presentation, those spaces can become very noticeable. **Kerning** is adjusting the space between two letters. Certain word processing and design programs let you adjust kerning any time. You can set other programs to automatically adjust kerning when the type is at least a certain size. In Microsoft Word, this feature is in the Advanced tab of the Font dialog box.

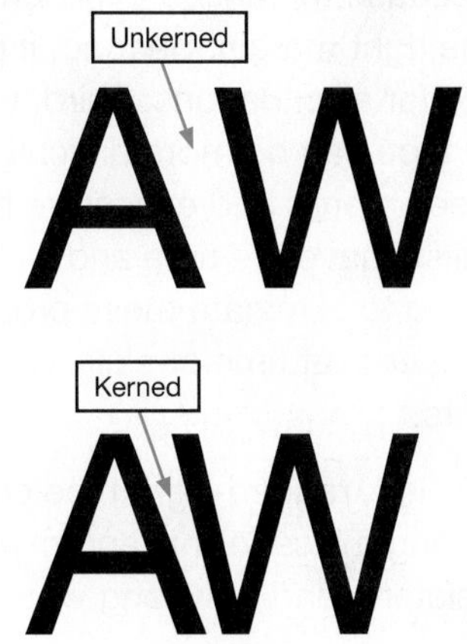

Figure 5.4
Kerning Example
In the top pair, kerning is not enabled. Although there is just a small amount of space between the letters, it looks like more because of their shapes. In the bottom pair, with kerning enabled, the letters are closer together. They still don't touch because of their shapes.

White Space

Any space free of text or artwork is considered **white space**. (Note that "white space" isn't necessarily white.) These unused areas provide visual contrast and important resting points for your readers. White space includes the open area surrounding headings, margins, and paragraph indents, plus the space around images, vertical space between columns, and horizontal space between paragraphs or lines of text. To increase the chance that readers will read your messages, be generous with white space; it makes pages and screens feel less intimidating and easier to read.

White space: An unused area that provides visual contrast and resting points for the reader.

Margins

A document's **margins** are the amounts of white space each edge of the printed page. A typical margin setting for a business letter or memo is 1" on all sides. This setting can be slightly increased or decreased as needed in most word processing programs for special purposes. For example, if a document almost fits on a single page but for one or two lines, decreasing the margins to 0.75" on each side may allow the document to fit. Or, to accommodate the extra space needed at the top of the page when printing on letterhead paper, you could increase the top margin to 2" (or some other amount, depending on the size of the letterhead graphic).

Margins: The white space around each edge of the printed page.

Paragraph Alignment

In addition to their width, the look and feel of margins are influenced by **paragraph alignment**, which can be set justified (which means they are flush, or aligned vertically, on both the left and the right); flush left with a ragged-right margin; flush right with a ragged-left margin; or centered. This paragraph is flush left with a ragged-right margin.

Paragraph alignment: The way the lines of a paragraph align with the margins: left, right, centered, or justified.

Magazines, newspapers, and books often use justified type because it can accommodate more text in a given space. However, justified type needs to be used with care and is not a good choice for most routine business documents.

First, it creates a denser look because the uniform line lengths decrease the amount of white space along the right margin. Second, it produces a more formal look that isn't appropriate for all situations. Third, unless it is formatted with skill and attention, justified type can be more difficult to read because it can produce large gaps between words and excessive hyphenation at the ends of lines. Publishing specialists have the time and skill needed to carefully adjust character and word spacing to eliminate these problems. Because most business communicators don't have that time or skill, it's best to avoid justified type in most business documents.

In contrast to justified type, flush-left, ragged-right type creates a more open appearance on the page, producing a less formal and more contemporary look. Spacing between words is consistent, and only long words that fall at the ends of lines are hyphenated.

Centered type is rarely used for text paragraphs but is commonly used for headings and subheadings. Flush-right, ragged-left type is rarely used.

Leading

Leading:
The amount of space between lines of text.

Leading is the amount of space between lines of text. Single-spacing has no leading; double-spacing has one extra line of space between line of text. In word processing programs you can specify other amounts of leading, such as 1.5 for leading halfway in-between single and double spacing. You can also indicate an amount of extra leading that should appear before or after a paragraph.

Widows and Orphans

Sometimes a paragraph breaks at the bottom of a page, so that part of the paragraph is on the next page. When there is just one line of the paragraph at the bottom of the page, it's known as an orphan. When there's just one line of the paragraph at the top of the next page, it's known as a widow. Both look unattractive and should be avoided. (You should also avoid hyphenating the last word on a page.) You can enable a feature in most word processing programs that will prevent widows and orphans from occurring.

Designing for Mobile Devices

In addition to making your content mobile-friendly using the writing tips in Chapter 4, you can follow these steps to format that content for mobile devices:

- **Think in small chunks.** Remember that mobile users consume information one screen at a time, so try to divide your message into independent, easy-to-consume bites. If readers have to scroll through a dozen screens to piece together your message, they might miss your point or just give up entirely.
- **Make generous use of white space.** White space is always helpful, but it's critical on small screens because are trying to get the point of every message as quickly as possible. Keep your paragraphs short (4–6 lines) and separate them with blank lines so the reader's eyes can easily jump from one point to the next.

- **Format simply.** Avoid anything that is likely to get in the way of fast, easy reading, including busy typefaces, complex graphics, and complicated layouts.
- **Consider horizontal and vertical layouts.** Most phones and tablets can automatically rotate their screen content from horizontal to vertical as the user rotates the device. A layout that doesn't work well with the narrow vertical perspective might be acceptable at the wider horizontal perspective.

Compare the two messages in Figure 5.5; notice how much more difficult the screen in Figure 5.5a is to read.

Figure 5.5 Designing for Mobile Devices

Even simple changes such as revising with shorter paragraphs, choosing cleaner typefaces, and making generous use of white space in and around the text can dramatically improve readability on mobile screens.

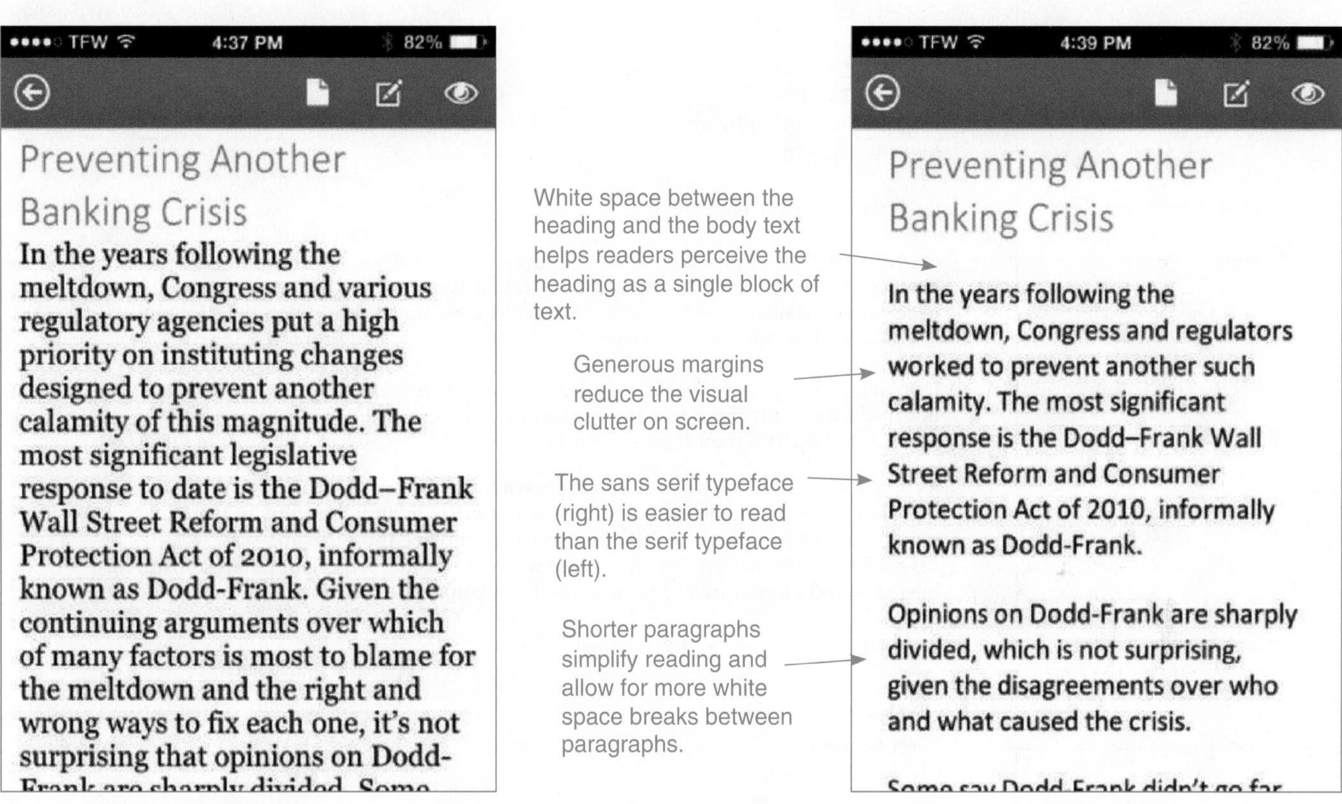

Figure 5.5a

Figure 5.5b

Business Letters, Envelopes, and Memos

All business letters, envelopes, and memos have certain elements in common. In the following sections you will learn about the basic layouts for these three essential forms of business correspondence.

Standard Letter Parts

The letter in Figure 5.6 shows the placement of standard letter parts. The writer of this business letter had no letterhead available but correctly included a heading. All business letters typically include these seven elements.

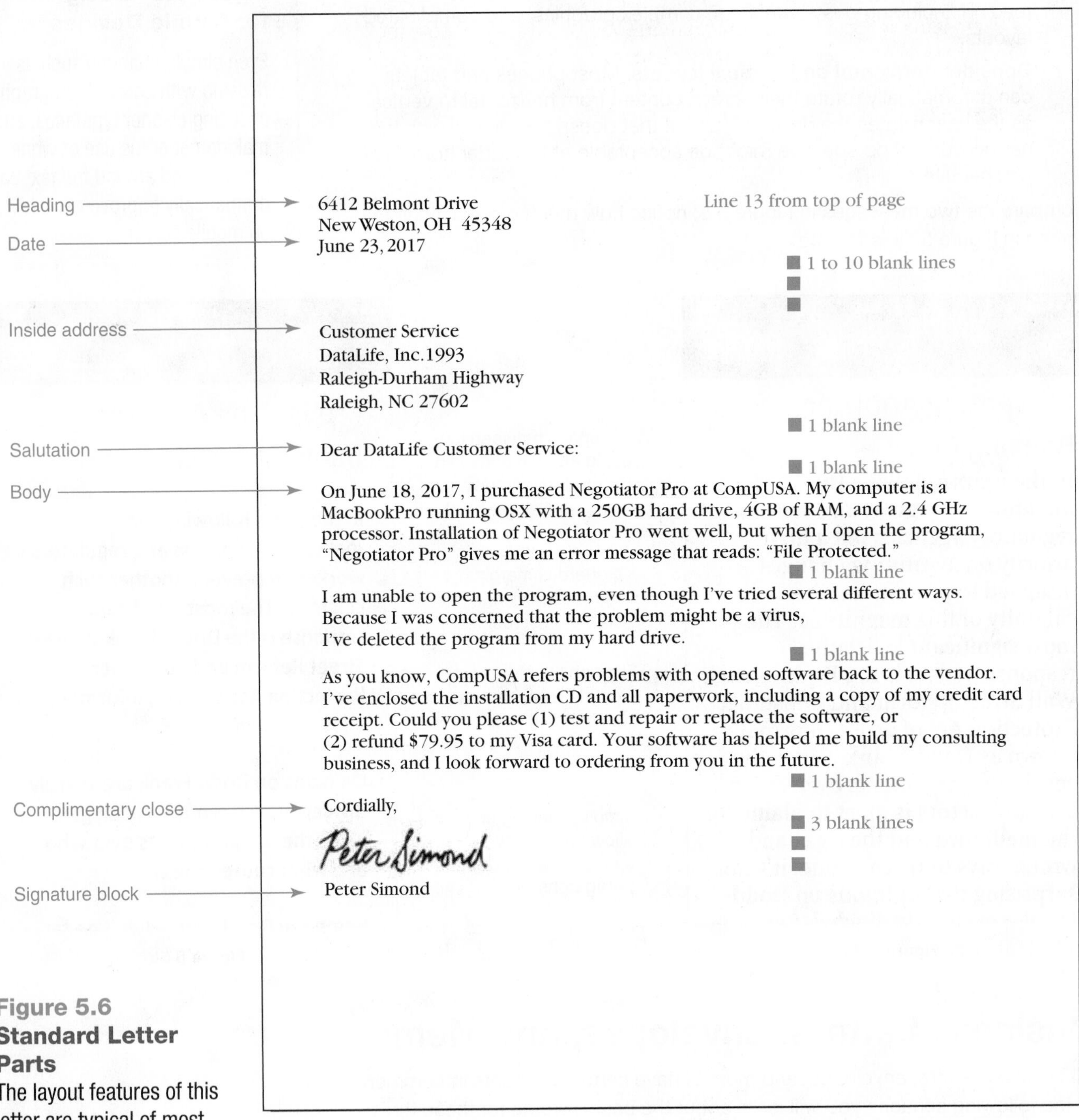

6412 Belmont Drive
New Weston, OH 45348
June 23, 2017

Customer Service
DataLife, Inc.1993
Raleigh-Durham Highway
Raleigh, NC 27602

Dear DataLife Customer Service:

On June 18, 2017, I purchased Negotiator Pro at CompUSA. My computer is a MacBookPro running OSX with a 250GB hard drive, 4GB of RAM, and a 2.4 GHz processor. Installation of Negotiator Pro went well, but when I open the program, "Negotiator Pro" gives me an error message that reads: "File Protected."

I am unable to open the program, even though I've tried several different ways. Because I was concerned that the problem might be a virus, I've deleted the program from my hard drive.

As you know, CompUSA refers problems with opened software back to the vendor. I've enclosed the installation CD and all paperwork, including a copy of my credit card receipt. Could you please (1) test and repair or replace the software, or (2) refund $79.95 to my Visa card. Your software has helped me build my consulting business, and I look forward to ordering from you in the future.

Cordially,

Peter Simond

Peter Simond

Figure 5.6 Standard Letter Parts
The layout features of this letter are typical of most business letters.

Letterhead: Pre-printed stationery containing the return addresses and sometimes other elements, such as a logo.

Heading

If **letterhead** stationery is not used, the heading includes a return address (but no name) and starts 13 lines from the top of the page, which leaves a 2-inch top margin. If letterhead is used, the heading is omitted.

Date

If you're using letterhead, place the date at least one blank line beneath the lowest part of the letterhead. Without letterhead, place the date immediately below the return address. The standard method of writing the date in the United States uses the full name of the month (no abbreviations), followed by the day (in numerals, without *st*, *nd*, *rd*, or *th*), a comma, and then the year: July 31, 2017. Many other countries use other formats (see Table 5.5), which can create confusion in international correspondence. To avoid misinterpretation in such cases, spell out the month.

Table 5.5 Common Date Formats

Convention	Order	Examples
US standard	Month day year	July 31, 2017 7/31/2017 7-31-2017
Japan	Year month day	17/07/31
Europe (most countries)	Day month year	31 July 2017 31/07/17 31.07.17
International (ISO) format	Year month day	2017-07-31

Inside Address

The **inside address** identifies the recipient of the letter. For US correspondence, begin the inside address at least one line below the date. Precede the addressee's name with a courtesy title, such as *Dr.*, *Mr.*, or *Ms*. The accepted courtesy title for women in business is Ms. If you're writing to a woman you know prefers Miss or Mrs., use it.

Inside address: The mailing address of the recipient of a letter, appearing near the top of the first page of the letter.

If you don't know—and can't find out—whether a person is a man or a woman, omit the courtesy title. For example, Terry Smith could be either a man or a woman. The first line of the inside address would be just Terry Smith, and the salutation would be Dear Terry Smith. The same is true if you know only a person's initials, as in S. J. Adams.

Spell out and capitalize titles that precede a person's name, such as Professor or General.

The person's organizational title, such as Director, may be included on this first line or on the line below; the name of a department may follow. In addresses and signature lines, don't forget to capitalize any professional title that follows a person's name:

Mr. Ray Johnson, Dean

or

Ms. Patricia T. Higgins

Assistant Vice President

Table 5.6: Forms of Address

Person	In Address	In Salutation
Personal Titles		
Man	Mr. [first & last name]	Dear Mr. [last name]:
Woman	Ms. [first & last name]	Dear Ms. [last name]:
Two men (or more)	Mr. [first & last name] and Mr. [first & last name]	Dear Mr. [last name] and Mr. [last name] or Messrs. [last name] and [last name]:
Two women (or more)	Ms. [first & last name] and Ms. [first & last name]	Dear Ms. [last name] and Ms. [last name] or Mses. [last name] and [last name]:
One woman and one man	Ms. [first & last name] and Mr. [first & last name]	Dear Ms. [last name] and Ms. [last name] or Mses. [last name] and [last name]:
Couple (married with same last name)	Mr. [husband's first name] and Mrs. [wife's first name] [couple's last name]	Dear Mr. and Mrs. [last name]:
Couple (married with different last name)	Mr. [first & last name of husband] Ms. [first & last name of wife]	Dear Mr. [husband's last name] and Ms. [wife's last name]: Dear [title in plural form] [last name]:
Couple (married professionals with same title and same last name)	[title in plural form] [husband's first name] and [wife's first name] [couple's last name]	Dear [title in plural form] [last name]:
Couple (married professionals with different titles and same last name)	[title] [first & last name of husband] and [title] [first & last name of wife]	Dear [title] and [title] [last name]:
Professional Titles		
President of a college or university	[title] [first & last name], President	Dear [title] [last name]:
Dean of a school or college	Dean [first & last name] or Dr., Mr., or Ms. [first & last name], Dean of [title]	Dear Dean [last name]: or Dear Dr., Mr., or Ms. [last name]:
Professor	Professor or Dr. [first & last name]	Dear Professor or Dr. [last name]:
Physician	[first & last name], M.D.	Dear Dr. [last name]:
Lawyer	Mr. or Ms. [first & last name], Attorney at Law	Dear Mr. or Ms. [last name]:
Military personnel	[full rank, first & last name, abbreviation of service designation] (add Retired if applicable)	Dear [rank] [last name]:
Company or corporation	[name of organization]	Ladies and Gentlemen: or Gentlemen and Ladies:
Governmental Titles		
President of the United States	The President	Dear Mr. or Madam President:
Senator of the United States	The Honorable [first & last name]	Dear Senator [last name]:
Cabinet member	The Honorable [first & last name]	Dear Mr. or Madam Secretary:
Attorney General	The Honorable [first & last name]	Dear Mr. or Madam Attorney General:
Mayor	The Honorable [first & last name], Mayor of [name of city]	Dear Mayor [last name]:
Judge	The Honorable [first & last name]	Dear Judge [last name]:

However, professional titles not appearing in an address or signature line are capitalized only when they directly precede the name:

President Kenneth Johanson will deliver the speech.

Maria Morales, president of ABC Enterprises, will deliver the speech.

The Honorable Helen Masters, senator from Arizona, will deliver the speech.

If the name of a specific person is unavailable, you may address the letter to the department or to a specific position within the department. Also, be sure to spell out company names in full, unless the company itself uses abbreviations in its official name.

Other address information includes the treatment of buildings, house numbers, and compass directions. The following example shows all the information that may be included in the inside address and its proper order for US correspondence:

Ms. Linda Coolidge, Vice President

Corporate Planning Department

Midwest Airlines

Kowalski Building, Suite 21-A

7279 Bristol Ave.

Toledo, OH 43617

Canadian addresses are similar, except that the name of the province is usually spelled out:

Dr. H. C. Armstrong

Research and Development

Commonwealth Mining Consortium

The Chelton Building, Suite 301

585 Second St. SW

Calgary, Alberta T2P 2P5

The order and layout of address information vary from country to country. So when addressing correspondence for other countries, carefully follow the format and information that appear in the company's letterhead. However, when you're sending mail *from* the United States, be sure that the name of the destination country appears on the last line of the address in capital letters. Use the English version of the country name so that your mail is routed from the United States to the right country. Then, to be sure your mail is routed correctly *within* the destination country, use the foreign spelling of the city name. For example, the following address uses the German spelling Köln instead of Cologne:

H. R. Veith, Director

Eisfieren Glaswerk

Blaubachstrasse 13 Street

Postfach 10 80 07

D-5000 Köln I District

GERMANY

Be sure to use organizational titles correctly when addressing international correspondence. Job designations vary around the world. In England, for example, a managing director is often what a US company would call its chief executive officer or president, and a British deputy is the equivalent of a vice president. In France, responsibilities are assigned to individuals without regard to title or organizational structure, and in China the title project manager has meaning, but the title sales manager may not. In addition, be aware that businesspeople in some countries sign correspondence without their names typed below. In Germany, for example, the belief is that employees represent the company, so it's inappropriate to emphasize personal names.

Salutation

Salutation:
The greeting in a letter, appearing just above the letter body.

In the **salutation** of your letter, follow the style of the first line of the inside address. If the first line is a person's name, the salutation is *Dear Mr.* or *Ms. Name*. The formality of the salutation depends on your relationship with the addressee. If in conversation you would say "Mary," your letter's salutation should be *Dear Mary*, followed by a colon. Otherwise, include the courtesy title and last name, followed by a colon. Presuming to write *Dear Lewis* instead of *Dear Professor Chang* demonstrates a disrespectful familiarity that the recipient may well resent.

If the first line of the inside address is a position title such as Director of Personnel, then use *Dear Director*. If the addressee is unknown, use a polite description, such as *Dear Alumnus*, *Dear SPCA Supporter*, or *Dear Voter*. If the first line is plural (a department or company), then use Ladies and Gentlemen (look again at Table 5.6). When you do not know whether you're writing to an individual or a group (for example, when writing a reference or a letter of recommendation), use *To whom it may concern*.

Salutopening:
An opening that omits the formal salutation but includes the recipient's name in the first paragraph.

In the United States some letter writers use a "salutopening" on the salutation line. A **salutopening** omits *Dear* but includes the first few words of the opening paragraph along with the recipient's name. After this line, the sentence continues a double space below as part of the body of the letter:

Thank you, Mr. Brown,

for your prompt payment of your bill.

Whether your salutation is informal or formal, be especially careful that names are spelled correctly. A misspelled name is glaring evidence of carelessness, and it belies the personal interest you're trying to express.

Body

The body of the letter is your message. Almost all letters are single-spaced, with one blank line before and after the salutation, between paragraphs, and before the complimentary close. The body may include indented lists and subheadings. Format these internal elements the same way every time you use them. If your company or department has a special format for all its letters, use it. company may select a format to use for all letters.

Complimentary Close

The **complimentary close** begins on the second line below the body of the letter. Alternatives for wording are available, but currently the trend seems to be toward using one-word closes, such as *Sincerely* and *Cordially*. In any case, the complimentary close reflects the relationship between you and the person you're writing to. Avoid cute closes, such as *Yours for bigger profits*. Your audience may not appreciate your sense of humor.

Complimentary close: The closing line of a letter, appearing below the letter body.

Signature Block

Leave three blank lines for a written signature below the complimentary close, and then include the **signature block** (unless it already appears in the letterhead). The person's title may appear on the same line as the name or on the line below:

Signature block: The writer's name and title, appearing just below the blank area where the writer will sign.

Cordially,

Raymond Dunnigan
Director of Personnel

If your name could be taken for either a man's or a woman's, you may include a courtesy title, with or without parentheses to indicate your gender. If you're a woman who prefers a particular courtesy title you may include it should include it in the same way:

Mrs. Nancy Winters

(Ms.) Juana Flores

Ms. Pat Li

(Mr.) Jamie Saunders

Additional Letter Parts

Some letters require additional information. The letter in Figure 5.7 shows how these additional parts should be arranged. The following elements may be used in any combination, depending on the requirements of the particular letter.

Figure 5.7
Additional Letter Parts
Not all letters contain these extra elements, but when they are required, they should be formatted using this example.

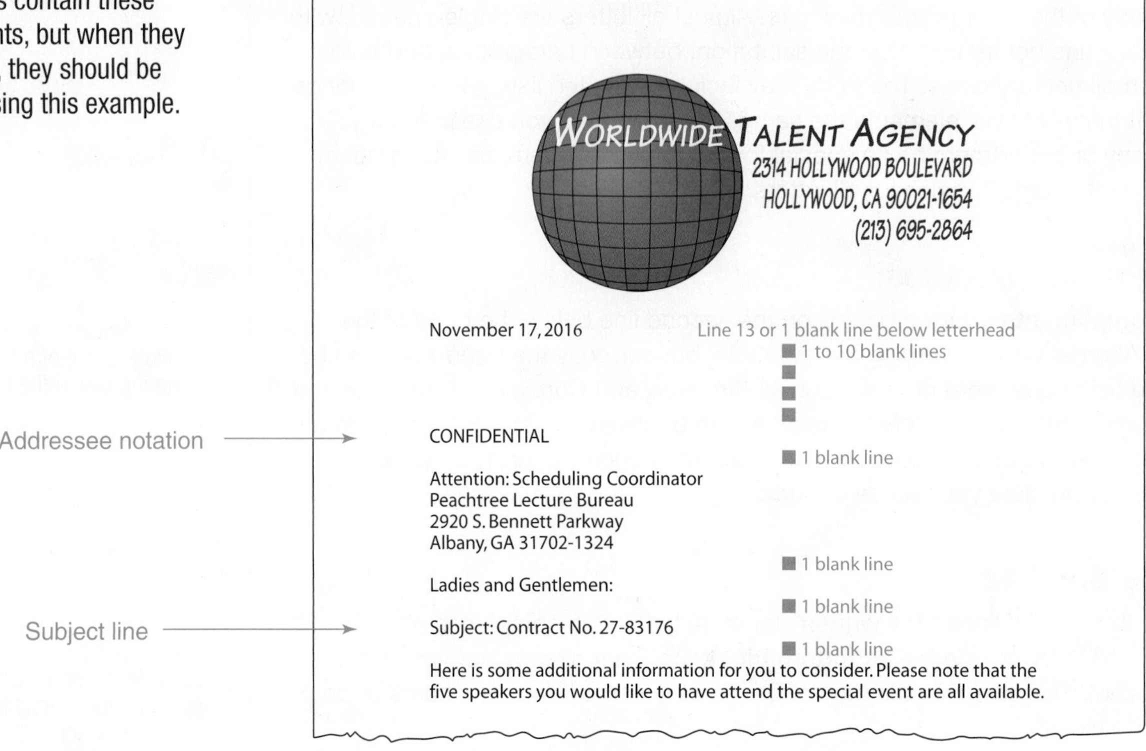

WORLDWIDE TALENT AGENCY
2314 HOLLYWOOD BOULEVARD
HOLLYWOOD, CA 90021-1654
(213) 695-2864

November 17, 2016

CONFIDENTIAL

Attention: Scheduling Coordinator
Peachtree Lecture Bureau
2920 S. Bennett Parkway
Albany, GA 31702-1324

Ladies and Gentlemen:

Subject: Contract No. 27-83176

Here is some additional information for you to consider. Please note that the five speakers you would like to have attend the special event are all available.

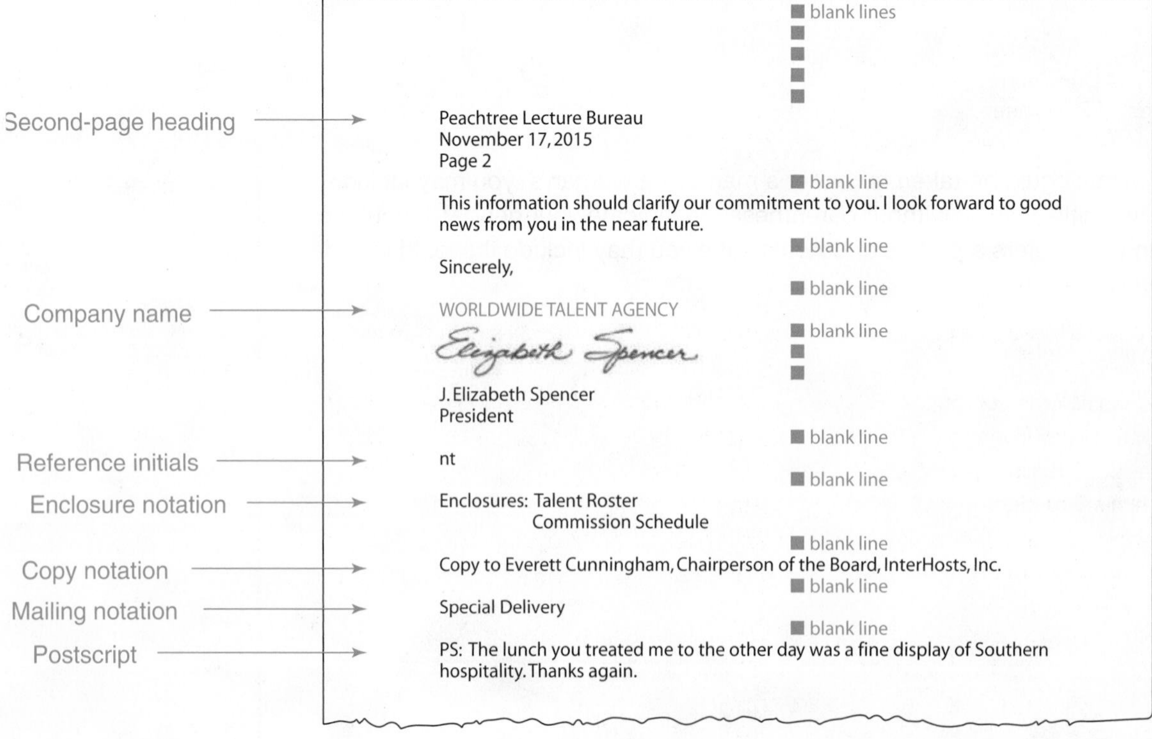

Peachtree Lecture Bureau
November 17, 2015
Page 2

This information should clarify our commitment to you. I look forward to good news from you in the near future.

Sincerely,

WORLDWIDE TALENT AGENCY

Elizabeth Spencer

J. Elizabeth Spencer
President

nt

Enclosures: Talent Roster
Commission Schedule

Copy to Everett Cunningham, Chairperson of the Board, InterHosts, Inc.

Special Delivery

PS: The lunch you treated me to the other day was a fine display of Southern hospitality. Thanks again.

Addressee Notation

Letters that have a restricted readership or that must be handled in a special way should include such addressee notations as *PERSONAL, CONFIDENTIAL*, or *PLEASE FORWARD*. This sort of notation appears a double space above the inside address, in all-capital letters.

Attention Line

Although not commonly used today, an attention line can be used if you know only the last name of the person you're writing to. It can also direct a letter to a position title or department. Place the attention line on the first line of the inside address and put the company name on the second.5 Match the address on the envelope with the style of the inside address. An attention line may take any of the following forms or variants of them:

Attention: Dr. McHenry

Attention: Director of Marketing

Attention: Marketing Department

Subject Line

The subject line tells recipients at a glance what the letter is about It usually appears below the salutation, either against the left margin, indented (as a paragraph in the body), or centered. Some businesses omit the word *Subject*, and some replace it with *Re*: or *In re*: (meaning "concerning" or "in the matter of"):

Subject: RainMaster Sprinklers

Re: Your February 2, 2016, order

In re: FALL 2017 SALES MEETING

Reference Order No. 27920

Second-page Heading

Use a second-page heading whenever an additional page is required. Some companies have second-page letterhead, with the company name and address on one line and in a smaller typeface. The heading provides the name (person or organization) from the first line of the inside address, the page number, the date, and perhaps a reference number. Leave two blank lines before the body. Make sure that at least two lines of a continued paragraph appear on the first and second pages. Never allow the closing lines to appear alone on a continued page. Precede the complimentary close or signature lines with at least two lines of the body.

All the following are acceptable forms for second-page headings:

Ms. Melissa Baker

May 10, 2017

Page 2

Ms. Melissa Baker, May 10, 2017, Page 2

Ms. Melissa Baker-2-May 10, 2017

Company Name

If you include the company's name in the signature block, put it a double space below the complimentary close. You usually include the company's name in the signature block only when the writer is serving as the company's official spokesperson or when letterhead has not been used.

Reference Initials

Reference initials: The initials of the person who produced the letter, if it is not the person signing it.

When one person dictates a letter and another person produces it, **reference initials** show that two people were involved. Place initials at the left margin, a double space below the signature block. When the signature block includes the writer's name, use only the preparer's initials. If the signature block includes only the department, use both sets of initials, usually in one of the following forms: *RSR/sm, RSR:sm*, or *RSR:SM* (writer/preparer).

Enclosure Notation

An enclosure notation lets the recipient know that something else is included with the letter. Enclosure notations appear at the bottom of a letter, one or two lines below the reference initials. Some common forms include the following:

Enclosure

Enclosures (2)

Enclosures:	Resume Photograph Brochure

Copy Notation

Copy notations may follow reference initials or enclosure notations. They indicate who's receiving a courtesy copy (cc). Recipients are listed in order of rank; if they are of equal rank, list them in alphabetical order.

Among the forms used are the following:

cc: David Wentworth, Vice President

Copy to Hans Vogel
748 Chesterton Road
Snohomish, WA 98290

Mailing Notation

You may place a mailing notation, such as Special Delivery or Registered Mail, at the bottom of the letter, after reference initials or enclosure notations (whichever is last), and before copy notations. Or you may place it at the top of the letter, either above the inside address on the left side or just below the date on the right side. For greater visibility, mailing notations may appear in capital letters.

Postscript

A postscript is presented as an afterthought to the letter, a message that requires emphasis, or a personal note. It is usually the last thing on any letter and may be preceded by *P.S.* A second afterthought would be designated *P.P.S.* (post postscript).

Letter Formats

A letter's format is the way its basic parts are arranged. Sometimes a company adopts a certain format as its policy; sometimes the individual letter writer or preparer is allowed to choose the most appropriate format. In the United States, three major letter formats are commonly used: Block, Modified Block, and Simplified.

Block Format

In **block format** each letter part begins at the left margin. The main advantage is quick and efficient preparation (see Figure 5.8).

Block format:
A traditional letter format in which each letter part begins at the left margin.

Modified Block Format

Modified block is similar to block format, except that the date, complimentary close, and signature block start near the center of the page (see Figure 5.9). The modified block format also permits indentions as an option. This format mixes preparation speed with traditional placement of some letter parts. It also looks more balanced on the page than the block format does.

Modified block format:
A traditional letter format in which most parts begin at the left margin, but certain parts begin at the horizontal center of the line.

Figure 5.8
Block Letter Format
In a block letter, all elements begin at the left margin.

Delauny Music
56 Commerce Circle • Davenport, IA 52806
(563) 555-4001 • delaunymusic.net

June 21, 2016 — Line 13 or one line below letterhead
■ 1 to 10 blank lines
■

Ms. Claudia Banks
122 River Heights Drive
Bettendorf, IA 52722

■ 1 blank line

Dear Ms. Banks:

■ 1 blank line

Thank you for your recent purchase. We wish you many years of satisfaction with your new Yamaha CG1 grand piano. The CG1 carries more than a century of Yamaha's heritage in design and production of world-class musical instruments and will give you many years of playing and listening pleasure.

■ 1 blank line

Our commitment to your satisfaction doesn't stop with your purchase, however. As a vital first step, please remember to call us sometime within three to eight months after your piano was delivered to take advantage of the Yamaha Servicebond℠ Assurance Program. This free service program includes a thorough evaluation and adjustment of the instrument after you've had some time to play your piano and your piano has had time to adapt to its environment.

■ 1 blank line

In addition to this important service appointment, a regular program of tuning is essential to ensure your piano's impeccable performance. Our piano specialists recommend four tunings during the first year and two tunings every year thereafter. As your local Yamaha dealer, we are ideally positioned to provide you with optimum service for both regular tuning and any maintenance or repair needs you may have.

Sincerely, — ■ 1 blank line

■ 3 blank lines
■
■

Madeline Delauny
Owner

tjr — ■ 1 blank line

■ 1 blank line

Charles Redburn
Sales Director

■ line 13 from top of page November 2, 2016
■ 1 to 10 blank lines
■

Ms. Eugenia Preston, President
Garden Valley High School PTA
P.O. Box 335
Garden Valley, ID 83622
■ 1 blank line
Dear Ms. Preston:
■ 1 blank line
Thank you for inviting us to participate in your "Day of Government" program. So that your honors students can experience state government firsthand, we will be delighted to provide one of our motor coaches next May at a 15% discount to transport up to 40 students and 7 advisers from Garden Valley to Boise and back.
■ 1 blank line
Our buses seat 47 passengers, are fully equipped with restrooms and reclining seats, and are climate controlled for year-round comfort. You can rely on us for your charter transportation needs:
■ 1 blank line

- Our intensive, ongoing driver-training program ensures your safety and satisfaction.
- Our competitive pricing allows us to compete both locally and nationwide.
- Our state-of-the-art maintenance facilities are located in all major U.S. cities to ensure quality, reliability, and excellent service.

■ 1 blank line
Please give me a call at (208) 997-4646 to discuss the specific date of your event, departure times, and the discounted price for your trip. Together, we'll make sure your students have a day that's not only fun and educational but safe and secure. I look forward to hearing from you.
■ 1 blank line
Sincerely,
■ 3 blank lines
■
■
Charles Redburn
Charles Redburn
Sales Director
■ 1 blank line
pf
■ 1 blank line
Enclosure

Figure 5.9 Modified Block Letter Format
A modified block format resembles block format except certain elements begin at the center of the page rather than at the left margin.

Simplified format:
A letter format that weaves the recipient name into the body rather than using a salutation, and does not include a complimenatry close.

Simplified Format

Instead of using a salutation, this format weaves the reader's name into the first line or two of the body and often includes a subject line in capital letters (see Figure 5.10). It does not include a complimentary close; the signature appears immediately below the body text. Because certain letter parts are eliminated, some line spacing is changed.

Figure 5.10 Simplified Letter Format
A simplified letter format omits several of the traditional elements, including a separate greeting line and complimentary close.

May 5, 2016

Line 13 from top of page
1 to 10 blank lines

Ms. Gillian Wiles, President
Scientific and Technical Contracts, Inc.
6348 Morehouse Dr.
San Diego, CA 92121

2 blank lines

NEW SERVICES

2 blank lines

Thank you, Ms. Wiles, for your recent inquiry about our services. Our complete line of staffing services offers high-level professionals with the skills you require. From the office to the factory, from the tech site to the trade show, from the law firm to the lab—we can provide you with the people and the expertise you need.

1 blank line

I have enclosed a package of information for your review, including specific information on our engineers, designers/drafters, and engineering support personnel. The package also contains reprints of customer reviews and a comparison sheet showing how our services measure up against those of competing companies. We identify qualified candidates and recruit through a network of professional channels to reach candidates whose skills match the specific engineering disciplines you require.

1 blank line

Please call me with any questions you may have. Whether you need a temporary employee for a day or an entire department staffed indefinitely, our staffing solutions give you the freedom you need to focus and the support you need to succeed. I will be glad to help you fill your staffing needs with Kelly professionals.

3 blank lines

Rudy Cohen

RUDY COHEN
CUSTOMER SERVICE SPECIALIST

1 blank line

jn

1 blank line

Enclosures

999 WEST BIG BEAVER ROAD • TROY, MICHIGAN 48084-4782
TELEPHONE (248) 362-4444

These three formats differ in the way paragraphs are indented, in the way letter parts are placed, and in some punctuation. However, the elements are always separated by at least one blank line, and the printed name is always separated from the line above by at least three blank lines to allow space for a signature. If paragraphs are indented, the indention is normally five spaces. The most common formats for intercultural business letters are the block style and the modified block style.

Punctuation Formats

In addition to these three letter formats, letters may also be classified according to their style of punctuation. Standard (also called mixed), punctuation uses a colon after the salutation (a comma if the letter is social or personal) and a comma after the complimentary close. Open punctuation uses no colon or comma after the salutation or the complimentary close. Although the most popular style in business communication is mixed punctuation, either style of punctuation may be used with block or modified block letter formats. Because the simplified letter format has no salutation or complimentary close, the style of punctuation is irrelevant.

Envelopes

The quality of the envelope is just as important as the quality of the stationery. Letterhead and envelopes should be of the same paper stock, have the same color ink, and be imprinted with the same address and logo.

Figure 5.11
Prescribed Envelope Format
These diagrams show the proper placement of the mailing address and return address.

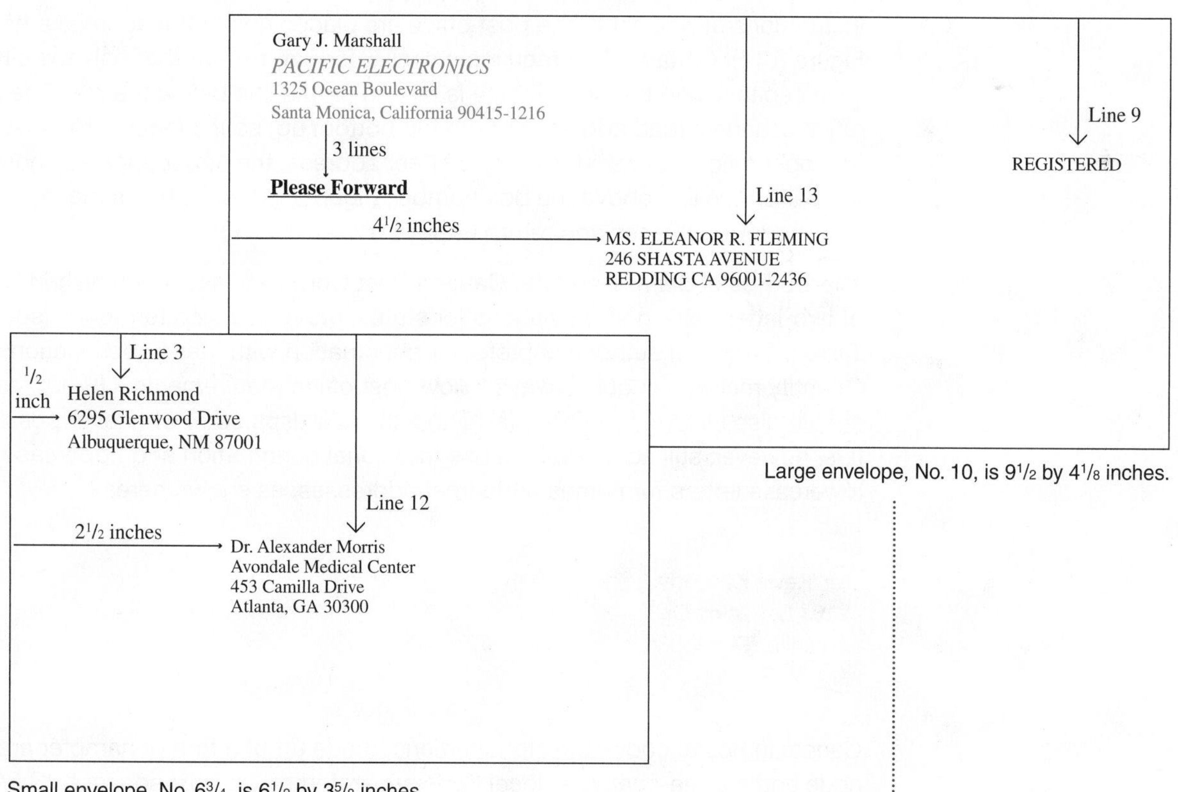

Large envelope, No. 10, is $9^1/_2$ by $4^1/_8$ inches.

Small envelope, No. $6^3/_4$, is $6^1/_2$ by $3^5/_8$ inches.

Most envelopes used by US businesses are No. 10 envelopes at 9 ½ inches long, they are sized accommodate an 8 ½-by-11-inch piece of paper folded in thirds. Some occasions call for a smaller, No. 6 ¾, envelope or for envelopes proportioned to fit special stationery. Figure 5.11 shows the two most common sizes.

Addressing an Envelope

No matter what size the envelope, the address is always single-spaced with all lines aligned on the left. The address on the envelope is in the same style as the inside address and presents the same information. The order to follow is from the smallest division to the largest:

- Name and title of recipient
- Name of department or subgroup
- Name of organization
- Name of building
- Street address and suite number, or post office box number
- City, state, or province, and zip code or postal code
- Name of country (if the letter is being sent abroad)

Because the US Postal Service uses optical scanners to sort mail, envelopes for quantity mailings, in particular, should be addressed in the prescribed format. Everything is in capital letters, no punctuation is included, and all mailing instructions of interest to the post office are placed above the address area (see Figure 5.11). Canada Post requires a similar format, except that only the city is all in capitals, and the postal code is placed on the line below the city. The post office scanners read addresses from the bottom up, so if a letter is to be sent to a post office box rather than to a street address, the street address should appear on the line above the box number. Figure 5.11 also shows the proper spacing for addresses and return addresses.

The US Postal Service and the Canada Post Corporation have published lists of two-letter mailing abbreviations for states, provinces, and territories (see Table 5.7). Postal authorities prefer no punctuation with these abbreviations. Quantity mailings should always follow post office requirements. US addresses should also include the ZIP+4 (available at www.usps.com) whenever possible. It is, however, still acceptable to use traditional punctuation and uppercase and lowercase letters for names and street addresses, as shown here:

Mr. Kevin Kennedy
2107 E. Packer Dr.
Amarillo, TX 79108

Canadian postal codes are alphanumeric, made up of a three-character area code and a three-character local code separated by a single space: K2P 5A5).

US Zip codes should be separated from the state name by one space. Canadian postal codes may be treated the same or may be positioned alone on the bottom line of the address.

Table 5.7 Two-Letter Mailing Abbreviations for the United States and Canada

State/Territory/Province	Abbreviation	State/Territory/Province	Abbreviation	State/Territory/Province	Abbreviation
United States		Massachusetts	**MA**	Tennessee	**TN**
Alabama	AL	Michigan	MI	Texas	TX
Alaska	AK	Minnesota	MN	Utah	UT
American Samoa	AS	Mississippi	MS	Vermont	VT
Arizona	AZ	Missouri	MO	Virginia	VA
Arkansas	AR	Montana	MT	Virgin Islands	VI
California	CA	Nebraskav	NE	Washington	WA
Canal Zone	CZ	Nevada	NV	West Virginia	WV
Colorado	CO	New Hampshire	NH	Wisconsin	WI
Connecticut	CT	New Jersey	NJ	Wyoming	WY
Delaware	DE	New Mexico	NM	**Canada**	
District of Columbia	DC	Maryland	MD	Alberta	AB
Florida	FL	New York	NY	British Columbia	BC
Georgia	GA	North Carolina	NC	Manitoba	MB
Guam	GU	North Dakota	ND	New Brunswick	NB
Hawaii	HI	North Mariana	MP	Newflondland and Labrador	NL
Idaho	ID	Ohio	OH	Northwest Territories	NT
Illinois	IL	Oklahoma	OK	Nova Scotia	NS
Indiana	**IN**	**Oregon**	OR	Nunavut	NU
Iowa	IA	Pennsylvania	PA	Ontairo	ON
Kansas	KS	Puerto Rico	PR	Prince Edward Island	PE
Kentucky	KY	Rhode island	RI	Quebec	QC
Louisiana	LA	South Carolina	SC	Saskatchewan	SK
Maine	ME	South Dakota	SD	Yukon Territory	YT

Memos

Electronic media have replaced most internal printed memos in many companies, but you may have occasion to send a printed memos from time to time. These can be simple announcements or messages, or they can be short reports using the memo format.

On your document, include a title such as *MEMO* or *INTEROFFICE CORRESPONDENCE*, in all captial letters, centered at the top of the page or aligned with the left margin. Next include the words *To*, *From*, *Date*, and *Subject*—followed by the appropriate information:

MEMO

TO:

FROM:

DATE:

SUBJECT:

Addressees

When sending a memo to a long list of people, include the notation See *distribution list* or *See below* in the *To* position at the top; then list the names at the end of the memo. Arrange this list alphabetically, except when high-ranking officials deserve more prominent placement. You can also address memos to groups of people—All Sales Representatives, Production Group, New Product Team.

Courtesy Titles

You need not use courtesy titles anywhere in an internal memo; first initials and last names, first names, or even initials alone are often sufficient. If you would use a courtesy title when speaking to a person face-to-face, however, it's best to include that title in your memo.

Subject Line

The subject line of a memo helps busy colleagues quickly find out what your memo is about, so take care to make it concise and compelling.

Body

Start the body of the memo on the second or third line below the heading. Like the body of a letter, it's usually single-spaced with blank lines between paragraphs. Indenting paragraphs is optional. Handle lists, important passages, and subheadings as you do in letters.

Second Page

If the memo carries over to a second page, head the second page just as you head the second page of a letter.

Writer's Initials

Unlike a letter, a memo doesn't require a complimentary close or a signature, because your name is already prominent at the top. You may initial the memo, however, either at the bottom of your memo or beside your name at the top.

Other Elements

Treat elements such as reference initials and copy notations just as you would in a letter. One difference is that while letters use the term *enclosure* to refer to other pieces included with the letter, memos usually use the word *attachment*.

Memos may be delivered by hand, by the post office (when the recipient works at a different location), or through interoffice mail. Interoffice mail may require the use of special reusable envelopes that have spaces for the recipient's name and department or room number; the name of the previous recipient is simply crossed out. If a regular envelope is used, the words *Interoffice Mail* appear where the stamp normally goes, so that it won't accidentally be stamped and mailed with the rest of the office correspondence. Informal, routine, or brief reports for distribution within a company are often presented in memo form. Don't include report parts such as a table of contents or appendix, but write the body of the memo report just as carefully as you would write a formal report.

Proofreading Your Message

Proofreading is the quality inspection stage for your documents. It is your last chance to make sure your document is ready to carry your message—and your reputation—to the intended audience. Even a small mistake can cost you credibility, so take proofreading seriously.

Look for two types of problems: undetected mistakes from the writing, design, and layout stages, and mistakes that crept in during production. Errors can include anything from inconsistent typefaces to problem web links to problems with the ink used in printing. Be particularly vigilant with complex documents and complex production processes that involve teams of people and multiple computers. Strange things can happen as files move from computer to computer, especially when lots of separate media elements are involved.

To be most effective, proofreading should be a methodical procedure in which you look for specific problems at specific times. Here is some advice from the pros:

- **Make multiple passes.** Go through the document several times, focusing on a different aspect each time. For instance, look for content errors the first time and layout errors the second time.
- **Use perceptual tricks.** To keep from missing errors that are "in plain sight," try reading pages out of order, placing your finger under each word as you read it to yourself, covering everything but the line you're currently reading, or reading the document aloud.
- **Focus on high-priority items.** Double-check names, titles, dates, addresses, and any number that could cause grief if incorrect.
- **Get some distance.** If possible, don't proofread immediately after you finish writing. Do something else for a while; then come back fresh later.
- **Stay focused and vigilant.** Block out distractions and focus as completely as possible on your proofreading. Avoid proofreading large amounts of material in one sitting and try not to proofread when you're tired.
- **Take your time.** Quick proofreading is not careful proofreading.

Table 5.8 offers some handy tips to improve your proofreading efforts.

Table 5.8 Proofreading Tips

Look for Writing and Typing Errors
✔ Typographical mistakes
✔ Misspelled words
✔ Grammatical errors
✔ Punctuation mistakes
✔ Missing or incorrect URLs, email addresses, or other contact information
Look for Design and Layout Errors
✔ Violation of company standards
✔ Page or screen layout errors (such as incorrect margins and column formatting)
✔ Clumsy page breaks or line breaks
✔ Inconsistent font usage (such as with headings and subheadings)
✔ Alignment problems (columns, headers, footers, and graphics)
✔ Missing or incorrect page and section numbers
✔ Missing or incorrect page headers or footers
✔ Missing or incorrect photos and other graphical elements
✔ Missing or incorrect source notes, copyright notices, or other reference items
Look for Production Errors
✔ Printing problems
✔ Browser compatibility problems
✔ Screen size or resolution issues for mobile devices
✔ Incorrect or missing tags on blog posts

Distributing Your Message

With the production finished, you're ready to distribute your message. You don't always have a choice about which distribution method to use, but if you do, consider the following factors:

- **Cost.** Cost isn't a concern for many messages, but for multiple copies of lengthy reports or multimedia productions, it might well be. Weigh the cost and the benefits before you decide. Be sure to consider the nonverbal message you send regarding cost as well. Overnight delivery of a printed report could look responsive in one instance and wasteful in another, for example.

- **Convenience.** Make sure your audience can conveniently access the material you send. For instance, sending a huge file may be fine on a fast office network, but receiving such files can be a major headache for remote colleagues who must download them over slower wireless networks.
- **Time.** How soon does the message need to reach the audience? Don't waste money on overnight delivery if the recipient won't read a report for a week.
- **Security and privacy.** Weigh the convenience offered by digital communication against security and privacy concerns. For the most sensitive messages, your company will probably restrict who is allowed to receive certain messages and the channels you can use to distribute them. In addition, computer users may be wary of opening certain types of attachments, particularly word processor files which are vulnerable to macro viruses and other risks. As an alternative, you can convert your documents to PDF files using Adobe Acrobat or an equivalent product.

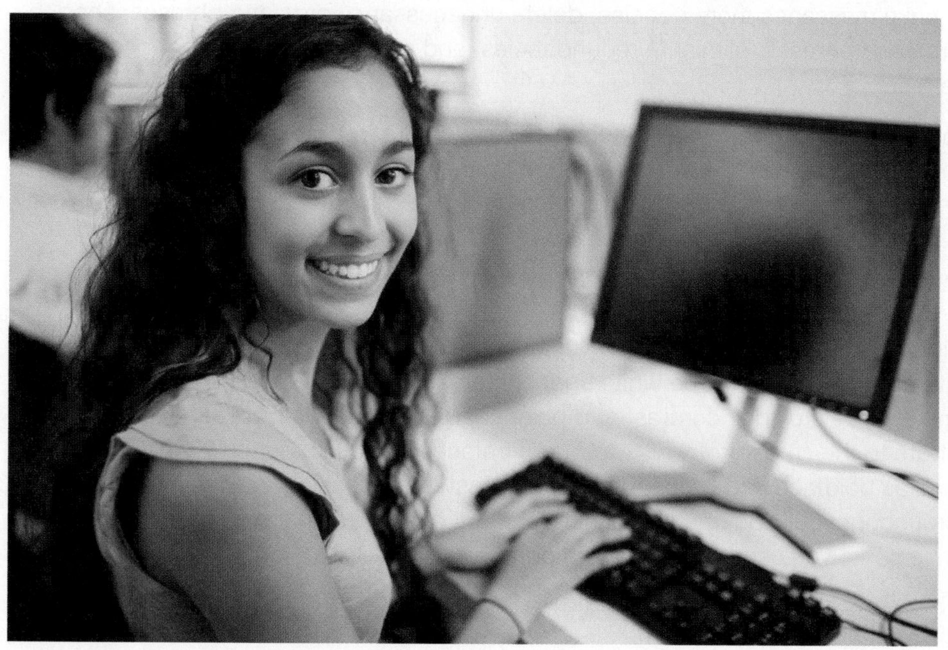

Figure 5.12 Distributing Your Message
What types of messages would you not want to send by email?

Chapter Summary

Revising Your First Draft

Revision is essential: it can nearly always make your first drafts tighter, clearer, and more compelling. Revision consists of three main tasks: evaluating content, organization, and tone; reviewing for readability; and editing for clarity and conciseness. After you revise your message, complete it by using design elements effectively, proofreading to ensure quality, and distributing it to your audience.

Four techniques that improve readability are varying sentence length, keeping paragraphs short, using bulleted and numbered lists, and adding headings and subheadings.

As you work to clarify your messages, break up overly long sentences, rewrite hedging sentences, impose parallelism, and correct dangling modifiers. Also, reword long noun sequences, replace camouflaged verbs, and clarify sentence structure, and awkward references. To make messages more concise, delete unnecessary words and phrases, shorten overly long words and phrases, eliminate redundancies, and reword sentences that begin with "It is" and "There are."

When asked to evaluate, edit, or revise someone else's work, recognize the dual responsibility that doing so entails: remember that your job is to help the other writer succeed at his or her task, and make sure you understand the writer's intent.

Designing Business Documents

Four key principles of effective design are consistency, balance, restraint, and detail. Major design elements of documents include white space, margins and justification, typefaces, and type styles. White space provides contrast and balance. Margins define the space around the text and contribute to the amount of white space. Typefaces influence the tone of the message. Type styles, such as boldface and italics, provide contrast or emphasis. Use design elements consistently throughout your document; balance text, art, and white space; show restraint in the number of elements you use; and pay attention to every detail.

Business Letters, Envelopes, and Memos

Business letters include standard parts that are always appropriate, and optional parts that are necessary only in certain situations. Every business letter includes a date, inside address, salutation, and body. Additional elements may include an attention line, a second-page heading, or an enclosure notation. A business letter can follow a block, modified block, or simplified format.

The envelope should match the letter's paper stock and design. Addresses contain required information and follow a specified format. You may have occasion to write a memo, which also follows a specified format. In many companies, electronic alternatives have replaced memos.

Proofreading Your Message

Proofreading is the quality inspection stage for your documents. It is your last chance to make sure your document is ready to carry your message—and your reputation—to the intended audience. Even a small mistake can damage effectiveness, so take proofreading seriously. Six tips for effective proofreading are to make multiple passes looking for specific problems each time, use perceptual tricks such as reading aloud, and focus on high priority. Also, try not to proofread immediately after you complete a document, stay focused and vigilant, and take your time.

Distributing Your Message

Consider cost, convenience, time, security, and privacy when choosing how to deliver a message. Security and privacy issues are especially important for messages that contain sensitive or confidential information.

Test Your Knowledge

1. What are the four main tasks involved in completing a business message?
2. What are your responsibilities when you review and edit the work of others?
3. What is parallel construction, and why is it important?
4. Why is proofreading an important part of the writing process?
5. What factors should you consider when choosing a method for distributing a message (when you have a choice)?

Apply Your Knowledge

1. Why is it essential to understand the writer's intent before you suggest or make changes to another person's document?
2. How can headings and bullets improve clarity?
3. How does white space help with readability on mobile screens?
4. What nonverbal signals can you send by your choice of distribution methods?

Practice Your Skills

1. **Revising for Clarity** Break the following sentences into shorter ones; revise as necessary to maintain sense and smooth flow.
   a. The next time you write something, check your average sentence length in a 100-word passage, and if your sentences average more than 16 to 20 words, see whether you can break up some of the sentences.
   b. Don't do what the village blacksmith did when he instructed his apprentice as follows: "When I take the shoe out of the fire, I'll lay it on the anvil, and when I nod my head, you hit it with the hammer." The apprentice did just as he was told, and now he's the village blacksmith.

c. Unfortunately, no gadget will produce excellent writing, but using spell checkers and grammar checkers can help by catching common spelling errors and raising grammatical points that writers might want to reconsider, such as suspect sentence structure and problems with noun–verb agreement.
d. Know the flexibility of the written word and its power to convey an idea, and know how to make your words behave so that your readers will understand.

2. **Revising for Conciseness** Eliminate unnecessary words in the following sentences.

   a. The board cannot act without a consensus of opinion.
   b. To surpass our competitors, we need new innovations both in products and in company operations.
   c. George McClannahan has wanted to be head of engineering a long period of time, and now he has finally gotten the promotion.
   d. Don't pay more than you have to; you can get our new fragrance for a price of just $50.

3. **Revising for Simplicity** Revise the following sentences, using shorter, simpler words.

   a. The antiquated calculator is ineffectual for solving sophisticated problems.
   b. It is imperative that the pay increments be terminated before an inordinate deficit is accumulated.
   c. There was unanimity among the executives that Ms. Jackson's idiosyncrasies were cause for a mandatory meeting with the company's personnel director.
   d. The impending liquidation of the company's assets was cause for jubilation among the company's competitors.

4. **Avoiding Long Phrases** Use infinitives as substitutes for the overly long phrases in the following sentences.

   a. For living, I require money.
   b. They did not find sufficient evidence for believing in the future.
   c. Bringing about the destruction of a dream is tragic.

5. **Reducing Wordiness** Condense the following sentences to as few words as possible; revise as needed to maintain clarity and sense.

   a. We are of the conviction that writing is important.
   b. In all probability, we're likely to have a price increase.
   c. Our goals include making a determination about that in the near future.
   d. When all is said and done at the conclusion of this experiment, I'd like to summarize the final windup.

6. **Reducing Modifiers** Remove all the unnecessary modifiers from the following sentences.

   a. Tremendously high pay increases were given to the extraordinarily skilled and extremely conscientious employees.
   b. The union's proposals were highly inflationary, extremely demanding, and exceptionally bold.

7. **Avoiding Hedging** Rewrite the following sentences so that they no longer contain any hedging.
   a. It would appear that someone apparently entered illegally.
   b. It may be possible that sometime in the near future the situation is likely to improve.
   c. Your report seems to suggest that we might be losing money.
   d. I believe Nancy apparently has somewhat greater influence over employees in the new-accounts department.

8. **Eliminating Indefinite Starters** Rewrite the following sentences to eliminate the indefinite starters (forms of *There are* or *It is*).
   a. There are several examples here to show that Elaine can't hold a position very long.
   b. It would be greatly appreciated if every employee would make a generous contribution to Mildred Cook's retirement party.
   c. It has been learned in Washington today from generally reliable sources that an important announcement will be made shortly by the White House.
   d. There is a rule that states that we cannot work overtime without permission.

9. **Imposing Parallelism** Revise the following sentences to fix the parallelism problems.
   a. Mr. Hill is expected to lecture three days a week, to counsel two days a week, and must write for publication in his spare time.
   b. She knows not only accounting, but she also reads Latin.
   c. Both applicants had families, college degrees, and were in their thirties, with considerable accounting experience but few social connections.
   d. This book was exciting, well written, and it kept me interested.

10. **Avoiding Awkward References** Revise the following sentences to delete the awkward references.
    a. The vice president in charge of sales and the production manager are responsible for funding the demo unit program and the loaner unit program, respectively.
    b. The demo unit program and the loaner unit program are funded from different budgets, with the former the responsibility of the vice president in charge of sales and the latter the responsibility of the production manager.
    c. The budgets for the demo unit program and the loaner unit program were increased this year, with the aforementioned budgets being increased 10 percent in both cases.
    d. A laser printer and an inkjet printer were delivered to John and Megan, respectively.

11. **Clarify Dangling Modifiers** Rewrite the following sentences to clarify the dangling modifiers.
    a. Running down the railroad tracks in a cloud of smoke, we watched the countryside glide by.
    b. Lying on the shelf, Ruby saw the seashell.
    c. In need of a major equipment upgrade, I think the factory would be a bad investment.
    d. Being cluttered and filthy, Sandy took the whole afternoon to clean up her desk.

12. **Reducing Noun Sequences** Rewrite the following sentences to eliminate the long strings of nouns.

    a. The focus of the meeting was a discussion of the bank interest rate deregulation issue.
    b. Following the government task force report recommendations, we are revising our job applicant evaluation procedures.
    c. The production department quality assurance program components include employee training, supplier cooperation, and computerized detection equipment.
    d. The supermarket warehouse inventory reduction plan will be implemented next month.

13. **Improving Sentence Structure** Rearrange each of the following sentences to bring the subjects closer to their verbs.

    a. Trudy, when she first saw the bull pawing the ground, ran.
    b. It was Terri who, according to Ted, who is probably the worst gossip in the office (Tom excepted), mailed the wrong order.
    c. William Oberstreet, in his book Investment Capital Reconsidered, writes of the mistakes that bankers through the decades have made.
    d. Judy Schimmel, after passing up several sensible investment opportunities, despite the warnings of her friends and family, invested her inheritance in a jojoba plantation.

14. **Repairing Camouflaged Verbs** Rewrite each of the follow ing sentences so that the verbs are no longer camouflaged.

    a. Adaptation to the new rules was performed easily by the employees.
    b. The assessor will make a determination of the tax due.
    c. Verification of the identity of the employees must be made daily.
    d. The board of directors made a recommendation that Mr. Ronson be assigned to a new division.

Activities

1. **Making Ethical Choices** The time and energy required for careful revision can often benefit you or your company directly. For example, reader-friendly product descriptions will increase the probability that website visitors will buy your products. But what about situations in which the quality of your writing and revision work really doesn't stand to benefit you directly?
   Say you know that an upcoming construction project at your manufacturing plant will seriously impact the people who live nearby; it will disrupt traffic and create noise and air pollution. The more people know about the project schedule, the more they can adjust their lives to minimize its negative impact.
   These people are not potential customers, however; your company does not sell its products locally. You could update the neighbors with a website notice, but doing so will take time away from your other responsibilities. Do you have an ethical obligation to keep the local community informed with accurate, up-to-date information? Why or why not? In a post on your class blog, explain your position on this question.

2. **Revising for Readability** Use what you know about readability to improve this paragraph:

   > Although major league baseball remains popular, more people are attending minor league baseball games because they can spend less on admission, snacks, and parking and still enjoy the excitement of America's pastime. Connecticut, for example, has three AA minor league teams, including the New Haven Ravens, who are affiliated with the St. Louis Cardinals; the Norwich Navigators, who are affiliated with the New York Yankees; and the New Britain Rock Cats, who are affiliated with the Minnesota Twins. These teams play in relatively small stadiums, so fans are close enough to see and hear everything, from the swing of the bat connecting with the ball to the thud of the ball landing in the outfielder's glove. Best of all, the cost of a family outing to see rising stars play in a local minor league game is just a fraction of what the family would spend to attend a major league game in a much larger, more crowded stadium.

3. **Structuring a Business Letter** Figure 5.13 on the next page contains all the elements for creating a business letter, but they are in the wrong order. Retype these elements into a new Modified Block letter in the correct order, with correct spacing between them. Use alignment, leading, and white space as needed. Select an appropriate font and size for the text, and set appropriate margins. Save your work and submit it to your instructor.

4. **Designing for Readability** Compare the home pages of Bloomberg and MarketWatch, two websites that cover financial markets. What are your first impressions of these two sites? How do their overall designs compare in terms of information delivery and overall user experience? Choose three pieces of information that a visitor to these sites would be likely to look for, such as a current stock price, news from international markets, and commentary from market experts. Which site makes it easier to find this information? Why? Present your analysis in a post for your class blog.

Figure 5.13 Text elements to include in Activity 3, "Structuring a Business Letter"

Body:
Thank you for your interest in renting the Centerville Sports Complex for your daughter's wedding reception. Unfortunately we are unable to accommodate your request for an estimate, as our facilities are not equipped for food service and we have no food handling nor liquor license.

If you have not yet secured a location, you may be interested in another nearby property, the Briar Rose Country Club, only one-half mile from our location. Mr. Fred Meyers, Manager, will be glad to provide a quote for you, and can be reached at 317-555-1199.

Complimentary closing:
Sincerely,

Copy line:
Copy to Mr. Fred Meyers, Manager, Briar Rose Country Club

Date:
Use today's date

Enclosure line:
Enclosure: Briar Rose Country Club brochure

Heading (return address)
Centerville Sports Complex
144 South Main St.
Macon, IL 62544

Mailing address:
Mrs. Christine Burrow
1555 River Heights Drive
Bettendorf, IA 52722

Salutation:
Dear Mrs. Burrow:

Signature
Todd Collins
General Manager

Typist initials
fw

Expand Your Skills

Identify a company website that in your opinion violates one or more of the principles of good design discussed on pages 150-154. Using whatever medium your instructor requests, write a one-page analysis of the site, citing specific elements from the website and support from the chapter.

CHAPTER

6

Crafting Messages for Digital Channels

After studying this chapter, you will be able to:

- Identify the major digital channels used for brief business messages.
- Describe the use of social networks in business communication.
- Explain how companies and business professionals can use information-and content-sharing websites.
- Describe the evolving role of email in business communication, and explain how to adapt the three-step writing process to email messages.
- Describe the business benefits of instant messaging (IM), and identify guidelines for effective IM in the workplace.
- Describe the use of blogging and microblogging in business communication, and briefly explain how to adapt the three-step process to blogging.
- Explain how to adapt the three-step process for writing podcasts.

Digital Media and Business Communication

The use of social media represents a fundamental shift in business communication. The shift is still taking place as more consumers adopt social and mobile media and as businesses experiment with the best ways to integrate these media and adapt them to their internal and external communication practices.

Social media:
Digital communication systems that empower individual users to participate by sharing content and responding to others.

Social media—such as Facebook—empowers people to view information and participate in creating the information environment. Users can share content, revise content, respond to content, and contribute new content. Many people rely on social media tools to get information of personal and professional interest. As a result, many consumers and professionals frequently engage in "content snacking," consuming large numbers of small pieces of information and bypassing larger documents that might require more than a few minutes or even a few seconds to read.

The amount of content employees and consumers access from mobile devices continues to rise. Because of this trend, communicators need to be more careful than ever to create audience-focused messages that are easy to find and use regardless of the access method.

With all these changes taking place, the field of business communication is a lot more interesting—but also a lot more complicated—than it was just a few years ago. In the past, only large companies could afford the marketing and public relations budgets to create a worldwide presence. Nowadays, however, smaller and newer companies can utilize social media to target customers just as effectively as larger companies do. Empowered consumers can also vote with their online voices and attention, promoting and encouraging companies that represent their ideas and values and punishing companies that do not. Social media also has the potential to increase transparency, with more eyes and ears to monitor business activities and more voices to demand accountability and change.

Smart companies have learned to adapt their communication efforts to welcome customers' participation. Social media are also revolutionizing internal communication, breaking down traditional barriers in the organizational hierarchy, promoting the flow of information and ideas, and enabling networks of individuals and organizations to collaborate on a global scale.

Increasingly, employees expect the leaders in their organizations to be active in social media. In one recent study, more than 80 percent of US employees agreed that CEOs who are able to use social media are better equipped to lead companies then their counterparts who don't have social media strategies. Moreover, roughly the same percentage are more likely to trust companies whose leadership teams engage with stakeholders via social media, and they would prefer to work for such companies as well.

Figure 6.1
Digital Channels
Businesses communicate with their customers using a variety of digital channels, including websites, social media, and mailing lists. These online channels enable communication with customers wherever they are, even outdoors.

Digital Media Options for Brief Messages

Social media are not the only options available for business communication, of course. For short-to-medium-length messages—those from a sentence or two to several pages long—individuals and companies have a broad range of options:

- Social networks
- Information and content sharing sites
- Email
- Instant messaging (IM)
- Text messaging
- Blogging and microblogging
- Podcasting

This chapter covers all of these media. Chapters 10 and 11 explore two other key media, websites and wikis, which are used for longer messages and documents.

As this list suggests, businesses use many of the same tools you use for personal communication. Generally speaking, companies are quick to jump on any communication platform where consumers are likely to congregate or that promise more efficient internal or external communication.

Although most of your business communication is likely to be digital, don't automatically dismiss the benefits of printed messages. Here are several situations in which you should use a printed message over digital alternatives:

- When you want to make a formal impression
- When you are legally required to provide information in printed form
- When you want to stand out from the flood of digital messages
- When you need a permanent, unchangeable, or secure record

Obviously, if you can't reach a particular audience through digital channels, you'll also need to use a printed message.

Compositional Modes for Digital Media

As you practice using digital media in this course, focus on the principles of communication and the fundamentals of planning, writing, and completing messages, on the specific details of any one medium or system. Fortunately, the basic communication skills required usually transfer from one system to another. You can succeed with written communication in virtually all digital media by using one of nine compositional modes:

- **Conversations.** IM is a great example of a written medium that mimics spoken conversation. The conversational mode works best for short, simple messages and more informal communication with an audience of one or two people.
- **Comments and critiques.** One of the most powerful aspects of social media is the opportunity for interested parties to express opinions and provide feedback, whether it's leaving comments on a blog post or reviewing products on an e-commerce site. Sharing helpful tips and insightful commentary is also a great way to build your personal brand. To be an effective commenter, focus on short chunks of information that a broad spectrum of other site visitors will find helpful. Rants, insults, jokes, and blatant self-promotion are usually of little benefit to other visitors.
- **Summaries.** At the beginning of an article or webpage, a summary functions as a miniature version of the document, giving readers all the key points while skipping over details. At the end of an article or webpage, a summary functions as a review, reminding readers of the key points they've just read. A series of key points extracted from an article or webpage can also serve as a summary.
- **Orientations.** The ability to help people find their way through an unfamiliar system or subject is a valuable writing skill and a talent that readers greatly appreciate. Unlike summaries, orientations don't give away the key points, but rather tell readers where to find those points. Writing effective orientations can be a delicate balancing act because you need to know the material well enough to guide others through it while being able to step back and view that information from the inexperienced perspective of a "newbie."
- **Reference materials.** One of the greatest benefits of the Internet is the access it can provide to vast quantities of reference materials. One of the challenges of writing reference material is that you can't always know how readers will use it. Will they read every word from beginning to end, or more likely skim through to find a particular data point or other detail? . Making the information accessible via search engines is an important step. Readers don't always know which search terms will yield the best results,

so consider an orientation and organize the material in logically with clear headings that promote skimming.

- **Narratives.** The storytelling techniques covered in Chapter 3 (page 104) can be effective in a wide variety of situations, from company histories to product reviews and demonstrations. Narratives work best when they have an intriguing beginning that piques readers' curiosity, a middle section that moves quickly through the challenges that an individual or company faced, and an inspiring or instructive ending that gives readers information they can apply in their own lives and jobs.
- **Teasers.** Teasers intentionally withhold key pieces of information as a way to pull readers or listeners into a story or other document. Teasers are widely used in marketing and sales messages, such as a bit of copy on the outside of an envelope that promises important information on the inside. In digital media, the space limitations and URL linking capabilities of Twitter and other microblogging systems make them a natural tool for the teaser approach. Be sure that the payoff, the information a teaser links to, is valuable and legitimate. You'll quickly lose credibility if readers think they are being tricked into clicking through to information they don't really want. *Tweetables* are Twitter-ready bites of information extracted from a blog post or other messages. They often serve as teasers, although a series of them can make an effective summary.
- **Status updates and announcements.** If you use social media frequently, much of your writing will involve status updates and announcements. However, don't post trivial information that only you are likely to find interesting. Post only those updates that readers will find useful, and include only the information they need.
- **Tutorials.** Given the community nature of social media, the purpose of many messages is to share how-to advice. Becoming known as a reliable expert is a great way to build customer loyalty for your company while enhancing your own personal value.

Creating Content for Social Media

No matter what media or compositional mode you use, writing for social media requires a different approach than for traditional media. Whether you're writing a blog or posting a product demonstration video to YouTube, consider these tips for creating successful content for social media:

- **Remember that it's a conversation, not a lecture or a sales pitch.** One of the great appeals of social media is the feeling of conversation, of people talking with one another instead of one person talking *at* everyone else. As more and more people gain a voice in the marketplace, companies that try to maintain the old "we talk, you listen" mindset are likely to be ignored in the social media landscape.
- **Write informally but not carelessly.** Write as a human being with a unique, personal voice. However, don't take this as a license to get sloppy; no one wants to slog through misspelled words and half-baked sentences to find your message.
- **Create concise, specific, and informative headlines.** The rise of content snacking and information overload make headlines extremely important in social media. Avoid the temptation to engage in clever wordplay when

writing headlines and teasers. This advice applies to all forms of business communication, of course, but it is essential for social media. Readers don't want to spend time figuring out what your witty headlines mean. Search engines won't know what they mean either, so fewer people will find your content.

- **Get involved and stay involved.** Social media makes some businesspeople nervous because it invites feedback the business can't control. However, don't hide from criticism. Take the opportunity to correct misinformation or explain how mistakes will be fixed.
- **Be transparent and honest.** Honesty is always essential, of course, but the social media environment is especially unforgiving. Attempts to twist the truth, withhold information, or hide behind a virtual barricade only invite attack in the "public square" of social media.
- **Think before you post!** Individuals and companies have been sued, employees have been fired, vital company secrets have been leaked, and business and personal relationships have been strained, all because of careless social media posts. Remember that you share the responsibility of keeping your company's and your customers' data private and secure. Assume that every message you send in any digital medium will be stored forever and might be read by people far beyond your original audience. Before you post, ask yourself two questions: First, "Would I say this to my audience face to face?" And second, "Am I comfortable with this message becoming a permanent part of my personal and professional communication history?"

Figure 6.2
Posting to Social Media
When you are representing your company, it is important to maintain the company's professional image in all your communications, including in social media.

Optimizing Content for Mobile Devices

Chapters 4 and 5 offer tips on writing and formatting messages for mobile devices. While you keep the limitations of small screens and alternative input methods in mind, look for opportunities to take advantage of mobile-specific capabilities via apps and mobile-friendly websites. Mobile expands your options as a content creator, and it gives your audience members a wider range of engaging ways to consume your content. These include:

- **Location-based services.** **Location-based services** tailor social networking features to the physical location of the device. Services like Yelp and Fandango all limit what you see based on where you—and your device—happen to be.

Location-based service: Software that uses a reader's reported location to customize content.

- **Gamification.** The addition of game-playing aspects to apps and web services, known as gamification, can increase audience engagement and encourage repeat use. Examples include Foursquare's "check-in" competitions and Bunchball's Nitro competitions for sales teams.
- **Augmented reality.** Superimposing data on live camera images can help consumers better predict the impact of a product or service. A dressing-room app might show you how a shirt would look on you in blue, when all the store has right now is red, for example. Another potential business use is enhanced, realistic on-the-job training.

Figure 6.3
Wearable Technology
Smartwatches and other wearable technologies can simplify and enhance everyday tasks.

- **Wearable technology.** From virtual-reality goggles to smartwatches to body-movement sensors, **wearable technology** pushes mobile to the next level. Some of these provide auxiliary screens and controls for other mobile devices; others are meant for independent use. Wearable technology can simplify and enhance everyday tasks for consumers and employees alike (see Figure 6.3).

Wearable technology: A computing device that the user can wear, such as a watch, wristband, or eyeglasses.

- **Mobile blogging.** Smartphones and tablets are ideal for mobile blogs, sometimes referred to as moblogs. The mobile capability is great for workers whose jobs keep them on the move and for special-event coverage such as live-blogging trade shows and industry conventions.
- **Mobile podcasting.** Similarly, smartphone-based podcasting tools make it easy to record audio and video on the go and post finished podcasts to your blog or website.

- **Cloud-based services.** Mobile communication is ideal for cloud-based services—digital services that rely on resources stored in the cloud.

Social Networks

Social network: A specific company or site that hosts a social media community.

Social networks—online services that help people and organizations form connections and share information—have become a major force in both internal and external business communication. They can be grouped into three categories:

- **Public, general-purpose networks.** Facebook is the largest such network, although Google+ is rapidly attracting many companies and brands. Additionally, regionally focused networks have significant user bases in some countries, such as China's Renren and Kaixin001.
- **Public, specialized networks.** Whereas Facebook and Google+ serve a wide audience with needs both personal and professional, other networks focus on a particular function or a particular audience. The most widely known of these is LinkedIn, with its emphasis on career- and sales-related networking. Other networks address the needs of entrepreneurs, small-business owners, specific professions, product enthusiasts, and other narrower audiences.
- **Private networks.** Some companies have built private social networks that are limited to their internal use. For example, the defense contractor Lockheed Martin created its Unity network, complete with a variety of social media applications, to meet the expectations of younger employees accustomed to social media and to capture the expert knowledge of older employees nearing retirement.

Regardless of the purpose and audience, social networks are most beneficial when all participants give and receive information, advice, support, and introductions—just as in offline social interaction. The following two sections describe how social networks are used in business communication and offer advice on using these platforms successfully.

Business Communication Uses of Social Networks

With their ability to reach virtually unlimited numbers of people through a variety of digital formats, social networks are a great fit for many business communication needs. Here are some of the key applications of social networks for internal and external business communication:

- **Integrating company workforces.** Just as public networks can bring friends and family together, internal social networks can help companies grow closer. They may help new employees navigate their way through the organization, finding experts, mentors, and other important contacts. Social networks can also facilitate unity following a reorganization or merger and help people from different parts of a company connect with each other.

- **Fostering collaboration.** Networks can help companies find pockets of knowledge and expertise within the organization, and give meeting or seminar participants a way to meet before an event and to maintain relationships afterward. Networking accelerates team development by helping members get to know each other, identify individual areas of expertise, and share information.
- **Building communities.** Social networks are a natural tool for bringing together communities of practice, people who engage in similar work, and communities of interest, people who share enthusiasm for a particular product or activity. Large and geographically dispersed companies can benefit greatly from communities of practice that connect experts who may work in different divisions or different countries. Communities of interest that form around a specific product are sometimes called **brand communities** and nurturing these communities can be a vital business communication task. A majority of consumers now trust their peers more than any other source of product information, so formal and informal brand communities are becoming an essential information source in consumer buying decisions.

Brand community: A community of people brought together by common interest in a particular product.

- **Socializing brands and companies.** According to one survey of company executives, socialization now accounts for more than half of a company or brand's global reputation. **Brand socialization** is a measure of how effectively a company engages with its various online stakeholders in a mutually beneficial exchange of information.

Brand socialization: A measure of how well a company engages its online stakeholders.

- **Understanding target markets.** With hundreds of millions of people expressing themselves via social media, you can be sure that smart companies are listening. When asked about the value of having millions of Facebook fans, Coca-Cola CEO Muhtar Kent replied, "The value is you can talk with them. They tell you things that are important for your business and brands." In addition, a number of tools now exist to gather market intelligence from social media more or less automatically.
- **Recruiting employees and business partners.** Companies use social networks to find potential employees, short-term contractors, subject-matter experts, product and service suppliers, and business partners. A key advantage here is that these introductions are made via trusted connections in a professional network. On LinkedIn, for example, members can recommend each other based on current or past business relationships, which helps remove the uncertainty of initiating business relationships with complete strangers.
- **Connecting with sales prospects.** A variety of sales-based networks let sales professionals identify potential buyers and ask for introductions through shared connections. Sales networking can reduce cold calling—phoning potential customers out of the blue—a practice that few people on either end of the conversation find pleasant.
- **Supporting customers.** Customer service is another of the fundamental areas of business communication that have been revolutionized by social media. Social customer service involves using social networks and other social media tools to give customers a more convenient way to get help from the company—and to help each other.

- **Extending the organization.** Social networking is also fueling the growth of *networked organizations*, sometimes known as virtual organizations, where companies supplement the talents of their employees with services from one or more external partners, such as a design lab, a manufacturing firm, or a sales and distribution company.

Strategies for Business Communication on Social Networks

Social networks offer lots of business communication potential, but with those opportunities comes a certain degree of complexity. And, the norms and practices of business social networking continue to evolve. Follow these guidelines to make the most of social networks for both personal branding and company communication:

- **Choose the best compositional mode for each message, purpose, and network.** As you visit various social networks, take some time to observe the variety of message types you see in different parts of each website. For example, the informal status update mode works well for Facebook wall posts but would be less effective for a company overviews and annual shareholder statements.
- **Offer valuable content to members of your online community.** People don't join social networks to be sales targets; they join looking for connections and information. **Content marketing** is the practice of providing free information that is valuable to community members but that also helps a company build closer ties with current and potential customers.

Content marketing: Providing free information that is valuable to consumers and builds ties with current and potential customers.

- **Join existing conversations.** Search for online conversations that are already taking place. Answer questions, solve problems, and respond to rumors and misinformation.
- **Anchor your online presence.** Although it's important to join conversations and be visible where your stakeholders are active, it's equally important to anchor your presence at your own central hub—a web presence you own and control. This can be a combination of a conventional website, a blog, and a company-sponsored online community, for example. Use your hub to connect the various pieces of your online "self " and make it easier for people to find and follow you. For example, you can link to your blog from your LinkedIn profile or automatically post your blog entries into the Notes tab on your Facebook page.
- **Facilitate community building.** Make it easy for customers and other audiences to connect with your company and with each other. For example, you can use the group feature on Google+, LinkedIn, and other social networks to create and foster special-interest groups. Groups are a great way to connect people who share interest in the same topic or own the same product.
- **Restrict conventional promotional efforts to the right time and place.** Persuasive communication efforts are still valid for specific communication tasks, such as regular advertising and the product information pages on a website, but efforts to inject blatant "salespeak" into social networking conversations will usually be rejected by the audience.

- **Maintain a consistent personality.** Each social network is a unique environment with particular norms of communication. For example, as a strictly business-oriented network, LinkedIn has a more formal "vibe" than Facebook and Google+, which cater to both consumers and businesses. However, while adapting to the expectations of each network, be sure to maintain a consistent personality across all the networks in which you are active.

Information and Media-Sharing Sites

Most social networks allow members to share information and media items as part of the networking experience, but a variety of systems have been designed specifically for sharing content. The field is diverse and still evolving, but the possibilities can be divided into user-generated content sites, content curation sites, and community Q&A sites.

User-Generated Content Sites

YouTube, Flickr, Yelp, and other **user-generated content (UGC) sites**, in which users rather than website owners contribute most or all of the content, have become serious business tools. On YouTube, for example, companies post everything from product demonstrations and TV commercials to company profiles and technical support explanations.

User-generated content (UGC) site:
A site or service in which users contribute most or all of the content.

As with other social media, the keys to effective user-generated content are making it valuable and making it easy. First, provide content that people want to see and share with colleagues. A video clip that explains how to use a product more effectively will be more popular than a clip that talks about how amazing the company behind the product is. Also, keep videos short, generally no longer than three to five minutes, if possible.

Second, make material easy to find, consume, and share. For example, a branded channel on YouTube lets a company organize all its videos in one place, making it easy for visitors to browse the selection or subscribe to get automatic updates of future videos. Sharing features let fans exchange videos through email or their accounts on Twitter, Facebook, and other platforms.

Content Curation Sites

Newsfeeds from blogs and other online publishers can be a great way to stay on top of developments in any field. However, anyone who has signed up for more than a few RSS feeds has probably experienced the "firehose effect" of getting so many feeds so quickly that it becomes impossible to stay on top of them. Moreover, when a highly active publisher feeds every new article, from the essential to the trivial, the reader is left to sort it all out every day.

An intriguing alternative to newsfeeds is **content curation**, in which someone with expertise or interest in a particular field collects and republishes material on a particular topic. Business Communication Headline News (http://bchn.businesscommunicationnetwork.com), for instance, was one of the earliest examples of content curation in the field of business communication.

Content curation:
The process of collecting and presenting information on a particular topic in a way that makes it convenient for target readers.

New curation tools, including Pinterest and Scoop.it!, make it easy to assemble attractive online magazines or portfolios on specific topics. Although it raises important issues regarding content ownership and message control,[24] curation has the potential to bring the power of community and shared expertise to a lot of different fields. Ultimately, curation could reshape audience behavior and the practice of business communication.

Community Q&A Sites

Community Q&A site: A site that enables visitors to answer questions posed by other visitors.

Community Q&A sites, on which visitors answer questions posted by other visitors, are a contemporary twist on the early ethos of computer networking, which was people helping each other. (Groups of like-minded people connected online long before the World Wide Web existed.) Community Q&A sites include dedicated customer support communities, such as those hosted on Get Satisfaction, and public sites like Quora and Yahoo! Answers.

Responding to questions on Q&A sites can be a great way to build your personal brand, demonstrate your company's commitment to customer service, and counter misinformation about your company and its products. Keep in mind that when you respond to an individual query on a community Q&A site, you are also "responding in advance" to every person in the future who comes to the site with the same question. In other words, you are writing a type of reference material in addition to corresponding with the original questioner, so keep the long time frame and wider audience in mind.

General-Purpose Social Networks

Most everyone is familiar with Facebook and Google+, and thousands of companies are active on these popular social networks. In addition, a number of social networks exist just for businesses and business professionals, including LinkedIn, the largest of the business networks. Kelly Financial Resources, part of the Kelly Services staffing company, maintains a profile on LinkedIn, as do several hundred of its employees.

Specialized Social Networks

A number of companies now host their own social networking sites, where product enthusiasts interact by sharing personal stories, offering advice, and commenting on products and company news—all brief-message functions that replace more traditional media options. For example, Specialized, a major bicycle manufacturer based in Morgan Hill, California, hosts the Specialized Riders Club, where customers can interact with each other and the professional riders the company sponsors. Similarly, using the Segway Social network, members can organize Segway polo matches and other events.

Figure 6.4
Real-Time Online Communication
Some jobs may involve talking to customers, vendors, and co-workers using real-time chat applications.

User-Generated Content

Many companies now encourage user-generated content as a way to engage stakeholders and provide additional value through shared expertise. The online shoe and apparel retailer Zappos, for example, invites customers to create and upload videos that communicate their experiences with Zappos and its products.

Email

Email has been an important communication tool for several decades. Early in its history, email offered a huge advantage in speed and efficiency over the printed or faxed media it usually replaced. Over the years, email grew in popularity; it was widely available and relatively easy for new users to learn. Now newer tools, such as instant messages, blogs, microblogs, social networks, and shared workspaces, have taken over specific tasks for which they are better suited. For example, instant messaging can be a better choice than email for conversational communication, and project management discussions and updates may work better via a wiki or other purpose-built system.

In addition to the widespread availability of better alternatives for many communication purposes, the indiscriminate use of email has lowered its appeal in the eyes of many professionals. In a sense, email is *too* easy to use—with a couple of clicks anyone can send low-value messages to multiple recipients or trigger long message chains that become impossible to follow as people chime in along the way. In fact, frustration with email is so high in some companies that managers are making changes to reduce or even eliminate its use for internal communication.

However, email still has compelling advantages that will keep it in steady use in many companies. First, email is universal. Anybody with an email address can reach anybody else with an email address, no matter which systems the senders and receivers use. Second, email is still the best medium for many private, short- to medium-length messages, particularly when the exchange is limited to two people. Unlike with microblogs or IM, for instance, midsize messages are easy to compose and easy to read on email. Third, email lets senders compose messages in private and on their own schedules, and it lets recipients read those messages when they choose.

Planning Email Messages

The solution to email overload starts in the planning step, by making sure every message has a useful, business-related purpose. Also, be aware that many companies now have formal email policies that specify how employees can use email, including restrictions against using company email service for personal messages, sending confidential information, or sending material that might be deemed objectionable. In addition, many employers now monitor email, either automatically with software programmed to look for sensitive content or manually via security staff actually reading selected email messages. Regardless of formal policies, though, every email user has a responsibility to avoid actions that could cause trouble, from opening virus-infected attachments to sending inappropriate photographs.

Even with fairly short messages, spend a moment or two on the message-planning tasks described in Chapter 3: analyzing the situation, gathering necessary information for your readers, and organizing your message. You'll save time in the long run because you will craft a more effective message on the first attempt. Your readers will get the information they need and won't have to generate follow-up messages asking for clarification or additional information.

Writing Email Messages

When you approach email writing on the job, recognize that business email is a more formal medium than you are probably accustomed to with email for personal communication (see Figure 6.5). The expectations of writing quality for business email are higher than for personal email, and the consequences of bad writing or poor judgment can be much more serious. For example, email messages and other digital documents have the same legal weight as printed documents, and they are often used as evidence in lawsuits and criminal investigations.

The email subject line might seem like a small detail, but it is actually one of the most important parts of an email message because it helps recipients decide which messages to read and when to read them. To capture your audience's attention, make your subject lines informative and compelling. Go beyond simply describing or classifying your message; use the opportunity to build interest with keywords, quotations, directions, or questions. For example, "July sales results" accurately describes the content of the message, but "July sales results: good news and bad news" is more intriguing. Readers will want to know why some news is good and some is bad.

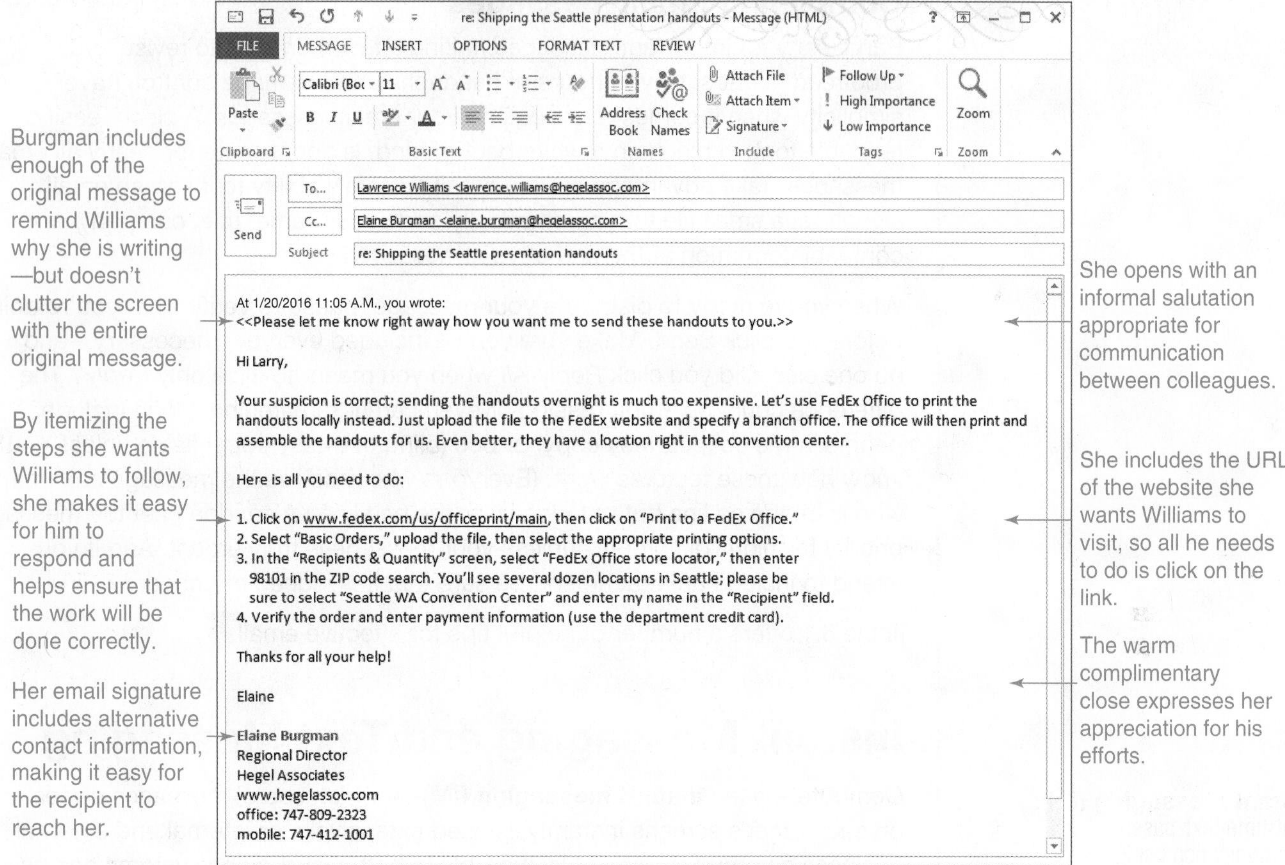

Figure 6.5
Email for Business Communication
In this response to an email query from a colleague, Elaine Burgman takes advantage of her email system's features to create an efficient and effective message.

Source: Microsoft Outlook 2013, Microsoft Corporation.

In addition, many email programs display the first few words or lines of incoming messages, even before the recipient opens them. In the words of social media public relations expert Steve Rubel, you can "tweetify" the opening lines of your email messages to make them stand out. In other words, choose the first few words carefully to grab your reader's attention. Think of the first sentence as an extension of your subject line.

Email can present challenges when you need to express particular emotional nuances, whether positive or negative. In casual conversations, users of email—and IM and text messaging—use emoticons and emoji to express or enhance emotion. (What's the difference? Emoticons are made of keyboard characters: —(is a sad face and ((())) means hugs, for example). Emoji are tiny cartoons users can insert into lines of text.)

In the past, the use of these symbols was widely regarded as unprofessional and therefore advised against in business communication. Some professionals do choose to use them, particularly for communication with close colleagues. Other professionals view the use of emojis as a sign of laziness or immaturity. In the face of these conflicting perspectives, the best advice is to use caution. Avoid emoticons and emoji, animated or otherwise, for formal internal messages and for all external business communication.

Completing Email Messages

Particularly for important messages, taking a few moments to revise and proofread might save you hours of headaches and damage control. Favor simplicity when it comes to producing your email messages. A clean, easily readable font, in black on a white background, is appropriate for nearly all email messages. Take advantage of your email system's ability to insert an email signature, a small file that automatically adds your name, title, company, and contact information at the end of your messages.

When you're ready to distribute your message, pause to verify what you're doing before you click Send. Make sure you've included everyone necessary—and no one else. Did you click *Reply All* when you meant to click only *Reply*? The difference could be embarrassing or even career threatening. Don't include people in the cc (courtesy copy) or bcc (blind courtesy copy) fields unless you know how these features work. (Everyone who receives the message can see who is on the cc line but not who is on the bcc line.) Also, don't set the message priority to "high" or "urgent" unless your message is truly urgent. And if you intend to include an attachment, be sure that it is indeed attached.

Table 6.1 offers a number of helpful tips for effective email.

Instant Messaging and Text Messaging

Instant messaging (IM): Real-time text-based communication using computing devices.

Computer-based **instant messaging (IM)**, in which users' messages appear on each other's screens instantly, is used extensively for internal and external business communication. IM is available in both stand-alone systems and as a function embedded in online meeting systems, collaboration systems, social networks, and other platforms. For conversational exchanges, it's hard to top the advantages of IM, which is replacing both email and voice-mail in many situations. Business-grade IM systems offer a range of capabilities, including basic chat, presence awareness (the ability to quickly see which people are at available to IM), and remote display of documents, videos. Some systems even let a remote user give a demonstration or check for a problem on another user's computer.

Text messaging: An instant message delivered via SMS, usually to a mobile device such as a smartphone

Text messaging refers to an instant message that is delivered via Simple Mail Service (SMS) to a mobile device such as a smartphone. Text messaging has a number of applications in business as well, including marketing (alerting customers about new sale prices, for example), customer service (such as airline flight status, package tracking, and appointment reminders), security (for example, authenticating mobile banking transactions), crisis management (such as updating all employees working at a disaster scene), and process monitoring (alerting computer technicians to system failures, for example).

As it becomes more tightly integrated with other communication media, text messaging is likely to find even more widespread use in business communication. For instance, texting is now integrated into systems such as

Table 6.1 Tips for Effective Email Messages

Tip	Why It's Important
When you request information or action, make it clear what you're asking for, why it's important, and how soon you need it; don't make your reader write back for details.	People will be tempted to ignore your messages if you aren't clear about what you want.
When you respond to a request, either paraphrase the request or include enough of the original message to remind the reader what you're replying to.	Some businesspeople get hundreds of email messages a day and may need reminding what your response is about.
If possible, avoid sending long, complex messages via email.	Long messages are easier to read as attached reports or web content. Adjust the level of formality to the message and the audience. Overly formal messages to colleagues can come across as stuffy and distant; overly informal messages to customers or top executives can be perceived as disrespectful.
Activate a signature file, which automatically pastes your contact information into every message you create.	A signature saves you the trouble of retyping vital information and ensures that recipients know how to reach you through other means.
Don't let unread messages pile up.	You'll miss important information and create the impression that you're ignoring other people.
Never type in all caps.	All caps are interpreted as shouting.
Don't overformat your messages with background colors, multicolored type, unusual fonts, and so on.	Such messages can be difficult and annoying to read on screen.
Remember that messages can be forwarded anywhere and saved forever.	Don't let a moment of anger or poor judgment haunt you for the rest of your career.
Use the "return receipt requested" feature only for the most critical messages.	This feature triggers a message back to you whenever someone receives or opens your message; some consider this an invasion of privacy.
Make sure your computer has up-to-date virus protection.	One of the worst breaches of "netiquette" is infecting other computers because you haven't bothered to protect your own system.
Pay attention to grammar, spelling, and capitalization.	Some people don't think email needs formal rules, but careless messages make you look unprofessional and can annoy readers.
Use acronyms sparingly.	Shorthand such as IMHO and LOL can be useful in informal correspondence with colleagues; leave them out of more formal messages.
Avoid using emoticons and emoji.	Many people view their use as immature and unprofessional.

Facebook Messages and Gmail, and branded "Star Star numbers" can deliver web-based content such as videos, software apps, and digital coupons to mobile phones. The following sections focus on IM, but many of the benefits, risks, and guidelines pertain to text messaging as well.

Benefits and Risks of IM

The benefits of IM include its capability for rapid response to urgent messages, lower cost than phone calls and email, ability to mimic conversation more closely than email, and availability on a wide range of devices. In addition, because it more closely resembles one-on-one conversation, IM doesn't get misused as a one-to-many broadcast method as often as email does.

The potential drawbacks of IM include security problems (computer viruses, network infiltration, and the possibility that sensitive messages might be intercepted by outsiders), the need for user authentication (making sure that online correspondents are really who they appear to be), the challenge of logging messages for later review and archiving (a legal requirement in some industries), incompatibility between competing IM systems, and spim (unsolicited commercial instant messages, similar to email spam). Fortunately, with the growth of IM systems designed for large-scale corporate use, known as enterprise instant messaging (EIM), many of these problems are being overcome.

Regardless of the system you're using, you can make IM more efficient and effective by heeding these tips:

- Be courteous; if you don't need an answer instantly, you can avoid interrupting someone by sending an email or other type of message instead.
- Unless a meeting is scheduled or you're expected to be available for other reasons, make yourself unavailable when you need to focus on other work.
- If you're not on a secure system, don't send confidential information using IM.
- Be extremely careful about sending personal messages—they have a tendency to pop up on other people's computers at embarrassing moments.
- Don't use IM for important but impromptu meetings if you can't verify that everyone concerned will be available.
- Don't use IM for lengthy, complex messages.
- Try to avoid carrying on multiple IM conversations at one time, to minimize the chance of sending messages to the wrong people or making one person wait while you tend to another conversation.
- Follow all security guidelines designed to keep your company's information and systems safe from attack.

Adapting the Three-Step Process for Successful IM

Although instant messages are often conceived, written, and sent within a matter of seconds, the principles of the three-step process still apply, particularly when with customers and other important audiences:

- **Planning instant messages.** Except for simple exchanges, take a moment to plan IM "conversations" in much the same way you would plan an important oral conversation. A few seconds of planning can help you deliver information in a coherent, complete way that minimizes the number of individual messages required.
- **Writing instant messages.** As with email, the appropriate writing style for business IM is more formal than the style you may be accustomed to with personal IM or text messaging (see Figure 6.6). Your company might discourage the use of IM acronyms—such as FWIW for "for what it's worth" or HTH for "hope that helps"—particularly with external audiences.
- **Completing instant messages.** The only task in the completing stage is to send your message. Just quickly scan it before sending, to make sure you don't have any missing or misspelled words and verify that your message is clear and complete.

Figure 6.6 Instant Messaging for Business Communication
Instant messaging is widely used in business, but you should not use the same informal style of communication you probably use for IM with your friends and family.

Eduardo Lopes – Hi Marcy, do you have a second?
← Lopes ask if DeLong is available for a chat, rather than launching right into his discussion on the assumption that she can chat this minute.

Marcy DeLong – You bet. What's up?

Eduardo Lopes – I have a favor to ask, and I'm afraid I'm on a tight deadline. We need to cut the Qualcomm bid by 5%. Can we reduce the consulting time by 80 or 100 hrs?
← He makes his request clearly and succinctly.

Marcy DeLong – That's a big chunk! I'm not sure we can cut that much, but I'll give it a try.
← DeLong expresses skepticism, which helps to set the expectations for what she can deliver. Note how her tone remains positive, however.

Eduardo Lopes – I really appreciate it. Any chance you can get to it by noon my time?
← He completes his request by providing a deadline. Note how he phrases it as a question, which is less jarring than a demand.

Marcy DeLong – No problem. I'll send you a revised bid sheet in an hour. Wish me luck...
← She concludes with a positive response while gently reiterating the difficulty of the task.

Blogging and Microblogging

Blogs are online journals that are easier to personalize and update than conventional websites. They have become a major force in business communication. Millions of business-oriented blogs are now in operation, and blogs have become an important source of information for consumers and professionals alike. Good business blogs and microblogs pay close attention to several important elements:

- **Communicating with personal style and an authentic voice.** Most business messages designed for large audiences are carefully scripted and written in a "corporate voice" that is impersonal and objective. In contrast, successful business blogs are written by individuals and exhibit their personal style. Audiences relate to this fresh approach and often build closer emotional bonds with the blogger's organization as a result.

- **Delivering new information quickly.** Blogging tools let you post new material as soon as you create it or find it. This feature not only allows you to respond quickly when needed—such as during a corporate crisis—but also lets your audiences know that active communication is taking place. Blogs that don't offer a continuous stream of new and interesting content are quickly ignored in today's online environment.
- **Choosing topics of peak interest to audiences.** Successful blogs cover topics that readers care about.
- **Encouraging audiences to join the conversation.** Not all blogs invite comments, although most do, and many bloggers consider comments to be an essential feature. Blog comments can be a valuable source of news, information, and insights. In addition, the informal nature of blogging seems to make it easier for companies to let their guard down and converse with their audiences. To protect against comments that are not helpful or appropriate, many bloggers review all comments and post only the most helpful or interesting ones.

Business Applications of Blogging

Blogs are a potential solution whenever you have a continuing stream of information to share with an online audience—and particularly when you want the audience to have the opportunity to respond. Here are some of the many ways businesses are using blogs for internal and external communication:

- **Anchoring the social media presence.** The multiple threads of any social media program should be anchored in a central hub the company or individual owns and controls. Blogs make an ideal social media hub.
- **Project management and team communication.** Using blogs is a good way to keep project teams up to date, particularly when team members are geographically dispersed. For instance, the trip reports that employees file after visiting customers or other external parties can be enhanced vividly with mobile blogs.
- **Company news.** Companies can use blogs to keep employees informed about general business matters, from facility news to benefit updates. Blogs also serve as online community forums, giving everyone in the company a chance to raise questions and voice concerns.
- **Customer support.** Customer support blogs answer questions, offer tips and advice, and inform customers about new products. Also, many companies monitor the blogosphere (and Twittersphere), looking for complaints and responding with offers to help dissatisfied customers.[42]
- **Public relations and media relations.** Many company employees and executives now share company news with both the general public and journalists via their blogs.
- **Recruiting.** Using a blog is a great way to let potential employees know more about your company, the people who work there, and the nature of the company culture. In the other direction, employers often find and evaluate the blogs and microblogs of prospective employees, making blogging is a great way to build a name for yourself within your industry or profession.

- **Policy and issue discussions.** Executive blogs in particular provide a public forum for discussing legislation, regulations, and other broad issues of interest to an organization.
- **Crisis communication.** A blog is a convenient way to provide up-to-the-minute information during emergencies, to correct misinformation, or respond to rumors.
- **Market research.** Blogs can be a clever mechanism for soliciting feedback from customers and experts in the marketplace. In addition to using their own blogs to solicit feedback, today's companies should monitor blogs that are likely to discuss them, their executives, and their products.
- **Brainstorming.** Online brainstorming via blogs offers a way for people to toss around ideas and build on each other's contributions.
- **Employee engagement.** Blogs can enhance communication across all levels of a company, giving lower-level employees a voice that they might not otherwise have and giving senior executives better access to timely information.
- **Customer education.** Blogs are a great way to help current and potential customers understand and use your products and services. This function can improve sales and support productivity as well, by reducing the need for one-on-one communication.
- **Word-of-mouth marketing.** Bloggers often make a point of providing links to other blogs and websites that interest them, giving marketers a great opportunity to have their messages spread by enthusiasts. (Online word-of mouth marketing is often called *viral marketing* in reference to the way biological viruses are transmitted from person to person. However, viral marketing is not really an accurate metaphor. Real viruses spread from host to host on their own, whereas word-of-mouth marketing spreads voluntarily from person to person. The distinction is critical, because you need to give people a good reason—good content, in other words—to pass along your message.)
- **Influencing traditional media news coverage.** Bloggers are frequently considered experts in their field, and are often called upon when journalists need insights into various topics.
- **Community building.** Blogging is a great way to connect people with similar interests, and popular bloggers often attract a community of readers who connect with one another through the commenting function.

The uses of blogs are limited only by your creativity, so be on the lookout for new ways you can use them to foster positive relationships with colleagues, customers, and other important audiences.

Adapting the Three-Step Process for Successful Blogging

The three-step writing process is easy to adapt to blogging tasks. The planning step is particularly important when you're launching a blog because you're planning an entire communication channel, not just a single message. Pay close attention to your audience, your purpose, and your scope:

- **Audience.** Except with team blogs and other efforts that have an obvious and well-defined audience, defining the target audience for a blog can be challenging. You want an audience large enough to justify the time you'll be investing but narrow enough that you can provide a clear focus for the blog. For instance, if you work for a firm that develops computer games, would you focus your blog on "hardcore" players, the types who spend thousands of dollars on super-fast PCs optimized for video games, or would you broaden the reach to include all video gamers? The decision often comes down to business strategy.
- **Purpose.** A business blog needs to have a business-related purpose that is important to your company and to your chosen audience. Moreover, the purpose has to "have legs"—that is, it needs to be something that can drive the blog's content for months or years—rather than focus on a single event or an issue of only temporary interest. For instance, if you're a technical expert, you might create a blog to give the audience tips and techniques for using your company's products more effectively—a never-ending subject that's important to both you and your audience. This would be the general purpose of your blog; each posting would have a specific purpose within the context of that general purpose. Finally, if you are not writing an official company blog but rather blogging as an individual employee, make sure you understand your employer's blogging guidelines. IBM, for example, gives its employees 12 specific social computing guidelines, such as identifying their role as IBM employees if they are discussing matters related to the company and respecting intellectual property laws.
- **Scope.** Defining the scope of your blog can be a bit tricky. You want to cover a subject area that is broad enough to provide discussion possibilities for months or years but narrow enough to have an identifiable focus.

Write Your Blog Posts

After you begin writing your blog, careful planning needs to continue with each message. Unless you're posting to a restricted-access blog, such as an internal blog on a company intranet, you can never be sure who might see your posts. Other bloggers might read a post months or years after you wrote it.

Use a comfortable, personal writing style. Blog audiences don't want to hear from your company; they want to hear from you. Bear in mind, though, that comfortable does not mean careless. Sloppy writing damages your credibility. Successful blog content also needs to be interesting, valuable to readers, and as brief as possible. In addition, although audiences expect you to be knowledgeable in the subject area your blog covers, you don't need to know everything about every topic. Instead, you can provide links to other blogs and websites that supply relevant information. In fact, *content curation* is one of the most valuable aspects of blogging. Just be sure the content you share is relevant to your readers and compatible with your communication goals.

Complete Your Blog Posts

Completing messages for your blog is usually quite easy. Evaluate the content and readability of your message, proofread to correct any errors, and post using your blogging system's tools. If you're using any contemporary blogging system, it should offer a newsfeed option so that your audience can automatically receive headlines and summaries of new blog posts. Really Simple Syndication (RSS) is the most common type of newsfeed.

Finally, make your material easier to find by **tagging** it with descriptive words. Your readers can then click on these "content labels" to find additional posts on those topics. Tags are usually displayed with each post, and they can also be groups in a tag cloud display, which shows all the tags in use on your blog.

Tag:
To mark a passage of text with descriptive words for ease of later lookup.

Table 6.2 Suggestions for Successful Blogging

Tip	Why It's Important
Don't blog without a clear plan.	Without a clear plan, your blog is likely to wander from topic to topic and fail to build a sense of community with your audience.
Post frequently; the whole point of a blog is fresh material.	If you won't have a constant supply of new information or new links, create a traditional website instead.
Make it about your audience and the issues important to them.	Readers want to know how your blog will help them, entertain them, or give them a chance to communicate with others who have similar interests.
Write in an authentic voice; never create an artificial character who supposedly writes a blog.	Flogs, or fake blogs, violate the spirit of blogging, show disrespect for your audience, and will turn audiences against you as soon as they uncover the truth. Fake blogs used to promote products are now illegal in some countries.
Link generously—but carefully.	Providing interesting links to other blogs and websites is a fundamental aspect of blogging, but make sure the links will be of value to your readers and don't point to inappropriate material.
Keep it brief.	Most online readers don't have the patience to read lengthy reports. Rather than writing long, report-style posts, you can write brief posts that link to in-depth reports.
Don't post anything you wouldn't want the entire world to see.	Future employers, government regulators, competitors, journalists, and community critics are just a few of the people who might eventually see what you've written.
Minimize marketing and sales messages.	Readers want information about them and their needs.
Take time to write compelling, specific headlines for your postings.	Readers usually decide within a couple of seconds whether to read your postings; boring or vague headlines will turn them away instantly.
Pay attention to spelling, grammar, and mechanics.	No matter how smart or experienced you are, poor-quality writing undermines your credibility with intelligent audiences.
Respond to criticism openly and honestly.	Hiding sends the message that you don't have a valid response to the criticism. If your critics are wrong, patiently explain why you think they're wrong. If they are right, explain how you'll fix the situation.
Listen and learn.	If you don't take the time to analyze the comments people leave on your blog or the comments other bloggers make about you, you're missing out on one of the most valuable aspects of blogging.
Respect intellectual property.	Improperly using material you don't own is not only unethical but can be illegal as well.
Be scrupulously honest and careful with facts.	Honesty is an absolute requirement for every ethical business communicator, of course, but you need to be extra careful online because inaccuracies (both intentional and unintentional) are likely to be discovered quickly and shared widely.
If you review products on your blog, disclose any beneficial relationships you have with the companies that make those products.	Bloggers who receive free products or other compensation from companies whose products they write about are now required to disclose the nature of these relationships.

Microblog:
A blog variation in which character count is sharply restricted.

Microblogging

A **microblog** is a variation on blogging in which messages are sharply restricted to specific character counts. Twitter is the best known of these systems, but many others exist. Some companies have private microblogging systems for internal use only; these systems are sometimes referred to as enterprise microblogging or internal micromessaging.[47]

Many of the concepts of regular blogging apply to microblogging as well, although the severe length limitations call for a different approach to composition. Microblog messages often involve short summaries or teasers that provide links to more information. In addition, microblogs tend to have a stronger social aspect that makes it easier for writers and readers to forward messages and for communities to form around individual writers.

Like regular blogging, microblogging quickly caught on with business users and is now a mainstream business medium. Microblogs are used for virtually all of the blog applications mentioned earlier. In addition, microblogs are often used for providing company updates, offering coupons and notice of sales, presenting tips on product usage, sharing relevant and interesting information from experts, announcing headlines of new blog posts, and serving as the backchannel in meetings and presentations. By following top names in your field, you can customize Twitter as your own real-time news source. Customer service is a popular use for Twitter as well, thanks to its ease, speed, and its option to switch between public tweets and private direct messages as the situation warrants. The social networking aspect of Twitter and other microblogs also makes them good for crowdsourcing research questions, asking followers for input or advice. Finally, the ease of retweeting, the practice of forwarding messages from other Twitter users, is the microblogging equivalent of sharing other content from other social media.

In addition to its usefulness as a stand-alone system, Twitter is also integrated with other social media systems and a variety of publishing and reading tools and services. Many of these systems use the Twitter feature known as the hashtag, the # symbol followed by a word or phrase. Hashtagging makes it easy for people to label and search for topics of interest and monitor ongoing Twitter conversations about particular topics.

Although microblogs are designed to encourage spontaneous, when you're using the medium for business communication, don't just tweet out whatever pops into your head. Make sure the messages you post are part of your overall communication strategy. Twitter followers consider tweets that are entertaining, surprising, informative, or engaging as the most valuable. In contrast, the least-valuable tweets tend to be complaints, conversations between the Twitter account owner and a specific follower, and relatively pointless messages such as saying "good morning."

Podcasting

Podcasting is the process of recording audio or video files and distributing them online via RSS subscriptions, in the same way that blog posts are automatically fed to subscribers. Podcasting combines the media richness of voice or visual communication with the convenience of portability. Audiences can listen to or watch podcasts on a blog or website, or download them to phones or portable music players to consume on the go. The hands-off, eyes-off aspect makes audio podcasts great for listening to while driving or exercising.

Podcasting: A digital audio or video file available on blogs or websites, or downloadable to phones or computers.

The most obvious use of podcasting is to replace existing audio and video messages, such as one-way teleconferences in which a speaker provides information without expecting to engage in conversation with the listeners. Training is another good use of podcasting. Podcasting is also a great way to offer free previews of seminars and training classes. Many business writers and consultants use podcasting to build their personal brands and to enhance their other product and service offerings. You can find a wide selection of business-related podcasts on iTunes, many of which are free. Go to the Podcasting section and select the Business category).

Although it might not seem obvious at first, the three-step writing process adapts quite nicely to podcasting. First, focus the planning step on analyzing the situation, gathering the information you'll need, and organizing your material. One vital planning step depends on whether you intend to create podcasts for limited use and distribution (such as a weekly audio update to your virtual team) or to create a wider, public **podcasting channel** with regular recordings on a consistent theme. As with planning a blog, if you intend to create a podcasting channel, be sure to think through the range of topics you want to address over time to verify that you have a sustainable purpose. If you bounce from one theme to another, you risk losing your audience. Maintaining a consistent schedule is also important; listeners will stop paying attention if they can't count on regular updates.

Podcasting channel: A set of regular recordings on a consistent theme

As you organize the content for a podcast, pay close attention to previews, transitions, and reviews. These steering devices are especially vital in audio recordings because audio lacks visual clues, such as headlines, that audiences rely on in print media. Particularly for more formal podcasts, start by revising your script or thinking through your speaking notes before you begin to record. The closer you can get to recording your podcasts in one take, the more productive you'll be.

Most personal computers, smartphones, and other devices now have basic audio recording capability, including built-in microphones, and free editing software such as Audacity is available online. These tools can be sufficient for creating informal podcasts for internal use, but to achieve the higher production quality expected in formal or public podcasts, you'll need additional pieces of hardware and software. These can include an audio processor (to filter out extraneous noise and otherwise improve the audio signal), a mixer (to combine multiple audio or video signals), a better microphone, more sophisticated recording and editing software, and perhaps some physical changes in your recording location to improve the acoustics.

Podcasts can be distributed in several ways, including media stores such as iTunes, by dedicated podcast hosting services, or on a blog with content that supports the podcast channel. If you distribute your podcast on a blog, you can provide additional information and use the commenting feature of the blog to encourage feedback from your audience.

Figure 6.7
Podcasts
Podcasts are being used more frequently in business. How could you use a podcast to market a new product?

CHAPTER SUMMARY

Digital Media and Business Communication

Digital media for short- to-medium length business messages include social networks, information and content sharing websites, email, instant messaging (IM), text messaging, blogging and microblogging, and podcasting. The nine compositional modes are conversations, comments and critiques, orientations, summaries, reference materials, narratives, teasers, status updates and announcements, and tutorials.

Social Networks

Businesses use a variety of social networks, including the well-known public networks such as Facebook and business-oriented networks such as LinkedIn. Companies have external networks for their customers and internal networks for their employees. Social networks help businesses collaborate, gather market intelligence, recruit employees, connect with business partners, market their products and services, and foster brand communities.

Information and Media-Sharing Sites

User-generated content sites such as YouTube allow companies to host media items (such as videos) that customers and other stakeholders can view, comment on, and share. Content curation sites allow professionals and consumers with expertise or interest in a particular field to collect and republish material on a particular topic. Community Q&A sites give individuals the opportunity to build their personal brands by providing expertise, and they give companies the chance to address customer complaints and correct misinformation.

Email

First, there was email. Businesses applied it to a broad range of tasks, whether or not it was well-suited for each. Over time, instant messages, blogs, and social networks have taken over some of these tasks. Still, email remains a vital medium that is appropriate for many private, short- to medium-length messages.

The three-step process adapts easily to email communication. One of the most important planning decisions is to make sure every message has a valuable purpose. Follow the chain of command in your organization; emailing over your boss's head is a good way to stir up resentment. Bear in mind that the expectations of writing quality and formality are higher in business email than in personal email. Also, pay close attention to the subject line; it often determines whether and when recipients open and read the message. The best subject lines are informative and compelling; they tell the readers what the message is about and give them a reason to read it. Completing email messages is straightforward. Proof and revise, stick with a clean design, use the email signature feature, and distribute the message to the right people.

Instant Messaging and Text Messaging

The benefits of IM include its capability for rapid response to urgent messages, lower cost than phone calls and email, ability to mimic conversation more closely than email, and availability on a wide range of devices.

As with email, business IM needs to be treated as a professional medium to ensure safe and effective communication. Be courteous in your use of IM to avoid interrupting others unnecessarily. Make yourself unavailable when you need to focus on other work, don't confidential information if you're not on a secure system, and don't send personal messages at work. Avoid IM for lengthy and complex messages. Don't carry on multiple conversations at once, follow security guidelines, and limit your use of abbreviations and emojis.

Blogging and Microblogging

Businesses use blogs for project management and team communication, company news, customer support, public relations, media relations, employee recruiting, policy and issue discussions, crisis communication, market research, brainstorming, and viral marketing, influencing traditional media news coverage, and community building. Twitter and other microblogs serve all these purposes; businesses also use microblogs to distribute coupons and sale announcements and answer customer service queries. Microblogs can also serve as the backchannel during meetings and presentations.

The three-step process adapts readily to blogging. In planning, pay particular care to defining your audience, identifying the overall purpose of your blog and specific purposes of each post, and establishing a scope that is narrow enough to be focused but broad enough to afford a steady supply of topics. In writing, be sure to write in a personal, authentic style, without slipping into overly familiar or careless writing. Completing involves the usual tasks of proofing and revising, along with the particular tasks needed to distribute your posts via newsfeeds.

Podcasting

The three-step process is also an effective way to develop podcasts. Focus the planning step on analyzing the situation, gathering the information you'll need, and organizing your material. If you plan to create an ongoing podcast channel on a given theme, make sure you've identified a range of topics extensive enough to keep you going over time. As you organize the words or images you'll use as content, pay close attention to previews, transitions, and reviews so that audiences don't get lost while they listen or watch. Good-quality podcasts usually require some specialized hardware and software.

Test Your Knowledge

1. What are three situations in which a printed memo or letter might be preferable to a digital message?
2. How do the compositional modes of orientations, summaries, and teasers differ?
3. Does the three-step writing process apply to IM? Why or why not?

Apply Your Knowledge

1. Given the strict limits on length, should all your microblogging messages function as teasers that link to more detailed information on a blog or website? Why or why not?
2. Can your company stay in control of messages on social media? Why or why not?
3. Is leveraging your connections on social networks for business purposes ethical? Why or why not?
4. If one of the benefits of blogging is the personal, intimate style of writing, is it a good idea to limit your creativity by adhering to conventional rules of grammar, spelling, and mechanics? Why or why not?
5. What are some ways the president of a hiking equipment company could use Twitter to engage potential customers without being overtly promotional?

Practice Your Skills

1. **Selecting Media** Working with at least two other students, identify the best medium to use for each of the following messages. For each of these message needs, choose a medium that you think would work effectively and explain your choice. (More than one medium could work in some cases; just be able to support your particular choice.)

    a. A technical support service for people trying to use their digital music players
    b. A message of condolence to the family of an employee who passed away recently
    c. A collection of infographics from a variety of sources on the state of the consumer electronics industry
    d. A series of observations on the state of the industry
    e. A series of messages, questions, and answers surrounding the work of a project team

2. **Writing Email Subject Lines** Using your imagination to make up whatever details you need, revise the following email subject lines to make them more informative:

    a. New budget figures
    b. Marketing brochure—your opinion
    c. Production schedule

Activities

1. **Addressing Complaints** You are in charge of public relations for a cruise line that operates out of Miami. You are shocked to read a letter in a local newspaper from a disgruntled passenger, complaining about the service and entertainment on a recent cruise. You will have to respond to these publicized criticisms in some way. What audiences will you need to consider in your response? For each of these audiences, which medium (or media) should you use to send your message?

2. **Blogging with Professionalism** You lead a project team that has enthusiastica embraced blogging as a communication medium. Unfortunately, as emotions heat up during the project, some of the blog postings are getting too casual, too personal, and

even sloppy. Because your boss and other managers around the company also read this project blog, you don't want the team to look unprofessional in anyone's eyes. Revise the following blog posting so that it communicates in a more businesslike manner while retaining the informal, conversational tone of a blog (be sure to correct any spelling and punctuation mistakes you find as well).

> Well, to the profound surprise of absolutely nobody, we are not going to be able meet the June 1 commitment to ship 100 operating tables to Southeast Surgical Supply. (For those of you who have been living in a cave the past six month, we have been fighting to get our hands on enough high-grade chromium steel to meet our production schedule.) Sure enough, we got news, this morning that we will only get enough for 30 tables. Yes, we look lik fools for not being able to follow through on promises we made to the customer, but no, this didn't have to happpen. Six month's ago, purchasing warned us about shrinking supplies and suggested we advance-buy as much as we would need for the next 12 months, or so. We naturally tried to followed their advice, but just asnaturally were shot down by the bean counters at corporate who trotted out the policy about never buying more than three months worth of materials in advance. Of course, it'll be us–not the bean counters who'll take the flak when everybody starts asking why revenues are down next quarter and why Southeast is talking to our friends at Crighton Manuf!!! Maybe, some day this company will get its head out of the sand and realize that we need to have some financial flexibility in order to compete.

3. **Revising Email** Use what you've learned about planning and writing business messages to revise this email. Remember these steps:
   - Determine the purpose.
   - Identify and analyze your audience.
   - Define the main idea.
   - Outline the major supporting points.
   - Choose between the direct and indirect approaches.
   - Don't forget to leave ample time for revision of your own work before you turn it in.

> TO: Felicia August <b_august@evertrust.com>
> SUBJECT: Compliance with new break procedure
>
> Some of you may not like the rules about break times; however, we determined that keeping track of employees while they took breaks at times they determined rather than regular breaks at prescribed times was not working as well as we would have liked it to work. The new rules are not going to be an option. If you do not follow the new rules, you could be docked from your pay for hours when you turned up missing, since your direct supervisor will not be able to tell whether you were on a "break" or not and will assume that you have walked away from your job. We cannot be responsible for any errors that result from your inattentiveness to the new rules. I have already heard complaints from some of you and I hope this memo will end this issue once and for all. The decision has already been made.

Starting Monday, January 1, you will all be required to take a regular 15-minute break in the morning and again in the afternoon, and a regular thirty-minute lunch at the times specified by your supervisor, NOT when you think you need a break or when you "get around to it."

There will be no exceptions to this new rule!

Felicia August
Manager
Billing and accounting

4. **Analyzing Instant Messaging Conversations** Review the following IM exchange and explain how the customer service agent could have handled the situation more effectively.

AGENT: Thanks for contacting Home Exercise Equipment. What's up?

CUSTOMER: I'm having trouble assembling my home gym.

AGENT: I hear that a lot! LOL

CUSTOMER: So is it me or the gym?

AGENT: Well, let's see <g>. Where are you stuck?

CUSTOMER: The crossbar that connects the vertical pillars doesn't fit.

AGENT: What do you mean doesn't fit?

CUSTOMER: It doesn't fit. It's not long enough to reach across the pillars.

AGENT: Maybe you assembled the pillars in the wrong place. Or maybe we sent the wrong crossbar.

CUSTOMER: How do I tell?

AGENT: The parts aren't labeled so could be tough. Do you have a measuring tape? Tell me how long your crossbar is.

5. **Analyzing Blog Posts** Read the following blog post. Analyze the strengths and weaknesses of each sentence, then revise according to the guidelines in this chapter.

[headline]

We're DOOMED!!!!!

[post]

I was at the Sikorsky plant in Stratford yesterday, just checking to see how things were going with the assembly line retrofit we did for them last year. I thinkl saw the future, and it ain't pretty. They were demo'ing a prototype robot from Motoman that absolutely blows our stuff out of the water. They wouldn't let me really see it, but based on the 10-second glimpse I got, it's smaller, faster, and more maneuverable than any of our units. And when I asked about the price, the guy just grinned. And it wasn't the sort of grin designed to make me feel good.

I've been saying for years that we need to pay more attention to size, speed, and maneuverability instead of just relying on our historical strengths of accuracy and payload capacity, and you'd have to be blind not to agree that this experience proves me right. If we can't at least show a design for a better unit within two or three months, Motoman is going to lock up the market and leave us utterly in the dust.

Believe me, being able to say "I told you so" right now is not nearly as satisfying as you might think!!

6. **Rewriting Blog Posts** The writer of this blog posting made plenty of mistakes. To analyze the post, ask yourself the following questions. Then use what you uncovered to rewrite it. Don't forget to revise your post before you turn it in.

   - What is the purpose of the post?
   - Who is your audience and what are their needs and concerns likely to be?
   - What is the main idea?
   - What are the main points that support the main idea?
   - Do you recommend a direct or an indirect approach?

[headline]

Get Ready!

[post]

We are hoping to be back at work soon, with everything running smoothly, same production
schedule and no late projects or missed deadlines. So you need to clean out your desk, put your stuff in boxes, and clean off the walls. You can put the items you had up on your walls in boxes, also.

We have provided boxes. The move will happen this weekend. We'll be in our new offices when you arrive on Monday.

We will not be responsible for personal belongings during the move.

7. **Microblogging** Busy knitters can go through a lot of yarn in a hurry, so most keep a sharp eye out for sales. You're on the marketing staff of Knitting Warehouse, and you like to keep your loyal shoppers up-to-date with the latest deals. Visit Knitting-Warehouse.com, select any on-sale product that catches your eye, and write a Twitter update that describes the product and the sale. Be sure to include a link back to the website so your Twitter followers can learn more. (Unless you are working on a private Twitter account that is accessible only by your instructor and your classmates, don't actually send this Twitter update. Email it to your instructor instead.)

8. **Podcasting** You've recently begun recording a weekly podcast to share information with your large and far-flung staff. After a month, you ask for feedback from several of your subordinates, and you're disappointed to learn that some people stopped listening to the podcast after the first couple weeks. Someone eventually admits that many staffers feel

that the recordings are too long and rambling and that the information they contain isn't valuable enough to justify the time it takes to listen. You aren't pleased, but you want to improve. An assistant transcribes the introduction to last week's podcast so you can review it. You immediately see two problems. Revise the introduction based on what you've learned in this chapter.

> So there I am, having lunch with Selma Gill, who just joined and took over the Northeast sales region from Jackson Stroud. In walks our beloved CEO with Selma's old boss at Uni-Plex; turns out they were finalizing a deal to co-brand our products and theirs and to set up a joint distribution program in all four domestic regions. Pretty funny, huh? Selma left Uni-Plex because she wanted sell our products instead, and now she's back selling her old stuff, too. Anyway, try to chat with her when you can; she knows the biz inside and out and probably can offer insight into just about any sales challenge you might be running up against. We'll post more info on the co-brand deal next week; should be a boost for all of us. Other than those two news items, the other big news this week is the change in commission reporting. I'll go into the details in minute, but when you log onto the intranet, you'll now see your sales results split out by product line and industry sector. Hope this helps you see where you're doing well and where you might beef things up a bit. Oh yeah, I almost forgot the most important bit. Speaking of our beloved CEO, Thomas is going to be our guest of honor, so to speak, at the quarterly sales meeting next week and wants an update on how petroleum prices are affecting customer behavior. Each district manager should be ready with a brief report. After I go through the commission reporting scheme, I'll outline what you need to prepare.

Expand Your Skills

1. **Writing Microblog Entries** Foursquare is one of the leading providers of location-based social networking services. Millions of people use Foursquare for social engagement and friendly competition, and many business owners are starting to recognize the marketing potential of having people who are on the move in local areas broadcasting their locations and sharing information about stores, restaurants, clubs, and other merchants.

   Your task: Review the information on Foursquare's Merchant Platform. Now write four brief messages, no more than 140 characters long (including spaces). The first should summarize the benefits to stores, restaurants, and other "brick and mortar" businesses of participating in Foursquare, and the next three messages should convey three compelling points that support that overall benefit statement. If your class is set up with private Twitter accounts, use your private account to send your messages. Otherwise, email your four messages to your instructor or post them on your class blog, as your instructor directs.

2. **Create an Employee-Use Policy** Employees who take pride in their work are a near-priceless resource for any business. When people come under criticism, however, that pride can sometimes manifest itself in negative ways—and public criticism is a fact of life in social media. Imagine that your company has experienced a rash of product

quality problems recently. The result is some unpleasant and occasionally unfair criticism on a variety of social media sites. Someone even set up a Facebook page specifically to give customers a place to vent their frustrations.

You and your public relations team jumped into action, responding to complaints with offers to replace defective products and help customers who have been affected by the quality problems. Everything seemed to be going well, when you checked industry blogs one evening and discovered that two engineers in your company's product design lab have responded to complaints on their own. They identified themselves as company employees and defended their products. They blamed the company's production department and even criticized several customers for lacking the skills needed to use such a sophisticated product. Within a matter of minutes, you see their harsh comments being retweeted and reposted on multiple sites, only fueling the fire of negative feedback against your firm. Needless to say, you are horrified.

Your task: You reach the engineers by private message and tell them to stop posting messages, but you realize you have a serious training issue on your hands. Write a post for the internal company blog that advises employees on how to respond appropriately when they represent the company online. Use your imagination to make up any details you need.

3. **Presenting a Professional Image with Social Networking** Social media can be a great way to socialize during your high school and college years. A possible downside is that today's employers often check up on the online activities of potential hires to avoid employees who may reflect poorly on the company.

   Your task: Team up with another student and review each other's public presence on Facebook, Twitter, Flickr, blogs, and any other website that an employer might check during the interview and recruiting process. Identify any photos, videos, messages, or other material that could raise a red flag with an employer. Write your teammate an email message that lists any risky material.

4. **Writing Professional Email** One-quarter of all motor vehicle accidents that involve children under age 12 are side-impact crashes. These crashes result in higher injury and fatality rates than those that involve front or rear impacts.

   Your task: You work in the consumer information department at Britax, a leading manufacturer of children's car safety seats. Your manager has asked you to prepare an email message that can be sent to parents who request information about side-impact crashes and the safety features of Britax seats. Start by researching side-impact crashes on the Britax website. Write a three-paragraph message that explains the seriousness of side-impact crashes, describes how injuries and fatalities can be minimized in these crashes, and describes how Britax's car seats are designed to help protect children in side-impact crashes.

5. **Press Releases for Small Screens** The size limitations of smartphone screens call for a different approach to writing and formatting documents.

   Your task: On the website of any company that interests you, find a news release (also called a press release) that announces the launch of a new product. Using Pages or any other writing app, revise and format the material in a way that would be effective on smartphone screens.

6. **Writing IM Scripts** High-definition television can be a joy to watch—but, a pain to buy. The field is cluttered with competing technologies and arcane terminology that is meaningless to most consumers. Moreover, it's nearly impossible to define one technical term without invoking two or three others, leaving consumers swimming in an alphabet soup of confusion. As a sales support manager for Crutchfield, a leading online retailer of audio and video systems, you understand the frustration buyers feel; your staff is deluged daily by their questions.

   Your task: To help your staff respond quickly to consumers who ask questions via Crutchfield's online IM chat service, you are developing a set of "canned" responses to common questions. When a consumer asks one of these questions, a sales adviser can simply click on the ready-made answer. Review the "Research and DIY" section on the Crutchfield website, and then write concise, consumer-friendly definitions of the following terms: 1080p, HDMI, 4K, and 3D TV.

7. **Writing an Instructional Blog Post** Tumblr has become a popular short-form blogging platform: it combines the simplicity of Twitter with the ability to share photos and other media easily.

   Your task: Write a 300- to 400-word post for your class blog that explains how to set up an account on Tumblr and get involved in the Tumblr community. The help pages on Tumblr are a good place to get more information about the service.

8. **Citing Sources in a Blog Post** Credit card debt can be a crippling financial burden with many side effects, from higher insurance and loan rates to difficulty getting a job or a promotion. It's also frighteningly easy to fall into, particularly for young people trying to get started in life with limited cash flow.

   Your task: Write a three- to five-paragraph blog post that warns college students about the dangers of credit card debt. Be sure to cite the sources you use in your research.

9. **Writing Tweets** A carefully constructed series of tweets can serve as a summary of a blog post, video, or other message or document.

   Your task: Find any article, podcast, video, or webpage on a business topic that interests you. Write four to six tweets that summarize the content of the piece. Restrict the first tweet to 120 characters to allow for a URL. Email the series to your instructor or publish them on Twitter if your instructor directs. If you use any direct quotes, be sure to use quotation marks and cite the source.

10. **Writing a Microblog Teaser** Twitter updates are a great way to alert people to helpful articles, videos, and other online resources.

    Your task: Find an online resource that offers some great tips to help college students prepare for job interviews. Write a teaser of no more than 120 characters that hints at the benefits other students can get from this resource. If your class is set up with private Twitter accounts, use your private account to send your message. Otherwise, email it to your instructor. Be sure to include the URL; if you're using a Twitter account, the system should shorten it to 20 characters to keep you within the 140-character limit.

11. **Scripting a Video Podcast** While writing the many messages that are part of the job search process, you find yourself wishing you could just talk to some of these companies so your personality could shine through. Well, you're in luck. One of the companies you've applied to has emailed you back, asking you to submit a two-minute podcast introducing yourself and explaining why you would be a good person to hire.

    Your task: Identify a company you'd like to work for after graduation and select a job that would be a good match for your skills and interests. Write a script for a two-minute podcast (two minutes represents roughly 250 words for most speakers). Introduce yourself and the position you're applying for, describe your background, and explain why you think you're a good candidate for the job. Make up any details you need. If your instructor asks you to do so, record the podcast and submit the audio file.

12. **Scripting and Recording a Podcast** Between this chapter and your own experience as a user of social media, you know enough about social media to offer some insights to other business communicators.

    Your task: Write a script for a two- to three-minute podcast (roughly 250 to 400 words) on any social media topic that you find compelling. Be sure to introduce your topic clearly and provide helpful transitions along the way. If your instructor asks you to do so, record the podcast and submit the file electronically.

CHAPTER

7

Writing Routine and Positive Messages

After studying this chapter, you will be able to:

- Outline an effective strategy for writing routine business requests.
- Describe three common types of routine requests.
- Outline an effective strategy for writing routine replies and positive messages.
- Describe six common types of routine replies and positive messages.

Making Routine Requests

Much of your daily business communication will involve routine and positive messages, including routine requests for information or action, replies on routine business matters, and positive messages such as good-news announcements and goodwill messages, from product operation hints and technical support to refunds and ordering glitches. These routine and positive messages are the focus of this chapter. Chapter 8 covers messages that convey negative information, and Chapter 9 addresses persuasive messages.

Making requests is a routine part of business. In most cases, your audience will be prepared to comply, as long as you're not being unreasonable or asking people to do something they would expect you to do yourself. By applying a clear strategy and tailoring your approach to each situation, you'll be able to generate effective requests quickly.

Like all other business messages, routine requests have three parts: an opening, a body, and a close. Using the direct approach, open with your main idea, which is a clear statement of your request. Use the body to give details and justify your request, and then close by requesting specific action.

Stating Your Request Up Front

With routine requests, you can make your request at the beginning of the message, but be careful that you don't come across as abrupt or tactless:

- **Pay attention to tone.** Instead of demanding action ("Send me the latest version of the budget spreadsheet"), show respect by using words such as *please* and *I would appreciate.*
- **Assume that your audience will comply.** Because the request is routine, you can generally assume that your readers will comply when they clearly understand the reason for your request.
- **Be specific.** State precisely what you want. For example, if you request the latest market data from your research department, be sure to say whether you want a 1-page summary or 100 pages of raw data.

Explaining and Justifying Your Request

Use the body of your message to explain your request. Make the explanation a smooth and logical outgrowth of your opening remarks. If complying with the request could benefit the reader, be sure to mention that. If you have multiple requests or questions, ask the most important questions first and deal with only one topic per question. If you have an unusual or complex request, break it down into specific, individual questions so that the reader can address each one separately. This consideration not only shows respect for your audience's time but also gets you a more accurate answer in less time.

Requesting Specific Action in a Courteous Close

Close your message with three important elements:

- a specific request that includes any relevant deadlines
- information about how you can be reached (if it isn't obvious)
- an expression of appreciation or goodwill; for example:

"Please send the March monthly sales figures by April 5 so that I can return first-quarter results to you before the April 15 board meeting. I appreciate your help."

Conclude your message with a sincere thanks. However, don't thank the reader "in advance" for cooperating; many people find that presumptuous.

Common Examples of Routine Requests

The most common types of routine messages ask for information or action, ask for a recommendation, and make a claim or request an adjustment.

Asking for Information or Action

Routine requests can have up to three basic elements:

- What you want to know or what you want your readers to do
- Why you're making the request (not required in all cases)
- Why it may be in your readers' interest to help you (not applicable in all cases)

For simple requests, using the direct approach gets the job done with a minimum of fuss. In more complex situations, you may need to provide more extensive reasons and justification for your request. If applicable, point out any benefits to the reader of complying with your request. Naturally, be sure to adapt your request to your audience and the situation (see Figure 7.1).

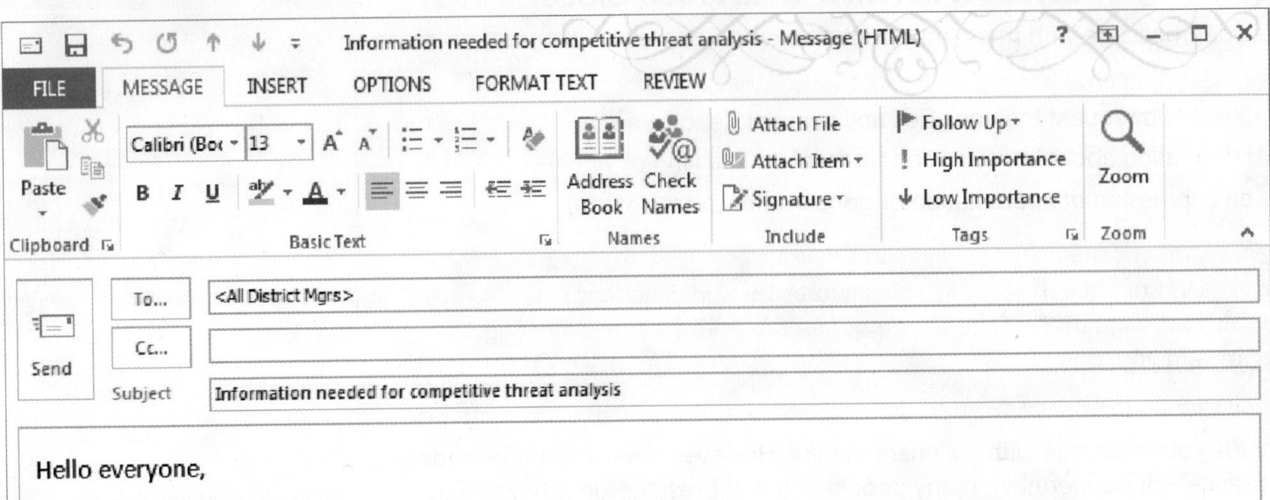

Hello everyone,

At last week's off-site meeting, Charles asked me to coordinate our company competitive threat analysis project. In order to devise a comprehensive strategic response that is sensitive to local market variations, we need your individual insights and advice.

To minimize the effort for you and to ensure consistent data collection across all regions, I've attached a template that identifies all the key questions we'd like to have answered. I realize this will require several hours of work on your part, but the result will be a truly nationwide look at our competitive situation. From this information, we can create a plan for next fiscal year that makes the best use of finite resources while adapting to your local district needs.

To allow sufficient time to compile your inputs before the November 13 board meeting, please email your responses to me by November 8. Thanks for your help and timely attention to this important project.

Helene

Helene H. Clausen
Director, Strategic Initiatives
Early Education Solutions, Inc.
14445 Lawson Blvd, Suite 455
Denver, CO 80201
Desk: 303-555-1200
Mobile: 303-555-9864
www.early-ed.com

Figure 7.1
Routine Message Requesting Action
In this email request to district managers across the country, Helene Clausen asks them to fill out an attached information collection form. Although the request is not unusual and responding to it is part of the managers' responsibility, Clausen asks for their help in a courteous manner and points out the benefits of responding.

Source: Microsoft Outlook 2013, Microsoft Corporation.

Asking for a Recommendation or Reference

References and recommendations are common in business. For example, before extending credit or awarding contracts, jobs, promotions, or scholarships, companies often ask applicants to supply references. Companies ask applicants to list references who can vouch for their ability, skills, integrity, character, and fitness for the job. Before you volunteer someone's name as a reference, ask permission to do so. Some people don't want you to use their names, perhaps because they don't know enough about you to feel comfortable writing a letter or because they or their employers have a policy of not providing recommendations.

Requests for recommendations and references are routine, so you can use the direct approach to organize your inquiry. Open your message by clearly stating why the recommendation is required (if it's not for a job, be sure to explain its purpose) and that you would like your reader to write the letter. If you haven't had contact with the person for some time, use the opening to trigger the reader's memory of the relationship you had.

Figure 7.2
Effective Request for a Recommendation
This writer uses a direct approach when asking for a recommendation from a former professor. Note how she takes care to refresh the professor's memory because she took the class a year and a half ago. She also indicates the date by which the letter is needed and points to the enclosure of a stamped, preaddressed envelope.

1181 Ashport Drive
Tate Springs, TN 38101
March 14, 2016

Professor Lyndon Kenton
School of Business
University of Tennessee, Knoxville
Knoxville, TN 37916

Dear Professor Kenton:

I recently interviewed with Strategic Investments and have been called for a second interview for their Analyst Training Program (ATP). They have requested at least one recommendation from a professor, and I immediately thought of you. May I have a letter of recommendation from you?

As you may recall, I took BUS 485, Financial Analysis, from you in the fall of 2011. I enjoyed the class and finished the term with an "A." Professor Kenton, your comments on assertiveness and cold-calling impressed me beyond the scope of the actual course material. In fact, taking your course helped me decide on a future as a financial analyst.

My enclosed résumé includes all my relevant work experience and volunteer activities. I would also like to add that I've handled the financial planning for our family since my father passed away several years ago. Although I initially learned by trial and error, I have increasingly applied my business training in deciding what stocks or bonds to trade. This, I believe, has given me a practical edge over others who may be applying for the same job.

If possible, Ms. Blackmon in Human Resources needs to receive your letter by March 30. For your convenience, I've enclosed a preaddressed, stamped envelope.

I appreciate your time and effort in writing this letter of recommendation for me. It will be great to put my education to work, and I'll keep you informed of my progress. Thank you for your consideration in this matter.

Sincerely,

Joanne Tucker

Joanne Tucker

Enclosure

The opening states the purpose of the letter and makes the request, assuming the reader will want to comply with the request.

Tucker includes information near the opening to refresh her professor's memory.

The body refers to the enclosed resume and mentions experience that could set the applicant apart from other candidates—information the professor could use in writing the recommendation.

She provides a deadline for response and includes information about the person who is expecting the recommendation.

The close mentions the preaddressed, stamped envelope to encourage a timely response.

Many employers contact references by phone or email. If an employer has specifically asked you for a letter of recommendation, use the body of your request to provide the information the reference will need to write it. Include the full name and address, or email address of the person to whom the recommendation should be sent. Consider including a resume to update the reference on your career advancement since your last contact.

Figure 7.3
Asking for a Reference
When applying for a job or to college, you might be asked to provide references or recommendations. Employers, teachers, and academic counselors are all appropriate to ask.

Making Claims and Requesting Adjustments

Claim: A formal complaint.

Adjustment: A settlement of a complaint.

If you're dissatisfied with a company's product or service, you can opt to make a **claim** (a formal complaint) or request an **adjustment** (a settlement of a claim). In either case, it's important to maintain a professional tone in all your communication, no matter how angry or frustrated you are. Keeping your cool will help you get the situation resolved sooner.

Open with a clear and calm statement of the problem and how you'd like it solved. In the body, give a complete, specific explanation of the details. Provide any information the recipient might need to verify your complaint. IBe prepared to back up your claim with invoices, sales receipts, canceled checks, dated correspondence, and any other relevant documents. Send copies and keep the originals for your files. In your close, politely request specific action or convey a sincere desire to find a solution. And, if appropriate, suggest that the business relationship will continue if the problem is solved satisfactorily.

If the remedy is obvious, tell your reader exactly what you expect from the company, such as exchanging incorrectly shipped merchandise for the right item or issuing a refund if the item is out of stock. In some cases, you might ask the recipient to resolve a problem. However, if you're uncertain about the precise nature of the trouble, you could ask the company to make an assessment and then advise you on how the situation could be fixed. Supply your contact information so that the company can discuss the situation with you, if necessary. Compare the poor and improved versions in Figure 7.4.

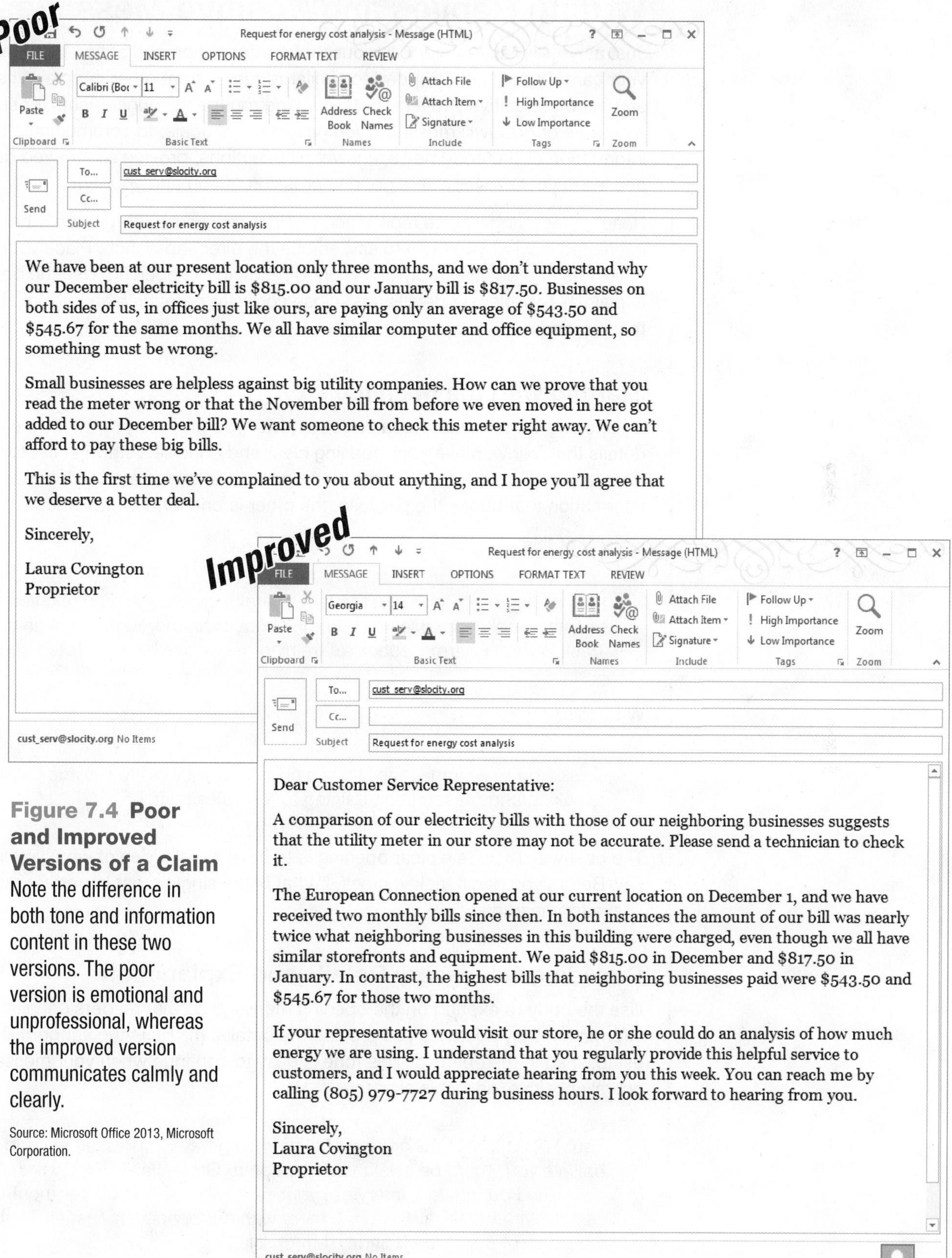

Figure 7.4 Poor and Improved Versions of a Claim
Note the difference in both tone and information content in these two versions. The poor version is emotional and unprofessional, whereas the improved version communicates calmly and clearly.

Source: Microsoft Office 2013, Microsoft Corporation.

Writing Replies and Positive Messages

Just as you'll make numerous requests for information and action throughout your career, you'll also respond to similar requests from other people. When you are respond positively to a request, sending routine announcements, or sending a positive or goodwill message, you have several goals: to communicate the information or the good news, answer all questions, provide all required details, and leave your reader with a good impression of you and your firm.

Readers receiving routine replies and positive messages will generally be interested in what you have to say, so use the direct approach. Place your main idea (the positive reply or the good news) in the opening. Use the body to explain all the relevant details, and close cordially, perhaps highlighting a benefit to your reader.

Starting with the Main Idea

By opening with the main idea or good news, you prepare your audience for the details that follow. Make your opening clear and concise. Although the following introductory statements make the same point, one is cluttered with unnecessary information that buries the purpose, the other is brief and to the point:

Instead of this:

> I am pleased to inform you that after careful consideration of a diverse and talented pool of applicants, each of whom did a thorough job of analyzing Trask Horton Pharmaceuticals's training needs, we have selected your bid.

Write this:

> Trask Horton Pharmaceuticals has accepted your bid to provide public speaking and presentation training to the sales staff.

The best way to write a clear opening is to have a clear idea of what you want to say. Before you begin, ask yourself, "What is the single most important message I have for the audience?"

Providing Necessary Details and Explanation

Use the body to expand on the opening message so that readers get all the information they need. As you provide the details, maintain the supportive tone established in the opening. This tone is easy to continue when your message is entirely positive, as in this example:

> Your educational background and internship have impressed us, and we believe you would be a valuable addition to Green Valley Properties. As discussed during your interview, your salary will be $4,300 per month, plus benefits. In that regard, you will meet with our benefits manager, Paula Sanchez, at 8 a.m. on Monday, March 21.

> She will assist you with all the paperwork necessary to tailor our benefit package to your family situation. She will also arrange various orientation activities to help you acclimate to our company.

However, if your routine message is mixed and must convey mildly disappointing information, put the negative portion of your message into as favorable a context as possible:

Instead of this:

> No, we no longer carry the Sportsgirl line of sweaters.

Write this:

> The new Olympic line has replaced the Sportsgirl sweaters you asked about. Olympic features a wider range of colors and sizes and more contemporary styling.

The more complete description is less negative and emphasizes how the audience can benefit from the change. If the negative news is likely to be a shock or particularly unpleasant for the reader, you'll want to use the indirect approach.

Ending with a Courteous Close

The close of routine replies and positive messages is usually short and simple, because you're leaving things on a neutral or positive note and not usually asking for the reader to do anything. Often, a simple thank you is all you need. However, if follow-up action is required or expected, use the close to identify who will do what and when that action will take place.

Common Examples of Routine Replies and Positive Messages

Most routine and positive messages fall into one of six categories: answers to routine requests, grants of claims or requests for adjustment, recommendations, routine informational messages, good-news announcements, and goodwill messages.

Answering Requests for Information or Action

Every professional answers requests for information or action from time to time. If the response is straightforward, the direct approach is appropriate. A prompt, gracious, and thorough response will positively influence how people view you and the organization you represent. When you're answering requests from a potential customer or other decision maker, look for subtle and respectful ways to encourage a decision in your favor.

Granting Claims and Requests for Adjustment

Even the best-run companies make mistakes, and each of these events represents a turning point in your relationship with your customer. If you handle the situation well, your customer is likely to be even more loyal than before because you've proven that you're serious about customer satisfaction. However, if a customer believes that you mishandled a complaint, you'll make the situation even worse. Dissatisfied customers often take their business elsewhere without notice and tell numerous friends and colleagues about the negative experience. A transaction that might be worth only a few dollars by itself could cost you many times that amount in lost business. In other words, every mistake is an opportunity to improve a relationship.

Your specific response to a customer complaint depends on your company's policies for resolving such issues and your assessment of whether the company, the customer, or some third party is at fault. In general, take the following steps:

- Acknowledge receipt of the customer's claim or complaint.
- Sympathize with the customer's inconvenience or frustration.
- Take (or assign) personal responsibility for setting matters straight.
- Explain precisely how you have resolved, or plan to resolve, the situation.
- Take steps to repair the relationship.
- Follow up to verify that your response was correct.

In addition to taking these positive steps, maintain a professional demeanor. Don't blame colleagues by name; don't make exaggerated, insincere apologies; don't imply that the customer is at fault; and don't promise more than you can deliver.

Communication about a claim is a delicate matter when the customer is clearly at fault. If you choose to grant the claim, open with that good news. However, the body needs special attention because you want to discourage similar claims in the future. Close in a courteous manner that expresses your appreciation for the customer's business (see Figure 7.5).

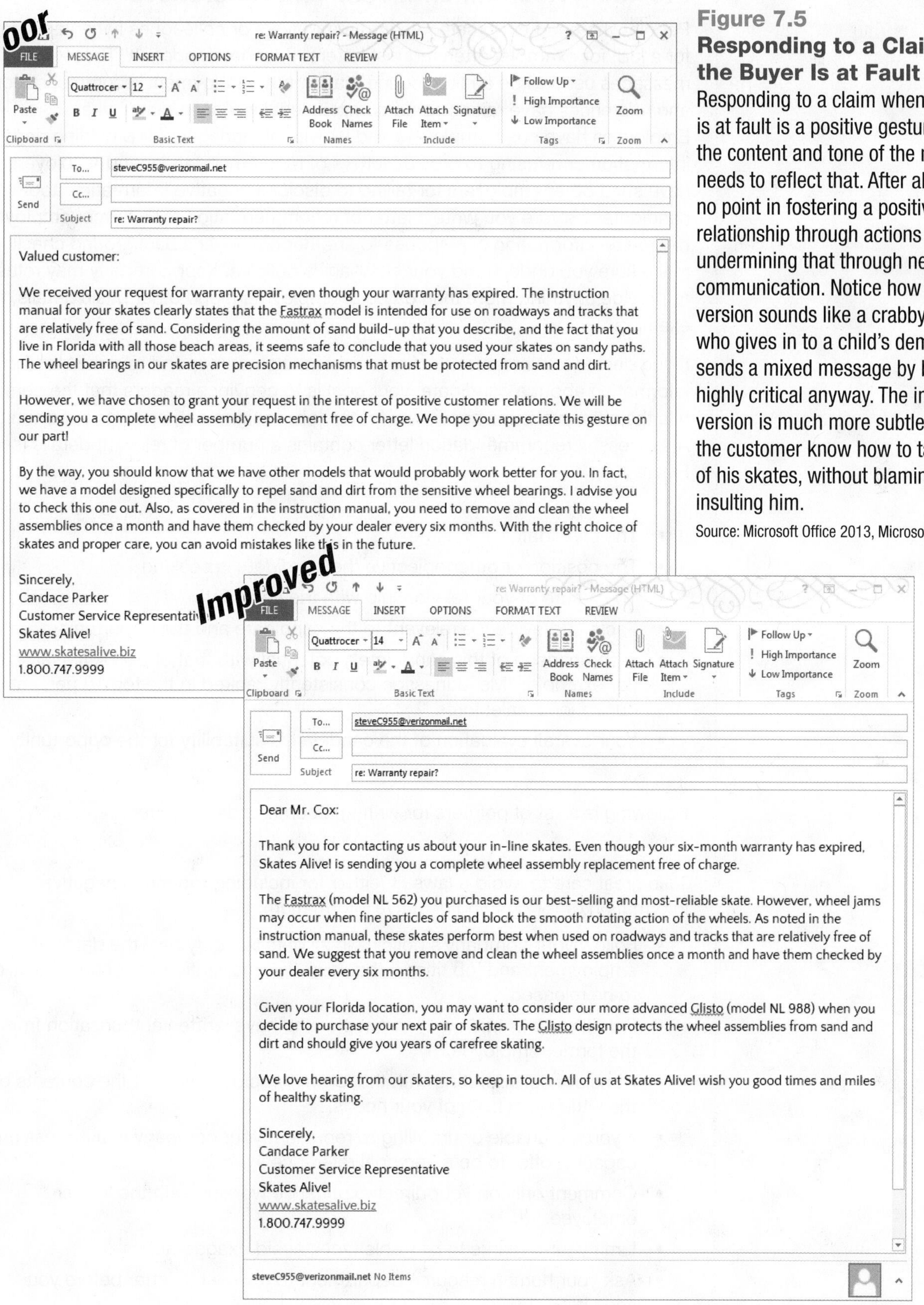

Poor

To... steveC955@verizonmail.net

Subject: re: Warranty repair?

Valued customer:

We received your request for warranty repair, even though your warranty has expired. The instruction manual for your skates clearly states that the Fastrax model is intended for use on roadways and tracks that are relatively free of sand. Considering the amount of sand build-up that you describe, and the fact that you live in Florida with all those beach areas, it seems safe to conclude that you used your skates on sandy paths. The wheel bearings in our skates are precision mechanisms that must be protected from sand and dirt.

However, we have chosen to grant your request in the interest of positive customer relations. We will be sending you a complete wheel assembly replacement free of charge. We hope you appreciate this gesture on our part!

By the way, you should know that we have other models that would probably work better for you. In fact, we have a model designed specifically to repel sand and dirt from the sensitive wheel bearings. I advise you to check this one out. Also, as covered in the instruction manual, you need to remove and clean the wheel assemblies once a month and have them checked by your dealer every six months. With the right choice of skates and proper care, you can avoid mistakes like this in the future.

Sincerely,
Candace Parker
Customer Service Representative
Skates Alive!
www.skatesalive.biz
1.800.747.9999

Improved

To... steveC955@verizonmail.net

Subject: re: Warranty repair?

Dear Mr. Cox:

Thank you for contacting us about your in-line skates. Even though your six-month warranty has expired, Skates Alive! is sending you a complete wheel assembly replacement free of charge.

The Fastrax (model NL 562) you purchased is our best-selling and most-reliable skate. However, wheel jams may occur when fine particles of sand block the smooth rotating action of the wheels. As noted in the instruction manual, these skates perform best when used on roadways and tracks that are relatively free of sand. We suggest that you remove and clean the wheel assemblies once a month and have them checked by your dealer every six months.

Given your Florida location, you may want to consider our more advanced Glisto (model NL 988) when you decide to purchase your next pair of skates. The Glisto design protects the wheel assemblies from sand and dirt and should give you years of carefree skating.

We love hearing from our skaters, so keep in touch. All of us at Skates Alive! wish you good times and miles of healthy skating.

Sincerely,
Candace Parker
Customer Service Representative
Skates Alive!
www.skatesalive.biz
1.800.747.9999

Figure 7.5
Responding to a Claim When the Buyer Is at Fault
Responding to a claim when the buyer is at fault is a positive gesture, so the content and tone of the message needs to reflect that. After all, there's no point in fostering a positive relationship through actions but then undermining that through negative communication. Notice how the poor version sounds like a crabby parent who gives in to a child's demand but sends a mixed message by being highly critical anyway. The improved version is much more subtle, letting the customer know how to take care of his skates, without blaming or insulting him.

Source: Microsoft Office 2013, Microsoft Corporation.

Providing Recommendations and References

People who need endorsements from employers or colleagues (when applying for a job, for example) often request letters of recommendation. These messages used to be a fairly routine matter, but employment recommendations and references have raised some complex legal issues in recent years. Employees have sued employers and individual managers for providing negative information or refusing to provide letters of recommendation, and employers have sued other employers for failing to disclose negative information about job candidates. Before you write a letter of recommendation for a former employee or provide information in response to another employer's background check, make sure you understand your company's policies. Your company may refuse to provide anything more than dates of employment and other basic details, for example.

If you decide to write a letter of recommendation or respond to a request for information about a candidate, your goal is to convince readers that the person has the characteristics necessary for the job, assignment, or other opportunity. A successful recommendation letter contains a number of relevant details (see Figure 7.6):

- The candidate's full name
- The position or other objective the candidate is seeking
- The nature of your relationship with the candidate
- Facts and evidence relevant to the candidate and the opportunity
- A comparison of this candidate's potential with that of peers, if available (for example, "Ms. Jonasson consistently ranked in the top 10 percent of our national salesforce.")
- Your overall evaluation of the candidate's suitability for the opportunity

Following is a list of pointers for writing recommendation letters:

Take great care to avoid a lawsuit (either for including too much negative information or for omitting negative information).

- Follow your company's policies in all details; verify only the dates of employment and job titles if that is all the information your company allows to be released.
- Release information only to people who have written authorization from the former employee.
- Consider collaborating with the former employee so that the contents of the letter meet both of your needs.
- If you are unable or unwilling to represent your company in a professional capacity, offer to be a personal reference instead.
- Comment only on your direct experience working with the former employee.
- Limit your remarks to provable facts; avoid exaggerations.
- Ask your human resource department to review the letter before you send it.

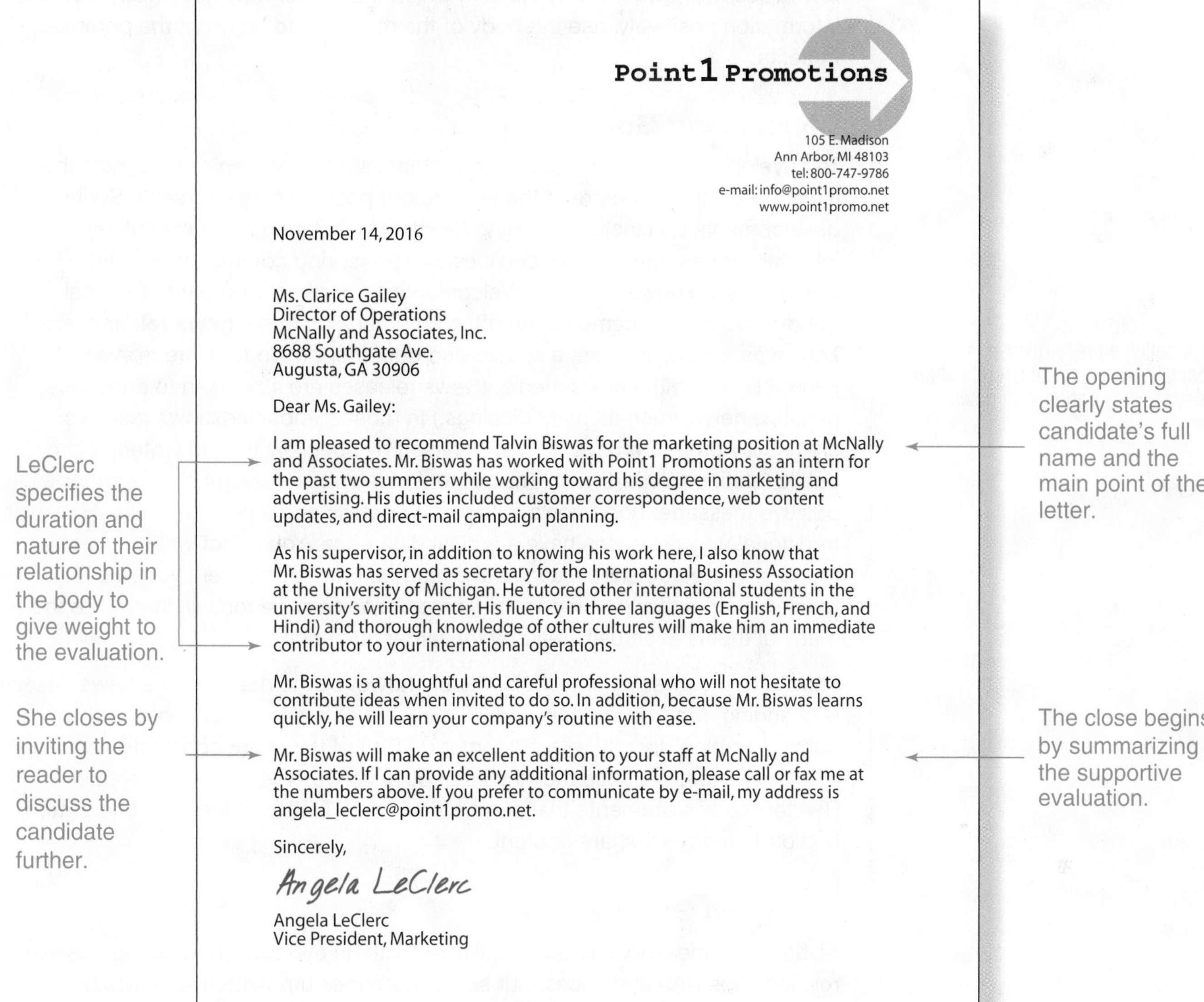

Point1 Promotions

105 E. Madison
Ann Arbor, MI 48103
tel: 800-747-9786
e-mail: info@point1promo.net
www.point1promo.net

November 14, 2016

Ms. Clarice Gailey
Director of Operations
McNally and Associates, Inc.
8688 Southgate Ave.
Augusta, GA 30906

Dear Ms. Gailey:

I am pleased to recommend Talvin Biswas for the marketing position at McNally and Associates. Mr. Biswas has worked with Point1 Promotions as an intern for the past two summers while working toward his degree in marketing and advertising. His duties included customer correspondence, web content updates, and direct-mail campaign planning.

As his supervisor, in addition to knowing his work here, I also know that Mr. Biswas has served as secretary for the International Business Association at the University of Michigan. He tutored other international students in the university's writing center. His fluency in three languages (English, French, and Hindi) and thorough knowledge of other cultures will make him an immediate contributor to your international operations.

Mr. Biswas is a thoughtful and careful professional who will not hesitate to contribute ideas when invited to do so. In addition, because Mr. Biswas learns quickly, he will learn your company's routine with ease.

Mr. Biswas will make an excellent addition to your staff at McNally and Associates. If I can provide any additional information, please call or fax me at the numbers above. If you prefer to communicate by e-mail, my address is angela_leclerc@point1promo.net.

Sincerely,

Angela LeClerc

Angela LeClerc
Vice President, Marketing

Figure 7.6 Effective Recommendation Letter

This letter clearly states the nature of the writer's relationship to the candidate and provides specific examples to support the writer's endorsements.

Sharing Routine Information

Many messages involve sharing routine information, such as project updates and order status notifications. Use the opening of these routine messages to state the purpose and briefly mention the nature of the information you are providing. Provide the necessary details in the body and end your message with a courteous close.

Most routine communications are neutral, so you don't have to take special steps in anticipation of emotional reactions from readers. However, some routine informative messages may require additional care. The announcement of a new policy, for example, may thrill management because of the money the company will save, while all the employees see are additional responsibilities. It might help to remind those employees that the savings may mean new resources—or even pay raises—for them. In instances in which the reader may not initially view the information positively, use the body of the message to highlight the potential benefits.

Announcing Good News

News release:
Also called a press release. A specialized document used to share relevant information with news media.

To develop and maintain good relationships, smart companies recognize that it's good business to spread the word about positive developments. Such developments can include opening new facilities, hiring a top executive, introducing new products or services, or sponsoring community events. Because good news is always welcome, use the direct approach. External good-news announcements are often communicated in a **news release**, also known as a *press release*, a specialized document used to share relevant information with the news media. (News releases are also used to announce negative news, such as plant closings.) In most companies, news releases are usually prepared or at least supervised by specially trained writers in the public relations department. The content follows the customary pattern for a positive message: good news followed by details and a positive close. However, traditional news releases have a critical difference: You're not writing directly to the ultimate audience (such as the readers of a newspaper); you're trying to interest an editor or a reporter in a story, and that person will then write the material that is eventually read by the larger audience.

Thanks to the Internet and social media, however, the nature of the news release is changing. Many companies now view them as a general-purpose tool for communicating directly with customers. Many of these are considered *social media releases*, because they include social networking links, "Tweetables" (Twitter-ready statements that can be shared on Twitter at the click of a button), and other ready-to-share content.

Fostering Goodwill

All business messages should be written with an eye toward fostering positive relationships with audiences, but some messages are written specifically to build goodwill. You can use these messages to enhance your relationships with customers, colleagues, and other businesspeople by sending friendly, even unexpected, notes with no direct business purpose. Whether you're thanking an employee for a job well done or congratulating a colleague for a personal or professional achievement, the small effort to send a goodwill message can have a positive and lasting effect on the people around you.

In addition to creating goodwill messages for a specific reason, you can craft almost any routine message in a way to build goodwill. Two ways to do so are by providing information that your readers might find helpful and by maintaining a positive tone throughout your message.

Sending Congratulations

A prime opportunity for sending goodwill messages is to congratulate individuals or companies for significant business achievements—perhaps for being promoted or for attaining product sales milestones (see Figure 7.6). Other reasons for sending congratulations include highlights in people's personal lives, such as weddings, births, graduations, and success in nonbusiness competitions. You may congratulate business acquaintances on their own achievements or on the accomplishments of a spouse or child. You may also take note of personal events, even if you don't know the reader well. If you're already friendly with the reader, a more personal tone is appropriate.

Sending Messages of Appreciation

An important leadership quality is the ability to recognize the contributions of employees, colleagues, suppliers, and other associates. Your praise does more than just make the person feel good; it encourages further excellence.

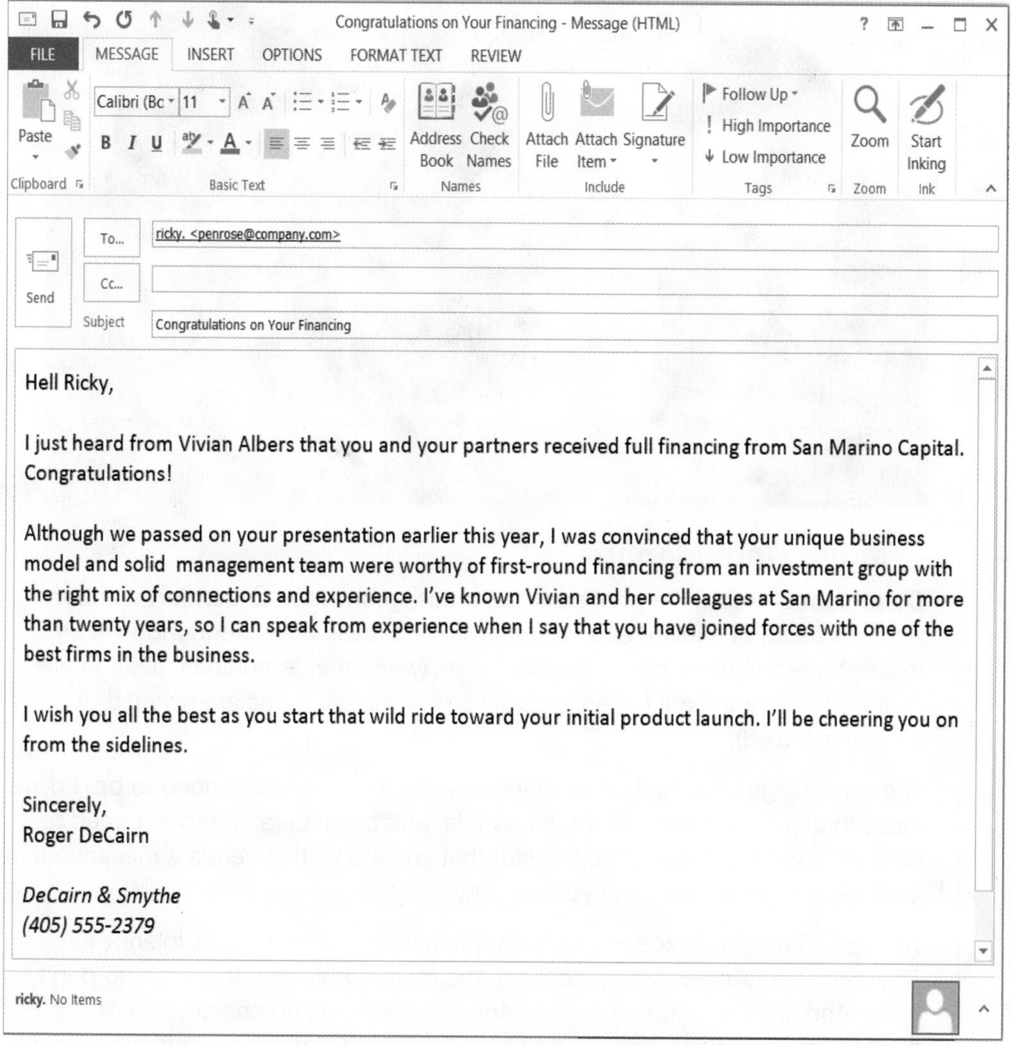

Congratulations on Your Financing - Message (HTML)

To... ricky. <penrose@company.com>

Cc...

Subject: Congratulations on Your Financing

Hell Ricky,

I just heard from Vivian Albers that you and your partners received full financing from San Marino Capital. Congratulations!

Although we passed on your presentation earlier this year, I was convinced that your unique business model and solid management team were worthy of first-round financing from an investment group with the right mix of connections and experience. I've known Vivian and her colleagues at San Marino for more than twenty years, so I can speak from experience when I say that you have joined forces with one of the best firms in the business.

I wish you all the best as you start that wild ride toward your initial product launch. I'll be cheering you on from the sidelines.

Sincerely,
Roger DeCairn

DeCairn & Smythe
(405) 555-2379

Figure 7.7
Goodwill Messages
Goodwill messages serve a variety of business functions. In this email message, investor Roger DeCairn congratulates an entrepreneur who had previously sought start-up capital from his firm but later secured funding from another firm. The message may ultimately benefit DeCairn and his company by building goodwill, but it doesn't serve an immediate business purpose.
Source: Microsoft Office 2013, Microsoft Corporation.

A message of appreciation may also become an important part of someone's personnel file, so provide specific information wherever possible, as in this example:

Hearing a sincere thank you can do wonders for morale. Moreover, in today's digital communication media environment, a handwritten thank-you note can be a particularly welcome acknowledgment.

Thank you and everyone on your team for the heroic efforts you took to bring our servers back up after last Friday's flood. We were able to restore business right on schedule first thing Monday morning. You went far beyond the level of contractual service in restoring our data center within 16 hours. I would especially like to highlight the contribution of networking specialist Julienne Marks, who worked for 12 straight hours to reconnect our Internet service. If I can serve as a reference in your future sales activities, please do not hesitate to ask.

Figure 7.8
Goodwill Messages
How can acknowledging good performance increase productivity?

Offering Condolences

Condolence letter:
A brief personal message written to comfort someone after the death of a loved one or other significant loss.

Condolence letters are brief personal messages written to comfort someone after the death of a loved one. You may have occasion to offer condolences to employees or other business associates (when the person has lost a family member) or to the family of an employee or business associate (when that person has died).

These messages can feel intimidating to write, but they don't need to be. Follow these three principles: be short, be simple, and be sincere. You don't need to produce a work of literary art; the fact that you are writing sends a message that is as meaningful as anything you can say.

Timing and media choice are important considerations with condolence letters. The sooner your message is received, the more comforting it will be, so don't delay. And unless circumstances absolutely leave you no choice, do not use digital formats. A brief, handwritten note on quality stationery is the way to go.

Open a condolence message with a simple expression of sympathy, such as "I am deeply sorry to hear of your loss" or "I am sorry for your loss." How you continue from there depends on the circumstances and your relationships with the deceased and the person to whom you are writing. For example, if you are writing to the husband of a colleague who recently died and you have never met him, you might continue with "Having worked with Janice for more than a decade, I know what a kind and caring person she was." Such a statement accomplishes two goals: explaining why you in particular are writing and letting the recipient know that his loved one was appreciated in the workplace.

Conversely, if you are writing to a colleague who recently lost a loved one, you might continue with "After meeting Warren at last year's company picnic and hearing your stories about his involvement with your son's soccer league and the many other ways he contributed to his community, I know what a special person he was." Sharing brief and positive memories like this adds meaning and depth to your expression of sympathy.

You can conclude with a simple statement such as "My thoughts are with you during this difficult time." If appropriate for the situation and your relationship, you might also include an offer of assistance. "Please call if there is anything I can do for you."

As you decide what to include in the message, keep two points in mind. First, make it a personal expression of sympathy, but don't make the whole message about you and your sense of loss. You might be grieving as well, but unless you, the deceased, and the reader were all personally close, don't say things like "I was so devastated to hear the news about Mollie."

Second, don't offer "life advice," and don't include trite sayings that you may have heard or read. At this point, soon after the loss, the recipient doesn't want your advice, only your sympathy. Also, don't bring religion into the discussion unless you have a close personal relationship with the recipient and religion is already a part of your relationship. Otherwise, you risk offending with unwelcome or inappropriate sentiments.

Condolence letters are the most personal business messages you may ever have to write, so they require the utmost in care and respect for your reader. By keeping the messages simple, short, and sincere, you will be able to achieve the right tone.

Chapter Summary

Writing Routine Requests

When writing a routine request, open by stating your specific request. Use the body to justify your request and explain its importance. Close routine requests by asking for specific action (including a deadline, if appropriate) and expressing goodwill. A courteous close contains three important elements: (1) a specific request, (2) information about how you can be reached (if it isn't obvious), and (3) an expression of appreciation or goodwill.

Common Examples of Routine Requests

The most common types of routine requests are asking for information or action, asking for recommendations, and making claims and requesting adjustments. Requests for information or action should explain what you want to know or what you want readers to do, why you're making the request, and why it may be in your readers' interest to help you (if applicable). Requests for recommendations should open by stating your request. The body should list all the information the recipient would need to write the letter, including your resume, if applicable. The close should contain an expression of appreciation and a deadline, if you have one. To make a claim (a formal complaint about a product or service) or request an adjustment (a settlement of a claim), open with a straightforward statement of the problem, use the body to give a complete explanation of the situation, and close with a polite request to resolve the situation.

Writing Routine Replies and Positive Messages

The direct approach works well for routine replies and positive messages because recipients are generally interested in what you have to say. Place your main idea (the positive reply or the good news) in the opening. Use the body to explain all the relevant details, and close cordially, perhaps by highlighting a benefit to your reader.

Common Examples of Routine Replies and Positive Messages

Most routine and positive messages fall into one of six categories: answers to requests for information and action, grants of claims and requests for adjustment, recommendations, routine informational messages, good-news announcements, and goodwill messages. Answering requests for information or action is a simple task, often assisted with form responses that can be customized as needed. Granting claims and requests for adjustments is more complicated, and the right response depends on whether the company, the customer, or a third party was at fault. Recommendations also require a careful approach to avoid legal complications; some companies prohibit managers from writing recommendation letters or providing anything beyond basic employment history. Routine announcements are often simple and straightforward, but some require extra care if the information affects recipients in a significant way. Good-news announcements are often handled inw news releases, which used to be sent exclusively to members of the news media but are now usually made available to the public as well. Social media releases enable easy sharing with blog- and Twitter-friendly bites of information. Finally, goodwill messages, meant to foster positive business relationships, include congratulations, thank-you messages, and messages of condolence.

Test Your Knowledge

1. What are three guidelines for asking a series of questions in a routine request?
2. Should you use the direct or indirect approach for most routine messages? Why?
3. If a message contains both positive and negative information, what is the best way to present the negative information?
4. How can you avoid sounding insincere when writing a goodwill message?
5. What are three principles to follow for writing condolence messages?

Apply Your Knowledge

1. Every time you send a routine request to Ted Jackson, he fails to comply. His lack of response is beginning to affect your job performance. Should you send Jackson an email message to ask what's wrong? Complain to your supervisor about Jackson's uncooperative attitude? Arrange a face-to-face meeting with Jackson? Bring up the problem at the next staff meeting? Explain.
2. Your company's error cost an important business customer a new client; you know it, and your customer knows it. Do you apologize, or do you refer to the incident in a positive light without admitting any responsibility? Briefly explain.
3. You've been asked to write a letter of recommendation for an employee who worked for you some years ago. You recall that the employee did an admirable job, but you can't remember any specific information at this point. How should you handle the situation?

Practice Your Skills

1. **Revising Email Messages** Revise the following short email messages so that they are more direct and concise; develop a subject line for each revised message.
   a. I'm contacting you about your recent order for a High Country backpack. You didn't tell us which backpack you wanted, and you know we make a lot of different ones. We have the canvas models with the plastic frames and vinyl trim, and we have the canvas
   models with leather trim, and we have the ones that have more pockets than the other ones. Plus they come in lots of different colors. Also they make the ones that are large for a big-boned person and the smaller versions for little women or kids.
   b. Thank you for contacting us about the difficulty you had collecting your luggage at the Denver airport. We are very sorry for the inconvenience this has caused you. Traveling can create problems of this sort regardless of how careful the airline personnel might be. To receive compensation, please send us a detailed list of the items that you lost and complete the following questionnaire. You can email it back to us.
   c. Sorry it took us so long to get back to you. We were flooded with resumes. Anyway, your resume made the final 10, and after meeting three hours yesterday, we've decided we'd like to meet with you. What is your schedule like for next week? Can you come in for an interview on June 15 at 3:00 p.m.? Please get back to us by the end of this work week and let us know if you will be able to attend. As you can imagine, this is our busy season.

2. **Revising Sentences** Rewrite the following so that they are direct and concise.
   a. We wanted to invite you to our special 40 percent off by-invitation-only sale. The sale is taking place on November 9.
   b. We wanted to let you know that we are giving an MP3 player with every $100 donation you make to our radio station.
   c. The director planned to go to the meeting that will be held on Monday at a little before 11:00 a.m.
   d. In today's meeting, we were happy to have the opportunity to welcome Paul Eccelson. He reviewed some of the newest types of order forms. If you have any questions about these new forms, feel free to call him at his office.

3. **Audience Analysis** With another student, conduct an audience analysis of an announcement that to avoid layoffs the company will institute a 10 percent salary reduction for the next six months.
   a. If the company is small and all employees work in the same location, which medium would you recommend for communicating this message?
   b. If the company is large and employees work in a variety of locations around the world, which medium would you recommend for communicating this message?
   c. How is the audience likely to respond to this message?
   d. Based on this audience analysis, would you use the direct or the indirect approach for this message? Explain your reasoning.

4. **Revising Closing Paragraphs** Rewrite each of the following closing paragraphs to be concise, courteous, and specific.
   a. I need your response sometime soon so I can order the parts in time for your service appointment. Otherwise your air-conditioning system may not be in tip-top condition for the start of the summer season.
   b. Thank you in advance for sending me as much information as you can about your products. I look forward to receiving your package in the very near future.
   c. To schedule an appointment with one of our knowledgeable mortgage specialists in your area, you can always call our hotline at 1-800-555-8765. This is also the number to call if you have more questions about mortgage rates, closing procedures, or any other aspect of the mortgage process. Remember, we're here to make the home-buying experience as painless as possible.

Activities

1. **Revising for Professional Tone** Analyze the strengths and weaknesses of this message and then revise it using this chapter's guidelines for routine requests for information:

> I'm fed up with the mistakes that our current accounting firm makes. I run a small construction company, and I don't have time to double-check every bookkeeping entry and call the accountants a dozen times when they won't return my messages. Please explain how your firm would do a better job than my current accountants. You have a

good reputation among home builders, but before I consider hiring you to take over my accounting, I need to know that you care about quality work and good customer service.

2. **Revising for Courtesy** Analyze the strengths and weaknesses of this message and, then revise it to follow this chapter's guidelines for routine requests for information:

I'm contacting you about your recent email request for technical support on your cable Internet service. Part of the problem we have in tech support is trying to figure out exactly what each customer's specific problem is so that we can troubleshoot quickly and get you back in business as quickly as possible. You may have noticed that in the online support request form, there are a number of fields to enter your type of computer, operating system, memory, and so on. While you did tell us you were experiencing slow download speeds during certain times of the day, you didn't tell us which times specifically, nor did you complete all the fields telling us about your computer. Please return to our support website and resubmit your request, being sure to provide all the necessary information; then we'll be able to help you.

3. **Revising a Request for Reference** Analyze the strengths and weaknesses of this message and then revise it to follow this chapter's guidelines for responding to requests for recommendations:

Your letter to Kunitake Ando, president of Sony, was forwarded to me because I am the human resources director. In my job as head of HR, I have access to performance reviews for all of the Sony employees in the United States. This means, of course, that I would be the person best qualified to answer your request for information on Nick Oshinski.

In your letter of the 15th, you asked about Nick Oshinski's employment record with us because he has applied to work for your company. Mr. Oshinski was employed with us from January 5, 2015, until March 1, 2016. During that time, Mr. Oshinski received ratings ranging from 2.5 up to 9.6, with 10 being the top score. As you can see, he must have done better reporting to some managers than to others. In addition, he took all vacation days, which is a bit unusual. Although I did not know Mr. Oshinski personally, I know that our best workers seldom use all the vacation time they earn. I do not know if that applies in this case.

In summary, Nick Oshinski performed his tasks well depending on who managed him.

4. **Revising a Request for Adjustment** Analyze the strengths and weaknesses of this message and then revise it to follow this chapter's guidelines for responding to requests for adjustments:

We read your letter, requesting your deposit refund. We couldn't figure out why you hadn't received it, so we talked to our maintenance engineer, as you suggested. He said you had left one of the doors off the hinges in your apartment in order to get a large sofa through the door. He also confirmed that you had paid him $50.00 to replace the door since you had to turn in the U-Haul trailer and were in a big hurry.

This entire situation really was caused by a lack of communication between our housekeeping inspector and the maintenance engineer. All we knew was that the door was off the hinges when it was inspected by Sally Tarnley. You know that our policy states that if anything is wrong with the apartment, we keep the deposit. We had no way of knowing that George just hadn't gotten around to replacing the door.

But we have good news. We approved the deposit refund, which will be mailed to you from our home office in Teaneck, New Jersey. I'm not sure how long that will take, however. If you don't receive the check by the end of next month, give me a call.

Next time, it's really a good idea to stay with your apartment until it's inspected, as stipulated in your lease agreement. That way, you'll be sure to receive your refund when you expect it. Hope you have a good summer.

5. **Writing a Positive Tweet** Locate an online announcement for a new product you find interesting or useful. Read enough about the product to be able to describe it to someone else, then write four Twitter tweets: one to introduce the product to your followers and three follow-up tweets, each describing a particularly compelling features or benefits of the product.

6. **Writing a Condolence Message** The husband of your coworker Chan Panich Papiboon was killed in a bus accident yesterday, along with 19 others. The bus skidded on icy pavement into a deep ravine, tipping over and crushing the occupants before rescuers could get to them.

   You met her husband, Surin, last year at a company banquet. You can still picture his warm smile and the easy way he joked with you and others, even though you were complete strangers to him. He was only 32 years old, and he left Chana with two children, a 12-year-old boy, Arsa, and a 10-year-old girl, Veera.

   Write the condolence letter in your own words. Use the following questions to help you thinking the advice through your choices before you begin writing:

   1. Which of the following sentences would make the best opening?
      a. I am sorry for your loss.
      b. What a terrible tragedy you have suffered.
      c. I was crushed by the horrible news about your husband.
      d. You and your children must be so upset, and who could blame you?
   2. In the body of the letter, you want to express something meaningful, but you are not familiar with her religious beliefs and you're not sure what's safe. Choose the best idea from the following:
      a. You could include a poetic quotation that doesn't mention any particular religion.
      b. You could express your deep sorrow for Chana's children.
      c. You could mention something positive about Surin you learned from your brief meeting.
      d. You could ask her close friends at work about her religious preferences and then do some research to come up with something appropriate to say.
   3. For your closing paragraph, which of these ideas is best?
      a. Express your thoughts about death and the hereafter.

b. Say that you are thinking of her during this difficult period and invite her to call if you or the company can assist her in any way.
c. Explain that you don't understand her religious beliefs and aren't sure what's appropriate to say at this time.
d. Any of the above.

4. In the following list, identify all the phrases you should avoid as you write:
   a. Life is for the living
   b. I am sorry for your loss
   c. Karma
   d. Unbearable pain

Expand Your Skills

1. **Requesting Information** You are writing a book about the advantages and potential pitfalls of using online collaboration systems for virtual team projects. You would like to include several dozen real-life examples from people in a variety of industries. Fortunately, you publish a highly respected blog on the subject, and you have several thousand regular readers.

   Your task: Write a post for your blog that asks readers to submit brief descriptions of their experiences using collaboration tools for team projects. Ask them to email stories of how well a specific system or approach worked for them. Explain that they will receive an autographed copy of the book as thanks, but they will need to sign a release form if their stories are to be included. In addition, emphasize that you would like to use real names—of people, companies, and software—but you can keep the anecdotes anonymous if readers require. To stay on schedule, you need to have these stories by May 20.

2. **Requesting a Recommendation** One of your colleagues, Katina Vander, was recently promoted to department manager and now serves on the company's strategic planning committee. At its monthly meeting next week, the committee will choose an employee to lead an important market research project that will help define the company's product portfolio for the next five years.

   You worked side by side with Katina for five years, so she knows your abilities well and has complimented your business insights on many occasions. You know that because she has only recently been promoted to manager, she needs to build credibility among her peers and will therefore be cautious about making such an important recommendation. On the other hand, making a stellar recommendation for such an important project would show that she has a good eye for talent—an essential leadership trait.

   Your task: Write an email message to Katina, telling her that you are definitely interested in leading the project and asking her to put in a good word for you with the committee. Mention four attributes that you believe would serve you well in the role: a dozen years of experience in the industry, an engineering degree that helps you understand the technologies involved in product design, a consistent record of excellent or exceptional ratings in annual employee evaluations, and your three years of experience in the company's customer support group, which gave you a firsthand look at customer satisfaction and quality issues. Make up any additional details you need to write the message.

3. **Requesting Information** Many companies now provide presales and postsales customer support through some form of instant messaging or online chat function. As a consumer looking for information, you'll get better service if you can frame your requests clearly and succinctly.

   Your task: Imagine that you need to replace your old laptop computer, but you're not sure whether to go with another laptop or switch to a tablet or perhaps one of the new tablet/ laptop hybrids. Think through the various ways you will use this new device, from researching and note-taking during class to watching movies and interacting with friends on social media. Now imagine you're in a chat session with a sales representative from a computer company, and this person has asked how he or she can help you. Draft a message (no more than 100 words) that summarizes your computing and media requirements and asks the representative to recommend the right type of device for you.

4. **Making Routine Requests** The vast Consumer Electronics Show (CES) is the premier promotional event in the electronics industry. More than 150,000 industry insiders from all over the world come to see new products on display from 3,000 companies—everything from video game gadgets to Internet-enabled refrigerators with built-in computer screens. You're there, and you've just stumbled on a video game controller that has a built-in webcam to allow networked gamers to see and hear each other while they play. Your company also makes game controllers, and you're worried that your customers will flock to this new controller-cam. You need to know how much buzz is circulating around the show: Have people seen the new controller-cam? What are they saying about it?

   Your task: Compose a text message to your colleagues at the show, alerting them to the new controller-cam and asking them to listen for any buzz that it might be generating among the attendees at the convention center and several nearby hotels. Your text messaging service limits messages to 160 characters, including spaces and punctuation, so keep your message within that limit.

5. **Keeping a Customer** Your company sells flower arrangements and gift baskets. Holidays are always a rush, and the overworked staff makes an occasional mistake. Last week, somebody made a big one. As a furious email message from a customer named Anders Ellison explains, he ordered a Valentine's Day bouquet for his wife, but the company sent a bereavement arrangement instead.

   Your task: Respond to Ellison's email message, apologizing for the error, promising to refund all costs that Ellison incurred, informing him that the correct arrangement will arrive tomorrow (and he won't be charged anything for it), and offering Ellison his choice of any floral arrangement or gift basket for free on his wife's birthday.

6. **Granting a Claim** Like many of the staff at Razer, you are an avid game player. You can therefore sympathize with a customer who got so excited during a hotly contested game that he slammed his Razer Anansi keyboard against his chair in celebration. Razer products are built for serious action, but no keyboard can withstand a blow like that. However, in the interest of building goodwill among the online gaming community you have approved a free replacement. This sort of damage is rare enough that the company isn't worried about unleashing a flood of similar requests.

Your task: Respond to the customer's email request for a replacement, in which he admitted to inflicting some abuse on this keyboard. Explain, tongue in cheek, that the company is "rewarding" him with a free keyboard in honor of his massive gaming win, but gently remind him that even the most robust electronic equipment needs to be used with care.

7. **Recording an Audio Podcast** As a training specialist in the human resources department at Winnebago Industries, you're always on the lookout for new ways to help employees learn vital job skills. You're watching a production worker page through a training manual on how to assemble a new recreational vehicle when you get an idea: record the assembly instructions as audio files that workers can listen to while they perform the steps. With audio instructions, they wouldn't have to shift their eyes between the product and the manual—and constantly lose their place. They could focus on the product and listen for each instruction. Plus, the new system wouldn't cost much at all; any computer can record the audio files, and you'd simply make them available on an intranet site for download onto digital music players.

   Your task: You immediately run your new idea past your boss, who has heard about podcasting but isn't sure it is appropriate for business training. He asks you to prove the viability of the idea by recording a demonstration. Choose a process that you engage in yourself—anything from replacing the strings on a guitar to sewing a quilt to changing the oil in a car—and write a brief (one page or less) description of the process that could be recorded as an audio file. Think carefully about the limitations of the audio format as a replacement for printed text. For instance, do you need to tell people to pause the audio while they perform each task? If your instructor asks you to do so, record your podcast and submit the audio file.

8. **Writing Routine Informational Messages** You are normally an easygoing manager who gives employees a lot of leeway in using their own personal communication styles. However, the weekly staff meeting this morning pushed you over the edge. People were interrupting one another, asking questions that had already been answered, sending text messages during presentations, and exhibiting just about every other poor listening habit imaginable.

   Your task: Review the advice in Chapter 2 on good listening skills, and then write a post for the internal company blog. Emphasize the importance of effective listening and list at least five steps your employees can take to become better listeners.

9. **Making an Announcement via Microblog** As a way to give back to the communities in which it does business, your company supports the efforts of the United Way, a global organization that works to improve lives through education, income stability, and healthy living choices. Each year, employees are encouraged to donate money to their local United Way agencies, and the company gives employees up to three paid days off to volunteer their time for the United Way. This year, you are in charge of the company's campaign.

   Your task: Compose a four-message sequence to be posted on the company's internal microblogging system (a private version of Twitter, essentially). The messages are limited to 200 characters, including spaces and punctuation. The first message will announce the company's annual United Way volunteering and fundraising campaign (make up any details you need); the other three messages will explain the United Way's efforts in the areas of education, income stability, and healthy living. Visit the United Way website to learn more about these three areas.

10. **Making an Announcement via Blog** Scoop.it! is one of the most popular platforms for content curation. One of the ways a company can use Scoop.it! is to find and present content of interest to its customers.

    Your task: Choose any company that interests you and imagine that you are in charge of its public communication efforts. Write a post for the company's internal blog, announcing that the company is now on Scoop.it!. Briefly describe Scoop.it! and explain how it will help the company connect with its customers. Visit the Scoop.it! website to learn more about it. Make up any information you need to complete your post.

11. **Writing a Letter of Recommendation** As a project manager at Orbitz, one of the largest online travel services in the world, you've seen plenty of college interns in action. However, few have impressed you as much as Maxine "Max" Chenault. For one thing, she learned how to navigate the company's content management system virtually overnight and always uses it properly, whereas other interns sometimes left things in a hopeless mess. She asked lots of intelligent questions about the business. You've been teaching her blogging and website design principles, and she's picked them up rapidly. Moreover, she has always been on time, professional, eager to assist, and she doesn't complain about mundane tasks. The only downside is that Max has a busy social life; early on, you often found her focused on her smartphone when she should have been working. To her credit, after you had a brief talk with her, the problem vanished. You'll be sorry to see Max leave when she returns to school in the fall, and you're pleased to write her a letter of recommendation. She's not sure where she'll apply for work after graduation or what career path she'll choose, so she asks you to keep the letter fairly general.

    Your task: Working with a team assigned by your instructor, discuss what should and should not be in the letter. Prepare an outline based on your discussion, then draft the letter.

12. **Sharing Good News** Amateur and professional golfers in search of lower scores want clubs that are optimized for their individual swings. This process of club fitting has gone decidedly high tech in recent years, with fitters using Doppler radar, motion-capture video, and other tools to evaluate golfers' swings and ball flight characteristics. Hot Stix Golf is a leader in this industry, having fitted more than 200 professionals and thousands of amateurs.

    Your task: Imagine that you are the communications director at the Indian Wells Golf Resort in Indian Wells, California. Your operation has just signed a deal with Hot Stix to open a fitting center on site. Write a three-paragraph message that could be posted on the resort blog. The first paragraph should announce the news that the Hot Stix center will open in six months, the second should summarize the benefits of club fitting, and the third should offer a brief overview of the services that will be available at the Indian Wells Hot Stix Center. Information on club fitting can be found on the Hot Stix website; make up any additional information you need to complete the post.

CHAPTER

8

Writing Negative Messages

After studying this chapter, you will be able to:

- Apply the three-step writing process to negative messages.
- Explain how to use the direct approach effectively when conveying negative news.
- Explain how to use the indirect approach effectively when conveying negative news, and explain how to avoid ethical problems when using this approach.
- Describe successful strategies for sending negative messages on routine business matters.
- Describe successful strategies for sending negative employment-related messages.
- List the important points to consider when conveying negative organizational news.
- Describe an effective strategy for responding to negative information in a social media environment.

Using the Three-Step Writing Process for Negative Messages

Delivering negative information is never enjoyable, but with some helpful guidelines, you can craft messages that minimize negative reactions. When you need to deliver bad news, you have five goals: to convey the bad news, to gain acceptance for it, to maintain as much good will as possible with your audience, to maintain a good image for your organization, and, if appropriate, to reduce or eliminate the need for future correspondence on the matter. Accomplishing all five goals requires careful attention to planning, writing, and completing your message.

Planning Negative Messages

When you need to convey negative news, you can't avoid the fact that your audience does not want to hear what you have to say. To minimize the damage to business relationships and to encourage acceptance of your message, plan carefully. With a clear purpose and your audience's needs in mind, gather the information your audience will need in order to understand and accept your message.

Selecting the right combination of medium and channel is critical. For instance, experts advise that bad news for employees be delivered in person whenever possible, both to show respect for the employees and to give them an opportunity to ask questions. Today, an increasing number of managers appear to be using email and other digital media to convey negative messages to employees.

Finally, the organization of a negative message requires particular care. One of the most critical planning decisions is choosing whether to use the direct or indirect approach (see Figure 8.1). A negative message using the direct approach opens with the bad news, proceeds to the reasons for the situation or decision, offers any additional information that may help the audience, and ends with a positive statement aimed at maintaining a good relationship with the audience. In contrast, the indirect approach opens with a buffer (see page 253), then builds up the reasons behind the bad news before presenting the bad news itself.

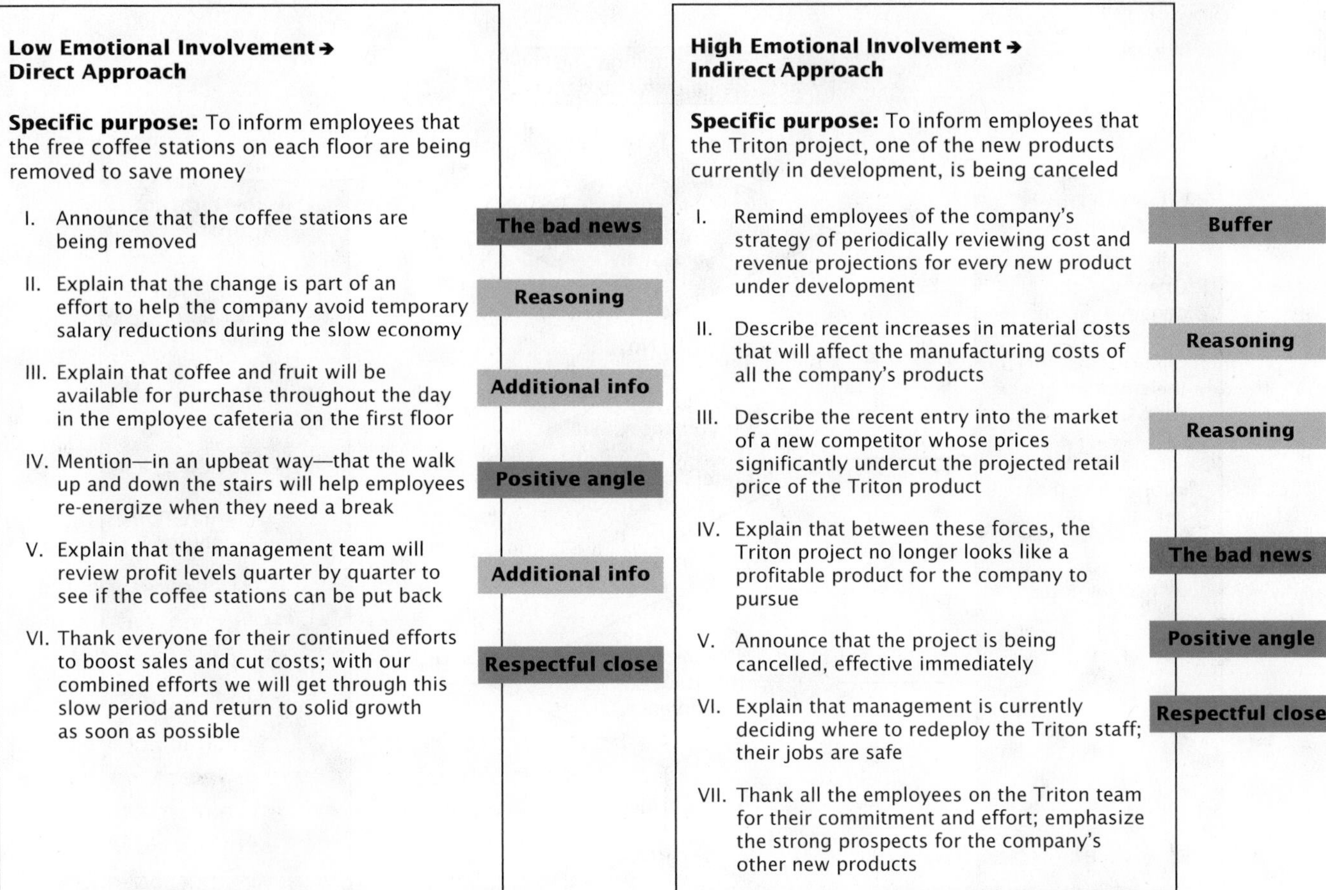

Figure 8.1 Comparing the Direct and Indirect Approaches for Negative Messages
Both these messages deal with changes made in response to negative financial developments, but the second example represents a much higher emotional impact for readers, so the indirect approach is called for in that case. Figure 8.2 explains how to choose the right approach for each situation.

To help decide which approach to take in a particular situation, ask yourself the following questions:

- **Do you need to get the reader's attention immediately?** If the situation is an emergency, or if someone has ignored repeated messages, the direct approach can help you get attention quickly.
- **Does the recipient prefer a direct style of communication?** Some recipients prefer the direct approach no matter what, so if you know this, go with direct.
- **How important is this news to the reader?** For minor or routine scenarios, the direct approach is nearly always best. However, if the reader has an emotional investment in the situation or the consequences to the reader are considerable, the indirect approach is often better, particularly if the bad news is unexpected.
- **Will the bad news come as a shock?** The direct approach is fine for many business situations in which people understand the possibility of receiving bad news. However, if the bad news might come as a shock to readers, use the indirect approach to help them prepare for it.

Figure 8.2 offers a convenient decision tree to help you decide which approach to use.

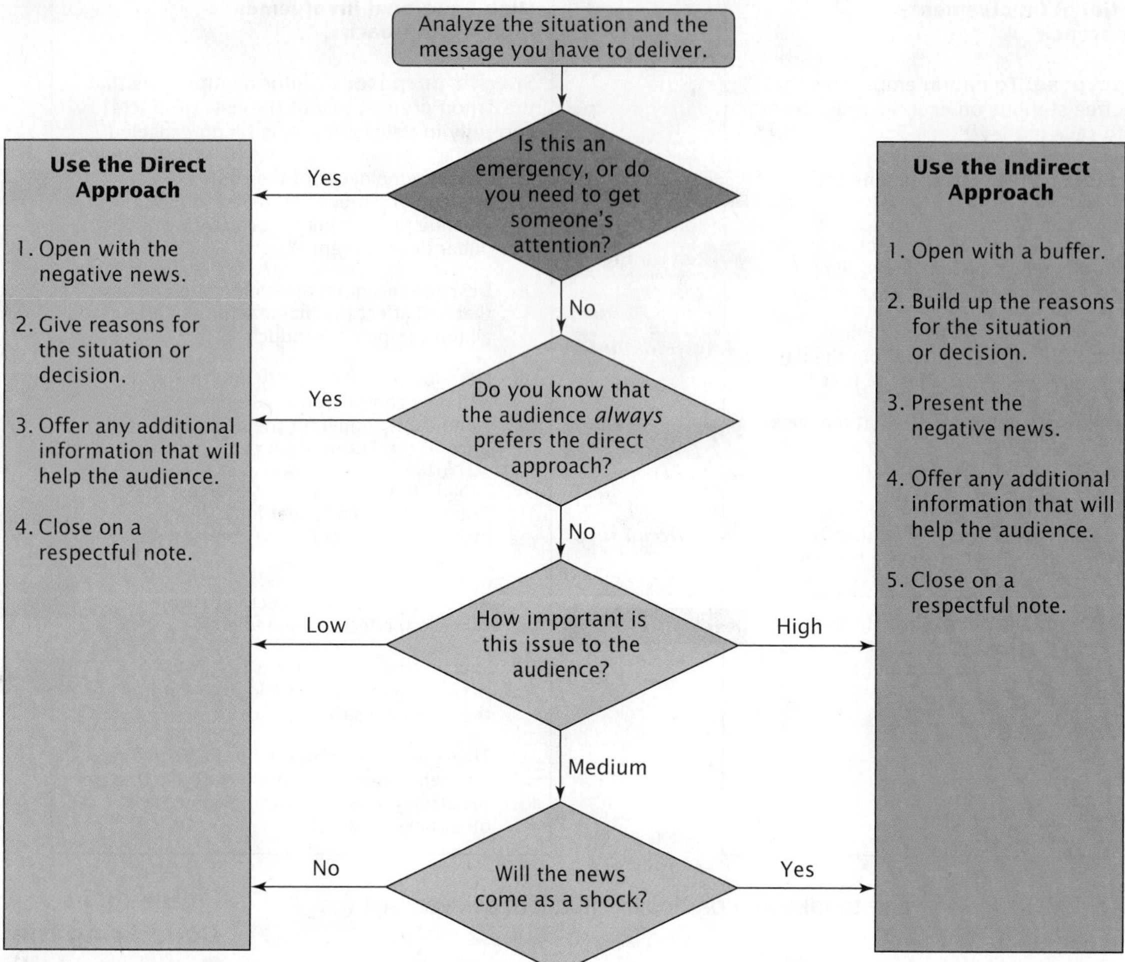

Figure 8.2
Choosing the Direct or Indirect Approach
Following this decision tree will help you decide whether the direct or indirect approach is better in a given situation. Use your best judgment as well. Your relationship with the audience could affect your choice of approaches, for example.

Writing Negative Messages

By writing clearly and sensitively, you can take some of the sting out of bad news and help your reader accept the decision and move on. If your credibility hasn't already been established with an audience, clarify your qualifications so recipients won't question your authority or ability.

When you use language that conveys respect and avoids an accusing tone, you protect your audience's pride. This kind of communication etiquette is always important, but it demands special care with negative messages. Moreover, you can ease the sense of disappointment by using positive words rather than negative, counterproductive ones (see Table 8.1).

Table 8.1 Choosing Positive Language

Negative Language	Positive Alternatives
Your request doesn't make any sense.	Please clarify your request.
The damage won't be fixed for a week.	The item will be repaired next week.
Although it wasn't our fault, there will be an unavoidable delay in your order.	We will process your order as soon as we receive an aluminum shipment from our supplier, which we expect within 10 days.
You are clearly dissatisfied.	I recognize that the product did not live up to your expectations.
I was shocked to learn that you're unhappy.	Thank you for sharing your concerns about your shopping experience.
The enclosed statement is wrong.	Please verify the enclosed statement and provide a correct copy.

Completing Negative Messages

The need for careful attention to detail continues as you complete your message. Revise your content to make sure everything is clear, complete, and concise—bearing in mind that even small flaws are likely to be magnified in readers' minds as they react to the negative news. Produce clean, professional documents and proofread carefully to eliminate mistakes. Finally, be sure to deliver messages promptly; withholding or delaying bad news can be unethical, and even illegal.

Using the Direct Approach for Negative Messages

A negative message using the direct approach opens with the bad news, proceeds to the reasons for the situation or decision, and ends with a positive statement aimed at maintaining a good relationship with the audience. Depending on the circumstances, the message may also offer alternatives or a plan of action to fix the situation. Stating the bad news at the beginning can have two advantages: It makes a shorter message possible, and it allows the audience to reach the main idea of the message in less time.

Opening with a Clear Statement of the Bad News

If you've chosen the direct approach to convey bad news, use the introductory paragraph of your message to share that information. To avoid being overly blunt, you can open with a neutral or positive statement that establishes common ground with the reader, then transition into the news. If necessary, remind the reader why you're writing.

Providing Reasons and Additional Information

In most cases, follow the direct opening with an explanation of why the negative thing is happening. The extent of your explanation depends on the nature of the news and your relationship with the reader. For example, if you want to preserve a long-standing relationship with an important customer, a detailed explanation could well be worth the extra effort. However, you will encounter some situations in which explaining negative news is neither appropriate nor helpful, such as when the reasons are confidential, excessively complicated, or irrelevant to the reader.

Should you apologize when delivering bad news? The answer isn't quite as simple as one might think, partly because the notion of apology is hard to pin down. To some people, it simply means an expression of sympathy that something negative has happened to another person. At the other extreme, it means admitting fault and taking responsibility for specific compensations or corrections to atone for the mistake.

Some experts contend that a company should never apologize, even when it knows it has made a mistake, as the apology might be taken as a confession of guilt that could be used against the company in a lawsuit. However, several states have laws that specifically prevent expressions of sympathy from being used as evidence of legal liability. In fact, judges, juries, and plaintiffs tend to be more forgiving of companies that express sympathy for wronged parties; moreover, an apology can help repair a company's reputation. Recently, some prosecutors have begun pressing executives to publicly admit guilt and apologize as part of the settlement of criminal cases—unlike the common tactic of paying a fine but refusing to admit any wrongdoing.

The best general advice in the event of a mistake or accident is to express sympathy immediately and sincerely and offer help, if appropriate, without admitting guilt; then seek the advice of your company's lawyers before elaborating. A straightforward, sincere apology can go a long way toward healing wounds and rebuilding relationships.

If you do apologize, make it a real apology. Don't say "I'm sorry if anyone was offended" by what you did—this statement implies that you're not sorry at all and that it's the other party's fault for being offended. For example, when Target's information systems were infiltrated in a hacking attack that exposed the personal data of tens of millions of customers, the CEO's apology to customers included the statement, "I know this breach has had a real impact on you, creating a great deal of confusion and frustration." Note that he did not say, "if this breach caused you any confusion or frustration."

Recognize that you can express sympathy for someone's plight without suggesting that you are to blame. For example, iif a business customer misused a product, broke it, and then lost money because he could no longer use it, you can say something along the lines of "I'm sorry to hear of your difficulties." This demonstrates sensitivity without accepting blame.

Closing on a Respectful Note

Afer you've explained the negative news, close the message in a manner that respects the impact the negative news is likely to have on the recipient. If appropriate, consider offering your readers an alternative solution—if you can and if doing so is a good use of your time. Look for opportunities to include positive statements, but avoid creating false hopes or writing in a way that seems to suggest that something negative didn't happen to the recipient. Ending on a false positive can leave readers feeling disrespected, disregarded, or deceived.

Using the Indirect Approach for Negative Messages

As noted earlier, the indirect approach helps readers prepare for the bad news by outlining the reasons for the situation before presenting the bad news itself. However, the indirect approach is not meant to obscure bad news, delay it, or limit your responsibility, it is meant to ease the blow and help readers accept the news. When poorly executed, the indirect approach can be disrespectful and even unethical. But when done well, it is a good example of audience-oriented communication crafted with attention to both ethics and etiquette. Showing consideration for the feelings of others is never dishonest.

Opening with a Buffer

Messages using the indirect approach open with a **buffer**, a neutral, noncontroversial statement that is closely related to the point of the message but doesn't convey the bad news. Depending on the circumstances, a good buffer can express your appreciation for being considered, assure the reader of your attention to their request, indicate your understanding of their needs, introduce the general subject matter, or simply establish common ground with your reader. A good buffer also needs to be relevant and sincere. In contrast, a poorly written buffer might trivialize the reader's concerns, divert attention from the problem with insincere flattery or irrelevant material, or mislead the reader into thinking your message actually contains good news.

Buffer:
A neutral, noncontroversial statement related to the point but not containing the bad news.

Consider these possible responses to a manager of the order-fulfillment department who requested temporary staffing help from your department—a request you won't be able to fulfill:

> Our department shares your goal of processing orders quickly and efficiently.
>
> As a result of the last downsizing, every department in the company is running shorthanded. You folks are doing a great job over there, and I'd love to be able to help out.
>
> Those new state labor regulations are driving me crazy over here; how about in your department?

Only the first of these buffers can be considered effective; the other three are likely to damage your relationship with the other manager. Table 8.2 provides several types of effective buffers you can use to open a negative message tactfully.

Table 8.2 Types of Buffers

Buffer Type	Strategy	Example
Agreement.	Find a point on which you and the reader share similar views.	We both know how hard it is to make a profit in this industry.
Appreciation	Express sincere thanks for receiving something.	Your check for $127.17 arrived yesterday. Thank you.
Cooperation	Convey your willingness to help in any way you realistically can.	Employee Services is here to assist all associates with their health insurance, retirement planning, and continuing education needs.
Fairness	Assure the reader that you've closely examined and carefully considered the problem, or mention an appropriate action that has already been taken.	For the past week, we have run our bandwidth monitoring tools around the clock to track your actual upload and download speeds.
Good news	Start with the part of your message that is favorable.	We have credited your account in the amount of $14.95 to cover the cost of return shipping.
Praise	Find an attribute or an achievement to compliment.	The Stratford Group clearly has an impressive record of helping clients resolve financial reporting problems.
Value	Favorably discuss the product or company related to the subject of the letter.	With their heavy-duty, full-suspension hardware and fine veneers, the desks and file cabinets in our Montclair line have long been popular with value-conscious professionals.
Understanding	Demonstrate that you understand the reader's goals and needs.	So that you can more easily find a printer with the features you need, we are enclosing a brochure that describes all the Epson printers currently available.

Providing Reasons and Additional Information

An effective buffer serves as a transition to the next part of your message, in which you build up the explanations and information that will culminate in your negative news. An ideal explanation section leads readers to your conclusion before you come right out and say it. By giving your reasons effectively, you help maintain focus on the issues at hand and defuse the emotions that accompany bad news. An effective way to do this is to start with positive or neutral points and move through progressively negative points. Provide enough detail for the audience to understand your reasons but be concise.

Avoid hiding behind company policy to cushion your bad news. If you say, "Company policy forbids our hiring anyone who does not have two years' supervisory experience," you imply that you won't consider anyone on his or her individual merits. Skilled and sympathetic communicators explain company policy (without referring to it as "policy") so that the audience can try to meet the requirements at a later time. Consider this response:

> Because these management positions are quite challenging, the human relations department has researched the qualifications needed to succeed in them. The findings show that the two most important qualifications are a bachelor's degree in business administration and two years' supervisory experience.

This paragraph does a good job of stating reasons for the refusal:

- It provides enough detail to logically support the refusal.
- It implies that the applicant is better off avoiding a position in which he or she might fail.
- It doesn't apologize for the decision, because no one is at fault.
- It avoids negative personal statements (such as "You do not meet our requirements").

Even valid, well-thought-out reasons won't convince every reader in every situation, but if you've done a good job of laying out your reasoning, then you've done everything you can to prepare the reader the negative news to come.

Continuing With a Clear Statement of the Bad News

After you've thoughtfully and logically established your reasons and readers are prepared to receive the bad news, you can use three techniques to convey the negative information as clearly and as kindly as possible. First, make sure you don't overemphasize the bad news:

- Minimize the space or time devoted to the bad news—without trivializing it or withholding important information. In other words, don't repeat it or belabor it.
- Subordinate bad news within a complex or compound sentence ("My department is already shorthanded, so I'll need all my staff for at least the next two months").
- Embed bad news in the middle of a paragraph or use parenthetical expressions ("Our profits, which are down, are only part of the picture").

However, keep in mind that it's possible to abuse this notion of deemphasizing bad news. For instance, if the primary point of your message is that profits are down, it would be inappropriate to marginalize that news by burying it in the middle of a sentence. State the negative news clearly, and then make a smooth transition to any positive news that might balance the story.

Second, if appropriate, use a conditional (*if* or *when*) statement to imply that the audience could have received, or might someday receive, a favorable answer under different circumstances ("When you have more managerial experience, you are welcome to apply for any openings that we may have in the future"). Such a statement could motivate applicants to improve their qualifications. However, you must avoid any suggestion that you might reverse the decision you've just made or any phrasing that could give a rejected applicant false hope.

Third, emphasize what you can do or have done rather than what you cannot do. Also, by implying the bad news, you may not need to actually state it, thereby making the bad news less personal ("Our development budget for next year is fully committed to our existing slate of projects"). However, make sure your audience understands the entire message—including the bad news. If an implied message might lead to uncertainty, state your decision in direct terms. Just be sure to avoid overly blunt statements that are likely to cause pain and anger.

Table 8.3 Choosing Language Carefully

Instead of This	Write This
Your request is denied.	Our development budget for next year is already fully committed.
You do not meet our qualifications.	Feel free to contact us again after you complete your four-year degree.
You are not invited to the convention.	I'll count on your help to keep the home office running smoothly while we are short-staffed.
We must turn down your extension request.	Please send in your payment by June 14.

As you follow these tips, be sure that what you say to soften the impact of your message doesn't confuse or mislead your audience. It's critical that they understand the entire message, including the bad news. If you're not certain they will, reconsider using the direct approach.

Closing on a Respectful Note

As in the direct approach, the close in the indirect approach offers an opportunity to emphasize your respect for your audience, even though you've just delivered unpleasant news. Express best wishes without ending on a falsely upbeat note. If you can find a positive angle that's meaningful to your audience, by all means consider adding it to your conclusion. However, don't try to pretend that the negative news didn't happen or that it won't affect the reader. If you've asked readers to decide between alternatives or to take some action, make sure that they know what to do, when to do it, and how to do it. Whatever type of conclusion you use, follow these guidelines:

- **Avoid an uncertain conclusion.** If the situation or decision is final, avoid statements that imply that the matter is open to discussion or negotiation, such as "I hope this decision meets with your approval."

- **Manage future correspondence.** Encourage additional communication only if you're willing to discuss your decision further. If you're not, avoid wording such as "If you have further questions, please write."
- **Express optimism, if appropriate.** If the situation might improve in the future, share that with your readers. Don't suggest the possibility of a positive change if you don't have insight that it might happen.
- **Be sincere.** Avoid clichés and insincere offers of assistance. If you can't help, don't say, "If we can be of any help, please contact us."

Keep in mind that the close can have a lasting impact on your audience. Even though they're disappointed, leave them with the impression that they were treated with respect.

Sending Negative Messages on Routine Business Matters

Professionals and companies receive a wide variety of requests and cannot respond positively to every single one. In addition, mistakes and unforeseen circumstances can lead to delays and other minor problems that occur in the course of business. Occasionally, companies must send negative messages to suppliers and other parties. Whatever the purpose, crafting routine negative responses and messages quickly and graciously is an important skill for every businessperson.

Making Negative Announcements

Many negative messages are written in response to requests from an internal or external correspondent, but on occasion managers need to make unexpected announcements of a negative nature. For example, a company might decide to consolidate its materials purchasing with fewer suppliers thereby need to tell several firms it will no longer be buying from them. Internally, management may need to announce the elimination of an employee benefit or other changes that employees will view negatively.

Although such announcements happen in the normal course of business, they are generally unexpected. Accordingly, except in the case of minor changes, the indirect approach is usually the better choice. Follow the steps outlined for indirect messages: open with a buffer that establishes some mutual ground between you and the reader, advance your reasoning, announce the change, and close with as much positive information and sentiment as appropriate under the circumstances.

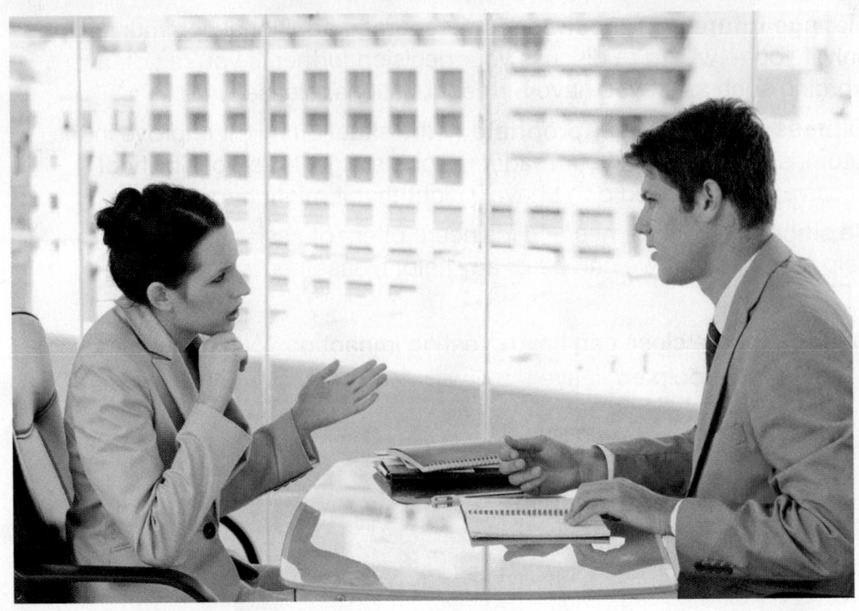

Figure 8.3
Negative Messages
When delivering bad news, consider the audience's likely response to the message and choose a direct or indirect approach accordingly.

Rejecting Proposals

Managers receive a variety of suggestions and proposals, both solicited and unsolicited, from internal and external sources. For an unsolicited proposal from an external source, you may not even need to respond if you don't already have a working relationship with the sender. However, if you need to reject a proposal you solicited, you owe the sender an explanation, and because the news will be unexpected, the indirect approach is better. In general, the closer your working relationship, the more thoughtful and complete you need to be in your response. For example, if you are rejecting a proposal from an employee, explain your reasons fully and carefully so that the employee can understand why the proposal was not accepted and so that you don't damage an important working relationship.

Refusing Routine Requests

When you are unable to meet a routine request, your primary communication challenge is to give a clear negative response without generating negative feelings or damaging either your personal reputation or the company's. As simple as these messages may appear to be, they can test your skills as a communicator because you often need to deliver negative information while maintaining a positive relationship with the other party.

The direct approach works best for most routine negative responses because it is simpler and more efficient. The indirect approach works best when the stakes are high for you or for the receiver, when you or your company has an established relationship with the person making the request, or when you're forced to decline a request that you might have accepted in the past (see Figure 8.4 on the next page).

Consider the following points as you develop routine negative messages:

- Manage your time carefully; focus on the most important relationships and requests.
- If the matter is closed, don't imply that it's still open by using phrases such as "Let me think about it and get back to you" as a way to delay saying no.
- Offer alternative ideas if you can, particularly if the relationship is important.
- Don't imply that other assistance or information might be available if it isn't.

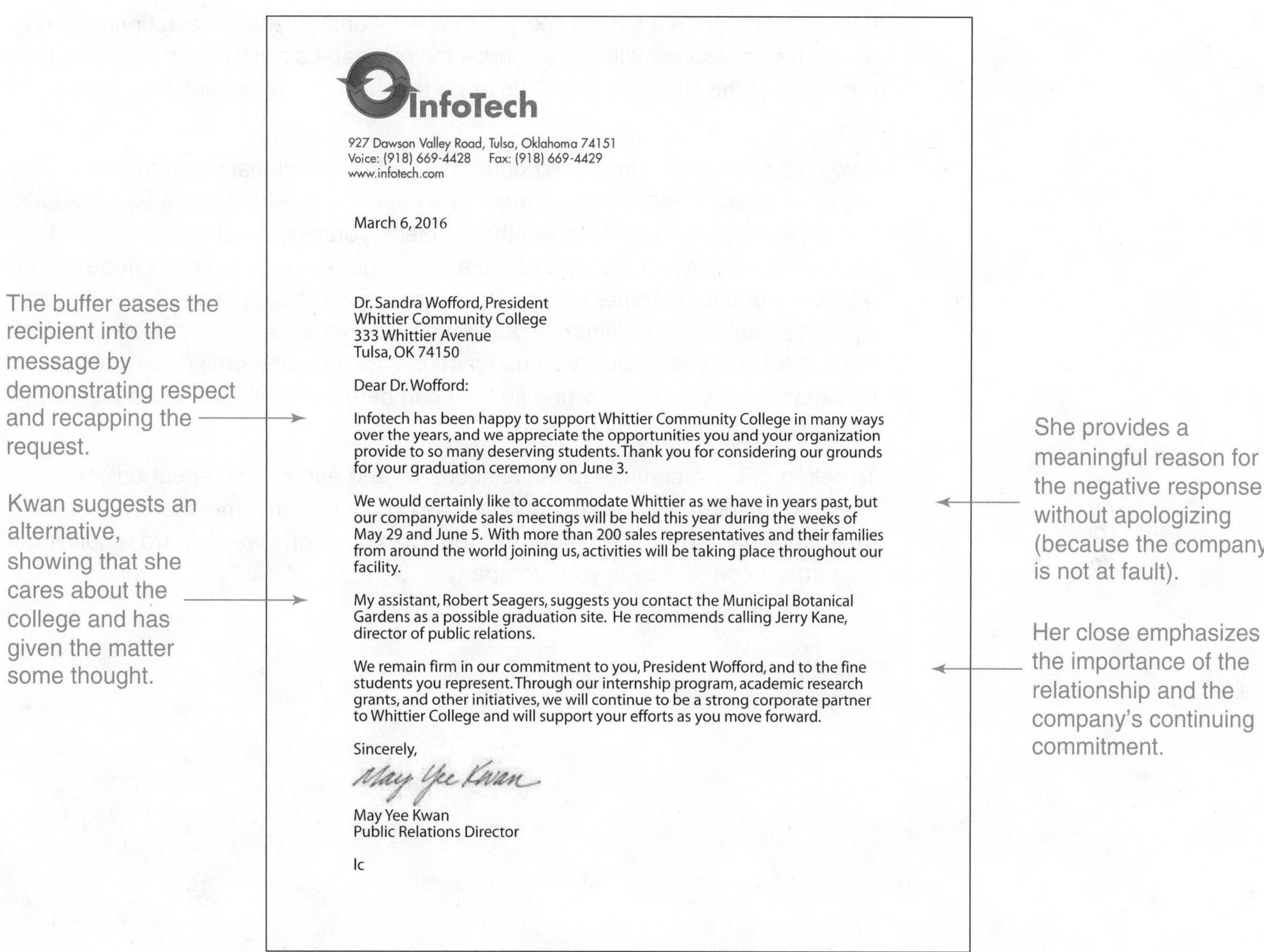

InfoTech

927 Dawson Valley Road, Tulsa, Oklahoma 74151
Voice: (918) 669-4428 Fax: (918) 669-4429
www.infotech.com

March 6, 2016

Dr. Sandra Wofford, President
Whittier Community College
333 Whittier Avenue
Tulsa, OK 74150

Dear Dr. Wofford:

Infotech has been happy to support Whittier Community College in many ways over the years, and we appreciate the opportunities you and your organization provide to so many deserving students. Thank you for considering our grounds for your graduation ceremony on June 3.

We would certainly like to accommodate Whittier as we have in years past, but our companywide sales meetings will be held this year during the weeks of May 29 and June 5. With more than 200 sales representatives and their families from around the world joining us, activities will be taking place throughout our facility.

My assistant, Robert Seagers, suggests you contact the Municipal Botanical Gardens as a possible graduation site. He recommends calling Jerry Kane, director of public relations.

We remain firm in our commitment to you, President Wofford, and to the fine students you represent. Through our internship program, academic research grants, and other initiatives, we will continue to be a strong corporate partner to Whittier College and will support your efforts as you move forward.

Sincerely,

May Yee Kwan

May Yee Kwan
Public Relations Director

lc

Figure 8.4 Effective Letter Declining a Routine Request
In declining a request to use her company's facilities, May Yee Kwan took note of the fact that her company has a long-standing relationship with the college and wants to maintain that positive relationship. Because the news is unexpected based on past experience, she chose an indirect approach to build up to her announcement.

Handling Bad News About Transactions

Bad news about transactions is always unwelcome and usually unexpected. When you send such messages, you have three goals: modify the customer's expectations, explain how you plan to resolve the situation, and repair whatever damage might have been done to the business relationship.

The specific content and tone of each message can vary widely, depending on the nature of the transaction and your relationship with the customer. Telling an individual consumer that his new sweater will be arriving a week later than you promised is a much simpler task than telling Toyota that 30,000 transmission parts will be a week late, especially when you know the company will be forced to idle a multimillion-dollar production facility as a result.

If you haven't done anything specific to set the customer's expectations—such as promising delivery within 24 hours—the message simply needs to inform the customer of the situation, with little or no emphasis on apologies (see Figure 8.5).

If you did set the customer's expectations and now find that you can't meet them, your task is more complicated. In addition to resetting those expectations and explaining how you'll resolve the problem, you may need to include an element of apology. The scope of the apology depends on the magnitude of the mistake. For the customer who ordered the sweater, a simple apology followed by a clear statement of when the sweater will arrive would probably be sufficient. For larger business-to-business transactions, the customer may also want an explanation of what went wrong so they can determine whether to do business with your company in the future.

To help repair the damage to the relationship and encourage repeat business, many companies offer discounts on future purchases, free merchandise, or other considerations. Even modest efforts can go a long way toward rebuilding a customer's confidence in your company.

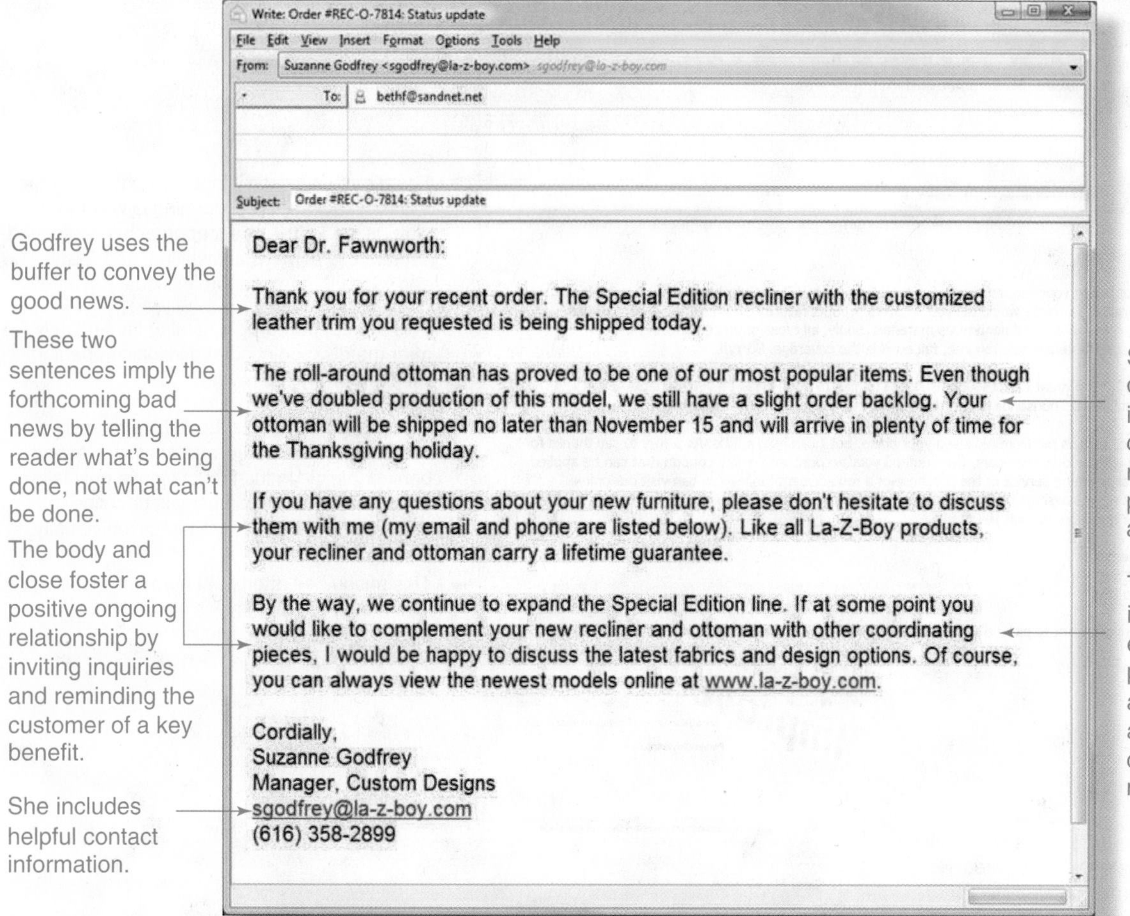

Write: Order #REC-O-7814: Status update

File Edit View Insert Format Options Tools Help

From: Suzanne Godfrey <sgodfrey@la-z-boy.com> sgodfrey@la-z-boy.com

To: bethf@sandnet.net

Subject: Order #REC-O-7814: Status update

Dear Dr. Fawnworth:

Thank you for your recent order. The Special Edition recliner with the customized leather trim you requested is being shipped today.

The roll-around ottoman has proved to be one of our most popular items. Even though we've doubled production of this model, we still have a slight order backlog. Your ottoman will be shipped no later than November 15 and will arrive in plenty of time for the Thanksgiving holiday.

If you have any questions about your new furniture, please don't hesitate to discuss them with me (my email and phone are listed below). Like all La-Z-Boy products, your recliner and ottoman carry a lifetime guarantee.

By the way, we continue to expand the Special Edition line. If at some point you would like to complement your new recliner and ottoman with other coordinating pieces, I would be happy to discuss the latest fabrics and design options. Of course, you can always view the newest models online at www.la-z-boy.com.

Cordially,
Suzanne Godfrey
Manager, Custom Designs
sgodfrey@la-z-boy.com
(616) 358-2899

Figure 8.5 Effective Negative Message Regarding a Transaction
This message, which is a combination of good and bad news, uses the indirect approach—with the good news serving as a buffer for the bad news. In this case, the customer wasn't promised delivery by a certain date, so the writer simply informs the customer when to expect the rest of the order. The writer also takes steps to repair the relationship and encourage future business with her firm.
Source: Microsoft Outlook 2013, Microsoft Corporation.

Refusing Claims and Requests for Adjustment

Customers who make a claim or request an adjustment tend to be emotionally involved, so the indirect approach is usually the better choice when you are denying such a request. Your delicate task as a writer is to avoid accepting responsibility for the unfortunate situation and yet avoid blaming or accusing the customer. To steer clear of these pitfalls, pay special attention to the tone of your letter. Demonstrate that you understand and have considered the complaint carefully, and then rationally explain why you are refusing the request. Close on a respectful and action-oriented note (see Figure 8.6). And be sure to respond quickly. With so many instantaneous media choices at their disposal, some angry consumers will take their complaints public if they don't hear back from a company within a few days—or even a few hours.

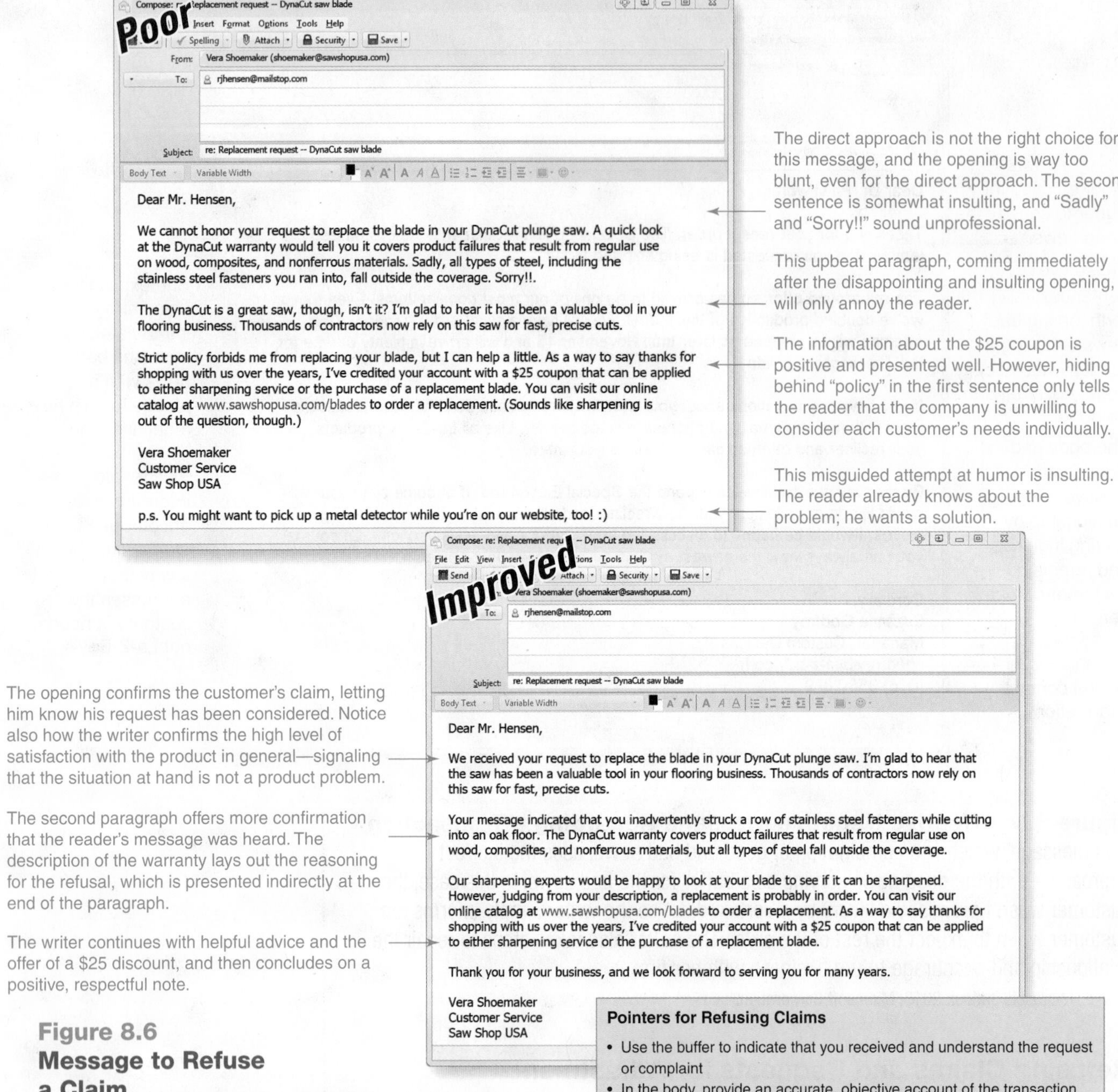

Poor

Compose: re: Replacement request – DynaCut saw blade

From: Vera Shoemaker (shoemaker@sawshopusa.com)

To: rjhensen@mailstop.com

Subject: re: Replacement request – DynaCut saw blade

Dear Mr. Hensen,

We cannot honor your request to replace the blade in your DynaCut plunge saw. A quick look at the DynaCut warranty would tell you it covers product failures that result from regular use on wood, composites, and nonferrous materials. Sadly, all types of steel, including the stainless steel fasteners you ran into, fall outside the coverage. Sorry!!.

The DynaCut is a great saw, though, isn't it? I'm glad to hear it has been a valuable tool in your flooring business. Thousands of contractors now rely on this saw for fast, precise cuts.

Strict policy forbids me from replacing your blade, but I can help a little. As a way to say thanks for shopping with us over the years, I've credited your account with a $25 coupon that can be applied to either sharpening service or the purchase of a replacement blade. You can visit our online catalog at www.sawshopusa.com/blades to order a replacement. (Sounds like sharpening is out of the question, though.)

Vera Shoemaker
Customer Service
Saw Shop USA

p.s. You might want to pick up a metal detector while you're on our website, too! :)

Improved

Compose: re: Replacement request – DynaCut saw blade

From: Vera Shoemaker (shoemaker@sawshopusa.com)

To: rjhensen@mailstop.com

Subject: re: Replacement request – DynaCut saw blade

Dear Mr. Hensen,

We received your request to replace the blade in your DynaCut plunge saw. I'm glad to hear that the saw has been a valuable tool in your flooring business. Thousands of contractors now rely on this saw for fast, precise cuts.

Your message indicated that you inadvertently struck a row of stainless steel fasteners while cutting into an oak floor. The DynaCut warranty covers product failures that result from regular use on wood, composites, and nonferrous materials, but all types of steel fall outside the coverage.

Our sharpening experts would be happy to look at your blade to see if it can be sharpened. However, judging from your description, a replacement is probably in order. You can visit our online catalog at www.sawshopusa.com/blades to order a replacement. As a way to say thanks for shopping with us over the years, I've credited your account with a $25 coupon that can be applied to either sharpening service or the purchase of a replacement blade.

Thank you for your business, and we look forward to serving you for many years.

Vera Shoemaker
Customer Service
Saw Shop USA

Figure 8.6
Message to Refuse a Claim

Vera Shoemaker diplomatically refuses this customer's request for a new saw blade. Without blaming the customer (even though the customer clearly made a mistake), she points out that the saw blade is not intended to cut steel, so the warranty doesn't cover a replacement.

Source: Microsoft Outlook 2013, Microsoft Corporation.

Pointers for Refusing Claims

- Use the buffer to indicate that you received and understand the request or complaint
- In the body, provide an accurate, objective account of the transaction.
- Make the refusal clear without being abrupt, insulting, or accusatory.
- Maintain an impersonal tone that doesn't offend the reader.
- Don't apologize for refusing, since your company hasn't done anything wrong.
- If appropriate, offer an alternative solution.
- Emphasize your continued desire for a positive relationship with the customer.
- Include resale information if appropriate.
- Make any suggested actions easy for the reader to follow.

Figure 8.7
Receiving a Negative Message
What factors should you consider when sending a negative message?

If you deal with enough customers over a long-enough period, chances are you'll get a request that is particularly outrageous. You may even be convinced that the person is not telling the truth. However, you must resist the temptation to call the person dishonest or incompetent. If you do, you could be sued for **defamation**, a false statement that damages someone's reputation. (Written defamation is called **libel;** spoken defamation is called **slander**.) To successfully sue for defamation, the aggrieved party must prove that the statement is false, that the language injures the person's reputation, and that the statement has been communicated to others.

Defamation: A false statement that damages someone's reputation

Libel: Written defamation.

Slander: Spoken defamation

To avoid accusations of defamation, follow these guidelines:

- Avoid using any kind of abusive language or terms that could be considered defamatory.
- Provide accurate information and stick to the facts.
- Never let anger or malice motivate your messages.
- Consult your company's legal advisers whenever you think a message might have legal consequences.
- Communicate honestly and make sure what you're saying is true.
- Emphasize a desire for a good relationship in the future.

Keep in mind that nothing positive can come out of antagonizing a customer, even one who has verbally abused you or your colleagues. Reject the claim or request for adjustment in a professional manner and move on to the next challenge.

Sending Negative Employment Messages

As a businessperson, you will find yourself in a variety of situations in which you have to convey bad news to individual employees or potential employees. Recipients have an emotional stake in these messages, so taking the indirect approach is usually advised. In addition, use great care in choosing your medium for each situation. For instance, email and other written forms let you control the message and avoid personal confrontation, but one-on-one conversations are often viewed as more sensitive and give both sides the opportunity to ask and answer questions.

Refusing Requests for References

When a person applies for a new job, the new employer often contacts previous employers for information about the candidate. Some companies share these details; many others only verify employment. Responses to these requests can be brief and direct:

> Our human resources department has authorized me to confirm that Yolanda Johnson worked for Tandy, Inc., for three years, from June 2013 to July 2016. Best of luck as you interview applicants.

This message doesn't need to say, "We cannot comply with your request." It simply gives the reader all the information that is allowable.

Imagine, however, that someone asks you to write them a letter of recommendation and you're not comfortable doing so. This is tricky; your refusal to cooperate can come across as a personal slight, even a threat to the applicant's future. Your careful preparation and diplomatic tone will help your reader:

> Thank you for letting me know about your job opportunity with Coca-Cola. Your internship there and the MBA you've worked so hard to earn should place you in an excellent position to land the marketing job.
>
> Although we do not send out formal recommendations here at PepsiCo, I can certainly send Coca-Cola a confirmation of your employment dates. And if you haven't considered this already, be sure to ask several of your professors to write evaluations of your marketing skills. Best of luck to you in your career.

This message tactfully avoids hurting the reader's feelings because it makes positive comments about the reader's recent activities, implies the refusal, suggests an alternative, and uses a polite close.

Refusing Social Networking Recommendation Requests

Making recommendations in a social networking environment is more complicated than with a traditional recommendation letter because the endorsements you give become part of *your* online profile. On a network such as LinkedIn, others can see whom you've recommended and what you've written about these people. Much more so than with traditional letters, the recommendations you make in a social network become part of your personal brand. Moreover, networks make it easy to find people and request recommendations, so chances are you will get more requests than you would have otherwise—and sometimes from people you don't know well.

Fortunately, social networks give you a bit more flexibility when it comes to responding to these requests. One option is to simply ignore or delete the request. Of course, if you do know a person, ignoring a request could create an uncomfortable situation, so you will need to decide each case based on your relationship with the requester. Another option is to refrain from making recommendations at all, and just let people know this policy when they ask. Whatever you decide, remember that it is your choice.

If you choose to make recommendations and want to respond to a request, you can write as much or as little about the person as you are comfortable sharing. And you don't need to write a complete letter. You can write a brief statement, even a single sentence that focuses on what you know—and feel comfortable sharing—about the person.

Rejecting Job Applications

Application rejections are routine communications, but saying no is never easy, and recipients are often emotionally invested in the decision. Moreover, companies must be aware of the possibility of employment discrimination lawsuits, which have been on the rise in recent years. Of course, a rejection must also be written in a way that doesn't inadvertently suggest any hint of discrimination. Expert opinions differ on the level of information to include in a rejection message, but the safest strategy is to avoid sharing any explanations for the company's decision and to avoid making or implying any promises of future consideration. Figure 8.7 shows an example.

Figure 8.7
Effective Message Rejecting a Job Applicant
This message rejecting a job applicant takes care to avoid making or implying any promises about future opportunities, beyond inviting the person to apply for positions that may appear in the future. Note that this would not be appropriate if the company did not believe the applicant was a good fit for the company in general.

Naturally, you should adjust your tactics to the circumstances. A simple and direct written message is fine when someone has only submitted a job application, but a phone call might be more appropriate for rejecting a candidate who has made it at least partway through the interview process.

Source: Microsoft Outlook 2013, Microsoft Corporation.

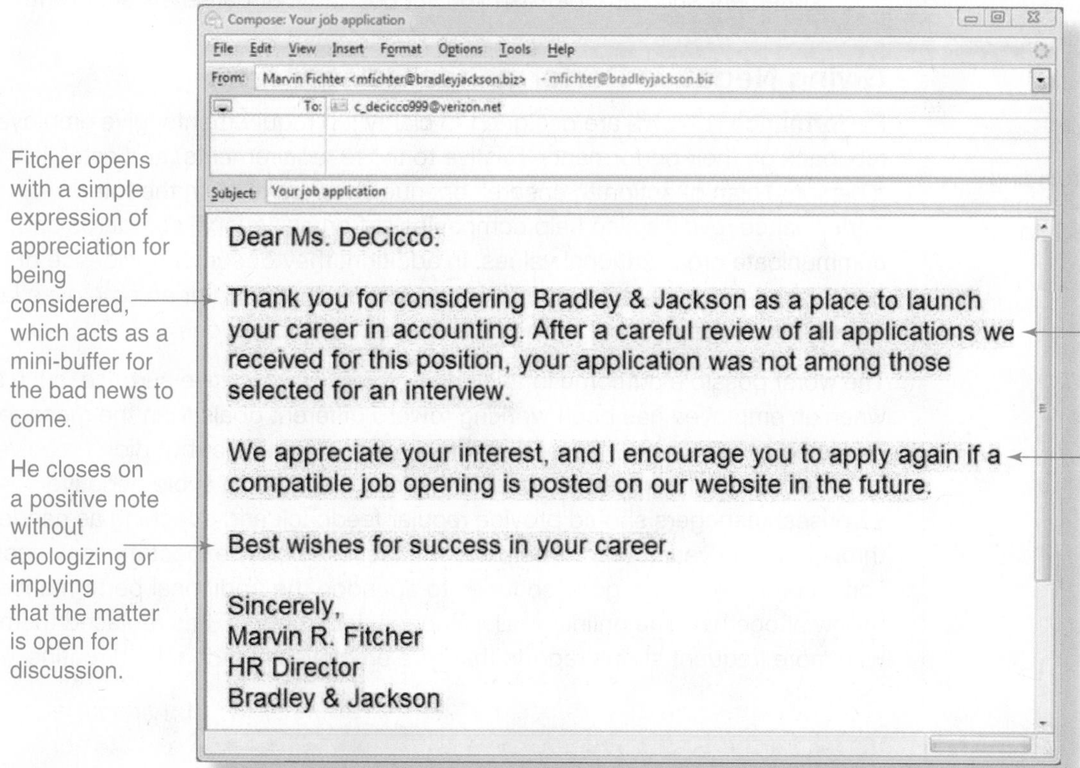

Here are some tips for writing negative job application messages:

- **Personalize the message by using the recipient's name.** "Dear Applicant" can make it sound as though you never bothered to read the application.
- **Open with a courteous expression of appreciation.** In a sense, this is like the buffer in an indirect message because it gives you an opportunity to begin the conversation without immediately and bluntly telling the reader that his or her application has been rejected.
- **Convey the negative news politely and concisely.** The passive voice is helpful in this situation because it depersonalizes the response. For example, "Your application was not among those selected for an interview" is less blunt than the active phrase "We have rejected your application."
- **Avoid explaining why an applicant was rejected or why other applicants were chosen instead.** Although it was once more common to offer such explanations, and some experts still advocate this approach, the simplest strategy from a legal standpoint is to avoid offering reasons for the decision. Avoiding explanations lowers the possibility that an applicant will perceive discrimination in the hiring decision or be tempted to challenge the reasons given.
- **Don't state or imply that the application will be reviewed at a later date.** Saying that "we will keep your resume on file for future consideration" can create false hopes for the recipient and leave the company vulnerable to legal complaints if a future hiring decision is made without actually reviewing this candidate's application again. If the candidate might be a good fit for another position in the company in the future, you can suggest he or she reapply if a new job opening is posted.
- **Close with positive wishes for the applicant's career success.** A brief statement such as "We wish you success in your career" is sufficient.

Giving Negative Performance Reviews

Performance review: An evaluation of an employee's work, providing feedback and establishing a personal plan of action for the future.

Performance reviews are designed to clarify job requirements, give employees feedback on their performance relative to those requirements, and establish a personal plan of action to ensure continued performance in the future. Performance reviews also help companies set organizational standards and communicate organizational values. In addition, they document evidence of performance in the event that disciplinary action is needed or an employee later disputes management decisions regarding pay or promotions.

The worst possible outcome in an annual review is a negative surprise, such as when an employee has been working toward different goals than the manager expected or has been underperforming throughout the year but didn't receive any feedback or improvement coaching along the way. To avoid negative surprises, managers should provide regular feedback and coaching as needed throughout the year if employee performance falls below expectations. In fact, some companies have gone so far as to abandon the traditional performance review altogether. The online retailer Zappos, for example, has replaced them with more frequent status reports that give employees feedback on routine job tasks.

Regardless of the specific approach a company takes, writing an effective performance review requires careful, objective assessment and a clear statement of how well an employee has done relative to agreed-upon goals. If you need to write a review that includes negative information, keep the following points in mind:

- **Document performance problems in detail as they happen.** You will need this information to write an effective appraisal and to support any decisions that need to be made about pay, promotions, or termination.
- **Evaluate all employees consistently.** Consistency is not only fair but also helps protect the company from claims of discriminatory practices.
- **Maintain a calm, objective tone.** Manage the emotions of the situation by maintaining professional reserve in your writing.
- **Focus on opportunities for improvement.** This information can serve as the foundation for an improvement plan for the coming year.
- **Keep job descriptions up to date.** If a job evolves over time in response to changes in the business, the employees' current activities may no longer match an outdated job description.

Terminating Employment

If an employee's performance cannot be brought up to company standards or if other factors such as declining sales cause a reduction in the workforce, a company often has no choice but to terminate employment. As with other negative employment messages, termination is fraught with emotions and legal ramifications, so careful planning, complete documentation, and sensitive writing are essential.

Termination messages should always be written with input from the company's legal staff, but here are general writing guidelines to bear in mind:

- Clearly present the reasons for this difficult action, whether it is the employee's performance or a business decision.
- Make sure the reasons are presented in a way that cannot be construed as unfair or discriminatory.
- Follow company policy, contractual requirements, and applicable laws to the letter.
- Avoid personal attacks or insults of any kind.
- Ask another manager to review the letter. An objective reviewer who isn't directly involved might spot troublesome wording or faulty reasoning.
- Deliver the termination letter in person if at all possible. Arrange a meeting that will ensure privacy and freedom from interruptions.

Any termination is clearly a negative outcome for the employee, but careful attention to content and tone in the termination message can help the employee move on gracefully and minimize the misunderstandings and anger that can lead to expensive lawsuits.

Sending Negative Organizational News

As a manager or business owner, you may at times need to issue negative announcements regarding some aspect of your products, services, or operations. Unlike routine announcements, these messages involve significant changes that negatively affect one or more groups (such as losing a major contract or canceling a popular product), announcements of workforce reductions, project cancelations, and crisis communication regarding environmental incidents, workplace accidents, or other traumatic situations (see Figure 8.8).

When making negative announcements, follow these guidelines:

- **Match your approach to the situation.** For example, in an emergency such as product tampering or a toxic spill, get to the point immediately and make sure all affected parties get the information they need.
- **Consider the unique needs of each affected group.** When a company or facility closes, for instance, employees need time to find new jobs, customers may need to find new suppliers, and community leaders may need to be prepared to help people who have lost their jobs.
- **Minimize the element of surprise whenever possible.** Give affected groups as much time as possible to prepare and respond.
- **If possible, give yourself enough time to plan and manage a response.** Make sure you're ready with answers to potential questions.
- **Look for positive angles but don't exude false optimism.** Laying off 10,000 people does not give them "an opportunity to explore new horizons." It's a traumatic event that can affect employees, their families, and their communities for years. The best you may be able to do is thank people for their past support and wish them well in the future.
- **Seek expert advice.** Many significant negative announcements have important technical, financial, or legal elements that require the expertise of lawyers, accountants, or other specialists.
- **Use multiple channels to reach out to affected audiences.** Provide information through your normal communication network, such as your company website, Facebook page, and Twitter account, but also reach out and participate in conversations that are taking place elsewhere in the social media landscape.
- **Be open and be transparent.** Be honest and share the whole truth as you know it—and are legally allowed to share. Now is not the time to backpedal on bad news or dodge unpleasant details."

Negative situations give you an opportunity to excel as a communicator and as a business leader. Inspirational leaders try to seize such situations as opportunities to reshape or reinvigorate the organization, and they offer encouragement to those around them.

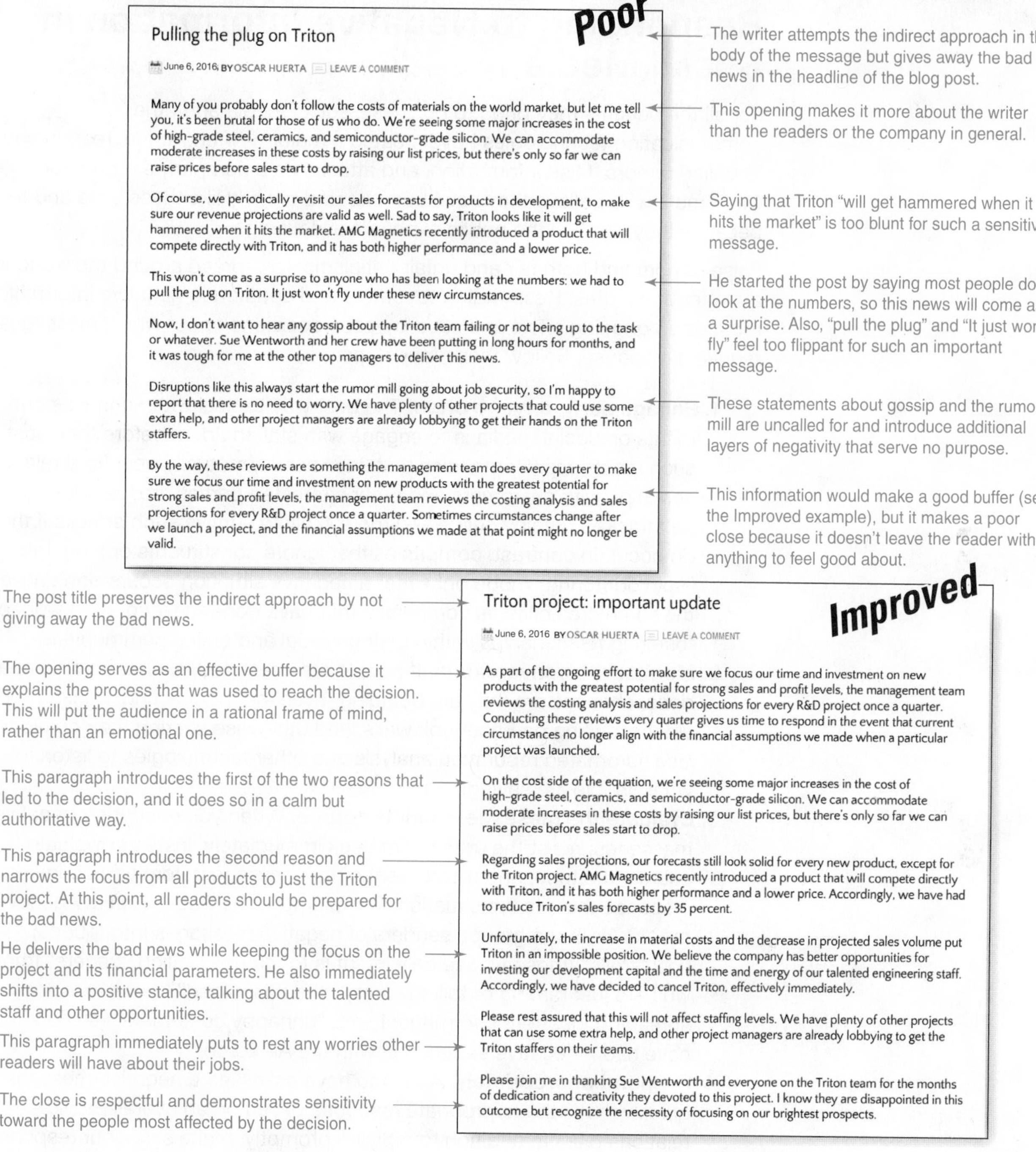

Figure 8.8 Internal Message Providing Bad News About Company Operations
The cancellation of a major development project before completion can be a traumatic event for a company's employees. People who worked on the project are likely to feel that all their time and energy was wasted and worry that their jobs are in jeopardy. Employees who didn't work on the project might worry about the company's financial health and the stability of their own jobs. Such messages are therefore prime candidates for the indirect approach. Note how much more effectively the revised version manages the reader's emotions from beginning to end.

Responding to Negative Information in Social Media

For all the benefits they bring to business, social media and other communication technologies have created a major new challenge: responding to online rumors, false information, and attacks on a company's reputation. Customers who believe they have been treated unfairly like these sites and tools because they can use the public exposure as leverage.

False rumors and both fair and unfair criticisms can spread around the world in a matter of minutes. Responding to rumors and countering negative information requires an ongoing effort and case-by-case decisions about which messages require a response. Follow these four steps:

1. **Engage early, engage often.** The best way to deal with negative comments on social media is to engage with stakeholders before they post such messages. Companies that have active, mutually beneficial relationships with customers and other interested parties are less likely to be attacked unfairly online and more likely to survive such attacks if they do occur. In contrast, companies that ignore constituents or jump into "spin doctoring" mode only after a negative situation occurs don't have the same credibility as companies that have done the long, hard work of fostering relationships within their physical and online communities.
2. **Monitor the conversation.** If people are interested in what your company does, chances are they are blogging, tweeting, podcasting, posting videos, writing on Facebook walls, and otherwise sharing their opinions. Use automated reputation analysis and other technologies to listen to what people are saying.
3. **Evaluate the message—and its source.** When you encounter negative messages, resist the urge to fire back immediately. Instead, evaluate the source, the tone, and the content of the message before you choose a response that fits the situation. For example, the Public Affairs Agency of the US Air Force groups senders of negative messages into four categories: "trolls" (those whose only intent is to stir up conflict), "ragers" (those who are just ranting or telling jokes), "the misguided" (those who are spreading incorrect information), and "unhappy customers" (those who have had a negative experience with the Air Force).
4. **Respond appropriately.** After you have assessed a negative message, quickly make the appropriate response based on an overall public relations plan. In addition to replying promptly, make sure your response won't make the situation even worse. For example, taking legal action against critics, even if technically justified, can rally people to their defense and create a public relations nightmare. In some instances, the best response can be to contact a critic privately (through direct messaging on Twitter, for example) to attempt a resolution away from the public forum.

Whatever you do, keep in mind that positive reputations are an important asset that need to be diligently guarded and defended. Everybody has a voice now, and some of those voices don't care to play by the rules of ethical communication.

Chapter Summary

Using the Three-Step Writing Process for Negative Messages

Because the way you say "no" can be even more damaging than the fact that you're saying it, planning negative messages is crucial. Make sure your purpose is specific and use an appropriate combination of medium and channel to fit the message. Collect all the facts necessary to support your negative decision, adapt your tone to the situation, and choose the direct or indirect approach. Use positive words to construct diplomatic sentences, and pay close attention to quality.

Using the Direct Approach for Negative Messages

The direct approach puts the bad news up front, follows with the reasons, and closes with a respectful statement that shares any positive aspects that are relevant. Even though it is direct, however, don't use the direct approach as a license to be rude or overly blunt.

Using the Indirect Approach for Negative Messages

The indirect approach begins with a buffer, explains the reasons, clearly states the negative news, and closes with a respectful statement. If the bad news is not unexpected, the direct approach is usually fine, but if the news is shocking or painful, the indirect approach is better. When using the indirect approach, pay careful attention to avoid obscuring the bad news, trivializing the audience's concerns, or even misleading your audience into thinking you're actually delivering good news. Remember that the purpose of the indirect approach is to cushion the blow, not to avoid delivering it.

Sending Negative Messages on Routine Business Matters

For making negative announcements on routine business matters, the indirect approach is usually preferred, unless the news has minor consequences for the audience. For rejecting suggestions or proposals when you requested the input or it came from someone you know, the indirect approach is the right choice because it allows you to gently reset the other party's expectations.

For refusing routine requests, the direct approach is usually sufficient, except when the matter at hand is significant, you or your company have an established relationship with the person making the request, or you're forced to decline a request that you might have accepted in the past.

When conveying bad news about transactions, you need to modify the customer's expectations, explain how you plan to resolve the situation, and repair whatever damage might have been done to the business relationship. Whether or not you also apologize depends on the magnitude of the situation and whether you previously established specific expectations about the transaction.

When refusing a claim or a request for adjustment, the indirect approach is usually preferred because the other party is emotionally involved and expects you to respond positively. Demonstrate that you understand and have considered the complaint carefully, and then rationally and calmly explain why you are refusing the request.

Sending Negative Employment Messages

The indirect approach is usually the better choice for negative employment messages because the recipient is always emotionally involved and the decisions are usually significant. When refusing requests from other employers for performance-related information about past employees, your message can be brief and direct. Simply provide whatever information your company allows to be shared in these situations. Refusing a recommendation request directly from a former employee feels much more personal for the recipient, however, so the indirect approach is better.

You have some flexibility when responding to requests for recommendations or endorsements on social networks. You can choose to ignore the request if you don't know the person, you can decline the request as a matter of personal policy, you can write a full recommendation if that matches your assessment of the person, or you can write a limited recommendation on just one or a few aspects of the person's capabilities.

Messages rejecting job applicants raise a number of emotional and legal issues and therefore must be approached with great care. Experts vary in their advice about how much information to include. The safest strategy is a brief message that opens with an expression of appreciation for being considered (which functions like a buffer in an indirect message), continues with a statement to the effect that the applicant was not chosen for the position applied for, and closes courteously without providing reasons for the rejection or making promises about future consideration.

Negative performance reviews should take care to document the performance problems, make sure that all employees are being evaluated consistently, be written in a calm and objective voice, and focus on opportunities for improvement. Moreover, they must be written with reference to accurate, current job descriptions that provide the basis for measuring employee performance.

Termination messages are the most challenging employment messages of all. They should clearly present the reasons for the decision, present those reasons in a way that cannot be construed as unfair or discriminatory, follow company policy and any relevant legal guidelines, and avoid personal attacks or insults of any kind.

Asking a manager not directly involved in the situation to review your message can help you avoid troublesome wording or faulty reasoning. Finally, try to deliver the written message in person if possible.

Sending Negative Organizational News

When communicating negative organizational news; 1) match your approach to the situation; 2) consider the unique needs of each group; 3) minimize the element of surprise whenever possible so that affected groups have time to prepare and respond; 4) give yourself as much time as possible to plan and manage a response; 5) look for positive angles but don't exude false optimism; 6) seek expert advice; 7) use multiple channels to reach out to affected audiences; and 8) be open and transparent.

Responding to Negative Information in a Social Media Environment

First, be sure you are engaged with important stakeholders before negative social media postings appear. Second, monitor the conversations taking place about your company and its products. Third, when you see negative messages, evaluate them before responding. Fourth, after evaluating negative messages, take the appropriate response based on an overall public relations plan. Some messages are better ignored, whereas others should be addressed immediately with corrective information.

Test Your Knowledge

1. What are the five general goals in delivering bad news?
2. What questions should you ask yourself when choosing between the direct and indirect approaches?
3. What is the sequence of elements in a negative message organized using the direct approach?
4. What is a buffer, and what is the advantage of using a respectful, ethical buffer?
5. Why is it important to be engaged with stakeholders before trying to use social media during a crisis or other negative scenario?

Apply Your Knowledge

1. Can you express sympathy with someone's negative situation without apologizing for the circumstances? Explain your answer.
2. Is intentionally deemphasizing bad news the same as distorting graphs and charts to deemphasize unfavorable data? Why or why not?
3. If your social media monitoring efforts pick up a tweet that accuses your customer service staff of lying and claims to have evidence to back it up, how would you respond?

Practice Your Skills

1. **Writing Negative Message** Select which approach you would use (direct or indirect) for the following negative messages.
    a. An email message to your boss, informing her that one of your key clients is taking its business to a different accounting firm
    b. An email message to a customer, informing her that one of the books she ordered from your website is temporarily out of stock
    c. A letter to a customer, explaining that the DVD burner he ordered for his new custom computer is on back order and that, as a consequence, the shipping of the entire order will be delayed

2. **Using Buffers** Answer the following questions about buffers.
    a. You have to tell a local restaurant owner that your plans have changed and you are canceling the 90-person banquet scheduled for next month. Do you need to use a buffer? Why or why not?
    b. Write a buffer for a letter declining an invitation to speak at an industry association's annual fund-raising event. Show your appreciation for being asked.
    c. Write a buffer for an email message rejecting an unsolicited proposal from a vendor with whom you have a positive and long-standing business relationship. Make up any details you need.

3. **Refusing Routine Requests** Working alone, revise the following statements to deemphasize the bad news without hiding it or distorting it. (Hint: Minimize the space devoted to the bad news, subordinate it, embed it, or use the passive voice.) Then team up with a classmate and read each other's revisions. Which approach seems to be most effective for each of the revised statements?
   a. The airline can't refund your money. The "Conditions" section on the back of your ticket states that there are no refunds for missed flights. Sometimes the airline makes exceptions, but only when life and death are involved. Of course, your ticket is still valid and can be used on a flight to the same destination.
   b. I'm sorry to tell you, we can't supply the custom decorations you requested. We called every supplier, and none of them can do what you want on such short notice. You can, however, get a standard decorative package on the same theme in time. I found a supplier that stocks these. Of course, it won't have quite the flair you originally requested.
   c. We can't refund your money for the malfunctioning MP3 player. You shouldn't have immersed the unit in water while swimming; the user's manual clearly states the unit is not designed to be used in adverse environments.

Activities

1. **Making Negative Announcements** Read the following document. Analyze the strengths and weaknesses of each sentence, and then revise the document so that it follows this chapter's guidelines.

> Your spring fraternity party sounds like fun. We're glad you've again chosen us as your caterer. Unfortunately, we have changed a few of our policies, and I wanted you to know about these changes in advance so that we won't have any misunderstandings on the day of the party.
>
> We will arrange the delivery of tables and chairs as usual the evening before the party. However, if you want us to set up, there is now a $100 charge for that service. Of course, you might want to get some of the brothers and pledges to do it, which would save you money. We've also added a small charge for cleanup. This is only $3 per person (you can estimate because I know a lot of people come and go later in the evening).
>
> Other than that, all the arrangements will be the same. We'll provide the skirt for the band stage, tablecloths, and of course, the barbecue. Will you have the tubs of ice with soft drinks again? We can do that for you as well, but there will be a fee.
>
> Please let me know if you have any problems with these changes and we'll try to work them out. I know it's going to be a great party.

2. **Refusing Routine Requests** As a customer service supervisor for a mobile phone company, you're in charge of responding to customers' requests for refunds. You've just received an email from a customer who unwittingly ran up a $550 bill for data charges after forgetting to disable his smartphone's WiFi hotspot feature. The customer says it wasn't his fault because he didn't know his roommates were using his phone to get free Internet access. However, you've dealt with this situation before and provided a notice to all customers to be careful about excess data charges resulting from the use of the hotspot capability. Draft a one-or two-sentence buffer for your email reply, sympathizing with the customer's plight but preparing him for the bad news (that company policy specifically prohibits refunds in such cases).

3. **Refusing Routine Requests** Read the following document, analyze the strengths and weaknesses of each sentence, and revise the message so that it follows this chapter's guidelines.

> I am responding to your letter of about six weeks ago asking for an adjustment on your wireless router, model WM39Z. We test all our products before they leave the factory; therefore, it could not have been our fault that your hub didn't work.
>
> If you or someone in your office dropped the unit, it might have caused the damage. Or the damage could have been caused by the shipper if he dropped it. If so, you should file a claim with the shipper. At any rate, it wasn't our fault. The parts are already covered by warranty. However, we will provide labor for the repairs for $50, which is less than our cost, since you are a valued customer.
>
> We will have a booth at the upcoming trade fair there and hope to see you or someone from your office. We have many new models of computing and networking accessories that we're sure you'll want to see. I've enclosed our latest catalog. Hope to see you there.

4. **Making Negative Announcements Involving Ethics** The insurance company where you work is planning to raise all premiums for healthcare coverage. Your boss has asked you to read a draft of her letter to customers, announcing the new, higher rates. The first two paragraphs discuss some exciting medical advances and the expanded coverage offered by your company. Only in the final paragraph do customers learn that they will have to pay more for coverage starting next year. What are the ethical implications of this draft? What changes would you suggest?

5. **Revising Negative Announcements** The following email message about travel budget cutbacks at Black & Decker contains numerous blunders. Using what you've learned in the chapter, read the message carefully and analyze its faults. Then revise the message with a stronger "you" attitude, including a more diplomatic opening and the use of lists to simplify reading. Since many employees will read it while traveling, be sure to make it mobile friendly.

Memo

FROM: M. Juhasz, Travel & Meeting Services

TO: mjuhasz@blackanddecker.com

SUBJECT: Travel Budget Cuts Effective Immediately

Dear Traveling Executives:

We need you to start using some of the budget suggestions we are going to issue as a separate memorandum. These include using videoconference equipment instead of traveling to meetings, staying in cheaper hotels, arranging flights for cheaper times, and flying from less-convenient but also less-expensive suburban airports.

The company needs to cut travel expenses by fifty percent, just as we've cut costs in all departments of Black & Decker. This means you'll no longer be able to stay in fancy hotels and make last-minute, costly changes to your travel plans.

You'll also be expected to avoid hotel WiFi surcharges. Hotels that charge for in-room Wifi often provide free WiFi in their lobbies, so do your work downstairs. And never return a rental car with an empty tank! That causes the rental agency to charge us a premium price for the gas they sell when they fill it up upon your return.

You'll be expected to make these changes in your travel habits immediately.

M. Juhasz

Travel & Meeting Services

6. **Refusing Routine Requests** The following letter rejecting a faucet manufacturer's product presentation contains many errors in judgment. Work with a team to create a more effective message. First, analyze and discuss the letter's flaws. Then rewrite it using the indirect approach.

July 15, 2017

Pamela Wilson,

Operations Manager

Sterling

Manufacturing

133 Industrial Avenue

Gary, IN 46403

Dear Ms. Wilson:

We regret to inform you that your presentation at Home Depot's recent product review sessions in St. Petersburg did not meet our expert panelists' expectations. We require new products that will satisfy our customers' high standards. Yours did not match this goal.

Our primary concern is to continue our commitment to product excellence, customer knowledge, and price competitiveness, which has helped make Home Depot a Fortune 500 company with more than a thousand stores nationwide. The panel found flaws in your design and materials. Also, your cost per unit was too high.

The product review sessions occur annually. You are allowed to try again; just apply as you did this year. Again, I'm sorry things didn't work out for you this time.

Sincerely,

Hilary Buchman, Assistant to the Vice President, Sales

7. **Negative Employment Messages** Read the following document, analyze the strengths and weaknesses of each sentence, and revise the message so that it follows this chapter's guidelines.

I regret to inform you that you were not selected for our summer intern program at Equifax. We had over a thousand resumes and cover letters to go through and simply could not get to them all. We have been asked to notify everyone that we have already selected students for the 25 positions based on those who applied early and were qualified.

We're sure you will be able to find a suitable position for summer work in your field and wish you the best of luck. We deeply regret any inconvenience associated with our reply.

Expand Your Skills

1. **Analyzing Negative News** Locate an example online of a negative-news message from any company. Possible examples include announcements of product recalls, poor financial results, layoffs, and fines or other legal troubles.

   Your task: Analyze the approach the company took; was it the most effective strategy possible? Did the company apologize, would doing so have been appropriate under the circumstances, and does the apology seem sincere? Does the tone of the message match the seriousness of the situation? Does the message end on a positive note, as appropriate? Using whatever medium your instructor requests, write a one-page brief analysis of the message, citing specific elements from the piece and support from the chapter.

2. **Refusing Claims and Requests for Adjustment** Your company markets a line of rugged smartphone cases designed to protect the sensitive devices from drops, spills, and other common accidents. Your guarantee states that you will reimburse customers for the cost of a new phone if the case fails to protect it from any of the following: a drop of no more than 6 feet onto any surface, spills of any beverage or common household chemical, being crushed by any object of up to 100 pounds, or being chewed on by dogs, cats, or other common household pets.

   Jack Simmons, a rancher from Wyoming, emailed your customer support staff, requesting a reimbursement after he dropped his iPhone in his hog barn and a 900-pound boar crushed it in a single bite.

   Your task: Write an email response to the customer, denying his request for a new phone.

3. **Rejecting Suggestions and Proposals** Knowing how much online product reviews can shape consumer behavior, the other cofounder of your company has just circulated an internal email message with the not-so-subtle hint that everyone in your small start-up should pose as happy customers and post glowing reviews of your new product on Amazon and other shopping sites. You're horrified at the idea—not only is this highly unethical, but if—or more likely when—the scheme is exposed, the company's reputation will be severely damaged.

   Your task: You would prefer to address this in a private conversation, but since your partner has already pitched the idea to everyone via email, you have no choice but to respond via email as well. You need to act quickly before anyone acts on the suggestion. Write a response, explaining why this is a bad idea and telling employees not to do it. Keep in mind that you are chastising your business partner in front of all your employees. Make up any names or other details you need.

4. **Making Routine Negative Announcements via Microblogging** Professional musicians do everything they can to keep the show going, particularly for tours that are scheduled months in advance. But illness and other unforeseeable circumstances can force an act to cancel shows, even after all the tickets have been sold.

Your task: Choose one of you favorite musical acts and assume that you are the tour manager who needs to tell 25,000 fans that an upcoming concert must be canceled because of illness. Ticket holders can apply for a refund at the artist's website or keep their tickets for a future concert date, which will be identified and announced as soon as possible. Write two tweets, one announcing the cancellation and one outlining the options for ticket holders. Make up any information you need, and send your tweets to your instructor via mail. (Don't actually tweet them!)

5. **Rejecting Suggestions and Proposals** Walter Joss is one of the best employees in your department. He's a smart, hard worker with a keen mind for business. His upbeat attitude has helped the entire department get through some rough times recently, and on a personal level, his wise counsel helped you grow into a leadership role when you were promoted to marketing manager several years ago.

   You generally welcome Joss's input on the department's operations, and you have implemented several of his ideas to improve the company's marketing efforts. But the proposal he emailed you yesterday was not his best work, to put it mildly. He proposed that the company dump the advertising agency it has used for a decade and replace it with some new agency you've never heard of. The only reasons he offered were that the agency "had become unresponsive" and that a "smaller agency could meet our needs better." He failed to address any of the other criteria that are used to select advertising agencies, such as costs, creative skills, technical abilities, geographic reach, research capabilities, and media experience. This is the first time you've heard any criticism of the agency, and in fact, their work has helped your company increase sales every year.

   Your task: Draft an email message to Joss, rejecting his proposal. (Note that in a real-life setting, you would want to discuss this with Joss in person, rather than through email, but use email for the purposes of this exercise.)

6. **Making Routine Negative Announcements** You've been proud of many things your gardening tool company has accomplished as it grew from just you working in your basement shop to a nationally known company that employs more than 200 people. However, nothing made you prouder than the company's Helping Our Hometown Grow program, in which employees volunteer on company time to help residents in your city start their own vegetable gardens, using tools donated by the company. Nearly 50 employees participated directly, helping some 500 families supplement their grocery budgets with home-grown produce. Virtually everyone in the company contributed; employees who didn't volunteer to help in the gardens pitched in to cover the work responsibilities of the volunteers.

   Sadly, 10 years after you launched the program, you have reached the inescapable conclusion that the company can no longer afford to keep the program going. With consumers around the country still struggling with the aftereffects of a recession, sales have dropped for the past three years—even as lower-cost competitors have stepped up their presence in the market. To save the program, you would have to lay off several employees, but your employees come first.

   Your task: Write an email to the entire company, announcing the cancelation of the program.

7. **Making Negative Announcements** Your company, PolicyPlan Insurance Services, is a 120-employee insurance claims processor based in Milwaukee. PolicyPlan has engaged Midwest Sparkleen for interior and exterior cleaning for the past five years. Midwest Sparkleen did exemplary work for the first four years, but after a change of ownership last year, the level of service has plummeted. Offices are no longer cleaned thoroughly, you've had to call the company at least six times to remind them to take care of spills and other messes they're supposed to address routinely, and they've left toxic cleaning chemicals in a public hallway on several occasions. You have spoken with the owner about your concerns twice in the past three months, but his assurances that service would improve have not resulted in any noticeable improvements. When the evening cleaning crew forgot to lock the lobby door last Thursday—leaving your entire facility vulnerable to theft from midnight until 8 a.m. Friday morning—you decided it was time for a change.

   Your task: Write a letter to Jason Allred, owner of Midwest Sparkleen, 4000 South Howell Avenue, Milwaukee, WI 53207, telling him that PolicyPlan will not be renewing its annual cleaning contract with Midwest Sparkleen when the current contract expires at the end of this month. Cite the examples identified previously, and keep the tone of your letter professional.

8. **Making Negative Announcements via Podcast** Offering an employee concierge seemed like a great idea when you added it as an employee benefit last year. The concierge handles a wide variety of personal chores for employees—everything from dropping off their dry cleaning to ordering event tickets to sending flowers. Employees love the service, and you know the time they save can be devoted to work or family activities. Unfortunately, profits are way down, and concierge use is up—up so far that you'll need to add a second concierge to keep up with the demand. As painful as it will be for everyone, you decide that the company needs to stop offering the service.

   Your task: Script a brief podcast announcing the decision and explaining why it was necessary. Make up any details you need. If your instructor asks you to do so, record your podcast and submit the file.

9. **Refusing Routine Requests via Email** Lee Valley Tools sells high-quality woodworking tools across Canada through its retail stores and around the world through its website and catalogs. Although weekend hobbyists can pick up a mass-produced hand plane (a tool for smoothing wood) for $20 or $30 at the local hardware store, serious woodworkers pay 5 or 10 times that much for one of Lee Valley's precision Veritas planes. For the price, they get top-quality materials, precision manufacturing, and innovative designs that help them do better work in less time.

   Lee Valley sells its own Veritas-brand tools and 5,000 tools made by other manufacturers. One of those companies has just emailed you to ask if Lee Valley would like to carry a new line of midrange hand planes that would cost more than the hardware-store models but less than Lee Valley's own Veritas models. Your job is to filter requests such as this, rejecting those that don't meet Lee Valley's criteria and forwarding those that do to the product selection committee for further analysis. After one quick read of this incoming email message, you realize there is no need to send this idea to the committee. Although these planes are certainly of decent quality, they achieve their lower cost through lower-quality steel that won't hold an edge as long and through thinner irons (the element that holds the cutting edge) that will be more prone to vibrate during use and thus produce a rougher finish. These planes have a market, to be sure, but they're not a good fit for Lee Valley's top-of-the-line product portfolio. Moreover, the planes don't offer any innovations in terms of ease of use or any other product attribute.

Your task: Reply to this email message, explaining that the planes appear to be decent tools, but they don't fit Lee Valley's strategy of offering only the best and most innovative tools. Support your decision with the three criteria described previously. Choose the direct or indirect approach carefully, taking into consideration your company's relationship with this other company.

10. **Sending Negative Employment Messages via Memo** Elaine Bridgewater, the former professional golfer you hired to oversee your golf equipment company's relationship with retailers, knows the business inside and out. As a former touring pro, she has unmatched credibility. She also has seemingly boundless energy, solid technical knowledge, and an engaging personal style. Unfortunately, she hasn't been quite as attentive as she needs to be when it comes to communicating with retailers. You've been getting complaints about voicemail messages going unanswered for days, confusing emails that require two or three rounds of clarification, and reports that are haphazardly thrown together. As valuable as Bridgewater's other skills are, she's going to cost the company sales if this goes on much longer. The retail channel is vital to your company's survival, and she's the employee most involved in the channel.

    Your task: Draft a brief (one page maximum, in memo format) informal performance appraisal and improvement plan for Bridgewater. Be sure to compliment her on the areas in which she excels, but don't shy away from highlighting the areas in which she needs to improve, too: punctual response to customer messages; clear writing; and careful revision, production, and proofreading. Use what you've learned in this course so far to supply any additional advice about the importance of these skills.

11. **Refusing Requests for Recommendations via Email** You're delighted to get a message from an old friend and colleague, Heather Lang. You're delighted right up to the moment you read her request that you write a recommendation about her web design and programming skills for her LinkedIn profile. You would do just about anything for Lang—anything except recommend her web design skills. She is a master programmer whose technical wizardry saved many client projects, but when it comes to artistic design, Lang simply doesn't have it. From gaudy color schemes to unreadable type treatment to confusing layouts, her design sense is as weak as her technical acumen is strong.

    Your task: First, write a brief email to Lang, explaining that you would be most comfortable highlighting her technical skills because that is where you believe her true strengths lie. Second, write a two-sentence recommendation that she could include in her LinkedIn profile, recommending Lang's technical skills. Make up or research any details you need.

12. **Refusing Requests for Recommendations** Daniel Sturgis, who quit last year just as you were planning to fire him for consistently failing to meet agreed-upon performance targets, has just emailed you from his new job, asking for a recommendation. He says his new job is awful and he regrets leaving your company. He knows you don't have any openings, but he would be grateful for a recommendation.

    Your task: Write an email message to Sturgis, explaining that you will not be able to write him a recommendation. Make up any details you need.

13. **Delivering Negative Organizational Messages via Blog** XtremityPlus is known for its outlandish extreme-sports products, and the Looney Launch is no exception. Fulfilling the dream of every childhood daredevil, the Looney Launch is an aluminum and fiberglass contraption that quickly unfolds to create the ultimate bicycle jump. The product has been selling as fast as you can make it, even though it comes plastered with warning labels proclaiming that its use is inherently dangerous.

    As XtremityPlus's CEO, you were nervous about introducing this product, and your fears were just confirmed: you've been notified of the first lawsuit by a parent whose child broke several bones after crash-landing off a Looney Launch.

    Your task: Write a post for your internal blog, explaining that the Looney Launch is being removed from the market immediately. Tell your employees to expect some negative reactions from enthusiastic customers and retailers, but explain that the company can't afford the risk of additional lawsuits and that even for XtremityPlus, the Looney Launch pushes the envelope a bit too far. The product is simply too dangerous to sell in good conscience.

14. **Responding to Rumors via Microblogging** Sheila Elliot, a well-known actress, appeared on a national talk show last night and claimed your company's Smoothstone cookware was responsible for her toddler's learning disability. Elliot said the nonstick surfaces of Smoothstone pots and pans contain a dangerous chemical that affected her child's cognitive development. There's just one problem with her story—well, three problems, actually: your company's cookware line is called Moonstone, not Smoothstone; Moonstone does not contain and never has contained the chemical Elliot mentioned; and the product she is really thinking of was called Smoothfire, which was made by another company and pulled off the market five years ago.

    Thousands of worried parents aren't waiting for the fact checkers, however. They took to the blogosphere and Twittersphere with a vengeance overnight, warning people to throw away anything made by your company, Tatum Housewares. Several television stations have already picked up the Twitter chatter and repeated the rumor. Retailers have begun calling your sales staff to cancel orders.

    Your task: Write a three-message sequence to be posted on your company's Twitter account, correcting the rumor and conveying the three points outlined above. Each message will include a URL linking to your company's website, so restrict each message to 120 characters, including spaces.

15. **Responding to Rumors and Public Criticism** The consumer reviews on Yelp can be a promotional boon to any local business—provided the reviews are positive, of course. Negative reviews, fair or not, can affect a company's reputation and drive away potential customers. Fortunately for business owners, sites like Yelp give them the means to respond to reviews, whether they want to apologize for poor service, offer some form of compensation, or correct misinformation in a review.

    Your task: Search Yelp for a negative review (one or two stars) on any business in any city. Find a review that has some substance to it, not just an angry rant. Now imagine that you are the owner of that business, and write a reply that could be posted via the "Add Owner Comment" feature. Use information you can find on Yelp about the company, and fill in any details by using your imagination. Remember that your comment will be visible to everyone who visits Yelp. Be sure you don't actually post the response; submit it to your instructor as required. Be sure you don't actually post the response; submit it to your instructor as required.

Responding to Rumors and Public Criticism. The [illegible]

[illegible]

CHAPTER

9

Writing Persuasive Messages

After studying this chapter, you will be able to:

- Apply the three-step writing process to persuasive messages.
- Describe an effective strategy for developing persuasive business messages.
- Identify the three most-common categories of persuasive business messages.
- Describe an effective strategy for developing marketing and sales messages, explain how to modify this approach for social media, and identify steps you can take to avoid ethical lapses in marketing and sales messages.

Using the Three-Step Writing Process for Persuasive Messages

Persuasion:
The attempt to change an audience's attitudes, beliefs, or actions.

For both internal messages to colleagues, employees, and managers and for external messages to customers, investors, and other outsiders, you'll use many of the same techniques of **persuasion**—the attempt to change an audience's attitudes, beliefs, or actions. Because persuasive messages ask audiences to give something of value (money in exchange for a product, for example) or take substantial action (such as changing a corporate policy), they are more challenging to write than routine messages. Successful professionals understand that persuasion is not about trickery or getting people to act against their own best interests; it's about letting audiences know they have choices and presenting your offering in the best possible light.

Planning Persuasive Messages

In today's information-saturated business environment, having a great idea or a great product is no longer enough. Every day, untold numbers of good ideas go unnoticed and good products go unsold simply because the messages meant to promote them aren't compelling enough to be heard above the competitive noise. Creating successful persuasive messages in these challenging situations demands careful attention to all four tasks in the planning step, starting with an insightful analysis of your purpose and your audience.

Analyzing the Situation

Purpose:
What you want to achieve.

In defining your **purpose**, make sure you're clear about what you really hope to achieve. Suppose you want to persuade company executives to support a particular research project. But what does "support" mean? Do you want them to pat you on the back and wish you well? Or do you want them to give you a staff of five researchers and a $1 million annual budget?

Assumptions:
Things that you take for granted to be true.

The best persuasive messages are closely connected to your audience's desires and interests (see Figure 9.1). Consider these important questions: Who is my audience? What are my **assumptions** about my audience members' needs? What do I want them to do? How might they resist? Are there alternative positions I need to examine? What does the decision-maker consider to be the most important issue? How might the organization's culture influence my strategy?

Demographics:
The quantifiable characteristics of people, such as age, gender, and occupation.

Psychographics:
The psychological characteristics of a person or group of people.

To understand and categorize audience needs, you can refer to specific information, such as **demographics** (the age, gender, occupation, income, education, and other quantifiable characteristics of the people you're trying to persuade) and **psychographics** (personality, attitudes, lifestyle, and other psychological characteristics). When analyzing your audiences, take into account their cultural expectations and practices. You don't want to undermine your persuasive message by using an inappropriate appeal or by organizing your message in a way that seems unfamiliar or uncomfortable to your readers.

Motivation:
The combination of forces that drive people to satisfy their needs.

If you aim to change someone's attitudes, beliefs, or actions, it is vital to understand his or her **motivation**—the combination of forces that drive people to satisfy their needs. Table 9.1 lists some of the needs that psychologists have identified or suggested as being important in influencing human motivation. Obviously, the more closely a persuasive message aligns with a recipient's existing motivation, the more effective the message is likely to be. For example, if you try to persuade consumers to purchase a product on the basis of its fashion appeal, that message will connect with consumers who are motivated by a desire to be in fashion, but it probably won't connect with consumers driven more by functional or financial concerns.

Table 9.1 Human Needs that Influence Motivation

Need	Implications for Communication
Basic physiological requirements: The needs for food, water, sleep, oxygen, and other essentials	Everyone has these needs, but the degree of attention an individual gives to them often depends on whether the needs are being met; for instance, an advertisement for sleeping pills will have greater appeal to someone suffering from insomnia than to someone who has no problem sleeping.
Safety and security: The needs for protection from bodily harm, for the safety of loved ones, and for financial security, protection of personal identity, career security, and other assurances	These needs influence both consumer and business decisions in a wide variety of ways; for instance, advertisements for life insurance often encourage parents to think about the financial security of their children and other loved ones.
Affiliation and belonging: The needs for companionship, acceptance, love, popularity, and approval	The need to feel loved, accepted, or popular drives a great deal of human behavior, from the desire to be attractive to potential mates to wearing the clothing style that a particular social group is likely to approve.
Power and control: The need to feel in control of situations or to exert authority over others	You can see many examples appealing to this need in advertisements: *Take control of your life, your finances, your future, your career,* and so on. Many people who lack power want to know how to get it, and people who have power often want others to know they have it.
Achievement: The need to feel a sense of accomplishment—or to be admired by others for accomplishments	This need can involve both *knowing* (when people experience a feeling of accomplishment) and *showing* (when people are able to show others that they've achieved success); advertising for luxury consumer products frequently appeals to this need.
Adventure and distraction: The need for excitement or relief from daily routine	People vary widely in their need for adventure; some crave excitement—even danger— whereas others value calmness and predictability. Some needs for adventure and distraction are met *virtually*, such as through horror movies, thriller novels, etc.
Knowledge, exploration, and understanding: The need to keep learning	For some people, learning is a means to an end, a way to fulfill some other need. For others, acquiring new knowledge is the goal in itself.
Aesthetic appreciation: The desire to experience beauty, order, symmetry, etc.	Although this need may seem "noncommercial" at first glance, advertisers appeal to it frequently, from the pleasing shape of a package to the quality of the gemstones in a piece of jewelry.
Self-actualization: The need to "be all that one can be," to reach one's full potential as a human being	Psychologists Kurt Goldstein and Abraham Maslow popularized self-actualization as the desire to make the most of one's potential, and Maslow identified it as one of the higher-level needs in his classic hierarchy; even if people met most or all of their other needs, they would still feel the need to self-actualize. An often-quoted example of appealing to this need is the US Army's one-time advertising slogan: "Be all that you can be."
Helping others: The need to believe that one is making a difference in the lives of other people	This need is the central motivation in fundraising messages and other appeals for charity.

Gathering Information

Once your situation analysis is complete, you need to gather the information necessary to create a compelling persuasive message. You'll learn more about the types of information to include in persuasive business messages and marketing and sales messages later in the chapter. Chapter 10 presents advice on how to find the information you need.

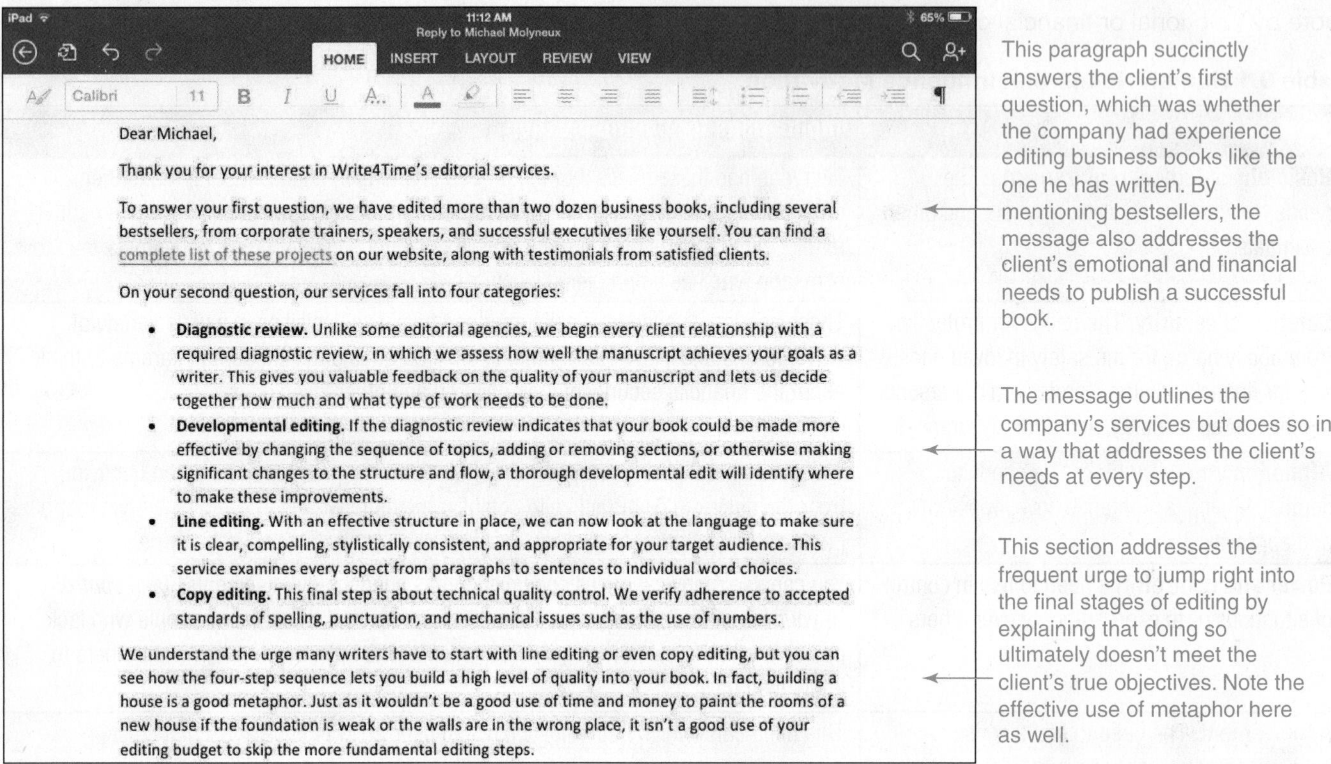

Dear Michael,

Thank you for your interest in Write4Time's editorial services.

To answer your first question, we have edited more than two dozen business books, including several bestsellers, from corporate trainers, speakers, and successful executives like yourself. You can find a complete list of these projects on our website, along with testimonials from satisfied clients.

On your second question, our services fall into four categories:

- **Diagnostic review.** Unlike some editorial agencies, we begin every client relationship with a required diagnostic review, in which we assess how well the manuscript achieves your goals as a writer. This gives you valuable feedback on the quality of your manuscript and lets us decide together how much and what type of work needs to be done.
- **Developmental editing.** If the diagnostic review indicates that your book could be made more effective by changing the sequence of topics, adding or removing sections, or otherwise making significant changes to the structure and flow, a thorough developmental edit will identify where to make these improvements.
- **Line editing.** With an effective structure in place, we can now look at the language to make sure it is clear, compelling, stylistically consistent, and appropriate for your target audience. This service examines every aspect from paragraphs to sentences to individual word choices.
- **Copy editing.** This final step is about technical quality control. We verify adherence to accepted standards of spelling, punctuation, and mechanical issues such as the use of numbers.

We understand the urge many writers have to start with line editing or even copy editing, but you can see how the four-step sequence lets you build a high level of quality into your book. In fact, building a house is a good metaphor. Just as it wouldn't be a good use of time and money to paint the rooms of a new house if the foundation is weak or the walls are in the wrong place, it isn't a good use of your editing budget to skip the more fundamental editing steps.

This paragraph succinctly answers the client's first question, which was whether the company had experience editing business books like the one he has written. By mentioning bestsellers, the message also addresses the client's emotional and financial needs to publish a successful book.

The message outlines the company's services but does so in a way that addresses the client's needs at every step.

This section addresses the frequent urge to jump right into the final stages of editing by explaining that doing so ultimately doesn't meet the client's true objectives. Note the effective use of metaphor here as well.

Figure 9.1 Appealing to Audience Needs

This draft of a response to an inquiry about an editorial company's services addresses the writer's concerns about the time, cost, and effectiveness of the company's services.

Source: Microsoft Office 2013.

Selecting the Right Combination of Medium and Channel

Media and channel choices are always important, of course, but these decisions are particularly sensitive with persuasive messages because such messages are often unexpected or even unwelcome. For instance, some people don't mind promotional email messages for products they're interested in; others resent every piece of commercial email they receive. Persuasive messages can be found in virtually every communication medium, from instant messages and podcasts to radio advertisements and skywriting. In fact, advertising agencies employ media specialists whose only job is to analyze the media options available and select the most cost-effective combination for each client and each advertising campaign.

Organizing Your Information

The nature of persuasion is to convince people to change their attitudes, beliefs, or actions, to produce a particular outcome or solution. Therefore, most persuasive messages use the indirect approach. That means you'll want to explain your reasons and build interest before asking for a decision or for action—or perhaps even before revealing your purpose. In some instances, such as when you have a close relationship with your audience and the message is welcome or at least neutral, the direct approach can be effective.

For persuasive business messages, the choice between the direct and indirect approaches is also influenced by the extent of your authority, expertise, or power in an organization. For example, if you are a highly regarded technical expert with years of experience, you might use the direct approach in a message to top executives. In contrast, if you aren't well known and therefore need to rely more on the strength of your message than the power of your reputation, the indirect approach will probably be more successful.

Writing Persuasive Messages

Encourage a positive response to your persuasive messages by using positive and polite language, understanding and respecting cultural differences, being sensitive to organizational cultures, and taking steps to establish your credibility.

Positive language usually happens naturally when you're promoting an idea or product you believe in. Just take care not to inadvertently insult your readers by implying that they've made poor choices in the past and that you're here to save them from their misguided ways.

Be sure to understand cultural expectations as well. For example, a message that seems forthright and direct in a low-context culture might seem brash and intrusive in a high-context culture. (See Chapter 1 for a review of high- and low-context cultures.)

Just as social culture affects the success of a persuasive message, so too does the culture within an organization. For instance, some organizations handle disagreement and conflict in an indirect, behind-the-scenes way, whereas others accept and even encourage open discussion and sharing of differing viewpoints.

Finally, if you are trying to persuade a skeptical or hostile audience, you must convince them you know what you're talking about and that you're not trying to mislead them. Use these techniques:

- Use simple language to avoid suspicions of fantastic claims and emotional manipulation.
- Provide objective evidence for the claims and promises you make.
- Identify your sources, especially if your audience already respects those sources.
- Establish common ground by emphasizing beliefs, attitudes, and background experiences you have in common with the audience.
- Be objective and present fair and logical arguments.
- Display your willingness to keep your audience's best interests at heart.
- Persuade with logic, evidence, and compelling narratives, rather than trying to coerce with high-pressure, "hard-sell" tactics.
- Whenever possible, try to build your credibility before you present a major proposal or ask for a major decision. That way, audiences don't have to evaluate both you and your message at the same time.

Completing Persuasive Messages

The pros know from experience that details can make or break a persuasive message, so they're careful not to skimp on this part of the writing process. For instance, advertisers may have a dozen or more people review a message before it's released to the public.

When you evaluate your content, try to judge your argument objectively and try not to overestimate your credibility. When revising for clarity and conciseness, carefully match the purpose and organization to audience needs. If possible, ask an experienced colleague who knows your audience well to review your draft. Your design elements must complement, not detract from, your argument. In addition, meticulous proofreading will identify any mechanical or spelling errors that would weaken your persuasive potential. Finally, make sure your distribution methods fit your audience's expectations as well as your purpose.

Developing Persuasive Business Messages

Your success as a businessperson is closely tied to your ability to encourage others to accept new ideas, change old habits, or act on your recommendations. Unless your career takes you into marketing and sales, most of your persuasive messages will be business messages designed to elicit a preferred response in a non-sales situation.

Even if you have the power to force others to do what you want them to do, persuading them is more effective. People who are forced into accepting a decision or plan are less motivated to support it and more likely to react negatively than if they're persuaded. Within the context of the three-step process, effective persuasion involves four essential strategies: framing your arguments, balancing emotional and logical appeals, reinforcing your position, and anticipating objections. (Note that the concepts in this section also apply to marketing and sales messages, which are covered later in the chapter.)

The AIDA Model

Many persuasive messages follow some variation of the indirect approach. One of the most commonly used variations is called the AIDA model, which organizes your message into four phases (see Figure 9.2):

- **Attention.** Your first objective is to encourage your audience to want to hear about your problem, idea, or new product—whatever your main idea is. Be sure to find some common ground on which to build your case.
- **Interest.** Provide additional details that prompt audience members to imagine how the solution might benefit them.
- **Desire.** Help audience members embrace your idea by explaining how the change will benefit them and answering potential objections.
- **Action.** Suggest the specific action you want your audience to take. Include a deadline, when applicable.

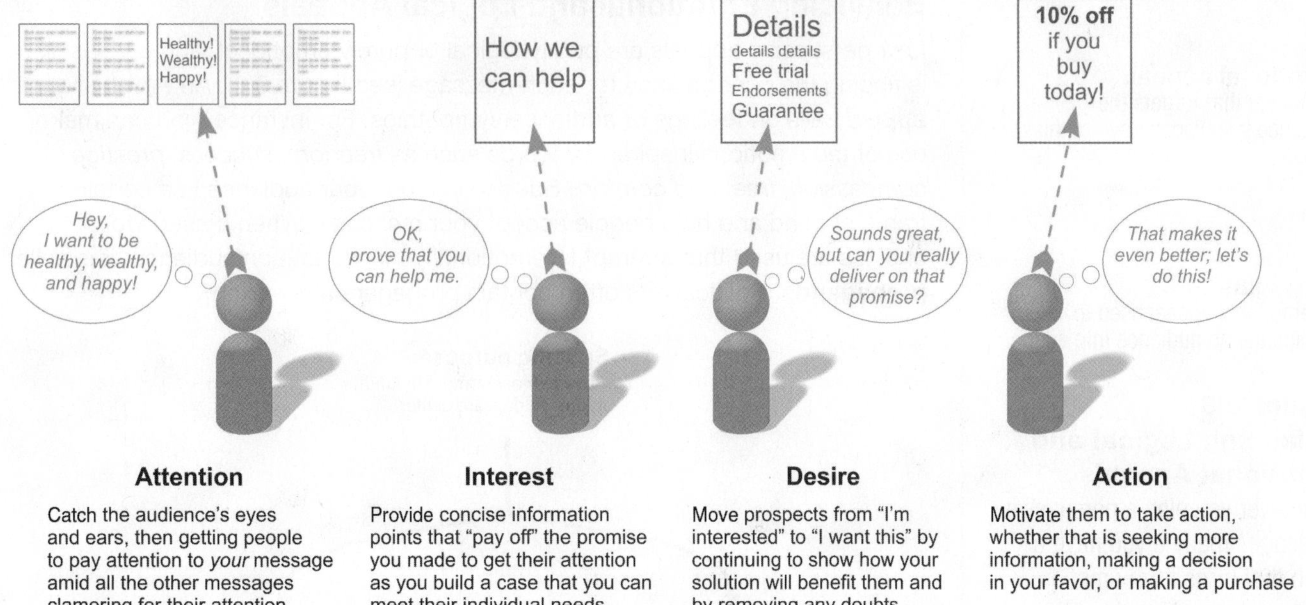

Figure 9.2
The AIDA Model for Persuasive Messages
With the AIDA model, you craft one or more messages to move recipients through four stages of attention, interest, desire, and action. The model works well for both persuasive business messages (such as persuading your manager to fund a new project) and marketing and sales messages.

The AIDA model, which saves your main idea for the action phase, is tailor-made for the indirect approach. It can also work with the direct approach, in which case you use your main idea as an attention-getter, build interest with your argument, create desire with your evidence, and emphasize your main idea in the action phase with the specific action you want your audience to take.

When your AIDA message uses the indirect approach and is delivered by memo or email, keep in mind that your subject line usually catches your reader's eye first. Your challenge is to make it interesting and relevant enough to capture reader attention without revealing your main idea. If you put your request in the subject line, you're likely to get a quick "no" before you've had a chance to present your arguments:

Instead of this:	Write this:
Request for development budget to add automated IM response system	Reducing the cost of customer support inquiries

With either the direct or indirect approach, AIDA and similar models do have limitations. First, AIDA is a unidirectional method that essentially talks *at* audiences, not *with* them. Second, AIDA is built around a single event, such as asking an audience for a decision, rather than on building a mutually beneficial, long-term relationship. AIDA is still a valuable tool for the right purposes, but as you'll read later in the chapter, a conversational approach is more compatible with today's social media.

Emotional appeal:
An appeal that targets the audience's feelings or sympathies.

Propaganda:
An emotional appeal used to manipulate an audience into action.

Balancing Emotional and Logical Appeals

Few persuasive appeals are purely logical or purely emotional, and a key skill is finding the right balance for each message (see Figure 9.3). An **emotional appeal** calls on feelings or audience sympathies. For instance, you can make use of the emotions inspired by words such as *freedom*, *success*, *prestige*, *compassion*, *free*, and *comfort*. Such words put your audience in a certain frame of mind and help people accept your message. When biased word choices are used that attempt to emotionally manipulate an audience, it is called **propaganda**. Political ads often contain propaganda, for example.

Specific purpose:
To persuade management to fund an on-site daycare center

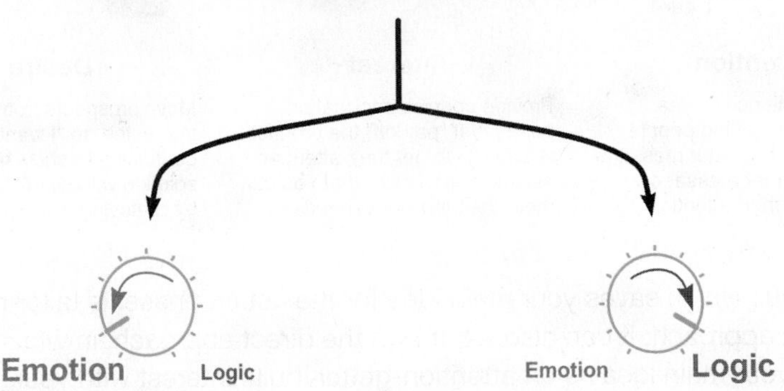

Proposal to improve employee satisfaction and work/life balance

Being separated during the day is stressful for both parents and children.

Many parents are now working more hours and second jobs to make ends meet, so the situation is getting worse.

The extra travel time every morning and evening to put children in daycare adds to the stress and cost of coming to work.

When parents need to leave work to pick up sick children from daycare or stay home with them, this often creates an unfair burden on other employees to pick up the slack.

Knowing that the company cares about them and their children would boost employee morale.

Therefore, the company should provide an on-site daycare facility with a separate infirmary where sick children could stay during the day.

Proposal to boost productivity and reduce absenteeism

Analysis of employee time records shows that employees with children under the age of 10 take unscheduled days off three times more often than employees without young children.

Daycare issues are cited as the number one reason for these unscheduled days off.

In the 98 exit interviews conducted last year, 24 departing employees mentioned the need to balance family and work commitments as the primary reason for leaving.

In the last six months, HR has logged 14 complaints from employees who say they have to take on extra work when colleagues leave the office to pick up sick children from daycare.

Research shows that on-site daycare can improve productivity by as much as 20 percent—among parents and nonparents alike.

Therefore, the company should provide an on-site daycare facility with a separate infirmary where sick children could stay during the day.

Figure 9.3
Balancing Logical and Emotional Appeals
Whenever you plan a persuasive message, imagine you have a knob that turns from emotion at one extreme to logic at the other, letting you adjust the relative proportions of each type of appeal. Compare these two outlines for a proposal that asks management to fund an on-site daycare center. The version on the left relies heavily on emotional appeals, whereas the version on the right uses logical appeals (inductive reasoning, specifically). Through your choice of words, images, and supporting details, you can adjust the emotional-logical ratio in every message.

Many marketing and sales messages rely heavily on emotional appeals, but most persuasive business messages rely more on logic. And even if your audience reaches a conclusion based on emotions, they'll look to you to provide logical support as well. A **logical appeal** uses one of three types of reasoning:

Logical appeal:
An appeal that is based on inductive reasoning, deductive reasoning, and/or analogy.

- **Analogy.** With **analogy**, you reason from specific evidence to specific evidence, in effect "borrowing" from something familiar to explain something unfamiliar. For instance, to convince management to add chat room capability to the company's groupware system, you could explain that it is like a neighborhood community center, only online.
- **Induction.** With **inductive reasoning**, you work from specific evidence to a general conclusion. To convince your boss to change a certain production process, you could point out that every company that has adopted it has increased profits.
- **Deduction.** With **deductive reasoning**, you work from a generalization to a specific conclusion. To persuade your boss to hire additional customer support staff, you might point to industry surveys that show how crucial customer satisfaction is to corporate profits.

Analogy:
Reasoning from specific evidence to specific evidence.

Inductive reasoning:
Working from specific evidence to a general conclusion.

Deductive reasoning:
Working from a generalization to a specific conclusion.

Every method of reasoning is vulnerable to misuse. To avoid faulty logic, follow these guidelines:

- **Avoid hasty generalizations.** Make sure you have plenty of evidence before drawing conclusions.
- **Avoid circular reasoning.** Circular reasoning is a logical fallacy in which you try to support your claim by restating it in different words. The statement "We know temporary workers cannot handle this task because temps are unqualified for it" doesn't prove anything because the claim and the supporting evidence are essentially identical.
- **Avoid attacking an opponent.** Attack the argument your opponent is making, not your opponent's character.
- **Avoid oversimplifying a complex issue.** For example, don't reduce a complex situation to a simple "either/or" statement if the situation isn't that simple or clear-cut.
- **Avoid mistaken assumptions of cause and effect.** If you can't isolate the impact of a specific factor, you can't assume that it's the cause of whatever effect you're discussing. You lowered prices, and sales went up. Were lower prices the cause? Maybe, but the sales increase might have been caused by a better advertising campaign, changes in the weather, or some other factor.
- **Avoid faulty analogies.** Be sure that the two objects or situations being compared are similar enough for the analogy to hold. For instance, explaining that an Internet firewall is like a prison wall is a poor analogy, because a firewall keeps things out, whereas a prison wall keeps things in.

Reinforcing Your Position

After you've worked out the basic elements of your argument, step back and look for ways to strengthen your position. Are all your claims supported by believable evidence? Would a quotation from a recognized expert help make your case?

Next, examine your language. Can you find more powerful words to convey your message? For example, if your company is in serious financial trouble, talking about fighting for survival is a more powerful emotional appeal than talking about ensuring continued operations. As with any other powerful tool, though, use vivid language and abstractions carefully and honestly.

In addition to examining individual word choices, consider using metaphors and other figures of speech. If you want to describe a quality-control system as being designed to detect every possible product flaw, you might call it a "spider web" to imply that it catches everything that comes its way. Similarly, anecdotes (brief stories) can help your audience grasp the meaning and importance of your arguments. Instead of just listing the number of times the old laptop computers in your department have failed, you could describe how you lost a sale when your computer broke down during a critical sales presentation.

Beyond specific words and phrases, look for other factors that can reinforce your position. When you're asking for something, your audience members will find it easier to grant your request if they stand to benefit from it as well.

Anticipating Objections

Even compelling ideas and exciting projects can encounter objections, if only as a consequence of people's natural tendency to resist change. Anticipate likely objections and address them before your audience can bring them up. By doing so, you can remove these potentially negative elements from the conversation and keep the focus on positive communication.

Note that you don't need to explicitly mention a particular concern. For instance, if your proposal to switch to lower-cost materials is likely to raise concerns about quality, you can emphasize that the new materials are just as good as existing materials. You'll not only get this issue out of the way sooner but also demonstrate a broad appreciation of the issue and imply confidence in your message.

If you expect a hostile audience that is biased against your plan, be sure to present all sides of the situation. As you cover each option, explain the pros and cons. You'll gain additional credibility if you mention these options before presenting your recommendation or decision. If you can, involve your audience in the design of the solution; people are more likely to support ideas they help create.

Avoiding Common Mistakes in Persuasive Communication

When you believe in a concept or project you are promoting, it's easy to get caught up in your own confidence and enthusiasm and thereby fail to see things from the audience's perspective. When putting together persuasive arguments, avoid these common mistakes (see Figure 9.4):

- **Using a hard sell.** Don't push. No one likes being pressured into making a decision, and communicators who take this approach can come across as being more concerned with meeting their own goals than with satisfying the needs of their audiences. In contrast, a "soft sell" is more like a comfortable conversation that uses calm, rational persuasion.
- **Resisting compromise.** Successful persuasion is often a process of give-and-take, particularly in the case of persuasive business messages, where you don't always get everything you asked for in terms of budgets, investments, and other commitments.

- **Relying solely on great arguments.** Great arguments are important, but connecting with your audience on the right emotional level and communicating through vivid language are just as vital. Sometimes a well-crafted story can be even more compelling than dry logic.
- **Assuming that persuasion is a one-shot effort.** Persuasion is often a process, not a one-time event. In many cases, you need to move your audience members along one small step at a time rather than try to convince them to say "yes" in one huge step.

Figure 9.4 Persuasive Argumentation

Imagine you're the marketing manager in a company that decided to speed up its new product launches but did too much too fast and wound up creating chaos. You decide enough is enough and write a memo to the company president advocating that the new program be shut down until the company can regroup—a suggestion you know will meet with resistance. Notice how the poor version doesn't quite use the direct approach but comes out swinging, so to speak, and is overly emotional throughout. The improved version builds to its recommendation indirectly, using the same information but in a calm, logical way. Because it sticks to the facts, it is also shorter.

Poor

It's time to call the Fast Track program what it truly is—a disaster. Everyone was excited last year when we announced the plan to speed up our development efforts and introduce at least one new product every month. We envisioned rapidly expanding market share and strong revenue growth in all our product lines. What we got instead is a nightmare that is getting worse with every launch.

As a company, we clearly underestimated the resources it would take to market, sell, and support so many new products. We can't hire and train fast enough, and our teams in every department are overwhelmed. Forced to jump from one new product to the next, with no time to focus, the sales and technical specialists can't develop the expertise needed to help buyers before the sale or support them after the sale. As a result, too many customers either buy the wrong product or buy the right product but then can't get knowledgeable help when they need it. We're losing credibility in the market, we're starting to lose sales, and it won't be long before we start losing employees who are fed up with the insanity.

To make matters even worse, some of the recent products were clearly rushed to market before they were ready, with hardware quality problems and buggy software. Returns and warranty costs are skyrocketing.

New products are the lifeblood of the company, to be sure, but there is no point in introducing products that only create enormous support headaches and cost more to support than they generate in profits. We need to put the Fast Track initiative on hold immediately so the entire company can regroup. The R&D lab can devote its time to fixing problems in the recent products, and the rest of us can catch our collective breath and figure out how to meet our sales and support goals with the current product portfolio and our current staffing levels.

The company has clearly staked a lot on this program, so opening by calling it a disaster will only put the reader on the defensive.

Word choices such as *nightmare* and *insanity* give the message an emotional, almost hysterical, tone that detracts from the serious message.

The writer mingles an observation that may be subjective (declining credibility), a hard data point (declining sales), and a prediction (possibility of employee defections).

The claim that recent products were "clearly rushed to market" is unnecessarily inflammatory (because it blames another department) and distracts the reader from the more immediate problems of poor quality.

The first sentence of the last paragraph is insulting to anyone with basic business sense—particularly the president of a company.

Improved

Everyone was excited last year when we launched the Fast Track program to speed up our development efforts and introduce at least one new product every month. We envisioned rapidly expanding market share and strong revenue growth in all our product lines.

While the R&D lab has met its goal of monthly releases, as a company, we clearly underestimated the resources it would take to market, sell, and support so many new products. We can't hire and train fast enough, and our teams in every department are overwhelmed. The sales and technical specialists haven't had time to develop the expertise needed to help buyers before the sale or support them after the sale. As a result, too many customers either buy the wrong product or buy the right product but then can't get knowledgeable help when they need it.

We're losing credibility in the market, and we're starting to lose sales. If the situation continues, I fear we will being losing employees, too.

In addition, some of the recent products are generating multiple reports of hardware quality problems and buggy software. Returns and warranty costs are climbing at an unprecedented rate.

With costs rising faster than revenues and our people getting overwhelmed, I believe it is time to put the Fast Track initiative on hold until the company can regroup. The hiatus would give R&D time to address the quality problems and give the marketing, sales, and tech support team the chance to re-assess our goals with the current product portfolio and our current staffing levels.

This neutral summary of events serves as an effective buffer for the indirect approach and provides a subtle reminder of the original goals of the program.

This paragraph contains the same information as the poor version, but does so in a calmer way that is less likely to trigger the reader's defense mechanisms and thereby keeps the focus on the facts.

Notice how the writer separates a personal hunch (about the possibility of losing employees) from an observation about the market and a measured data point.

The information about the quality problems is introduced without directing blame.

With the evidence assembled, the writer introduces the main idea of putting the program on hold. The recommendation is a judgment call and a suggestion to a superior, so the hedging clause *I believe* is appropriate.

Figure 9.5
Persuasive Message Using the AIDA Model
This message uses the AIDA model in a persuasive message about a program that would try to reduce Host Marriott's annual plastics costs and curtail consumer complaints about the company's recycling record. Note how the writer "sells the problem" before attempting to sell the solution. Few people are interested in hearing about solutions to problems they don't know about or don't believe exist. The interest section introduces an additional, unforeseen problem with plastic product containers.
Source: Microsoft Office 2013.

Common Examples of Persuasive Business Messages

Throughout your career, you'll have numerous opportunities to write persuasive messages—for example, when suggesting more-efficient operating procedures, asking for cooperation from other departments, pitching investors on a new business idea, or requesting adjustments that go beyond a supplier's contractual obligations. In addition, many of the routine requests you studied in Chapter 7 can become persuasive messages if you want a nonroutine result or believe that you haven't received fair treatment. Most of these messages can be divided into persuasive requests for action, persuasive presentation of ideas, and persuasive claims and requests for adjustment.

Persuasive Requests for Action

The bulk of your persuasive business messages will involve requests for action. In some cases, your request will be anticipated, so the direct approach is fine. In others, you'll need to introduce your intention indirectly, and the AIDA model or a similar approach is ideal for this purpose (see Figure 9.5).

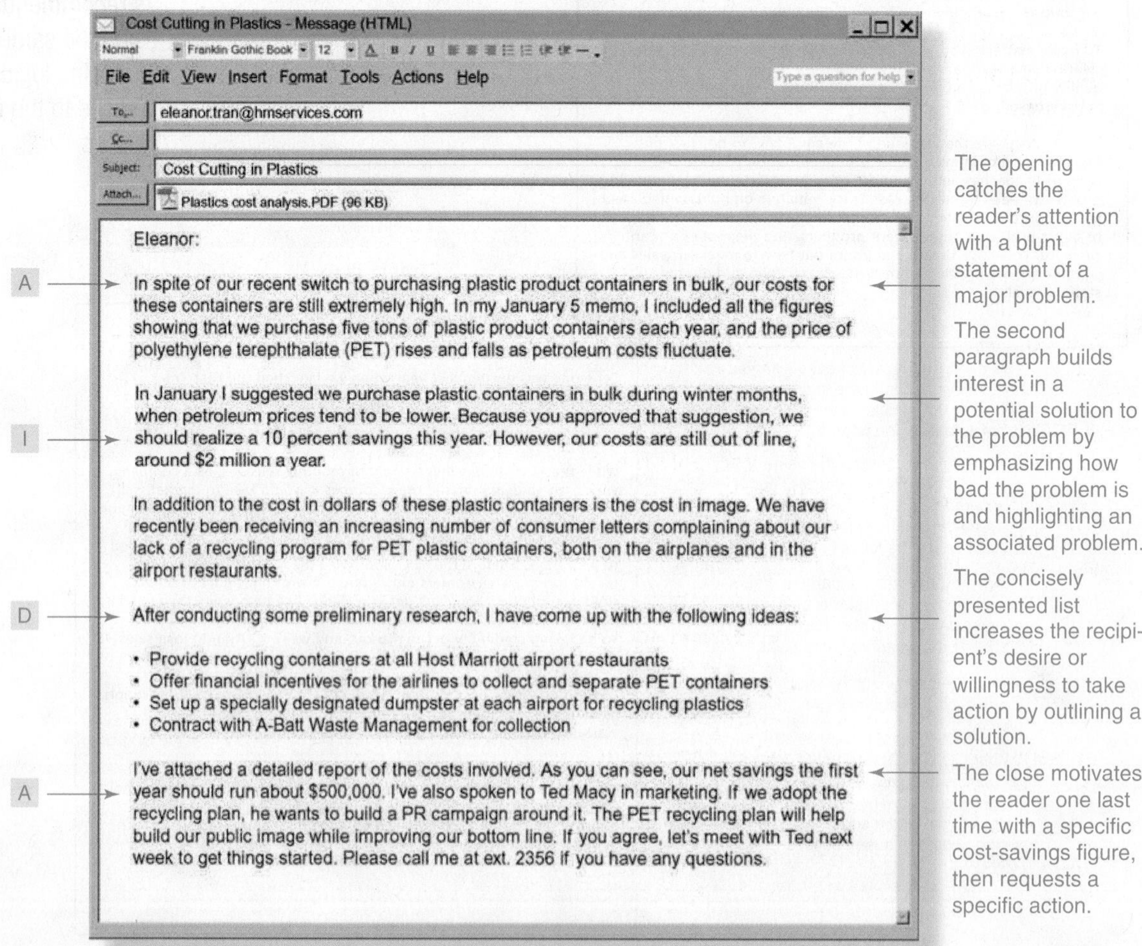

Cost Cutting in Plastics - Message (HTML)

File Edit View Insert Format Tools Actions Help

To: eleanor.tran@hmservices.com
Cc:
Subject: Cost Cutting in Plastics
Attach: Plastics cost analysis.PDF (96 KB)

Eleanor:

A → In spite of our recent switch to purchasing plastic product containers in bulk, our costs for these containers are still extremely high. In my January 5 memo, I included all the figures showing that we purchase five tons of plastic product containers each year, and the price of polyethylene terephthalate (PET) rises and falls as petroleum costs fluctuate.

I → In January I suggested we purchase plastic containers in bulk during winter months, when petroleum prices tend to be lower. Because you approved that suggestion, we should realize a 10 percent savings this year. However, our costs are still out of line, around $2 million a year.

In addition to the cost in dollars of these plastic containers is the cost in image. We have recently been receiving an increasing number of consumer letters complaining about our lack of a recycling program for PET plastic containers, both on the airplanes and in the airport restaurants.

D → After conducting some preliminary research, I have come up with the following ideas:

- Provide recycling containers at all Host Marriott airport restaurants
- Offer financial incentives for the airlines to collect and separate PET containers
- Set up a specially designated dumpster at each airport for recycling plastics
- Contract with A-Batt Waste Management for collection

A → I've attached a detailed report of the costs involved. As you can see, our net savings the first year should run about $500,000. I've also spoken to Ted Macy in marketing. If we adopt the recycling plan, he wants to build a PR campaign around it. The PET recycling plan will help build our public image while improving our bottom line. If you agree, let's meet with Ted next week to get things started. Please call me at ext. 2356 if you have any questions.

Open with an attention-getting device and show readers that you understand their concerns. Use the interest and desire sections of your message to demonstrate that you have good reason for making such a request and to cover what you know about the situation: the facts and figures, the benefits of helping, and any history or experience that will enhance your appeal. Your goals are to gain credibility (for yourself and your request) and to make your readers believe that helping you will indeed help solve a significant problem. Close with a request for some specific action, and make that course of action as easy to follow as possible to maximize the chances of a positive response.

Persuasive Presentation of Ideas

You may encounter situations in which you simply want to change attitudes or beliefs about a particular topic, without asking the audience to decide or do anything—at least not yet. The goal of your first message might be nothing more than convincing your audience to reexamine long-held opinions or to admit the possibility of new ways of thinking.

For instance, the World Wide Web Consortium, a global association that defines many of the guidelines and technologies behind the World Wide Web, launched a campaign called the Web Accessibility Initiative. Although the consortium's ultimate goal is making websites more accessible to people who have disabilities or age-related limitations, a key interim goal is simply making website developers more aware of the need. As part of this effort, the consortium has developed a variety of presentations and documents that highlight the problems many web visitors face.

Persuasive Claims and Requests for Adjustments

Most claims are routine messages and use the direct approach discussed in Chapter 7. However, consumers and business professionals sometimes encounter situations in which they believe they haven't received a fair deal by following normal procedures. These situations require a more persuasive message.

The key ingredients of a good persuasive claim are a complete and specific review of the facts and a confident and positive tone based on your right to be satisfied with every transaction. Begin persuasive claims by outlining the problem and continue by reviewing what has been done about it so far, if anything. The recipient might be juggling numerous claims and other demands on his or her attention, so be clear, calm, and complete when presenting your case. Be specific about how you would like to see the situation resolved.

Next, give your reader a good reason for granting your claim. Show how the individual or organization is responsible for the problem, and appeal to your reader's sense of fair play, goodwill, or moral responsibility. Explain how you feel about the problem, but don't get carried away and don't make threats. People generally respond most favorably to requests that are calm and reasonable. Close on a respectful note that reflects how a successful resolution of the situation will repair or maintain a mutually beneficial working relationship.

Developing Marketing and Sales Messages

Marketing and sales messages use the same basic techniques as other persuasive messages, with emphasis on of encouraging someone to participate in a commercial transaction. Although the terms marketing message and sales message are often used interchangeably, there is an important difference: **Marketing messages** usher potential buyers through the purchasing process without asking them to make an immediate decision. **Sales messages** take over at that point, encouraging potential buyers to make a purchase decision then and there.

Marketing message: A message that ushers potential buyers through the purchase process without asking for an immediate decision.

Sales message: A message that encourages potential buyers to make a purchase decision immediately.

Marketing messages focus on such tasks as introducing new brands to the public and encouraging customers to visit websites for more information, whereas sales messages make an explicit request for people to buy a specific product or service. (The text of marketing and sales messages is usually referred to as "copy," by the way.) Most marketing and sales messages, particularly in larger companies, are created and delivered by professionals with specific training in marketing, advertising, sales, or public relations. However, you may be called on to review the work of these specialists or even to write such messages; having a good understanding of how these messages work will help you be a more effective manager.

Figure 9.6
Effective Marketing Messages
The ideal marketing message catches people's attention and makes them want to learn more about the product or service.

Planning Marketing and Sales Messages

Everything you've learned about planning messages applies in general to marketing and sales messages, but the planning steps for these messages have some particular aspects to consider as well:

- **Assessing audience needs.** As with every other business message, successful marketing and sales messages start with an understanding of audience needs. Depending on the product and the market, these considerations can range from a few functional factors (such as the size, weight, and finish of office paper) to a complicated mix of emotional and logical issues (all the factors that play into buying a house, for example).

- **Analyzing your competition.** Marketing and sales messages nearly always compete with messages from other companies trying to reach the same audience. When Nike plans a marketing campaign to introduce a new shoe model to current customers, the company knows its audience has also been exposed to messages from Adidas, New Balance, Reebok, and numerous other shoe companies. Finding a unique message in crowded markets can be quite a challenge.
- **Determining key selling points and benefits.** With some insight into audience needs and the alternatives offered by your competitors, the next step is to decide which features and benefits to highlight. Selling points are the most attractive features of a product, whereas benefits are the particular advantages purchasers can realize from those features. In other words, selling points focus on what the product does. Benefits focus on what the user experiences or gains. Benefits can be practical, emotional, or a combination of the two. For example, the feature of a thin, flexible sole in a running shoe offers the practical benefit of a more natural feel while running. In contrast, the visual design features of the shoe offer no practical benefits but can offer the emotional benefit of wearing something stylish or unusual.
- **Anticipating purchase objections.** Marketing and sales messages usually encounter objections, and, as with persuasive business messages, the best way to handle them is to identify and address these objections up front. Objections can range from high price or low quality to a lack of compatibility with existing products or a perceived risk involved with the product. By identifying potential objections up front, you can craft your promotional messages in ways that address those concerns. If price is a likely objection, for instance, you can look for ways to increase the perceived value of the purchase and decrease the perception of high cost. When promoting a home gym, you might say that it costs less than a year's worth of health club dues. Of course, any attempts to minimize perceptions of price or other potential negatives must be done ethically.

Writing Conventional Marketing and Sales Messages

Conventional marketing and sales messages are often prepared using the AIDA model or some variation of it. (See the next section on crafting messages for social media.) Here are the key points of using the AIDA model for these messages:

- **Getting the reader's attention.** By looking and listening during any given day, you'll notice the many ways advertisers try to get your attention. For example, a headline might offer an exciting product benefit, a piece of interesting news, an appeal to your emotions or sense of financial value, or a unique solution to a common problem. Of course, words aren't the only attention-getting devices. Depending on the medium, marketers can use evocative images, music, animation, or video. "Cutting through the clutter" to get the audience's attention is one of the biggest challenges with marketing and sales messages.

- **Building interest.** After catching the reader's or viewer's attention, your next step is to build interest in the product, company, or idea you are promoting. A common technique is to "pay off" the promise made in the headline by explaining how you can deliver those benefits. For example, if the headline offers a way to "Get Fit for $2 a Day," the first paragraph could explain that the home gyms your company sells start at less than $700, which works out to less than $2 a day over the course of a year.
- **Increasing desire.** Now that you've given the audience some initial information to start building interest, the next step is to boost desire for the product by expanding on your explanation of its benefits. Think carefully about the sequence of support points and use plenty of subheadings, hyperlinks, video demonstrations, and other devices to help people quickly find the information they need. By keeping the focus on potential customers and their practical and emotional needs, you can layer on information that helps convince people that your product really is the best solution for them. You can also use a variety of techniques to address potential objections and minimize doubts, including testimonials from satisfied users, articles written by industry experts, competitive comparisons, offers of product samples or free demonstrations, independent test results, and money-back guarantees.
- **Motivating action.** The final step in the AIDA model is persuading the audience to take action, such as encouraging people to pick up the phone to place an order or visit an online app store to download your software. The keys to a successful call to action are making it easy and as risk-free as possible. If the process is confusing or time-consuming, you'll lose potential customers.

If you analyze the advertisements you encounter day to day, you'll see variations on these techniques used again and again.

Writing Promotional Messages for Social Media

The AIDA model and similar approaches have been successful with marketing and sales messages for decades, but in the social media landscape, consumers are more apt to look for product information from other consumers, not from the companies marketing those products. Consequently, your emphasis should shift to encouraging and participating in online conversations. Follow these guidelines:

- **Facilitate community building.** Give customers and other audiences an opportunity to connect with you and one another, such as on your Facebook page or through members-only online forums.
- **Listen at least as much as you talk.** Listening is just as essential for online conversations as it is for in-person conversations.
- **Initiate and respond to conversations within the community.** Through content on your website, blog postings, social network profiles and messages, newsletters, and other tools, make sure you provide the information customers need in order to evaluate your products and services. Use an objective, conversational style; people in social networks want useful information, not "advertising speak."

- **Provide information people want.** Whether it's industry-insider news, in-depth technical guides to using your products, or brief answers to questions posted on community Q&A sites, fill the information gaps about your company and its products.
- **Identify and support your champions.** In marketing, champions are enthusiastic fans of your company and its products. Champions are so enthusiastic they help spread your message (through their blogs, for instance), defend you against detractors, and help other customers use your products.
- **Be real.** Social media audiences respond positively to companies that are open and conversational about themselves, their products, and subjects of shared interest. In contrast, if a company is serving its stakeholders poorly with shoddy products, bad customer service, or unethical behavior, an attempt to improve its reputation by adopting social media without fixing the underlying problems is likely to fail as soon as audiences see through the superficial attempt to "be social."
- **Integrate conventional marketing and sales strategies at the right time and in the right places.** AIDA and similar approaches are still valid for specific communication tasks, such as conventional advertising and the product promotion pages on your website.

Creating Promotional Messages for Mobile Devices

Mobile advertising and mobile commerce (sometimes referred to as m-commerce) are two of the hottest developments in marketing communications. Mobile advertising is already a multibillion-dollar business, with nearly 70 percent of ad dollars spent on Google and Facebook ads. The types of marketing and sales messages created for mobile audiences range from short, simple text ads that appear next to search engine results to mobile-optimized video—the most common form of content marketing in the mobile arena.

Companies are putting so much emphasis on mobile marketing because mobile devices now play such a big role in consumer buying behavior. Smartphone owners tend to use their devices for many shopping-related tasks, from searching for product reviews to finding stores and service businesses, looking for coupons and other promotions, and doing in-store price comparisons. In fact, some 80 percent of smartphone-equipped consumers use their devices to get shopping-related information.

If you are involved with creating mobile marketing or sales messages, keep two essential points in mind. First, like all mobile messages, promotional messages need to be kept short and simple. Second, the mobile experience needs to be fast and straightforward. Mobile users are often time-constrained, and they will quickly abandon websites that don't load quickly or are confusing to navigate.

Maintaining High Ethical and Legal Standards

The word *persuasion* has negative connotations for some people, especially in a marketing or sales context. However, ethical businesspeople view persuasion as a positive force, a way to align their own interests with what is best for their audiences. They influence audience members by providing information and aiding understanding, which allows audiences the freedom to choose.

As marketing and selling grow increasingly complex, so do the legal ramifications of marketing and sales messages. In the United States, the Federal Trade Commission (FTC) and other federal, state, and local authorities can penalize advertisers that violate standards for truthful advertising and other regulations. All marketers need to understand these basic legal aspects of promotional communication:

- Marketing and sales messages must be truthful and nondeceptive. The FTC considers messages to be deceptive if they (a) include statements that are likely to mislead reasonable customers and the statements are an important part of the purchasing decision, (b) fail to include important information, or (c) imply deceptive claims without actually making them.
- You must back up your claims with evidence. According to the FTC, offering a money-back guarantee or providing letters from satisfied customers is not enough; you must still be able to support your claims with objective evidence such as a survey or scientific study.
- Reducing the cost of customer support inquiries.
- "Bait and switch" advertising is illegal. Trying to attract buyers by advertising a product that you don't intend to sell—and then trying to sell them another (and usually more expensive) product—is illegal.
- Marketing messages and websites aimed at children are subject to special rules. For example, online marketers must obtain consent from parents before collecting personal information about children under age 13.
- Marketing and sales messages are considered binding contracts in many states. If you imply or make an offer and then can't fulfill your end of the bargain, you can be sued for breach of contract.
- In most cases, you can't use a person's name, photograph, or other identity without permission. Doing so is considered an invasion of privacy. You can use images of people considered to be public figures as long as you don't unfairly imply that they endorse your message.
- Marketers also need to be up to date on the latest regulations affecting "spam" (unsolicited bulk email), customer privacy, and data security.

Chapter Summary

Using the Three-Step Writing Process for Persuasive Messages

To plan persuasive messages, carefully clarify your purpose to make sure you focus on a single goal. Understand audience needs, which can involve research to identify relevant demographic and psychographic variables and to assess audience motivations. Persuasive messages usually ask people to give up time, money, or other resources, so gathering the right information to convince readers of the benefits of responding is essential. Media choices need to be considered carefully, particularly with marketing and sales messages in a social media landscape. For organizing persuasive messages, you will usually want to choose the indirect approach in order to establish awareness and interest before asking the audience to take action.

When writing persuasive messages, use positive and polite language, understand and respect cultural differences, be sensitive to organizational cultures when writing persuasive business messages, and take steps to establish your credibility. Seven common ways to establish credibility in persuasive messages are using simple language, supporting your claims, identifying your sources, establishing common ground, being objective, displaying good intentions, and avoiding the hard sell.

The steps for completing persuasive messages are the same as for other types of messages, but accuracy and completeness are especially important because they send signals about your credibility—a crucial element in persuasive messages.

Developing Persuasive Business Messages

Within the context of the three-step process, effective persuasion involves four essential strategies: framing your arguments, balancing emotional and logical appeals, reinforcing your position, and anticipating objections. One of the most commonly used methods for framing a persuasive argument is the AIDA model, in which you open your message by getting the audience's attention; build interest with facts, details, and additional benefits; increase desire by providing more evidence and answering possible objections; and motivate a specific action. Persuasive business messages combine emotional appeals (which call on feelings and sympathies) and logical appeals (which call on reason, using analogy, induction, or deduction). To reinforce your position, look for ways to add convincing evidence, quotations from experts, or other support material.

By identifying potential objections and addressing them as you craft your message, you can help prevent audience members from gravitating toward negative answers before you have the opportunity to ask them for a positive response. You can often resolve these issues before the audience has a chance to go on the defensive.

Common Examples of Persuasive Business Messages

There are three common types of persuasive business messages. In the persuasive request for action, you ask the recipient to make a decision or engage in some activity. In the persuasive presentation of ideas, you aren't necessarily looking for a decision or action but rather would like the audience to consider a different way of looking at a particular topic. When you make a persuasive claim for adjustments, you believe you have not received fair treatment under an organization's standard policies and would like the recipient to give your case fresh consideration.

Developing Marketing and Sales Messages

Marketing and sales messages use the same basic techniques as other persuasive messages, with the emphasis on encouraging someone to participate in a commercial transaction. Marketing messages do this indirectly, whereas sales messages do it directly. The basic strategy for creating these messages includes assessing audience needs; analyzing your competition; determining key selling points and benefits; anticipating purchase objections; applying the AIDA model; adapting your writing to social media, if appropriate; and maintaining high standards of ethical and legal compliance.

To use social media for promotional communication, start by engaging audiences with efforts to build networked communities of potential buyers and other interested parties. Listen to conversations taking place about your company and its products. Initiate and respond to conversations within these communities, being sure to use an objective, conversational style. Provide the information interested parties want. Identify and support the enthusiastic product champions who want to help spread your message. Be authentic and transparent in all your communication. Speak directly to customers so you don't have to rely on the news media. Finally, continue to use the AIDA model or similar approaches, but only at specific times and places.

Effective and ethical persuasive communicators focus on aligning their interests with the interests of their audiences. They help audiences understand how their proposals will provide benefits to the audience, using language that is persuasive without being manipulative. They choose words that are less likely to be misinterpreted and take care not to distort the truth. Throughout, they maintain a "you" attitude with honest concern for the audience's needs and interests.

Test Your Knowledge

1. What are some questions to ask when gauging the audience's needs during the planning of a persuasive message?
2. How do emotional appeals differ from logical appeals?
3. What three types of reasoning can you use in logical appeals?
4. What is the AIDA model, and what are its limitations?
5. Why do promotional messages need to be short and simple on mobile devices?

Apply Your Knowledge

1. When writing persuasive messages, why is it so important to give special attention to the analysis of your purpose and audience?
2. Is the "hard-sell" approach unethical? Why or why not?
3. What is likely to happen if a promotional message starts immediately with a call to action? Why?
4. Are emotional appeals ethical? Why or why not?

Practice Your Skills

1. **Analyzing a Persuasive Message** With another student, analyze the persuasive email message from Figure 9.5 on page 296 by answering the following questions.
   a. What techniques are used to capture the reader's attention?
   b. Does the writer use the direct or indirect organizational approach? Why?
   c. Is the subject line effective? Why or why not?
   d. Does the writer use an emotional appeal or a logical appeal? Why?
   e. What reader benefits are included?
   f. How does the writer establish credibility?
   g. What tools does the writer use to reinforce his position?

2. **Writing Persuasive Business Messages for Mobile Channels** Compose effective subject lines for the following email messages. Make sure they are mobile-friendly.
   a. A recommendation to your branch manager to install wireless networking throughout the facility. Your primary reason is that management has encouraged more teamwork, and the teams often congregate in meeting rooms, the cafeteria, and other places that lack network access, without which they can't do much of the work they are expected to do.
   b. A sales brochure to be sent to area residents, soliciting customers for your new business, "Meals à la Car," a carryout dining service that delivers from most local restaurants. Diners place orders online, and individual households can order from up to three restaurants at a time to accommodate different tastes. The price is equal to the standard menu prices plus a 10 percent delivery charge.
   c. A special request to the company president to allow managers to carry over their unused vacation days to the following year. Apparently, many managers canceled their fourth-quarter vacation plans to work on the installation of a new company computer system. Under their current contract, vacation days not used by December 31 can't be carried over to the following year.

3. **Rewriting Marketing and Sales Messages** Determine whether the following sentences focus on features or benefits; rewrite them as necessary to focus on benefits.
   a. All-Cook skillets are coated with a durable, patented non-stick surface.
   b. You can call anyone and talk as long you like on Saturdays and Sundays with this new mobile phone plan.
   c. With 8-millisecond response time, the Samsung LS-S4095D 40" LCD TV delivers fast video action that is smooth and crisp.

Activities

1. **Planning an Online Marketing Campaign** You have been asked to plan and implement a web and social media marketing campaign for a friend who is running for your local city council. Make some notes to prepare for your initial meeting with him, identifying ideas and strategies in the following areas:

   - **Assumptions:** What do you assume about the target audience? What are they like? What motivates them?
   - **Purpose:** What do you want the audience to do?
   - **Outcome:** What is the desired overall outcome?
   - **Key issues:** What does the target audience care about? What are their issues?
   - **Techniques:** How can the candidate best target the audience with persuasive rhetoric?

2. **Revising Persuasive Business Messages** Read the following message. Analyze the strengths and weaknesses of each sentence, and then revise the document so that it follows this chapter's guidelines.

   > Dear TechStar Computing:
   >
   > I'm writing to you because of my disappointment with my new multimedia PC display. The display part works all right, but the audio volume is also set too high and the volume knob doesn't turn it down. It's driving us crazy. The volume knob doesn't seem to be connected to anything but simply spins around. I can't believe you would put out a product like this without testing it first.
   >
   > I depend on my computer to run my small business and want to know what you are going to do about it. This reminds me of every time I buy electronic equipment from what seems like any company. Something is always wrong. I thought quality was supposed to be important, but I guess not.
   >
   > Anyway, I need this fixed right away. Please tell me what you want me to do.

3. **Analyzing Persuasive Business Messages** The following persuasive request for adjustment contains numerous flaws. Read the message carefully and analyze its faults. Then determine whether to use the direct or indirect approach and write an improved message.

March 22, 2017

Mr. Robert Bechtold, Manager
Kukyendahl Joint, Inc.88
North Park RoadHouston, TX 77005

Re: Last Warning

Dear Mr. Bechtold:

Enclosed is a summary of recent ETS-related court cases in which landlords and owners were held responsible for providing toxin-free air for their tenants. In most of these cases, owners were also required to reimburse rents and pay damages for the harm done before the environmental tobacco smoke problem was remedied.

We've been plagued with this since we moved in on January 2, 2016. You haven't acted on our complaints, or responded to our explanations that secondhand smoke is making us sick, filtering in from nearby offices. You must act now or you will be hearing from our lawyers. We've told you that we were forced to hire contractors to apply weather stripping and seal openings. This cost us $3,000 (bills attached) and we expect reimbursement. But the smoke is still coming in. We also want a refund for the $9,000 we've paid you in rent since January. Call us immediately at (832) 768-3899, or our attorneys will be calling you.

Cigarette smoke from tenants on either side of us, and perhaps above and below as well, has been infiltrating our space and you have done nothing, despite our pleas, to stop it. This is unacceptable. This is a known human carcinogen. Ask the Environmental Protection Agency, which classified it as this Group A toxin. It causes lung, breast, cervical, and endocrine cancer in nonsmokers. You wouldn't want to breathe it, either.

One employee already quit who suffered from asthma. Another is threatening because he's a high risk for heart attack. Migraines, bronchitis, respiratory infections—all caused by the 4,600 chemicals in ETS, including poisons such as cyanide, arsenic, formaldehyde, carbon monoxide, and ammonia. We've had them all—the illnesses, that is.

Secondhand smoke is even more dangerous than what smokers inhale, since the inhalation process burns off some of the toxins. Sick time has already cost CMSI valuable business and lowered productivity. Plus many of us are considering finding other jobs unless our office air becomes safe to breathe again. But as the court cases prove, the responsibility for fixing this problem is yours.

We expect you to live up to that responsibility immediately. Frankly, we're fed up with your lack of response.

Kathleen Thomas

Manager

4. **Analyzing Marketing and Sales Messages** Read the following message. Analyze the strengths and weaknesses of each sentence, and then revise the document so that it follows this chapter's guidelines.

> At Tolson Auto Repair, we have been in business for over 25 years. We stay in business by always taking into account what the customer wants. That's why we are writing. We want to know your opinions to be able to better conduct our business.
>
> Take a moment right now and fill out the enclosed questionnaire. We know everyone is busy, but this is just one way we have of making sure our people do their job correctly. Use the enclosed envelope to return the questionnaire.
>
> And again, we're happy you chose Tolson Auto Repair. We want to take care of all your auto needs.

5. **Revising Marketing and Sales Messages** Read the following message. Analyze the strengths and weaknesses of each sentence, and then revise the document so that it follows this chapter's guidelines.

> I am considered the country's foremost authority on employee health insurance programs. My clients offer universally positive feedback on the programs I've designed for them. They also love how much time I save them—hundreds and hundreds of hours. I am absolutely confident that I can thoroughly analyze your needs and create a portfolio that realizes every degree of savings possible. I invite you to experience the same level of service that has generated such comments as "Best advice ever!" and "Saved us an unbelievable amount of money."

6. **Revising Marketing and Sales Messages** Use what you know about sales messages to analyze the flaws in this promotional brochure, and then revise it to produce a better version.

We are pleased to announce that ScrubaDub has added a new service, the Car Care Club.

It costs $5.95 for a lifetime membership (your car's lifetime) and features our computer automation. You'll be given a bar-coded sticker for your windshield so our computers can identify you as a club member when you pull in. If you sign up within the next 30 days we will grant you a SuperWash for free.

The new club offers the standard ScrubaDub Touchless systems to protect your finishes, our private formula Superglo detergent to clean your car safely and thoroughly, wheel sensors to prescribe the right treatment for whitewalls, wire, or chrome, soft, heated well water to eliminate spots, soft-cloth drying for final gloss. We also recycle our water and grant you a free car wash on your birthday.

In addition, club members only will have access to a 48-hour guarantee (free rewashes) or 4 days if you purchased the premium Super Wash, Luxury Wash, Special or Works Wash. After ten washes, our computer will award you a free wash. Also available only to club members are $5 rebates for foam waxes (Turtle Wax, Simonize, or Blue Coral). Some additional specials will be granted by us to car club members, on an unplanned basis

We can handle special requests if you inquire of our Satisfaction Supervisors. We honor our customers with refunds if they remain unsatisfied after a rewash. This is our Bumper to Bumper Guarantee.

7. **Making Ethical Choices** Your boss has asked you to post a message on the company's internal blog, urging everyone in your department to donate money to the company's favorite charity, an organization that operates a summer camp for children with physical challenges. You wind up writing a lengthy posting packed with facts and heartwarming anecdotes about the camp and the children's experiences. When you must work that hard to persuade your audience to take an action such as donating money to a charity, aren't you being manipulative and unethical? Explain.

Expand Your Skills

1. **Writing Persuasive Business Messages on Twitter** You've been trying for months to convince your boss, company CEO Will Florence, to start using Twitter. You've told him that top executives in numerous industries now use Twitter as a way to connect with customers and other stakeholders without going through the filters and barriers of formal corporate communications, but he doesn't see the value.

   Your task: You come up with the brilliant plan to demonstrate Twitter's usefulness using Twitter itself. First, find three executives from three different companies who are on Twitter (choose any companies and executives you find interesting). Study their tweets to get a feel for the type of information they share.

   Write four tweets to demonstrate the value of executive microblogging: one that summarizes the value of having a company CEO use Twitter and three support tweets, each one summarizing how your three real-life executive role models use Twitter. If your class is set up with private Twitter accounts, use your private account to send your messages. Otherwise, email your four messages to your instructor or post them on your class blog, as your instructor directs.

2. **Writing Persuasive Email Messages** As someone who came of age in the "post email" world of blogs, wikis, social networks, and other technologies, you were rather disappointed to find your new employer solidly stuck in the age of email. You use email, of course, but it is only one of the tools in your communication toolbox. From your high school years, you have hands-on experience with a wide range of social media tools. You've used them to collaborate on school projects, to become involved in your local community, to learn more about various industries and professions, and to research potential employers during your job search. (In fact, without social media, you might never have heard about your current employer in the first place.) Moreover, your use of social media on the job has already paid several important dividends. You've found potential sales contacts at several large companies, connected with peers in other companies to share ideas for working more efficiently, and learned about some upcoming legislative matters in your state that could profoundly hamper your company's current way of doing business.

   You hoped that your example would encourage your new colleagues and company management to adopt social media tools at work, but just the opposite has happened. Waiting in your email inbox this morning was a message from the CEO, announcing that the company is now cutting off access to social networking websites and banning the use of any social media at work. The message says using company time and company computers for socializing is highly inappropriate and might be considered grounds for dismissal in the future if the problem gets out of hand.

   Your task: You are stunned by the message. You fight the urge to fire off a hotly worded reply to straighten out the CEO's misperceptions. Instead, you wisely decide to send a message to your immediate superior first, explaining why you believe the new policy should be reversed. Using your boss's favorite medium (email, of course!), write a persuasive message, explaining why Facebook, Twitter, and other social networking technologies are valid—and valuable—business tools. Bolster your argument with examples from other companies and advice from communication experts.

3. **Writing Persuasive Business Letters** The coffee shop across the street from your apartment is your haven away from home—great beverages, healthy snacks, free wireless, and an atmosphere that is fun but not so lively that you can't focus on homework. It lacks only one thing: some way to print out your homework and other files when you need hard copy. Your school's libraries and computer labs provide printers, but you live three miles from campus, and it's a long walk or an inconvenient bus ride.

   Your task: Write a letter to the owner of the coffee shop, encouraging her to set up a printing service to complement the free wireless access. Propose that the service run at break-even prices, just enough to pay for paper, ink cartridges, and the cost of the printer itself. The benefit to the shop would be enticing patrons to spend more time—and therefore more of their coffee and tea money—in the shop. You might also mention that you had to take the bus to school to print this letter, so you bought your afternoon latte somewhere else.

4. **Writing Persuasive Blog Posts** As a strong advocate for the use of social media in business, you are pleased by how quickly people in your company have taken up blogging, wiki writing, and other new-media activities. You are considerably less excited

by the style and quality of what you see in the writing of your colleagues. Many seem to have interpreted "authentic and conversational" to mean "anything goes." Several Twitter users in the company seem to have abandoned any pretense of grammar and spelling. A few managers have dragged internal disagreements about company strategy out into public view, arguing with each other through comments on various industry-related forums. Production demonstration videos have been posted to the company's YouTube channel virtually unedited, making the whole firm look unpolished and unprofessional. The company CEO has written some blog posts that bash competitors with coarse and even crude language.

You pushed long and hard for greater use of these tools, so you feel a sense of responsibility for this situation. In addition, you are viewed by many in the company as the resident expert on social media, so you have some "expertise authority" on this issue. On the other hand, you are only a first-level manager, with three levels of managers above you, so while you have some "position authority" as well, you can hardly dictate best practices to the managers above you.

Your task: Working with two other students, write a post for the company's internal blog (which is not viewable outside the company), outlining your concerns about these communication practices. Use the examples mentioned above, and make up any additional details you need. Emphasize that although social media communication is often less formal and more flexible than traditional business communication, it shouldn't be unprofessional. You are thinking of proposing a social media training program for everyone in the company, but for this message you just want to bring attention to the problem.

5. **Writing Persuasive Email Messages** Whole Foods Market has grown into a nationwide chain by catering to consumer desires for healthier foods and environmentally sensitive farming methods. Along with selling these products, the company makes a commitment "to be active participants in our local communities." Whole Foods not only donates five percent of after-tax profits to not-for-profit organizations but also financially supports employees who volunteer their time for community service projects. Many Whole Foods stores donate food and household supplies to food banks in their local communities.

You are the manager of the Whole Foods Market on Ponce de Leon Avenue in Atlanta. You developed a program for donating surplus food to local food banks. Because of the success of that program, top executives have asked you to help other Whole Foods stores coordinate this effort into a chain-wide food donation program, "Whole Foods for Life." Ideally, by streamlining the process chain-wide, the company would be able to increase the number of people it helps and to get more of its employees involved.

You have a limited budget for the program, so the emphasis has to be on using resources already available to the stores and tapping into employees' creativity to come up with locally relevant ideas.

Your task: Write a persuasive email message to all managers at Whole Foods Market, explaining the new program and requesting that they help by pooling ideas they've gleaned from their local experience. Even if they don't have food-donation programs currently in place, you want to hear ideas from them and their employees for this charitable project. With their help, you'll choose the best ideas to develop the new Whole Foods for Life program.

6. **Writing Requests for Action** Managing a new-product launch can be an aggravating experience as you try to coordinate a wide variety of activities and processes while barreling toward a deadline that is often defined more by external factors than a realistic assessment of whether you can actually meet it. You depend on lots of other people to meet their deadlines, and if they fail, you fail. The pressure is enough to push anybody over the edge. Unfortunately, that happened to you last week. After a barrage of bad news from suppliers and the members of the team you lead, you lost your cool in a checkpoint meeting. Shouting at people and accusing them of slacking off was embarrassing enough, but the situation got a hundred times worse this morning when your boss suggested you needed some low-pressure work for a while and removed you as the leader of the launch team.

   Your task: Write an email message to your boss, Sunil, requesting to be reinstated as the project team leader. Make up any information you need.

7. **Writing Email Requests for Action** You appreciate how important phones are to your company's operations, but the amount of conversational chatter in your work area has gotten so bad that it's hard to concentrate on your work. You desperately need at least a few quiet hours every day to engage in the analytical thinking your job requires.

   Your task: Write an email message to the division vice president, Jeri Ross, asking her to designate one of the conference rooms as a quiet-zone work room. It would have WiFi so that employees can stay connected to the corporate network, but it would not have any phone service, either landline or mobile. (Mobile reception is already weak in the conference rooms, but you will propose to equip the room with a mobile signal jammer to ensure that no calls can be made or received.) In addition, conversation of any kind would be strictly forbidden. Make up any details you need.

8. **Writing Persuasive Email Messages** Your new company, WorldConnect Language Services, started well and is going strong. However, to expand beyond your Memphis, Tennessee, home market, you need a one-time infusion of cash to open branch offices in other cities around the Southeast. At the Entrepreneur's Lunch Forum you attended yesterday, you learned about several angels, as they are called in the investment community—private individuals who invest money in small companies in exchange for a share of ownership. One such angel, Melinda Sparks, told the audience she is looking for investment opportunities outside high technology, where angels often invest their money. She also indicated that she looks for entrepreneurs who know their industries and markets well, who are passionate about the value they bring to the marketplace, who are committed to growing their businesses, and who have a solid plan for how they will spend an investor's money. Fortunately, you meet all of her criteria.

   Your task: Draft an email message to Sparks, introducing yourself and your business and asking for a meeting at which you can present your business plan in more detail. Explain that your Memphis office was booked to capacity within two months of opening, thanks to the growing number of international business professionals looking for translators and interpreters. You've researched the entire Southeast region and identified at least 10 other cities that could support language services offices such as yours. Making up whatever other information you need, draft a four-paragraph message following the AIDA model, ending with a request for a meeting within the next four weeks. You know Sparks tends to read email on her phone, so craft your message to be mobile-friendly.

9. **Writing Requests for Information** As a motivated, ambitious employee, you naturally care about your performance on the job—and about making sure your performance is being fairly judged and rewarded. Unfortunately, the company has gone through a period of turmoil over the past several years, and you have reported to seven managers during the past five years. One year, your annual performance review was done by someone who had been your boss for only three weeks and knew almost nothing about you or your work. Last year, your boss was fired the day after he wrote your review, and you can't help but wonder whether you got a fair review from someone in that situation. Overall, you are worried that your career progression and wage increases have been hampered by inconsistent and ill-informed performance reviews.

   The company allows employees to keep copies of their reviews, but you haven't been diligent about doing so. You would like to get copies of your last five reviews, but you heard from a colleague that the human resources department will not release copies of past reviews without approval from the managers who wrote them. In your case, however, three of the managers who reviewed you are no longer with the company, and you do not want your current boss to know you are concerned about your reviews.

   Your task: Write an email message to the director of human resources, Leon Sandes, requesting copies of your performance reviews over the past five years. Use the information included above and make up any additional details you need.

10. **Writing Persuasive Marketing and Sales Messages** Water polo is an active sport that provides great opportunities for exercise and for learning the collaborative skills involved in teamwork. You can learn more at the USA Water Polo website (www.usawaterpolo.org).

    Your task: Write a one-page letter to parents of 10- to 14-year-old boys and girls, promoting the health and socialization benefits of water polo and encouraging them to introduce their children to the sport through a local club. Tell them they can learn more about the sport and find a club in their area by visiting the USA Water Polo website.

11. **Promoting an Invention Online** You never intended to become an inventor, but you saw a way to make something work more easily, so you set to work. You developed a model, found a way to mass-produce it, and set up a small manufacturing studio in your home. You know that other people are going to benefit from your invention. Now all you need to do is reach that market.

    Your task: Team up with other students assigned by your instructor and imagine a useful product that you might have invented—perhaps something related to a hobby or sporting activity. List the features and benefits of your imaginary product, and describe how it helps customers. Then write the copy for a webpage that would introduce and promote this product, using what you've learned in this chapter and making up details as you need them. As your instructor indicates, submit the copy as a word processor file or as a webpage using basic HTML formatting.

12. **Promoting a Musical Act Online** Convincing people to give their music a try is one of the toughest challenges new bands and performers face.

    Your task: Imagine you've taken on the job of promoting an amazing new band or performer you just discovered. Choose someone you've heard live or online and write 100 to 200 words of webpage copy describing the music in a way that will convince people to listen to a few online samples.

13. **Promoting a Product with Microblogging** Effective microblogging messages emphasize clarity and conciseness—and so do effective sales messages.

    Your task: Find the website of any product that can be ordered online (any product you find interesting and that is appropriate to use for a class assignment). Adapt the information on the website, using your own words, and write four tweets to promote the product. The first should get your audience's attention (with an intriguing benefit claim, for example); the second should build audience interest by providing some support for the claim you made in the first message; the third should increase readers' desire to have the product by layering on one or two more buyer benefits; and the fourth should motivate readers to take action to place an order. Your first three tweets can be up to 140 characters, but the fourth should be limited to 120 to accommodate a URL (you don't need to include the URL in your message, however).

    If your class is set up with private Twitter accounts, use your private account to send your messages. Otherwise, email your four messages to your instructor or post them on your class blog, as your instructor directs.

CHAPTER 10

Understanding and Planning Reports and Proposals

After studying this chapter, you will be able to:

- Adapt the three-step writing process to reports and proposals.
- Describe an effective process for conducting business research, explain how to evaluate the credibility of an information source, and identify the five ways to use research results.
- Explain the role of secondary research and describe the two major categories of online research tools.
- Document sources in the commonly accepted format appropriate to the subject matter.
- Explain the role of primary research and identify the two most common forms of primary research for business communication purposes.
- Explain how to plan informational reports and website content.
- Identify the three most common ways to organize analytical reports.
- Explain how to plan proposals.

Applying the Three-Step Writing Process to Reports and Proposals

In previous chapters, you learned to use the three-step writing process for developing shorter business messages; now it's time to apply those skills to longer messages. Reports fall into three basic categories (see Figure 10.1):

- Informational reports offer data, facts, feedback, and other types of information, without analysis or recommendations.
- Analytical reports offer both information and analysis and can also include recommendations.
- Proposals present persuasive recommendations to internal or external audiences, often involving investments or purchases.

Figure 10.1
Common Business Reports and Proposals
You will have the opportunity to read and write many types of reports in your career; here are some of the most common.

Informational Reports
Offer data, facts, feedback, and other types of information, without analysis or recommendations

- **Reports to Monitor and Control Operations**
  Provide feedback and other information for decision making (plans, operating reports, personal activity reports)
- **Reports to Implement Policies and Procedures**
  Communicate organizational rules and positions (guidelines, position papers)
- **Reports to Demonstrate Compliance**
  Provide information to show regulators or other authorities that the company meets formal requirements
- **Reports to Document Progress**
  Provide managers or customers with information on project status

Analytical Reports
Offer information and analysis; can also include recommendations

- **Reports to Assess Opportunities**
  Explain the risks and rewards of choosing a course of action (market analysis reports, due diligence reports)
- **Reports to Solve Problems**
  Analyze problems and (optionally) suggest solutions (troubleshooting reports, failure analysis reports)
- **Reports to Support Decisions**
  Judge the merits of past or future decisions (feasibility reports, justification reports)

Proposals
Feature persuasive requests for decisions or action

- **Internal Proposals**
  Request decisions from managers within the organization (funding proposals, general project proposals)
- **External Proposals**
  Request decisions from parties outside the organization (investment proposals, grant proposals, sales proposals)

Try to view every business report as an opportunity to demonstrate your understanding of your audience's challenges and your ability to contribute to your organization's success. The three-step process is easily adapted to reports and, in fact, makes these larger projects easier to produce by ensuring a methodical, efficient approach to planning, writing, and completing.

Analyzing the Situation

Reports can be complex, time-consuming projects, so be sure to analyze the situation carefully before you begin to write. Pay special attention to your **statement of purpose**, which explains *why* you are preparing the report and *what* you plan to deliver.

Statement of purpose: A statement of why you are preparing the report and what you plan to deliver.

The most useful way to phrase your purpose statement is to begin with an infinitive phrase (*to* plus a verb), which helps pin down your general goal (*to inform, to identify, to analyze,* and so on). For instance, in an informational report, your statement of purpose can be as simple as one of these:

To identify potential markets for our new phone-based videogames

To update the board of directors on the progress of the research project

To submit required information to the Securities and Exchange Commission

The statement of purpose for an analytical report often needs to be more comprehensive. For example, if you were asked to find ways of reducing employee travel and entertainment (T&E) costs, you might phrase your statement of purpose like this:

To analyze the T&E budget, evaluate the impact of recent changes in airfares and hotel costs, and suggest ways to tighten management's control over T&E expenses

A proposal must also be guided by a clear statement of purpose to help you focus on crafting a persuasive message. Here are several examples:

To secure funding in next year's budget for new conveyor systems in the warehouse

To get management approval to reorganize the North American sales force

To secure $2 million from outside investors to start production of the new titanium mountain bike

Work plan:
A plan that describes the scope and tasks involved in a project.

In addition to considering your purpose carefully, you will want to prepare a **work plan** for most reports and proposals in order to make the best use of your time. For simpler reports, the work plan can be an informal list of tasks and a simple schedule. However, if you're preparing a lengthy report, particularly when you're collaborating with others, you'll want to develop a more detailed work plan (see Figure 10.2).

The problem statement clearly and succinctly defines the problem the writers intend to address.

STATEMENT OF THE PROBLEM
The rapid growth of our company over the past five years has reduced the sense of community among our staff. People no longer feel like part of an intimate organization that values teamwork.

This paragraph identifies exactly what will be covered by the research and addressed in the final report.

PURPOSE AND SCOPE OF WORK
The purpose of this study is to determine whether social networking technology such as Facebook and Socialtext would help rebuild a sense of community within the workforce and whether encouraging the use of such tools in the workplace will have any negative consequences. The study will attempt to assess the impact of social networks in other companies in terms of community-building, morale, project communication, and overall productivity.

This section explains how the researchers will find the data and information they need.

SOURCES AND METHODS OF DATA COLLECTION
Data collection will start with secondary research, including a review of recently published articles and studies on the use of social networking in business and a review of product information published by technology vendors. Primary research will focus on an employee and management survey to uncover attitudes about social networking tools. We will also collect anecdotal evidence from bloggers and others with experience using networks in the workplace.

The preliminary outline has enough detail to guide the research and set reader expectations.

PRELIMINARY OUTLINE
The preliminary outline for this study is as follows:

I. What experiences have other companies had with social networks in the workplace?
   A. Do social networks have a demonstrable business benefit?
   B. How do employees benefit from using these tools?
   C. Has network security and information confidentiality been an issue?
II. Is social networking an appropriate solution for our community-building needs?
   A. Is social networking better than other tools and methods for community building?
   B. Are employees already using social networking tools on the job?
   C. Will a company-endorsed system distract employees from essential duties?
   D. Will a company system add to managerial workloads in any way?
III. If we move ahead, should we use a "business-class" network such as Socialtext or a consumer tool such as Facebook?
   A. How do the initial and ongoing costs compare?
   B. Do the additional capabilities of a business-class network justify the higher costs?
IV. How should we implement a social network?
   A. Should we let it grow "organically," with employees choosing their own tools and groups?
   B. Should we make a variety of tools available and let employees improvise on their own?
   C. Should we designate one system as the official company social network and make it a permanent, supported element of the information technology infrastructure?
V. How can we evaluate the success of a new social network?
   A. What are the criteria of success or failure?
   B. What is the best way to measure these criteria?

The assignments and schedule section clearly lists responsibilities and due dates.

TASK ASSIGNMENTS AND SCHEDULE
Each phase of this study will be completed by the following dates:

Secondary research: Hank Waters	September 15, 2013
Employee and management survey: Julienne Cho	September 22, 2013
Analysis and synthesis of research: Hank Waters/Julienne Cho	October 6, 2013
Comparison of business and consumer solutions: Julienne Cho	October 13, 2013
Comparison of implementation strategies: Hank Waters	October 13, 2013
Final report: Hank Waters	October 20, 2013

Figure 10.2 Work Plan for a Report
A formal work plan such as this is a vital tool for planning and managing complex writing projects. The preliminary outline here helps guide the research; the report writers may well modify the outline when they begin writing the report.

Gathering Information

Obtaining the information needed for many reports and proposals requires careful planning—you may even need to do a separate research project just to acquire the data and information you need. To stay on schedule and on budget, be sure to review both your statement of purpose and your audience's needs so that you can prioritize your information needs and focus on the most important questions.

Selecting the Right Combination of Media and Channels

In addition to the general media and channel selection criteria discussed in Chapter 3, consider several points for reports and proposals. First, for many reports and proposals, audiences have specific media requirements, and you might not have a choice. For instance, executives in many corporations now expect to review many reports via their in-house intranets, sometimes in conjunction with an **executive dashboard**, a customized graphical presentation of key performance parameters (see Figure 10.3). Second, consider how your audience members will want to provide feedback on your report or proposal. Do they prefer to write comments on a printed document or edit a wiki article? Third, will people need to be able to search through your document or update it in the future? Fourth, bear in mind that your choice of medium and channel sends a message. For instance, a routine sales report dressed up in expensive multimedia may look like a waste of valuable company resources.

Executive dashboard: A customized graphical presentation of key performance parameters.

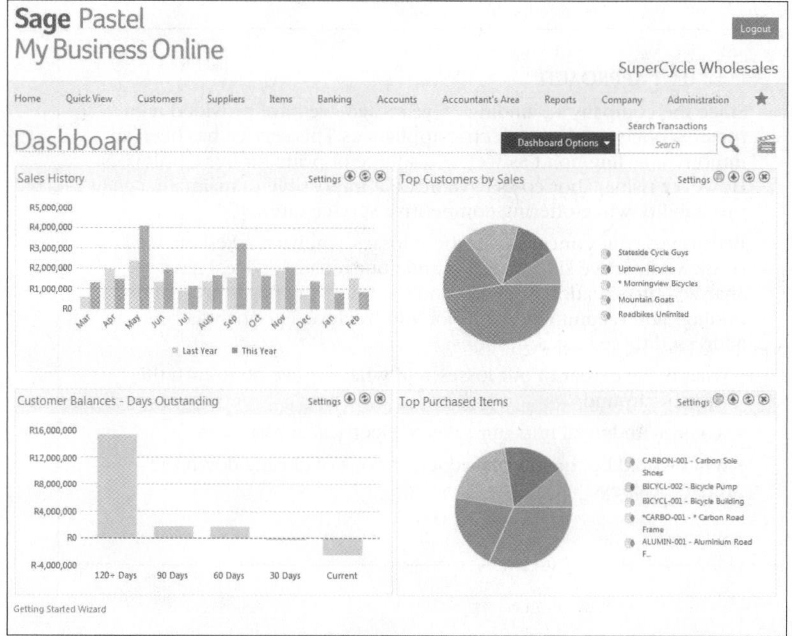

Figure 10.3
Executive Dashboards
Executive dashboards are super-summarized operating reports that present key business figures in graphical format.

Organizing Your Information

The direct approach is often used for reports because it is efficient and easy to follow (see Figure 10.4). When your audience is likely to be receptive or at least open-minded, use the direct approach: lead with a summary of your key findings, conclusions, recommendations, or proposal, whichever is relevant.

This "up-front" arrangement saves time and makes the rest of the report easier to follow. For those readers who have questions or want more information, later parts of the report provide complete findings and supporting details.

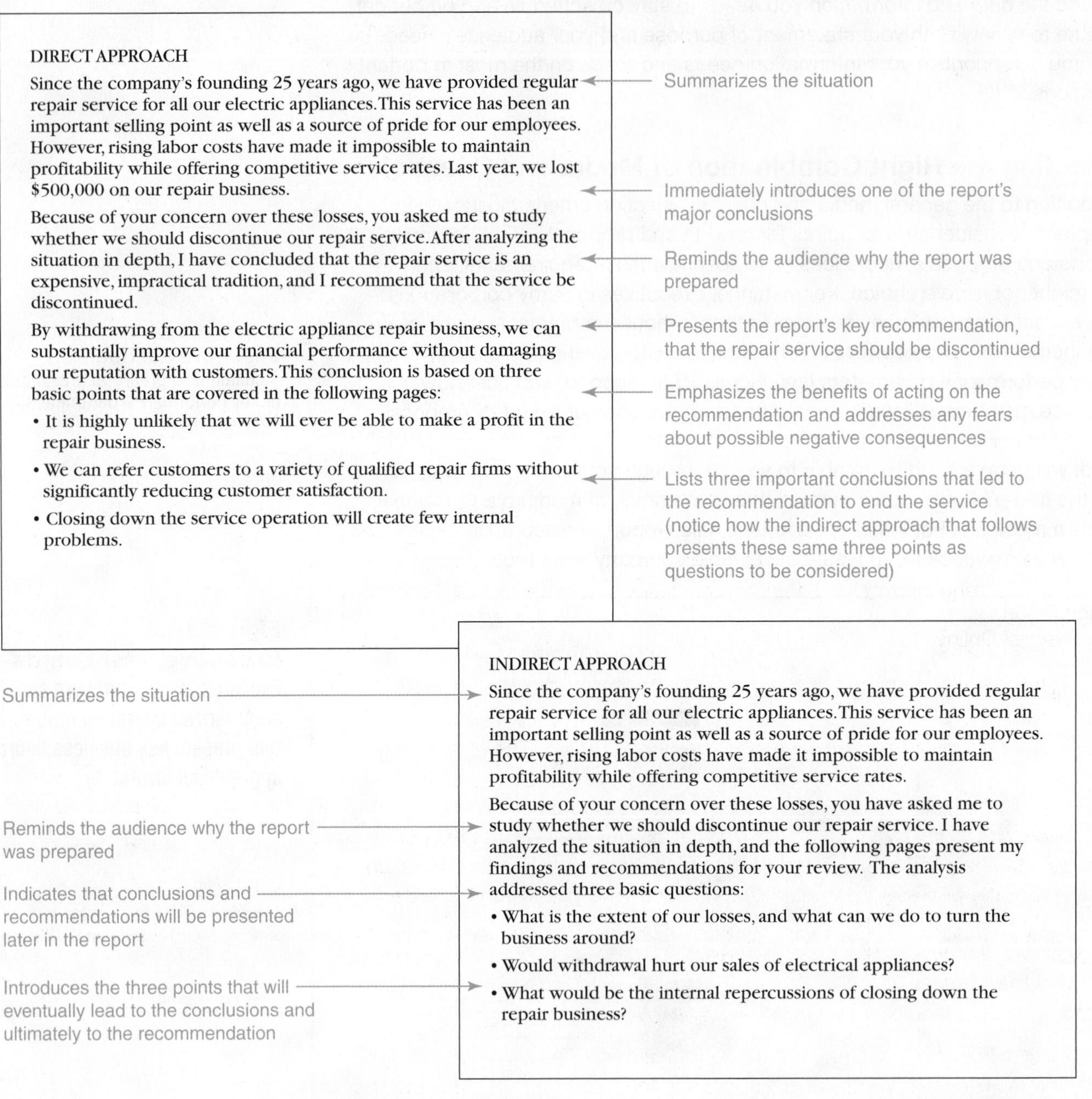

Figure 10.4

Direct Approach Versus Indirect Approach in an Introduction

In the direct version of this introduction, the writer quickly presents the report's recommendation, followed by the conclusions that led to that recommendation. In the indirect version, the same topics are introduced in the same order, but no conclusions are drawn about them; the conclusions and the ultimate recommendation appear later, in the body of the report.

If the audience is unsure about your credibility or is not ready to accept your main idea without first seeing some reasoning or evidence, the indirect approach is a better choice because it gives you a chance to prove your points and gradually overcome audience reservations. To enable the use of AIDA-style persuasion, unsolicited proposals in particular often use the indirect approach. Bear in mind, though, that the longer the document, the less effective the indirect approach is likely to be.

Supporting Your Messages with Reliable Information

Effective research involves a lot more than simply typing a few terms into a search engine. Save time and get better results by using a clear process:

1. **Plan your research.** Planning is the most important step of any research project; a solid plan yields better results in less time.
2. **Locate the data and information you need.** Figure out where the data and information are and how to access them.
3. **Process the data and information you located.** The data and information you find probably won't be in a form you can use immediately and may require statistical analysis or other processing.
4. **Apply your findings.** You can apply your research findings in three ways: summarizing information, drawing conclusions, and developing recommendations.
5. **Manage information efficiently.** Many companies strive to maximize the return on the time and money invested in business research by collecting and sharing research results in a variety of computer-based systems, known generally as **knowledge management systems**.

Knowledge management system: A computer-based system for collecting and sharing research results.

Planning Your Research

Start by developing a **problem statement** that defines the purpose of your research—the decision you need to make or the conclusion you need to reach at the end of the process. Next, identify the information you need to in order to make that decision or reach that conclusion. You can then begin to generate the questions that will constitute your research. Chances are you will have more questions than you have time or money to answer, so prioritize your information needs.

Problem statement: A statement of the decision you need to make or the conclusion you need to reach.

Before any research project, remember that research carries significant ethical responsibilities. Your research tactics affect the people you gather data and information from, the people who read your results, and the people who are affected by the way you present those results. To avoid ethical lapses, follow these guidelines:

- Keep an open mind so that you don't skew the research toward answers you want or expect to see.
- Respect the privacy of your research participants, and don't mislead people about the purposes of your research.

- Document sources and give appropriate credit.
- Respect your sources' *intellectual property rights* (the ownership of unique ideas that have commercial value in the marketplace).
- Don't distort information from your sources.
- Don't misrepresent who you are or what you intend to do with the research results.

In addition to ethics, research etiquette deserves careful attention. For example, respect the time of anyone who agrees to be interviewed or to be a research participant, and maintain courtesy throughout the interview or research process.

Locating Data and Information

The range of sources available to business researchers today can be overwhelming. The good news is that if you have a question about an industry, a company, a market, a new technology, or a financial topic, somebody else has probably already researched the subject. Research done previously for another purpose is considered **secondary research**; sources for such research information include magazines, newspapers, public websites, books, and other reports. Don't let the name *secondary* fool you, though. You want to start with secondary research because it can save you considerable time and money for many projects. In contrast, **primary research** involves the collection of new data through surveys, interviews, and other techniques.

Secondary research: Research that someone else has already collected and made available.

Primary research: The collection of new data through surveys, interviews, and other techniques.

Evaluating Information Sources

The process of analyzing primary and secondary sources is important. It is your responsibility to separate quality information from unreliable junk so that you don't taint your results, damage your reputation, or deliver incorrect information in a presentation, whether formal or informal. Social media tools have complicated this challenge by making many new sources of information available. On the positive side, independent sources communicating through blogs, Twitter and other microblogging sites, wikis, user-generated content sites, and podcasting channels can provide valuable and unique insights, including input from experts whose voices might never be heard otherwise. On the negative side, these nontraditional information sources often lack the editorial boards and fact checkers commonly used in traditional publishing. You cannot assume that the information you find in blogs and other sources is accurate, objective, and current. Answer the following questions about each piece of material:

- Does the source have a reputation for honesty and reliability? For example, try to find out how the source accepts articles and whether it has an editorial board, conducts peer reviews, or follows fact-checking procedures.
- Is the source potentially biased? To interpret an organization's information, you need to know its point of view.
- What is the purpose of the material? For instance, was the material designed to inform others of new research, to advance a political position,

or to promote a product?

- Is the author credible? Is the author a professional journalist or merely someone with an opinion?
- Where did the source get its information? Try to find out who collected the data and the methods used.
- Can you verify the material independently? Verification is particularly important when the information goes beyond simple facts to include projections, interpretations, and estimates.
- Is the material current and complete? Make sure you are using the most current information available. Have you accessed the entire document or only a selection from it?
- Does the information make sense? Step back and determine whether the information stands up to logical scrutiny.

You probably won't have time to conduct a thorough background check on all your sources, so focus your efforts on the most important or most suspicious pieces of information. And if you can't verify critical facts or figures, be sure to let your readers know that.

Using Your Research Results

After you've collected your data and information, the next step is to transform this raw material into the specific content you need. This step can involve quoting, paraphrasing, or summarizing textual material; drawing conclusions; and making recommendations.

Quoting, Paraphrasing, and Summarizing Information

You can use textual information from secondary sources in three ways. *Quoting* a source means you reproduce the material exactly as you found it (giving full credit to the source, of course). Use direct quotations when the original language will enhance your argument or when rewording the passage would reduce its impact. However, be careful with direct quotes: using too many creates a choppy patchwork of varying styles and gives the impression that all you've done is piece together the work of other people. When quoting sources, set off longer passages (generally, five lines or more) as separate, indented paragraphs.

You can often maximize the impact of secondary material in your own writing by *paraphrasing* it: restating it in your own words and with your own sentence structures. Paraphrasing helps you maintain consistent tone while using vocabulary that's familiar to your audience. Of course, you still need to credit the originator of the information, but you don't need quotation marks or indented paragraphs.

Summarizing is similar to paraphrasing but presents the gist of the material in fewer words than the original by leaving out details, examples, and less important information (see Figure 10.5). Like quoting and paraphrasing, summarizing also requires complete documentation of sources. Summarizing is not always a simple task, and your audience will judge your ability to separate significant issues from less significant details.

Original: 116 words

Our facilities costs spiraled out of control last year. The 23 percent jump was far ahead of every other cost category in the company and many times higher than the 4 percent average rise for commercial real estate in the Portland metropolitan area. The rise can be attributed to many factors, but the major factors include repairs (mostly electrical and structural problems at the downtown office), energy (most of our offices are heated by electricity, the price of which has been increasing much faster than for oil or gas), and last but not least, the loss of two sublease tenants whose rent payments made a substantial dent in our cost profile for the past five years.

Analyze the text to find main idea, major supporting points, and details

Main idea → Our facilities costs spiraled out of control last year. The 23 percent jump

Major support points → was far ahead of every other cost category in the company and many times higher than the 4 percent average rise for commercial real estate in the Portland metropolitan area. The rise can be attributed to many factors, but the major factors include repairs (mostly electrical and structural problems at the downtown office), energy (most of our offices are heated by electricity, the price of which has

Details → been increasing much faster than for oil or gas), and last but not least, the loss of two sublease tenants whose rent payments made a substantial dent in our cost profile for the past five years.

45-word summary

Our facilities costs jumped 23 percent last year, far ahead of every other cost category in the company and many times higher than the 4 percent local average. The major factors contributing to the increase are repairs, energy, and the loss of two sublease tenants.

22-word summary

Our facilities costs jumped 23 percent last year, due mainly to rising repair and energy costs and the loss of sublease income.

Figure 10.5
Summarizing Effectively
To summarize a section of text, first analyze it to find the main idea, the major support points, and the less-important details. Then assemble the appropriate pieces with additional words and phrases as needed to ensure a smooth flow.

Plagiarism:
Presenting someone else's words or other creative product as your own.

Conclusion:
A logical interpretation of facts and other information.

Recommendation:
A suggestion about what to do with the available information.

Of course, all three approaches require careful attention to ethics. When quoting directly, take care not to distort the original intent of the material by quoting selectively or out of context. And never resort to **plagiarism**—presenting someone else's words as your own, such as copying material from an online source and dropping it into a report without giving proper credit.

Drawing Conclusions

A **conclusion** is a logical interpretation of facts and other information. In addition to being logically sound, a conclusion should be based only on the information provided or at least referred to in the report. Reaching good conclusions is one of the most important skills you can develop in your business career. In fact, the ability to see patterns and possibilities that others can't is one of the hallmarks of innovative business leaders.

Making Recommendations

Whereas a conclusion interprets information, a **recommendation** suggests what to do about the information. The following example shows the difference between a conclusion and a recommendation:

Conclusion	Recommendation
On the basis of its track record and current price, I believe that this company is an attractive buy.	I recommend that we offer to buy the company at a 10 percent premium over the current market value of its stock.

To be credible, recommendations must be practical and based on sound logical analysis. State your recommendation clearly so that readers aren't left wondering what happens next.

Conducting Secondary Research

Even if you intend to eventually conduct primary research, start with a review of any available secondary research. Inside your company, you might be able to find a variety of helpful reports and other documents. Outside the company, business researchers can choose from a wide range of print and online resources, both in libraries and online.

Finding Information at a Library

Figure 10.6
Library Research
Your school's library can provide access to a wide variety of resources, including books, magazines, audio and video recordings, and digital archives. Most cities also have public libraries that can also provide research materials.

Public, corporate, and school libraries offer printed sources with information that is not available online, as well as online sources that are available only by subscription. Libraries are also where you'll find one of your most important resources: librarians. Reference librarians are trained in research techniques and can often help you find obscure information you can't find on your own. They can also direct you to the typical library's many sources of business information:

- **Newspapers and periodicals.** Libraries offer access to a wide variety of popular magazines, general business magazines, trade journals (which provide information about specific professions and industries), and academic journals (which provide research-oriented articles from researchers and educators).
- **Business books.** Although less timely than newspapers, periodicals, and online sources, business books provide in-depth coverage and analysis that often can't be found anywhere else.
- **Directories.** Thousands of directories are published in print and digital formats in the United States, and many include membership information for all kinds of professions, industries, and special-interest groups.
- **Almanacs and statistical resources.** Almanacs are handy guides to factual and statistical information about countries, politics, the labor force, and so on. One of the most extensive is the *Statistical Abstract of the United States* (available online and in print).

- **Government publications.** You can often find information on laws, court decisions, tax questions, regulatory issues, and other governmental concerns in collections of government documents.
- **Databases.** Databases offer vast collections of computer-searchable information, often in specific areas such as business, law, science, technology, and education. Some of these are available only by institutional subscription, so the library may be your only way to gain access to them. Some libraries offer remote online access to some or all databases; for others, you'll need to visit in person.
- **Technical documentation.** A library may offer reference books that provide technical information about using and/or servicing specific products or general classes of products.

Finding Information Online

The Internet can be a tremendous source of business information, provided you know where to look and how to use the tools available. Roughly speaking, the tools fall into two categories: those you can use to actively search for existing information and those you can use to monitor selected sources for new information. (Some tools can perform both functions.)

Online Search Tools

The most familiar search tools are general-purpose search engines, such as Google and Bing. Search engines scan millions of websites to identify individual webpages that contain a specific word or phrase and then attempt to rank the results from most useful to least useful. Website owners use **search engine optimization** techniques to help boost their rankings in the results, but the ranking algorithms are kept secret to prevent unfair manipulation of the results.

Search engine optimization: Web development technique that increase a page's chance of being found by a search engine.

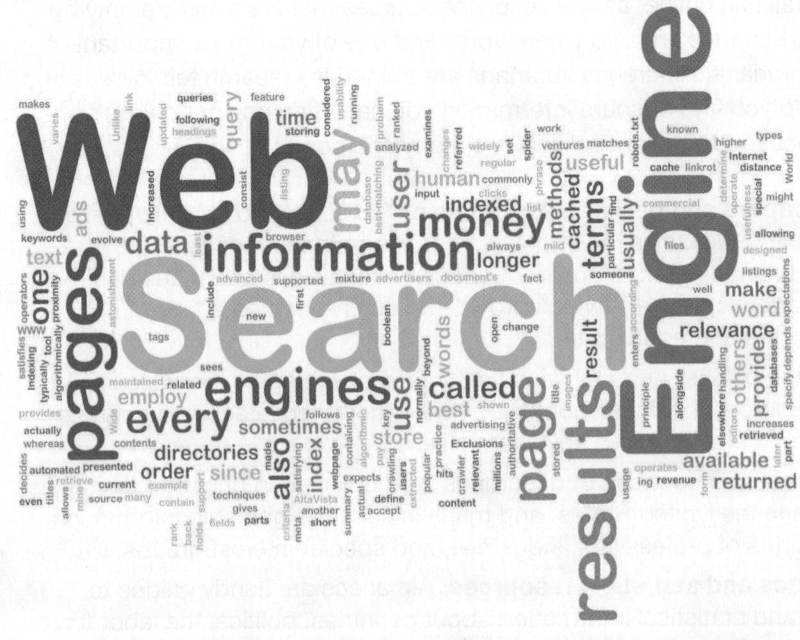

Figure 10.7
Online Research
A great deal of the information that is traditionally found in school and public libraries is also available online. By using both free and paid commercial research sources, you can find the sources you need without leaving your home or office.

For all their ease and power, conventional search engines have three primary shortcomings: no human editors are involved to evaluate the quality or ranking of the search results; various engines use different search techniques, so they often find different material; and search engines can't reach all the content on some websites. (This part of the internet is sometimes called the *hidden Internet*, the *invisible Internet*, and the *Dark Web*.)

A variety of tools can overcome these weaknesses of general-purpose search engines, and you should consider one or more of them in your business research. First, **web directories**, such as the Open Directory Project, use human editors to categorize and evaluate websites. A variety of other directories focus on specific media types, such as blogs or podcasts.

Web directory:
A searchable website database generated by human editors.

Second, **metasearch engines** help overcome the differences among search engines by formatting your search request for multiple search engines, making it easy to find a broader range of results. With a few clicks, you can compare results from multiple search engines to make sure you are getting a broad view of the material.

Metasearch engine:
A search engine that returns results from multiple databases.

Third, **online databases** help address the challenge of the hidden Internet by offering access to newspapers, magazines, journals, digital copies of books, and other resources often not available with standard search engines. Some of these databases offer free access to the public, but others require a subscription (check with your library). Also, a variety of specialized search engines now exist to reach various parts of the hidden Internet.

Online database:
A database of information stored on a web server and accessed online.

When appropriate, you may also want to reference online technical documentation. Such documentation is often in PDF format, rather than traditional web (HTML) format, so it may not appear in search results from search engines. One effective way to find such documentation is to visit the website of the product's manufacturer and look for a Support section of the website. There you may find a special version of a search engine that searches only that company's support documents. Look up a product by model number to locate its user manual, service manual, parts list, and other documents that may be of assistance to your project.

Online Monitoring Tools

One of the most powerful aspects of online research is the ability to automatically monitor selected sources for new information. The possibilities include subscribing to newsfeeds from blogs, following people on Twitter and other microblogs, setting up alerts on search engines and online databases, and using specialized monitors such as TweetBeep and TweetDeck to track tweets that mention specific companies or other terms.

Search Tips

Search engines, web directories, and databases work in different ways, so make sure you understand how to optimize your search and interpret the results for each tool you're using. With a **keyword search**, the engine or database attempts to find items that include all the words you enter. A **Boolean search** lets you define a query with greater precision, using such operators as AND (the search must include two terms linked by AND), OR (it can include either or both

Keyword search:
A search performed by entering one or more keywords related to the subject.

Boolean search:
A keyword search that combines terms with operators such as AND, OR, and NOT.

Natural language search: A search that accepts a question in everyday language as input.

Forms-based search: A search performed by completing an online form.

words), or NOT (the search ignores items with whatever word comes after NOT). **Natural language searches** let you ask questions in everyday English. **Forms-based searches** help you create powerful queries by simply filling out an online form.

To make the best use of any search tool, keep the following points in mind:

- **Think before you search.** The neatly organized results you get from a search engine can create the illusion that the Internet is an orderly warehouse of all the information in the universe, but the reality is far different. The Internet is an incomplete, unorganized hodge-podge of millions of independent websites with information that ranges in value from priceless to utter rubbish. After you have identified what you need to know, spend a few moments thinking about where that information might be found, how it might be structured, and what terms various websites might use to describe it.
- **Read instructions and pay attention to details.** A few minutes of learning can save hours of inefficient search time.
- **Review search and display options carefully** so you don't misinterpret the results; some of these settings can make a huge difference in the results you see.
- **Try variations of your terms**, such as *adolescent* and *teenager* or *management* and *managerial*.
- **User fewer search terms to find more results**; use more search terms to find fewer results.
- **Look beyond the first page of results.** Don't assume that the highest-ranking results are the best sources for you. For example, materials that haven't been optimized for search engines won't rank as highly (meaning they won't show up in the first few pages of results), but they may be far better for your purposes.

Search technologies continue to evolve rapidly, so look for new ways to find the information you need. Some new tools search specific areas of information (such as Twitter) in better ways, whereas others approach search in new ways. For instance, Yolink finds webpages like a regular search engine does but then also searches through documents and webpages that are linked to those first-level results.

Other powerful search tools include *desktop search engines* that search all the files on your personal computer, *enterprise search engines* that search all the computers on a company's network, *research and content managers* such as Zotero, *social tagging* or *bookmarking sites* such as Reddit, and media curation sites such as Pinterest and Scoop.it!.

Documenting Your Sources

Documentation gives readers the means for checking your findings and pursuing the subject further. Also, documenting your report is the accepted way to give credit to the people whose work you have drawn from.

Documentation is necessary for books, articles, tables, charts, diagrams, song lyrics, scripted dialog, letters, speeches—anything you take from someone else, including ideas and information you've re-expressed through paraphrasing or summarizing. However, you do not have to cite a source for knowledge that's generally known among your readers, such as the fact that Microsoft is a large software company or that computers are pervasive in business today.

What style should you use to document your report? Experts recommend various forms, depending on your field or discipline. Moreover, your employer or client may use a form different from those the experts suggest. Don't let this discrepancy confuse you. If your employer specifies a form, use it. If the choice of form is left to you, adopt one of the styles described here. Whatever style you choose, be consistent within any given report, using the same order, punctuation, and format from one reference citation or bibliography entry to the next.

A wide variety of style manuals provide detailed information on documentation. These publications explain the three most commonly used styles:

- American Psychological Association, *Publication Manual of the American Psychological Association*, 6th ed. (Washington, D.C.: American Psychological Association, 2009). Details the author-date system, which is preferred in the social sciences and often in the natural sciences as well.
- *The Chicago Manual of Style*, 16th ed. (Chicago: University of Chicago Press, 2010). Often referred to only as "Chicago" and widely used in the publishing industry; provides detailed treatment of source documentation and many other aspects of document preparation.
- Joseph Gibaldi, *MLA Style Manual and Guide to Scholarly Publishing*, 3rd ed. (New York: Modern Language Association, 2008). Serves as the basis for the note and bibliography style used in much academic writing and is recommended in many college textbooks on writing term papers; provides a lot of examples in the humanities.

All of these are simply different ways to arrange the same information: the author or authors of the work you used, the name of that work, the publisher, the publication date, and the relevant page range.

The following sections summarize the major conventions for documenting sources in three styles: *The Chicago Manual of Style* (Chicago), the *Publication Manual of the American Psychological Association* (APA), and the *MLA Style Manual* (MLA).

Figure 10.7
Documenting Your Sources
By providing information about your sources, you improve your own credibility as well as the credibility of the facts and opinions you present.

Chicago Humanities Style

The Chicago Manual of Style recommends two types of documentation systems. The *documentary-note system*, also called the *humanities* system gives bibliographic citations in notes—either footnotes (printed at the bottom of a page) or endnotes (printed at the end of the report). The humanities system is often used in literature, history, and the arts. The other system recommended by *Chicago* is the *author-date system*, which cites the author's last name and the date of publication in the text, usually in parentheses, reserving full documentation for the reference list or bibliography. This section concentrates on the humanities system, which is described in detail in *Chicago*.

In-Text Citation: Chicago Humanities Style

To document report sources in text, the humanities system relies on superscripts—Arabic numerals placed just above the line of type at the end of the reference:

> Toward the end of his speech, Myers sounded a note of caution, saying that even though the economy is expected to grow, it could easily slow a bit.[10]

The superscript lets the reader know to look for source information in either a footnote or an endnote. Some readers prefer footnotes so that they can simply glance at the bottom of the page for information. Others prefer endnotes so that they can read the primary text without a clutter of notes on the page (see Figure 10.8). Also, endnotes relieve the writer from worrying about how long each note will be and how much space it will take away from the page. Today's word processing software handles both footnotes and endnotes automatically.

NOTES

Journal article with volume and issue numbers

1. Jonathan Clifton, “Beyond Taxonomies of Influence,” *Journal of Business Communication* 46, no. 1 (2009): 57–79.

Brochure

2. BestTemp Staffing Services, *An Employer’s Guide to Staffing Services,* 2d ed. (Denver: BestTemp Information Center, 2014), 31.

Newspaper article, no author

3. “Might Be Harder Than It Looks,” *Los Angeles Times,* 30 January 2013, sec. A, p. 22.

Annual report

4. The Walt Disney Company, *2012 Annual Report* (Burbank, Calif.: The Walt Disney Company, 2013), 48.

Magazine article

5. Kerry A. Dolan, “A Whole New Crop” *Forbes*, 2 June 2013, 72–75.

Television broadcast

6. Daniel Han, “Trade Wars Heating Up Around the Globe,” *CNN Headline News* (Atlanta: CNN, 5 March 2013).

Internet, World Wide Web

7. “Intel—Company Capsule,” Hoover’s Online [cited 19 June 2011], 3 screens; available from www.hoovers.com/intel/-ID_13787-/free-co-factsheet.xhtml.

Book, component parts

8. Sonja Kuntz, “Moving Beyond Benefits,” in *Our Changing Workforce,* ed. Randolf Jacobson (New York: Citadel Press, 2001), 213–27.

Unpublished dissertation or thesis

9. George H. Morales, “The Economic Pressures on Industrialized Nations in a Global Economy” (Ph.D. diss., University of San Diego, 2001), 32–47.

Paper presented at a meeting

10. Charles Myers, “HMOs in Today’s Environment” (paper presented at the Conference on Medical Insurance Solutions, Chicago, Ill., August 2001), 16–17.

Online magazine article

11. Leo Babauta, “17 Tips to Be Productive with Instant Messaging,” in *Web Worker Daily* [online] (San Francisco, 2011 [updated 14 November 2012; cited 14 February 2013]); available from http://webworkerdaily.com.

Interview

12. Georgia Stainer, general manager, Day Cable and Communications, interview by author, Topeka, Kan., 2 March 2011.

Newspaper article, one author

13. Evelyn Standish, “Global Market Crushes OPEC’s Delicate Balance of Interests,” *Wall Street Journal,* 19 January 2002, sec. A, p. 1.

Book, two authors

14. Miriam Toller and Jay Fielding, *Global Business for Smaller Companies* (Rocklin, Calif.: Prima Publishing, 2001), 102–3.

Government publication

15. U.S. Department of Defense, *Stretching Research Dollars: Survival Advice for Universities and Government Labs* (Washington, D.C.: GPO, 2002), 126.

Figure 10.8
Sample Endnotes: *Chicago* Humanities Style

For the reader's convenience, you can use footnotes for content notes that supplement your main text with asides about a particular issue or event, provide a cross-reference to another section of your report, or direct the reader to a related source. Then you can use endnotes for source notes, which document direct quotations, paraphrased passages, and visual aids. Consider which type of note is most common in your report, and then choose whether to present these notes all as endnotes or all as footnotes. Regardless of the method you choose, all, notes for visual aids are placed on the same page as the visual.

Bibliography: Chicago Humanities Style

The humanities system may or may not be accompanied by a bibliography, because the notes give all the necessary bibliographic information. However, endnotes are arranged in order of appearance in the text, so an alphabetical bibliography can be valuable to your readers. The bibliography may be titled *Bibliography, Reference List, Sources, Works Cited* (if you include only those sources you actually cited in your report), or *Works Consulted* (if you include uncited sources as well). This list of sources may also serve as a reading list for those who want to pursue the subject of your report further, so you may want to annotate each entry—that is, comment on the subject matter and viewpoint of the source, as well as on its usefulness to readers. Annotations may be written in either complete or incomplete sentences. You may choose to classify your bibliography, which means divide it into categories, either by type of reference or by subject matter. Following are the major conventions for developing a bibliography according to Chicago style (see Figure 10.9):

- Exclude any page numbers that may be cited in source notes, except for journals, periodicals, and newspapers.
- Alphabetize entries by the last name of the lead author (listing last name first). The names of second and succeeding authors are listed in normal order. Entries without an author name are alphabetized by the first important word in the title.
- Format entries as hanging indents (indent second and succeeding lines three to five spaces).
- Arrange entries in the following general order: author name, title information, publication information, date, periodical page range.
- Use quotation marks around the titles of articles from magazines, newspapers, and journals. Capitalize the first and last words, as well as all other important words (except prepositions, articles, and coordinating conjunctions).
- Use italics to set off the names of books, newspapers, journals, and other complete publications. Capitalize the first and last words, as well as all other important words.
- For journal articles, include the volume number and the issue number (if necessary). Include the year of publication inside parentheses and follow with a colon and the page range of the article: *Journal of Business Communication* 46, no. 1 (2009): 57–79. (In this source, the volume is 46, the number is 1, and the page range is 57–79.)

BIBLIOGRAPHY

Online magazine article	Babauta, Leo. "17 Tips to Be Productive with Instant Messaging," In *Web Worker Daily* [online], San Francisco, 2011 [updated 14 November 2012, cited 14 February 2013]. Available from http://webworkerdaily.com.
Brochure	BestTemp Staffing Services. *An Employer's Guide to Staffing Services.* 2d ed. Denver: BestTemp Information Center, 2014.
Journal article with volume and issue numbers	Clifton, Jonathan. "Beyond Taxonomies of Influence." *Journal of Business Communication* 46, no. 1 (2009): 57–79.
Magazine article	Dolan, Kerry A. "A Whole New Crop," *Forbes*, 2 June 2013, 72–75.
Television broadcast	Han, Daniel. "Trade Wars Heating Up Around the Globe." *CNN Headline News.* Atlanta: CNN, 5 March 2013.
Internet, World Wide Web	"Intel—Company Capsule." *Hoover's Online* [cited 19 June 2011]. 3 screens; Available from www.hoovers.com/intel/-ID_13787-/free-co-factsheet.xhtml.
Book, component parts	Kuntz, Sonja. "Moving Beyond Benefits." In *Our Changing Workforce*, edited by Randolf Jacobson. New York: Citadel Press, 2001.
Newspaper article, no author	"Might Be Harder Than It Looks." *Los Angeles Times,* 30 January 2013, sec. A, p. 22.
Unpublished dissertation or thesis	Morales, George H. "The Economic Pressures on Industrialized Nations in a Global Economy." Ph.D. diss., University of San Diego, 2001.
Paper presented at a meeting	Myers, Charles. "HMOs in Today's Environment." Paper presented at the Conference on Medical Insurance Solutions, Chicago, Ill., August 2001.
Interview	Stainer, Georgia, general manager, Day Cable and Communications. Interview by author. Topeka, Kan., 2 March 2011.
Newspaper article, one author	Standish, Evelyn. "Global Market Crushes OPEC's Delicate Balance of Interests." *Wall Street Journal,* 19 January 2002, sec. A, p. 1.
Book, two authors	Toller, Miriam, and Jay Fielding. *Global Business for Smaller Companies.* Rocklin, Calif.: Prima Publishing, 2001.
Government publication	U.S. Department of Defense. *Stretching Research Dollars: Survival Advice for Universities and Government Labs.* Washington, D.C.: GPO, 2002.
Annual report	The Walt Disney Company, *2012 Annual Report,* Burbank, Calif.: The Walt Disney Company, 2013.

Figure 10.9 Sample Bibliography: *Chicago* Humanities Style

- Use brackets to identify all electronic references: [Online database] or [CD-ROM].
- Explain how electronic references can be reached: Available from www.spaceless.com.
- Give the citation date for online references: Cited 23 August 2016.

APA Style

The *American Psychological Association* (APA) recommends the author-date system of documentation, which is popular in the physical, natural, and social sciences. When using this system, you simply insert the author's last name into the text discussion of the material cited. Include a page number if you use a direct quotation. This approach briefly identifies the source so that readers can locate complete information in the alphabetical reference list at the end of the report. The author-date system is both brief and clear, saving readers time and effort.

In-Text Citation: APA Style

To document report sources in text using APA style, insert the author's surname and the date of publication at the end of a statement. Enclose this information in parentheses. If the author's name is referred to in the text itself, then the name can be omitted from parenthetical material.

> Some experts recommend both translation and backtranslation when dealing with any non-English-speaking culture (Clifton, 2009).
>
> Toller and Fielding (2001) make a strong case for small companies succeeding in global business.

Personal communications and interviews conducted by the author would not be listed in the reference list at all. Such citations would appear in the text only.

> Increasing the role of cable companies is high on the list of Georgia Stainer, general manager at Day Cable and Communications (personal communication, March 2, 2011).

List of References: APA Style

For APA style, list only those works you actually cite in the text, not those for background or further reading. Following are the major conventions for developing a reference list according to APA style (see Figure 10.10):

- Format entries as hanging indents.
- List all author names in reversed order (last name first), and use only initials for the first and middle names.
- Arrange entries in the following general order: author name, date, title information, publication information, periodical page range.
- Follow the author name with the date of publication in parentheses.
- List titles of articles from magazines, newspapers, and journals without underlines or quotation marks. Capitalize only the first word of the title, any proper nouns, and the first word to follow an internal colon.
- Italicize titles of books, capitalizing only the first word, any proper nouns, and the first word to follow a colon.
- Italicize titles of magazines, newspapers, journals, and other complete publications. Capitalize all the important words in the title.

REFERENCES

Online magazine article	Babauta, L. (2007, November 14). 17 tips to be productive with instant messaging. *Web Worker Daily*. Retrieved from http://webworkerdaily.com
Brochure	BestTemp Staffing Services. (2014). *An employer's guide to staffing services* (2nd ed.) [Brochure]. Denver, CO: BestTemp Information Center.
Journal article with volume and issue numbers	Clifton, J. (2009). Beyond taxonomies of influence. *Journal of Business Communication, 46*(1), 57.
Magazine article	Dolan, K. A. (2013, June 2). A whole new crop. *Forbes*, 72–75.
Television broadcast	Han, D. (2013, March 5). Trade wars heating up around the globe. *CNN Headline News* [Television broadcast]. Atlanta, GA: CNN.
Internet, World Wide Web	Hoover's Online. (2011). *Intel—company capsule*. Retrieved from http://www.hoovers.com/intel/-ID_13787-/free-co-factsheet.xhtml
Book, component parts	Kuntz, S. (2001). Moving beyond benefits. In Randolph Jacobson (Ed.), *Our changing workforce* (pp. 213–227). New York, NY: Citadel Press.
Newspaper article, no author	Might be harder than it looks. (2013, January 30). *Los Angeles Times,* p. A22.
Unpublished dissertation or thesis	Morales, G. H. (2001). *The economic pressures on industrialized nations in a global economy*. Unpublished doctoral dissertation, University of San Diego.
Paper presented at a meeting	Myers, C. (2001, August). *HMOs in today's environment*. Paper presented at the Conference on Medical Insurance Solutions, Chicago, IL.
Interview	*Cited in text only, not in the list of references.*
Newspaper article, one author	Standish, E. (2002, January 19). Global market crushes OPEC's delicate balance of interests. *Wall Street Journal*, p. A1.
Book, two authors	Toller, M., & Fielding, J. (2001). *Global business for smaller companies*. Rocklin, CA: Prima Publishing.
Government publication	U.S. Department of Defense. (2002). *Stretching research dollars: Survival advice for universities and government labs*. Washington, DC: U.S. Government Printing Office.
Annual report	The Walt Disney Company. (2013). *2012 Annual report,* Burbank, CA: The Walt Disney Company.

Figure 10.10 Sample Reference: APA Style

- For journal articles, include the volume number (in italics) and, if necessary, the issue number (in parentheses). Include the page range of the article: *Journal of Business Communication*, 46(1), 57–79. (In this example, the volume is 46, the number is 1, and the page range is 57–79.)
- Include personal communications (such as letters, memos, email, and conversations) only in text, not in reference lists.
- Electronic references include author, date of publication, title of article, name of publication, volume, date of retrieval (month, day, year), and the source.
- Use the abbreviation *n.d.* for any source that shows no publication date.
- For webpages with extremely long URLs, use your best judgment to determine which URL from the site to use. For example, rather than giving the URL of a specific news release with a long URL, you can provide the URL of the "Media relations" webpage.
- APA citation guidelines for social media are still evolving. For the latest information, visit the APA Style Blog.
- For online journals or periodicals that assign a digital object identifier (DOI), include that instead of a conventional URL. If no DOI is available, include the URL of the publication's home page.

MLA Style

The style recommended by the *Modern Language Association of America* is used widely in the humanities, especially in the study of language and literature. Like APA style, MLA style uses brief parenthetical citations in the text. Instead of including author name and year, however, MLA citations include author name and page reference.

In-Text Citation: MLA Style

To document report sources in text using MLA style, insert the author's last name and a page reference inside parentheses following the cited material: (Matthews 63). If the author's name is mentioned in the text reference, the name can be omitted from the parenthetical citation: (63). The citation indicates that the reference came from page 63 of a work by Matthews. With the author's name, readers can find complete publication information in the alphabetically arranged list of works cited that comes at the end of the report.

List of Works Cited: MLA Style

> Some experts recommend both translation and backtranslation when dealing with any non-English-speaking culture (Clifton 57).
>
> Toller and Fielding make a strong case for small companies succeeding in global business (102–03).

The *MLA Style Manual* recommends preparing the list of works cited first so that you will know what information to give in the parenthetical citation (for example, whether to add a short title if you're citing more than one work by the same author, or whether to give an initial or first name if you're citing two authors who have the same last name). The list of works cited appears at the end of your report, contains all the works that you cite in your text, and lists them in alphabetical order. Following are the major conventions for developing a reference list according to MLA style (see Figure 10.11):

WORKS CITED

Source type	Entry
Online magazine article	Babauta, Leo. "17 Tips to Be Productive with Instant Messaging," *Web Worker Daily* 14 Nov. 2012. 14 Feb. 2013. http://webworkerdaily.com
Brochure	BestTemp Staffing Services. *An Employer's Guide to Staffing Services*. 2d ed. Denver: BestTemp Information Center, 2014.
Journal article with volume and issue numbers	Clifton, Jonathan. "Beyond Taxonomies of Influence." *Journal of Business Communication* 46, 1 (2009): 57–79.
Magazine article	Dolan, Kerry A. "A Whole New Crop" *Forbes*, 2 June 2013: 72–75.
Television broadcast	Han, Daniel. "Trade Wars Heating Up Around the Globe." *CNN Headline News*. CNN, Atlanta. 5 Mar. 2013.
Internet, World Wide Web	"Intel—Company Capsule." *Hoover's Online*. 2011. Hoover's Company Information. 19 June 2011 http://www.hoovers.com/intel/-ID_13787/free-co-factsheet.xhtml
Book, component parts	Kuntz, Sonja. "Moving Beyond Benefits." *Our Changing Workforce*. Ed. Randolf Jacobson. New York: Citadel Press, 2001. 213–27.
Newspaper article, no author	"Might Be Harder Than It Looks." *Los Angeles Times*, 30 Jan. 2013: A22.
Unpublished dissertation or thesis	Morales, George H. "The Economic Pressures on Industrialized Nations in a Global Economy." Diss. U of San Diego, 2001.
Paper presented at a meeting	Myers, Charles. "HMOs in Today's Environment." Conference on Medical Insurance Solutions. Chicago. 13 Aug. 2001.
Interview	Stainer, Georgia, general manager, Day Cable and Communications. Telephone interview. 2 Mar. 2011.
Newspaper article, one author	Standish, Evelyn. "Global Market Crushes OPEC's Delicate Balance of Interests." *Wall Street Journal*, 19 Jan. 2002: A1.
Book, two authors	Toller, Miriam, and Jay Fielding. *Global Business for Smaller Companies*. Rocklin, CA: Prima Publishing, 2001.
Government publication	United States. Department of Defense. *Stretching Research Dollars: Survival Advice for Universities and Government Labs*. Washington: GPO, 2002.
Annual report	The Walt Disney Company, *2012 Annual Report*. Burbank, Calif.: The Walt Disney Company, 2013.

Figure 10.11 Sample Works Cited: MLA Style

- Format entries as hanging indents.
- Arrange entries in the following general order: author name, title information, publication information, date (or n.d. if no publication date is provided), periodical page range.

- List the lead author's name in reverse order (last name first), using either full first names or initials. List second and succeeding author names in normal order.
- Use quotation marks around the titles of articles from magazines, newspapers, and journals. Capitalize all important words.
- Italicize the names of books, newspapers, journals, and other complete publications, capitalizing all main words in the title.
- For journal articles, include the volume number and the issue number (if necessary). Include the year of publication inside parentheses and follow with a colon and the page range of the article: *Journal of Business Communication* 46, 1 (2009): 57. (In this source, the volume is 46, the number is 1, and the page is 57.)
- Electronic sources and their online addresses often change; a link you include today may not work in a month. Include enough additional information for your reader to find your in the event of a broken link.
- The date for electronic sources should contain both the date assigned in the source and the date accessed by the researcher.
- The URL for electronic sources must be as accurate and complete as possible, from access-mode identifier (such as http or ftp) to all relevant directory and file names. If the URL is extremely long, use the URL of the website's home page or the URL of the site's search page if you used the site's search function to find the article. The *MLA Style Manual* no longer requires writers to include URLs for materials retrieved online. However, follow whatever guidelines your instructor gives you in this regard.
- MLA style requires you to indicate the medium of publication. For most sources, this will be "Web" or "Print," but you may also cite "CD-ROM" and other media, as appropriate.

Conducting Primary Research

If secondary research can't provide the information and insights you need, you may need to gather the information with primary research. The two most common primary research methods for report writing are surveys and interviews. Other primary techniques are observations (including tracking the behavior of website visitors) and experiments (in special situations such as test marketing), but they're less commonly used for day-to-day business research.

Conducting Surveys

Surveys can provide invaluable insights, but only if they are *reliable* (would produce identical results if repeated under similar conditions) and *valid* (measure what they're supposed to measure). To conduct a survey that generates reliable and valid results, you need to choose research participants carefully and develop an effective set of questions. For surveys on strategically important topics with lots at stake, you're usually better off hiring a research specialist who knows how to avoid errors during planning, execution, and analysis. To develop an effective survey questionnaire, follow these tips:

- Provide clear instructions to make sure people can answer every question correctly.

- Don't ask for information that people can't be expected to remember, such as how many times they went grocery shopping in the past year.
- Keep the questionnaire short and easy to answer; don't expect people to give you more than 10 or 15 minutes of their time.
- Whenever possible, formulate questions to provide answers that are easy to analyze. Numbers and facts are easier to summarize than opinions, for instance.
- Avoid leading questions that could bias your survey. If you ask, "Do you prefer that we stay open in the evenings for customer convenience?" you'll no doubt get a "yes." Instead, ask, "What time of day do you normally do your shopping?"
- Avoid ambiguous descriptors such as "often" or "frequently." Such terms mean different things to different people.
- Avoid compound questions such as "Do you read books and magazines?"

When selecting people to participate in a survey, the most critical task is getting a **representative sample** of the entire population in question. For instance, if you want to know how US consumers feel about something, you can't just survey a few hundred people in a shopping mall. Different types of consumers shop at different times of the day and different days of the week, and many consumers rarely, if ever, shop at malls. The online surveys you see on many websites potentially suffer from the same **sampling bias**: they capture only the opinions of people who visit the sites and who want to participate, which might not be a representative sample of the population. A good handbook on survey research will help you select the right people for your survey, including selecting enough people to have a statistically valid survey.

Representative sample:
A sample that fairly represents the group you are trying to survey.

Sampling bias:
The tendency of a survey to capture only the opinions of people who are available and willing to be surveyed.

Conducting Interviews

Getting in-depth information straight from an expert, customer, or other interested party can be a great method for collecting primary information. Interviews can have a variety of formats, from email exchanges to group discussions.

Ask **open-ended questions** (such as "Why do you believe that South America represents a better opportunity than Europe for this product line?") to solicit opinions, insights, and information. Ask **closed questions** to elicit a specific answer, such as yes or no. However, don't use too many closed questions in an interview, or the experience will feel more like a simple survey and won't take full advantage of the interactive interview setting.

Open-ended question:
A question that is intentionally broad or vague in scope, designed to elicit creative answers.

Closed question:
A question that is designed to elicit a specific narrow range of answers, such as *Yes* or *No*.

Think carefully about the sequence of your questions and the potential answers so you can arrange them in an order that helps uncover layers of information. Also consider providing each subject with a list of questions at least a day or two before the interview, especially if you'd like to quote your subjects in writing or if your questions might require people to conduct research or think extensively about the answers. If you want to record interviews, ask ahead of time; never record without permission.

Planning Informational Reports

Informational reports provide the feedback that employees, managers, and others need to make decisions, take action, and respond to changes. As Figure 10.1 on page 316 indicates, informational reports can be grouped into four general categories:

- **Reports to monitor and control operations.** Managers rely on a wide range of reports to see how well their companies are functioning. *Plans* establish expectations and guidelines to direct future action. Among the most important of these are *business plans*, which summarize a proposed business venture and describe the company's goals and plans for each major functional area. *Operating reports* provide feedback on a wide variety of an organization's functions, including sales, inventories, expenses, shipments, and so on. *Personal activity* reports provide information regarding an individual's experiences during sales calls, industry conferences, and other activities.
- **Reports to implement policies and procedures.** *Policy reports* range from brief descriptions of business procedures to manuals that run dozens or hundreds of pages. *Position papers*, sometimes called *white papers* or *backgrounders*, outline an organization's official position on issues that affect the company's success.
- **Reports to demonstrate compliance.** Businesses are required to submit a variety of *compliance reports*, from tax returns to reports describing the proper handling of hazardous materials.
- **Reports to document progress.** Supervisors, investors, and customers frequently expect to be informed of the progress of projects and other activities. *Progress reports* range from simple updates in memo form to comprehensive status reports.

Organizing Informational Reports and Technical Documentation

In most cases, the direct approach is the best choice for informational reports and technical documentation because you are simply conveying information. For example, technical documentation for a company's newest product might include sections such as setting up the product, using the product, maintaining the product, and troubleshooting the product. However, if the information is disappointing, indicating that the project is behind schedule or over budget, you might consider using the indirect approach to build up to the bad news.

Most informational reports use a **topical organization**, arranging material in one of the following ways:

Topical organization:
A direct type of organization that arranges material into logical topics or groupings.

- **Comparison.** Showing similarities and differences (or advantages and disadvantages) between two or more entities
- **Importance.** Building up from the least important item to the most important (or from most important to the least, if you don't think your audience will read the entire report)
- **Sequence.** Organizing the steps or stages in a process or procedure
- **Typical Order of Usage.** Organizing topics in the order in which most people will want to reference them.
- **Chronology.** Organizing a chain of events in order from oldest to newest or vice versa

- **Geography.** Organizing by region, city, state, country, or other geographic unit
- **Category.** Grouping by topical category, such as sales, profit, cost, or investment

When developing technical documents such as a manual or informational reference guide, it is important to analyze the audience, their needs, and level of understanding on the subject.

Organizing Website Content

Many websites, particularly company websites, function as informational reports, offering sections with information about the company and its history, products and services, executive team, and so on. Most of what you've already learned about informational reports applies to website writing, but the online environment requires some special considerations:

- **Web readers are demanding.** If they can't find what they're looking for in a few minutes, most site visitors will click away to another site.
- **Reading online can be difficult.** Studies show that reading speeds are about 25 percent slower on a monitor than on paper. Reading from computer screens can also be exhausting and a source of physical discomfort.
- **The web is a nonlinear, multidimensional medium.** Readers of online material move around in any order they please; there often is no beginning, middle, or end.

In addition, many websites have to perform more than one communication function and have more than one purpose. Each of these individual purposes needs to be carefully defined and then integrated into an overall statement of purpose for the entire website.

Moreover, many websites also have multiple target audiences, such as potential employees, customers, investors, and the news media. You need to analyze each group's unique information needs and find a logical way to organize all that material. Website designers use the term **information architecture** to describe the structure and navigational flow of all the parts of a website. As you develop the site architecture, you can begin to simulate how various audiences will enter and explore the site. Accommodating multiple entry points is one of the most difficult tasks in site design.

Information architecture: The structure and navigational flow of all parts of a website.

To organize your site effectively, keep the following advice in mind:

- If you know that a sizable percentage of your target audience will access your site with mobile devices, take a *mobile-first* approach: design the site to work with tablets and smartphones, then make sure it functions well on conventional computer screens as well.
- Plan your site structure and navigation before you write.
- Let your readers be in control by creating links and pathways that let them explore on their own.
- Help online readers scan and absorb information by breaking it into self-contained, easily readable chunks that are linked together logically.

Planning Analytical Reports

The purpose of analytical reports is to analyze, to understand, or to explain—to think through a problem or an opportunity and explain how it affects an organization and how the organization should respond. In many cases, you'll also be expected to make a recommendation based on your analysis. As you saw in Figure 10.1, analytical reports fall into three basic categories:

- **Reports to assess opportunities.** Every business opportunity carries some degree of risk and requires a variety of decisions and actions to capitalize on the opportunity. You can use analytical reports to assess both risk and required decisions and actions. For instance, *market analysis reports* are used to judge the likelihood of success for new products or sales. *Due diligence reports* examine the financial aspects of a proposed decision, such as acquiring another company.
- **Reports to solve problems.** Managers often assign *troubleshooting reports* when they need to understand why something isn't working properly and how to fix it. A variation, the *failure analysis report*, studies events that happened in the past, with the hope of learning how to avoid similar failures in the future.
- **Reports to support decisions.** *Feasibility reports* explore the potential ramifications of a decision that managers are considering, and *justification reports* explain a decision that has already been made.

Writing analytical reports presents a greater challenge than writing informational reports, for three reasons. First, you're doing more than simply delivering information—you're also analyzing a situation and presenting your conclusions. Second, when your analysis is complete, you need to present your thinking in a compelling and persuasive manner. Third, analytical reports often convince other people to make significant financial and personnel decisions, and these reports carry the added responsibility of the consequences of such decisions.

Focusing on Conclusions

When planning reports for audiences that are likely to accept your conclusions—either because they've asked you to perform an analysis or they trust your judgment—consider using the direct approach, focusing immediately on your conclusions. This structure communicates the main idea quickly, but it does present some risks. Even if audiences trust your judgment, they may have questions about your data or the methods you used. Moreover, starting with a conclusion may create the impression that you have oversimplified the situation. To give readers the opportunity to explore the thinking behind your conclusion, support that conclusion with solid reasoning and evidence (see Figure 10.12).

Focusing on Recommendations

A slightly different approach is useful when your readers want to know what they ought to *do* in a given situation (as opposed to what they ought to conclude). The actions you want your readers to take become the main subdivisions of your report.

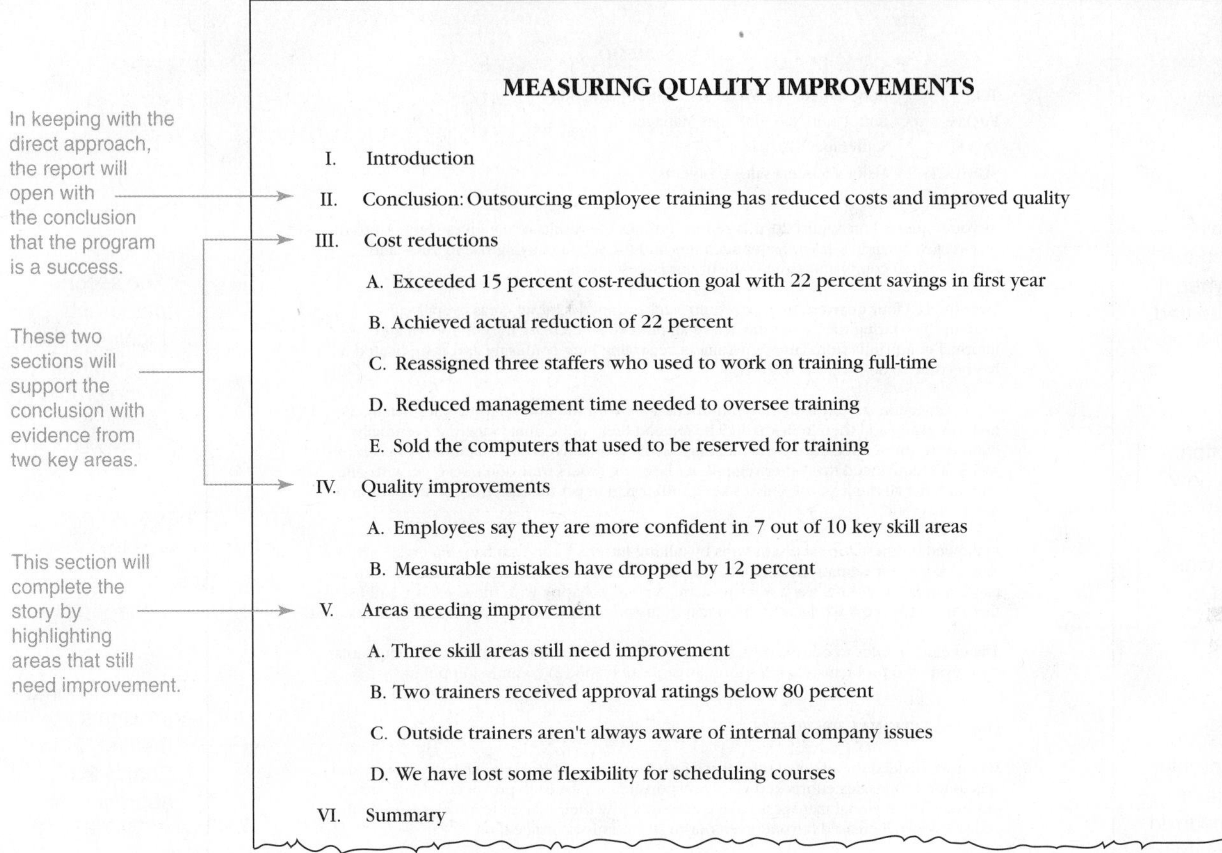

Figure 10.12 Preliminary Outline of a Research Report Focusing on Conclusions

A year after a bank decided to have an outside firm handle its employee training, an analyst was asked to prepare a report evaluating the results. The analysis shows that the outsourcing experiment was a success, so the report opens with that conclusion but supports it with clear evidence. Readers who accept the conclusion can stop reading, and those who desire more information can continue with solid reasoning and evidence.

When structuring a report around recommendations, use the direct approach, as you would for a report that focuses on conclusions. Then unfold your recommendations using a series of five steps:

1. Establish the need for action in the introduction by briefly describing the problem or opportunity.
2. Introduce the benefit(s) that can be achieved if the recommendation is adopted, along with any potential risks.
3. List the steps (recommendations) required to achieve the benefit, using action verbs for emphasis.
4. Explain each step more fully, giving details on procedures, costs, and benefits; if necessary, also explain how risks can be minimized.
5. Summarize your recommendations.

Focusing on Logical Arguments

When readers are potentially skeptical or hostile, consider using the indirect approach to logically build toward your conclusion or recommendation. If you guide these readers along a rational path toward the answer, they are more likely to accept it when they encounter it. The two most common logical approaches are known as the *2 + 2 = 4 approach*, in which you convince readers by demonstrating that everything adds up to your conclusion, and the *yardstick approach*, in which you use a number of criteria to decide which option to select from two or more possibilities (see Figure 10.13).

MEMO

TO:	Robert Mendoza, Vice President of Marketing
FROM:	Binh Phan, National Sales Manager BP
DATE:	September 12, 2016
SUBJECT:	Major accounts sales problems

The first paragraph verifies who requested the report, when it was requested, and who wrote it.

As you requested on August 20, this report outlines the results of my investigation into the recent slowdown in sales to major accounts and the accompanying rise in sales- and service-related complaints from some of our largest customers.

The second paragraph highlights the serious nature of the problem.

Over the last four quarters, major account sales dropped 12%, whereas overall sales were up 7%. During the same time, we've all noticed an increase in both formal and informal complaints from larger customers, regarding how confusing and complicated it has become to do business with us.

This section explains how the information used in the analysis was collected.

My investigation started with in-depth discussions with the four regional sales managers, first as a group and then individually. The tension I felt in the initial meeting eventually bubbled to the surface during my meetings with each manager. Staff members in each region are convinced that other regions are booking orders they don't deserve, with one region doing all the legwork only to see another region get the sale, the commission, and the quota credit.

I followed up these formal discussions by talking informally and exchanging email with several sales representatives from each region. Virtually everyone who is involved with our major national accounts has a story to share. No one is happy with the situation, and I sense that some reps are walking away from major customers because the process is so frustrating.

The decline in sales to our major national customers and the increase in their complaints stem from two problems: (1) sales force organization and (2) commission policy.

Organizational problems are the first "2" in Phan's 2 + 2 = 4 approach.

ORGANIZATIONAL PROBLEMS

Phan describes the first problem and explains how it occurred, without blaming anyone personally.

When we divided the national sales force into four geographical regions last year, the idea was to focus our sales efforts and clarify responsibilities for each prospective and current customer. The regional managers have gotten to know their market territories very well, and sales have increased beyond even our most optimistic projections.

However, while solving one problem, we have created another. In the past 12 to 18 months, several regional customers have grown to national status, and a few retailers have taken on (or expressed interest in) our products. As a result, a significant portion of both current sales and future opportunities lies with these large national accounts.

I uncovered more than a dozen cases in which sales representatives from two or more regions found themselves competing with each other by pursuing the same customers from different locations. Moreover, the complaints from our major accounts about overlapping or nonexistent account coverage are a direct result of the regional organization. In some cases, customers aren't sure which of our representatives they're supposed to call with problems and orders. In other cases, no one has been in contact with them for several months.

Figure 10.13
Analytical Report Focusing on Logical Arguments

As national sales manager of a New Hampshire sporting goods company, Binh Phan was concerned about his company's ability to sell to its largest customers. His boss, the vice president of marketing, shared these concerns and asked Phan to analyze the situation and recommend a solution. In this troubleshooting report, his main idea is that the company should establish separate sales teams for these major accounts, rather than continuing to service them through the company's four regional divisions. However, Phan knew his plan would be controversial because it required a big change in the company's organization and in the way sales reps are paid. His thinking had to be clear and easy to follow, so he focused on logical argumentation.

Phan brings the first problem to life by complementing the general description with a specific example.

2

For example, having retail outlets across the lower tier of the country, AmeriSport received pitches from reps out of our West, South, and East regions. Because our regional offices have a lot of negotiating freedom, the three were offering different prices. But all AmeriSport buying decisions were made at the Tampa headquarters, so all we did was confuse the customer. The irony of the current organization is that we're often giving our weakest selling and support efforts to the largest customers in the country.

Commission problems are the second "2" in Phan's 2 + 2 = 4 approach.

COMMISSION PROBLEMS

In discussing the second problem, he simplifies the reader's task by maintaining a parallel structure: a general description followed by a specific example.

The regional organization problems are compounded by the way we assign commissions and quota credit. Salespeople in one region can invest a lot of time in pursuing a sale, only to have the customer place the order in another region. So some sales rep in the second region ends up with the commission on a sale that was partly or even entirely earned by someone in the first region. Therefore, sales reps sometimes don't pursue leads in their regions, thinking that a rep in another region will get the commission.

For example, Athletic Express, with outlets in 35 states spread across all four regions, finally got so frustrated with us that the company president called our headquarters. Athletic Express has been trying to place a large order for tennis and golf accessories, but none of our local reps seem interested in paying attention. I spoke with the rep responsible for Nashville, where the company is headquartered, and asked her why she wasn't working the account more actively. Her explanation was that last time she got involved with Athletic Express, the order was actually placed from their L.A. regional office, and she didn't get any commission after more than two weeks of selling time.

Phan concludes the 2 + 2 = 4 approach: organizational problems + commission problems = the need for a new sales structure.

RECOMMENDATIONS

Our sales organization should reflect the nature of our customer base. To accomplish that goal, we need a group of reps who are free to pursue accounts across regional borders—and who are compensated fairly for their work. The most sensible answer is to establish a national account group. Any customers whose operations place them in more than one region would automatically be assigned to the national group.

He explains how his recommendation (a new organizational structure) will solve both problems.

In addition to solving the problem of competing sales efforts, the new structure will also largely eliminate the commission-splitting problem because regional reps will no longer invest time in prospects assigned to the national accounts team. However, we will need to find a fair way to compensate regional reps who are losing long-term customers to the national team. Some of these reps have invested years in developing customer relationships that will continue to yield sales well into the future, and everyone I talked to agrees that reps in these cases should receive some sort of compensation. Such a "transition commission" would also motivate the regional reps to help ensure a smooth transition from one sales group to the other. The exact nature of this compensation would need to be worked out with the various sales managers.

He acknowledges that the recommended solution does create a temporary compensation problem but expresses confidence that a solution to that can be worked out.

3

SUMMARY

The summary concisely restates both the problem and the recommended solution.

The regional sales organization is effective at the regional and local levels but not at the national level. We should establish a national accounts group to handle sales that cross regional boundaries. Then we'll have one set of reps who are focused on the local and regional levels and another set who are pursuing national accounts.

To compensate regional reps who lose accounts to the national team, we will need to devise some sort of payment to reward them for the years of work invested in such accounts. This can be discussed with the sales managers once the new structure is in place.

Figure 10.13
Analytical Report Focusing on Logical Arguments (continued)

Planning Proposals

Proposals can be grouped into two general categories. *Internal proposals* (see Figure 10.14) request decisions from managers within the organization. *External proposals* request decisions from parties outside the organization. For example, *investment proposals* request funding from outside investors, *grant proposals* request funds from government agencies and other sponsoring organizations, and *sales proposals* present solutions for potential customers and request purchase decisions.

A subject line with a compelling promise catches the reader's attention.

"The Solution" explains the proposed solution in enough detail to make it convincing, without burdening the reader with excessive detail.

"The Problem" describes the current situation and explains why it should be fixed.

Listing a number of compelling benefits as subheadings builds reader interest in the proposed solution.

MEMO

TO: Jamie Engle
FROM: Shandel Cohen SC
DATE: July 8, 2016
SUBJECT: Saving $145k/year with an automated email response system

THE PROBLEM:
Expensive and Slow Response to Customer Information Requests

Our new product line has been very well received, and orders have surpassed our projections. This very success, however, has created a shortage of printed brochures, as well as considerable overtime for people in the customer response center. As we introduce upgrades and new options, our printed materials quickly become outdated. If we continue to rely on printed materials for customer information, we have two choices: Distribute existing materials (even though they are incomplete or inaccurate) or discard existing materials and print new ones.

THE SOLUTION:
Automated Email Response System

With minor additions and modifications to our current email system, we can set up an automated system to respond to customer requests for information. This system can save us time and money and can keep our distributed information current.

Automated email response systems have been tested and proven effective. Many companies already use this method to respond to customer information requests, so we won't have to worry about relying on untested technology. Using the system is easy, too: Customers simply send a blank email message to a specific address, and the system responds by sending an electronic copy of the requested brochure.

Benefit #1 : Always-Current Information

Rather than discard and print new materials, we would only need to keep the electronic files up to date on the server. We could be able to provide customers and our field sales organization with up-to-date, correct information as soon as the upgrades or options are available.

Benefit #2: Instantaneous Delivery

Almost immediately after requesting information, customers would have that information in hand. Electronic delivery would be especially advantageous for our international customers. Regular mail to remote locations sometimes takes weeks to arrive, by which time the information may already be out of date. Both customers and field salespeople will appreciate the automatic mail-response system.

Benefit #3: Minimized Waste

With our current method of printing every marketing piece in large quantities, we discard thousands of pages of obsolete catalogs, data sheets, and other materials every year. By maintaining and distributing the information electronically, we would eliminate this waste. We would also free up a considerable amount of expensive floor space and shelving that is required for storing printed materials.

Figure 10.14 Internal Proposal

Shandel Cohen's internal proposal seeks management's approval to install an automatic mail-response system. She lays out the problem concisely, describes her proposed solution, itemizes the four benefits it would provide, and provides a clear analysis of the financial impact.

She acknowledges one potential shortcoming with the new approach but provides a convincing solution to that as well.

2

Of course, some of our customers may still prefer to receive printed materials, or they may not have access to electronic mail. For these customers, we could simply print copies of the files when we receive such requests. The new Xerox DocuColor printer just installed in the Central Services building would be ideal for printing high-quality materials in small quantities.

Benefit #4: Lower Overtime Costs

In addition to saving both paper and space, we would also realize considerable savings in wages. Because of the increased interest in our new products, we must continue to work overtime or hire new people to meet the demand. An automatic mail response system would eliminate this need, allowing us to deal with fluctuating interest without a fluctuating workforce.

Cost Analysis

The necessary equipment and software costs approximately $15,000. System maintenance and upgrades are estimated at $5,000 per year. However, those costs are offset many times over by the predicted annual savings:

A detailed breakdown of cost savings provides credible support for the $145k/year claim made in the subject line.

Printing	$100,000
Storage	25,000
Postage	5,000
Wages	20,000
Total	**$150,000**

Based on these figures, the system would save $130,000 the first year and $145,000 every year after that.

Her conclusion summarizes the benefits and invites further discussion.

CONCLUSION

An automated email response system would yield considerable benefits in both customer satisfaction and operating costs. If you approve, we can have it installed and running in 6 weeks. Please give me a call if you have any questions.

Figure 10.14
Internal Proposal (continued)

The most significant factor in planning a proposal is whether the recipient has asked you to submit a proposal. *Solicited proposals* are generally prepared at the request of external parties that require a product or a service, but they may also be requested by such internal sources as management or the board of directors. Some organizations prepare a formal invitation to bid on their contracts, called a **request for proposals**, or RFP. The RFP specifies exactly the type of work to be performed or products to be delivered, along with budgets, deadlines, and other requirements. Other companies then respond with proposals that show how they would meet those needs. In most cases, organizations that issue RFPs also provide strict guidelines on what the proposals should include, and you need to follow these guidelines carefully in order to be considered.

Request for proposals (RFP):
A formal invitation to bid ona contract.

Unsolicited proposals offer more flexibility but a completely different sort of challenge because recipients aren't expecting to receive them. In fact, your audience may not be aware of the problem or opportunity you are addressing, so before you can propose a solution, you might first need to convince your readers that a problem or an opportunity exists. Consequently, the indirect approach is often the wise choice for unsolicited proposals.

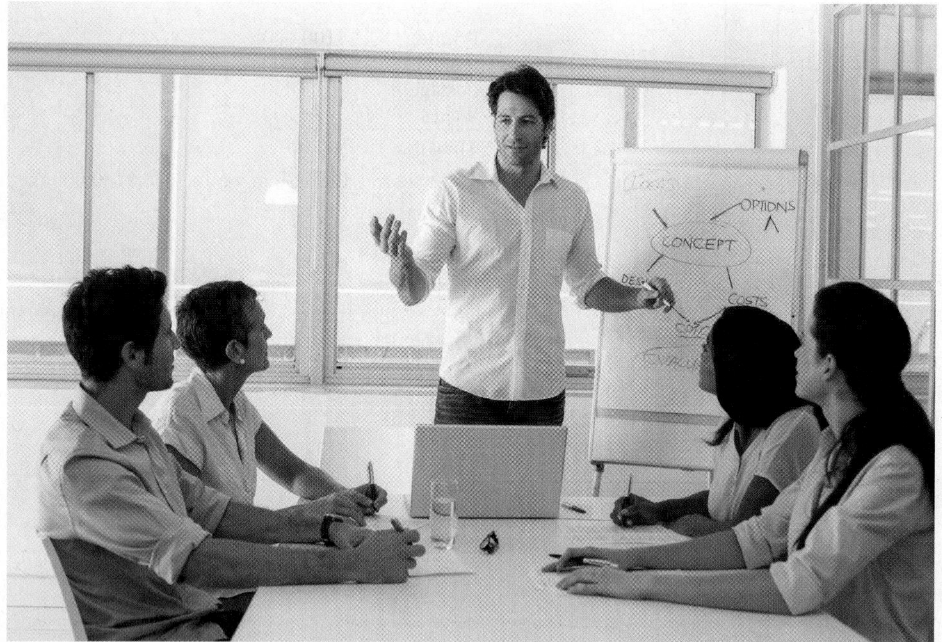

Figure 10.15
Preparing a Proposal
Regardless of its format and structure, a good proposal explains what a project or course of action will involve, how much it will cost, and how the recipient and his or her organization will benefit.

Chapter Summary

Applying the Three-Step Writing Process to Reports and Proposals

To adapt the three-step process to reports and proposals, apply what you learned in Chapters 3 through 5, with particular emphasis on clearly identifying your purpose, preparing a work plan, determining whether a separate research project might be needed, choosing the medium and channel, and selecting the best approach for the specific type of report.

Supporting Your Messages with Reliable Information

Begin the research process with careful planning to make sure you focus on the most important questions. Then locate the data and information, using primary and secondary research as needed. Process the results of your research, and apply your findings by summarizing information, drawing conclusions, or developing recommendations. Finally, manage information effectively so that you and others can retrieve it later and reuse it in other projects.

Evaluating the credibility of an information source can involve eight questions: 1) Does the source have a reputation for honesty and reliability? 2) Is the source potentially biased? 3) What is the purpose of the material? 4) Is the author credible? 5) Where did the source get its information? 6) Can you verify the material independently? 7) Is the material current and complete? 8) Does the information make sense?

Three ways to use research results are quoting, paraphrasing or summarizing textual material; drawing conclusions; and making recommendations.

Conducting Secondary Research

Secondary research—research via secondary sources—generally comes first, both to save time in case someone else has already gathered the information needed and to offer additional insights into your research questions. The two major categories of online research tools are tools used for searching (including various types of search engines, web directories, and online databases) and tools used for automatically monitoring for new information.

Documenting Your Sources

Three citation formats are common in business and academic research citations: *American Psychological Association* (APA), *Chicago Manual of Style* (Chicago), and *Modern Language Association* (MLA). Each has its own specifications for both in-text and bibliographical citation.

Conducting Primary Research

Primary research involves the collection of new data. Conduct it when secondary research does not provide you with the information you need. The two most common primary research methods for business communication purposes are surveys and interviews.

Planning Informational Reports

Informational reports focus on the delivery of facts, figures, and other types of information. Most informational reports use a topical organization, arranging material by comparison, importance, sequence, chronology, geography, or category.

When developing online reports and websites in general, plan the structure and navigation paths first, then write the content. Make sure you give readers navigational flexibility they need to control their online experience. Break your information in chunks that can be scanned and absorbed quickly.

Planning Analytical Reports

Analytical reports assess a situation or problem and recommend a course of action in to address it. The three most common ways to organize analytical reports are by focusing on conclusions, focusing on recommendations, and focusing on logical arguments.

Planning Proposals

The most significant factor in planning a proposal is whether the proposal is solicited or unsolicited. Solicited proposals are obviously expected and welcomed by the recipient, but they often must follow a specific organization, particularly when they are submitted in response to a request for proposals (RFP). For unsolicited proposals, the writer has flexibility in choosing the most effective organization, format, and content. However, because unsolicited proposals are unexpected, the writer often needs to explain why the solution offered in the proposal is even necessary for the reader to consider. Because of this, the indirect approach is usually preferred for unsolicited proposals.

Test Your Knowledge

1. What are the three basic categories of reports?
2. What is typically covered in the work plan for a report?
3. How does a conclusion differ from a recommendation?
4. Should you use primary research before or after secondary research?
5. How do proposal writers use an RFP?

Apply Your Knowledge

1. Companies occasionally make mistakes that expose confidential information, such as when employees lose laptop computers containing sensitive data files or webmasters forget to protect confidential webpages from search engine indexes. If your online research turned up competitive information on webpages that were clearly intended to be private, what would you do? Explain your answer.
2. Can you use the same approach for planning website content as you use for planning printed reports? Why or why not?
3. If you were writing a recommendation report for an audience that doesn't know you, would you use the direct approach, focusing on the recommendation, or the indirect approach, focusing on logic? Why?

Activities

1. **Analyzing the Situation** South by Southwest (SXSW) is a group of conferences and festivals in Austin, Texas, that showcases some of the world's most creative talents in music, interactive media, and film. In addition to being a major entertainment venue for a week every March, SXSW is also an increasingly important trade show, an opportunity for companies to present products and services to potential customers and business partners. You work for a company that makes music training equipment, such as an electronic keyboard with an integrated computer screen that guides learners through every step of learning to play the keyboard. Your manager has asked you to look into whether the company should rent an exhibition booth at SXSW next year. Prepare a work plan for an analytical report that will assess the promotional opportunities at SXSW and make a recommendation on exhibiting. Include the statement of purpose, a problem statement for any research you will conduct, a description of what will result from your investigation, the sources and methods of data collection, and a preliminary outline. Visit the SXSW website for more information.

2. **Documenting Sources** Select five business articles from a combination of print and online sources. Develop a resource list.

3. **Conducting Secondary Research** Using an online, database, or printed sources, find the following information. Be sure to properly cite your sources.

   - Contact information for the American Management Association
   - Current market share for Perrier water
   - Performance ratios for office supply retailers
   - Annual stock performance for Hewlett-Packard (HP)
   - Number of franchise outlets in the United States
   - Composition of the US workforce by profession

   Collect this information in a Word document, and then email that file to your instructor.

4. **Conducting Secondary Research** Select any public company and find the following information. Be sure to properly cite your sources.

   - Names and titles of the company's current officers
   - List of the company's products or services (or, if the company has a large number of products, the product lines or divisions)
   - Three important current issues in the company's industry
   - The outlook for the company's industry as a whole

   Collect this information in a Word document, and then email that file to your instructor.

5. **Referencing Technical Documentation** A friend needs to know how to do a hard reset for his iPhone 6s. Go to the Apple website, locate the Support section, and find the reset information for the iPhone 6s. Copy the step-by-step information about doing a hard reset into a Word document or email message to send to your friend.

6. **Citing Sources** Choose a topic that has been heavily reported on in the business news in the last week. Use news.google.com to find business-related news articles on that topic. Write a two-paragraph summary of the key facts, including APA-formatted citations from at least three sources you found online. Include at least one direct quotation from an article, and at least one paraphrased idea.

7. **Conducting Primary Research** You work for a movie studio that is producing a young director's first motion picture, the story of a group of unknown musicians finding work and making a reputation in a competitive industry. Unfortunately, some of your friends leave the screening saying that the 182-minute movie is simply too long. Others say they can't imagine any sequences to cut out. Your boss wants to test the movie on a typical audience and ask viewers to complete a questionnaire that will help the director decide whether edits are needed and, if so, where. Design a questionnaire that you can use to solicit valid answers for a report to the director about how to handle the audience's reaction to the movie. Use this data to build an informal presentation to be delivered to your boss and 2-3 coworkers. The presentation should focus on your findings, and your recommendations for how to proceed with edits to the movie.

8. **Conducting Primary Research** You're conducting an information interview with a manager in another division of your company. Partway through the interview, the manager shows clear signs of impatience. How should you respond? What might you do differently to prevent this from happening in the future? Explain your answers.

9. **Analyzing Informational Reports** The Securities and Exchange Commission (SEC) requires all public companies to file a comprehensive annual report (form 10-K) electronically. Many companies post links to these reports on their websites, along with links to other company reports. Visit Dell's website (www.dell.com) and find the company's most recent annual 10-K and Year in Review reports. Compare the style and format of the two reports. For which audience(s) is the Year in Review targeted? Who besides the SEC might be interested in form 10-K? Which report do you find easier to read? More interesting? More detailed?

10. **Outlining Informational Reports** You're the vice president of operations for a Florida fast-food chain. In the aftermath of a major hurricane, you're drafting a report on the emergency procedures to be followed by personnel in each restaurant when storm warnings are in effect. Answer who, what, when, where, why, and how, and then prepare a one-page outline of your report. Make up any details you need.

11. **Analyzing Informational Reports** From your library or company websites, find the annual reports recently released by two corporations in the same industry. Analyze each report and be prepared to discuss the following questions in class.

    - What organizational differences, if any, do you see in the way each corporation discusses its annual performance? Are the data presented clearly so that shareholders can draw conclusions about how well the company performed?
    - What goals, challenges, and plans do top managers emphasize in their discussion of results?
    - How do the format and organization of each report enhance or detract from the information being presented?

12. **Planning Informational Reports** A college president has received many student complaints about campus parking problems. You are appointed to chair a student committee organized to investigate the problems and recommend solutions. The president gives you a file labeled "Parking: Complaints from Students," and you jot down the essence of the complaints as you inspect the contents. Your notes are:

    - Inadequate student spaces at critical hours
    - Poor night lighting near the computer center
    - Inadequate attempts to keep resident neighbors from occupying spaces
    - Dim marking lines
    - Motorcycles taking up full spaces
    - Discourteous security officers
    - Spaces (usually empty) reserved for college officials
    - Relatively high parking fees
    - Full fees charged to night students even though they use the lots only during low-demand periods
    - Vandalism to cars and a sense of personal danger
    - Inadequate total space
    - Harassment of students parking on the street in front of neighboring houses

    Now prepare an outline for an informational report to be submitted to committee members. Use a topical organization for your report that categorizes this information.

13. **Planning Analytical Reports** Of the organizational approaches introduced in the chapter, which is best suited for writing a report that answers the following questions? Briefly explain why.

    a. In which market segment—energy drinks or traditional soft drinks—should Fizz Drinks, Inc., introduce a new drink to take advantage of its enlarged research and development budget?

    b. Should Major Manufacturing, Inc., close down operations of its antiquated Bellville, Arkansas, plant despite the adverse economic impact on the town that has grown up around the plant?

    c. Should you and your partner adopt a new accounting method to make your financial statements look better to potential investors?

    d. Should Grand Canyon Chemicals buy disposable test tubes to reduce labor costs associated with cleaning and sterilizing reusable test tubes?

    e. What are some reasons for the recent data loss at the college computer center, and how can we avoid similar problems in the future?

14. **Team Project: Planning a Report** Break into small groups and identify an operational problem occurring at your campus—perhaps involving registration, food services, parking, or library services. Then develop a workable solution to that problem. Finally, develop a list of pertinent facts that your team will need to gather to convince readers that the problem exists and that your solution will work.

15. **Evaluating a Website** Company websites function as multidimensional informational reports, with numerous sections and potentially endless ways for visitors to navigate through all the various pages. Locate at the website of a public corporation with a fairly complex website. Imagine that you are approaching the site as (a) a potential employee, (b) a potential investor (purchaser of stock), (c) a member of one of the local communities in which this company operates, and (d) a potential customer of the company's products and services. Analyze how easy or difficult it is to find the information each of these four visitors would typically be seeking. Using whatever medium your instructor requests, write a brief analysis of the information architecture of the website, describing what works well and what doesn't.

Expand Your Skills

1. **Citing Sources with Citation Management Software** Full-featured word processing programs like Microsoft Word can help users format citations according to the criteria prescribed by the different citation formats. Using the citation features in these programs, writers are freed from having to remember the formatting and spacing required for different kinds of sources.

   Your task: Research the initial public offering (IPO) of a technology company that happened within the last 30 days using a news site such as news.google.com. Suppose your supervisor has asked you to collect information about this IPO. Write a one-to-two page summary of the facts about the IPO that you learned in your research, and document the sources using Chicago citation format. If available, use Microsoft Word, and use the features on the References tab, in the Citations & Bibliography group, to enter the sources and generate a bibliography.

2. **Reviewing Informational Reports** Concern is growing in many youth sports about the negative consequences of existing approaches to player development and competition. The long-term athlete development (LTAD) approach aims to instill methods and mindsets that will make athlete development more successful in the long run while making sports more enjoyable for kids. The American Development Model (ADM) used by USA Hockey is one example of the LATD approach in a specific sport.

   Your task: Visit USA Hockey's website and review the information on ADM. Write a one- to two-page informational report on the ADM concept, including the rationale behind it and the benefits it offers youth athletes.

3. **Writing Informational Reports** Anyone contemplating stock market investing is likely to shudder at least a little bit at the market's penchant for taking a tumble now and again.

   Your task: Write a brief informational report that contains a chart of one of the major stock market indices (such as the Dow Jones Industrial Average or the S&P 500) over the past twenty years. Pick out four significant drops in the index during this time period and investigate economic or political events that occurred immediately before or during these declines. Briefly describe the events and their likely effect on the stock market.

4. **Team Project: Writing Informational Reports** The use of social networks by employees during work hours remains a controversial topic, with some companies encouraging networking, some at least allowing it, and others prohibiting it.

   Your task: Using the free wiki service offered by Zoho or a comparable system, collaborate on a report that summarizes the potential advantages and disadvantages of allowing social network use in the workplace.

5. **Developing Technical Documentation** Clear documentation is important for a product or service because it increases consumer satisfaction and decreases technical support phone calls. If your company develops a new product or adds a new service, you may be tasked with writing the documentation that will be distributed with the product or provided online to customers.

   Your task: Using a smartphone or tablet, find and download a simple app that functions as a timer. Write a one- to two-page document explaining how to set and cancel the timer.

6. **Team Project: Writing Informational Reports** If you're like many other students, your first year in high school was more than you expected: more difficult, more fun, more frustrating, more exhausting, more rewarding—more of everything, positive and negative.

   Your task: With several other students, identify five or six things you wish you would've realized or understood better before you started your first year of high school. These can relate to your school life (such as "I didn't realize how much work I would have for my classes" or "I should've asked for help as soon as I got stuck") and your personal and social life ("I wish I had been more open to meeting people"). Use these items as the foundation of a brief informational report you could post on a blog that is read by high school students and their families. Your goal with this report is to help the next generation of students make a successful and rewarding transition to high school.

7. **Writing Analytical Reports** Your company develops a mobile phone apps that helps people get detailed technical information about products while they are shopping. The original plan was to incorporate Quick Reference (QR) codes into the app, so that people could scan QR stickers placed on product displays in retail stores. After decoding the QR code, the app would then pull up information about the product on display. You have, however, recently learned about near-field communication, a short-range radio technology that might able to accomplish the same thing in a way that is simpler for consumers to use.

   Your task: Research the prospects for QR codes and NFC technology and write a short comparative report. Draw a conclusion about which technology you think will dominate in the coming years.

8. **Writing Analytical Reports** Mistakes can be wonderful learning opportunities if we're honest with ourselves and receptive to learning from them.

   Your task: Identify a mistake you've made—something significant enough to have cost you a lot of money, wasted a lot of time, harmed your health, damaged a relationship, created problems at school, prevented you from pursuing what could've been a rewarding opportunity, or otherwise had serious consequences. Now figure out why you made that mistake. Did you let emotions get in the way of clear thinking? Did you make a serious financial blunder because you didn't take the time to understand the consequences of a decision? Were you too cautious? Not cautious enough? Perhaps several factors led to a poor decision.

   Write a brief analytical report to your instructor that describes the situation and outlines your analysis of why the failure occurred and how you can avoid making a similar mistake in the future. If you can't think of a significant mistake or failure that you're comfortable sharing with your instructor, write about a mistake that a friend or family member made (without revealing the person's identify or potentially embarrassing him or her).

9. **Writing Analytical Letters** Imagine you are a consultant hired to improve the customer service of a restaurant or store in your community.

   Your task: Visit the location and look critically at its operations. Then draft a letter that could be sent to the manager, offering recommendations that would help the facility service customers more effectively, perhaps suggesting products it should carry, hours that it should remain open, or added services that would attract more student traffic. Be sure to support your recommendations.

10. **Writing Analytical Reports** Spurred in part by the success of numerous do-it-yourself (DIY) TV shows, homeowners across the country are redecorating, remodeling, and rebuilding. Many people are content with superficial changes, such as new paint or new accessories, but some are more ambitious. These homeowners want to move walls, add rooms, redesign kitchens, convert garages to home theaters—the big stuff.

    Publishers try to create magazines that appeal to carefully identified groups of potential readers and the advertisers who'd like to reach them. Numerous magazines already serve the DIY market, but you see an opportunity in the homeowners who tackle the heavy-duty projects. Case Tables 10.1 through 10.3 summarize the results of some preliminary research you asked your company's research staff to conduct.

    One additional way to capture information about your customers is through a focus group. A focus group is a time where a moderator (someone asking the questions) gathers a group of potential customers—either in person or virtually—to ask them questions and observe the potential customers' reactions to certain questions.

    Your task: You think the data shows a real opportunity for a "big projects" DIY magazine, although you'll need more extensive research to confirm the size of the market, obtain input from the focus group observation, and refine the editorial direction of the magazine. Prepare a brief analytical report that presents the data you have, identifies the opportunity or opportunities you've found (suggest your own ideas, based on the data in the tables), and requests funding from the editorial board to pursue further research.

Case Table 10.1 Rooms Most Frequently Remodeled by DIYers

Room	Percentage of Homeowners Surveyed Who Have Tackled or Plan to Tackle at Least a Partial Remodel
Kitchen	60
Bathroom	48
Home office/study	44
Bedroom	38
Media room/home theater	31
Den/recreation room	28
Living room	27
Dining room	12
Sun room/solarium	8

Case Table 10.2 Average Amount Spent on Remodeling Projects

Estimated Amount	Percentage of Surveyed Homeowners
Under $5k	5
$5k–$10k	21
$10k–$20k	39
$20k–$50k	22
More than $50k	13

Case Table 10.3 Tasks Performed by Homeowner on a Typical Remodeling Project

Tasks	Percentage of Surveyed Homeowners Who Perform or Plan to Perform Most or All of This Task Themselves
Conceptual design	90
Technical design/architecture	34
Demolition	98
Foundation work	62
Framing	88
Plumbing	91
Electrical	55
Heating/cooling	22
Finish carpentry	85
Tile work	90
Painting	100
Interior design	52

11. **Writing Proposals** One of the problems of apartment living is residents who don't care about the condition of their shared surroundings. They might leave trash all over the place, dent walls when they move furniture, spill food and beverages in common areas, destroy window screens, and otherwise degrade living conditions for everyone. Landlords obviously aren't thrilled about this behavior, either, because it raises the costs of cleaning and maintaining the facility.

    Your task: Assume you live in a fairly large apartment community. Write an email proposal you could send to your landlord, suggesting that fostering a sense of stronger community among residents in your building might help reduce incidents of vandalism and neglect. Propose that the little-used storage area in the basement of the building be converted to a community room, complete with a simple kitchen and a large-screen television. By attending Super Bowl parties and other events there, residents could get to know one another and perhaps forge bonds that would raise the level of shared concern for their living environment. You can't offer any proof of this in advance, of course, but share your belief that a modest investment in this room could pay off long term in lower repair and maintenance costs. Moreover, it would be an attractive feature to entice new residents.

12. **Writing Proposals** Select a product you are familiar with and imagine you are the manufacturer, trying to get a local retail outlet to carry it. Use the Internet and other resources to gather information about the product.

    Your task: Write an unsolicited sales proposal in letter format to the owner or manager of the store, proposing that they carry your item. Use the information you gathered to describe some of the product's features and benefits. Then make up some reasonable figures, highlighting what the item costs, what it can be sold for, and what services your company provides (return of unsold items, free replacement of unsatisfactory items, necessary repairs, and so on).

CHAPTER

11

Writing and Completing Reports and Proposals

After studying this chapter, you will be able to:

- List the topics commonly covered in the introduction, body, and close of informational reports, analytical reports, and proposals.
- Identify six guidelines for drafting effective website content and offer guidelines for becoming a valuable wiki contributor.
- Discuss six principles of graphic design that can improve the quality of your visuals and identify the major types of business visuals.
- Summarize the four tasks involved in completing business reports and proposals.

Writing Reports and Proposals

This chapter focuses on writing and completing reports, along with creating content for websites, collaborating on wikis, and creating graphical elements to illustrate messages of all kinds. All the writing concepts and techniques you learned in Chapter 4 apply to the longer format of business reports. The length and complexity of reports call for special attention to several issues, starting with adapting to your audience.

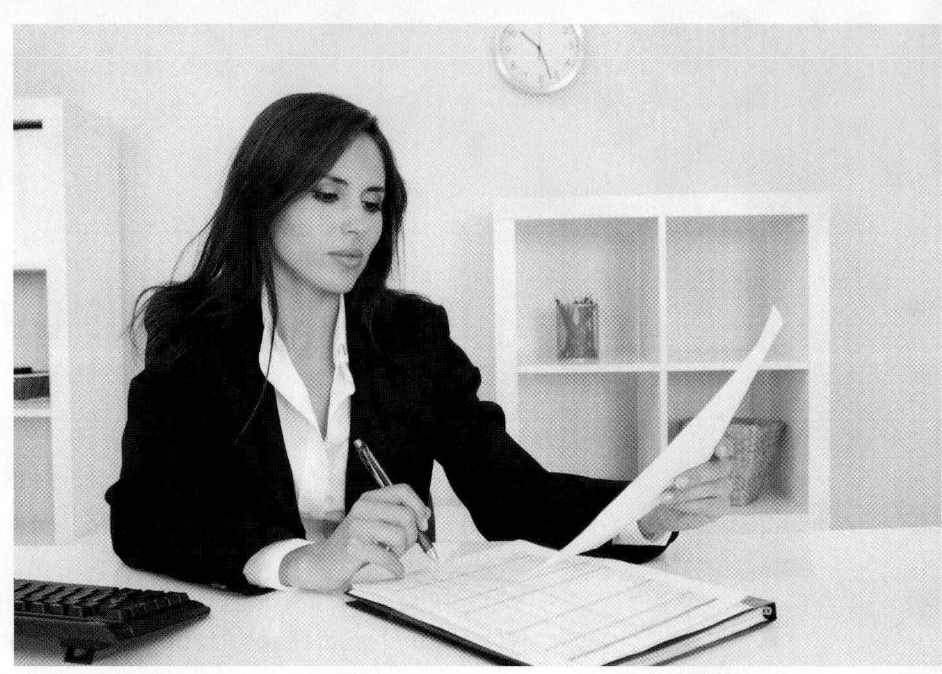

Figure 11.1
Business Report Writing
Along with routine day-to-day short documents, you may also be tasked with writing longer reports and proposals. These have their own set of customary structures and formats, which you will become familiar with in this chapter.

Adapting to Your Audience

Reports and proposals can put heavy demands on your readers, so the "you" attitude is especially important with these long messages. In general, try to strike a balance between being overly informal (which can be perceived as trivializing important issues) and overly formal (which can put too much distance between writer and reader). If you know your readers reasonably well and your report is likely to meet with their approval, you can generally adopt an informal tone. To make your tone less formal, speak to readers in the first person, refer to them as you, and refer to yourself as I (or we if there are multiple report authors).

To make your tone more formal, use the impersonal journalism style: emphasize objectivity, avoid personal opinions, and build your argument on provable facts (see Figure 11.2). Eliminate all personal pronouns (including I, you, we, us, and our). Avoid humor, and be careful with your use of similes, metaphors, and particularly colorful adjectives or adverbs. However, you don't need to make the writing monotonous. For example, you can still create interest by varying the types of sentences to create a pleasing rhythm.

Take into account that communicating with people in other cultures often calls for more formality in reports, both to respect cultural preferences and to reduce the risk of miscommunication. Informal elements such as humor and casual language tend to translate poorly from one culture to another.

Executive Summary

Long and somewhat rigorous sentences help give the report its formal tone. For a more consumer-oriented publication, this writing could certainly be simplified.

Eating and physical activity patterns that are focused on consuming fewer calories, making informed food choices, and being physically active can help people attain and maintain a healthy weight, reduce their risk of chronic disease, and promote overall health. The *Dietary Guidelines for Americans, 2010* exemplifies these strategies through recommendations that accommodate the food preferences, cultural traditions, and customs of the many and diverse groups who live in the United States.

By law (Public Law 101-445, Title III, 7 U.S.C. 5301 et seq.), *Dietary Guidelines for Americans* is reviewed, updated if necessary, and published every 5 years. The U.S. Department of Agriculture (USDA) and the U.S. Department of Health and Human Services (HHS) jointly create each edition. *Dietary Guidelines for Americans, 2010* is based on the *Report of the Dietary Guidelines Advisory Committee on the Dietary Guidelines for Americans, 2010* and consideration of Federal agency and public comments.

Dietary Guidelines recommendations traditionally have been intended for healthy Americans ages 2 years and older. However, *Dietary Guidelines for Americans, 2010* is being released at a time of rising concern about the health of the American population. Poor diet and physical inactivity are the most important factors contributing to an epidemic of overweight and obesity affecting men, women, and children in all segments of our society. Even in the absence of overweight, poor diet and physical inactivity are associated with major causes of morbidity and mortality in the United States. Therefore, the *Dietary Guidelines for Americans, 2010* is intended for Americans ages 2 years and older, including those at increased risk of chronic disease.

Dietary Guidelines for Americans, 2010 also recognizes that in recent years nearly 15 percent of American households have been unable to acquire adequate food to meet their needs.[1] This dietary guidance can help them maximize the nutritional content of

1. Nord M, Coleman-Jensen A, Andrews M, Carlson S. Household food security in the United States, 2009. Washington (DC): U.S. Department of Agriculture, Economic Research Service. 2010 Nov. Economic Research Report No. ERR-108. Available from http://www.ers.usda.gov/publications/err108.

viii DIETARY GUIDELINES FOR AMERICANS, 2010

A less-formal report might've said something along the lines of "Poor diet and physical inactivity are killing U.S. citizens" instead of the more formal (and more precise) "are associated with major causes of morbidity and mortality."

This paragraph mentions the troubling statistic that 15 percent of U.S. households can't afford to meet basic nutritional requirements, but because the report is presenting dietary recommendations and not public policy statements about economics or other issues, the tone is objective and dispassionate.

Figure 11.2
Achieving the Appropriate Tone for a Report

This report excerpt (part of the executive summary of the Dietary Guidelines for Americans published by the US Department of Agriculture and the US Department of Health and Human Services), uses a number of techniques to create a formal tone. Its intended readers are educators, government regulators, and others charged with using the information to help inform consumers. If the document had been written with consumers in mind, you can imagine how the tone might have been lighter and less formal.

Drafting Report Content

You can simplify report writing by breaking the job into three main sections: an introduction (or opening), a body, and a close. Table 11.1 summarizes the goals of each section and lists elements to consider including in each as well. You can use this table as a handy reference whenever you need to write a report in school or on the job.

At a minimum, an effective *introduction* accomplishes these four tasks:

- It helps the reader understand the context of the report by tying it to a problem or an assignment.
- It introduces the subject matter and indicates why it is important.
- It previews the main idea (if you're using the direct approach).
- It establishes the tone and the writer's relationship with the audience.

The *body* presents, analyzes, and interprets the information gathered during your investigation and supports your recommendations or conclusions. The length and content of the body can vary widely based on the subject matter.

The *close* has three important functions:

- It summarizes your key points.
- It emphasizes the benefits to the reader if the document suggests a change or some other course of action.
- It brings all the action items together in one place.

To serve the needs of your readers and build your reputation as a careful and insightful professional, make sure your content in every section is accurate, complete, balanced, clear, and logical. As always, be sure to properly document all your sources (see Chapter 10).

In addition, help today's time-pressed readers find what they're looking for and stay on track as they navigate through your documents. First, write clear headings and subheadings that let readers follow the structure of your document and help them pick up the key points of your message. Second, use plenty of transitions to tie together ideas and show how one thought is related to another. Third, include preview sections to help readers get ready for new information and review sections after a body of material to summarize key points.

Finally, make the process as easy on yourself as possible by taking advantage of all available productivity tools. For example, the size and complexity of many reports make templates and style sheets particularly helpful. If you include graphics, spreadsheets, or database records produced in other programs, make sure you know how your writing software handles the file connection. You might have the choice to maintain a "live" connection with these included files, so that any changes in the original automatically show up in your report. And be sure to explore your media and channel options. Video clips, animation, presentation slides, screencasts (recordings of on-screen activity), and other media elements can enhance the communication and persuasion powers of the written word.

Table 11.1 Content Elements to Consider for Reports and Proposals

Reports	Proposals
Introduction: Establish the context, identify the subject, preview main ideas (if using the direct approach), establish tone and reader relationship.	**Introduction**: Identify the problem you intend to solve or the opportunity you want to pursue.
• Authorization. Reiterate who authorized the report, if applicable. • Problem/purpose. Explain the reason for the report's existence and what the report will achieve. • Scope. Describe what will and won't be covered in the report. • Background. Review historical conditions or factors that led up to the report. • Sources and methods. Discuss the primary and secondary sources consulted and methods used. • Definitions. List terms and their definitions, including any terms that might be misinterpreted. Terms may also be defined in the body, explanatory notes, or glossary. • Limitations. Discuss factors beyond your control that affect report quality (but do not use this as an excuse for poor research or a poorly written report). • Report organization. Identify the topics to be covered and in what order.	• Background or statement of the problem. Briefly review the situation at hand, establish a need for action, and explain how things could be better. In unsolicited proposals, convince readers that a problem or an opportunity exists. • Solution. Briefly describe the change you propose, highlighting your key selling points and their benefits to show how your proposal will solve the reader's problem. • Scope. State the boundaries of the proposal—what you will and will not do. • Report organization. Orient the reader to the remainder of the proposal and call attention to the major divisions of thought.
Body: Present relevant information and support your recommendations or conclusions.	**Body**: Give complete details on the proposed solution and describe anticipated results.
• Explanations. Give complete details of the problem, project, or idea. • Facts, statistical evidence, and trends. Lay out the results of studies or investigations. • Analysis of action. Discuss potential courses of action. • Pros and cons. Explain advantages, disadvantages, costs, and benefits of a particular course of action. • Procedures. Outline steps for a process. • Methods and approaches. Discuss how you've studied a problem (or gathered evidence) and arrived at your solution (or collected your data). • Criteria. Describe the benchmarks for evaluating options and alternatives. • Conclusions and recommendations. Discuss what you believe the evidence reveals and what you propose should be done about it. • Support. Give the reasons behind your conclusions or recommendations.	• Facts and evidence to support your conclusions. Give complete details of the proposed solution and anticipated results. • Proposed approach. Describe your concept, product, or service. Stress reader benefits and emphasize any advantages you have over your competitors. • Work plan. Describe how you'll accomplish what must be done (unless you're providing a standard, off-the-shelf item). Explain the steps you'll take, their timing, the methods or resources you'll use, and the person(s) responsible. State when work will begin, how it will be divided into stages, when you'll finish, and whether follow-up will be needed. • Statement of qualifications. Describe your organization's experience, personnel, and facilities—relating it all to readers' needs. Include a list of client references. • Costs. Prove that your costs are realistic—break them down so that readers can see the costs of labor, materials, transportation, travel, training, and other categories.
Close: Summarize key points, emphasize benefits of any recommendations, list action items; label as "Summary" or "Conclusions and Recommendations."	**Close**: Summarize key points, emphasize the benefits and advantages of your proposed solution, ask for a decision from the reader.
• For direct approach. Summarize key points (except in short reports), listing them in the order in which they appear in the body. Briefly restate your conclusions or recommendations, if appropriate. • For indirect approach. If you haven't done so at the end of the body, present your conclusions or recommendations. • For motivating action. Spell out exactly what should happen next and provide a schedule with specific task assignments.	• Review of argument. Briefly summarize the key points. • Review of reader benefits. Briefly summarize how your proposal will help the reader. • Review of the merits of your approach. Briefly summarize why your approach will be more effective than alternatives. • Restatement of qualifications. For external proposals, briefly reemphasize why you and your firm should do the work. • Request. Ask for a decision from the reader.

Drafting Proposal Content

All of the guidelines for writing reports also apply to proposals, plus there are some additional considerations. As Chapter 10 notes, the most important factor is whether the proposal is solicited or unsolicited, because this can affect your organization, content, and tone.

The general purpose of any proposal is to persuade readers to do something, so your writing approach should be similar to that used for persuasive messages, perhaps including the use of the AIDA model to gain attention, build interest, create desire, and motivate action. Here are some additional strategies to strengthen your argument:

- Demonstrate your knowledge.
- Provide concrete information and examples.
- Research the competition so you know what other proposals your audience is likely to read.
- Demonstrate that your proposal is appropriate and feasible for your audience.
- Relate your product, service, or personnel to the reader's unique needs.

Moreover, make sure your proposal is error-free, visually inviting, and easy to read. Readers will prejudge the quality of your products, services, or capabilities by the quality of your proposal. Errors, omissions, and inconsistencies will work against you—and might even cost you important career and business opportunities.

Consider using proposal-writing software if you and your company need to submit proposals as a routine part of doing business. These programs can automatically personalize proposals, ensure proper structure (making sure you don't forget any sections, for instance), organize storage of all your **boilerplate** text, integrate contact information from sales databases, scan RFPs (request for proposal) to identify questions (and even assign them to content experts), and fill in preliminary answers to common questions from a centralized knowledge base.

Boilerplate:
A standard way of saying something that can be used in multiple contexts.

Writing for Websites and Wikis

In addition to standalone reports and proposals, you may be asked to write in-depth content for websites or to collaborate on a wiki. The basic principles of report writing apply to both formats, but each has some unique considerations as well.

Drafting Website Content

Major sections on websites, particularly those that are fairly static (unlike, say, a blog) function in much the same way as reports. The skills you've developed for report writing adapt easily to this environment, as long as you keep a few points in mind:

- Because readers can be skeptical of online content, take special care to build trust with your intended audiences. Make sure your content is accurate, current, complete, and authoritative.
- As much as possible, adapt your content for a global audience. Translating content is expensive, so some companies compromise by *localizing* the homepage while keeping the deeper, more detailed content in its original language.
- In an environment that presents many reading challenges, compelling, reader-oriented content is a key to success. Wherever you can, use the *inverted pyramid style*, in which you cover the most important information briefly at first and then gradually reveal successive layers of detail—letting readers choose to see those additional layers if they want to.
- Present your information in a concise, skimmable format (see Figure 11.3). Effective websites use a variety of means to help readers skim pages quickly, including lists, use of color and boldface, informative headings, and helpful summaries that give readers the option of learning more if they choose to do so.
- Write effective links that serve for both site navigation and content skimming. Above all, clearly identify where a link will take readers. Don't resort to cute wordplay that obscures the content, and don't force readers to click through and try to figure out where they're going.
- Make your website a "living" document by regularly adding fresh content and deleting content that is out of date or no longer relevant to your target audience. Over time, websites can accumulate many pages of outdated information that get in the way and send a negative message about the company's efforts to stay on top of user needs.

Figure 11.3
Writing for the Web
This page from the Google Help feature for Gmail demonstrates several important points about effective web writing.

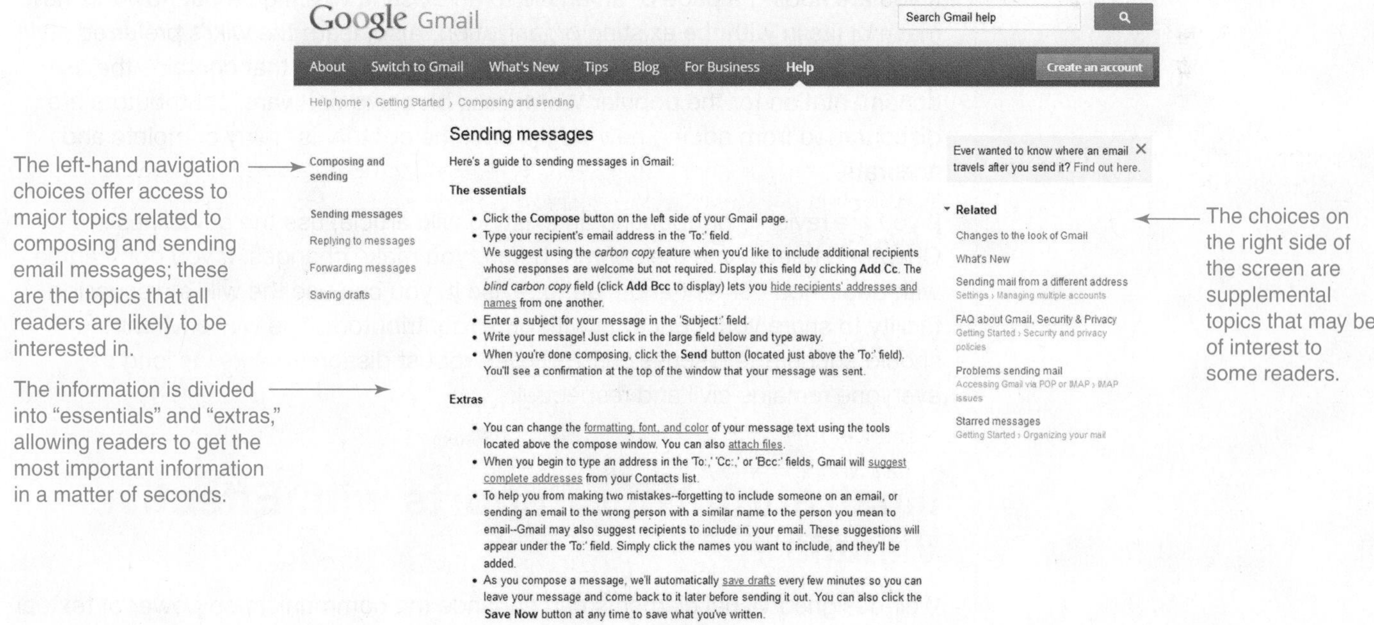

Collaborating on Wikis

As Chapter 2 points out, wikis are a great way for teams and other groups to collaborate on writing projects, from brief articles to long reports and reference works. Although wikis have many benefits, they do require a unique approach to writing. To be a valuable wiki contributor, keep these points in mind:

- Let go of traditional expectations of authorship, including individual recognition and control.
- Encourage all team members to improve each other's work.
- Use page templates and other formatting options to make sure your content matches the rest of the wiki.
- Use the separate editing and discussion capabilities appropriately.
- Take advantage of the sandbox, if available; this is a "safe," nonpublished section of the wiki where team members can practice editing and writing.

Wikis usually have guidelines to help new contributors integrate their work into the group's ongoing effort. Be sure to read and understand these guidelines, and don't be afraid to ask for help.

If you are creating a new wiki, think through your long-term purpose carefully, just as you would with a new blog or podcast channel. Doing so will help you craft appropriate guidelines, like editorial oversight and security policies. For instance, the PlayStation development team at Sony uses a wiki to keep top managers up to date on new products; because this information is highly confidential, access to the wiki is tightly controlled.

If you are adding a page or an article to an existing wiki, figure out how this new material fits in with the existing organization. Also, learn the wiki's preferred style for handling works in progress. For example, on the wiki that contains the user documentation for the popular WordPress blogging software, contributors are discouraged from adding new pages until the content is "fairly complete and accurate."

If you are revising or updating an existing wiki article, use the guidelines in Chapter 5 to evaluate the content before you make changes. If you don't agree with published content and plan to revise it, you can use the wiki's discussion facility to share your concerns with other contributors. The wiki environment should encourage discussions and even robust disagreements, as long as everyone remains civil and respectful.

Illustrating Your Reports with Effective Visuals

Well-designed visual elements can enhance the communication power of textual messages and, in some instances, even replace textual messages. Generally speaking, in a given amount of time, effective images can convey much more information than text. Using pictures is also a helpful way to communicate with multilingual audiences.

Figure 11.4
Incorporating Visuals
Longer business documents can be boring to read, but graphics make them more interesting and easier to understand.

Given the importance of visuals in today's business environment, **visual literacy**—the ability (as a sender) to create effective images and (as a receiver) to correctly interpret visual messages—has become a key business skill. The following six design principles will help you be a more effective visual communicator:

Visual literacy: The ability to create effective images and correctly interpret visual messages.

- **Consistency.** Think of consistency as *visual parallelism*, similar to parallel structure in writing, which helps audiences understand and compare a series of ideas. You can achieve visual parallelism through the consistent use of color, shape, size, texture, position, scale, or typeface.
- **Contrast.** To emphasize differences, depict items in contrasting colors, such as red and blue or black and white. To emphasize similarities, make color differences more subtle.
- **Balance.** Visual balance can be either *formal*, in which the elements in the images are arranged symmetrically around a central point, or *informal*, in which elements are not distributed evenly, but stronger and weaker elements are arranged in a way that achieves an overall effect of balance. Formal balance tends to feel calming and serious, whereas informal balance tends to feel dynamic and engaging, (which is why most advertising uses this approach.
- **Emphasis.** Audiences usually assume that the dominant element in a design is the most important, so make sure that the visually dominant element really does represent the most important information.
- **Convention.** Just as written communication is guided by spelling, grammar, punctuation, and usage conventions, visual communication is guided by generally accepted rules or conventions that dictate virtually every aspect of design. In every culture, for instance, certain colors and shapes have specific meanings.
- **Simplicity.** When you're designing graphics for your documents, limit the number of colors and design elements and take care to avoid *chartjunk*—decorative elements that clutter documents without adding any relevant information. Think carefully about using some of the chart features available in your software, too. Many of these features can actually get in the way of effective visual communication. For example, three-

dimensional bar charts, cones, and pyramids can look appealing, but the third dimension usually adds no additional information and can be visually confusing.

Choosing the Right Visual for the Job

After you've identified which points would benefit most from visual presentation, your next decision is to choose the types of visuals to use. As you can see in Figure 11.5, you have many choices for business graphics. For certain kinds of information, the decision is usually obvious. If you want to present a large set of numeric values or detailed textual information, for example, a table is the obvious choice in most cases. Also, certain visuals are commonly used for certain applications; so, for example, your audience is likely to expect line charts and bar charts to show trends. (Note that *chart* and *graph* are used interchangeably for most of the display formats discussed here.)

Tables

Table:
A systematic arrangement of data in columns and rows.

When you need to present detailed, specific information, choose a **table**, a systematic arrangement of data in columns and rows. Tables are ideal when your audience needs information that would be either difficult or tedious to handle in the main text.

Follow these guidelines to create clear, effective tables:

- Use common, understandable units and clearly identify them: dollars, percentages, price per ton, and so on.
- Express all items in a column in the same unit and round off for simplicity, if doing so doesn't distort the meaning.
- Label column headings clearly and use subheads if necessary.
- Separate columns or rows with lines, extra space, or colors to make the table easy to follow. Make sure the intended reading direction—down the columns or across the rows—is obvious, too.
- Keep online tables small enough to read comfortably on screen.
- Document the source of data using the same format as a text footnote (see Chapter 10).

Figure 11.5 Selecting the Best Visual
You often have more than one option for communicating data and information visually; choose the best visual for each situation based on audience needs, the medium you'll use for your report, and your graphics capabilities.

Communication Challenge	Effective Visual Choice

Presenting Data

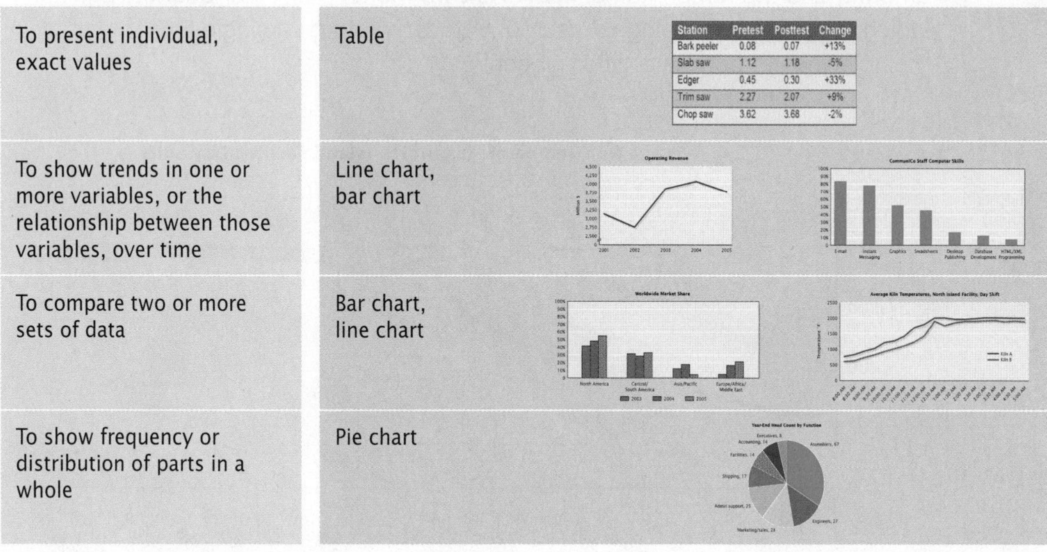

Communication Challenge	Effective Visual Choice
To present individual, exact values	Table
To show trends in one or more variables, or the relationship between those variables, over time	Line chart, bar chart
To compare two or more sets of data	Bar chart, line chart
To show frequency or distribution of parts in a whole	Pie chart

Station	Pretest	Posttest	Change
Bark peeler	0.08	0.07	+13%
Slab saw	1.12	1.18	-5%
Edger	0.45	0.30	+33%
Trim saw	2.27	2.07	+9%
Chop saw	3.62	3.68	-2%

Presenting Information, Concepts, and Ideas

Communication Challenge	Effective Visual Choice
To show geographic relationships or comparisons	Map
To illustrate processes or procedures	Flowchart, diagram
To show conceptual or spatial relationships (simplified)	Drawing
To tell a data-driven story visually	Infographic
To show spatial relationships (realistic)	Photograph
To show processes, transformations, and other activities	Animation, video

Line Charts and Surface Charts

Line chart:
A chart that illustrates trends over time or plots the relationship of two variables using one or more lines.

A **line chart** (see Figure 11.6) illustrates trends over time or plots the relationship of two variables. In line charts that show trends, the vertical, or *y*, axis shows the amount, and the horizontal, or *x*, axis shows the time or other quantity against which the amount is being measured. You can plot just a single line or overlay multiple lines to compare different entities.

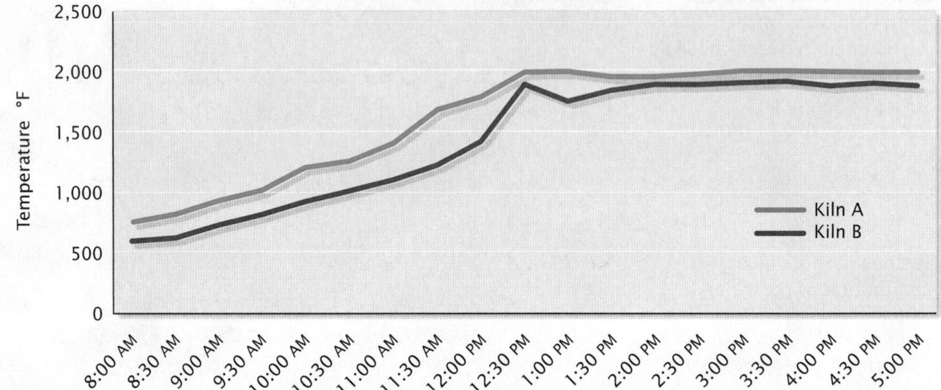

Figure 11.6
Line Chart
This two-line chart compares the temperatures measured inside two cement kilns every half hour from 8:00 A.M. to 5:00 P.M.

Surface chart (area chart):
A variant of the line chart that shows a cumulative effort.

A **surface chart**, also called an **area chart**, is a form of line chart that shows a cumulative effect; all the lines add up to the top line, which represents the total (see Figure 11.7). This type of chart helps you illustrate changes in the composition of something over time.

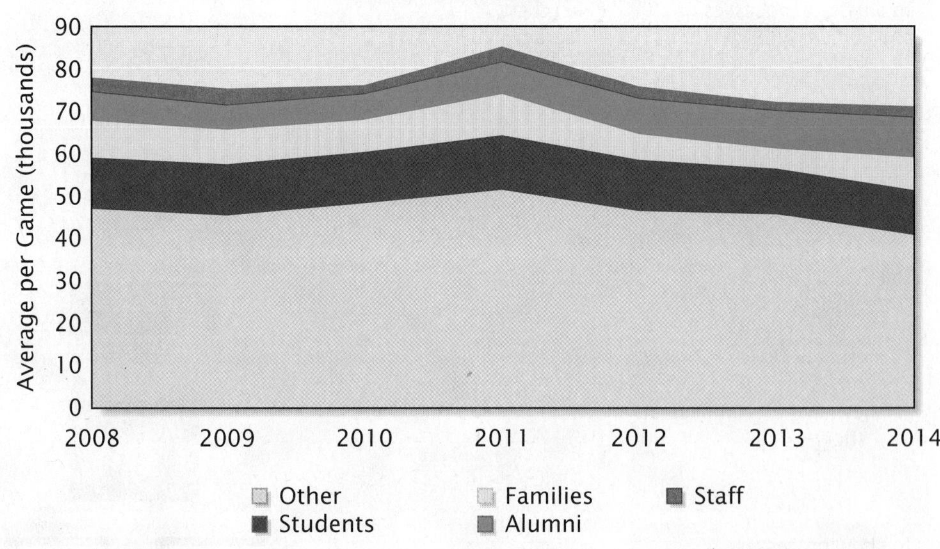

Figure 11.7
Surface Chart
Surface or area charts can show a combination of trends over time and the individual contributions of the components of a whole.

Bar Charts and Pie Charts

A **bar chart** portrays numbers with the height or length of its rectangular bars, making a series of numbers easy to grasp quickly. Bars can be oriented horizontally or vertically (in which case they are sometimes referred to as *column charts*). Bar charts are particularly valuable when you want to show or compare quantities over time. As the charts in Figure 11.8 suggest, bar charts can appear in various forms. Specialized bar charts such as *timelines* and *Gantt charts* are used often in project management, for example.

Bar chart:
A chart using the height or length of rectangular bars to represent data.

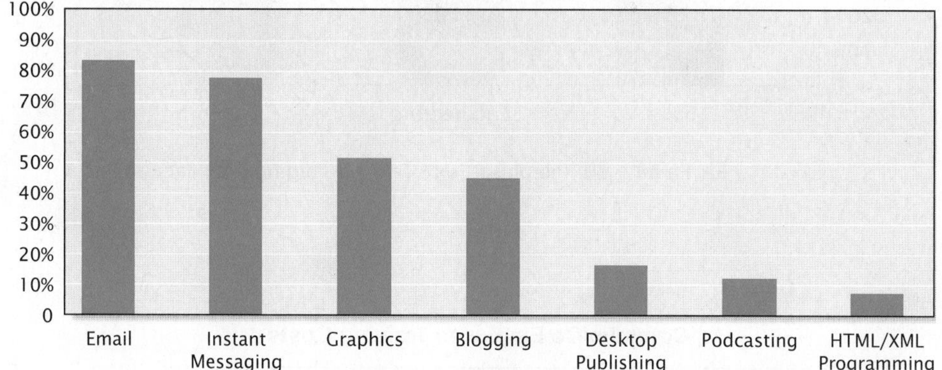

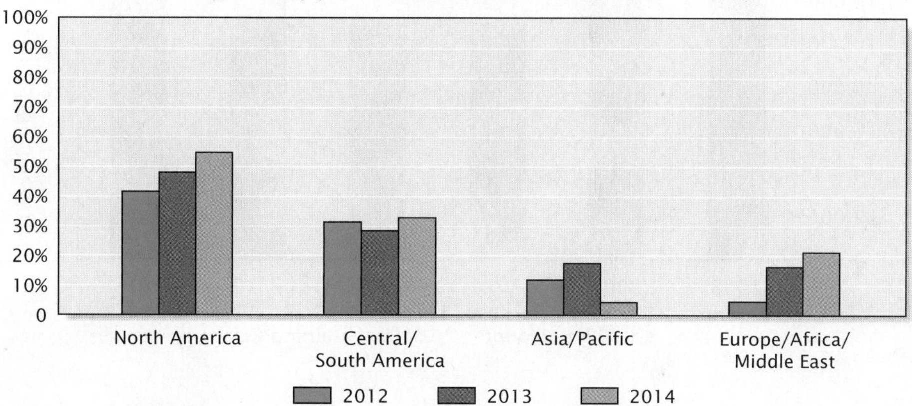

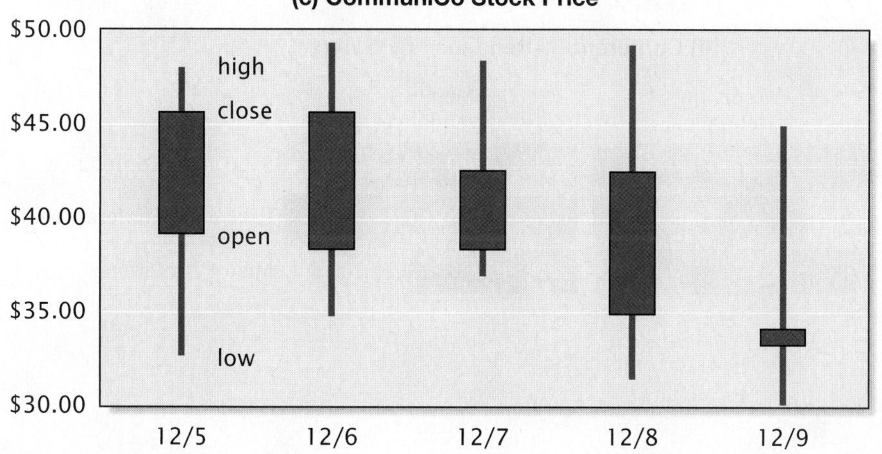

Figure 11.8
The Versatile Bar Chart
Here are six of the dozens of variations possible with bar charts: singular (11.9a), grouped (11.9b), stock (11.9c), stacked (11.9d), combination (11.9e), and paired (11.9f).

Figure 11.8
The Versatile Bar Charts (continued)

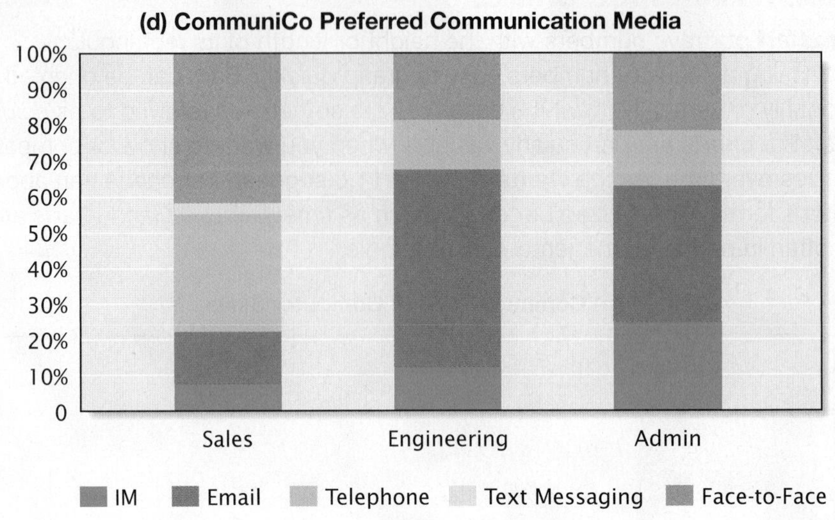

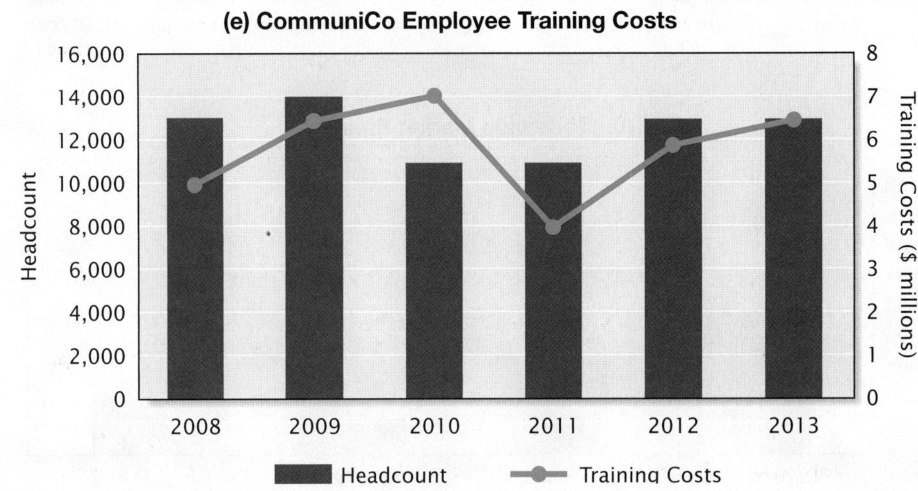

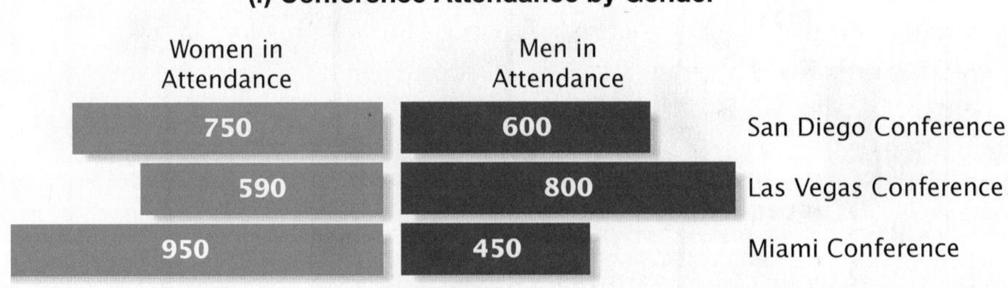

A **pie chart** is a commonly used tool for showing how the parts of a whole are distributed. Although pie charts are popular and can quickly highlight the dominant parts of a whole, they are often not as effective as bar charts or tables. For example, comparing percentages accurately is often difficult with a pie chart but can be fairly easy with a bar chart (see Figure 11.9). Making pie charts easier to read with accuracy can require labeling each slice with data values, in which case a table might serve the purpose more effectively.

Pie chart:
A type of graph in which a circle is divided into sectors that each represent a proportion of the whole.

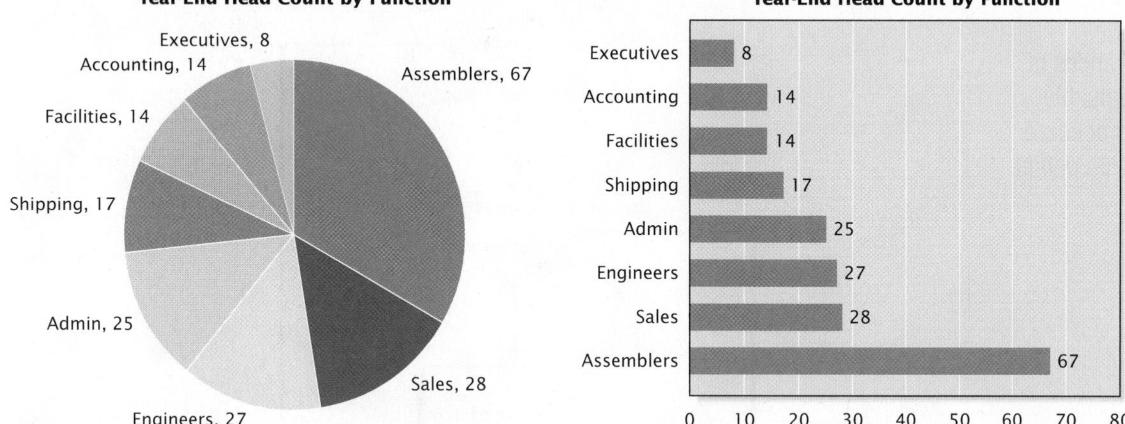

Figure 11.9
Pie Charts Versus Bar Charts
Pie charts are used frequently, but they aren't necessarily the best choice for many data presentations. This pie chart does make it easy to see that assemblers are the largest employee category, but other comparisons of slice sizes (such as Sales, Engineers, and Admin) are not as easy to make and require a numerical rather than a visual comparison. In contrast, the bar chart gives a quick visual comparison of every data point.

Data Visualization

Conventional charts and graphs are limited in several ways: most types can show only a limited number of data points before becoming too cluttered to interpret, they often can't show complex relationships among data points, and they can represent only numeric data. As computer technologies continue to generate large amounts of data that can be combined and connected in endless ways, a diverse class of display capabilities known as **data visualization** work to overcome all these drawbacks. In some instances, data visualization is less about clarifying individual data points and more about extracting broad meaning from giant masses of data or putting the data in context.

Data visualization has become an important tool for companies working with *big data*, a term used to describe massive collections of data from a variety of sources piling up at high speeds. Interactive apps let users "drill down" into data sets to find details or look at data collections from a variety of perspectives.

In addition to displaying large data sets and linkages within data sets, other kinds of visualization tools combine data with textual information to communicate complex or dynamic data much faster than conventional presentations can. For example, a tag cloud shows the relative frequency of tags (content labels), in an article, a blog, a website, survey data, or another collection of text.

Data visualization:
Using summary graphics to create meaning from raw data.

Flowcharts and Organization Charts

A **flowchart** (see Figure 11.10) illustrates a sequence of events from start to finish; it is indispensable when illustrating processes, procedures, and sequential relationships. For general business purposes, you don't need to be too concerned about the specific shapes on a flowchart; just be sure to use them consistently. However, you should be aware that there is a formal flowchart

Flowchart:
A chart that illustrates a sequence of events from start to finish.

"language," in which each shape has a specific meaning (diamonds are decision points, rectangles are process steps, and so on). If you're communicating with computer programmers and others who are accustomed to formal flowcharting, make sure you use the correct symbols to avoid confusion.

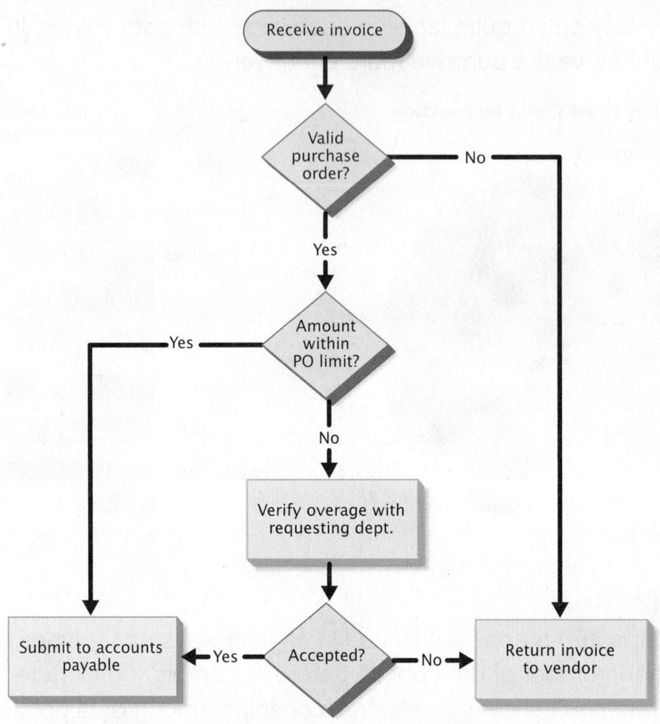

Figure 11.10
Flowchart
Flowcharts show sequences of events and are most valuable when the process or procedure has a number of decision points and variable paths.

As the name implies, an **organization chart** illustrates the positions, units, or functions in an organization and the ways they interrelate (see Figure 11.11). Organization charts can be used to portray almost any hierarchy, in fact, including the topics, subtopics, and supporting points you need to organize for a report.

Organization chart: A chart that illustrates the positions, units, or functions in an organization and the ways they interrelate.

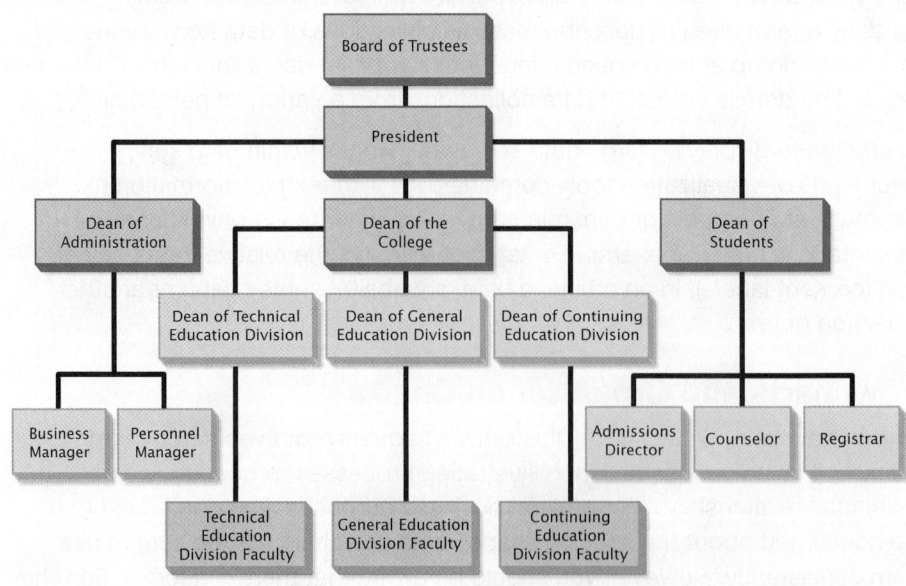

Figure 11.11
Organization Chart
An organization chart is the expected way to illustrate the hierarchy of positions in an organization.

Maps, Drawings, Diagrams, Infographics, Figures, and Photographs

Maps can show location, distance, points of interest (such as competitive retail outlets), and geographic distribution of data, such as sales by region or population by state. In addition to presenting facts and figures, maps are useful for showing market territories, distribution routes, and facilities locations. When combined with databases and aerial or satellite photography in *geographic information systems (GIS)*, maps become extremely powerful visual reporting tools.

Drawings and diagrams can show an endless variety of business concepts, such as the network of suppliers in an industry, the flow of funds through a company, or the process for completing payroll each week. More complex diagrams can convey technical topics, such as the operation of a machine or repair procedures.

You can create drawings and diagrams in a variety of applications. For simple drawings, you might use the drawing tools in applications such as Microsoft PowerPoint or Microsoft Word. For more complicated drawings, you might use Microsoft Visio, or a full-featured drawing program such as Adobe Illustrator.

Infographics are a special class of diagrams that can convey both data and concepts or ideas. In addition, infographics contain enough visual and textual information to function as independent, standalone documents. Broadly speaking, there are two types of infographics, those that are stylized collections of charts or graphs and those that have a structured narrative. The first types, represented by Figure 11.12a, don't necessarily convey any more information than basic charts and graphs in a conventional report would; their communication value lies in their ability to catch the audience's attention and the ease with which they can be distributed online. The second types, represented by Figure 11.12b, go beyond this to take full advantage of the visual medium to tell stories or show interconnected processes. These infographics can be powerful communication tools, even to the point of replacing conventional reports. You can create simple infographics using the SmartArt feature in Microsoft Office applications, or by using a drawing program.

Infographics: Graphic visual representations of information or data intended to present information quickly and clearly.

When a graphic is referenced by name or number in the text, it is commonly called a figure. For example, in this book, each graphic has a number (such as Figure 11.12) and a caption. A figure can be any type of graphic, such as a drawing, diagram, infographic, map, or photograph. To create your own figures, use an appropriate application for the type of figure you want. Then in the word processing or desktop publishing program you are working with, use the Caption feature to add numbered descriptive captions for you figures.

Figure 11.12
Infographics
Roughly speaking, infographics can be divided into simple presentations of data (Figure 11.12a) and visual narratives (Figure 11.12b) that use the full power of the medium to tell stories or illustrate processes.

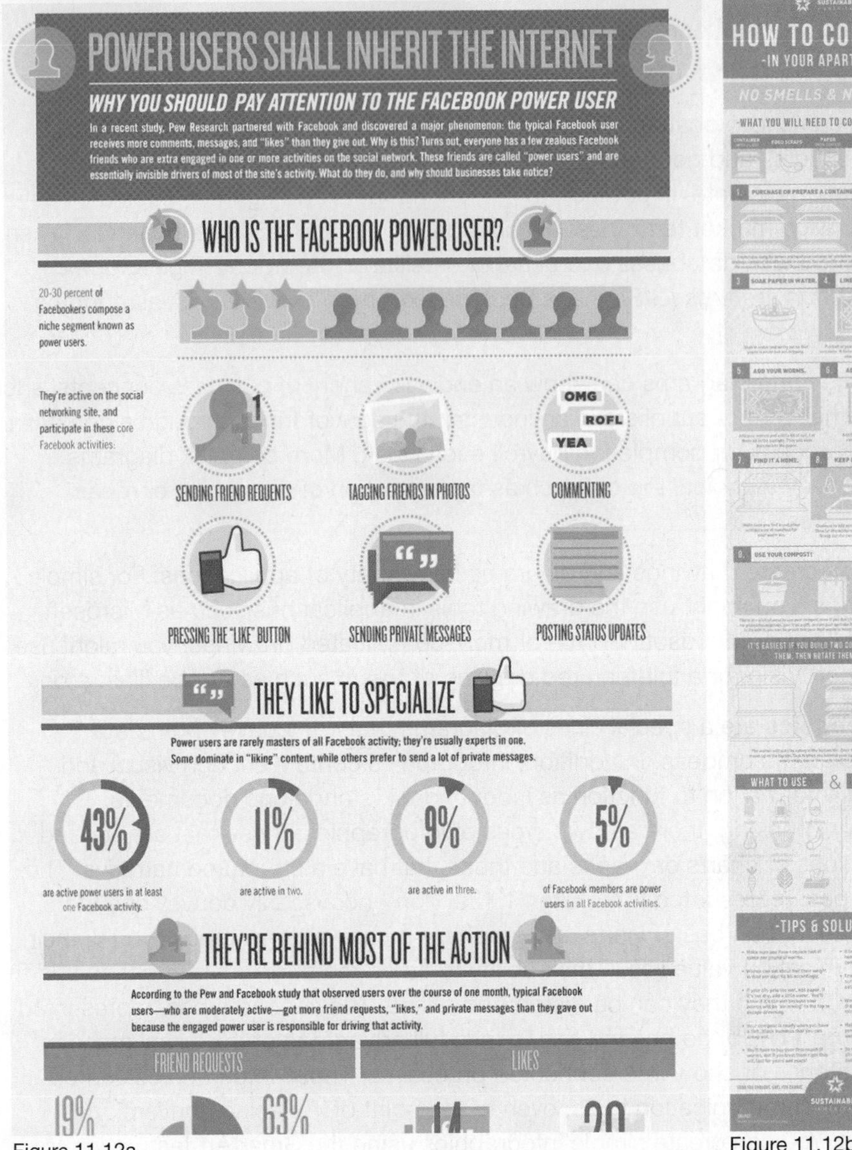

Figure 11.12a

Figure 11.12b

Photographs offer both functional and decorative value, and nothing can top a photograph when you need to show exact appearances. However, in some situations, a photograph can show too much detail, which is one reason repair manuals frequently use drawings instead of photos. Because audiences expect photographs to show literal visual truths, you must take care when using image-processing tools such as Adobe Photoshop.

Animation and Video

Computer animation and video can offer unparalleled visual impact when they offer appropriate content in a well-produced package. At a simple level, you can animate shapes and text on presentation slides. At a more sophisticated level, software such as Adobe Flash enables the creation of multimedia files that include computer animation, digital video, and other elements.

The combination of simple digital video recording and video-sharing websites such as YouTube has spurred a revolution in business video applications in recent years. Product demonstrations, company overviews, promotional presentations, and training seminars are among the most popular applications of business video. *Branded channels* on YouTube allow companies to present their videos as an integrated collection in a customized user interface.

Designing Effective Visuals

Computers make it easy to create great visuals and even easier to create awful ones. Following the design principles on page 367 will help you create basic visuals that are attractive and effective. If possible, have a professional designer set up a template for the various types of visuals you and your colleagues need to create. By specifying color palettes, typeface selections, slide layouts, and other choices, design templates have three important benefits: they help ensure better designs, they promote consistency across the organization, and they save everyone time by eliminating repetitive decision making.

Remember that the style and quality of your visuals communicate a subtle message about your relationship with the audience. A simple sketch might be fine for a working meeting but inappropriate for a formal presentation or report. On the other hand, elaborate, full-color visuals may be viewed as extravagant for an informal report but may be entirely appropriate for a message to top management or influential outsiders.

In addition to being well designed, visuals need to be well integrated with text. First, try to position your visuals so that your audience won't have to flip back and forth in printed documents or scroll on screen between visuals and the text that discusses them. If space constraints prevent you from placing visuals close to relevant text, include pointers such as "Figure 2 (on the following page)" to help readers locate the image quickly. Second, clearly refer to visuals by number in the text of your report and help your readers understand the significance of visuals by referring to them before readers encounter them in the document or on screen. Third, write effective titles, captions, and legends to complete the integration of your text and visuals. A **title** provides a short description that identifies the content and purpose of the visual. A **caption** usually offers additional discussion of the visual's content and can be several sentences long, if appropriate. A **legend** helps readers "decode" the visual by explaining what various colors, symbols, or other design choices mean.

Title:
A short description that identifies the content and purpose of the item.

Caption:
Text accompanying a graphic or chart that offers additional discussion of its content.

Legend:
A table or key that helps the reader decode a visual by explaining what various colors, symbols, or design choices mean.

Be sure to check your visuals carefully for accuracy. Check for mistakes such as typographical errors, inconsistent color treatment, confusing or undocumented symbols, and misaligned elements. Make sure that your computer hasn't done something unexpected, such as arranging chart bars in an order you don't want or plotting line charts in confusing colors. Make sure your visuals are properly documented. Most important, make sure your visuals are honest—that they don't intentionally or unintentionally distort the truth.

Finally, step back and consider the ethical implications of your visuals. Visuals are easy to misuse, intentionally or unintentionally. To avoid ethical lapses in your visuals, consider all possible interpretations, provide enough background information for readers to interpret your visuals correctly, and don't hide or minimize visual information that readers need in order to make informed judgments.

Designing Effective Page Layouts

In addition to using graphics to improve a page's appearance, you can also use a variety of design and layout conventions. Here are some basic elements of graphic design that should be considered:

- **Headings.** Break up a text-heavy page by adding headings that summarize the content of the text beneath them. For example, if your report outlines three strategies, include a heading for each of the strategies.
- **Multiple columns.** You can break up the text on a page into multiple newspaper-style columns. If you use a desktop publishing application or word processing application that supports multiple columns, the text will automatically flow between the linked columns, as in Figure 11.13, making

Figure 11.13
Effective page layout
An effective page layout makes the content accessible to the reader visually. A plain page of text can be enhanced with elements such as headings, multiple columns, graphics, typography, and text wrapping.

This page title is enhanced by an underline, a large font, and colored text.

GS-400 Garden Tiller/Cultivator

This picture is set so that text wraps tightly around it.

Stop struggling with heavy, difficult-to-use tillers! The GS-400 tiller/cultivator is a lightweight tiller that makes gardening easier. Featuring premium soft-grip handles for maximum control and comfort, a palm-controlled safety switch, and multiple speed control options, this tiller offers superior ease of operation.

The GS-400 tiller/cultivator is the **easiest-to-handle** small tiller on the market. Designed for home gardeners like you, the GS-400 tiller is a single solution powerhouse for all your gardening tasks. It's easy to lift, easy to carry, and easy to move around the yard.

At only 25 pounds, the GS-400 tiller is the **lightest weight** tiller available. Its sought-after features, combined with classic ruggedness and dependability, make the GS-400 tiller the ultimate home gardening solution for

the back-breaking drudgery of hand-digging or the budget-busting inconvenience of renting a hard-to-handle professional model. Your garden chores will get some faster and easier than you ever dreamed possible, from weeding around delicate plants to busting tough clods of sod, and even digging planting holes. The GS-400 tiller **does it all**.

A commercial grade engine is at the heart of each GS-400 tiller, paired with a durable power train that features our exclusive precision gear system and heavy-duty aluminum housing. It produces **exceptional power**, turning specialized spring-steel serpentine tines at up to 250 RPM for maximum performance. Reversing the tines produces a unit delicate enough for weeding, making the GS-400 tiller a lightweight **premium cultivator**. Most gardens can be weeded in under 20 minutes, saving both time and effort.

Rather than using headings, this layout uses typography to draw attention to certain words.

The two-column layout breaks up the text into easier-to-read segments.

- **Text wrap.** You can set text to wrap around a graphic, as in Figure 11.13. Most desktop publishing and word processing applications enable you to adjust the wrap in relation to the image. If you move the image around in the document, the text wrap changes automatically.
- **Typography.** The typeface and font size you choose can make a page much more or less readable, as you learned in Chapter 5. Choose a font size of at least 10 points for body text. You can also use typography as a graphical element, as in Figure 11.13, to create interest on the page.
- **Repetition.** For consistency, consider repeating key elements on every page, such as the document's title or the company name in the header and footer of each page.
- **Proximity.** Make sure that any graphics, charts, tables, or infographics you use are placed nearby the reference to them in the text. If they get too far away, the reader may not understand the connection.
- **Figure numbering.** It may be appropriate to number the figure captions, and to refer to the numbers in the text discussion.
- **White space.** You can make a page easier to read by creating intentional areas of white space. Readers will find a page more appealing if it is not stuffed over-full of text.
- **Contrast.** Make sure that the color of the paper or background contrasts sharply with the color of the text.

Completing Reports and Proposals

When you have finished the first draft of a report or proposal, you need to perform four tasks to complete it: revise, produce, proofread, and distribute. The revision process is essentially the same for reports as for other business messages, although it may take considerably longer, depending on the length and complexity of your documents. Evaluate your organization, style, and tone to make sure your content is clear, logical, and reader oriented. Then work to improve the report's readability by varying sentence length, keeping paragraphs short, using lists and bullets, and adding headings and subheadings. Remember that even minor mistakes can affect your credibility.

Tight, efficient writing that is easy to skim is always a plus, but it's especially important for impatient online audiences. Review online content carefully; strip out all information that doesn't meet audience needs and condense everything else as much as possible. Audiences will gladly return to sites that deliver quality information quickly—and they'll avoid sites that don't.

After assembling your report or proposal in its final form, review it thoroughly one last time, looking for inconsistencies, errors, and missing components. Don't forget to proof your visuals thoroughly and make sure they are positioned correctly. For online reports, make sure all links work as expected and all necessary files are active and available. If you need specific tips on proofreading documents, look back at Chapter 5.

Producing Formal Reports and Proposals

Formal reports and proposals can include a variety of features beyond the text and visuals (see Table 11.2). Most of these provide additional information; a few are more decorative and add a degree of formality

Table 11.2 Production Elements to Consider for Formal Reports and Proposals

Reports	Proposals
Prefatory elements (before the introduction)	Prefatory elements (before the introduction)
• Cover. Include a concise title that gives readers the information they need to grasp the purpose and scope of the report. For a formal printed report, choose heavy, high-quality cover stock. • Title fly. Some formal reports open with a plain sheet of paper that has only the title of the report on it, although this is certainly not necessary. • Title page. Typically includes the report title, name(s) and title(s) of the writer(s), and date of submission; this information can be put on the cover instead. • Letter of authorization. If you received written authorization to prepare the report, you may want to include that letter or memo in your report. • Letter of transmittal. "Cover letter" that introduces the report and can include scope, methods, limitations, highlights of the report; offers to provide follow-on information or assistance; and acknowledges help received while preparing the report. • Table of contents. List all section headings and major subheadings to show the location and hierarchy of the information in the report. • List of illustrations. Consider including if the illustrations are particularly important, and you want to call attention to them. • Synopsis or executive summary. See discussion on page 381.	• Cover, title fly, title page. Same uses as with reports; be sure to follow any instructions in the RFP (request for proposal), if relevant. • Copy of or reference to the RFP. Instead of having a letter of authorization, a solicited proposal should follow the instructions in the RFP. Some will instruct you to include the entire RFP in your proposal; others may want you to simply identify it by a name and tracking number. • Synopsis or executive summary. These components are less common in formal proposals than in reports. In an unsolicited proposal, your letter of transmittal will catch the reader's interest. In a solicited proposal, the introduction will provide an adequate preview of the contents. • Letter of transmittal. If the proposal is solicited, treat the transmittal letter as a positive message, highlighting those aspects of your proposal that may give you a competitive advantage. If the proposal is unsolicited, the transmittal letter should follow the advice for persuasive messages (see Chapter 9)—the letter must persuade the reader that you have something worthwhile to offer that justifies reading the proposal.
Supplementary elements (after the close)	Supplementary elements (after the close)
• Appendixes. Additional information related to the report but not included in the main text because it is too lengthy or lacks direct relevance. List appendixes in your table of contents and refer to them as appropriate in the text. • Bibliography. List the secondary sources you consulted; see Chapter 10. • Index. List names, places, and subjects mentioned in the report, along with the pages on which they occur.	• Appendixes. Same uses as with reports; be sure to follow any instructions in the RFP, if relevant. • Resumes of key players. For external proposals, resumes can convince readers that you have the talent to achieve the proposal's objectives.

One of the most important elements to consider is an introductory feature that helps time-pressed readers either get a sense of what's in the document or even get all the key points without reading the document. A **synopsis**, sometimes called an **abstract**, is a brief overview (one page or less) of a report's most important points. The phrasing of a synopsis can be *informative* (presenting the main points in the order in which they appear in the text) if you're using the direct approach or *descriptive* (simply describing what the report is about, without "giving away the ending") if you're using the indirect approach. As an alternative to a synopsis or an abstract, a longer report may include an **executive summary,** a fully developed "mini" version of the report, for readers who lack the time or motivation to read the entire document.

Synopsis (abstract): A brief overview of a report's most important points.

Executive summary: A fully developed mini version of a report, for readers who lack the time or motivation to read the entire document.

For an illustration of how the various parts of a report fit together, see Figure 11.14.

Figure 11.14
Analyzing an Effective Formal Report

The "how-to" tone of Moreno's title is appropriate for an action-oriented report that emphasizes recommendations. A more neutral title, such as "An Analysis of Electrovision's Travel and Entertainment Costs," would be more suitable for an informational report.

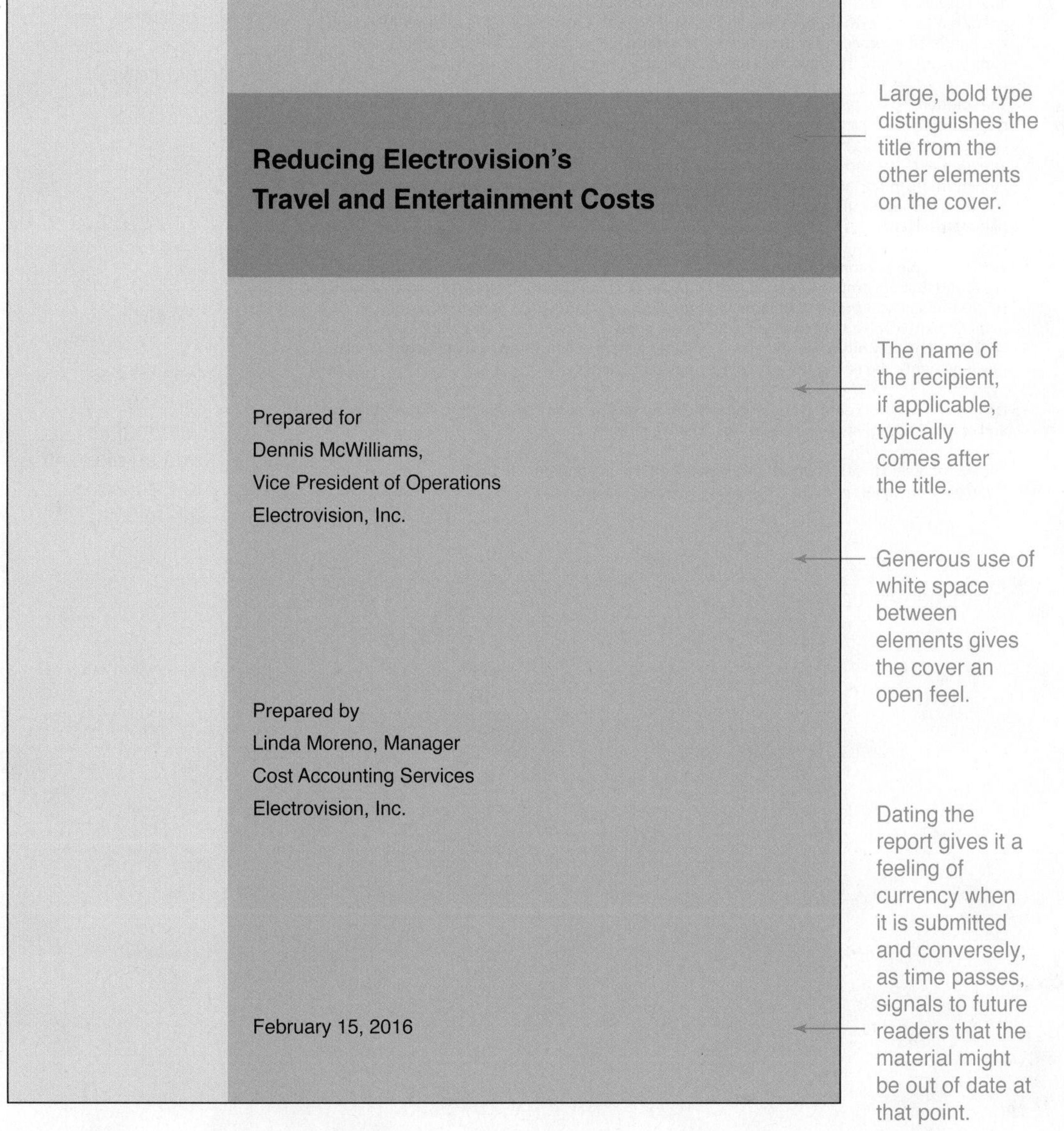

Reducing Electrovision's
Travel and Entertainment Costs

Prepared for
Dennis McWilliams,
Vice President of Operations
Electrovision, Inc.

Prepared by
Linda Moreno, Manager
Cost Accounting Services
Electrovision, Inc.

February 15, 2016

Large, bold type distinguishes the title from the other elements on the cover.

The name of the recipient, if applicable, typically comes after the title.

Generous use of white space between elements gives the cover an open feel.

Dating the report gives it a feeling of currency when it is submitted and conversely, as time passes, signals to future readers that the material might be out of date at that point.

In this report, Moreno decided to write a brief memo of transmittal and include a separate executive summary. Short reports (fewer than 10 pages) often combine the synopsis or executive summary with the memo or letter of transmittal.

The memo format is appropriate for this internal report; the letter format would be used for transmitting an external report.

MEMORANDUM

TO: Dennis McWilliams, Vice President of Operations
FROM: Linda Moreno, Manager of Cost Accounting LM
DATE: Services February 15, 2016
SUBJECT: Reducing Electrovision's Travel and Entertainment Costs

Here is the report you requested January 28 on Electrovision's travel and entertainment costs.

Moreno expects a positive response, so she presents her main conclusion right away.

Your suspicions were right. We are spending far too much on business travel. Our unwritten policy has been "anything goes," leaving us with no real control over T&E expenses. Although this hands-off approach may have been understandable when Electrovision's profits were high, we can no longer afford the luxury of going first class.

The tone is conversational yet still businesslike and respectful.

The solutions to the problem seem rather clear. We need to have someone with centralized responsibility for travel and entertainment costs, a clear statement of policy, an effective control system, and a business-oriented travel service that can optimize our travel arrangements. We should also investigate alternatives to travel, such as videoconferencing. Perhaps more important, we need to change our attitude. Instead of viewing travel funds as a bottomless supply of money, all traveling employees need to act as if they were paying the bills themselves.

Getting people to economize is not going to be easy. In the course of researching this issue, I've found that our employees are deeply attached to their generous travel privileges. I think some would almost prefer a cut in pay to a loss in travel status. We'll need a lot of top management involvement to sell people on the need for moderation. One thing is clear: People will be very bitter if we create a two-class system in which top executives get special privileges while the rest of the employees make the sacrifices.

Acknowledging help given by others is good etiquette and a way to foster positive working relationships.

I'm grateful to Mary Lehman and Connie McIlvain for their considerable help in rounding up and sorting through five years' worth of expense reports.

Thanks for giving me the opportunity to work on this assignment. It's been a real education. If you have any questions about the report, please give me a call.

She closes graciously, with thanks and an offer to discuss the results.

Moreno decided to include an executive summary because her report is aimed at a mixed audience, some of whom are interested in the details of her report and others who just want the "big picture." The executive summary is aimed at the second group, giving them enough information to make a decision without burdening them with the task of reading the entire report.

Her writing style matches the serious nature of the content without sounding distant or stiff. Moreno chose the formal approach because several members of her audience are considerably higher up in the organization, and she did not want to sound too familiar. In addition, her company prefers the impersonal style for formal reports.

The executive summary begins by stating the purpose of the report.

Moreno presents the points in the executive summary in the same order as they appear in the report, using subheadings that summarize the content of the main sections of the report.

EXECUTIVE SUMMARY

This report analyzes Electrovision's travel and entertainment (T&E) costs and presents recommendations for reducing those costs.

Travel and Entertainment Costs Are Too High

Travel and entertainment is a large and growing expense category for Electrovision. The company spends over $16 million per year on business travel, and these costs have been increasing by 12 percent annually. Company employees make roughly 3,390 trips each year at an average cost per trip of $4,720. Airfares are the biggest expense, followed by hotels, meals, and rental cars.

The nature of Electrovision's business does require extensive travel, but the company's costs are excessive: our employees spend more than twice the national average on travel and entertainment. Although the location of the company's facilities may partly explain this discrepancy, the main reason for our high costs is a management style that gives employees little incentive to economize.

Cuts Are Essential

Electrovision management now recognizes the need to gain more control over this element of cost. The company is currently entering a period of declining profits, prompting management to look for every opportunity to reduce spending. At the same time, rising airfares and hotel rates are making T&E expenses more significant.

Electrovision Can Save $6 Million per Year

Fortunately, Electrovision has a number of excellent opportunities for reducing T&E costs. Savings of up to $6 million per year should be achievable, judging by the experience of other companies. A sensible travel-management program can save companies as much as 35 percent a year (Gilligan 39–40), and we should be able to save even more, since we purchase many more business-class tickets than the average. Four steps will help us cut costs:

1. Hire a director of travel and entertainment to assume overall responsibility for T&E spending, policies, and technologies, including the hiring and management of a national travel agency.
2. Educate employees on the need for cost containment, both in avoiding unnecessary travel and reducing costs when travel is necessary.
3. Negotiate preferential rates with travel providers.
4. Implement technological alternatives to travel, such as virtual meetings.

As necessary as these changes are, they will likely hurt morale, at least in the short term. Management will need to make a determined effort to explain the rationale for reduced spending. By exercising moderation in their own travel arrangements, Electrovision executives can set a good example and help other employees accept the changes. On the plus side, using travel alternatives such as web conferencing will reduce the travel burden on many employees and help them balance their business and personal lives.

iv

Her audience is receptive, so the tone in the executive summary is forceful; a more neutral approach would be better for hostile or skeptical readers.

The executive summary uses the same font and paragraph treatment as the text of the report.

The page numbering in the executive summary continues with Roman numerals.

In her brief introduction, Moreno counts on topic sentences and transitions to indicate that she is discussing the purpose, scope, and limitations of the study.

A color bar highlights the report title and the first-level headings; a variety of other design treatments are possible as well.

REDUCING ELECTROVISION'S TRAVEL AND ENTERTAINMENT COSTS

INTRODUCTION

The introduction opens by establishing the need for action.

Electrovision has always encouraged a significant amount of business travel. To compensate employees for the stress and inconvenience of frequent trips, management has authorized generous travel and entertainment (T&E) allowances. This philosophy has been good for morale, but last year Electrovision spent $16 million on travel and entertainment—$7 million more than it spent on research and development.

This year's T&E costs will affect profits even more, due to increases in airline fares and hotel rates. Also, the company anticipates that profits will be relatively weak for a variety of other reasons. Therefore, Dennis McWilliams, Vice President of Operations, has asked the accounting department to explore ways to reduce the T&E budget.

The purpose of this report is to analyze T&E expenses, evaluate the effect of recent hotel and airfare increases, and suggest ways to tighten control over T&E costs. The report outlines several steps that could reduce Electrovision's expenses, but the precise financial impact of these measures is difficult to project. The estimates presented here provide a "best guess" view of what Electrovision can expect to save.

Moreno mentions her sources and methods to increase credibility and to give readers a complete picture of the study's background.

In preparing this report, the accounting department analyzed internal expense reports for the past five years to determine how much Electrovision spends on travel and entertainment. These figures were then compared with average statistics compiled by Dow Jones (publisher of the Wall Street Journal) and presented as the Dow Jones Travel Index. We also analyzed trends and suggestions published in a variety of business journal articles to see how other companies are coping with the high cost of business travel.

THE HIGH COST OF TRAVEL AND ENTERTAINMENT

Although many companies view travel and entertainment as an incidental cost of doing business, the dollars add up. At Electrovision the bill for airfares, hotels, rental cars, meals, and entertainment totaled $16 million last year. Our T&E budget has increased by 12 percent per year for the past five years. Compared to the average U.S. business traveler, Electrovision's expenditures are high, largely because of management's generous policy on travel benefits.

A *running footer* that contains the report title and page number appears on every page.

Reducing Electrovision's Travel and Entertainment Costs Page 1

Moreno opens the first main section of the body with a topic sentence that introduces an important fact about the subject of the section. Then she orients the reader to the three major points developed in the section.

$16 Million per Year Spent on Travel and Entertainment

Electrovision's annual budget for travel and entertainment is only 8 percent of sales. Because this is a relatively small expense category compared with such things as salaries and commissions, it is tempting to dismiss T&E costs as insignificant. However, T&E is Electrovision's third-largest controllable expense, directly behind salaries and information systems.

Last year Electrovision personnel made about 3,390 trips at an average cost per trip of $4,720. The typical trip involved a round-trip flight of 3,000 miles, meals, and hotel accommodations for two or three days, and a rental car. Roughly 80 percent of trips were made by 20 percent of the staff—top management and sales personnel traveled most, averaging 18 trips per year.

Figure 1 illustrates how the T&E budget is spent. The largest categories are airfares and lodging, which together account for $7 out of $10 that employees spend on travel and entertainment. This spending breakdown has been relatively steady for the past five years and is consistent with the distribution of expenses experienced by other companies.

The visual is placed as close as possible to the point it illustrates.

Figure 1
Airfares and Lodging Account for Over Two-Thirds of Electrovision's T&E Budget

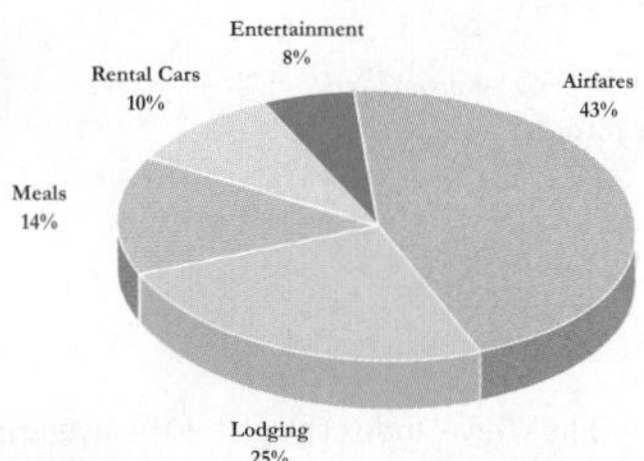

Although the composition of the T&E budget has been consistent, its size has not. As mentioned earlier, these expenditures have increased by about 12 percent per year for the past five years, roughly twice the rate of the company's sales growth (see Figure 2). This rate of growth makes T&E Electrovision's fastest-growing expense item.

Each visual has a title that clearly indicates what it's about; titles are consistently placed to the left of each visual.

Figure 2
T&E Expenses Continue to Increase as a Percentage of Sales

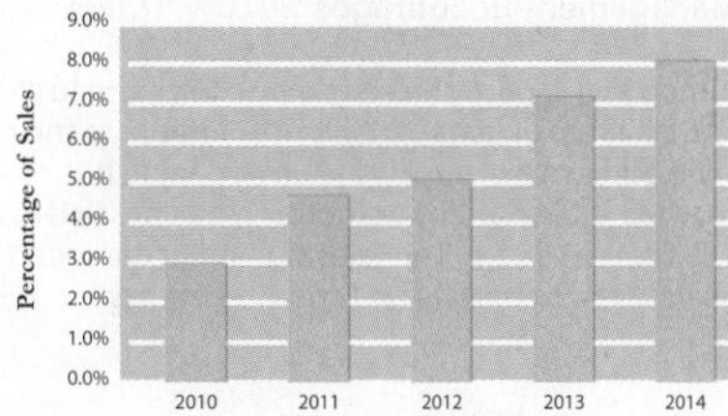

The chart in Figure 3 is simple but effective; Moreno includes just enough data to make her point. Notice how she is as careful about the appearance of her report as she is about the quality of its content.

Electrovision's Travel Expenses Exceed National Averages

Much of our travel budget is justified. Two major factors contribute to Electrovision's high T&E budget:

- With our headquarters on the West Coast and our major customer on the East Coast, we naturally spend a lot of money on cross-country flights.
- A great deal of travel takes place between our headquarters here on the West Coast and the manufacturing operations in Detroit, Boston, and Dallas. Corporate managers and division personnel make frequent trips to coordinate these disparate operations.

Even though a good portion of Electrovision's travel budget is justifiable, the company spends considerably more on T&E than the average business (see Figure 3).

Moreno introduces visuals before they appear and indicates what readers should notice about the data.

The visuals are numbered consecutively and referred to by their numbers in the text.

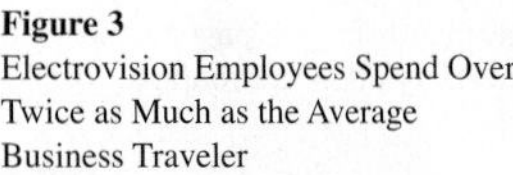

Figure 3
Electrovision Employees Spend Over Twice as Much as the Average Business Traveler

Source: *Wall Street Journal* and company records

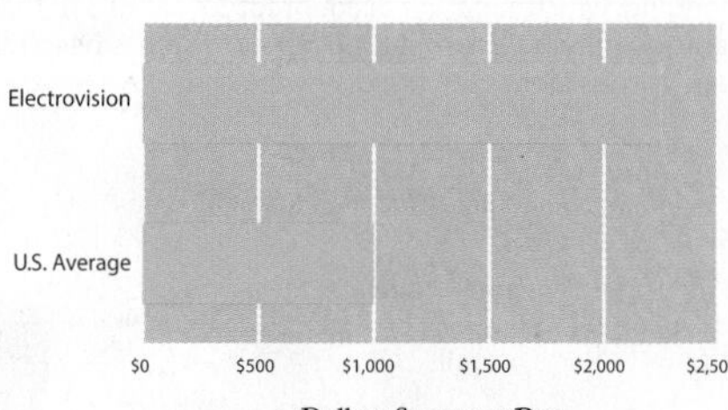

The Dow Jones Travel Index calculates the average cost per day of business travel in the United States, based on average airfare, hotel rates, and rental car rates. The average fluctuates weekly as travel companies change their rates, but it has been running at about $1,000 per day for the last year or so. In contrast, Electrovision's average daily expense over the past year has been $2,250—a hefty 125 percent higher than average. This figure is based on our average trip cost of $4,720 listed earlier and an average trip length of 2.1 days.

Management Encourages Luxury Travel

Although a variety of factors may contribute to this differential, Electrovision's relatively high T&E costs are at least partially attributable to the company's philosophy and management style. Since many employees do not enjoy business travel, management has tried to make the trips more pleasant by authorizing business-class airfare, luxury hotel accommodations, and full-size rental cars. The sales staff is encouraged to entertain clients at top restaurants and to invite them to cultural and sporting events.

Moreno designed her report to include plenty of white space so even those pages that lack visuals are still attractive and easy to read.

A bulleted list makes it easy for readers to identify and distinguish related points.

The cost of these privileges is easy to overlook, given the weakness of Electrovision's system for keeping track of T&E expenses:

- The monthly financial records do not contain a separate category for travel and entertainment; the information is buried under Cost of Goods Sold and under Selling, General, and Administrative Expenses.
- Each department head is given authority to approve any expense report, regardless of how large it may be.
- Receipts are not required for expenditures of less than $100.
- Individuals are allowed to make their own travel arrangements.
- No one is charged with the responsibility for controlling the company's total spending on travel and entertainment.

Informative headings focus reader attention on the main points. Such headings are appropriate when a report uses the direct order and is intended for a receptive audience. However, descriptive headings are more effective when a report uses the indirect order and readers are less receptive.

GROWING IMPACT ON THE BOTTOM LINE

During the past three years, the company's healthy profits have resulted in relatively little pressure to push for tighter controls over all aspects of the but we all know that situation is changing. We're projecting flat to declining profits for the next two years, a situation that has prompted all of us to search for ways to cut costs. At the same time, rising airfares and hotel rates have increased the impact of T&E expenses on the company's financial results.

Lower Profits Underscore the Need for Change

The next two years promise to be difficult for Electrovision. After several years of steady increases in spending, the Postal Service is tightening procurement policies for automated mail-handling equipment. Funding for the A-12 optical character reader has been canceled. As a consequence, the marketing department expects sales to drop by 15 percent. Although Electrovision is negotiating several other promising R&D contracts, the marketing depart- ment does not foresee any major procurements for the next two to three years.

At the same time, Electrovision is facing cost increases on several fronts. As we have known for several months, the new production facility now under construction in Salt Lake City, Utah, is behind schedule and over budget. Labor contracts in Boston and Dallas will expire within the next six months, and plant managers there anticipate that significant salary and benefits concessions may be necessary to avoid strikes.

Moreover, marketing and advertising costs are expected to increase as we attempt to strengthen these activities to better cope with competitive pressures. Given the expected decline in revenues and increase in costs, the Executive Committee's prediction that profits will fall by 12 percent in the coming fiscal year does not seem overly pessimistic.

Reducing Electrovision's Travel and Entertainment Costs Page 4

Moreno creates a forceful tone by using action verbs in the third-level subheadings of this section. This approach is appropriate to the nature of the study and the attitude of the audience. In an even more status-conscious organization, the imperative verbs might sound a bit too presumptuous coming from a junior member of the staff.

Moreno supports her argument with objective facts and sound reasoning.

Airfares and Hotel Rates Are Rising

Business travelers have grown accustomed to frequent fare wars and discounting in the travel industry in recent years. Excess capacity and aggressive price competition, particularly in the airline business, made travel a relative bargain.

That situation has changed as weaker competitors have been forced out and the remaining players have grown stronger and smarter. Airlines and hotels are better at managing inventory and keeping occupancy rates high, which translates into higher costs for Electrovision. Last year saw some of the steepest rate hikes in years. Business airfares (tickets most likely to be purchased by business travelers) jumped more than 40 percent in many markets. The trend is expected to continue, with rates increasing another 5 to 10 percent overall (Phillips 331; "Travel Costs Under Pressure" 30; Dahl B6).

Given the fact that air and hotel costs account for almost 70 percent of our T&E budget, the trend toward higher prices in these two categories will have serious consequences unless management takes action to control these costs.

The recommendations are realistic, noting both the benefits and the risks of taking action.

METHODS FOR REDUCING T&E COSTS

By implementing a number of reforms, management can expect to reduce Electrovision's T&E budget by as much as 40 percent. This estimate is based on the general assessment made by American Express (Gilligan 39) and on the fact that we have an opportunity to significantly reduce air travel costs by eliminating business-class travel. However, these measures are likely to be unpopular with employees. To gain acceptance for such changes, management will need to sell employees on the need for moderation in T&E allowances.

Four Ways to Trim Expenses

By researching what other companies are doing to curb T&E expenses, the accounting department has identified four prominent opportunities that should enable Electrovision to save about $6 million annually in travel-related costs.

Institute Tighter Spending Controls

A single individual should be appointed director of travel and entertainment to spearhead the effort to gain control of the T&E budget. More than a third of all US companies now employ travel managers ("Businesses Use Savvy Managers" 4). The director should be familiar with the travel industry and should be well versed in both accounting and information technology. The director should also report to the vice president of operations. The director's first priorities should be to establish a written T&E policy and a cost-control system.

Electrovision currently has no written policy on travel and entertainment, a step that is widely recommended by air travel experts (Smith D4). Creating a policy would clarify management's position and serve as a vehicle for communicating the need for moderation.

Moreno takes care not to overstep the boundaries of her analysis. For instance, she doesn't analyze the value of the seminars that employees attend every year, so she avoids any absolute statements about reducing travel to seminars.

In addition to making key points easy to find, bulleted lists help break up the text to relieve the reader's eye.

At a minimum, the policy should include the following:

- All travel and entertainment should be strictly related to business and should be approved in advance.
- Except under special circumstances to be approved on a case-by-case basis, employees should travel by coach and stay in mid-range business hotels.
- The T&E policy should apply equally to employees at all levels.

To implement the new policy, Electrovision will need to create a system for controlling T&E expenses. Each department should prepare an annual T&E budget as part of its operating plan. These budgets should be presented in detail so that management can evaluate how T&E dollars will be spent and can recommend appropriate cuts. To help management monitor performance relative to these budgets, the director of travel should prepare monthly financial statements showing actual T&E expenditures by department.

Moreno lists the steps needed to implement her recommendations.

The director of travel should also retain a business-oriented travel service that will schedule all employee business trips and look for the best travel deals, particularly in airfares. In addition to centralizing Electrovision's reservation and ticketing activities, the agency will negotiate reduced group rates with hotels and rental car firms.
The agency selected should have offices nationwide so that all Electrovision facilities can channel their reservations through the same company. This is particularly important in light of the dizzying array of often wildly different airfares available between some cities. It's not uncommon to find dozens of fares along commonly traveled routes (Rowe 30). In addition, the director can help coordinate travel across the company to secure group discounts whenever possible (Barker 31; Miller B6).

Reduce Unnecessary Travel and Entertainment

One of the easiest ways to reduce expenses is to reduce the amount of traveling and entertaining that occurs. An analysis of last year's expenditures suggests that as much as 30 percent of Electrovision's travel and entertainment is discretionary. The professional staff spent $2.8 million attending seminars and conferences last year. Although these gatherings are undoubtedly beneficial, the company could save money by sending fewer representatives to each function and perhaps by eliminating some of the less valuable seminars.

Similarly, Electrovision could economize on trips between headquarters and divisions by reducing the frequency of such visits and by sending fewer people on each trip. Although there is often no substitute for face-to-face meetings, management could try to resolve more internal issues through telephone, electronic, and written communication.

Electrovision can also reduce spending by urging employees to economize. Instead of flying business class, employees can fly coach class or take advantage of discount fares.

Reducing Electrovision's Travel and Entertainment Costs Page 6

Note how Moreno makes the transition from section to section. The first sentence under the second heading on this page refers to the subject of the previous paragraph and signals a shift in thought.

By pointing out possible difficulties and showing that she has considered all angles, Moreno builds reader confidence in her judgment.

Obtain Lowest Rates from Travel Providers

Apart from urging employees to economize, Electrovision can also save money by searching for the lowest available airfares, hotel rates, and rental car fees. Currently, few employees have the time or knowledge to seek out travel bargains. When they need to travel, they make the most convenient and comfortable arrangements. A professional travel service will be able to obtain lower rates from travel providers.

Judging by the experience of other companies, Electrovision may be able to trim as much as 30 to 40 percent from the travel budget simply by looking for bargains in airfares and negotiating group rates with hotels and rental car companies. Electrovision should be able to achieve these economies by analyzing its travel patterns, identifying frequently visited locations, and selecting a few hotels that are willing to reduce rates in exchange for guaranteed bussiness. At the same time, the company should be able to save up to 40 percent on rental car charges by negotiating a corporate rate.

The possibilities for economizing are promising; however, making the best travel arrangements often requires trade-offs such as the following:

- The best fares might not always be the lowest. Indirect flights are usually cheaper, but they take longer and may end up costing more in lost work time.
- The cheapest tickets often require booking 14 or even 30 days in advance, which is often impossible for us.
- Discount tickets are usually nonrefundable, which is a serious drawback when a trip needs to be canceled at the last minute.

Replace Travel with Technological Alternatives

Online meeting systems such as WebEx and GoTo Meeting offer a compelling alternative to many instances of business travel. With webcam video, application/screen sharing, and collaboration tools such as virtual whiteboards, they have made great strides toward replicating the in-person meeting experience.

As effective as they can be, though, they shouldn't automatically replace every in-person meeting. When establishing a business relationship, for example, meeting face to face is an important part of building trust and getting past the uncertainties of working with a new partner. Part of the new travel director's job would be to draft guidelines for choosing travel or on-line meeting options.

Note how Moreno calls attention in the first paragraph to items in the following table, without repeating the information in the table.

An informative title in the table is consistent with the way headings are handled throughout this report, and it is appropriate for a report to a receptive audience.

The in-text reference to the table highlights the key point the reader should get from the table.

Including financial estimates helps management envision the impact of the suggestions, even though the estimated savings are difficult to project accurately.

The Impact of Reforms

By implementing tighter controls, reducing unnecessary expenses, negotiating more favorable rates, and exploring alternatives to travel, Electrovision should be able to reduce its T&E budget significantly. As Table 1 illustrates, the combined savings should be in the neighborhood of $6 million, although the precise figures are somewhat difficult to project.

Table 1
Electrovision Can Trim Travel and Entertainment Costs by an Estimated $6 Million per Year

SOURCE OF SAVINGS	ESTIMATED SAVINGS
Switching from business-class to coach airfare	$2,300,000
Negotiating preferred hotel rates	940,000
Negotiating preferred rental car rates	460,000
Systematically searching for lower airfares	375,000
Reducing interdivisional travel	675,000
Reducing seminar and conference attendance	1,250,000
TOTAL POTENTIAL SAVINGS	**$6,000,000**

To achieve the economies outlined in the table, Electrovision will incur expenses for hiring a director of travel and for implementing a T&E cost-control system. These costs are projected at $115,000: $105,000 per year in salary and benefits for the new employee and a one-time expense of $10,000 for the cost-control system. The cost of retaining a full-service travel agency is negligible, even with the service fees that many are now passing along from airlines and other service providers.

The measures required to achieve these savings are likely to be unpopular with employees. Electrovision personnel are accustomed to generous T&E allowances, and they are likely to resent having these privileges curtailed. To alleviate their disappointment

- Management should make a determined effort to explain why the changes are necessary.
- The director of corporate communication should be asked to develop a multifaceted campaign that will communicate the importance of curtailing T&E costs.
- Management should set a positive example by adhering strictly to the new policies.
- The limitations should apply equally to employees at all levels in the organization.

Moreno doesn't introduce any new facts in this section. In a longer report she might have divided this section into subsections, labeled "Conclusions" and "Recommendations," to distinguish between the two.

She uses a descriptive heading for the last section of the text. In informational reports, this section is often called "Summary"; in analytical reports, it is called "Conclusions" or "Conclusions and Recommendations."

Moreno summarizes her conclusions in the first two paragraphs—a good approach because she organized her report around conclusions and recommendations, so readers have already been introduced to them.

CONCLUSIONS AND RECOMMENDATIONS

Electrovision is currently spending $16 million per year on travel and entertainment. Although much of this spending is justified, the company's costs are high relative to competitors' costs, mainly because Electrovision has been generous with its travel benefits.

Electrovision's liberal approach to travel and entertainment was understandable during years of high profitability, but the company is facing the prospect of declining profits for the next several years. Management is therefore motivated to cut costs in all areas of the business. Reducing T&E spending is particularly important because the bottom-line impact of these costs will increase as airline fares increase.

Electrovision should be able to reduce T&E costs by as much as 40 percent by taking four important steps:

Presenting the recommendations in a list gives each one emphasis.

1. Institute tighter spending controls. Management should hire a director of travel and entertainment who will assume overall responsibility for T&E activities. Within the next six months, this director should develop a written travel policy, institute a T&E budget and a cost-control system, and retain a professional, business-oriented travel agency that will optimize arrangements with travel providers.

2. Reduce unnecessary travel and entertainment. Electrovision should encourage employees to economize on T&E spending. Management can accomplish this by authorizing fewer trips and by urging employees to be more conservative in their spending.

3. Obtain lowest rates from travel providers. Electrovision should also focus on obtaining the best rates on airline tickets, hotel rooms, and rental cars. By channeling all arrangements through a professional travel agency, the company can optimize its choices and gain clout in negotiating preferred rates.

4. Replace some travel with technological alternatives. Online meeting systems are adequate for most of our tactical meetings with established clients and for most internal communication as well.

Because these measures may be unpopular with employees, management should make a concerted effort to explain the importance of reducing travel costs. The director of corporate communication should be given responsibility for developing a plan to communicate the need for employee cooperation.

MLA style lists references alphabetically by the author's last name, and when the author is unknown, by the title of the reference.

WORKS CITED

Barker, Julie. "How to Rein in Group Travel Costs." Successful Meetings Feb. 2014: 31. Print.

"Businesses Use Savvy Managers to Keep Travel Costs Down." Christian Science Monitor 17 July 2013: 4. Print.

Dahl, Jonathan. "2000: The Year Travel Costs Took Off." Wall Street Journal 29 Dec. 2007: B6. Print.

Gilligan, Edward P. "Trimming Your T&E Is Easier Than You Think." Managing Office Technology Nov. 2013: 39–40. Print.

Miller, Lisa. "Attention, Airline Ticket Shoppers." Wall Street Journal 7 July 2013: B6. Print.

Phillips, Edward H. "Airlines Post Record Traffic." Aviation Week & Space Technology 8 Jan. 2014: 331. Print.

"Product Overview: Cisco WebEx Meeting Center," Webex.com. WebEx, n.d. 2 Feb. 2014. Web.

Rowe, Irene Vlitos. "Global Solution for Cutting Travel Costs." European Business 12 Oct. 2011: 30. Print.

Smith, Carol. "Rising, Erratic Airfares Make Company Policy Vital." Los Angeles Times 2 Nov. 2012: D4. Print.

Solheim, Shelley. "Web Conferencing Made Easy." eWeek 22 Aug. 2012: 26. Web.

"Travel Costs Under Pressure." Purchasing 15 Feb. 2012: 30. Print.

Moreno's list of references follows the style recommended in the *MLA Style Manual.* The box below shows how these sources would be cited following *American Psychological Associations* (APA) style.

REFERENCES

Barker, J. (2014, February). How to rein in group travel costs. Successful Meetings, p. 31.

Businesses use savvy managers to keep travel costs down. (2012, July 17). Christian Science Monitor, p. 4.

Dahl, J. (2007, December 29). 2000: The year travel costs took off. Wall Street Journal, B6.

Gilligan, E. (2013, November). Trimming your T&E is easier than you think. Managing Office Technology, pp. 39–40.

Miller, L. (2013, July 7). Attention, airline ticket shoppers. Wall Street Journal, B6.

Phillips, E. (2014, January 8). Aviation Week & Space Technology, p. 331.

Rowe, I. (2011, October 12). Global solution for cutting travel costs. European, p. 30.

Smith, C. (2012, November 2). Rising, erratic airfares make company policy vital. Los Angeles Times, D4.

Solheim, S. (2012, August 22). Web conferencing made easy. eWeek, p. 26.

Travel costs under pressure. (2012, February 15). Purchasing, p. 30.

WebEx.com. (2014). Cisco WebEx Meeting Center. Retrieved from http://www.webex.com/product-overview/index.html

Just as with reports, the text of a proposal is composed of an introduction, a body, and a close. The introduction presents and summarizes the problem you intend to solve and your solution for it, plus the benefits the reader will receive from that solution. The body explains the complete details of the solution: how the job will be done, how it will be broken into tasks, what method will be used to do it (including the required equipment, material, and personnel), when the work will begin and end, how much the work will cost, and why your company is qualified (for external proposals). The close emphasizes the benefits readers will realize from your solution and ends with a persuasive call to action (see Figure 11.15).

Distributing Reports and Proposals

For physical distribution of important printed reports or proposals, consider spending the extra money for a professional courier or package delivery service. Doing so can help you stand out in a crowd, and it lets you verify receipt. Alternatively, if you've prepared the document for a single person or small group in your office or the local area, delivering it in person will give you the chance to personally "introduce" the report and remind readers why they're receiving it.

For digital distribution, unless your audience specifically requests a word processor file, provide documents as portable document format (PDF) files. Using Adobe Acrobat or similar products, you can quickly convert reports and proposals to PDF files that are easy to share online. PDFs are generally considered safer than word processor files, but they can also be used to transmit computer viruses.

If your company or client expects you to distribute your reports via cloud storage, a web-based content management system, a shared workspace, or some other online location, double-check that you've uploaded the correct files to the correct location. Verify the on-screen display of your reports after you've posted them, making sure graphics, charts, links, and other elements are in place and operational.

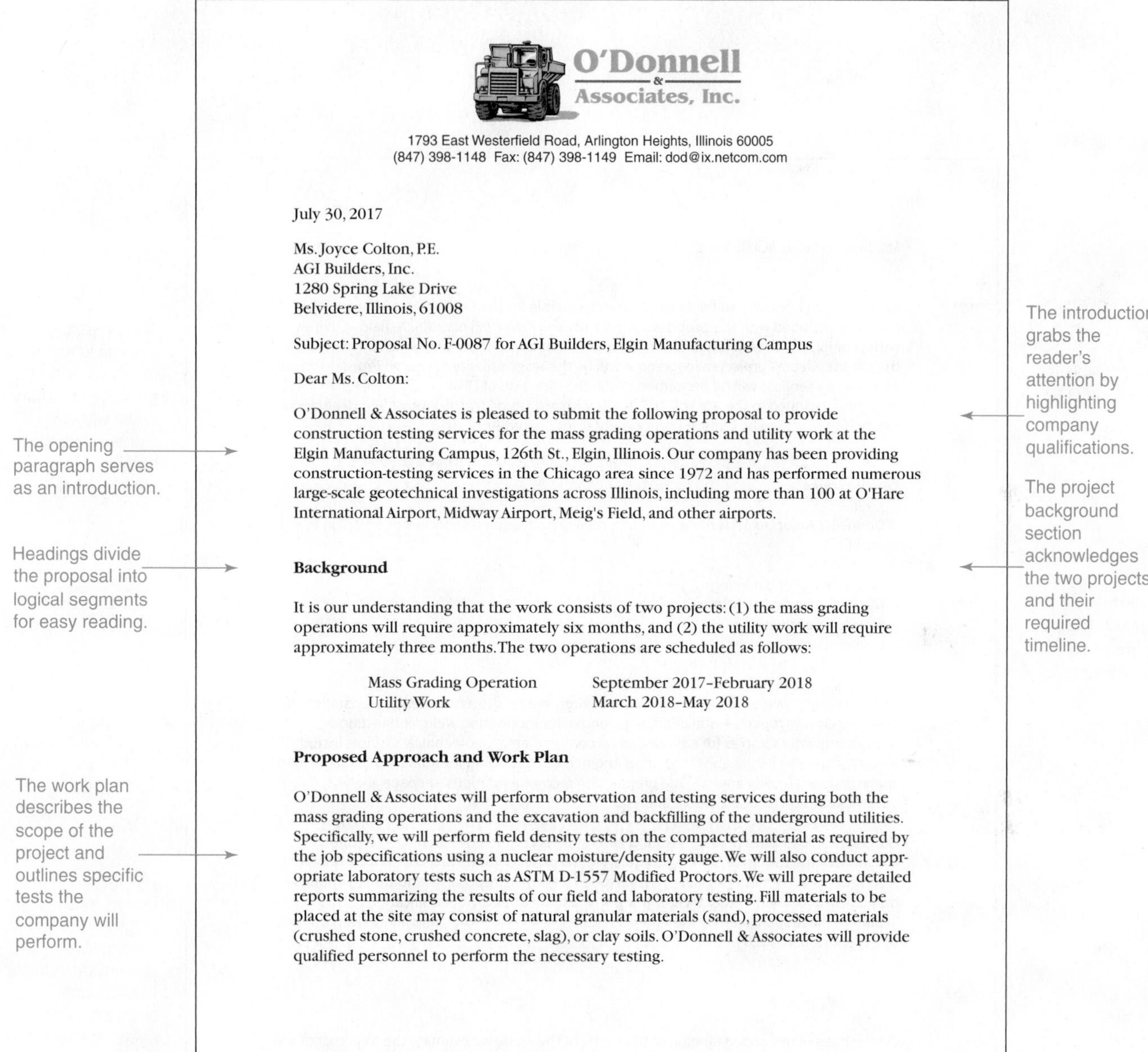

Figure 11.15
External Solicited Proposal

This proposal was submitted by Dixon O'Donnell, vice president of O'Donnell & Associates, a geotechnical engineering firm that conducts a variety of environmental testing services. The company is bidding on the mass grading and utility work specified by AGI Builders. As you review this document, pay close attention to the specific items addressed in the proposal's introduction, body, and closing.

The work plan also explains who will be responsible for the various tasks.

The project leader's resume is attached to the proposal, providing additional detail without cluttering up the body of the proposal.

Ms. Joyce Colton, AGI Builders Page 2 July 30, 2017

Kevin Patel will be the lead field technician responsible for the project. A copy of Mr. Patel's resume is included with this proposal for your review. Kevin will coordinate field activities with your job site superintendent and make sure that appropriate personnel are assigned to the job site. Overall project management will be the responsibility of Joseph Proesel. Project engineering services will be performed under the direction of Dixon O'Donnell, P.E. All field personnel assigned to the site will be familiar with and abide by the Project Site Health and Safety Plan prepared by Carlson Environmental, Inc., dated April 2012.

Qualifications

The qualifications section grabs attention by mentioning compelling qualifications.

O'Donnell & Associates has been providing quality professional services since 1972 in the areas of

- Geotechnical engineering
- Materials testing and inspection
- Pavement evaluation
- Environmental services
- Engineering and technical support (CADD) services

The company provides Phase I and Phase II environmental site assessments, preparation of LUST site closure reports, installation of groundwater monitoring wells, and testing of soil/groundwater samples for environmental contaminants. Geotechnical services include all phases of soil mechanics and foundation engineering, including foundation and lateral load analysis, slope stability analysis, site preparation recommendations, seepage analysis, pavement design, and settlement analysis.

O'Donnell & Associates materials testing laboratory is certified by AASHTO Accreditation Program for the testing of Soils, Aggregate, Hot Mix Asphalt and Portland Cement Concrete. A copy of our laboratory certification is included with this proposal. In addition to in-house training, field and laboratory technicians participate in a variety of certification programs, including those sponsored by the American Concrete Institute (ACI) and Illinois Department of Transportation (IDOT).

Describing *certifications* (approvals by recognized industry associations or government agencies) helps build the company's credibility.

Costs

On the basis of our understanding of the scope of the work, we estimate the total cost of the two projects to be $100,260.00, as follows:

A clear and complete itemization of estimated costs builds confidence in dependability of the project's financial projections.

Ms. Joyce Colton, AGI Builders   Page 3   July 30, 2017

Cost Estimates

Cost Estimate: Mass Grading	**Units**	**Rate ($)**	**Total Cost ($)**
Field Inspection			
Labor	1,320 hours	$38.50	$ 50,820.00
Nuclear Moisture Density Meter	132 days	35.00	4,620.00
Vehicle Expense	132 days	45.00	5,940.00
Laboratory Testing			
Proctor Density Tests (ASTM D-1557)	4 tests	130.00	520.00
Engineering/Project Management			
Principal Engineer	16 hours	110.00	1,760.00
Project Manager	20 hours	80.00	1,600.00
Administrative Assistant	12 hours	50.00	600.00
Subtotal			**$ 65,860.00**
Cost Estimate: Utility Work	**Units**	**Rate ($)**	**Total Cost ($)**
Field Inspection			
Labor	660 hours	$ 38.50	$ 25,410.00
Nuclear Moisture Density Meter	66 days	5.00	2,310.00
Vehicle Expense	66 days	45.00	2,970.00
Laboratory Testing			
Proctor Density Tests (ASTM D-1557)	2 tests	130.00	260.00
Engineering/Project Management			
Principal Engineer	10 hours	110.00	1,100.00
Project Manager	20 hours	80.00	1,600.00
Administrative Assistant	15 hours	50.00	750.00
Subtotal			**$ 34,400.00**
Total Project Costs			**$100,260.00**

This estimate assumes full-time inspection services. However, our services may also be performed on an as-requested basis, and actual charges will reflect time associated with the project. We have attached our standard fee schedule for your review. Overtime rates are for hours in excess of 8.0 hours per day, before 7:00 a.m., after 5:00 p.m., and on holidays and weekends.

To give the client some budgetary flexibility, the proposal offers an alternative to the fixed-fee approach—which may lower any resistance to accepting the bid.

The brief close emphasizes the bidder's qualifications and asks for a decision.

Ms. Joyce Colton, AGI Builders Page 4 July 30, 2017

Authorization

With a staff of over 30 personnel, including registered professional engineers, resident engineers, geologists, construction inspectors, laboratory technicians, and drillers, we are confident that O'Donnell & Associates is capable of providing the services required for a project of this magnitude.

If you would like our firm to provide the services as outlined in this proposal, please sign this letter and return it to us along with a certified check in the amount of $10,000 (our retainer) by August 14, 2017. Please call me if you have any questions regarding the terms of this proposal or our approach.

The call to action clarifies the steps needed to put the project in motion.

Sincerely,

Dixon O'Donnell

Dixon O'Donnell
Vice President

Enclosures

Accepted for AGI BUILDERS, INC.

By____________________ Date ____________________

The customer's signature will make the proposal a binding contract.

Chapter Summary

Writing Reports and Proposals

The introduction of a report identifies who authorized the report and highlights its purpose and scope, the sources or methods used to gather information, important definitions, any limitations, and the order in which the various topics are covered. The body provides enough information to support its conclusion and recommendations, which can range from explanations of problems or opportunities to results of studies or investigations. The close summarizes key points, restates conclusions and recommendations if appropriate, and lists action items.

To a large extent, the content of proposals is dictated by the circumstances, particularly by whether the proposal is solicited or unsolicited. Proposals submitted in response to an RFP (request for proposal) should always follow its instructions. The introduction commonly includes a background or statement of the problem, an overview of the proposed solution (or, for indirect proposals, a statement that a solution is about to be presented), the scope of the proposals, and a description of how the proposal is organized. The body usually includes a description of the proposed solution, a work plan that outlines how and when the work will be accomplished, a statement of qualifications of the individual or organization presenting the proposal, and a discussion of costs. The close summarizes the key points, emphasizes the benefits that readers will realize from the proposed solution, summarizes the merits of your approach, restates why you and your firm are a good choice, and asks for a decision from the reader.

Writing for Websites and Wikis

Follow these six guidelines to draft effective online content: 1) Build trust by being accurate, current, complete, and authoritative; 2) adapt content to global audiences; 3) write web-friendly content that is compact and efficient; 4) present information in a concise, skimmable format; 5) make effective use of links; and 6) make the website a "living" document by adding fresh content and deleting content that is out of date or no longer relevant.

To become a valuable wiki contributor, let go of traditional expectations of authorship, including individual recognition and control, and don't be afraid to edit and improve existing content. Use page templates and other formatting options to make sure your content is formatted in the same style as the rest of the wiki; keep edits and comments separate by using the "talk page" to discuss content, rather than inserting comments directly into the text. Finally, take advantage of the sandbox to learn how use the wiki's writing and editing tools; and understand and follow the wiki's contributor guidelines.

Illustrating Your Reports with Effective Visuals

When preparing visuals, 1) use elements of design consistently; 2) use color and other elements to show contrast effectively; 3) strive for visual balance, either formal or informal, that creates a feel that is appropriate for your overall message; 4) use design choices to draw attention to key elements; 5) understand and follow design conventions; and 6) strive for simplicity in your visuals.

The major types of business visuals include tables; line charts and surface charts; bar charts and pie charts; data visualization; flowcharts and organization charts; maps, drawings, diagrams, infographics, and photographs; and animation and video.

Completing Reports and Proposals

The four completion tasks of revising, producing, proofreading, and distributing all need to be accomplished with care, given the size and complexity of many reports. The production stage for a formal report or proposal can involve creating a number of elements not found in most other business documents. Possible prefatory parts (those coming before the main text of the report or proposal) include a cover, a title fly, a title page, a letter of authorization, a letter of transmittal, a table of contents, a list of illustrations, and a synopsis or an executive summary. Possible supplemental parts (those coming after the main text of the report or proposal) include one or more appendixes, a bibliography, and an index.

Test Your Knowledge

1. Why must the introduction of an unsolicited proposal include a statement of the problem or opportunity that the proposal addresses?
2. What navigational elements can you use to help readers follow the structure and flow of information in a long report?
3. How can you use the inverted pyramid style of writing to craft effective online content?
4. How do you check a visual for quality?
5. How does a synopsis differ from an executive summary?

Apply Your Knowledge

1. Should the most experienced member of a department have final approval of the content for the department's wiki? Why or why not?
2. If you wanted to compare average monthly absenteeism for five divisions in your company over the course of a year, which type of visual would you use? Explain your choice.
3. If a company receives a solicited formal proposal outlining the solution to a particular problem, is it ethical for the company to adopt the proposal's recommendations without hiring the firm that submitted the proposal? Why or why not?
4. Is an executive summary a persuasive message? Explain your answer.

Activities

1. **Team Project: Reviewing Informational Reports** You and a classmate are helping Linda Moreno prepare her report on Electrovision's travel and entertainment costs (see Figure 11.14). This time, however, the report is to be informational rather than analytical, so it will not include recommendations. Review the existing report and determine what changes would be needed to make it an informational report. Be as specific as possible. For example, if your team decides the report needs a new title, what title would you use? Draft a transmittal memo for Moreno to use in conveying this informational report to Dennis McWilliams, Electrovision's vice president of operations.

2. **Reviewing Informational Reports** Review a long business article from a print or online source. Highlight examples of how the article uses headings, transitions, previews, and reviews to help the readers find their way.

3. **Preparing Analytical Reports** Your boss has asked you to prepare a feasibility report to determine whether the company should advertise its custom-crafted cabinetry in the weekly neighborhood newspaper. Based on your primary research, you think it should. As you draft the introduction to your report, however, you discover that the survey administered to the neighborhood newspaper subscribers was flawed. Several of the questions were poorly written and misleading. You used the survey results, among other findings, to justify your recommendation. The report is due in three days. What actions might you want to take, if any, before you complete your report?

4. **Creating Visuals** You work for C & S Holdings, a company that operates coin-activated, self-service car washes. Research shows that the farther customers live from a car wash, the less likely they are to visit. You know that 50 percent of customers at each of your car washes live within a four-mile radius of the location, 65 percent live within six miles, 80 percent live within eight miles, and 90 percent live within 10 miles. C & S's owner wants to open two new car washes in your city and has asked you to prepare a report recommending locations. Using a map of your city from an online or printed source, choose two possible locations for car washes and create a visual that depicts the customer base surrounding each location (make up whatever population data you need).

5. **Team Project: Creating Visuals** As directed by your instructor, team up with other students, making sure that at least one of you has a digital camera or camera phone capable of downloading images to your word processing software. Find a busy location at school or in the surrounding neighborhood, someplace with lots of signs, storefronts, pedestrians, and traffic. Scout out two different photo opportunities, one that maximizes the visual impression of crowding and clutter, and one that minimizes this impression.

   For the first, assume that you are someone who advocates reducing the crowding and clutter, so you want to show how bad it is. For the second, assume that you are a real estate agent or someone else who is motivated to show people that even though the location offers lots of shopping, entertainment, and other attractions, it's actually a rather calm and quiet neighborhood. Insert the two images in a word processing document and write a caption for each that emphasizes the two opposite messages just described. Finally, write a brief paragraph, discussing the ethical implications of what you've just done. Have you distorted reality or just presented it in ways that work to your advantage? Have you prevented audiences from gaining the information they would need to make informed decisions?

6. **Improving Page Layout** You are a graphic design consultant who has been asked to look at some reports and offer suggestions for improvement. Locate a very dull page layout (in a textbook, magazine, book, or webpage), and print it out or make a copy of it. Then write or sketch suggestions for improving its layout on the page.

7. **Producing Formal Reports** You are president of the Friends of the Library, a not-for-profit group that raises funds and provides volunteers to support your local library. Every February, you send a report of the previous year's activities and accomplishments to the County Arts Council, which provides an annual grant of $1,000 toward your group's summer reading festival. Now it's February 6, and you've completed your formal report.

   Here are the highlights:

   - Back-to-school book sale raised $2,000.
   - Holiday craft fair raised $1,100.
   - Promotion and prizes for summer reading festival cost $1,450.
   - Materials for children's program featuring local author cost $125.
   - New reference databases for library's career center cost $850.
   - Bookmarks promoting library's website cost $200.

   Write a letter of transmittal to Erica Maki, the council's director. Because she is expecting this report, you can use the direct approach. Be sure to express gratitude for the council's ongoing financial support.

8. **Analyzing Website Reports** Download the latest issue of the International Trade Update from http://trade.gov. What techniques does the report use to help readers find their way through the document or direct readers to other sources of information? What techniques are used to highlight key points in the document? Are these techniques effective? Using whatever medium your instructor requests, write a brief summary of your analysis.

Expand Your Skills

1. **Summarizing Data in Informational Reports** You've been in your new job as human resources director for only a week, and already you have a major personnel crisis on your hands. Some employees in the marketing department got their hands on a confidential salary report and learned that, on average, marketing employees earn less than engineering employees. In addition, several top performers in the engineering group make significantly more than anybody in marketing. The report was instantly passed around the company by email, and now everyone is discussing the situation. You'll deal with the data security issue later; for now, you need to address the dissatisfaction in the marketing group.

   Case Table 11.1 lists the salary and employment data you were able to pull from the employee database. You also had the opportunity to interview the engineering and marketing directors to get their opinions on the pay situation; their answers are listed in Case Table 11.2.

Case Table 11.1 Selected Employment Data for Engineers and Marketing Staff

Employment Statistic	Engineering Department	Marketing Department
Average number of years of work experience)	18.2	16.3
Average number of years of experience in current profession	17.8	8.6
Average number of years with company	12.4	7.9
Average number of years of college education	6.9	4.8
Average number of years between promotions	6.7	4.3
Salary range	$58-165k	$45-$85k
Median salary	$77k	$62k

Case Table 11.2 Selected Statements From Department Director Interview

Question	Engineering Director	Marketing Director
Should engineering and marketing professionals receive roughly similar pay?	In general, yes, but we need to make allowances for the special nature of the engineering profession. In some cases, it's entirely appropriate for an engineer to earn more than a marketing person.	Yes.
Why or why not?	Several reasons: (1) Top engineers are extremely hard to find, and we need to offer competitive salaries; (2) the structure of the engineering department doesn't provide as many promotional opportunities, so we can't use promotions as a motivator the way marketing can; (3) many of our engineers have advanced degrees, and nearly all pursue continuous education to stay on top of the technology.	Without marketing, the products the engineers create wouldn't reach customers, and the company wouldn't have any revenue. The two teams make equal contributions to the company's success.
If we decide to balance pay between the two departments, how should we do it?	If we do anything to cap or reduce engineering salaries, we'll lose key people to the competition.	If we can't increase payroll immediately to raise marketing salaries, the only fair thing to do is freeze raises in engineering and gradually raise marketing salaries over the next few years.

Your task: The CEO has asked for a short report, summarizing whatever data and information you have on engineering and marketing salaries. Feel free to offer your own interpretation of the situation as well (make up any information you need), but keep in mind that because you are a new manager with almost no experience in the company, your opinion might not have a lot of influence. Use charts, figures, typographic elements, fonts, and infographics to present the data as you deem appropriate.

2. **Writing Comparative Reports** Your company develops a mobile phone app that helps people get detailed technical information about products while they are shopping. The original plan was to incorporate Quick Reference (QR) codes into the app, so that people could scan QR stickers placed on product displays in retail stores. After decoding the QR code, the app would then pull up information about the product on display. You have recently learned about near-field communication (NFC), a short-range radio technology that might able to accomplish the same thing in a way that is simpler for consumers to use.

   Your task: Research the prospects for QR codes and NFC technology, and write a short comparative report. Draw a conclusion about which technology you think will dominate in the coming years.

3. **Team Project: Researching and Writing Analytical Reports** Anyone looking at the fragmented 21st-century landscape of media and entertainment options might be surprised to learn that poetry was once a dominant medium for not only creative literary expression but also philosophical, political, and even scientific discourse.

   Your task: With a team of fellow students, your challenge is to identify opportunities to increase sales of poetry—any kind of poetry, in any medium. The following suggestions may help you get started:

   - Research recent bestsellers in the poetry field and try to identify why they have been popular.
   - Interview literature professors, professional poets, librarians, publishers, and bookstore personnel.
   - Consider art forms and venues in which verse plays an essential role, including popular music and poetry slams.
   - Conduct surveys and interviews to find out why consumers don't buy more poetry.
   - Review professional journals that cover the field of poetry, including *Publishers Weekly* and *Poets & Writers*, from both business and creative standpoints.

   Summarize your findings in a brief formal report; assume that your target readers are executives in the publishing industry.

4. **Writing Short Analytical Reports** After several false starts, tablet computers have finally caught on among business users. In addition to Apple's popular iPad, seemingly every computer company on the planet is looking to get a share of the tablet market. Will they be a passing fad? A cool toy or a serious business tool?

   Your task: Prepare a short analytical report that compares the advantages and disadvantages of tablet computers for traveling salespeople.

5. **Summarizing Survey Results** Your company is the largest private employer in your metropolitan area, and the 43,500 employees in your workforce have a tremendous impact on local traffic. A group of city and county transportation officials recently approached your CEO with a request to explore ways to reduce this impact. The CEO has assigned you the task of analyzing the workforce's transportation habits and attitudes as a first step toward identifying potential solutions. He's willing to consider anything from subsidized bus passes to company-owned shuttle buses to telecommuting, but the decision requires a thorough understanding of employee transportation needs. Case Tables 11.3 through 11.7 summarize data you collected in an employee survey.

   Your task: Present the results of your survey in an informational report, using the data provided in the tables. Use desktop publishing tools to create charts, figures, or infographics to make the data more accessible. Use typographic and design elements.

Case Table 11.3 Employee Carpool Habits

Frequency of Use: Carpooling	Portion of Workforce
Every day, every week	10,138 (23%)
Certain days, every week	4,361 (10%)
Randomly	983 (2%)
Never	28,018 (64%)

Case Table 11.4 Use of Public Transportation

Frequency of Use: Public Transportation	Portion of Workforce
Every day, every week	23,556 (54%)
Certain days, every week	2,029 (5%)
Randomly	5,862 (13%)
Never	12,053 (28%)

Case Table 11.5 Effect of Potential Improvements to Public Transportation

Which of the Following Would Encourage You to Use Public Transportation More Frequently (check all that apply)	Portion of Respondents
Increased perception of safety	4,932 (28%)
Improved cleanliness	852 (5%)
Reduced commute times	7,285 (41%)
Greater convenience: fewer transfers	3,278 (18%)
Greater convenience: more stops	1,155 (6%)
Lower (or subsidized) fares	5,634 (31%)
Nothing could encourage me to take public transportation	8,294 (46%)

Case Table 11.6 Distant Traveled To/From Work

Distance You Travel to Work (one way)	Portion of Workforce
Less than 1 mile	531 (1%)
1–3 miles	6,874 (16%)
4–10 miles	22,951 (53%)
11–20 miles	10,605 (24%)
More than 20 miles	2,539 (6%)

Case Table 11.7 Is Telecommuting an Option?

Does the Nature of Your Work Make Telecommuting a Realistic Option?	Portion of Workforce
Yes, every day	3,460 (8%)
Yes, several days a week	8,521 (20%)
Yes, random days	12,918 (30%)
No	18,601 (43%)

6. **Researching and Writing Analytical Reports** As a student and an active consumer, you may have considered one or more of the following questions at some point in the past few years:

   - What criteria distinguish the top-rated MBA programs in the country? How well do these criteria correspond to the needs and expectations of business? Are the criteria fair for students, employers, and business schools?
   - Which of three companies you might like to work for has the strongest corporate ethics policies?
   - What will the music industry look like in the future? What's next after online stores such as Apple's iTunes and digital players such as the iPod?
   - Which industries and job categories are forecast to experience the greatest growth—and therefore the greatest demand for workers—in the next 10 years?
   - What has been the impact of Starbucks's aggressive growth on small, independent coffee shops? On midsized chains or franchises? In the United States or in another country?
   - How large is the "industry" of major college sports? How much do the major football or basketball programs contribute—directly or indirectly—to other parts of a typical university?
   - How much have minor league sports—baseball, hockey, arena football—grown in small- and medium-market cities? What is the local economic impact when these municipalities build stadiums and arenas?

   Your task: Answer one of the preceding questions using secondary research sources for information. Be sure to document your sources, using the format your instructor indicates. Give conclusions and offer recommendations where appropriate.

7. **Writing Analytical Reports** An observer who surveys the current consumer electronics landscape and sees Apple products everywhere might be surprised to learn that during part of the company's history, it was regarded by some as a fairly minor player in the computer industry—and at times a few pundits even wondered whether the company would survive.

   Your task: In a two- to three-page report, identify the reasons Apple has been successful and explain how other companies can apply Apple's strategies and tactics to improve their business results.

8. **Writing Proposals** Presentations can make—or break—both careers and businesses. A good presentation can bring in millions of dollars in new sales or fresh investment capital. A bad presentation might cause any number of troubles, from turning away potential customers to upsetting fellow employees to derailing key projects. To help business professionals plan, create, and deliver more effective presentations, you offer a three-day workshop that covers the essentials of good presentations:

   - Understanding your audience's needs and expectations
   - Formulating your presentation objectives
   - Choosing an organizational approach
   - Writing openings that catch your audience's attention
   - Creating effective graphics and slides
   - Practicing and delivering your presentation
   - Leaving a positive impression on your audience
   - Avoiding common mistakes with presentation slides
   - Making presentations online using webcasting tools
   - Handling questions and arguments from the audience
   - Overcoming the top 10 worries of public speaking (including *How can I overcome stage fright?* and *I'm not the performing type; can I still give an effective presentation?*)

   Workshop benefits: Students will learn how to prepare better presentations in less time and deliver them more effectively.

   Who should attend: Top executives, project managers, employment recruiters, sales professionals, and anyone else who gives important presentations to internal or external audiences.

   Your qualifications: 18 years of business experience, including 14 years in sales and 12 years of public speaking. Experience speaking to audiences as large as 5,000 people. More than a dozen speech-related articles published in professional journals. Have conducted successful workshops for nearly 100 companies.

   Workshop details: Three-day workshop (9 a.m. to 3:30 p.m.) that combines lectures, practice presentations, and both individual and group feedback. Minimum number of students: 6. Maximum number of students per workshop: 12.

   Pricing: The cost is $3,500, plus $100 per student; 10 percent discount for additional workshops.

Other information: Each attendee will have the opportunity to give three practice presentations that will last from 3 to 5 minutes. Everyone is encouraged to bring PowerPoint files containing slides from actual business presentations. Each attendee will also receive a workbook and a digital video recording of his or her final class presentation on DVD. You'll also be available for phone or email coaching for six months after the workshop.

Your task: Identify a company in your local area that might be a good candidate for your services. Learn more about the company by visiting its website so you can personalize your proposal. Using the information listed above, prepare a sales proposal that explains the benefits of your training and what students can expect during the workshop.

9. **Writing Formal Proposals** For years, a controversy has been brewing over the amount of junk food and soft drinks being sold through vending machines in local schools. Schools benefit from revenue-sharing arrangements, but many parents and health experts are concerned about the negative effects of these snacks and beverages. You and your friend have almost a decade of experience running juice stands in malls and on street corners, and you'd love to find some way to expand your business into schools. After a quick brainstorming session, the two of you craft a plan that makes good business sense while meeting the financial concerns of school administrators and the nutritional concerns of parents and dietitians. Here are the notes from your brainstorming session:

   - Set up portable juice bars on school campuses, offering healthy fruit and vegetable drinks along with simple, healthy snacks
   - Offer schools 30 percent of profits in exchange for free space and long-term contracts
   - Provide job-training opportunities for students (during athletic events, etc.)
   - Provide detailed dietary analysis of all products sold
   - Establish a nutritional advisory board composed of parents, students, and at least one certified health professional
   - Assure schools and parents that all products are safe (e.g., no stimulant drinks, no dietary supplements)
   - Support local farmers and specialty food preparers by buying locally and giving these vendors the opportunity to test-market new products at your stands

   Your task: Based on the ideas listed, draft a formal proposal to the local school board, outlining your plan to offer healthier alternatives to soft drinks and prepackaged snack foods. Invent any details you need to complete your proposal.

10. **Team Project: Writing Proposals** It seems like everybody in your firm is frustrated. On the one hand, top executives complain about the number of lower-level employees who want promotions but just don't seem to "get it" when it comes to dealing with customers and the public, recognizing when to speak out and when to be quiet, knowing how to push new ideas through the appropriate channels, and performing other essential but difficult-to-teach tasks. On the other hand, ambitious employees who'd like to learn more feel that they have nowhere to turn for career advice from people who've been there. In between, a variety of managers and midlevel executives are overwhelmed by the growing number of mentoring requests they're getting, sometimes from employees they don't even know.

    You've been assigned the challenge of proposing a formal mentoring program—and a considerable challenge it is:

    - The number of employees who want mentoring relationships far exceeds the number of managers and executives willing and able to be mentors; how will you select people for the program?
    - The people most in demand for mentoring also tend to be some of the busiest people in the organization.
    - After several years of belt tightening and staff reductions, the entire company feels overworked; few people can imagine adding another recurring task to their seemingly endless to-do lists.
    - What's in it for the mentors? Why would they be motivated to help lower-level employees?
    - How will you measure the success or failure of the mentoring effort?

    Your task: With a team assigned by your instructor, identify potential solutions to the issues (make up any information you need), and draft a proposal to the executive committee for a formal, companywide mentoring program that would match selected employees with successful managers and executives.

CHAPTER 12

Developing and Delivering Business Presentations

After studying this chapter, you will be able to:

- Highlight the importance of presentations in your business career and explain how to adapt the planning step of the three-step process to presentations.
- Describe the tasks involved in developing a presentation.
- Describe the six major design and writing tasks required to enhance your presentation with effective visuals.
- Outline three special tasks involved in completing a presentation.
- Describe four important aspects of delivering a presentation in today's social media environment.

Planning a Presentation

Presentations, delivered in person or online, offer important opportunities to put all your communication skills on display, including research, planning, writing, visual design, and interpersonal and nonverbal communication. Presentations also let you demonstrate your ability to think on your feet, grasp complex business issues, and handle challenging situations—all attributes that executives look for when searching for talented employees to promote.

While there are many types of presentations, two of the most common are formal and informal presentations. A formal presentation is delivered according to a detailed outline—or even a script—and are often done to a larger number of people in a setting such as an auditorium. An informal presentation also has an outline, but is usually delivered to a smaller group of people in a more informal setting such as a small conference room. Informal presentations tend to be more conversational in nature, with the audience often asking questions throughout the presentation. Both presentation formats—formal and informal—require that data supports points within the presentation.

In a professional setting and presentation, it is important to ensure that the points and conclusions you present are supported by information and data. Having well supported conclusions within your presentation—either formal or informal—enhances your credibility, and thus the acceptance of the presentation. In a professional setting, the emphasis should be on the information delivered—and the supporting evidence—so that the audience can draw an informed conclusion. When the presentation points are supported by data, the audience will be much more likely to accept any opinions or recommendations within the presentation.

Figure 12.1
The Three-Step Process for Developing Oral and Online Presentations
Although you rarely "write" a presentation or speech in the sense of composing every word ahead of time, the tasks in the three-step writing process adapt quite well to the challenge of planning, creating, and delivering oral and online presentations.

1 Plan →

Analyze the Situation
Define your purpose and develop a profile of your audience, including their likely emotional states and language preferences.

Gather Information
Determine audience needs and obtain the information necessary to satisfy those needs.

Choose Medium and Channel
Identify the best combination for the situation, message, and audience, including handouts and other support materials.

Organize the Information
Define your main idea, limit your scope and verify timing, select the direct or indirect approach, and outline your content.

2 Write →

Adapt to Your Audience
Adapt your content, presentation style, and room setup to the audience and the specific situation. Be sensitive to audience needs and expectations with a "you" attitude, politeness, positive emphasis, and bias-free language. Plan to establish your credibility as required.

Compose Your Presentation
Outline an attention-getting introduction, body, and close. Prepare supporting visuals and speaking notes.

3 Complete

Revise the Message
Evaluate your content and speaking notes.

Master Your Delivery
Choose your delivery mode and practice your presentation.

Prepare to Speak
Verify facilities and equipment, including online connections and software setups. Hire an interpreter if necessary.

Overcome Anxiety
Take steps to feel more confident and appear more confident on stage.

Planning presentations, both formal and informal, is much like planning other business messages: You analyze the situation, gather information, select the best media and channels, and organize the information (see Figure 12.1). Gathering information for presentations is essentially the same as it is for written communication projects. The other three planning tasks have some special applications when it comes to oral presentations; they are covered in the following sections.

On the subject of planning, be aware that preparing a professional-quality business presentation can take a considerable amount of time. Not every one-hour presentation justifies a week or two of preparation, of course, but the important presentations that can make your career or your company certainly can.

Analyzing the Situation

As with written communications, analyzing the situation involves defining your purpose and developing an audience profile (see Table 12.1). The purpose of most of your presentations will be to inform or to persuade, although you may occasionally need to make a collaborative presentation, such as when you're leading a problem-solving or brainstorming session.

Table 12.1 Analyzing Audiences for Business Presentations

To determine audience size and composition	• Estimate how many people will attend (in person and online). • Identify what they have in common and how they differ. • Analyze the mix of organizational position, professions, language fluencies, and other demographic factors that could influence your content and delivery choices.
To predict the audience's probable reaction	• Analyze why audience members are attending the presentation. • Determine the audience's general attitude toward the topic: interested, moderately interested, unconcerned, open-minded, or hostile. • Analyze your audience's likely mood when you speak to them. • Find out what kind of supporting information will help the audience accept and respond to your message: technical data, historical information, financial data, demonstrations, samples, and so on. • Consider whether the audience has any biases that might work against you. • Anticipate possible objections or questions.
To gauge the audience's experience	• Analyze whether everybody has the same background and level of understanding. • Determine what the audience already knows about the subject. • Consider whether the audience is familiar with the vocabulary you intend to use. • Analyze what the audience expects from you. • Think about the mix of general concepts and specific details you will need to present.

In addition to following the audience analysis advice in Chapter 3, try to anticipate the likely emotional state of your audience members. Figure 12.2 offers tips for dealing with a variety of audience mindsets.

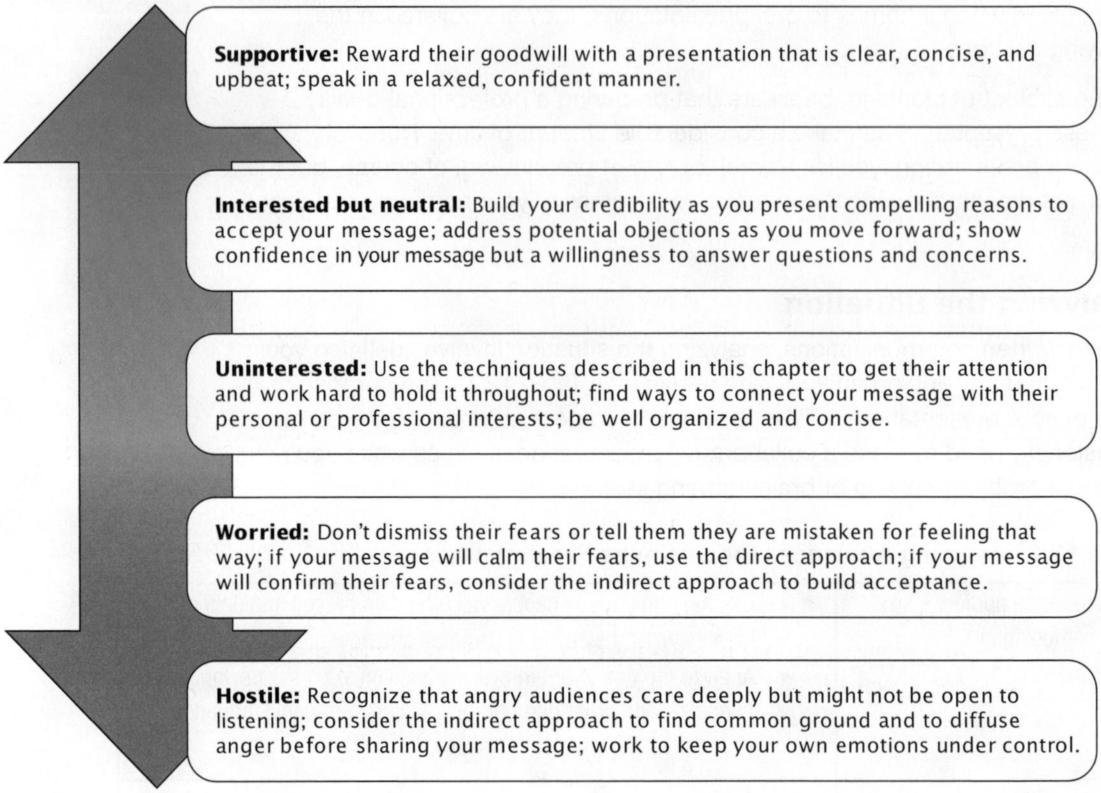

Supportive: Reward their goodwill with a presentation that is clear, concise, and upbeat; speak in a relaxed, confident manner.

Interested but neutral: Build your credibility as you present compelling reasons to accept your message; address potential objections as you move forward; show confidence in your message but a willingness to answer questions and concerns.

Uninterested: Use the techniques described in this chapter to get their attention and work hard to hold it throughout; find ways to connect your message with their personal or professional interests; be well organized and concise.

Worried: Don't dismiss their fears or tell them they are mistaken for feeling that way; if your message will calm their fears, use the direct approach; if your message will confirm their fears, consider the indirect approach to build acceptance.

Hostile: Recognize that angry audiences care deeply but might not be open to listening; consider the indirect approach to find common ground and to diffuse anger before sharing your message; work to keep your own emotions under control.

Figure 12.2
Planning for Various Audience Mindsets
Try to assess the emotional state of your audience ahead of time so you can plan your presentation approach accordingly.

As you analyze the situation, also consider the circumstances. If some or all of the audience members will be in the same room with you, how will they be seated? Can you control the environment to minimize distractions? What equipment will you need? If some or all your audience members will be online, how will the meeting system you're using affect their ability to hear and see you and your presentation materials? Such variables can influence not only the style of your presentation but the content itself.

Keep your presentation's purpose in mind as you are selecting the appropriate form of media in which to deliver your presentation. After selection, format your presentation in the way that best suits your purpose and which delivers your information most effectively.

Selecting the Best Media and Channels

For some presentations, you'll be expected to use whatever media and channels your audience, your boss, or the circumstances require. For example, you might be required to use specific presentation software and a conference room's built-in display system or your company's online meeting software.

For other presentations, though, you might be able to choose from an array of choices for presentations, from live, in-person presentations to webcasts (online presentations that people either view live or download later from the web), screencasts (recordings of activity on computer displays with audio voiceover), or twebinars (the use of Twitter as a backchannel for real-time conversation during a web-based seminar).

Organizing a Presentation

The possibilities for organizing a business presentation fall into two basic categories, **linear** or **nonlinear**. Linear presentations are like printed documents in the sense that they are outlined like conventional messages and follow a predefined flow from start to finish. The linear model is appropriate for speeches, technical and financial presentations, and other presentations in which you want to convey your message point by point or build up to a conclusion following logical steps.

Linear presentations: These are outlined like conventional messages and follow a predefined flow from start to finish.

Nonlinear presentations: These do not flow in a particular direction; gives the presenter the option to move back and forth between topics.

In contrast, a nonlinear presentation doesn't flow in any particularly direction but rather gives the presenter the option to move back and forth between topics and up and down in terms of level of detail. Nonlinear presentations can be useful when you want to be able to show complicated relationships between multiple ideas or elements, to zoom in and out between the "big picture" and specific details, to explore complex visuals, or to have the flexibility to move from topic to topic in any order.

The difference between the two styles can be seen in the type of software typically used to create and deliver a presentation. Microsoft PowerPoint, Apple Keynote, and similar packages use sequences of individual slides, often referred to as a slide deck. They don't necessary need to be presented in a strict linear order, because the presenter does have the option of jumping out of the predefined order, but in most presentations using slides the speaker moves from start to finish in that order.

Prezi is the best-known nonlinear presentation software and doesn't use the concept of individual slides. Instead, you start from a main screen, or canvas, which often presents the big picture overview of your topic. From there, you add individual objects (including blocks of text, photos, or videos) that convey specific information points. When you present, you can zoom in and out, discussing the individual objects and their relationship to the big picture and each other. You can also define a narrative flow by defining a path from one object to the next, which also lets people view the presentation on their own[3] (and effectively turns a Prezi presentation into a linear presentation). Prezi is sometimes viewed as a more dynamic and engaging way to present, and it certainly has that potential.

However, keep several points in mind if you have a choice of which approach to take and which software to use. First, match the tool to the task, not the other way around. A detailed technical discussion might need a linear presentation, whereas a freeform brainstorming session might benefit from a nonlinear approach. Second, if they are used well, software features can help you tell your story, but your story is what matters—not the software. If they are used poorly, software features only get in the way. (Overuse of zooming in Prezi is a good example of this.) Third, in spite of their reputation, PowerPoint and other slide programs aren't limited to creating boring, linear flows of bullet points (see "Choosing Structured or Free-Form Slides" on page 427).

Defining Your Main Idea

Regardless of which overall approach you take, a successful presentation starts with a clear idea of the main idea you who want to share with your audience. Start by composing a one-sentence summary that links your subject and purpose to your audience's frame of reference. Here are some examples:

> Convince management that reorganizing the technical support department will improve customer service and reduce employee turnover.
>
> Convince the board of directors that we should build a new plant in Texas to eliminate manufacturing bottlenecks and improve production quality.
>
> Address employee concerns regarding a new healthcare plan by showing how the plan will reduce costs and improve the quality of their care.

Each of these statements puts a particular slant on the subject, one that directly relates to the audience's interests. By focusing on your audience's needs and using the "you" attitude, you help keep their attention and convince them your points are relevant.

Limiting Your Scope

Limiting your scope is important with any message, but it's particularly vital with presentations, for two reasons. First, for most presentations, you must work within strict time limits. Second, the longer you speak, the more difficult it is to hold the audience's attention levels, and the more difficult it is for your listeners to retain your key points.

The only sure way to know how much material you can cover in a given time is to practice your presentation after you complete it. As an alternative, if you're using conventional structured slides (see page 428) you can figure on three or four minutes per slide as a rough guide. Of course, be sure to factor in time for introductions, coffee breaks, demonstrations, question-and-answer sessions, and anything else that takes away from your speaking time.

Approaching time constraints as a creative challenge can actually help you develop more effective presentations. Limitations can force you to focus on the most essential message points that are important to your audience.[7]

Choosing Your Approach

With a well-defined main idea to guide you and a clear idea about the scope of your presentation, you can begin to arrange your message. If you have 10 minutes or less, consider organizing your presentation much as you would a letter or other brief message: use the direct approach if the subject involves routine information or good news and use the indirect approach if the subject involves bad news or persuasion. Plan your introduction to arouse interest and to give a preview of what's to come. For the body of the presentation, be prepared to explain the who, what, when, where, why, and how of your subject.

In the final section, review the points you've made and close with a statement that will help your audience remember the subject of your speech (see Figure 12.3).

Progress Update: August 2017

Purpose: To update the Executive Committee on our product development schedule.

I. Review goals and progress.
  A. Mechanical design:
    1. Goal: 100%
    2. Actual: 80%
    3. Reason for delay: Unanticipated problems with case durability
  B. Software development:
    1. Goal: 50%
    2. Actual: 60%
  C. Material sourcing:
    1. Goal: 100%
    2. Actual: 45% (and materials identified are at 140% of anticipated costs)
    3. Reason for delay: Purchasing is understaffed and hasn't been able to research sources adequately.

II. Discuss schedule options.
  A. Option 1: Reschedule product launch date.
  B. Option 2: Launch on schedule with more expensive materials.

III. Suggest goals for next month.

IV. Q&A

Figure 12.3
Effective Outline for a 10-Minute Presentation
Here is an outline of a short presentation that updates management on the status of a key project; the presenter has some bad news to deliver, so she opted for an indirect approach to lay out the reasons for the delay before sharing the news of the schedule slip.

Longer presentations are often organized more like reports. If the purpose is to motivate or inform, you'll typically use the direct approach and a structure imposed naturally by the subject: comparison, importance, sequence, chronology, geography, or category (as discussed in Chapter 10). If your purpose is to analyze, persuade, or collaborate, organize your material around conclusions and recommendations or around a logical argument. Use the direct approach if the audience is receptive and the indirect approach if you expect resistance.

No matter what the length, look for opportunities to integrate storytelling into the structure of your presentation. The dramatic tension (not knowing what will happen to the "hero") at the heart of effective storytelling is a great way to capture and keep the audience's attention.

Preparing Your Outline

An outline helps you organize your message, and it serves as the foundation for delivering your speech. Prepare your outline in several stages:

- State your purpose and main idea and then use these elements to guide the rest of your planning.

- Organize your major points and subpoints in logical order, expressing each major point as a single, complete sentence.
- Identify major points in the body first, then outline the introduction and close.
- Identify transitions between major points or sections, then write these transitions in full-sentence form.
- Prepare your bibliography or source notes; highlight those sources you want to identify by name during your talk.
- Choose a compelling title. Make it brief, action oriented, and focused on what you can do for the audience.

Many speakers like to prepare both a detailed planning outline (see Figure 12.4) and a simpler speaking outline that provides all the cues and reminders they need in order to present their material.

Figure 12.4
Effective Outline for a 30-Minute Presentation
This outline clearly identifies the purpose and the distinct points to be made in the introduction, body, and close. Notice also how the speaker has written her major transitions in full-sentence form to be sure she can clearly phrase these critical passages when it's time to speak.

OUR TRAVEL AND ENTERTAINMENT COSTS ARE OUT OF CONTROL

A clear statement of purpose helps the presenter stay focused on her message while she develops her outline.

Purpose: To explain why Electrovision's travel and entertainment (T&E) costs are so high and to propose a series of changes to bring them under control.

INTRODUCTION

The introduction starts by highlighting the problem she will address.

I. Our T&E costs are way above average, and they pose a threat to the company's financial health; fortunately, we can fix the problem in four straightforward steps that could save as much as $6 million a year.

The introduction continues with a description of the investigation she undertook; this will enhance her credibility by showing that the research was thorough and objective.

II. How we approached the investigation
   A. We analyzed internal expense reports.
   B. We compared our cost data with nationwide averages.
   C. We analyzed published information on trends and cost-control suggestions.

(Transition: This presentation reviews Electrovision's spending patterns, analyzes the impact on company profits, and recommends four steps for reducing the budget.)

BODY

The organization of the body is clear and logical, moving from one key point to the next.

Part I of the body identifies the nature, scope, and causes of the problem.

I. Analysis of spending patterns
   A. The amount we've been spending on T&E:
      1. Airfares, hotels, rental cars, restaurants, and entertainment totaled $16 million last year.
      2. T&E budget increased by 12 percent per year for the past five years.
   B. Where the money goes:
      1. We took 3,390 trips last year at an average cost per trip of $4,725.
      2. Airfares and lodging represent 70 percent of T&E expenses.
   C. How our spending compares with national averages:
      1. Facilities and customers spread from coast to coast force us to spend a lot on travel.
      2. However, we spend 125 percent more than the national average for every day of travel. (Source: Dow Jones)
   D. Why do we spend so much?
      1. First-class travel has been viewed as compensation for the demands of extensive travel.
      2. The sales staff is encouraged to entertain clients.
      3. T&E costs are hard for managers to view and study.
      4. No one has central responsibility for controlling costs.

(Transition: We need to control spending for two reasons: (1) profits are projected to be flat or declining over the next two years, and (2) hotel rates and airfares continue to rise sharply.)

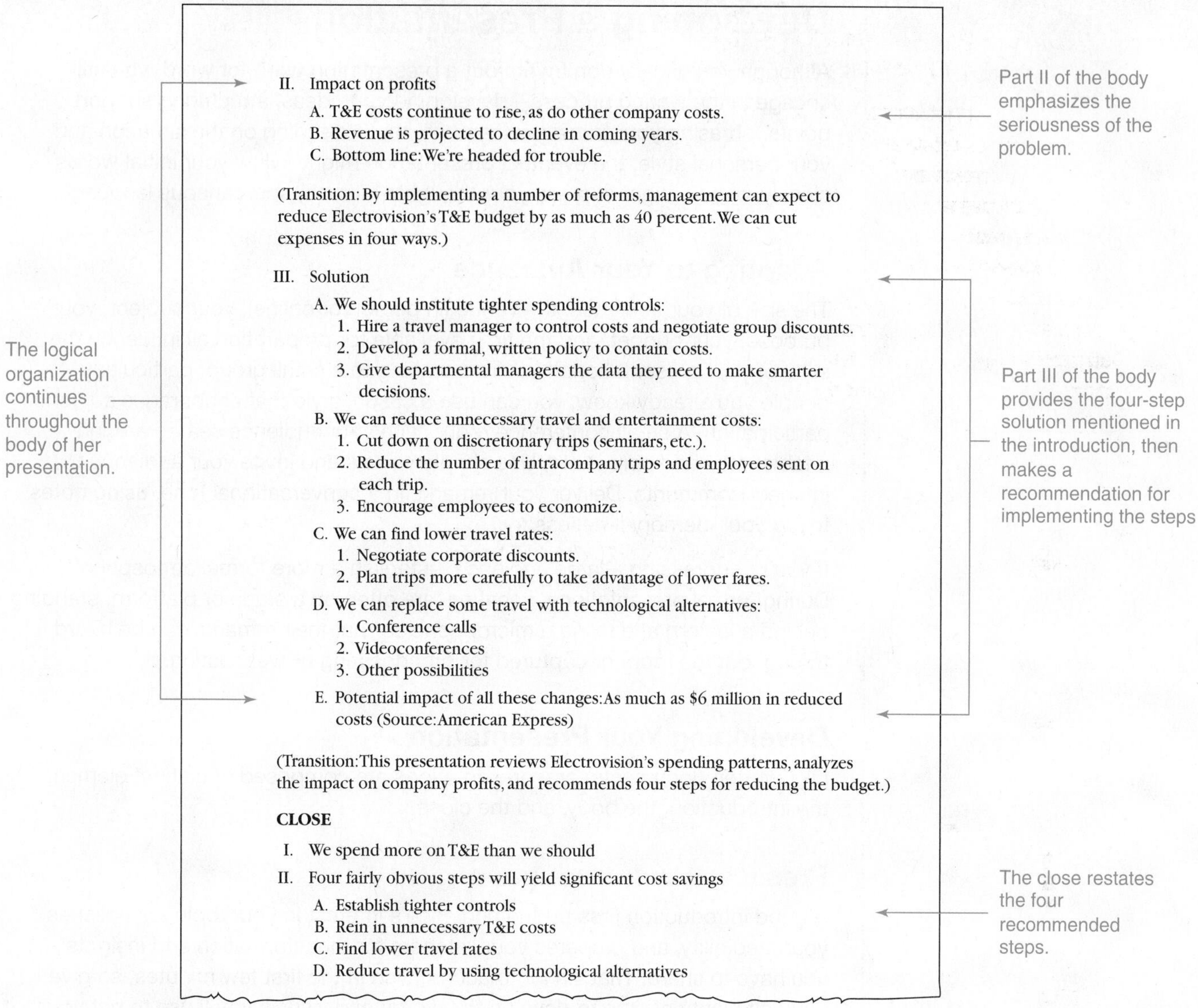

II. Impact on profits

A. T&E costs continue to rise, as do other company costs.
B. Revenue is projected to decline in coming years.
C. Bottom line: We're headed for trouble.

(Transition: By implementing a number of reforms, management can expect to reduce Electrovision's T&E budget by as much as 40 percent. We can cut expenses in four ways.)

III. Solution

A. We should institute tighter spending controls:
1. Hire a travel manager to control costs and negotiate group discounts.
2. Develop a formal, written policy to contain costs.
3. Give departmental managers the data they need to make smarter decisions.

B. We can reduce unnecessary travel and entertainment costs:
1. Cut down on discretionary trips (seminars, etc.).
2. Reduce the number of intracompany trips and employees sent on each trip.
3. Encourage employees to economize.

C. We can find lower travel rates:
1. Negotiate corporate discounts.
2. Plan trips more carefully to take advantage of lower fares.

D. We can replace some travel with technological alternatives:
1. Conference calls
2. Videoconferences
3. Other possibilities

E. Potential impact of all these changes: As much as $6 million in reduced costs (Source: American Express)

(Transition: This presentation reviews Electrovision's spending patterns, analyzes the impact on company profits, and recommends four steps for reducing the budget.)

CLOSE

I. We spend more on T&E than we should

II. Four fairly obvious steps will yield significant cost savings

A. Establish tighter controls
B. Rein in unnecessary T&E costs
C. Find lower travel rates
D. Reduce travel by using technological alternatives

To prepare an effective speaking outline, follow these steps:

- Start with the planning outline and then strip away anything you don't plan to say directly to your audience.
- Condense points and transitions to key words or phrases.
- Add delivery cues, such as places where you plan to pause for emphasis or use visuals.
- Arrange your notes on numbered cards or use the notes capability in your presentation software.

Developing a Presentation

Although you usually don't write out a presentation word for word, you still engage in the writing process—developing your ideas, structuring support points, phrasing your transitions, and so on. Depending on the situation and your personal style, the eventual presentation might follow your initial words closely, or you might express your thoughts in fresh, spontaneous language.

Adapting to Your Audience

The size of your audience, the venue (in person or online), your subject, your purpose, your budget, and the time available for preparation all influence the style of your presentation. If you're speaking to a small group, particularly people you already know, you can use a casual style that encourages audience participation. A small conference room, with your audience seated around a table, may be appropriate. Use simple visuals and invite your audience to interject comments. Deliver your remarks in a conversational tone, using notes to jog your memory if necessary.

If you're addressing a large audience, establish a more formal atmosphere. During formal presentations, speakers are often on a stage or platform, standing behind a lectern and using a microphone so that their remarks can be heard throughout the room or captured for broadcasting or webcasting.

Developing Your Presentation

Like written documents, oral presentations are composed of distinct elements: the introduction, the body, and the close.

Presentation Introduction

A good introduction fires up the audience's interest in your topic, establishes your credibility, and prepares your listeners for the information and insights you have to share. That's a lot to accomplish in the first few minutes, so give yourself plenty of time to develop the words and visuals you'll use to get your presentation off to a great start.

Getting Your Audience's Attention

Figure 12.5
Engage the Audience
Before you begin delivering the body of your message, make a connection with your audience by sharing a story, asking a question, or taking an informal poll.

Some subjects are naturally more interesting to some audiences than others. If your presentation involves the health, wealth, or happiness of your listeners, most people will be interested, regardless of how you begin. With other subjects, though, you need to use some imagination to pull people in. Here are six ways to arouse audience interest:

- Unite the audience around a common goal.
- Tell a compelling story that illustrates an important and relevant point. If your entire presentation is structured as a story, of course, you'll want to keep the interest high by not giving away the ending yet.
- Pass around an example or otherwise appeal to listeners' senses.
- Ask a question that will get your audience thinking about your message.
- Share an intriguing, unexpected, or shocking detail.
- Open with an amusing observation about yourself, the subject matter of the presentation, or the circumstances surrounding the presentation—but make sure any humorous remarks are relevant, appropriate, and not offensive to anyone in the audience.

Regardless of which technique you choose, make sure you can give audience members a reason to care and to believe that the time they're about to spend listening to you will be worth their while.

Building Your Credibility

Audiences tend to decide within a few minutes whether you're worth listening to, so establishing your credibility quickly is vital. If you're not a well-known expert or haven't already earned your audience's trust in other situations, you'll need to build credibility in your introduction. If someone else will introduce you, he or she can present your credentials. If you will be introducing yourself, keep your comments brief, but don't be afraid to mention your accomplishments. Your listeners will be curious about your qualifications, so tell them briefly who you are, why you're there, and how they'll benefit from listening to you. You might say something like this:

> I'm Karen Whitney, a market research analyst with Information Resources Corporation. For the past five years, I've specialized in studying high-technology markets. Your director of engineering, John LaBarre, asked me to talk about recent trends in computer-aided design so that you'll have a better idea of how to direct your development efforts.

This speaker establishes credibility by tying her credentials to the purpose of her presentation. By mentioning her company's name, her specialization and position, and the name of the audience's boss, she lets her listeners know immediately that she is qualified to tell them something they need to know.

Previewing Your Message

In addition to getting the audience's attention and establishing your credibility, a good introduction gives your audience a preview of what's ahead. Your preview should summarize the main idea of your presentation, identify major supporting points, and indicate the order in which you'll develop those points. By giving listeners the framework of your message, you help them process the information you'll be sharing, Of course, if you're using the indirect approach, you'll have to decide how much of your main idea to give away in the introduction.

Presentation Body

The bulk of your presentation is devoted to a discussion of the main points in your outline. No matter what organizational pattern you're using, your goals are to make sure that the organization is clear and that you hold the audience's attention.

Planning Verbal and Nonverbal Strategies

As you set out to accomplish your purpose, such as informing or persuading, you will want to employ both verbal and nonverbal strategies. Whether the presentation is formal or informal, nonverbal strategies can help support your points as well as better engage the audience. Verbal means using words, either spoken or written. Some examples of verbal strategies include:

- Speaking personally about the topic
- Playing a recording of someone else speaking about the topic
- Providing a handout containing references or additional information in text form
- Displaying a slide or other visual aid that contains text

Nonverbal communication are signals that play a vital role in communication. They can strengthen a verbal message (when the nonverbal signals match the spoken words), weaken a verbal message (when nonverbal signals don't match the words), or replace words entirely. The following are the major categories of nonverbal expression:

- Facial expressions
- Gestures and postures
- Vocal characteristics
- Personal appearance
- Touch
- Use of time and personal space

In Figure 12.6, notice the difference in the appeals between the verbal delivery in slide 12.6a and the nonverbal delivery in slide 12.6b.

Figure 12.6
Words vs. Pictures
In Figure 12.6a, the appeal is rational and verbal; the slide provides information using words. In Figure 12.6b, a picture conveys the message emotionally.

Why Donate to Helping Hands?

- We serve nutritious meals to over 2,000 people a day
- Our food pantry supplies over 300 families a month with essential grocery items
- Our community gardens make fresh vegetables available to more than 50 participating local families

Figure 12.6a

Figure 12.6b

Connecting Your Ideas

In written documents, you can show how ideas are related with a variety of design clues: headings, paragraph indentions, white space, and lists. With oral communication—particularly when you aren't using visuals for support—you have to rely primarily on spoken words to link various parts and ideas.

For the links between sentences and paragraphs, use one or two transitional words: therefore, because, in addition, in contrast, moreover, for example, consequently, nevertheless, or finally. To link major sections of a presentation, use complete sentences or paragraphs, such as "Now that we've reviewed the problem, let's take a look at some solutions." Every time you shift topics, be sure to stress the connection between ideas by summarizing what's been said and previewing what's to come. The longer your presentation, the more important your transitions. Your listeners need clear transitions to guide them to the most important points. Furthermore, they'll appreciate brief interim summaries to pick up any ideas they may have missed.

Holding Your Audience's Attention

A successful introduction will have grabbed your audience's attention; now the body of your presentation needs to hold that attention. Here are a few helpful tips for keeping the audience tuned into your message:

- Keep relating your subject to your audience's needs.
- Anticipate—and answer—likely questions as you move along so people don't get confused or distracted.
- Use clear, vivid language and throw in some variety; repeating the same words and phrases over and over puts people to sleep.
- Show how your subject is related to ideas that audience members already understand, and give people a way to categorize and remember your points.
- If appropriate, encourage participation by asking for comments or questions.
- Illustrate your ideas with visuals, which enliven your message, help you connect with audience members, and help them remember your message more effectively.

Presentation Close

The close of a speech or presentation has two critical jobs to accomplish: making sure your listeners leave with the key points from your talk clear in their minds, and putting your audience in the appropriate emotional state. For example, if the purpose of your presentation is to warn managers that their out-of-control spending threatens the company's survival, you want them to leave with that message ringing in their ears—and with enough concern for the problem to stimulate changes in their behavior.

Restating Your Main Points

Use the close to succinctly restate your main points, emphasizing what you want your listeners to do or to think. For example, to close a presentation on your company's executive compensation program, you could repeat your specific recommendations and then conclude with a memorable statement to motivate your audience to take action. Repetition of key ideas, as long as you don't overdo it, greatly improves the chance that your audience will hear your message in the way you intended.

> We can all be proud of the way our company has grown. If we want to continue that growth, we need to take four steps to ensure that our best people don't start looking for opportunities elsewhere:
>
> First, increase the overall level of compensation
>
> Second, establish a cash bonus program
>
> Third, offer a variety of stock-based incentives
>
> Fourth, improve our health insurance and pension benefits
>
> By taking these steps, we can ensure that our company retains the management talent it needs to face our industry's largest competitors.

Ending with Clarity and Confidence

If you've been successful with the introduction and body of your presentation, your listeners now have the information they need, and they're in the right frame of mind to put that information to good use. Now you're ready to end on a strong note that confirms expectations about any actions or decisions that will follow the presentation—and to bolster the audience's confidence in you and your message one final time.

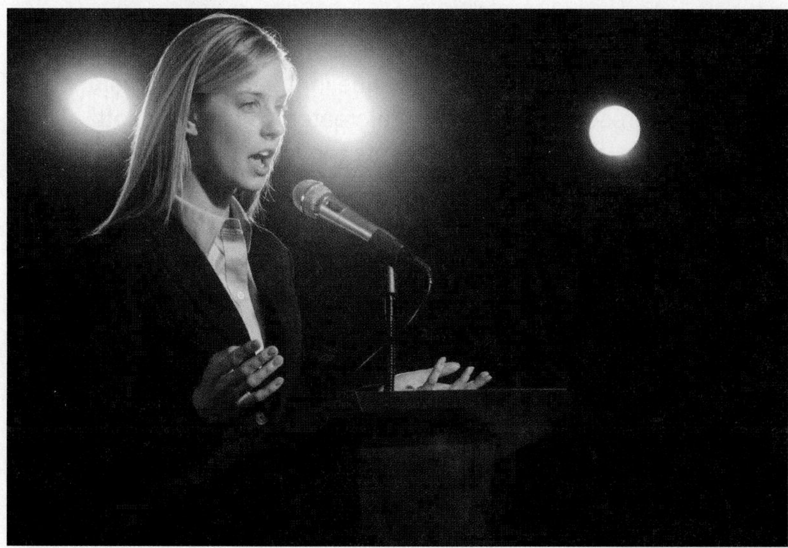

Figure 12.7
A Strong Conclusion
As you conclude your presentation, restate and emphasize what you want the audience to remember.

Some presentations require the audience to reach a decision or agree to take specific action, in which case the close should provide a clear wrap-up. If the audience reached agreement on an issue covered in the presentation, briefly review the consensus. If they didn't agree, make the lack of consensus clear by saying something like, "We seem to have some fundamental disagreement on this question." Then be ready to suggest a method of resolving the differences.

If you expect any action to occur as a result of your speech, be sure to identify who is responsible for doing what. List the action items and, if possible within the time you have available, establish due dates and assign responsibility for each task.

Make sure your final remarks are memorable and expressed in a tone that is appropriate to the situation. For example, if your presentation is a persuasive request for project funding, you might emphasize the importance of this project and your team's ability to complete it on schedule and within budget. Expressing confident optimism will send the message that you believe in your ability to perform. Conversely, if your purpose is to alert the audience to a problem or risk, false optimism will undermine your message.

Whatever final message is appropriate, think through your closing remarks carefully before stepping in front of the audience. You don't want to wind up on stage with nothing to say but "Well, I guess that's it."

Enhancing Your Presentation with Effective Visuals

Slides and other visuals can improve the quality and impact of your presentation by creating interest, illustrating points that are difficult to explain in words alone, adding variety, and increasing the audience's ability to absorb and remember information.

You can select from a variety of visuals to enhance presentations. Don't overlook "old-school" technologies such as overhead transparencies, chalkboards, whiteboards, and flipcharts—they can all have value in the right circumstances. However, most business presentation visuals are created using Microsoft PowerPoint, Apple Keynote, or Google Documents for linear presentations and Prezi for nonlinear presentations. Presentation slides and Prezis are easy to edit and update; you can add sound, photos, video, and animation; they can be incorporated into online meetings, webcasts, and webinars; and you can record self-running presentations for trade shows, websites, and other uses.

Presentation slides are practically universal in business today, but their widespread use is not always welcome. You may have already heard the expression "death by PowerPoint," the agonizing experience of sitting through too many poorly conceived and poorly delivered slide shows.

The good news is that both linear and nonlinear presentations can be an effective communication medium and an experience that is satisfying, and sometimes even enjoyable, for presenter and audience alike. Start with the mindset of simplicity and authenticity (talking with your audience about things they care about, rather that talking *at* them or trying to be a performer), and you'll be well on your way to becoming an effective presenter.

Choosing Structured or Free-Form Slides

For linear presentations, the most important design choice you face when creating slides is whether to use conventional, bullet point-intensive structured slides or the looser, visually oriented free-form slides that many presentation specialists now advocate. Compare the two rows of slides in Figure 12.8. The structured slides in the top row follow the same basic format throughout the presentation. In fact, they're based directly on the templates built into PowerPoint, which tend to feature lots and lots of bullet points.

The free-form slides in the bottom row don't follow a rigid structure. However, free-form designs should not change randomly from one slide to the next. Effectively designed slides should still be unified by design elements such as color and font selections, as can be seen in Figures 12.8c and 12.8d. Also, note how Figure 12.8d combines visual and textual messages to convey the point about listening without criticizing. This complementary approach of pictures and words is a highlight of free-form design.

Figure 12.8
Structured Versus Free-Form Slide Design
Compare the rigid, predictable design of the two slides in the top row with the more dynamic free-form designs in the bottom row. Although the two free-form slides don't follow the same design structure, they are visually linked by color and font choices. (Note that Figure 12.8d is a humorous way of conveying the first bullet point in Figure 12.8b.)

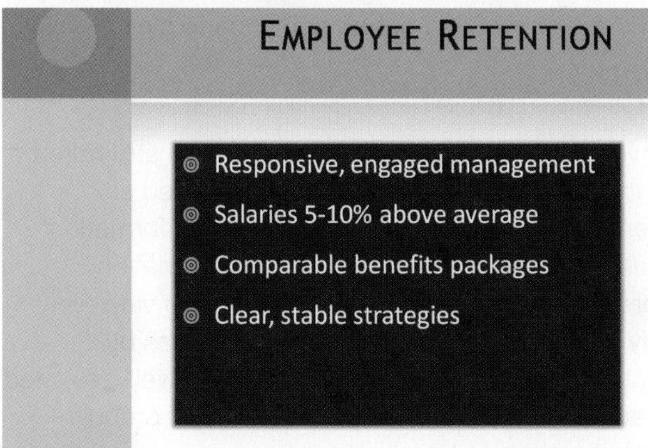

Figure 12.8a

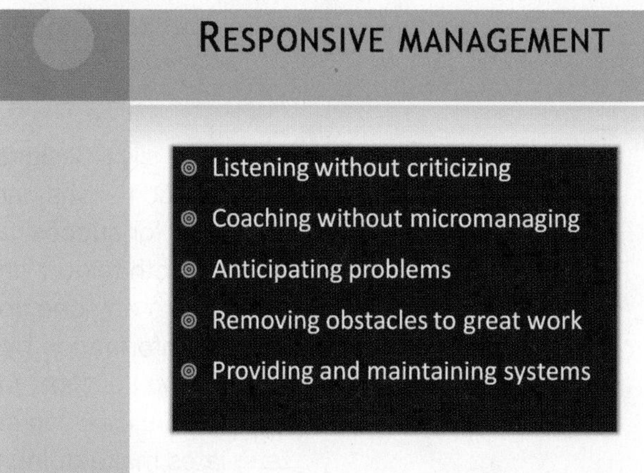

Figure 12.8b

Figure 12.8c

Figure 12.8d

Advantages and Disadvantages of Structured Slides

Structured slides have the advantage of being easy to create; you simply choose an overall design scheme for the presentation, select a template for a new slide, and start typing. If you're in a schedule crunch, going the structured route might save the day because at least you'll have something ready to show. Given the speed and ease of creating them, structured slides can be a more practical choice for routine presentations such as project status updates.

Also, because more information can usually be packed on each slide, carefully designed structured slides can be more effective at conveying complex ideas or sets of interrelated data to the right audiences. For example, if you are talking to a group of executives who must decide where to make budget cuts across the company's eight divisions, at some point in the presentation they probably will want to see summary data for all eight divisions on a single slide for easy comparison. Such a slide would be overcrowded by the usual definition, but this might be the only practical way to get a "big picture" view of the situation. (The best solution is probably some high-level, summary slides supported by a detailed handout, as "Creating Effective Handouts" on page 435 explains.)

The primary disadvantage of structured design is that they can be boring, caused by text-heavy slides that all look alike. Slide after slide of dense, highly structured bullet points with no visual relief can put an audience to sleep.

Advantages and Disadvantages of Free-Form Slides

Free-form slide designs can overcome the drawbacks of text-heavy structured design. Such slides can fulfill three criteria researchers have identified as important for successful presentations: providing complementary information through both textual and visual means, limiting the amount of information delivered at any one time to prevent cognitive overload, and helping viewers process information by identifying priorities and connections, such as by highlighting the most important data points in a graph. (Of course, well-designed structured slides can also meet these criteria, but the constraints of prebuilt templates make doing so more of a challenge.)

With appropriate imagery, free-form designs can also create a more dynamic and engaging experience for the audience. Given their ability to excite and engage, free-form designs are particularly good for motivational, educational, and persuasive presentations—particularly when the slides will be used multiple times and can compensate for the extra time and effort required to create them.

Free-form slides have several potential disadvantages, however. First, effectively designing slides with both visual and textual elements is more creatively demanding and more time consuming than simply typing text into preformatted templates. The emphasis on visual content also requires more images, which take time to find.

Second, because far less textual information tends to be displayed on screen, the speaker is responsible for conveying more of the content. Ideally, of course, this is how a presentation should work, but presenters sometimes find themselves in less than ideal circumstances, such as being asked to fill in for a colleague on short notice.

Third, if not handled carefully, the division of information into smaller chunks can make it difficult to present complex subjects in a cohesive, integrated manner. For instance, if you're discussing a business problem that has five interrelated causes, it might be helpful to insert a conventional bullet-point slide as a summary and reminder after discussing each problem on its own.

Designing Effective Slides

Despite complaints about "death by PowerPoint," the problem is not with that software itself (or with Apple Keynote or any other presentation program). It is just a tool, and, like other tools, can be used well or poorly. Unfortunately, lack of design awareness, inadequate training, schedule pressures, and the instinctive response of doing things the way they've always been done can lead to ineffective slides and lost opportunities to really connect with audiences. And although Prezi is sometimes promoted as the antidote to PowerPoint, using Prezi does not guarantee you'll end up with an effective presentation. Like any presentation tool, it can be misused and wind up creating a barrier between the speaker and the audience.

Another reason for ineffective slides is the practice of treating slide sets as standalone documents that can be read on their own, without a presenter. (The emergence of websites such as SlideShare might be contributing to this, too, by making it so easy to share slide sets.) These "slideument" hybrids that try to function as both presentation visuals and printed documents don't work well as either: They often have too much information to be effective visuals and too little to be effective reports (in addition to being clumsy to read).

As "Creating Effective Handouts" on page 435 explains, the ideal solution is to create an effective slide set and a separate handout document that provides additional details and supporting information. This way, you can optimize each piece to do the job it is really meant to do. An alternative is to use the notes field in your presentation software to include your speaking notes for each slide. Anyone who gets a copy of your slides can at least follow along by reading your notes, although you will probably need to edit and embellish them to make them understandable by others.

However, if creating slideuments is your only option for some reason, be sure to emphasize clarity and simplicity. If you have to add more slides to avoid packing individual slides with too much text, by all means do so. Having a larger number of simpler slides is a better compromise all around than a smaller number of jam-packed slides. Remember that the primary purpose of the slides is supporting your presentation, so make sure your slides work well for that purpose.

Designing Slides Around a Key Visual

With any type of presentation, it is often helpful to structure specific slides around a key visual that helps organize and explain the points you are trying to make. For example, a pyramid suggests a hierarchical relationship, and a circular flow diagram emphasizes that the final stage in a process loops back to the beginning of the process. Figure 12.9 shows six of the many types of visual designs you can use to organize information on a slide.

Figure 12.9
Using a Key Visual to Organize Points on a Slide
Simple graphical elements such as these SmartArt images in Microsoft PowerPoint make it easy to organize slide content using a key visual. Whether you're trying to convey the relationship of ideas in a hierarchy, a linear process, a circular process, or just about any other configuration, a key visual can work in tandem with your written and spoken messages to help audiences get your message.

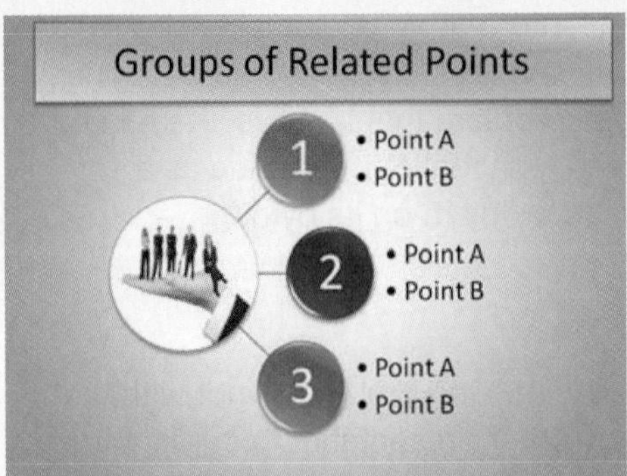

Figure 12.9a

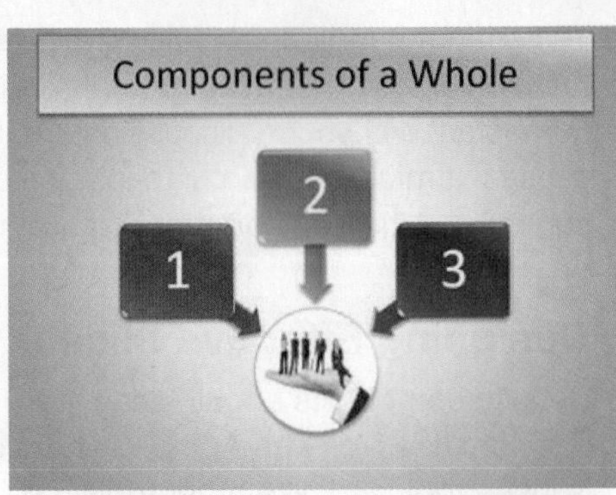

Figure 12.9b

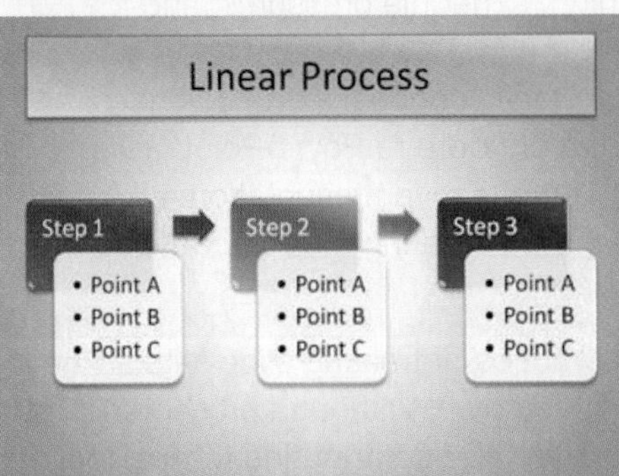

Figure 12.9c

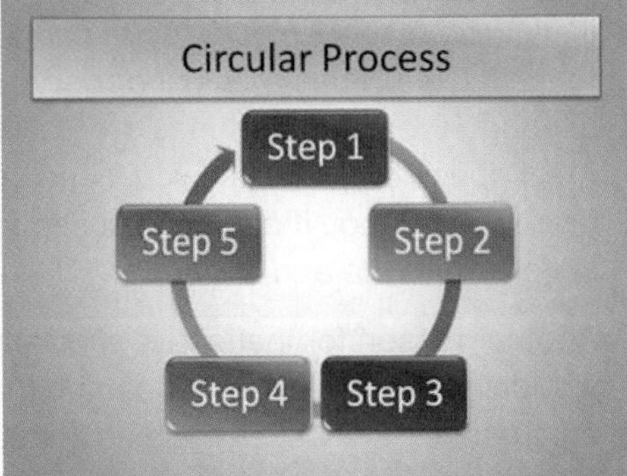

Figure 12.9d

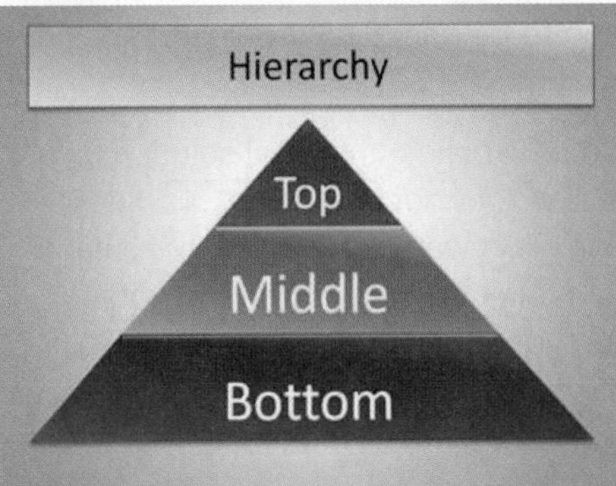

Figure 12.9e

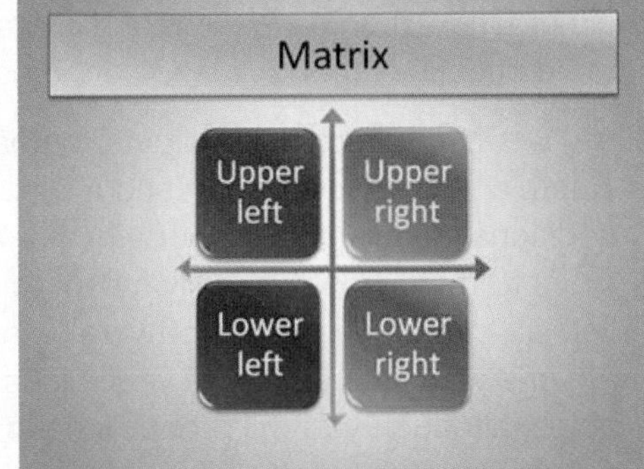

Figure 12.9f

Writing Readable Content

One of the most common mistakes beginners make—and one of the chief criticisms leveled at structured slide designs in general—is stuffing slides with too much text. Doing so overloads the audience with too much information too fast, takes attention away from the speaker by forcing people to read more, and requires the presenter to use smaller type.

Effective text slides supplement your words and help the audience follow the flow of ideas (see Figure 12.10). Use text to highlight key points, summarize and preview your message, signal major shifts in thought, illustrate concepts, or help create interest in your spoken message.

Writing Readable Content

To choose effective words and phrases, think of the text on your slides as guides to the content, not the content itself. In a sense, slide text serves as the headings and subheadings for your presentation. Accordingly, choose words and short phrases that help your audience follow the flow of ideas, without forcing people to read in depth. You primarily want your audience to *listen*, not to *read*. Highlight key points, summarize and preview your message, signal major shifts in thought, illustrate concepts, or help create interest in your spoken message.

Figure 12.7a

Writing Readable Content

- Text should be a guide to your content
- Use bullets like headings and subheadings
- Help audience follow the flow of ideas
- Encourage audience to *listen*, not *read*
- Highlight, summarize, preview, illustrate

Figure 12.7b

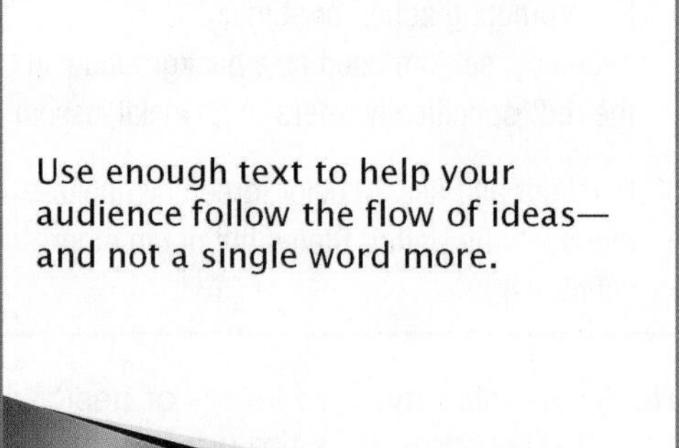

Figure 12.7c

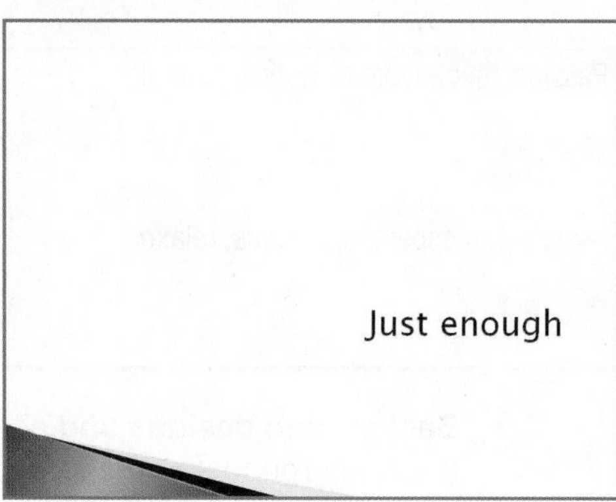

Figure 12.7d

Figure 12.10
Writing Text for Slides
Effective text slides are clear, simple guides that help the audience understand and remember the speaker's message. Notice the progression toward simplicity in these slides: Figure 12.10a is a paragraph that would distract the audience for an extended period of time. Figure 12.10b offers concise, readable bullets, although too many slides in a row in this structured design would become tedious. Figure 12.10c distills the message down to a single thought that is complete on its own but doesn't convey all the information from the original and would need embellishment from the speaker. Figure 12.10d pushes this to the extreme, with only the core piece of the message to serve as an "exclamation point" for the spoken message.
Figure 12.10c—and especially Figure 12.10d—could be even more powerful with a well-chosen visual that illustrates the idea of following the flow.

Creating Charts and Tables for Slides

Charts and tables for presentations need to be simpler than visuals for printed documents. Detailed images that look fine on the printed page can be too dense and too complicated for presentations. Remember that your audience will view your slides from across the room—not from a foot or two away, as you do while you create them. Keep the level of detail to a minimum, eliminating anything that is not absolutely essential. If necessary, break information into more than one chart or table. It may also be useful to provide detailed versions of charts and tables in a handout.

Selecting Design Elements

As you create slides, pay close attention to the interaction of color, background and foreground designs, artwork, typefaces, and type styles.

- **Color.** Color is a critical design element that can grab attention, emphasize important ideas, create contrast, influence acceptance of your ideas, improve retention, and stimulate a variety of emotions (see Table 12.2). Color is powerful, so use it carefully.

Table 14.2 Color and Emotion

Color	Emotional Associations (for US audiences)	Best Uses
Blue	Peaceful, soothing, tranquil, cool, trusting	Background for electronic business presentations (usually dark blue); safe and conservative
White	Neutral, innocent, pure, wise	Font color of choice for most electronic business presentations with a dark background
Yellow	Warm, bright, cheerful, enthusiastic	Text bullets and subheadings with a dark background
Red	Passionate, dangerous, active, painful	For promoting action or stimulating the audience; seldom used as a background ("in the red" specifically refers to financial losses)
Green	Assertive, prosperous, envious, relaxed	Highlight and accent color (green symbolizes money in the United States but not in other countries).

- **Background designs and artwork.** All visuals have two layers of design: the background and the foreground. The background is the equivalent of paper in a printed document, and the elements in the foreground are the essential content of your slides. Make sure the background stays in the background and doesn't distract viewers or compete with the foreground. (Note that many of the template designs in presentation software have backgrounds that are too distracting for serious business use.)
- **Foreground designs and artwork.** The foreground contains the unique text and graphic elements that make up each individual slide. Foreground elements can be either functional or decorative. Functional artwork includes photos, technical drawings, charts, and other visual elements containing information that's part of your message. In contrast, decorative artwork simply enhances the look of your slides and should be using sparingly, if at all.
- **Typefaces and type styles.** Type is harder to read on-screen than on the printed page, so you need to choose fonts and type styles with care. Sans serif fonts are usually easier to read than serif fonts. Use both uppercase and lowercase letters, with generous space between lines of text, and limit the number of fonts to one or two per slide. Choose font sizes that are easy to read from anywhere in the room, usually between 28 and 36 points, and test them in the room if possible. A clever way to test readability at your computer is to stand back as many feet from the screen as your screen size in inches (17 feet for a 17-inch screen, for example). If the slides are readable at this distance, you're probably in good shape.

Maintaining design consistency is critical because audiences start to assign meaning to visual elements beginning with the first slide. For instance, if yellow is used to call attention to the first major point in your presentation, viewers will expect the next occurrence of yellow to also signal an important point. The slide master feature makes consistency easy to achieve because it applies consistent design choices to every slide in a presentation.

Adding Animation and Multimedia

Today's presentation software offers many options for livening up your slides, including sound, animation, video clips, transition effects, hyperlinks, and zooming. Think about the impact that all these effects will have on your audience, and use only those special effects that support your message.

Functional animation involves motion that is directly related to your message, such as a highlight arrow that moves around the screen to emphasize specific points in a technical diagram. Such animation is also a great way to demonstrate sequences and procedures. In contrast, decorative animation, such as having a block of text cartwheel in from offscreen or many instances of the zooming and panning capabilities in Prezi, needs to be used with great care. These effects don't add any functional value, and they easily distract audiences.

Slide transitions control how one slide replaces another, such as having the current slide gently fade out before the next slide fades in. Subtle transitions like this can ease your viewers' gaze from one slide to the next, but many of the transition effects now available are little more than distractions and are best avoided. **Slide builds** control the release of text, graphics, and other elements on individual slides. With builds, you can make key points appear one at a time rather than having all of them appear on a slide at once, thereby making it easier for you and the audience to focus on each new message point.

Slide transition:
A movement from one slide to the next slide using an animated effect.

Slide build:
Animation within a single slide that controls the gradual appearance of text, graphics, and other elements.

A *hyperlink* instructs your computer to jump to another slide in your presentation, to a website, or to another program entirely. Using hyperlinks is also a great way to build flexibility into your presentations so that you can instantly change the flow of your presentation in response to audience feedback.

Multimedia elements offer the ultimate in active presentations. Using audio and video clips can be a great way to complement your textual message. Just be sure to keep these elements brief and relevant, as supporting points for your content, not as replacements for it.

Integrating Mobile Devices in Presentations

Smartphones and tablets offer a variety of ways to enhance presentations for presenters as well as audience members. For example, you can get around the problem of everyone in the audience having a clear view of the screen with systems that broadcast your slides to tablets and smartphones. In fact, these systems can eliminate a conventional projection system entirely; everyone in the audience can view your slides on their mobile devices. You can also broadcast a live presentation to mobile users anywhere in the world. Each time you advance to a new slide, it is sent to the phone or tablet of everyone who is subscribed to your presentation.

Completing a Presentation

The completion step for presentations involves a wider range of tasks than most printed documents require. Make sure you allow enough to time to test your presentation slides, verify equipment operation, practice your speech, and create handout materials. With a first draft of your presentation in hand, revise your slides to make sure they are readable, concise, consistent, and fully operational (including transitions, builds, animation, and multimedia). Complete your production efforts by finalizing your slides, creating handouts, choosing your presentation method, and practicing your delivery.

Finalizing Your Slides

Electronic presentation software can help you throughout the editing and revision process. For example, the slide sorter view (different programs have different names for this feature) lets you see some or all of the slides in your presentation on a single screen. Use this view to add and delete slides, reposition slides, check slides for design consistency, and verify the operation of any effects. Moreover, the slide sorter is a great way to review the flow of your story.

In addition to using content slides, you can help your audience follow the flow of your presentation by creating slides for your title, agenda and program details, and navigation:

- **Title slide(s).** You can make a good first impression with one or two title slides, the equivalent of a report's cover and title page.
- **Agenda and program details.** These slides communicate the agenda for your presentation and any additional information the audience might need such as hashtags and WiFi log-in information.
- **Navigation slides.** To tell your audience where you're going and where you've been, you can use a series of **navigation slides**. A simple way to do this is to repeat your agenda slide at the beginning of each major section in your presentation, with the upcoming section highlighted in some way. (The two navigation slides in Figure 12.11 show a more stylized way of showing the audience where you are in the presentation.)

Navigation slide:
A slide that serves as a table of contents to the presentation.

Figure 12.11 illustrates some of the many options you have for presenting various types of information. Note that although these slides don't follow a rigid structure of text-heavy bullet points, they are unified by the color scheme (silver background and bold color accents) and typeface selections.

Left: This stylized bar graph sends a stark visual message about how bad the company's turnover really is.

Right: This slide is essentially a bullet list, with three groups of two bullets each. Repeating the photo element from the introductory slide emphasizes the message about employee turnover.

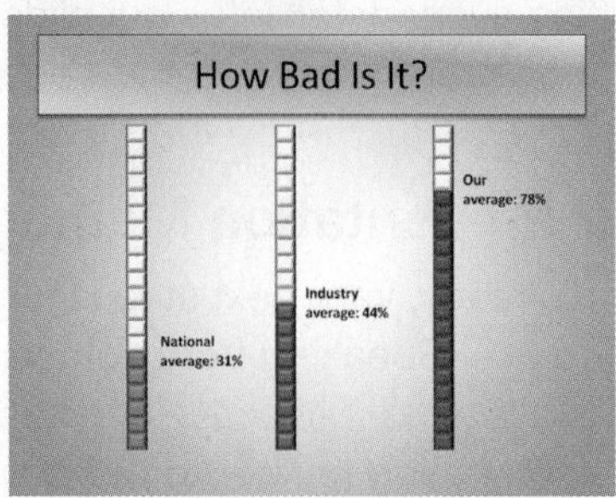

These two *navigation slides* show one way to introduce each of the four subtopics in this particular section. As the highlight moves around the central circle, the audience is reminded of which subtopics have been covered and which subtopic is going to be covered next. And each time it is shown, the message is repeated that all these problems are the "true cost of chaos" in the company's employment practices.

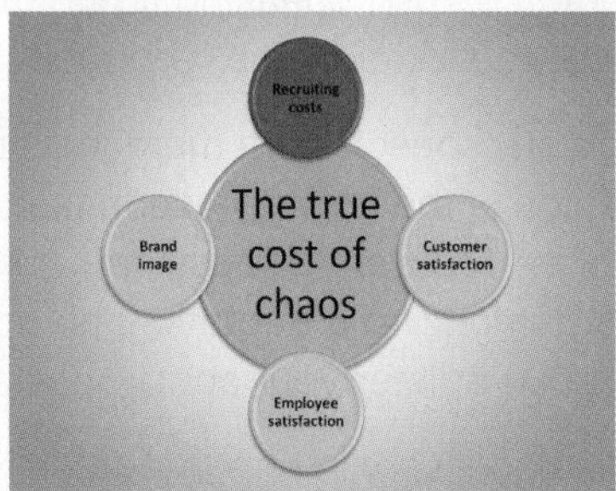

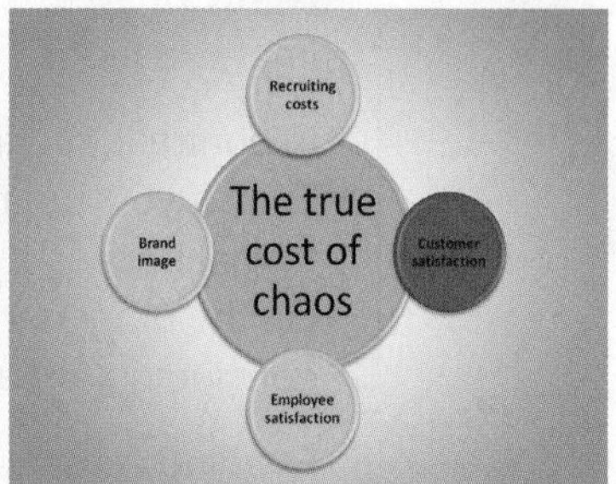

Left: This slide introduces three key points the speaker wants to emphasize in this particular section.

Right: This slide shows a linear flow of ideas, each with bulleted subpoints. This slide could be revealed one section at a time to help the speaker keep the audience's attention focused on a single topic.

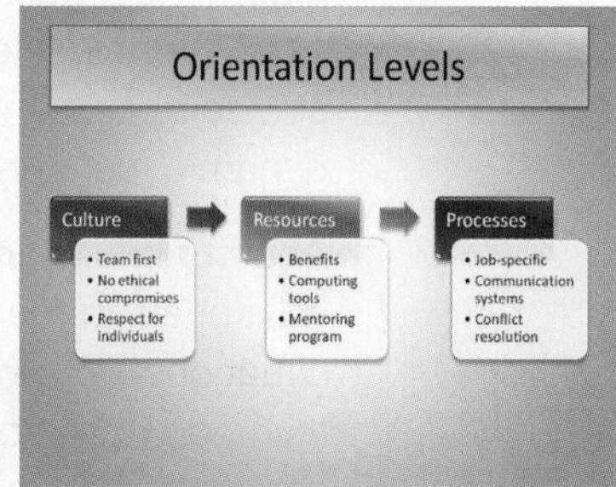

Left: This flowchart packs a lot of information onto one slide, but seeing the sequence of events in one place is essential.

Right: This simple visual highlights the presenter's spoken message about being careful to choose the right tasks to focus on and them completing them quickly.

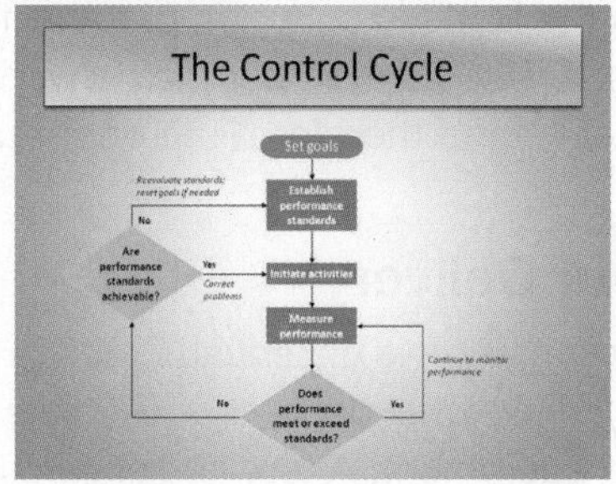

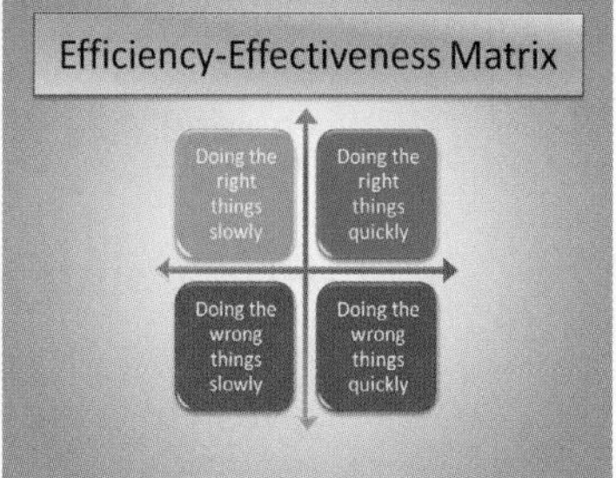

Figure 12.11
Designing Effective Visuals: Selected Slides
These slides, from a presentation that addresses a company's high employee turnover rate, illustrate the wide variety of design options you have for creating effective, appealing slides. (All the slides were created using features in PowerPoint.)

Creating Effective Handouts

Handouts—any printed materials you give the audience to supplement your talk—should be considered an integral part of your presentation strategy. Handouts can include detailed charts and tables, case studies, research results, magazine articles, and anything else that supports the main idea of your presentation.

Plan your handouts as you develop your presentation so that you use each medium as effectively as possible. Your presentation should paint the big picture, convey and connect major ideas, set the emotional tone, and rouse the audience to action (if that is relevant to your talk). Your handouts can then carry the rest of the information load, providing the supporting details that audience members can consume at their own speed, on their own time. You won't need to worry about stuffing every detail into your slides because you have the more appropriate medium of printed documents to do that.

Choosing Your Presentation Method

With all your materials ready, your next step is to decide which method of speaking you want to use. Speaking from notes, rather than from a fully written script, is nearly always the most effective and easiest delivery mode. This approach gives you something to refer to as you progress while still allowing for plenty of eye contact, a natural speaking flow, interaction with the audience, and improvisation in response to audience feedback.

In contrast, reciting your speech from memory is nearly always a bad idea. Even if you can memorize the entire presentation, you will sound stiff and overly formal because you are "delivering lines," rather than talking to your audience. On the other hand, memorizing a quotation, an opening statement, or a few concluding remarks can bolster your confidence and strengthen your delivery.

Reading a speech is necessary in rare instances, such as when delivering legal information, policy statements, or other messages that must be conveyed in an exact manner. However, for all other business presentations, reading is a poor choice because it limits your interaction with the audience and lacks the fresh, dynamic feel of natural talking.

Another important decision at this point is preparing the venue where you will speak. In many instances, you won't have much of a choice, and in some situations, you won't even be able to visit the venue ahead of time. However, if you do have some control over the environment, think carefully about the seating for the audience, your position in the room, and the lighting. For instance, dimming the lights is common practice for many presenters, but dimming the lights too far can hamper the nonverbal communication between you and your audience and therefore limit opportunities for interaction.

Practicing Your Delivery

Practicing your presentation is essential. Practice boosts your confidence, gives you a more professional demeanor, and lets you verify the operation of your visuals and equipment. A test audience can tell you if your slides are understandable and whether your delivery is effective. A day or two before you're ready to step on stage for an important talk, make sure you and your presentation are ready:

- Can you present your material naturally, without reading your slides?
- Could you still make a compelling and complete presentation if you experience an equipment failure and have to proceed without using your slides at all?
- Is the equipment working, and do you know how to work it?
- Is your timing on track?
- Can you easily pronounce all the words you plan to use?
- Have you anticipated likely questions and objections?

If you're addressing an audience that doesn't speak your language, consider using an interpreter. Send your interpreter a copy of your speech and visuals as far in advance of your presentation as possible. If your audience is likely to include persons with hearing impairments, be sure to team up with a sign language interpreter as well.

When you deliver a presentation to people from other cultures, you may need to adapt the content of your presentation. It is also important to take into account any cultural differences in appearance, mannerisms, and other customs. Your interpreter or host will be able to suggest appropriate changes for a specific audience or occasion.

Delivering a Presentation

It's show time. This section offers practical advice on four important aspects of delivery: overcoming anxiety, handling questions responsively, embracing the backchannel, and giving presentations online.

Figure 12.12
Public Speaking Stress
There's no magic formula for overcoming stage fright, but being well-prepared and practicing in front of friends and allies can help.

Overcoming Anxiety

Even seasoned pros get a little nervous before a big presentation—and that is a good thing. Nervousness is an indication that you care about your audience, your topic, and the occasion. These techniques will help you convert anxiety into positive energy:

- **Stop worrying about being perfect.** Successful speakers focus on making an authentic connection with their listeners, rather than on trying to deliver a note-perfect presentation.
- **Know your subject.** The more familiar you are with your material, the less panic you'll feel.
- **Practice, practice, practice.** The more you rehearse, the more confident you will feel.

- **Visualize success.** Visualize mental images of yourself in front of the audience, feeling confident, prepared, and able to handle any situation that might arise. Remember that your audience wants you to succeed, too.
- **Remember to breathe.** Tension can lead people to breathe in a rapid and shallow fashion, which can create a lightheaded feeling. Breathe slowly and deeply to maintain a sense of calm and confidence.
- **Be ready with your opening line.** Have your first sentence memorized so you don't have to improvise your opening.
- **Be comfortable.** Dress appropriately but as comfortably as possible. Drink plenty of water ahead of time to hydrate your voice, and take a bottle of water with you to the actual presentation.
- **Take a three-second break if you need to.** If you sense that you're starting to race, pause and arrange your notes or perform some other small task while taking several deep breaths. Then start again at your normal pace.
- **Concentrate on your message and your audience, not on yourself.** When you're busy thinking about your subject and observing your audience's response, you tend to forget your fears.
- **Maintain eye contact with friendly audience members.** Eye contact not only makes you appear sincere, confident, and trustworthy but can give you positive feedback as well.
- **Keep going.** Things usually get better as you move along, with each successful minute giving you more and more confidence.

Handling Questions Responsively

Whether you take them during a formal question-and-answer (Q&A) period or as they come up during your presentation, questions are often one of the most important parts of a presentation. They give you a chance to obtain important information, to emphasize your main idea and supporting points, and to build enthusiasm for your point of view. When you're speaking to high-ranking executives in your company, the Q&A period will often consume most of the time allotted for your presentation.

Whether or not you can establish ground rules for questions depends on the audience and the situation. If you're presenting to a small group of upper managers or potential investors, for example, you will probably have no say in the matter: audience members will likely ask as many questions as they want, whenever they want, to get the information they need. On the other hand, if you are presenting to your peers or a large public audience, establish some guidelines, like when and for how long you'll be able to answer questions.

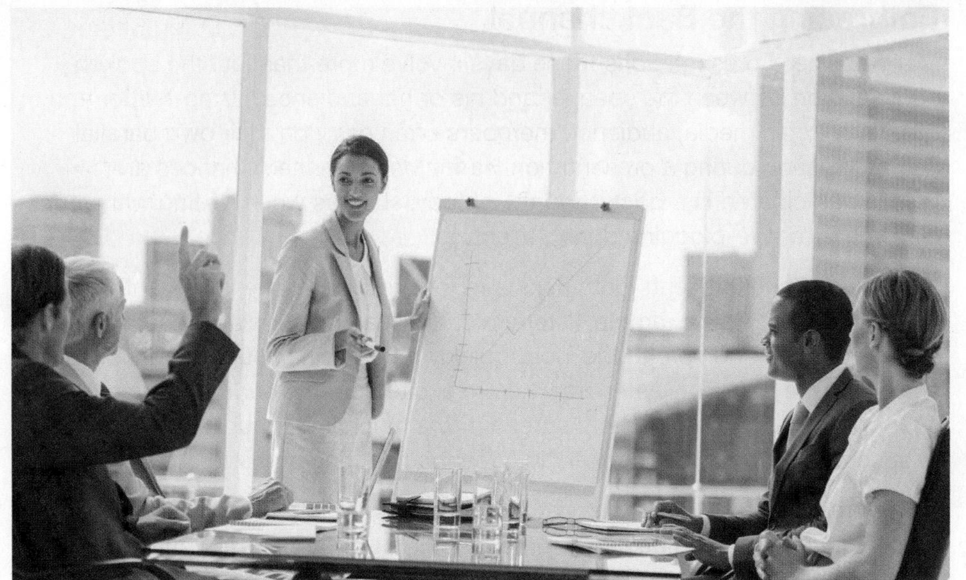

Figure 12.13
Taking Questions
When someone asks a question, answer it as clearly and concisely as possible, but look out for hidden agendas and nonverbal signals.

Don't assume you can handle whatever comes up without some preparation. Learn enough about your audience members to get an idea of their concerns and think through answers to potential questions.

When people ask questions, pay attention to nonverbal signals to help determine what each person really means. Repeat the question to confirm your understanding and to ensure that the entire audience has heard it. If the question is vague or confusing, ask for clarification; then give a simple, direct answer.

If you are asked a difficult or complex question, avoid the temptation to sidestep it. Offer to meet with the questioner afterward if the issue isn't relevant to the rest of the audience or if giving an adequate answer would take too long. If you don't know the answer, don't pretend you do. Instead, offer to get a complete answer as soon as possible.

Be on guard for audience members who use questions to make impromptu speeches or to take control of your presentation. Without offending anyone, find a way to stay in control. You might admit that you and the questioner have differing opinions and offer to get back to the questioner after you've done more research.

If a question ever puts you on the hot seat, respond honestly but keep your cool. Look the person in the eye, answer the question as well as you can, and keep your emotions under control. Defuse hostility by paraphrasing the question and asking the questioner to confirm that you've understood it correctly. Maintain a businesslike tone of voice and a pleasant expression.

Backchannel:
A line of communication in which the audience for a presentation connects with other audience members, with or without the knowledge of the speaker.

Embracing the Backchannel

Many business presentations these days involve more than just the spoken conversation between the speaker and his or her audience. Using Twitter and other electronic media, audience members often carry on their own parallel communication during a presentation via the backchannel. Chances are you've participated in a **backchannel** already, such as when texting with your classmates or live-blogging during a lecture.

The backchannel presents both risks and rewards for business presenters. On the negative side, for example, listeners can research your claims the instant you make them and spread the word quickly if they think your information is shaky. On the plus side, listeners who are excited about your message can build support for it, expand on it, and spread it to a much larger audience in a matter of seconds. You can also get valuable feedback during and after presentations.

By embracing the backchannel, rather than trying to fight it or ignore it, presenters can use this powerful force to their advantage. Follow these tips to make the backchannel work for you:

- **Integrate social media into the presentation process.** For example, you can create a website for the presentation so that people can access relevant resources during or after the presentation, create a Twitter hashtag that everyone can use when sending tweets, or display the Twitterstream during Q&A so that everyone can see the questions and comments on the backchannel.
- **Monitor and ask for feedback.** Using a free service such as TweetDeck, which organizes tweets by hashtag and other variables, you can monitor comments from people in the audience. To avoid trying to monitor the backchannel while speaking, you can schedule "Twitter breaks," during which you review comments and respond as needed.
- **Review comments point by point to improve your presentation.** After a presentation is over, review comments on audience members' Twitter accounts and blogs to see which parts confused them, which parts excited them, and which parts seemed to have little effect (based on few or no comments).
- **Automatically tweet key points from your presentation while you speak.** Add-ons for presentation software can send out prewritten tweets as you show specific slides during a presentation. By making your key points readily available, you make it easy for listeners to retweet and comment on your presentation.

Evaluating Presentations

In addition to giving your own presentations, you may also be a part of the audience when other people do so. These presentations may be in a formal business setting, or in an informal context such as at a trade show or all-employee meeting.

When listening to other people's presentations, employ critical listening skills (critical thinking applied to listening) to evaluate what you hear. Ask yourself whether the claims made are believable and backed up by objective facts. Listen not only for the verbal message, but for nonverbal subtext. Pay attention to the presenter's tone of voice, gestures, and level of enthusiasm. You can also apply these same critical listening skills to evaluate yourself in your own formal and non-formal presentations; ask a friend to record a video of your speech that you can evaluate later to improve.

Giving Presentations Online

Online presentations offer many benefits, including the opportunity to communicate with a geographically dispersed audience at a fraction of the cost of travel and the ability for a project team or an entire organization to meet at a moment's notice. However, this format also presents some challenges for the presenter, thanks to that layer of technology between you and your audience. Many of those "human moments" that guide and encourage you through an in-person presentation won't travel across the digital divide. For instance, it's often difficult to tell whether audience members are bored or confused, because your view of them is usually confined to small video images at best..

To ensure successful online presentations, keep the following advice in mind:

- **Consider sending preview study materials ahead of time.** Doing so allows audience members to familiarize themselves with any important background information. Also, by using a free service such as SlideShare, you can distribute your presentation slides to either public or private audiences, and you can record audio narrative to make your presentations function on their own. Some presenters advise against giving out your slides ahead of time, however, because doing so gives away the ending of your presentation.
- **Keep your presentation as simple as possible.** Break complicated slides down into multiple slides if necessary, and keep the direction of your discussion clear so that no one gets lost.
- **Ask for feedback frequently.** You won't have as much of the visual feedback that alerts you when audience members are confused, and many online viewers will be reluctant to call attention to themselves by interrupting you to ask for clarification. Setting up a backchannel via Twitter or as part of your online meeting system will help in this regard.
- **Consider the viewing experience from the audience members' point of view.** Will they be able to see what you think they can see? For instance, webcast video is typically displayed in a small window on-screen, so viewers may miss important details.
- **Allow plenty of time for everyone to get connected and familiar with the screen they're viewing.** Build extra time into your schedule to ensure that everyone is connected and ready to start.

Last but not least, don't get lost in the technology. Use these tools whenever they'll help, but remember that the most important aspect of any presentation is getting the audience to receive, understand, and embrace your message.

CHAPTER SUMMARY

Planning a Presentation

Presentations give you the opportunity to use all your communication skills, from research to writing to speaking. They also demonstrate your ability to think quickly, to adapt to challenging situations, and to handle touchy questions and complex issues.

The tasks in planning presentations are generally the same as with any other business message, but three tasks require special consideration. First, when analyzing the situation, in addition to understanding the audience's information needs, you also need to anticipate the likely emotional states of your listeners during the presentation. Second, although some presentations consist only of a speaker addressing an audience, others integrate a variety of electronic media. Third, to organize your presentation, you need to decide whether to create a conventional linear presentation (using PowerPoint or similar software) or a nonlinear presentation (using Prezi or a similar system). With any format, limiting the scope is particularly vital, because many presentations must fit strict time limits, and keeping presentations as short as possible is always a good idea in order to keep from losing the audience's attention.

Developing a Presentation

Although you usually don't write out a presentation word for word, you still engage in the writing process—developing your ideas, structuring support points, phrasing your transitions, and so on. Adapting to the audience is crucial because presentation audiences and venues can vary widely, from small, informal gatherings to formal keynote speeches in large auditoriums to virtual presentations given entirely online. To compose a presentation, break it down into three essential parts: an introduction that arouses the audience's interest in your topic, establishes your credibility, and prepares the audience for what will follow; a body that conveys your information in a way that maintains audience interest and makes it easy to connect one idea to the next; and a close that restates your main points, wraps up any unfinished business, and lets you end with clarity and confidence.

Enhancing Your Presentation with Effective Visuals

First, choose between structured and free-form slides. Structured slides follow the same design plan for most or all the slides in a presentation, are often created by using the templates provided with presentation software, and tend to convey most of their information through bullet points. In contrast, visually oriented free-form slides do not follow any set design scheme from slide to slide, although they should have a unified sense of color, font selection, and other design elements. Second, look for opportunities to design slides around a key visual that unites and explains important points. Third, for any slides that have textual content, be sure to strictly limit the word count and keep the font size large enough to read easily. Fourth, make sure any graphic elements are simple and clear enough to be easily grasped from anywhere in the room. Fifth, choose and use design elements—color, background and foreground designs, artwork, typefaces, and type styles—in a way that enhances, not obscures, your message. Sixth, add animation and multimedia elements if they will help build audience interest and understanding.

Completing a Presentation

The completion stage for presentations requires a wider range of tasks than printed documents. Three tasks require particular attention. First, finalize your slides and support materials using the slide sorter to get a big picture view of your presentation and creating title slide(s), agenda and program detail slides, and navigation slides. Second, choose your presentation method: memorizing your material word for word, reading a printout of your material, or speaking from notes. Speaking from notes is the best choice for most presentations. Third, practice your delivery. Practice helps ensure a smooth presentation and boosts your confidence.

Delivering a Presentation

First, take steps to reduce your anxiety, which include: not trying to be perfect; preparing more material than is necessary; practicing extensively; visualizing success; breathing deeply and slowly; being ready with an opening line; dressing as comfortably as appropriate; taking a deliberate pause if you're rushing; concentrating on your message; maintaining eye contact; and plowing ahead no matter what happens.

Second, handle questions responsively. Determine whether you can set boundaries for the Q&A period. Prepare answers to potential questions. Pay attention to nonverbal signals and be sure to respond to all questions. Don't let questioners take control of the presentation. Face hostile questions head-on without getting defensive. Finally, alert the audience when the Q&A period is almost over.

Third, embrace the backchannel, the parallel conversation that might be going on among audience members on Twitter and other media. To take advantage of the backchannel, you can integrate social media into your presentation, monitor and ask for feedback, review point by point comments to improve your presentation, automatically tweet key points from your presentation while you speak, and establish expectations with the audience.

Fourth, to ensure a successful online presentation, consider sending preview materials ahead of time, keep your content and presentation as simple as possible, ask for feedback frequently, consider the viewing experience from the audience's side, and give participants time to get connected.

Test Your Knowledge

1. What skills do presentations give you the opportunity to practice and demonstrate?
2. How do linear and nonlinear presentations differ?
3. What three goals should you accomplish during the introduction of a presentation?
4. What techniques can you use to get an audience's attention during your introduction?
5. What three tasks should you accomplish in the close of your presentation?
6. What steps can you take to ensure success with online presentations?

Apply Your Knowledge

1. You just gave an in-depth presentation on the company's new marketing programs, intended for the specialists in the marketing department. The marketing manager then asked you to give a shorter version of the presentation to the company's top executives. Generally speaking, how should you modify the scope of your presentation for this new audience?
2. Is it ethical to use design elements and special effects to persuade an audience? Why or why not?
3. Why is speaking from notes usually the best method of delivery?

Activities

1. **Planning and Delivering a Presentation** Select one of the following topics:

   a. The town you live in suffers from a great deal of juvenile vandalism. Explain to a group of community members why juvenile recreational facilities should be built instead of a juvenile detention complex.
   b. You are speaking to a group of first-year medical students. Support or oppose the use of animals for medical research purposes.
   c. You are talking to civic leaders of your community. Convince them to build an art gallery that features artwork from populations that are traditionally under-represented in mainstream art galleries.
   d. You are speaking to a first-grade class at an elementary school. Explain why they should brush their teeth after meals.
   e. You are speaking to a group of traveling salespeople. Convince them that they should wear seatbelts while driving.
   f. You are speaking to a group of elderly people. Convince them to adopt an exercise program.
   g. You are speaking to a group of 18-year-olds. Convince them to register to vote, and explain how to register.
   h. Explain the process of applying for and receiving a mortgage to people who are interested in buying their first home.
   i. Explain how the Social Security system works to young entry-level employees who are new to the workforce.
   j. Explain the process of becoming a foster parent to young adults who are interested in being foster parents.
   k. Explain an interesting new technology that has lately been in the news to your classmates.
   l. Explain how the Electoral College works, to people who are applying for US citizenship. Assume that most in the audience are not native speakers of English.
   m. Explain the basic rules of your favorite team sport to someone who has never seen or heard of it.

   Research your topic as needed and prepare two 10-minute presentations—one formal and one informal. Describe the differences between the two presentations. Prepare to deliver the information presentation to your class. Include a two-minute question-and-answer session at the end.

When preparing a presentation—either formal or informal—make sure you take into account the audience, occasion, and purpose of the speech. Revise and edit your presentation to fit your audience. Use the information you gather to support your main points, making sure you provide citations for your research sources. As you do your research, remember to use media literacy strategies to analyze and evaluate your primary and secondary sources, such as recognizing bias, misinformation, untruths, and source credibility. Identify up to three nonverbal strategies that would enhance your formal presentation and three nonverbal strategies that would enhance your informal presentation.

2. **Performing Self-Evaluation** When you are finished with your presentation from Activity 1, write a one-page self-evaluation report. What do you think you did well in preparing the presentation? In delivering it? What would you do differently?

3. **Evaluating Presentations** Participate as an audience member in other people's presentations in Activity 1. Apply critical-listening strategies, and evaluate the effectiveness of the presentation in each case. Participate in question-and-answer sessions following each presentation, and ask thoughtful, relevant questions. After evaluating several people's presentations, write a one- to two-page summary of the experience of being an audience member. What did you learn from other people's successes and mistakes that will change how you do your own presentations?

4. **Overcoming Apprehension** Create a five-minute presentation directed at people who are nervous about public speaking. Cover techniques for managing communication apprehension and building self-confidence. (Research this topic online if needed; cite your sources appropriately.) Then use these techniques yourself to minimize your own nervousness as you present this information to a small group of your classmates. Afterwards, write down your impressions of the exercise, or discuss them with your classmates. Did the recommended techniques help?

5. **Creating Strong Introductions (Team Project)** You've been asked to give an informative 10-minute talk on vacation opportunities in your home state. Draft your introduction, which should last no more than two minutes. Then pair up with a classmate and analyze each other's introductions. How well do these two introductions arouse the audience's interest, build credibility, and preview the presentation? Suggest how these introductions might be improved.

6. **Evaluating a Professional Speech** Locate the transcript of a speech, either online or through your school library. Good sources include Yahoo's directory of commencement speeches and the publication Vital Speeches of the Day. (Recent years of Vital Speeches of the Day are available in the ProQuest database; ask at your library.) Many corporate websites also have archives of executives' speeches; look in the "investor relations" section. Examine both the introduction and the close of the speech you've chosen, and then analyze how these two sections work together to emphasize the main idea. What action does the speaker want the audience to take? Next, identify the transitional sentences or phrases that clarify the speech's structure for the listener, especially those that help the speaker shift between supporting points. Using these transitions as clues, list the main message and supporting points; then indicate how each transitional phrase links the current supporting point to the succeeding one. Prepare a two- to three-minute presentation summarizing your analysis for your class.

7. **Designing Presentation Visuals** Look through recent issues (print or online) of *Bloomberg Businessweek*, *Fortune*, or other business publications for articles discussing challenges that a specific company or industry is facing. Using the articles and the guidelines discussed in this chapter, create a short Prezi or three to five slides summarizing these issues. Include at least one table and one chart.

8. **Analzying Presentation Visuals** Find a business-related slide presentation on SlideShare and analyze the design. Do you consider it structured or free form? Does the design help the audience understand and remember the message? Why or why not? What improvements would you suggest to the design?

9. **Analyzing Nonverbal Signals** Observe and analyze the delivery of a speaker in a school, work, or other setting. What type of delivery did the speaker use? Was this delivery appropriate for the occasion? What nonverbal signals did the speaker use to emphasize key points? Were these signals effective? Which nonverbal signals would you suggest to further enhance the delivery of this oral presentation? Why?

10. **Persuading with Verbal and NonVerbal Signals** Prepare a 5-minute presentation that will persuade your classmates to donate to the charity of your choice. Use both intellectual and emotional appeals to make your case, and both verbal and nonverbal signals. Present your presentation to a small group of your classmates. Afterwards, ask your classmates for feedback. Were they convinced? Which of the strategies you used were particularly effective?

11. **Developing a Supporting Backchannel for a Presentation** In a team of six students, develop a 10-minute Prezi or slide presentation on any topic that interests you. Nominate one person to give the presentation; the other five will participate via a Twitter backchannel. Create a webpage that holds at least one downloadable file that will be discussed during the presentation. Practice using the backchannel, including using a hashtag for the meeting and having the presenter ask for audience feedback during a "Twitter break." Be ready to discuss your experience with the entire class.

12. **Evaluating Presentations** Visit the TED website at www.ted.com/talks and listen to any presentation that interests you. Compare the speaker's delivery and visual support materials with the concepts presented in this chapter. What works? What doesn't work? Using whatever medium your instructor requests, write a brief summary of your analysis.

Expand Your Skills

1. **Planning a Presentation** Pecha-kucha is a style of presentation that might be the ultimate in creative constraint: The speaker is limited to 20 slides, each of which is displayed for exactly 20 seconds before automatically advancing. Pecha-kucha Nights, which are open to the public, are now put on in cities all over the world. Visit www.pecha-kucha.org for more information on these events or to view some archived presentations.

Your task: Select one of the subjects from Activity 12.1 and develop a pecha-kucha style presentation with 20 slides, each designed to be displayed for 20 seconds. Use the slide timing capabilities in your presentation software to control the timing. Make sure you practice before presenting to your class so that you can hit the precise timing requirements.

2. **Planning a Presentation** You know those times when you're craving Thai food or the perfect fruit smoothie, but you don't know where to go? Or when you're out shopping and want to let your friends know where you are? Foursquare's location-based services connect you with friends and companies that offer products and services of interest.

   Your task: Create a brief presentation explaining the Foursquare concept and its features and benefits. Using a table, list at least two Foursquare competitors and give a brief assessment of which you would recommend to your classmates.

3. **Planning, Designing, and Creating Presentation Slides** Not long ago, snowboarding seemed to be on pace to pass skiing as the country's favorite way to zoom down snowy mountains, but the sport's growth has cooled off in recent years.

   Your task: Research and prepare a 10-minute presentation on participation trends in snowboarding and skiing, including explanations for the relative popularity of both sports. Include at least three quotations to emphasize key points in your presentation. Use either structured or free-form slides.

4. **Planning, Designing, and Creating Presentation Slides** Many companies publish stories of their founding and early years. The computer company Hewlett-Packard (HP), for example, tells the story of how founders Bill Hewlett and Dave Packard started the company in a garage in Palo Alto, California, in 1938, doing anything they could to "bring in a nickel." That garage is now preserved as "the birthplace of Silicon Valley," which helps maintain HP's image as a technology pioneer.

   Your task: Choose a company that has been in business for at least two decades and prepare a 10-minute presentation on its history.

5. **Planning a Presentation (Team Project)** In your job as a business development researcher for a major corporation, you're asked to gather and process information on a wide variety of subjects. Management has gained confidence in your research and analysis skills and would now like you to begin making regular presentations at management retreats and other functions. Topics are likely to include the following:

   - Offshoring of US jobs
   - Foreign ownership of US firms
   - Employment issues involving workers from other countries
   - Tax breaks offered by local and state governments to attract new businesses
   - Economic impact of environmental regulations

Your task: With a team assigned by your instructor, choose one of the topics from the list and conduct enough research to familiarize yourself with the topic. Identify at least three important issues that anyone involved with this topic should know about. Prepare a 10-minute presentation that introduces the topic, comments on its importance to the US economy, and discusses the issues you've identified. Assume that your audience is a cross-section of business managers who don't have any particular experience in the topic you've chosen. Use appropriate presentation visuals, including tables, charts, and figures.

6. **Designing Presentation Visuals** Depending on the sequence your instructor chose for this course, you've probably covered many chapters at this point and learned or improved many valuable skills. Think through your progress and identify five business communication skills that you've either learned for the first time or developed during this course.

   Your task: Create a Prezi or slide presentation that describes each of the five skills you've identified. Be sure to explain how each skill could help you in your career. Use any visual style that you feel is appropriate for the assignment.

7. **Designing Presentation Visuals** On SlideShare or any other source, find a business presentation on any topic that interests you.

   Your task: Re-create the first five slides in the presentation in a manner that will make them more mobile-friendly. Create as many additional slides as you need.

CHAPTER 13

Building Careers and Writing Resumes

After studying this chapter, you will be able to:

- List eight key steps to finding the ideal opportunity in today's job market.
- Explain the process of planning your resume, including how to choose the best resume organization.
- Describe the tasks involved in writing your resume and list the sections to consider including in your resume.
- Characterize the completing step for resumes, including the six most common resume formats.

Finding the Ideal Opportunity in Today's Job Market

Figure 13.1
Your Job Search
Finding the right job can be a full-time endeavor in itself, involving many hours of research, paperwork, and interviewing.

Identifying and landing a job can be a long and challenging process. Fortunately, the skills you're developing in this course will give you a competitive advantage. This section offers a general job-search strategy with advice that applies to just about any career path you might want to pursue. As you craft your personal strategy, keep these three guidelines in mind:

- **Get organized.** Your job search could last many months and involve multiple contacts with dozens of companies. You need to keep all the details straight to ensure that you don't miss opportunities or make mistakes such as losing someone's email address or forgetting an appointment.
- **Start now and stick to it.** Even if you are a year or more away from graduation, now is not too early to get started with some of the essential research and planning tasks. If you wait until the last minute, you will miss opportunities and you won't be as prepared as other candidates.
- **Look for stepping-stone opportunities.** Particularly in today's tough job market, you might not find the opportunity you're looking for right away. You might need to take a job that doesn't meet your expectations while you keep looking to get on the right track. But view every job as an opportunity to learn workplace skills, observe effective and ineffective business practices, and fine-tune your sense of how you'd like to spend your career.

Writing the Story of You

Writing or updating your resume is a great opportunity to step back and think about where you've been and where you'd like to go. Do you like the path you're on, or is it time for a change? Are you focused on a particular field, or do you need some time to explore?

You might find it helpful to think about the "story of you," the things you are passionate about, your skills, your ability to help an organization reach its goals, the path you've been on so far, and the path you want to follow in the future (see Figure 13.2). Think in terms of an image or a theme you'd like to project. Are you academically gifted? An effective leader? A well-rounded professional with wide-ranging talents? A creative problem solver? A technical wizard? Writing your story is a valuable planning exercise that helps you think about where you want to go and how to present yourself to target employers.

My Story

Where I Have Been

- Honor student and all around big shot in high school
- Have worked several part-time jobs; only thing that really appealed to me in any of them was making improvements, making things work better

What experiences from your past give you insight into where you would like to go in the future?

Where I Am Now

- Junior; on track to graduate in 2018
- Enjoy designing creative solutions to challenging problems
- Not a high-end techie in an engineering sense, but I figure most things out eventually
- Not afraid to work hard, whatever it takes to get the job done
- I can tolerate some routine, as long as I have the opportunity to make improvements if needed
- Tend to lead quietly by example, rather than by visibly and vocally taking charge
- Knowing that I do good work is more important than getting approval from others
- I tend not to follow fads and crowds; sometimes I'm ahead of the curve, sometimes I'm behind the curve

Where do you stand now in terms of your education and career, and what do you know about yourself?

Where I Want to Be

- Get a college degree; not sure what subject area yet, though
- Haven't really settled on one industry or profession yet; working with systems of any kind is more appealing than any particular profession that I've learned about so far
- Develop my leadership and communication skills to become a more "obvious" leader
- Collaborate with others while still having the freedom to work independently (may be become an independent contractor or consultant at some point?)
- Have the opportunity to work internationally, at least for a few years
- I like the big bucks that corporate executives earn, but I don't want to live in the public eye like that or have to "play the game" to get ahead
- Believe I would be good manager, but not sure I want to spend all my time just managing people
- What to be known as an independent thinker and creative problem solver, as somebody who can analyze tough situations and figure out solutions that others might not consider
- Are there jobs where I could focus on troubleshooting, improving processes, or designing new systems?

What would you like your future to be? What do you like and dislike? What would you like to explore? If you haven't figured everything out yet, that's fine—as long as you've started to think about the future.

Figure 13.2 Writing the Story of You

Writing the "story of you" is a helpful way to think through where you've been in your life and career so far, where you are now, and where you would like to go from here. Remember that this is a private document designed to help you clarify your thoughts and plans, although you probably will find ways to adapt some of what you've written to various job-search documents, including your resume.

Learning to Think Like an Employer

When you know your side of the hiring equation a little better, switch sides and look at it from an employer's perspective. To begin with, recognize that companies take risks with every hiring decision—the risk that the person hired won't meet expectations and the risk that a better candidate has slipped through their fingers. Many companies judge the success of their recruiting efforts by quality of hire, a measure of how closely new employees meet the company's needs. Given this perspective, what steps can you take to present yourself as the low-risk, high-reward choice?

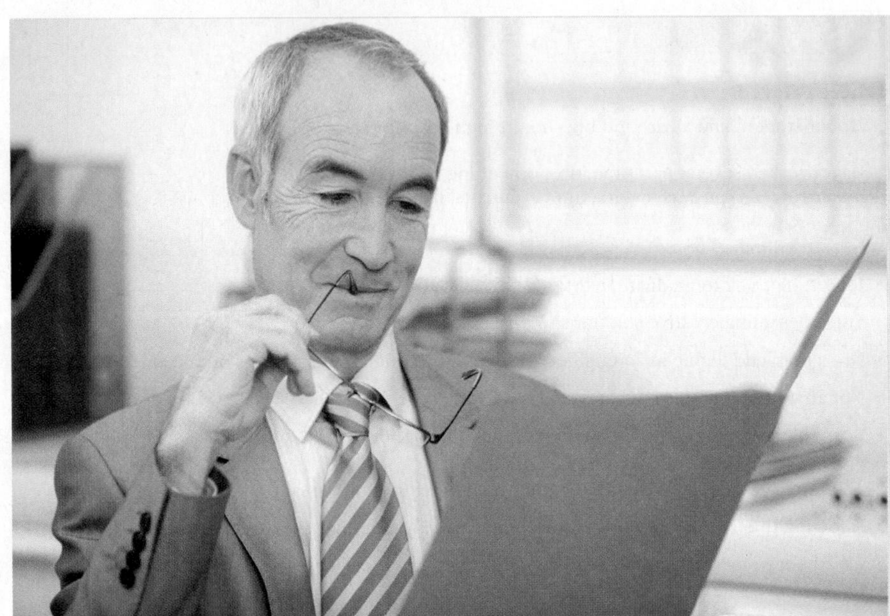

Figure 13.3
What Employers Want
An employer is looking for someone with the skills, experience, and personality to succeed in the open position and to represent the company professionally.

Of course, your ability to perform the job is an essential part of your quality as a new hire. But hiring managers consider more than just your ability to meet those minimum requirements. They want to know if you'll be reliable and motivated—if you're somebody who "gets it" when it comes to being a professional in today's workplace. A great way to get inside the heads of corporate recruiters is to "listen in" on their professional conversations by reading periodicals such as *Workforce Management* and blogs such as Fistful of Talent and The HR Capitalist.

Researching Industries and Companies of Interest

Learning more about professions, industries, and individual companies is a vital step in your job search. It also impresses employers, particularly when you go beyond the easily available sources such as a company's own website.

Table 13.1 lists some of the many websites where you can learn more about companies and find job openings. Start with the Riley Guide, which offers advice for online job searches as well as links to hundreds of specialized websites that post openings in specific industries and professions. Your school's career center placement office probably maintains an up-to-date list as well.

Table 13.1 Selected Job-Search Websites

Website*	URL	Highlights
Riley Guide	www.rileyguide.com	Vast collection of links to both general and specialized job sites for every career imaginable
TweetMyJobs.com	http://tweetmyjobs.com	The largest Twitter job board, with thousands of channels segmented by geography, job type, and industry
CollegeRecruiter.com	www.collegerecruiter.com	Focused on opportunities for graduates with less than three years of work experience
Monster	www.monster.com	One of the most popular job sites, with hundreds of thousands of openings, many from hard-to-find small companies; extensive collection of advice on the job search process
MonsterCollege	http://college.monster.com	Focused on job searches for new college grads
CareerBuilder	www.careerbuilder.com	One of the largest job boards; affiliated with more than 150 newspapers around the country
Jobster	www.jobster.com	Uses social networking to link employers with job seekers
USAJOBS	www.usajobs.gov	The official job search site for the US government, featuring everything from jobs for economists to astronauts to border patrol agents
IMDiversity	www.imdiversity.com	Good resource on diversity in the workplace, with job postings from companies that have made a special commitment to promoting diversity in their workforces
Dice.com	www.dice.com	One of the best sites for high-technology jobs
Net-Temps	www.net-temps.com	Popular site for contractors and freelancers looking for short-term assignments
Internship Programs.com	http://internshipprograms.com	Posts listings from companies looking for interns in a wide variety of professions
Simply Hired	www.simplyhired.com	Specialized search engines that look for job postings on hundreds of websites worldwide; they find many postings that aren't listed on job board sites such as Monster
Indeed	www.indeed.com	Search by job title or keyword(s) and location for listings from thousands of websites worldwide
*Note: This list represents only a small fraction of the hundreds of job-posting sites and other resources available online; be sure to check with your school's career center for the latest information.		

To learn more about contemporary business topics, browse some of these leading business periodicals and newspapers with significant business sections. (In some cases, you may need to go through your library's online databases in order to access back issues.)

In addition, thousands of bloggers, microbloggers, and podcasters offer news and commentary on the business world. AllTop is another good resource for finding people who write about topics that interest you. In addition to learning more about professions and opportunities, this research will help you get comfortable with the jargon and buzzwords currently in use in a particular field, including essential keywords to use in your resume (see page 467).

Take advantage of job search apps as well, including those offered by job posting websites and major employers. You can use them to learn more about the company as well as specific jobs.

Translating Your General Potential into a Specific Solution for Each Employer

An important aspect of the employer's quality-of-hire challenge is trying to determine how well a candidate's attributes and experience will translate into the demands of a specific position. As a job candidate, customizing your resume to each job opening is an important step in showing employers that you will be a good fit. As you can see from the sample resumes in Figures 13.14 through 13.16 on pages 473-475, customizing your resume is not difficult if you have done your research. From your initial contact all the way through the interviewing process, in fact, you will have opportunities to impress recruiters by explaining how your general potential translates to the specific needs of the position.

Taking the Initiative to Find Opportunities

When it comes to finding the right opportunities for you, the easiest ways are not always the most productive ways. The major job boards such as Monster and classified services such as Craigslist might have thousands of openings, but thousands of job seekers are looking at and applying for these same openings. Moreover, posting job openings on these sites is often a company's last resort, after it has exhausted other possibilities.

Figure 13.4
Job Search
Most job searches begin with employment ads, either in print publications or, increasingly, online. However, many jobs are never even posted, but are filled from within the company or through recommendations and referrals.

To maximize your chances, take the initiative and go find opportunities. Identify the companies you want to work for and focus your efforts on them. Get in touch with their human resources departments (or individual managers, if possible), describe what you can offer the company, and ask to be considered if any opportunities come up. Reach out to company representatives on social networks. Your message might appear right when a company is busy looking for someone but hasn't yet advertised the opening to the outside world.

Building Your Network

Networking is the process of making informal connections with mutually beneficial business contacts. Networking takes place wherever and whenever people talk: at industry functions, at social gatherings, at alumni reunions—and all over the Internet, from LinkedIn and Twitter to Facebook and Google+. In addition to making connections through social media tools, you might get yourself noticed by company recruiters.

Networking:
The process of making informal connections with mutually beneficial business contacts.

Networking is more essential than ever, because the vast majority of job openings are never advertised to the general public. To avoid the time and expense of sifting through thousands of applications and the risk of hiring complete strangers, most companies prefer to ask their employees for recommendations first. The more people you know, the better chance you have of being recommended for one of these hidden job openings.

Start building your network now, before you need it. Your classmates could end up being some of your most valuable contacts, if not right away then possibly later in your career. Then branch out by identifying people with similar interests in your target professions, industries, and companies. Read news sites, blogs, and other online sources. Follow industry leaders on Twitter. You can also follow individual executives at your target companies to learn about their interests and concerns. Be on the lookout for career-oriented *Tweetups*, in which people who've connected on Twitter get together for in-person networking events. Connect with people on LinkedIn and Facebook, particularly in groups dedicated to particular career interests. Depending on the system and the settings on individual users' accounts, you may be able to introduce yourself via public or private messages. Just make sure you are respectful of people, and don't take up much of their time.

Figure 13.5
Professional Social Networking
Social networking is not just for fun; sites like LinkedIn help people refer and connect one another for business and career purposes.

Participate in student business organizations, especially those with ties to professional organizations. Visit trade shows to learn about various industries and rub shoulders with people who work in those industries. Don't overlook volunteering; you not only meet people but also demonstrate your ability to solve problems, manage projects, and lead others. You can do some good while creating a network for yourself.

Remember that networking is about people helping each other, not just about other people helping you. Pay close attention to networking etiquette: try to learn something about the people you want to connect with; don't overwhelm others with too many messages or requests; be succinct in all your communication efforts; don't give out other people's names and contact information without their permission; never email your resume to complete strangers; and remember to thank everyone who helps you.

To become a valued network member, you need to be able to help others in some way. You may not have any influential contacts yet, but because you're researching industries and trends as part of your own job search, you probably have valuable information you can share via your online and offline networks. Or you might simply be able to connect one person with another who can help. The more you network, the more valuable you become in your network—and the more valuable your network becomes to you.

Finally, be aware that your online network reflects on who you are in the eyes of potential employers, so exercise some judgment in making connections. Also, many employers now contact people in a candidate's public network for background information, even if the candidate doesn't list those people as references.

Exploring Training, Education, and Certification Opportunities

Potential employers look not only for relevant experience, but also for education and training. Formal education includes high school diplomas and college degrees. While you are still in high school, you may be able to enroll in classes at your local community college to jump-start your higher education. Some high schools also cross-list courses with local colleges, so a class you take at your high school may also count as college credit. Make sure you include such classes on your resume.

In addition to formal academic education, potential employers also look at skills training classes you have attended and certificates of completion you have earned. For example, you might attend training for a safety certification such as Hazardous Waste Operations and Emergency Response (HAZWOPER) or take a set of exams that measure your skill using a particular computer program, such as Microsoft Office Specialist. Check with your local community college to see what classes are available. Some community colleges offer non-credit courses for the general public that award Continuing Education Units (CEUs).

Internships, Mentorships, and Job Shadowing Opportunities

In addition to education and training, employers also look for real-world experiences. Having an actual job in the field is preferable, of course, but there are other ways to get practical experience in a field without being employed in that field.

For example, participating in an internship may increase your value to a potential employer. An **internship** is a short-term educational opportunity in which the student works for a company in the his or her field of interest, contributing to real-world projects. Some internships are unpaid; others pay a minimal amount. Interns work alongside experienced professionals, and are typically assigned to complete simple, well-defined tasks under close supervision.

Internship:
A short-term educational opportunity in which the student works for a company and contributes to real-world projects.

Job shadowing consists of following around someone who has the job you would like to have, observing what they say and do and what responsibilities they have, but not participating in the work yourself. Job shadowing can help you decide if you would enjoy a particular job before you spend a lot of time preparing for it.

Job shadowing:
Following and observing someone in a particular job, to learn first-hand what that job entails.

A **mentor** is an experienced person who advises a less-experienced person in a particular area. Having a mentor in a field that interests you can give you perspective about the realities of a particular job or field. Your mentor may also be able to suggest companies to apply to and training opportunities that will help you prepare, and may even write letters of recommendation for you.

Mentor:
An experienced person who advises a less-experienced person in a particular area.

Seeking Career Counseling

Your school's career center probably offers a wide variety of services, including individual counseling, job fairs, on-campus interviews, and job listings. Counselors can advise on career planning and provide workshops on job search techniques, resume preparation, job readiness training, interview techniques, self-marketing, and more. You can also find career planning advice online. Many of the websites listed in Table 13.1 offer articles and online tests to help you choose a career path, identify essential skills, and prepare to enter the job market.

Avoiding Mistakes

While you're making all these positive moves to show employers you will be a quality hire, take care to avoid simple blunders that can torpedo a job search. These include not catching mistakes in your resume, misspelling the name of a manager you're writing to, showing up late for an interview, tweeting something unprofessional, failing to complete application forms correctly, asking for information that you can easily find yourself on a company's website, or making any other error that could flag you as someone who is careless or disrespectful. Busy recruiters will seize on these errors as a way to narrow the list of candidates they need to spend time on, so don't give them a reason to toss out your resume.

Figure 13.6
Job Interview Skills; Making a Good First Impression
Your personal appearance and behavior during an interview can mean the difference between a job offer and a rejection letter.

Also, assume that every employer will conduct an online search on you, because most do. They want to know what your LinkedIn profile looks like and whether you've posted anything career-damaging on Twitter, YouTube, or other sites. If they don't like what they see or if what they see doesn't match what they read on your resume, you won't be invited for an interview.

Planning Your Resume

Although you will create many messages during your career search, your resume will be the most important document in this process. You will be able to use it directly in many instances, adapt it to a variety of uses such an e-portfolio or a social media resume, and reuse pieces of it in social networking profiles and online application forms. Even if you apply to a company that doesn't want to see resumes from applicants, the process of developing your resume will prepare you for interviewing and preemployment testing.

Developing a resume is one of those projects that really benefits from multiple planning, writing, and completing sessions spread out over several days or weeks. You are trying to summarize a complex subject (yourself!) and present a compelling story to strangers in a brief document. Follow the three-step writing process (see Figure 13.7) and give yourself plenty of time.

1 Plan →

Analyze the Situation
Recognize that the purpose of your resume is to get an interview, not to get a job.

Gather Information
Research target industries and companies so that you know what they're looking for in new hires; learn about various jobs and what to expect; learn about the hiring manager, if possible.

Select the Right Medium
Start with a traditional paper resume and develop scannable, electronic plain-text, PDF, and online versions, as needed. Consider using PowerPoint and video for your e-portfolio.

Organize the Information
Choose an organizational model that highlights your strengths and downplays your shortcomings; use the chronological approach unless you have a strong reason not to.

2 Write →

Adapt to Your Audience
Plan your wording carefully so that you can catch a recruiter's eye within seconds; translate your education and experience into attributes that target employers find valuable.

Compose the Message
Write clearly and succinctly, using active, powerful language that is appropriate to the industries and companies you're targeting; use a professional tone in all communications.

3 Complete

Revise the Message
Evaluate content and review readability and then edit and rewrite for conciseness and clarity.

Produce the Message
Use effective design elements and suitable layout for a clean, professional appearance; seamlessly combine text and graphical elements. When printing, use quality paper and a good printer.

Proofread the Message
Review for errors in layout, spelling, and mechanics; mistakes can cost you interview opportunities.

Distribute the Message
Deliver your resume, carefully following the specific instructions of each employer or job board website.

Figure 13.7
Three-Step Writing Process for Resumes
Following the three-step writing process will help you create a successful resume in a short time. Remember to pay particular attention to the "you" attitude and presentation quality; your resume will probably get tossed aside if it doesn't speak to audience needs or if it contains mistakes.

Before you dive into your resume, be aware that you will find a wide range of opinions about resumes, regarding everything from appropriate length, content, design, distribution methods, and acceptable degrees of creativity to whether it even makes sense to write a traditional resume in this age of online applications. For example, you may encounter a prospective employer that wants you to tweet your resume or submit all the links that make up your online presence, rather than submitting a conventional resume. You may run across examples of effective resumes that were produced as infographics, interactive videos, simulated search engine results, puzzles, games, graphic novels—you name it, somebody has probably tried it.

When you hear conflicting advice or see trendy concepts that you might be tempted to try, remember the most important question in business communication: what is the most effective way to adapt your message to the individual needs of each member of your audience? An approach that is wildly successful with one company or in one industry could be a complete disaster in another industry. To forge your own successful path through this maze of information, get inside the heads of the people you are trying to reach—try to think the way they think—and then apply the principles of effective communication you are learning in this course.

Fallacy	Fact
The purpose of a resume is to list all your skills and abilities.	The purpose of a resume is to kindle employer interest and generate an interview.
A good resume will get you the job you want.	All a resume can do is get you in the door.
Your resume will always be read carefully and thoroughly.	In most cases, your resume needs to make a positive impression within a few seconds; only then will someone read it in detail. Moreover, it will likely be screened by a computer looking for keywords first—and if it doesn't contain the right keywords, a human being may never see it.
The more good information you present about yourself in your resume, the better, so stuff your resume with every positive detail.	Recruiters don't need that much information about you at the initial screening stage, and they probably won't read it.

Analyzing Your Purpose and Audience

Planning an effective resume starts with understanding its true function—as a brief, persuasive business message intended to stimulate an employer's interest in meeting you and learning more about you. In other words, the purpose of a resume is not to get you a job but rather to get you an interview.

As you conduct your research on various professions, industries, companies, and individual managers, learn as much as you can about the individuals who may be reading your resume. Many professionals and managers are bloggers, Twitter users, and LinkedIn members, for example, so you can learn more about them online even if you've never met them. Any bit of information can help you craft a more effective message.

If employers ask to see your "CV," they're referring to your *curriculum vitae*, the term used instead of resume in academic professions and in many countries outside the United States. Resumes and CVs are essentially the same, although CVs can be much more detailed and include personal information that is not included in a resume.

Gathering Pertinent Information

If you haven't started an employment portfolio already, you may need to do some research on yourself at this point. Gather all the pertinent personal history you can think of, including specific dates, duties, and accomplishments from any previous jobs you've held. Compile all your educational accomplishments, including formal degrees, training certificates, professional and technical certifications, academic awards, and scholarships. Also, gather information about school or volunteer activities that might be relevant to your job search, including offices you have held in any club or professional organization, presentations given, and online or print publications. Figure 13.8 shows an example. You probably won't use every piece of information you come up with, but you'll want to have it at your fingertips.

<u>Things I Have to Offer an Employer</u>

High School diploma

Bilingual (Spanish and English)

Keyboarding 60 words per minute

Microsoft Windows proficiency

Macintosh OS X proficiency

Word processing training certificate

Experience answering office phone at lumber yard

Cashier experience

Good work ethic

Volunteer experience at Helping Hands food pantry

Adventure Scout Mentor

Figure 13.8
Make a List of Your Strengths and Experiences
As you prepare to write your resume, jot down a list of your "selling points"—that is, the qualities, skills, and abilities you have that might interest an employer. You will figure out how to phrase them and in what order to place them on the resume later.

Selecting the Best Media and Channels

You should expect to produce your resume in several media and formats. "Producing Your Resume" on page 476 discusses your options.

Organizing Your Resume Around Your Strengths

Although there are a number of ways to organize a resume, most are some variation of chronological, functional, or a combination of the two. The right choice depends on your background and your goals.

The Chronological Resume

In a **chronological resume**, the work experience section dominates and is placed immediately after your contact information and introductory statement. The chronological approach is the most common way to organize a resume, and many employers prefer this format because it presents your professional history in a clear, easy-to-follow arrangement. If you're just graduating from high school or college and have limited professional experience, you can vary this chronological approach by putting your educational qualifications before your experience.

Chronological resume: A resume in which the work experience section dominates and appears immediately after the contact information and introductory statement.

Develop your work experience section by listing your jobs in reverse chronological order, beginning with the most recent one and giving more space to the most recent positions you've held. For each job, start by listing the company name and location, your official job title, and the dates you held the position. Write "to present" if you are still in your most recent job. Next, in a short block of text, highlight your accomplishments in a way that is relevant and understandable to your readers. If the general responsibilities of the position are not obvious from the job title, provide a little background to help readers understand what you did.

The Functional Resume

Functional resume: A resume that emphasizes skills and capabilities, identifying employers and academic experience in subordinate sections.

A **functional resume**, sometimes called a skills resume, emphasizes your skills and capabilities, identifying employers and academic experience in subordinate sections. This arrangement stresses individual areas of competence rather than job history. The functional approach has three benefits: without having to read through job descriptions, employers can get an idea of what you can do for them; you can emphasize earlier job experience through the skills you gained in those positions; and you can deemphasize any lengthy unemployment or lack of career progress. However, you should be aware that because the functional resume can obscure your work history, many employment professionals are suspicious of it. Moreover, it lacks the evidence of job experience that supports your skills claims. If you don't believe the chronological format will work for you, consider the combination resume instead.

The Combination Resume

Combination resume: A resume that meshes the skills focus of the functional format with the job history focus of the chronological format.

A **combination resume** meshes the skills focus of the functional format with the job history focus of the chronological format. The chief advantage of this format is that it allows you to highlight your capabilities and education when you don't have a long or steady employment history, without raising concerns that you might be hiding something about your past.

As you look at a number of sample resumes, you'll probably notice many variations on the three basic formats presented here. Study these other options in light of the effective communication principles you've learned in this course and the unique circumstances of your job search. If you find one that seems like the best fit for your unique situation, by all means use it.

Addressing Areas of Concern

Many people have gaps in their careers or other issues that could be a concern for employers. Here are some common issues and suggestions for handling them in a resume:

- **Frequent job changes.** If you've had a number of short-term jobs of a similar type, such as independent contracting and temporary assignments, you can group them under a single heading. Also, if past job positions were eliminated as a result of layoffs or mergers, find a subtle way to convey that information (if not in your resume, then in your cover letter). Reasonable employers understand that many professionals have been forced to job hop by circumstances beyond their control.
- **Gaps in work history.** Mention relevant experience and education you gained during employment gaps, such as volunteer or community work.

- **Inexperience.** Mention related volunteer work and membership in professional groups. List relevant course work and internships.
- **Overqualification.** Tone down your resume, focusing exclusively on the experience and skills that relate to the position.
- **Long-term employment with one company.** Itemize each position held at the firm to show growth within the organization and increasing responsibilities along the way.
- **Job termination for cause.** Be honest with interviewers and address their concerns with proof, such as recommendations and examples of completed projects.
- **Criminal record.** You don't necessarily need to disclose a criminal record or time spent incarcerated on your resume, but you may be asked about it on job application forms. Laws regarding what employers may ask (and whether they can conduct a criminal background check) vary by state and profession, but if you are asked and the question applies to you, you are legally bound to answer truthfully. Use the interview process to explain any mitigating circumstances and to emphasize your rehabilitation and commitment to being a law-abiding, trustworthy employee.

Writing Your Resume

With the necessary information and a good plan in hand, you're ready to begin writing. If you feel uncomfortable writing about yourself, you're not alone. Many people, even accomplished writers, can find it difficult to write their own resumes. If you get stuck, imagine you are somebody else, writing a resume for ta stranger. By being your own client in this sense, you might find the words and idea flow more easily. You can also find a classmate or friend who is writing a resume and swap projects for a while. Working on each other's resumes might speed up the process for both of you.

Keeping Your Resume Honest

Estimates vary, but one comprehensive study uncovered lies about work history in more than 40 percent of the resumes tested. And dishonest applicants are getting bolder all the time—going so far as to buy fake diplomas online, pay a computer hacker to insert their names into prestigious universities' graduation records, and sign up for services that offer phony employment verification.

Applicants with integrity know they don't need to stoop to lying. If you are tempted to stretch the truth, bear in mind that professional recruiters have seen all sorts of fraud by job applicants, and frustrated employers are working aggressively to uncover the truth. Nearly all employers do some form of background checking, from contacting references and verifying employment to checking criminal records and sending resumes through verification services. Employers are also beginning to craft certain interview questions specifically to uncover dishonest resume entries.

More than 90 percent of companies that find lies on resumes refuse to hire the offending applicants, even if that means withdrawing formal job offers. And if you do sneak past these filters and get hired, you'll probably be exposed on the job when you can't live up to your own resume. Given the networked nature of today's job market, lying on a resume could haunt you for years—and you could be forced to keep lying throughout your career to hide the misrepresentations on your original resume.

Adapting Your Resume to Your Audience

The importance of adapting your resume to your target readers' needs and interests cannot be overstated. In a competitive job market, the more you look like a good fit—a quality hire—the better your chances of securing interviews. Address your readers' business concerns by showing how your capabilities meet the demands and expectations of the position and the organization as a whole.

For example, an in-house public relations (PR) department and an independent PR agency perform many of the same tasks, but the outside agency must also sell its services to multiple clients. Consequently, it needs employees who are skilled at attracting and keeping paying customers, in addition to being skilled at PR. If you are applying for both in-house and agency PR jobs, you need to adapt your resume for each of these audiences.

An essential step in adapting your resume is using the same terminology as the employer uses to describe job responsibilities and professional accomplishments. In Figures 13.4 through 13.6 starting on page 473, you can see how the sample resumes do this, echoing key terms and phrases from the job postings. With the rise of automated **applicant tracking systems**, matching your language to the employer's will help you get past the keyword filters these systems use to rank incoming resumes.

Applicant tracking system (ATS): A software application that enables the electronic handling of recruitment needs.

If you are applying for business positions after military service or moving from one industry to another, you may need to "translate" your experience into the language of your target employers. For instance, military experience can help you develop many skills that are valuable in business, but military terminology can sound like a foreign language to people who aren't familiar with it. Isolate the important general concepts and present them in the business language your target employers use.

Composing Your Resume

Write your resume using a simple and direct style. Use short, crisp phrases instead of whole sentences and focus on what your reader needs to know. Avoid using the word *I*, which can sound both self-involved and repetitious by the time you outline all your skills and accomplishments. Instead, start your phrases with strong action verbs such as these:

accomplished	coordinated	initiated	participated	set up
achieved	created	installed	performed	simplified
administered	demonstrated	introduced	planned	sparked
approved	developed	investigated	presented	streamlined
arranged	directed	launched	proposed	strengthened
assisted	established	maintained	raised	succeeded
assumed	explored	managed	recommended	supervised
budgeted	forecasted	motivated	reduced	systematized
chaired	generated	negotiated	reorganized	targeted
changed	identified	operated	resolved	trained
compiled	implemented	organized	saved	transformed
completed	improved	oversaw	served	upgraded

For example, you might say, "Created a campus organization for students interested in entrepreneurship" or "Managed a fast-food restaurant and four employees." Whenever you can, quantify the results so that your claims don't come across as empty. Don't just say that you're a team player or detail oriented—show that you are by offering concrete proof. Here are some examples of phrasing accomplishments using active statements that show results:

Instead of This	Write Active Statements That Show Results
Responsible for developing a new filing system	Developed a new filing system that reduced paperwork by 50 percent
I was in charge of customer complaints and all ordering problems	Handled all customer complaints and resolved all product order discrepancies
I won a trip to Europe for opening the most new customer accounts in my department	Generated the highest number of new customer accounts in my department
Member of special campus task force to resolve student problems with existing cafeteria assignments	Assisted in implementing new campus dining program that balances student wishes with cafeteria capacity

Providing specific supporting evidence is vital, but make sure you don't go overboard with small details. Carefully select the most compelling evidence so that your message clear and immediate.

In addition to clear writing with specific examples, the particular words and phrases used throughout your resume are critically important. The majority of resumes are now subjected to *keyword searches* in an applicant tracking system or other database, in which a recruiter searches for resumes most likely to match the requirements of a particular job. Resumes that don't match the requirements closely may never be seen by a human reader, so it is essential to use the words and phrases that a recruiter is most likely to search on. Although most experts used to advise including a separate *keyword summary* as a standalone list, the trend nowadays is to incorporate your keywords into your introductory statement and other sections of your resume.

Identifying these keywords requires some research, but you can uncover many of them while you are researching various industries and companies. In particular, study job descriptions carefully. In contrast to the action verbs that catch a human reader's attention, keywords that catch a computer's attention are usually nouns that describe the specific skills, attributes, and experiences an employer is looking for in a candidate. Keywords can include the business and technical terms associated with a specific profession, industry-specific jargon, names or types of products or systems used in a profession, job titles, and degrees.

Name and Contact Information

Your name and contact information (see Figure 13.9) constitute the heading of your resume, and should include the following:

- Name
- Address (both permanent and temporary, if you're likely to move during the job search process)
- Email address
- Phone number(s)
- The URL of your personal webpage, e-portfolio, or social media resume (if you have one)

Emma Gomes
(847) 555-2153
emma.gomes@mailsystem.net
emmawrites.blogspot.com

Address:	**Permanent Address:**
860 North 8th Street, Terre Haute, IN 47809	993 Church Street, Barrington, IL 60010

Figure 13.9
Name and Contact Information
You should provide a variety of ways you can be reached, including postal mail, phone, and email.

If the only email address you have is through your current employer, get a free personal email address from one of the many services that offer them. It's not fair to your current employer to use company resources for a job search, and doing so sends a bad signal to potential employers. Also, if your personal email address is anything like *precious.princess@something.com* or *PsychoDawg@something.com*, get a new email address for your business correspondence.

Introductory Statement

Of all the parts of a resume, the brief introductory statement that follows your name and contact information probably generates the most disagreement. You can put one of three things here:

- **Career objective.** A career objective identifies either a specific job you want to land or a general career track you would like to pursue. Some experts advise against including a career objective because it can categorize you so narrowly that you miss out on interesting opportunities, and it is essentially about fulfilling your desires, not about meeting the employer's needs. In the past, most resumes included a career objective, but in recent years more job seekers are using a qualifications summary or a career summary. If you have little or no work experience in your target profession, a career objective might be your best option. If you do opt for an objective, word it in a way that relates your qualifications to employer needs.
- **Qualifications summary.** A qualifications summary (as in Figure 13.10) offers a brief view of your key qualifications. The goal is to let a reader know within a few seconds what you can deliver. You can title this section generically as "Qualifications Summary" or "Summary of Qualifications," or, if you have one dominant qualification, you can use that as the title. Consider using a qualifications summary if you have one or more important qualifications but don't yet have a long career history. Also, if you haven't been working long but your academic classes have given you a dominant professional "theme," such as multimedia design or statistical analysis, you can craft a qualifications summary that highlights your educational preparedness.

Summary of Qualifications

- In-depth academic preparation in marketing analysis techniques
- Intermediate skills with a variety of analytical tools, including Microsoft Excel and Google Analytics
- Front-line experience with consumers and business owners
- Multiple research and communication projects involving the business applications of social media

Figure 13.10 Qualifications Summary
The qualifications summary is one of three possible summaries that can appear near the top of your resume. A qualifications summary recaps the facts about you that make you qualified for the position, and can include a combination of education and career experience.

- **Career summary.** A career summary offers a brief recap of your career with the goal of presenting increasing levels of responsibility and performance. A career summary can be particularly useful for managers who have demonstrated the ability to manage increasingly larger and more complicated business operations—a key consideration when companies look to hire upper-level executives.

Whichever option you choose, make sure it includes many of the essential keywords you identified in your research—and adapt these words and phrases to each job opportunity as needed.

Education

If you're still in school or have recently graduated, education is probably your strongest selling point. Present your educational background in depth, choosing facts that support your professional theme. Give this section a heading such as "Education," "Technical Training," or "Academic Preparation," as appropriate. Then, starting with the most recent, list the name and location of each school you have attended, the month and year of your graduation (say "anticipated graduation: ______" if you haven't graduated yet), your major and minor fields of study, significant skills and abilities you've developed in your course work, and the degrees or certificates you've earned. Fine-tune your message by listing courses that are most relevant to each job opening, and indicate any scholarships, awards, or academic honors you've received.

The education section (shown in Figure 13.11) should also include relevant training sponsored by business or government organizations. Mention high school or military training only if the associated achievements are pertinent to your career goals, or unless high school is the highest level of education you have completed..

Figure 13.11
Education Section
List all degrees and diplomas, plus relevant training you have received. Depending on your strengths, this section may be alternatively titled Technical Training, Academic Preparation, or something similar. If you took specific classes or did special projects that prepared you for the position, list them as well.

Education

B.S. in Marketing (Marketing Management Track), Indiana State University, Terre Haute, IN, anticipated graduation: May 2017

Whether you list your grade point average depends on the job you want and the quality of your grades. If you don't show your GPA on your resume—and there's no rule saying you have to—be prepared to answer questions about it during the interview process. If you choose to show a grade point average, be sure to mention the scale, especially if it isn't a four-point scale. If your grades are better within your major than in other courses, you can also list your GPA as "Major GPA" and include only those courses within your major.

Work Experience, Skills, and Accomplishments

This section can be called "Work Experience," "Professional Experience," or "Work and Volunteer Experience," if you have limited work experience and want to bolster that with volunteer experience. Figure 13.12 shows an example. Like the education section, the work experience section should show how your past can contribute to an employer's future. Use keywords to call attention to the skills you've developed on the job and to your ability to handle responsibility. Emphasize what you accomplished in each position, not just the generic responsibilities of the job.

Figure 13.12
Work and Volunteer Experience
List all work you have done, both paid and unpaid. Include your job title, the dates, and your major responsibilities. If you won any performance awards, such as Employee of the Month, include that also.

Work and Volunteer Experience

Independent math tutor, 2009-present. Assist students with a variety of math courses at the elementary, junior high, and high school level; all clients have achieved combined test and homework score improvements of at least one full letter grade, with an average improvement of 38 percent

Volunteer, LeafSpring Food Bank, Terre Haute, IN (weekends during college terms, 2012–present). Stock food and supply pantries; prepare emergency baskets for new clients; assist director with public relations activities, including website updates and social media news releases.

Customer care agent, Owings Ford, Barrington, IL (summers, 2011–2013). Assisted the service and sales managers of this locally owned car dealership with a variety of customer-service tasks; scheduled service appointments; designed and implemented improvements to service-center waiting room to increase guest comfort; convinced dealership owners to begin using Twitter and Facebook to interact with current and potential customers.

List your jobs in reverse chronological order, starting with the most recent. Include military service and any internships and part-time or temporary jobs related to your career objective. Include the name and location of the employer, and if readers are unlikely to recognize the organization, briefly describe what it does. When you want to keep the name of your current employer confidential, you can identify the firm by industry only *a large video game developer*. If an organization's name or location has changed since you worked there, state the current name and location and include the old information preceded by *formerly*. Before or after each job listing, state your job title and give the years you worked in the job; use the phrase *to present* to denote current employment. Indicate whether a job was part-time.

Devote the most space to the jobs that are most recent or most closely related to your target position. If you were personally responsible for something significant, be sure to mention it. Facts about your skills and accomplishments are the most important information you can give a prospective employer, so quantify them whenever possible.

One helpful exercise is to write a 30-second "commercial" for each major skill you want to highlight. How would the commercial prove that you really do possess each skill? For your resume, distill the commercials down to brief phrases; you can use the more detailed proof statements in cover letters and as answers to interview questions.

If you have a number of part-time, temporary, or entry-level jobs that don't relate to your career objective, you have to use your best judgment when it comes to including or excluding them. Too many minor and irrelevant work details can clutter your resume, particularly if you've been in the professional workforce for a few years. If you don't have a long employment history, including these jobs shows your ability and willingness to keep working.

Activities and Achievements

This optional section can be used to highlight activities and achievements outside of a work or educational context—but only if they make you a more attractive job candidate. For example, traveling, studying, or working abroad and fluency in multiple languages could weigh heavily in your favor with employers who do business internationally. Depending on the context, you might use a different name for this section, such as Professional Engagement (as in Figure 13.13). You might also have a separate Awards section if you have received any.

Professional Engagement

- Collegiate member, American Marketing Association; helped establish the AMA Collegiate Chapter at Indiana State
- Participated in AMA International Collegiate Case Competition, 2011-2012

Figure 13.13
Professional Engagement Section
This section includes any memberships in professional societies, conferences attended, competitions, and other professional experiences you have had that may not have fit well in the previous sections.

Because many employers are involved in their local communities, they tend to look positively on applicants as well. Consider including community service activities that suggest leadership, teamwork, communication skills, technical aptitude, or other valuable attributes.

You should generally avoid indicating membership or significant activity in religious or political organizations (unless, of course, you're applying to such an organization) because doing so might raise concerns for people with differing beliefs or affiliations. If you want to highlight skills you developed while involved with such a group, you can refer to it generically as a "not-for-profit organization."

Finally, if you have little or no job experience and not much to discuss outside of your education, indicating involvement in athletics or other organized student activities lets employers know that you don't spend all your free time hanging around your house playing video games. Also consider mentioning publications, projects, and other accomplishments that required relevant business skills.

Personal Data and References

In nearly all instances, your resume should not include any personal data beyond the information described in the previous sections. When applying to US companies, never include any of the following: physical characteristics, age, gender, marital status, sexual orientation, religious or political affiliations, race, national origin, salary history, reasons for leaving jobs, names of previous supervisors, names of references, Social Security number, or student ID number.

Be aware that standards can vary in other countries. For example, some international employers might require you to include your citizenship, nationality, or marital status.

The availability of references is assumed, so you don't need to put "References available upon request" at the end of your resume. However, be sure to have a list of several references ready when you begin applying for jobs. Prepare your reference sheet with your name and contact information at the top. For a finished look, use the same design and layout you use for your resume. Then list three or four people who have agreed to serve as references. Include each person's name, job title, organization, address, telephone number, email address (if the reference prefers to be contacted by email), and the nature of your relationship.

Figures 13.14 through 13.16 show how a job applicant can put these guidelines to work in three job-search scenarios:

- **Scenario 1: Positioning Yourself for an Ideal Opportunity** (when you've found a job opening that aligns closely with your career goals and your academic and professional credentials)
- **Scenario 2: Positioning Yourself for an Available Opportunity** (when you can't find a job in your chosen field and need to adapt to whatever opportunities are available)
- **Scenario 3: Positioning Yourself for More Responsibility** (after you have some experience in your field and want to apply for positions of greater responsibility)

Figure 13.14

Crafting Your Resume, Scenario 1: Positioning Yourself for an Ideal Opportunity

Even when your qualifications closely match the job opening, you still need to adapt your resume content to the specific language of the job description.

The Scenario

You are about to graduate and have found a job opening that is in your chosen field. You don't have any experience in this field, but the courses you've taken in pursuit of your degree have given you a solid academic foundation for this position.

The Opportunity

The job opening is for an associate market analyst with Living Social, the rapidly growing advertising and social commerce service that describes itself as "the online source for discovering valuable local experiences." (A market analyst researches markets to find potentially profitable business opportunities.)

The Communication Challenge

You don't have directly relevant experience as a market analyst, and you might be competing against people who do. Your education is your strongest selling point, so you need to show how your coursework relates to the position.

Don't let your lack of experience hold you back; the job posting makes it clear that this is an entry-level position. For example, the first bullet point in the job description says "Become an expert in market data . . .," and the required skills and experience section says that "Up to 2 years of experience with similar research and analysis is preferred." The important clues here are *become* (the company doesn't expect you to be an expert already) and *preferred* (experience would be great if you have it, but it's not required).

Keywords and Key Phrases

You study the job posting and highlight the following elements:

1. Working in a team environment
2. Research, including identifying trendy new businesses
3. Analyzing data using Microsoft Excel
4. Managing projects
5. Collaborating with technical experts and sales staff
6. Creating new tools to help maximize revenue and minimize risks
7. Bachelor's degree is required
8. Natural curiosity and desire to learn
9. Detail oriented
10. Hands-on experience with social media

Emma Gomes
(847) 555-2153
emma.gomes@mailsystem.net
emmawrites.blogspot.com

Address:
860 North 8th Street, Terre Haute, IN 47809

Permanent Address:
993 Church Street, Barrington, IL 60010

Summary of Qualifications

- ❷ In-depth academic preparation in marketing analysis techniques
- ❸ Intermediate skills with a variety of analytical tools, including Microsoft Excel and Google Analytics
- Front-line experience with consumers and business owners
- ❷ ❿ Multiple research and communication projects involving the business applications of social media

Education

❼ B.S. in Marketing (Marketing Management Track), Indiana State University, Terre Haute, IN, anticipated graduation: May 2014

Program coursework

- ❸ ❻ 45 credits of core business courses, including Business Information Tools, Business Statistics, Principles of Accounting, and Business Finance
- ❷ 27 credits of marketing and marketing management courses, including Buyer Behavior, Marketing Research, Product and Pricing Strategy, and seminars in e-commerce and social media

Special projects

- ❷ "Handcrafting a Global Marketplace: The Etsy Phenomenon," in-depth analysis of how Etsy transformed the market for handmade craft items by bringing e-commerce capabilities to individual craftspeople
- ❶ ❷ ❸ ❹ ❻ "Hybrid Communication Platforms for Small Businesses," team service project for five small businesses in Terre Haute, recommending best practices for combining traditional and social-media methods of customer engagement and providing a customized measurement spreadsheet for each company

Work and Volunteer Experience

Independent math tutor, 2009-present. Assist students with a variety of math courses at the elementary, junior high, and high school level; all clients have achieved combined test and homework score ❾ improvements of at least one full letter grade, with an average improvement of 38 percent

Volunteer, LeafSpring Food Bank, Terre Haute, IN (weekends during college terms, 2012–present). Stock food and supply pantries; prepare emergency baskets for new clients; assist director with public relations ❿ activities, including website updates and social media news releases.

❺ **Customer care agent, Owings Ford, Barrington, IL (summers, 2011–2013)**. Assisted the service and sales managers of this locally owned car dealership with a variety of customer-service tasks; scheduled service ❹ appointments; designed and implemented improvements to service-center waiting room to increase ❿ guest comfort; convinced dealership owners to begin using Twitter and Facebook to interact with current and potential customers.

Professional Engagement

- ❽ Collegiate member, American Marketing Association; helped establish the AMA Collegiate Chapter at Indiana State
- Participated in AMA International Collegiate Case Competition, 2011-2012

Awards

- ❽ Dean's List: 2012, 2013
- Forward Youth award, Barrington Chamber of Commerce, 2010

Gomes includes phone and email contacts, along with a blog that features academic-oriented writing.

Using a *summary of qualifications* for her opening statement lets her target the resume and highlight her most compelling attributes.

Her education is a much stronger selling point than her work experience, so she goes into some detail—carefully selecting course names and project descriptions to echo the language of the job description.

She adjusts the descriptions and accomplishments of each role to highlight the aspects of her work and volunteer experience that are relevant to the position.

The final sections highlight activities and awards that reflect her interest in marketing and her desire to improve her skills.

Notice how Gomes adapts her resume to mirror the keywords and phrases from the job posting:

❶ Offers concrete evidence of teamwork (rather than just calling herself a "team player," for example)

❷ Emphasizes research skills and experience in multiple instances

❸ Calls out Microsoft Excel, as well as Google Analytics, a key online tool for measuring activity on websites

❹ Indicates the ability to plan and carry out projects, even if she doesn't have formal project management experience

❺ Indicates some experience working in a supportive or collaborative role with technical experts and sales specialists (the content of the work doesn't translate to the new job, but the concept does)

❻ Suggests the ability to work with new analytical tools

❼ Displays her B.S. degree prominently

❽ Demonstrates a desire to learn and to expand her skills

❾ Tracking the progress of her tutoring clients is strong evidence of a detail-oriented worker—not to mention someone who cares about results and the quality of her work

Figure 13.15
Crafting Your Resume, Scenario 2: Repositioning Yourself for Available Opportunities

If you can't find an ideal job opening, you'll need to adjust your plans and adapt your resume to the openings that are available.

The Scenario

You are about to graduate but can't find job openings in the field you'd like to enter. However, you have found an opening that is in a related field, and it would give you the chance to get some valuable work experience.

The Opportunity

The job opening is for a seller support associate with Amazon, the online retail giant. Employees in this position work with merchants that sell products through the Amazon e-commerce system to make sure merchants are successful. In essence, it is a customer service job, but directed at these merchants, not the consumers who buy on Amazon.

The Communication Challenge

This isn't the job you ultimately want, but it is a great opportunity with a well-known company.

You note that the position does not require a college degree, so in that sense you might be a bit overqualified. However, you also see a strong overlap between your education and the responsibilities and required skills of the job, so be sure to highlight those.

Keywords and Phrases

You study the job posting and highlight the following elements:

1. Be able to predict and respond to merchant needs; good business sense with the ability to appreciate the needs of a wide variety of companies
2. Strong written and oral communication skills
3. High degree of professionalism
4. Self-starter with good time management skills
5. Logically analyze problems and devise solutions
6. Comfortable with computer-based tools, including Microsoft Excel
7. Desire to expand business and technical skills
8. Customer service experience
9. Collaborate with fellow team members to resolve difficult situations
10. Record of high performance regarding quality of work and personal productivity

---

Emma Gomes
(847) 555-2153
emma.gomes@mailsystem.net
emmawrites.blogspot.com

Address:
860 North 8th Street, Terre Haute, IN 47809

Permanent Address:
993 Church Street, Barrington, IL 60010

Summary of Qualifications

- (8) Front-line customer service experience with consumers and business owners
- Strong business sense based on work experience and academic preparation
- (6) Intermediate skills with a variety of software tools, including Microsoft Excel and Google Analytics
- (10) Record of quality work in both business and academic settings

Gomes modified her summary of qualifications to increase emphasis on customer service.

Education

B.S. in Marketing (Marketing Management Track), Indiana State University, Terre Haute, IN, expected graduation May 2014

Program coursework

- (6) 45 credits of core business courses, including Business Information Tools, Business Statistics, Principles of Accounting, and Business Finance
- (1) 27 credits of marketing and marketing management courses, including Marketing Fundamentals, Buyer Behavior, Marketing Research, Retail Strategies and seminars in e-commerce and social media

She adjusts the selection of highlighted courses to reflect the retail and e-commerce aspects of this particular job opening.

Special projects

- (1) (2) "Handcrafting a Global Marketplace: The Etsy Phenomenon," in-depth analysis of how the Etsy e-commerce platform helps craftspeople and artisans become more successful merchants
- (1) (2) (9) "Hybrid Communication Platforms for Small Businesses," team service project for five small businesses in Terre Haute, recommending best practices for combining traditional and social-media methods of customer engagement and providing a customized measurement spreadsheet for each company

She adjusts the wording of this Etsy project description to closely mirror what Amazon is—an e-commerce platform serving a multitude of independent merchants.

Work and Volunteer Experience

(3) (4) (10) **Independent math tutor, 2009-present.** Assist students with a variety of math courses at the elementary, junior high, and high school level; all clients have achieved combined test and homework score improvements of at least one full letter grade, with an average improvement of 38 percent

(2) **Volunteer, LeafSpring Food Bank, Terre Haute, IN (weekends during college terms, 2012–present).** Stock food and supply pantries; prepare emergency baskets for new clients; assist director with public relations activities, including website updates and social media news releases.

(8) **Customer care agent, Owings Ford, Barrington, IL (summers, 2011–2013).** Assisted the service and sales managers of this locally owned car dealership with a variety of customer-service tasks; scheduled service appointments; designed and implemented improvements to service-center waiting room to increase (5) guest comfort; convinced dealership owners to begin using Twitter and Facebook to interact with current and potential customers.

She provides more detail regarding her customer support experience.

Professional Engagement

- (7) Collegiate member, American Marketing Association; helped establish the AMA Collegiate Chapter at Indiana State
- Participated in AMA International Collegiate Case Competition, 2011-2012

Awards

- (3) (4) (10) Dean's List: 2012, 2013
- (1) Forward Youth award, Barrington Chamber of Commerce, 2010

The final sections are still relevant to this job opening, so she leaves them unchanged.

Notice how Gomes adapts her resume to mirror the keywords and phrases from the job posting:

1. Suggests strong awareness of the needs of various businesses
2. Examples of experience with written business communication; she can demonstrate oral communication skills during phone, video, or in-person interviews
3. Results-oriented approach to tutoring business suggests high degree of professionalism, as do the two awards
4. The ability to work successfully as an independent tutor while attending high school and college is strong evidence of self-motivation and good time management
5. Indicates ability to understand problems and design solutions
6. Suggests the ability to work with a variety of software tools
7. Demonstrates a desire to learn and to expand her skills
8. Highlights customer service experience
9. Offers concrete evidence of teamwork (rather than just calling herself a "team player," for example)
10. Tracking the progress of her tutoring clients is strong evidence of someone who cares about results and the quality of her work; Dean's List awards also suggest quality of work; record of working while attending high school and college suggests strong productivity

Figure 13.16 Crafting Your Resume, Scenario 3: Positioning Yourself for More Responsibility

When you have a few years of experience under your belt, your resume strategy should shift to emphasize work history and accomplishments.

The Scenario

Moving forward from Figures 13.4 and 13.5, let's assume you have worked in both those positions, first for two years as a seller support associate at Amazon and then for almost three years an associate market analyst at Living Social. You believe you are now ready for a bigger challenge, and the question is how to adapt your résumé for a higher-level position now that you have some experience in your chosen field. (Some of the details from the earlier résumés have been modified to accommodate this example.)

The Opportunity

The job opening is for a senior strategy analyst for Nordstrom. The position is similar in concept to the position at Living Social, but at a higher level and with more responsibility.

The Communication Challenge

This job is an important step up; a senior strategy analyst is expected to conduct in-depth financial analysis of business opportunities and make recommendations regarding strategy changes, merchandising partnerships with other companies, and important decisions.

You worked with a wide variety of retailers in your Amazon and Living Social jobs, including a number of fashion retailers, but you haven't worked directly in fashion retailing yourself.

Bottom line: You can bring a good set of skills to this position, but your financial analysis skills and retailing insights might not be readily apparent, so you'll need to play those up.

Keywords and Key Phrases

You study the job posting and highlight the following elements:

1. Provide research and analysis to guide major business strategy decisions
2. Communicate across business units and departments within Nordstrom
3. Familiar with retail analytics
4. Knowledge of fashion retailing
5. Qualitative and quantitative analysis
6. Project management
7. Strong communication skills
8. Bachelor's required; MBA preferred
9. Advanced skills in financial and statistical modeling
10. Proficient in PowerPoint and Excel

Emma Gomes
(847) 555-2153
emma.gomes@mailsystem.net
Twitter: www.twitter.com/emmagomes
1605 Queen Anne Avenue North, Seattle, WA 98109

Market and Strategy Analyst

- ❶ ❸ Five years of experience in local and online retailing, with three years of focus on market opportunity analysis
- ❹ Strong business sense developed through more than 60 marketing programs across a range of retail sectors, including hospitality, entertainment, and fashion
- ❶ ❺ Recognized by senior management for ability to make sound judgment calls in situations with incomplete or conflicting data
- ❷ ❻ Adept at coordinating research projects and marketing initiatives across organizational boundaries and balancing the interests of multiple stakeholders
- ❾ ❿ Advanced skills with leading analysis and communication tools, including Excel, PowerPoint, and Google Analytics

Gomes stays with a summary of qualifications as her opening statement but gives it a new title to reflect her experience and to focus on her career path as a market analyst.

Professional Experience

Associate Market Analyst, LivingSocial, Seattle, WA (July 2011-present). Analyzed assigned markets for ❶ such factors as consumer demand, merchandising opportunities, and seller performance; designed, ❹ launched, and managed marketing initiatives in 27 retailing categories, including fashions and accessories; ❼ met or exceeded profit targets on 90 percent of all marketing initiatives; appointed team lead/trainer in ❸ ❺ recognition of strong quantitative and qualitative analysis skills; utilized both established and emerging ❼ social media tools and helped business partners use these communication platforms to increase consumer engagement in local markets.

Seller support associate, Amazon, Seattle, WA (July 2009–June 2011). Worked with more than 300 ❹ product vendors, including many in the fashion and accessories sectors, to assure profitable retailing activities on the Amazon e-commerce platform; resolved vendor issues related to e-commerce ❼ operations, pricing, and consumer communication; anticipated potential vendor challenges and assisted in ❸ the development of more than a dozen new selling tools that improved vendor profitability while reducing Amazon's vendor support costs by nearly 15 percent.

Work experience is now her key selling point, so she shifts to a conventional chronological resume that puts employment ahead of education. She also removes the part-time jobs she had during high school and college.

Education

❽ **Evening MBA program, University of Washington, Seattle, WA; anticipated graduation: May 2015.** Broad-based program combining financial reporting, marketing strategy, competitive strategy, and supply chain ❶ management with individual emphasis on quantitative methods, financial analysis, and marketing decision ❾ models.

❾ **B.S. in Marketing (Marketing Management Track), Indiana State University, Terre Haute, IN, May 2009.** Comprehensive coursework in business fundamentals, accounting and finance, marketing fundamentals, retailing, and consumer communications.

She updates the Education section with a listing for the MBA program she has started (selecting points of emphasis relevant to the job opening) and reduces the amount of detail about her undergraduate degree.

Professional Engagement

- Member, American Marketing Association
- Member, International Social Media Association
- ❹ Active in National Retail Federation and Retail Advertising & Marketing Association

Awards

- Living Social Top Ten Deals (monthly employee achievement award for designing the most profitable couponing deals); awarded seven times, 2011—2013
- Social Commerce Network's Social Commerce Innovators: 30 Under 30; 2012

She updates the Professional Engagement and Awards section with timely and relevant information.

Notice how Gomes adapts her resume to mirror the keywords and phrases from the job posting:

❶ Highlights her experience in market and business analysis and her continuing education in this area
❷ Mentions skill at coordinating cross-functional projects
❸ Lists experiences that relate to the collection and analysis of retail data
❹ Emphasizes the work she has done with fashion-related retailing and retailing in general
❺ Identifies experience and education that relates to quantitative and qualitative analysis (this point overlaps #1 and #3 to a degree)
❻ Mentions project management experience
❼ Lists areas that suggest effective communication skills
❽ Lists education, with emphasis on coursework that relates most directly to the job posting
❾ Mentions work experience and educational background related to these topics
❿ Includes these programs in the list of software tools she uses

Completing Your Resume

Completing your resume involves revising it for optimum quality, producing it in the various forms and media you'll need, and proofreading it for any errors before distributing it or publishing it online.

Revising Your Resume

Revising your resume for clarity and conciseness is essential. Recruiters and hiring managers want to find key pieces of information about you, including your top skills, your current job, and your education, in a matter of seconds. Many are overwhelmed with resumes, and if they have to work to find or decode this information, chances are they'll toss yours aside and move on to the next one in the pile. Remember the fundamental purpose of the resume—which is to get you an interview, not to get you a job. Weed out details and irrelevant information until your resume is tight, clear, and focused.

The ideal length of your resume depends on the depth of your experience and the level of the positions for which you are applying. As a general guideline, if you have fewer than five years of professional experience, keep your conventional resume to one page. For online resume formats, you can always provide links to additional information. If you have more experience and are applying for a higher-level position, you may need to prepare a somewhat longer resume. For highly technical positions, longer resumes are often the norm as well because the qualifications for such jobs can require more description.

Producing Your Resume

No matter how many media and formats you eventually choose for producing your resume, a clean, professional-looking design is a must. Recruiters and hiring managers want to skim your essential information in a matter of seconds, and anything that distracts or delays them will work against you.

Choosing a Design Strategy

You'll find a wide range of resume designs in use today, from text-only examples that follow a conventional layout to full-color infographics with unique designs. As with every type of business message, keep your audience, your goals, and your resources in mind. Don't choose a style just because it seems trendy, flashy, or different. For example, you can find a lot of eye-catching infographic resumes online, but many of those are created by graphic designers applying for visual jobs in advertising, fashion, web design, and other areas in which graphic design skills are a must. In other words, the intended audience expects an applicant to have design skills, and the resume is a good opportunity to demonstrate those. In contrast, a colorful, graphically intense resume might just look odd to recruiters in finance, engineering, or other professions.

The sample resumes in Figures 13.14 through 13.16 use a classic, conservative design that will serve you well for most business opportunities. Notice how they feature simplicity, an easy-to-read layout, effective use of white space, and clear typefaces. Recruiters can pick out the key pieces of information in a matter of seconds.

You can certainly enhance your resume beyond this style, but do so carefully and always with an eye on what will help the reader. Make subheadings easy to find and easy to read. Avoid big blocks of text, and use lists to itemize your most important qualifications. Color is not necessary by any means, but if you add color, make it subtle and sophisticated. Above all, don't make the reader work to find the key points of story. Your resume should be a high-efficiency information-delivery system, not a treasure hunt.

Depending on the companies you apply to, you might want to produce your resume in as many as six formats (all are explained in the following sections):

- Printed traditional resume
- Printed scannable resume
- Electronic plain-text file
- Microsoft Word file
- Online resume
- PDF file

Unfortunately, no single format or medium will work for all situations, and employer expectations continue to change as technology evolves. Find out what each employer or job posting expects, and provide your resume in that specific format.

Considering Photos, Videos, Presentations, and Infographics

As you produce your resume in various formats, you may wonder whether to include a photograph of yourself on or with your resume. For print or electronic documents that you will submit to employers or job websites, the safest advice is to avoid photos. The reason is that seeing visual cues of the age, ethnicity, and gender of candidates early in the selection process exposes employers to complaints of discriminatory hiring practices. In fact, some employers won't even look at resumes that include photos, and some applicant tracking systems automatically discard resumes with any kind of attachment. Photographs are acceptable and expected for social media resumes and other online formats that are not directed to a specific employer.

Some applicants create PowerPoint or Prezi presentations, videos, or infographics to supplement a conventional resume. Two key advantages of a presentation supplement are flexibility and multimedia capabilities. For instance, you can present a menu of choices on the opening screen and allow viewers to click through to sections of interest. (Note that most of the things you can accomplish with a presentation can be done with an online resume, which is probably more convenient for most readers.)

A video resume can be a compelling supplement as well, but be aware that some employment law experts advise employers not to view videos, at least not until after candidates have been evaluated solely on their credentials. The reason for this caution is the same as with photographs. In addition, videos are more cumbersome to evaluate than paper or electronic resumes, and some recruiters refuse to watch them. Not all companies share this concern over videos, so you'll have to research their individual preferences. In fact, the online retailer Zappos encourages applicant videos and provides a way to upload videos on its job application webpage.

An infographic resume conveys a person's career development and skill set through a visual metaphor such as a timeline or subway map or as a poster with array of individual elements. A well-designed infographic could be an intriguing element of the job-search package for candidates in certain situations and professions; it can definitely stand out from traditional resumes and can show a high level of skill in visual communication. But infographics may not work with most applicant tracking systems—or with the screening habits of most recruiters. While you might stand out with an infographic, you might also get tossed out if you try to use an one in place of a conventional resume. In virtually every situation, an infographic should complement a conventional resume, not replace it. In addition, successful infographics require skills in graphical design, and if you lack those skills, you'll need to hire a designer.

Producing a Traditional Printed Resume

Even though much of your application activity will take place online, a conventional printed resume is important for job fairs, interviews, and other events. Many interviewers expect you to bring a printed resume to the interview, even if you applied online. The resume can serve as a note-taking form or discussion guide, and it is tangible evidence of your attention to professionalism and detail. When printing a resume, choose a heavier, higher-quality paper designed specifically for resumes and other important documents. White or slightly off-white is the best color choice. Avoid papers with borders or backgrounds.

Printing a Scannable Resume

Scannable resume: A resume that is formatted to be compatible with optical scanning systems that convert printed documents to electronic text.

You might encounter a company that prefers **scannable resumes**, which are specially formatted to be compatible with optical scanning systems that convert printed documents to electronic text. These systems were quite common just a few years ago, but their use appears to be declining rapidly as more employers prefer email delivery or website application forms. A scannable resume differs from the traditional format in two major ways: it should always include a keyword summary, and it should be formatted in a simpler fashion that avoids underlining, special characters, and other elements that can confuse the scanning system. If you need to produce a scannable resume, search online for "formatting a scannable resume" to get detailed instructions.

Creating a Plain-Text File of Your Resume

Plain-text resume: An electronic version of a resume that has no formatting applied.

A **plain-text resume** (sometimes known as an ASCII text resume) is an electronic version of your resume that has no font formatting, no bullet symbols, no colors, no lines or boxes, or other special formatting. The plain-text version can be used in two ways. First, you can include it in the body of an email message, for employers who want email delivery but don't want file attachments. Second, you can copy and paste the sections into the application forms on an employer's website.

A plain-text version is easy to create with your word processor. Start with the file you used to create your resume, use the "Save As" choice to save it as "plain text" or whichever similarly labeled option your software has, and verify the result by using a basic text editor (such as Notepad or TextEdit). If necessary, reformat the page manually, moving text and inserting space as needed. For simplicity's sake, left-justify all your headings rather than trying to center them manually.

Creating a Word File of Your Resume

In some cases, an employer or job-posting website will want you to upload a Microsoft Word file or attach it to an email message. (Although there is certainly other word processing software on the market, Microsoft Word is the standard in business.) This method of transferring information preserves the design and layout of your resume and saves you the trouble of creating a plain-text version. Before you submit a Word file to anyone, make sure your computer is free of viruses. Infecting a potential employer's computer will not make a good first impression. To ensure your document contrains no macro viruses, save it in a macro-free format such as .docx, rather than a macro-enabled one such as .docm.

Creating a PDF Version of Your Resume

PDFs preserve the formatting of your resume and are less vulnerable to viruses than word-processer files. Creating a PDF file is a simple procedure, but you need the right software. Adobe Acrobat (not the free Adobe Reader) to create PDF files use Adobe's online service to create PDFs without buying software.

Creating an Online or Social Media Resume

A variety of online resume formats, referred to as *e-portfolios*, *interactive resumes*, or *social media resumes*, provide the opportunity to create a dynamic, multimedia presentation of your qualifications. You can expand on the information contained in your basic resume with links to projects, publications, screencasts, online videos, course lists, blogs, social networking profiles, and other elements that give employers a more complete picture of who you are and what you can offer (see Figure 13.17).

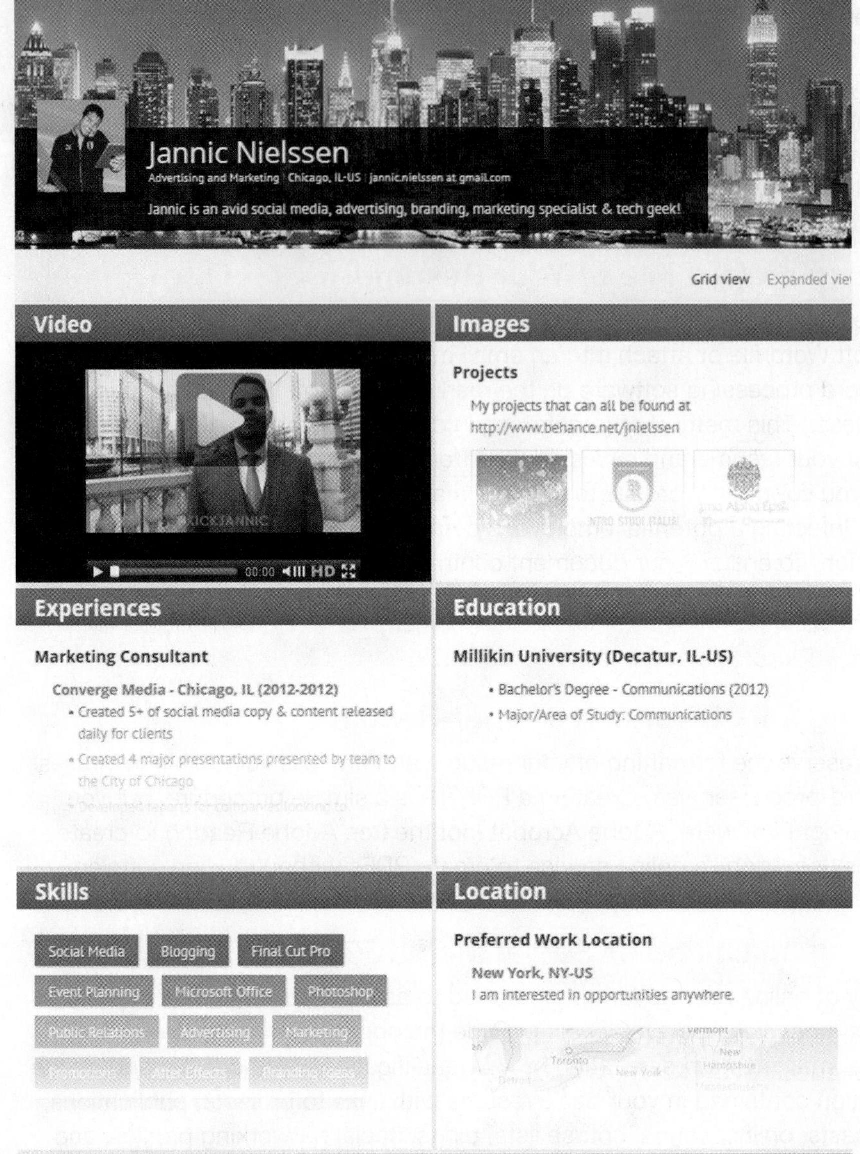

Figure 13.17
Social Media Resume
Gozaik is one of several services that allow you to create and post a social media resume.

You have a number of options for hosting an online resume. Start with your school's career center; many offer hosting for e-portfolios, for example, where you can showcase your academic achievements. You can also choose one of the commercial resume hosting services, such as LinkedIn, VisualCV, and Gozaik. In addition to being free (for basic services, at least), these sites provide easy-to-use tools for creating your online profile. You can also use them to peruse examples of various resumes, from students just about to enter the workforce full-time all the way up to corporate CEOs.

Regardless of the approach you take to creating an online resume, keep these helpful tips in mind:

- Remember that your online presence is a career-management tool. The way you are portrayed online can work for you or against you, and it's up to you to create a positive impression.

- Take advantage of social networking. Use whatever tools are available to direct people to your online resume, such as including your URL in your Twitter profile.
- During the application process, don't expect or ask employers to retrieve a resume from a website. Submit your resume using whatever method and medium each employer prefers. If employers then want to know more about you, they will likely do a web search on you and find your site, or you can refer them to your site in your resume or application materials.

Proofreading Your Resume

Employers view your resume as a concrete example of your attention to quality and detail. Your resume doesn't need to be good or pretty good—it needs to be *perfect*. Although it may not seem fair, just one or two errors in a job application package are enough to doom a candidate's chances.

Your resume is one of the most important documents you'll ever write, so don't rush or cut corners when it comes to proofreading. Check all headings and lists for clarity and parallelism, and be sure your grammar, spelling, and punctuation are correct. Double-check all dates, phone numbers, email addresses, and other essential data. Ask at least three other people to read it, too. As the creator of the material, you could stare at a mistake for weeks and not see it.

Distributing Your Resume

How you distribute your resume depends on the number of employers you target and their preferences for receiving resumes. Employers usually list their requirements on their websites, so verify this information and follow it carefully. Beyond that, here are some general distribution tips:

- **Mailing printed resumes.** Take some care with the packaging. Spend a few extra cents to mail these documents in a flat 9 × 12 envelope, or better yet, use a Priority Mail flat-rate envelope, which gives you a sturdy cardboard mailer and faster delivery for just a few dollars more.
- **Emailing your resume.** Some employers want applicants to include the text of their resumes in the body of an email message; others prefer an attached Microsoft Word or PDF file. If you have a reference number or a job ad number, include it in the subject line of your email message.
- **Submitting your resume to an employer's website.** Many employers, including most large companies, now prefer or require applicants to submit their resumes online. In some instances, you will be asked to upload a complete file. In others, you will need to copy and paste sections of your resume into individual boxes in an online application form.

- **Posting your resume on job websites.** You can post your resume on general-purpose job websites such as Monster and CareerBuilder, on more specialized websites such as Jobster or Jobfox, or with staffing services such as Volt. Roughly 100,000 job boards are now online, so you'll need to spend some time looking for sites that specialize in your target industries, regions, or professions. Before you upload your resume to any site, however, learn about its privacy protection. Some sites allow you to specify levels of confidentiality, such as letting employers search your qualifications without seeing your personal contact information or preventing your current employer from seeing your resume. Don't post your resume to any website that doesn't give you the option of restricting the display of your contact information. Only employers that are registered clients of the service should be able to see your contact information.

Figure 13.18
Preparing a Resume
You want your resume to describe you in a way that makes the employer want to meet you. A well-written resume will help you to get an interview. How can you make a positive impression and show you are serious and qualified for the job?

Chapter Summary

Finding the Ideal Opportunity in Today's Job Market

The eight steps discussed in this chapter include writing the story of you, which involves describing where you have been in your career so far and where you would like to go in the future, and learning to think like an employer so you can present yourself as a quality hire. Next, research industries and companies of interest to identify promising opportunities and to learn the language of the hiring managers. Translate your general potential into a specific solution for each employer so that you look like a good fit for each opening. Take the initiative to approach interesting companies even if they haven't yet posted any job openings. Build your network so you and your connections can help each other in the job search process, seek career counseling if appropriate, and avoid mistakes that can ruin your chances of getting a job.

Planning Your Resume

Planning a resume starts with recognizing what it is: a persuasive message designed to get you job interviews. Gathering the necessary information involves learning about target industries, professions, companies, and specific positions, as well as gathering information about yourself. How you organize your resume depends on your background and your goals. A chronological resume helps employers easily locate necessary information, highlights your professional growth and career progress, and emphasizes continuity and stability. If you can use the chronological format, you should; it it is the approach employers tend to prefer. A functional resume helps employers easily see what you can do for them, allows you to emphasize specific job experience, and lets you downplay any lengthy periods of unemployment or a lack of career progress—but many employers are suspicious of functional resumes for this very reason. The combination approach uses the best features of the other two and is often the best choice for recent graduates.

Writing Your Resume

Adapting to the audience is crucial, because readers are looking to see how well you understand their businesses and can present a solution to their talent needs. The major sections to consider including in your resume are your name and contact information; an introductory statement, which can be a career objective, a qualifications summary, or a career summary; your education; your work experience; and activities and achievements that are professionally relevant. Most resumes do not need to include any personal data.

Completing Your Resume

Quality is paramount with resumes, so the tasks of revising and proofing are particularly important. The six common resume formats are traditional printed resume, scannable resume, electronic plain-text file, Microsoft Word file, PDF, and online resume (which might be called a personal webpage, an e-portfolio, or a social media resume).

Test Your Knowledge

1. Why is networking an essential part of your lifelong career planning?
2. What is the purpose of a resume?
3. Why do most employers prefer chronological resumes over functional resumes?
4. Why is it important to find and use relevant keywords in your resume?

Apply Your Knowledge

1. If you were a team leader at a summer camp for children with special needs, should you include this in your employment history if you are applying for work that is unrelated? Explain your answer.
2. Can you use a qualifications summary if you don't yet have extensive professional experience in your desired career? Why or why not?
3. Some people don't have a clear career path when they enter the job market. If you're in this situation, how would your uncertainty affect the way your write your resume?
4. Select a professional communications career that interests you and research professional groups, organizations, and associations that represents that career. Collect as much information as you can, such as the type, purpose, dynamics, processes, effectiveness, roles of members, and leadership style for each group. Use the information to compile a chart or table you can use to compare the groups.

Practice Your Skills

1. **Researching Career Opportunities** Based on the academic, professional, and personal qualities you have to offer, perform an online search for a career opportunity that matches your interests and qualifications (starting with any of the websites listed in Table 13.1). Draft a one-page report indicating how the career you select and the job openings you find match your strengths and preferences.

2. **Researching Certifications and Training** Choose one of the following careers, and find out what certifications and training are available that would help you prepare for that career. Create a table that lists at least three possible training programs or classes you could take in your area.

   - Microsoft Office applications specialist
   - PC repair technician
   - Computer network installer
   - Construction project manager
   - Database administrator

3. **Planning a Resume** Identify a position in an interesting career field for which you might qualify. Using at least three different sources, including the description in an online job posting, create a list of 10 keywords that should be included in a resume customized for this positioning.

4. **Writing a Resume** Rewrite this resume so that it follows the guidelines presented in this chapter.

Sylvia Manchester

765 Belle Fleur Blvd.

New Orleans, LA 70113

(504) 312-9504

smanchester@rcnmail.com

Personal: Single, excellent health, 5'7", 136 lbs.; hobbies include cooking, dancing, and reading.

Job Objective: To obtain a responsible position in marketing or sales with a good company.

Education: BA degree in biology, University of Louisiana, 1998. Graduated with a 3.0 average. Member of the varsity cheerleading squad. President of Panhellenic League. Homecoming queen.

Work Experience

Fisher Scientific Instruments, 2014 to now, field sales representative. Responsible for calling on customers and explaining the features of Fisher's line of laboratory instruments. Also responsible for writing sales letters, attending trade shows, and preparing weekly sales reports.

Fisher Scientific Instruments, 2011–2013, customer service representative. Was responsible for handling incoming phone calls from customers who had questions about delivery, quality, or operation of Fisher's line of laboratory instruments. Also handled miscellaneous correspondence with customers.

Medical Electronics, Inc., 2008–2011, administrative assistant to the vice president of marketing. In addition to handling typical secretarial chores for the vice president of marketing, I was in charge of compiling the monthly sales reports, using figures provided by members of the field sales force. I also was given responsibility for doing various market research activities.

New Orleans Convention and Visitors Bureau, 2005–2008, summers, tour guide. During the summers of my college years, I led tours of New Orleans for tourists visiting the city. My duties included greeting conventioneers and their spouses at hotels, explaining the history and features of the city during an all-day sightseeing tour, and answering questions about New Orleans and its attractions. During my fourth summer with the bureau, I was asked to help train the new tour guides. I prepared a handbook that provided interesting facts about the various tourist attractions, as well as answers to the most commonly asked tourist questions. The Bureau was so impressed with the handbook they had it printed up so that it could be given as a gift to visitors.

University of Louisiana, 2005–2008, part-time clerk in admissions office. While I was a student in college, I worked 15 hours a week in the admissions office. My duties included filing, processing applications, and handling correspondence with high school students and administrators.

5. **Writing a Resume (Team Project)** Working with another student, change the following statements to make them more effective for a resume by using action verbs and concrete keywords.
   a. Have some experience with database design.
   b. Assigned to a project to analyze the cost accounting methods for a large manufacturer.
   c. I was part of a team that developed a new inventory control system.
   d. Am responsible for preparing the quarterly department budget.
   e. Was a manager of a department with seven employees working for me.
   f. Was responsible for developing a spreadsheet to analyze monthly sales by department.
   g. Put in place a new program for ordering supplies.

6. **Writing a Resume** Using your team's answers to Activity 5, make the statements stronger by quantifying them (make up any numbers you need).

7. **Communication Ethics when Writing a Resume** Assume that you achieved all the tasks shown in Activity 5, not as an individual employee but as part of a work team. In your resume, must you mention other team members? Explain your answer.

8. **Analyzing a Resume** Locate an example of an online resume (a sample or an actual resume). Analyze the resume following the guidelines presented in this chapter. Using whatever medium your instructor requests, write a brief analysis (no more than one page) of the resume's strengths and weaknesses, citing specific elements from the resume and support from the chapter. If you are analyzing a real resume, do not include any personally identifiable data, such as the person's name, email address, or phone number, in your report.

Expand Your Skills

1. **Researching Career Opportunities** Knowing the jargon and "hot button" issues in a particular profession or industry can give you a big advantage when it comes to writing your resume and participating in job interviews. You can fine-tune your resume for both human readers and applicant tracking systems, sound more confident and informed in interviews, and present yourself as a professional-class individual with an inquiring mind.

   Your task: Imagine a specific job category in a company that has an informative, comprehensive website (to facilitate the research you'll need to do). This doesn't have to be a current job opening, but a position you know exists or is likely to exist in this company, such as a business systems analyst at Apple or a brand manager at Unilever.

   Explore the company's website and other online sources to find the following: 1) a brief description of what this job entails, with enough detail that you could describe it to a fellow student; 2) some of the terminology used in the profession or industry, both formal terms that might serve as keywords on your resume and informal terms and phrases that insiders are likely to use in publications and conversations; 3) an ongoing online conversation among people in this profession, such as a LinkedIn Group, a popular industry or professional blog that seems to get quite a few comments, or an industry or professional publication that attracts a lot of comments; and 4) at least one significant issue that will affect people in this profession or companies in this industry over the next few years. For example, if your chosen profession involves accounting in a publicly traded corporation, upcoming changes in international financial reporting standards would be a significant issue. Similarly, for a company in the consumer electronics industry, the recycling and disposal of e-waste is an issue. Write a brief email message summarizing your findings and explaining how you could use this information on your resume and during job interviews.

2. **Researching Career Opportunities** Perhaps you won't be able to land your ultimate dream job right out of school, but that doesn't mean you shouldn't start planning right now to make that dream come true.

   Your task: Using online job search tools, find a job that sounds just about perfect for you, even if you're not yet qualified for it. It might even be something that would take 10 or 20 years to reach. Don't settle for something that's not quite right—find a job that is so "you" and so exciting that you would jump out of bed every morning, eager to go to work. Start with the job description you found online and then supplement it with additional research so that you get a good picture of what this job and career path are all about. Compile a list of all the qualifications you would need in order to have a reasonable chance of landing such a job. Now compare this list with your current resume. Write a brief email message to your instructor that identifies all the areas in which you would need to improve your skills, work experience, education, and other qualifications in order to land your dream job.

3. **Planning a Resume (Team Project)** If you haven't begun your professional career yet or you are pursuing a career change, the employment history section on your resume can sometimes be a challenge to write. A brainstorming session with your classmates could help.

   Your task: In a team assigned by your instructor, help each other evaluate your employment histories and figure out the best way to present your work backgrounds on a resume. First, each member of the team should compile his or her work history, including freelance projects and volunteer work if relevant, and share this information with the team. If you haven't any work experience, focus on volunteer or extracurricular activities. After allowing some time for everyone to review each other's information, meet as a team. Discuss each person's history, pointing out strong spots and weak spots, and then brainstorm the best way to present each person's employment history.

   Note: If there are aspects of your employment history you would rather not share with your teammates, substitute a reasonably similar experience of the same duration.

4. **Writing a Resume (Team Project)** The introductory statement of a resume requires some careful thought, both in deciding which of the three types of introductory statement (see page 469) to use and what information to include in it. Getting another person's perspective on this communication challenge can be helpful. In this activity, in fact, someone else is going to write your introductory statement for you, and you will return the favor.

Your task: Pair with a classmate. Provide each other with the basic facts about your qualifications, work history, education, and career objectives. Then meet for an informal interview in which you ask each other questions to flesh out the information you have on each other. Assume that each of you has chosen to use a qualifications summary for your resume. Now write each other's qualifications summary and then trade them for review. As you read what your partner wrote about you, ask yourself if this feels true to what you believe about yourself and your career aspirations. Do you think it introduces you effectively to potential employers? What might you change about it?

5. **Completing a Resume** Creating presentations and other multimedia supplements can be a great way to expand on the brief overview that a resume provides.

   Your task: Starting with any version of a resume you've created for yourself, create a PowerPoint presentation that expands on your resume information to give potential employers a more complete picture of what you can contribute. Include samples of your work, testimonials from current or past employers and colleagues, videos of speeches you've made, and anything else that tells the story of the professional "you." If you have a specific job or type of job in mind, focus your presentation on that. Otherwise, present a more general picture that shows why you would be a great employee for any company to consider. Be sure to review the information from Chapter 12 about creating professional-quality presentations.

6. **Completing a Resume** In the right circumstances, brief videos can be an effective complement to a traditional job-search communication package.

   Your task: Find a job opening that interests you (something you are at least partially qualified for at this stage of your career) and produce a two-minute video profile of yourself, highlighting the skills mentioned in the job description. For tips on producing effective videos, visit www.indie-film-making.com.

CHAPTER

14

Applying and Interviewing for Employment

After studying this chapter, you will be able to:

- Explain the purposes of application letters and describe how to apply the AIDA organizational approach to them.
- Describe the typical sequence of job interviews, the major types of interviews, and the attributes employers look for during an interview.
- List six tasks you need to complete to prepare for a successful job interview.
- Explain how to succeed in all three stages of an interview.
- Identify the most common messages that follow an interview and explain when you would use each one.

Submitting Your Resume

Your resume (see Chapter 13) is the centerpiece of your job search package, but it needs support from several other employment messages, including application letters, job-inquiry letters, application forms, and follow-up notes.

Write an Application Letter

Application letter: A letter accompanying a resume providing a context for sending it.

Whenever you mail, email, hand-deliver, or upload your resume, you should include an **application letter**, also known as a cover letter. (Even when it is electronic, not printed, these are still referred to as letters.) An application letter tells your reader what you're sending, why you're sending it, and how they will benefit from reading it. Take the same care with each application letter that you took with your resume. A poorly written application letter can prompt an employer to skip over your resume, even if you are a good fit for a job.

The best approach for an application letter depends on whether you are applying for an identified job opening or are *prospecting*—taking the initiative to write to companies even though they haven't announced a job opening that is right for you. In many ways, the difference between the two is like the difference between solicited and unsolicited proposals. Figure 14.1 shows an application message written in response to a posted job opening. The writer knows exactly what qualifications the organization is seeking and can "echo" those attributes back in his letter.

Prospecting letters are more challenging to write; you don't have the clear target you have with a solicited letter, and your message will arrive unexpected. You will need to do more research to identify the qualities that a company will probably seek for the position you hope to occupy (see Figure 14.2). Search for news items that involve the company, its customers, the profession, or the individual manager to whom you are writing. Using this information in your application letter helps you establish common ground with your reader—and it shows that you are tuned in to what's going on in the industry.

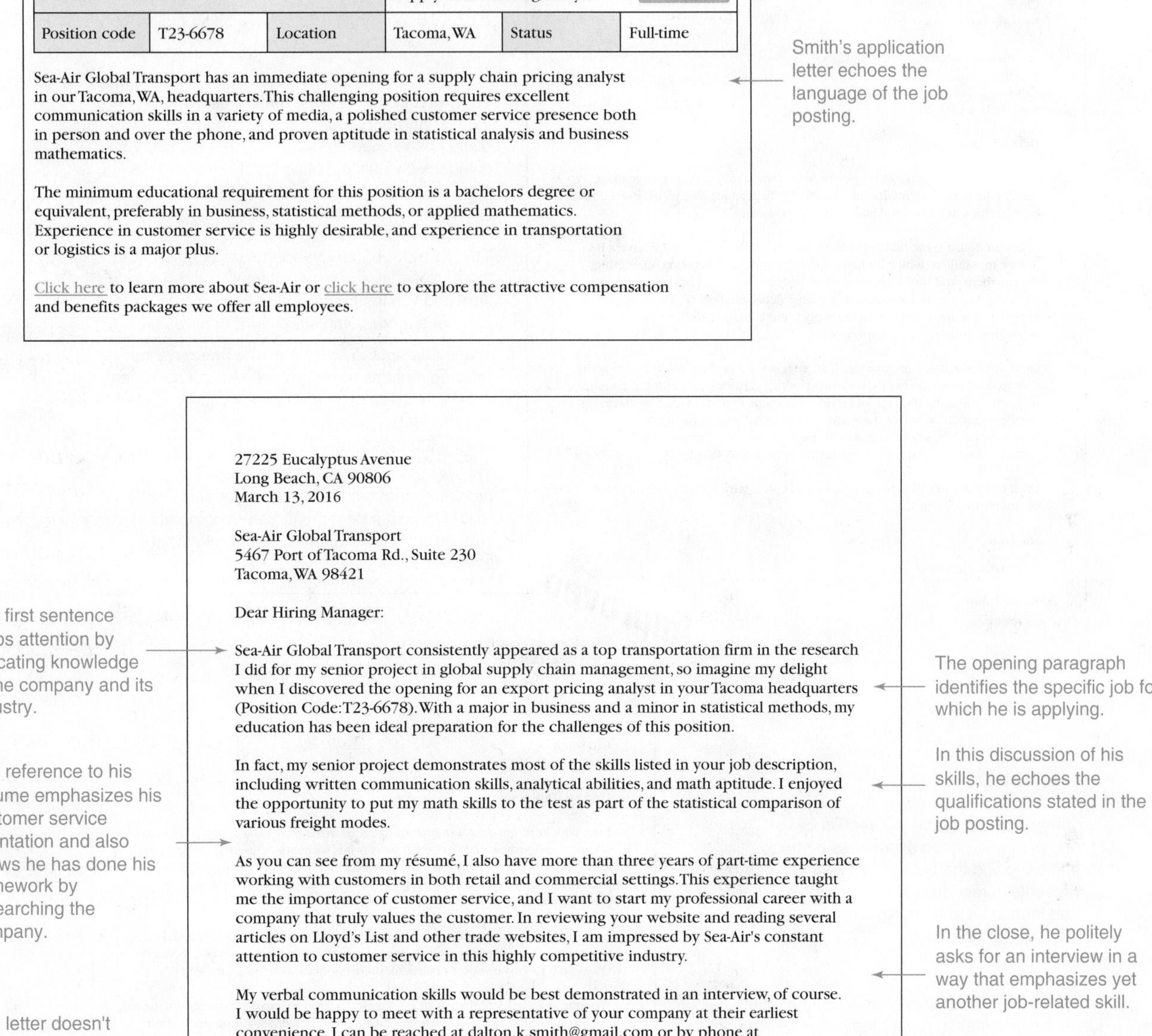

Position			Supply Chain Pricing Analyst		Apply
Position code	T23-6678	Location	Tacoma, WA	Status	Full-time

Sea-Air Global Transport has an immediate opening for a supply chain pricing analyst in our Tacoma, WA, headquarters. This challenging position requires excellent communication skills in a variety of media, a polished customer service presence both in person and over the phone, and proven aptitude in statistical analysis and business mathematics.

The minimum educational requirement for this position is a bachelors degree or equivalent, preferably in business, statistical methods, or applied mathematics. Experience in customer service is highly desirable, and experience in transportation or logistics is a major plus.

Click here to learn more about Sea-Air or click here to explore the attractive compensation and benefits packages we offer all employees.

Smith's application letter echoes the language of the job posting.

27225 Eucalyptus Avenue
Long Beach, CA 90806
March 13, 2016

Sea-Air Global Transport
5467 Port of Tacoma Rd., Suite 230
Tacoma, WA 98421

Dear Hiring Manager:

Sea-Air Global Transport consistently appeared as a top transportation firm in the research I did for my senior project in global supply chain management, so imagine my delight when I discovered the opening for an export pricing analyst in your Tacoma headquarters (Position Code:T23-6678). With a major in business and a minor in statistical methods, my education has been ideal preparation for the challenges of this position.

In fact, my senior project demonstrates most of the skills listed in your job description, including written communication skills, analytical abilities, and math aptitude. I enjoyed the opportunity to put my math skills to the test as part of the statistical comparison of various freight modes.

As you can see from my résumé, I also have more than three years of part-time experience working with customers in both retail and commercial settings. This experience taught me the importance of customer service, and I want to start my professional career with a company that truly values the customer. In reviewing your website and reading several articles on Lloyd's List and other trade websites, I am impressed by Sea-Air's constant attention to customer service in this highly competitive industry.

My verbal communication skills would be best demonstrated in an interview, of course. I would be happy to meet with a representative of your company at their earliest convenience. I can be reached at dalton.k.smith@gmail.com or by phone at (562) 555-3737.

Sincerely,

Dalton Smith

The first sentence grabs attention by indicating knowledge of the company and its industry.

The opening paragraph identifies the specific job for which he is applying.

The reference to his resume emphasizes his customer service orientation and also shows he has done his homework by researching the company.

In this discussion of his skills, he echoes the qualifications stated in the job posting.

In the close, he politely asks for an interview in a way that emphasizes yet another job-related skill.

The letter doesn't include a handwritten signature because it was uploaded to a website along with his resume.

Figure 14.1
Solicited Application Message
In this response to an online job posting, Dalton Smith highlights his qualifications while mirroring the requirements specified in the posting. Following the AIDA model, he grabs attention immediately by letting the reader know he is familiar with the company and the global transportation business.

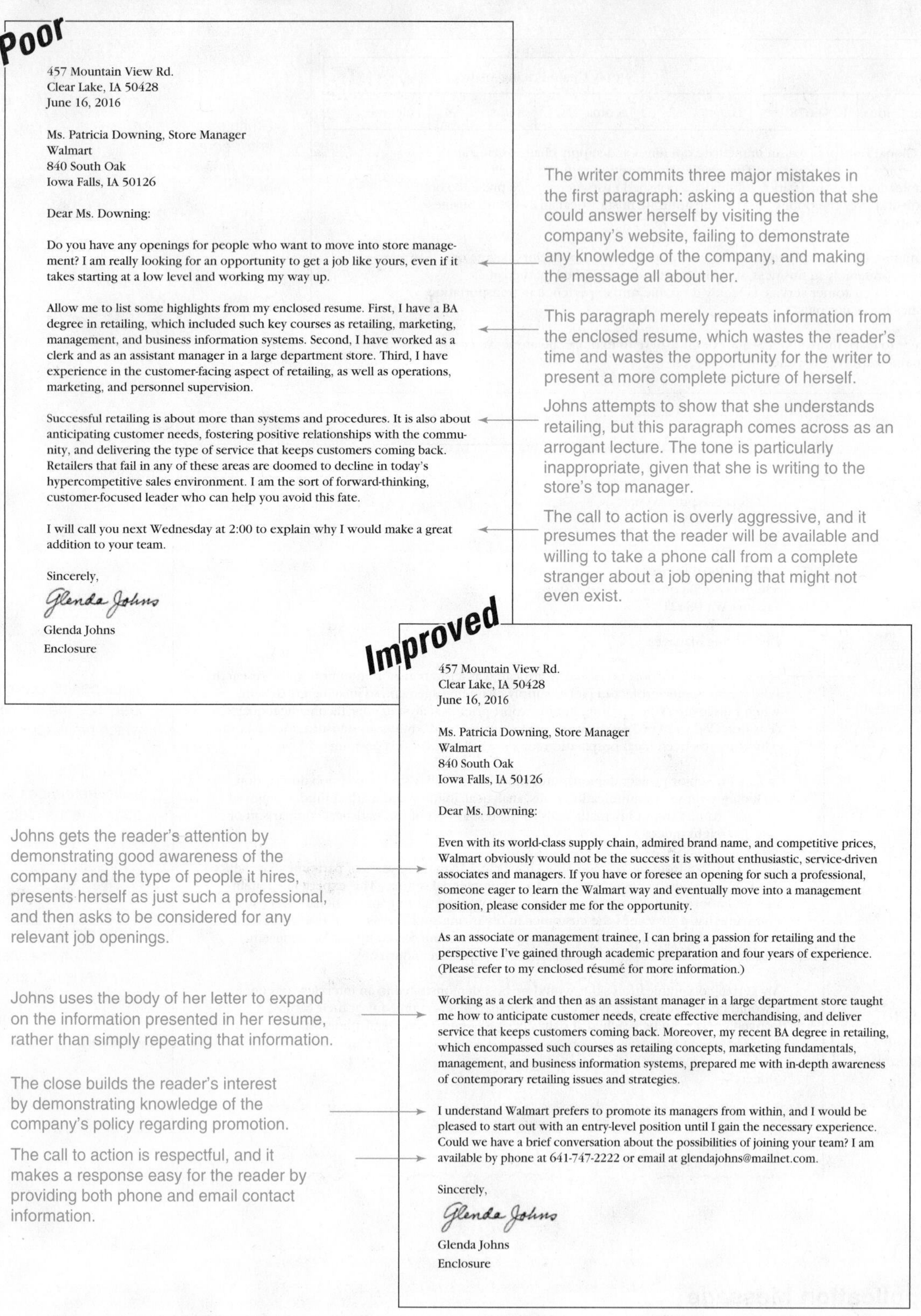

Figure 14.2
Unsolicited Application Letter: Poor and Improved
Demonstrating knowledge of the employer's needs and presenting your qualifications accordingly are essential steps in an unsolicited application letter.

For either type of letter, follow these tips to be more effective:

- If you can find the name of an individual manager, address your letter to that person. (And be sure you do, because other applicants will.) Search LinkedIn, the company's website, industry directories, Twitter, and anything else you can think of to locate an appropriate name. Ask the people in your network if they know a name. If you can't find one, addressing your letter to "Dear Hiring Manager" is perfectly acceptable.
- Clearly identify the opportunity you are applying for or expressing interest in.
- Show that you understand the company and its marketplace.
- Never volunteer salary history or requirements unless an employer has asked for this information.
- Keep it short—no more than three or four brief paragraphs. Remember that all you are trying to do at this point is move the conversation one step.
- Show some personality while maintaining a business-appropriate tone. The letter gives you the opportunity to balance the facts-only tone of your resume.
- Project confidence but not arrogance.
- Don't just repeat information from your resume; use the conversational tone of the letter to convey additional professional and personal qualities and your reasons you want this particular job.

Because application letters are persuasive messages, the AIDA approach you learned in Chapter 9 is ideal, as the following sections explain.

Getting Attention

The opening paragraph of your application letter must accomplish two essential tasks: it explains why you are writing and it gives the recipient a reason to keep reading. Give that reason by demonstrating that you have immediate potential for meeting the company's needs. Consider this opening:

> With the recent slowdown in corporate purchasing, I can certainly appreciate the challenge of new fleet sales in this business environment. With my high energy level and 16 months of new-car sales experience, I believe I can produce the results you listed as vital in the job posting on your website.

This applicant does a smooth job of echoing the company's stated needs while highlighting his personal qualifications and providing evidence that he understands the broader market. He balances his relative lack of experience with enthusiasm and knowledge of the industry. Table 14.1 suggests some other ways you can spark interest and grab attention in your opening paragraph.

Table 14.1 Tips for Getting Attention in Application Letters

Tip	Example
Show how your strongest skills will benefit the organization.	If you need a regional sales specialist who consistently meets sales targets while fostering strong customer relationships, please consider my qualifications.
Describe your understanding of the job's requirements and show how well your qualifications fit them.	Your annual report stated that improving manufacturing efficiency is one of the company's top priorities for next year. Through my postgraduate research in systems engineering and consulting work for several companies in the industry, I've developed reliable methods for quickly identifying ways to cut production time while reducing resource use.
Mention the name of a person known to and highly regarded by the reader.	When Janice McHugh of your franchise sales division spoke to our business communication class last week, she said you often need promising new marketing graduates at this time of year.
Refer to publicized company activities, achievements, changes, or new procedures.	Today's issue of the Detroit News reports that you may need the expertise of computer programmers versed in robotics when your Lansing tire plant automates this spring.
Use a question to demonstrate your understanding of the organization's needs.	Can your fast-growing market research division use an interviewer with two years of field survey experience, a B.A. in public relations, and a real desire to succeed? If so, please consider me for the position.
Use a catchphrase opening if the job requires ingenuity and imagination.	Haut monde—whether referring to French, Italian, or Arab clients, it still means "high society." As an interior designer for your Beverly Hills showroom, not only could I serve and sell to your distinguished clientele, but I could do it in all these languages. I speak, read, and write them fluently.
Identify where you discovered the job opening; describe what you have to offer.	Your job posting on Monster.com for a cruise-line social director caught my eye. My eight years of experience as a social director in the travel industry would equip me to serve your new Caribbean cruise division well.

Build Interest and Increase Desire

The middle section of your letter presents your strongest selling points in terms of their potential benefit to the organization. This builds interest in you and creating a desire to interview you. Be specific and back up your assertions with convincing evidence:

> Poor: I completed three college courses in business communications, earning an A in each course, and have worked for the past years at Imperial Construction.

> Improved: Using the skills I gained from three semesters of college training in business communciations, I developed a collection systen for Imperial Construction that reduced annual bad-debt losses by 25 percent.

In a solicited letter, be sure to discuss each major requirement listed in the job posting. If you are deficient in any of these requirements, stress other solid selling points to help strengthen your overall presentation. Don't restrict your message to just core job duties, either. Also highlight personal characteristics that apply to the targeted position, such as your ability to work hard or handle responsibility:

> While I attended college full-time, I worked part-time during the school year and up to 60 hours a week each summer in order to be totally self-supporting. I can offer your organization the same level of effort and perseverance percent.

Mention your salary requirements only if the organization has asked you to state them. If you don't know the salary that's appropriate for the position and someone with your qualifications, you can find typical salary ranges at the Bureau of Labor Statistics website, www.bls.gov, or on a number of commercial websites. If you do state a target salary, tie it to the value you would offer:

> For the past two years, I have been helping a company similar to yours organize its database marketing efforts. I would therefore like to receive a salary in the same range—the mid-60s—for helping your company set up a more efficient customer database.

Toward the end of this section, refer the reader to your resume by citing a specific fact or general point covered there:

> As you can see in the attached resume, I've been worked part-time with a local publisher since my sophomore year. During that time, I've used client interactions as an opportunity to build strong customer service skills.

Motivate Action

The final paragraph of your application letter has two important functions: to ask the reader for a specific action, usually an interview, and to facilitate a reply. Offer to come to the employer's office at a convenient time or, if the firm is some distance away, to meet with its nearest representative or arrange a telephone or Skype interview. Include your email address and phone number, as well as the best times to reach you:

> After you have reviewed my qualifications, I would like to discuss the possibility of putting my marketing skills to work for your company. I am available at (360) 555-7845 from 2 PM to 10 PM Monday to Friday or by email at john.wagner462@gmail.com.

Follow Up After Submitting a Resume

Deciding if, when, and how to follow up after you submit your resume and application letter is one of the trickiest parts of a job search. First and foremost, keep in mind that employers continue to evaluate your communication efforts and professionalism during this phase, so don't say or do anything that might leave a negative impression. Second, adhere to whatever instructions the employer has provided. If a job posting says "no calls," for example, don't call. Third, if the job posting lists a close date, don't call or write before then; the company is still collecting applications and will not have made a decision about inviting people for interviews. Wait a week or so after the close date. If no close date is given and you have no other information to suggest a timeline, you can generally contact the company starting a week or two after submitting your resume.

When you follow up by email or telephone, try to share an additional piece of information that links your qualifications to the position. Mention any late-breaking news about the company, and ask a question about the hiring process as a way to gather information about your status. Good questions to ask include:

- Has a hiring decision been made yet?
- Can you tell me what to expect next in terms of the hiring process?
- What is the company's timeframe for filling this position?
- Could I follow up in another week if you haven't had the chance to contact me yet?
- Can I provide any additional information regarding my qualifications for the position?

Whatever the circumstances, a follow-up message can demonstrate that you're sincerely interested in working for the organization, persistent in pursuing your goals, and committed to upgrading your skills.

If you don't land a job at your dream company on the first attempt, don't give up. You can apply again if a new opening appears. If you have gained additional experience, taken a relevant course, or otherwise improved your skill set, you can send an updated resume with a new application letter. Many employers take note of applicants who came close but didn't quite make it; they may extend offers when positions open up in the future.

Understanding the Interviewing Process

An **employment interview** is a meeting during which both you and the prospective employer ask questions and exchange information. The employer's objective is to find the best talent to fill available job openings. Your objective is to find the right match for your goals and capabilities.

Employment interview: A meeting with a prospective employer to ask questions and exchange information.

As you get ready to begin interviewing, keep two points in mind. First, the process takes time. Start your preparation and research early; the best job offers usually go to the best-prepared candidates. Second, don't limit your options by looking at only a few companies. Explore a wide range of firms and positions. You might uncover great opportunities that you would not have found otherwise. You'll increase the odds of getting more job offers, too.

Figure 14.3 Employment Interviews
An employment interview helps you show a potential employer who you are and what you have to offer the company.

The Typical Sequence of Interviews

Most employers interview an applicant multiple times before deciding to make a job offer. At the most selective companies, you might have a dozen or more individual interviews across several stages. Depending on the company and the position, the process may stretch out over many weeks, or it may be completed in a matter of days.

Employers start with the screening stage, in which they filter out applicants who are unqualified or otherwise not a good fit for the position. Screening can take place on your school's campus, at company offices, via telephone or video chat, or through a computer-based screening system. Time is limited in screening interviews, so keep your answers short while you provide a few key points that confirm your fit for the position. If your screening interview will take place by phone, schedule it for a time when you can be focused and free from interruptions.

The next stage of interviews, the selection stage, helps the organization identify the top candidates from all those who qualify. During these interviews, show keen interest in the job, relate your skills and experience to the organization's needs, listen attentively, and ask insightful questions that show you've done your research.

If the interviewers agree that you're a good candidate, you may receive a job offer, either on the spot or a few days later by phone, mail, or email. In other instances, you may be invited back for a final evaluation, often by a higher-ranking executive. The objective of the final stage is often to sell you on the advantages of joining the organization.

Common Types of Interviews

Be prepared to encounter a variety of interviewing approaches. These vary in structure, the number of people involved, and the purpose of the interview.

Structured versus Unstructured Interviews

Structured interview: An interview in which the applicant is asked a series of questions in a predetermined order.

In a **structured interview**, the interviewer—or a computer program—asks a series of questions in a predetermined order. Structured interviews help employers identify candidates who don't meet basic job criteria, and they allow the interview team to compare answers from multiple candidates.

Open-ended interview: An interview in which the interviewer adapts his or her line of questioning based on the answers given and the questions the applicant asks.

In contrast, in an **open-ended interview**, the interviewer adapts his or her line of questioning based on the answers you give and the questions you ask. Even though it may feel like a conversation, remember that it's still an interview, so keep your answers focused and professional.

Figure 14.4 The Interview Conversation
Open-ended interviews allow job candidates and employers a chance to assess compatibility in a less rigid way than in a structured interview.

Panel and Group Interviews

Although one-on-one interviews are the most common, some employers use panel or group interviews as well. In a **panel interview**, you meet with several interviewers at once. In these, try to make a connection with each person on the panel. Keep in mind that each person has a different perspective, so tailor your responses accordingly. For example, an upper-level manager is likely to be interested in your overall business sense and strategic perspective; a potential colleague might be more interested in your technical skills and ability to work in a team. In a **group interview**, one or more interviewers meet with several candidates simultaneously. A key purpose of a group interview is to observe how the candidates interact. Group interviews can be tricky; you want to stand out, but you also want to come across as a supportive team player. Be sure to treat your fellow candidates with respect while you look for opportunities to demonstrate the depth of knowledge you have about the company and its needs.

Panel interview: An interview in which a single applicant meets with several interviewers at once.

Group interview: An interview in which one or more interviewers meet with several candidates simultaneously.

Figure 14.5 Panel and Group Interviews
Interviews are not always one-on-one meetings. Panel and group interviewers may include multiple candidates and/or multiple interviewers.

Behavioral, Situational, Working, and Stress Interviews

Interviewing techniques also vary based on the types of questions you are asked. Perhaps the most common type of interview these days is the **behavioral interview**, in which you are asked to relate specific incidents and experiences from your past. In contrast to generic questions that can often be answered with "canned" responses, behavioral questions require candidates to use their own experiences and attributes to craft answers. Studies show that behavioral interview questions are a much better predictor of success on the job than traditional interview questions. To prepare for a behavioral interview, review your work or school experiences. Think of instances in which you demonstrated important job-related attributes or dealt with challenges, such as uncooperative team members or heavy workloads. Get ready with responses that quickly summarize the situation, the actions you took, and the outcome of those actions.

Behavioral interview: An interview in which an applicant is asked to relate specific incidents and experiences from their past.

Situational interview: An interview in which questions focus on how the applicant would handle various hypothetical situations on the job.

Working interview: An interview in which the applicant performs a job-related activity.

Stress interview: An interview in which questions are asked designed to unsettle the applicant to see how they will react to stress.

A **situational interview** is similar to a behavioral interview except that the questions focus on how you would handle various hypothetical situations on the job. The situations will likely relate closely to the job you're applying for, so the more you know about the position, the better prepared you'll be.

A **working interview** is the most realistic type of interview: you actually perform a job-related activity during the interview. You may be asked to lead a brainstorming session, solve a business problem, engage in role-playing, or even make a presentation.

The most unnerving type of interview is the **stress interview**. During one of these, you might be asked questions designed to unsettle you, or you might be subjected to long periods of silence, criticism, interruptions, or even a hostile reaction from the interviewer. The theory behind this approach is that you'll reveal how well you handle stressful situations, although some experts find the technique of dubious value. If you find yourself in a stress interview, recognize what is happening and collect your thoughts before you respond.

You might encounter two or more types of interview questions within a single interview, so stay alert and try to understand the type of question you're facing before you answer each one.

Interview Media

Expect to be interviewed through a variety of media. As employers cut travel costs and the demands on staff time, they now interview candidates via telephone, email, virtual online systems, and videoconferencing, in addition to traditional face-to-face meetings.

To succeed at a telephone interview, make sure you treat it as seriously as an in-person interview. Be prepared with a copy of all the materials you have sent to the employer, including your resume and any correspondence. In addition, prepare some note cards with key message points you'd like to make and questions you'd like to ask. Remember that you won't be able to use a pleasant smile, a firm handshake, or other nonverbal signals to create a good impression. A positive, alert tone of voice is therefore vital.

Email is sometimes used in the screening stage. Although you have almost no opportunity to send and receive nonverbal signals with this format, you do have the advantage of being able to review and edit each response before you send it. Maintain a professional style in your responses, and be sure to ask questions that demonstrate your knowledge of the company and the position.

Many employers use video technology for interviews. The online retailer Zappos uses video interviews on Skype to select the top two or three finalists for each position, then invites those candidates for in-person interviews. Recruiters can also use mobile apps for interviews. With recorded video interviews, an online system asks a set of questions and records the respondent's answers. Recruiters then watch the videos as part of the screening process. Prepare for a video interview as you would for an in-person interview—including dressing and grooming—and take the extra steps needed to become familiar with the equipment and the process. If you're interviewing from home, arrange your space so that the webcam doesn't pick up anything distracting or embarrassing in the background. During any video interview, remember to sit up straight and focus on the camera.

Figure 14.6
Remote Interviews
Digital interviews can save time and money for both employers and candidates. If an initial interview goes well via phone or video chat, you may be invited for an in-person meeting.

What Employers Look for in an Interview

Interviews give employers the chance to go beyond the basic data of your resume to get to know you and to answer two essential questions. The first is whether you can handle the responsibilities of the position. Naturally, the more you know about the demands of the position, and the more you've thought about how your skills match those demands, the better you'll be able to respond.

The second essential question is whether you will be a good fit with the organization and the target position. All good employers want people who are confident, dedicated, positive, curious, courteous, ethical, and willing to commit to something larger than their own goals. Companies also look for fit with their individual cultures. Just like people, companies have different personalities. Some are intense; others are more laid back. Some emphasize teamwork; others expect employees to forge their own way and even to compete with one another. Expectations also vary from job to job within a company and from industry to industry. An outgoing personality is essential for sales but less so for research, for instance.

Preemployment Testing and Background Checks

In an effort to improve the predictability of the selection process, many employers now conduct a variety of preemployment evaluations and investigations.

Here are types of assessments you may encounter during your job search:

- Integrity tests attempt to measure how truthful and trustworthy a candidate is likely to be.
- Personality tests are designed to gauge such aspects as attitude toward work, interests, managerial potential, dependability, commitment, and motivation.
- Cognitive tests measure a variety of attributes involved in acquiring, processing, analyzing, using, and remembering information. Typical tests involve reading comprehension, mathematics, problem solving, and decision making.
- Language proficiency tests measure your ability to read and write
- Job knowledge and skills tests measure knowledge and abilities you'll need in a particular position. If you're an accounting candidate, for example, you might take a knowledge test of accounting principles and legal matters or be given a skills test in which you create a simple balance sheet or income statement.
- A majority of companies perform some level of drug testing. Many employers believe such testing is necessary to maintain workplace safety, ensure productivity, and protect companies from lawsuits. Others view it as an invasion of employee privacy.
- Many companies conduct background checks. An employer might review your credit record, check to see whether you have a criminal history, and verify your education. You should also assume that every employer will conduct a general online search on you. To prevent a background check from tripping you up, look for any mistakes or outdated information in your credit and academic records. Plug your name into multiple search engines to see whether anything embarrassing shows up, and scour your social network profiles and connections for potential problems.

Figure 14.7
Pre-Employment Testing
Many employers screen job candidates using personality tests, cognitive assessments, and knowledge and skills exams.

Preemployment assessments are a complex and controversial aspect of workforce recruiting. For instance, even though personality testing is widely used, some research suggests that commonly used tests are not a reliable predictor of job success. Expect to see innovation in this area and greater use of testing in general as companies try to reduce the risks and costs of poor hiring decisions.

If you're concerned about any preemployment test, ask the employer for more information or ask your school's career center for advice. You can also get more information from the Equal Employment Opportunity Commission at www.eeoc.gov.

Preparing for a Job Interview

Now that you're armed with insights into the interviewing and assessment process, you're ready to begin preparing for your interviews. Preparation will help you feel more confident and perform better under pressure. It starts with learning about the organization.

Learning about the Organization

Employers expect serious candidates to demonstrate an understanding of the company's operations, its markets, and its strategic and tactical challenges. You've already done some initial research to identify companies of interest, but when you're invited to an interview, it's time to dig a little deeper (see Table 14.2). Making this effort demonstrates your interest in the company, and it identifies you as a business professional who knows the importance of investigation and analysis.

In addition to the company and the job opening, learn as much as you can about the managers who will be interviewing you. It's perfectly acceptable to ask your contact at the company for the names and titles of the people who will be interviewing you, then research them on LinkedIn. As you find information, think about ways to use it during your interview. For example, if an interviewer lists membership in a particular professional organization, you might ask whether the organization is a good forum for people to learn about vital issues in the profession or industry. This question gives the interviewer an opportunity to talk about his or her own interests and experiences for a moment, which builds rapport and might reveal vital insights into the career path you are considering. Just make sure your questions are sincere and not uncomfortably personal.

Table 14.2 Investigating an Organization and a Job Opportunity

Where to Look and What You Can Learn
Company website, blogs, and social media accounts: Overall information about the company, including key executives, products and services, locations and divisions, employee benefits, job descriptions
Competitors' websites, blogs, and social media accounts: Similar information from competitors, including the strengths these companies claim to have
Industry-related websites and blogs: Objective analysis and criticism of the company, its products, its reputation, and its management
Marketing materials (print and online): The company's marketing strategy and customer communication style
Company publications (print and online): Key events, stories about employees, new products
Your social network contacts: Names and job titles of potential contacts within a company
Points to Learn About the Organization
Full name
Location (headquarters and divisions, branches, subsidiaries, or other units)
Ownership (public or private; whether it is owned by another company)
Brief history
Products and services
Industry position (whether the company is a leader or a minor player; whether it is an innovator or more of a follower)
Key financial points (such as stock price and trends, if a public company)
Growth prospects (whether the company is investing in its future through research and development; whether it is in a thriving industry)
Points to Learn About the Position
Title
Functions and responsibilities
Qualifications and expectations
Possible career paths
Salary range
Travel expectations and opportunities
Relocation expectations and opportunities

Thinking Ahead About Questions

Planning ahead for the interviewer's questions will help you handle them more confidently and successfully. You'll also want to prepare insightful questions of your own.

Plan for the Employer's Questions

Many general interview questions are "stock" queries you can expect to hear again and again during your interviews. Get ready to face these six at the very least:

- **What is the hardest decision you've ever had to make?** Be prepared with a good example that isn't too personal. Be ready to explain why the decision was difficult, how you made the choice you made, and what you learned from the experience.
- **What is your greatest weakness?** This question seems to be a favorite of some interviewers, although it rarely yields useful information. One good strategy is to mention a skill or attribute you haven't had the opportunity to develop yet but would like to in your next position. Another option is to discuss a past shortcoming you took steps to correct.
- **Where do you want to be five years from now?** This question tests whether you're merely using this job as a stopover until something better comes along and whether you've given thought to your long-term goals. Your answer should reflect your desire to contribute to the employer's long-term goals, not just your own goals. Whether this question often yields useful information is also a matter of debate, but be prepared to answer it.
- **What didn't you like about previous jobs you've held?** Answer this one carefully: the interviewer is trying to predict whether you'll be an unhappy or difficult employee. Describe something that you didn't like in a way that puts you in a positive light, such as having limited opportunities to apply your skills or education. Avoid making negative comments about former employers or colleagues.
- **Tell me something about yourself.** One good strategy is to briefly share the "story of you" (see page 452)—quickly summarizing where you have been and where you would like to go—in a way that aligns your interests with the company's. Or you can focus on a specific skill you know is valuable to the company, share something business-relevant that you are passionate about, or offer a short summary of what colleagues or customers think about you. Whatever tactic you choose, this is not the time to be shy or indecisive; be ready with a confident, memorable answer.
- **How do you spend your free time?** This question can pop up late in an interview, after the interviewer has covered the major work-related questions and wants to get a better idea of what sort of person you are. Prepare an answer that is honest and that puts you in a positive light. Don't reveal anything that could suggest that you might not fit in the corporate culture. Sports, hobbies, reading, spending time with family, and volunteer work are all safe answers here.

Continue your preparation by planning a brief answer to each question in Table 14.

Table 14.3 Twenty-Five Common Interview Questions

Questions about School
1. What courses in school did you like most? Least? Why?
2. Do you think your extracurricular activities in school were worth the time you spent on them? Why or why not?
3. When did you choose your major (if applicable)? Did you ever change your major? If so, why?
4. Do you feel you did the best scholastic work you are capable of?
5. How has your education prepared you for this position?
Questions about Employers and Jobs
6. Why did you leave your last job?
7. Why did you apply for this job opening?
8. Why did you choose your particular field of work?
9. What are the disadvantages of your chosen field?
10. What do you know about our company?
11. What do you think about how this industry operates today?
12. Why do you think you would like this particular type of job?
Questions about Work Experiences and Expectations
13. What was your biggest failure?
14. Describe an experience in which you learned from one of your mistakes.
15. What motivates you? Why?
16. What do you think determines a person's progress in a good organization?
17. Are you a leader or a follower?
18. What have you done that shows initiative and willingness to work?
19. Why should I hire you?
Questions about Work Habits
20. Do you prefer working with others or by yourself?
21. What type of boss do you prefer?
22. Have you ever had any difficulty getting along with colleagues or supervisors? With instructors? With other students?
23. What would you do if you were given an unrealistic deadline for a task or project?
24. How do you feel about overtime work?
25. How do you handle stress or pressure on the job?

As you prepare your answers, look for ways to frame your responses as quick stories rather than simple declarative answers. Cohesive stories tend to stick in the listener's mind more effectively than disconnected facts and statements.

Plan Questions of Your Own

Remember that an interview is a two-way conversation in which the questions you ask are just as important as the answers you provide. When you ask insightful questions, you demonstrate your understanding of the organization, steer the discussion into areas that allow you to present your qualifications to best advantage, and verify for yourself whether this is a good opportunity. Plus, interviewers expect you to ask questions and look negatively on candidates who don't have any questions to ask. For good questions that you might use as a starting point, see Table 14.4

Table 14.4 Ten Questions to Consider Asking an Interviewer

Question	Reason for Asking
1. What are the job's major responsibilities?	A vague answer could mean that the responsibilities have not been clearly defined, which is almost guaranteed to cause frustration if you take the job.
2. What qualities do you want in the person who fills this position?	This will help you go beyond the job description to understand what the company really wants.
3. How do you measure success for someone in this position?	A vague or incomplete answer could mean that the expectations you will face are unrealistic or ill defined.
4. What is the first problem that needs the attention of the person you hire?	Not only will this help you prepare, but it can signal whether you're about to jump into a problematic situation.
5. Would relocation be required now or in the future?	If you're not willing to move often or at all, you need to know those expectations now.
6. Why is this job now vacant?	If the previous employee got promoted, that's a good sign. If the person quit, that might not be such a good sign.
7. What makes your organization different from others in the industry?	The answer will help you assess whether the company has a clear strategy to succeed in its industry and whether top managers communicate this to lower-level employees.
8. How would you define your organization's managerial philosophy?	You want to know whether the managerial philosophy is consistent with your own working values.
9. What is a typical workday like for you?	The interviewer's response can give you clues about daily life at the company.
10. What are the next steps in the selection process? What's the best way to follow up with you?	Knowing where the company is in the hiring process will give you clues about following up after the interview and possibly give you hints about where you stand.

Boosting Your Confidence

Interviewing is stressful for everyone and some nervousness is natural, but there are steps you can take to build confidence. Start by reminding yourself that you have value to offer the employer, and the employer already thinks highly enough of you to invite you to an interview.

If some aspect of your appearance or background makes you uneasy, correct or offset it by emphasizing your positive traits: your warmth, wit, intelligence, or charm. Instead of dwelling on your weaknesses, focus on your strengths. Instead of worrying about how you will perform in the interview, focus on how you can help the organization succeed. As with public speaking, the more prepared you are, the more confident you'll be.

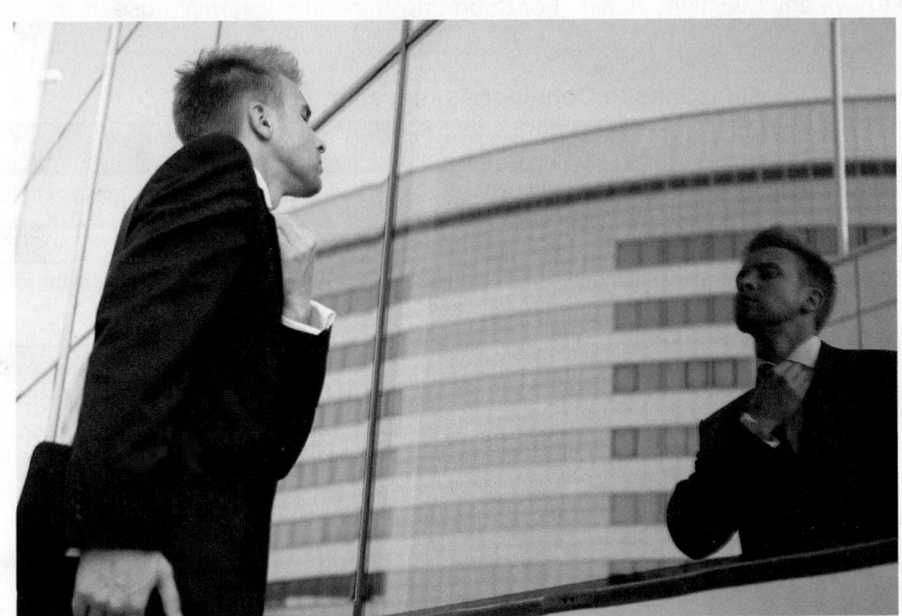

Figure 14.8
Making a Good Impression
A desirable job candidate projects confidence and professionalism, but not arrogance.

Polish Your Interview Style

Competence and confidence are the foundation of your interviewing style, and you can enhance them by displaying poise, good manners, and good judgment. Develop your interviewing style by staging mock interviews with a friend or using an interview simulator on your phone or tablet. Record these sessions so you can evaluate yourself. Your school's career center may have computer-based systems for practicing interviews as well.

After you practice, look for opportunities to improve. Have your mock interview partner critique your performance, or critique using the list of warning signs shown in Table 14.5. Pay close attention to the length of your planned answers. Interviewers want you to give complete answers, but they don't want you to take up valuable time or test their patience chatting about minor or irrelevant details.

Table 14.5 Warning Signs: 25 Attributes Interviewers Don't Like to See

1. Poor personal appearance
2. Overbearing, overaggressive, or conceited demeanor; a "superiority complex"; a know-it-all attitude
3. Inability to express ideas clearly; poor voice, diction, or grammar
4. Lack of knowledge or experience
5. Poor preparation for the interview
6. Lack of interest in the job
7. Lack of planning for career; lack of purpose or goals
8. Lack of enthusiasm; passive and indifferent demeanor
9. Lack of confidence and poise; appearance of being nervous and ill at ease
10. Insufficient evidence of achievement
11. Failure to participate in extracurricular activities
12. Overemphasis on money; interest only in the best offer
13. Poor scholastic record
14. Unwillingness to start at the bottom; expecting too much too soon
15. Tendency to make excuses
16. Evasive answers; hedging on unfavorable factors in record
17. Lack of tact
18. Lack of maturity
19. Lack of courtesy and common sense, including answering mobile phones, texting, or chewing gum during the interview
20. Being critical of past or present employers
21. Lack of social skills
22. Marked dislike for schoolwork
23. Lack of vitality
24. Failure to look interviewer in the eye
25. Limp, weak handshake

In addition to reviewing your answers, evaluate your nonverbal behavior as well. Include your posture, eye contact, facial expressions, and hand gestures and movements. Do you come across as alert and upbeat or passive and withdrawn? Pay close attention to your speaking voice. If you tend to speak in a monotone, for instance, practice speaking in a livelier style, with more inflection and emphasis. And watch out for "filler words" such as *uh* and *um*. Many people start sentences with a filler without being conscious of doing so. Train yourself to pause silently for a moment instead as you gather your thoughts and plan what to say.

Present a Professional Image

Clothing and grooming are important elements of preparation; they reveal something about a candidate's personality, professionalism, and ability to sense the unspoken rules of a situation. Your research into various industries and professions should give you insight into expectations for business attire. If you're not sure what to wear, ask someone who works in the same industry or visit the company at the end of the day to see what employees are wearing as they leave the office. You don't need to spend a fortune on interview clothes, but your clothes must be clean, pressed, and appropriate.

Figure 14.9 Choosing Interview Clothes
Even if the position for which you are interviewing has a casual dress code, you should wear your best and most professional business attire to an interview.

The following look will serve you well in just about any interview situation:

- Neat, "adult" hairstyle
- For more formal environments, a conservative business suit (for women, that means no exposed midriffs, short skirts, or plunging necklines) in dark solid color or a subtle pattern such as pinstripes; white shirt and understated tie for men; coordinated blouse for women
- For less formal environments, smart-looking "business casual," including a pressed shirt or blouse and nice slacks or a skirt
- Limited jewelry (men, especially, should wear very little jewelry)
- No visible piercings other than one or two earrings for women only
- No visible tattoos
- Stylish but professional-looking shoes; no extreme high heels or casual shoes
- Clean hands and nicely trimmed fingernails
- Little or no perfume or cologne (some people are allergic and many people are put off by strong smells)
- Subtle makeup for women
- Exemplary personal hygiene

An interview is not the place to express your individuality or to let your inner rebel run wild. Send a clear signal that you understand the business world and know how to adapt to it. You won't be taken seriously otherwise.

Arrive Prepared

When you go to your interview, take a small notebook, a pen, a list of the questions you want to ask, several copies of your resume (protected in a folder), an outline of what you have learned about the organization, and your past correspondence about the position. You may also want to take a small calendar, a transcript of your school coursework and grades, a list of references, and a portfolio containing samples of your work, performance reviews, and certificates of achievement. Think carefully if you plan to use a tablet computer or any other device for note-taking or reference during an interview. You don't want to waste the interviewer's time fumbling with it. And turn off your mobile phone; in a recent survey of hiring professionals, texting or answering a call during an interview was identified as the most common mistake job candidates made.

Be sure you know when and where the interview will be held. The worst way to start any interview is to be late. Verify the route and time required to get there, even if that means traveling there ahead of time. Plan to arrive early, but don't approach the reception desk until five minutes or so before your appointed time. Chances are the interviewer won't be ready to receive you until the scheduled time.

If you have to wait for the interviewer, use this time to review the key messages about yourself you want to get across in the interview. Conduct yourself professionally while you wait. Show respect for everyone you encounter, and avoid chewing gum, eating, or drinking. Anything you do or say at this stage may get back to the interviewer, so make sure your best qualities show from the moment you enter the premises.

Interviewing for Success

At this point, you have a good sense of the overall process and know how to prepare for your interviews. The next step is to get familiar with the three stages of every interview: the warm-up, the question-and-answer session, and the close.

The Warm-Up

Of the three stages, the warm-up is the most important, even though it may account for only a small fraction of the time you spend in the interview. Studies suggest that many interviewers make up their minds within the first 20 seconds of contact with a candidate. Don't let your guard down if the interviewer engages in what feels like small talk; these exchanges are every bit as important as structured questions.

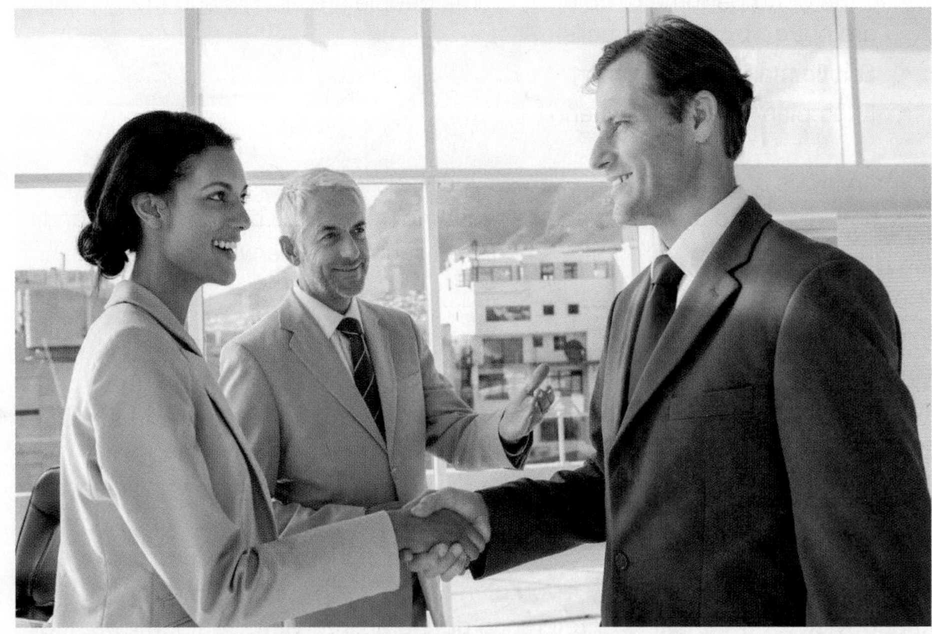

Figure 14.10
Initial Contact
At the beginning of the interview, it is customary for the interviewer and candidate to shake hands and introduce themselves.

Body language is crucial at this point. Stand or sit up straight, maintain regular but natural eye contact, and don't fidget. When the interviewer extends a hand, respond with a firm but not overpowering handshake. Repeat the interviewer's name when you're introduced ("It's a pleasure to meet you, Ms. Litton"). Wait until you're asked to be seated or until the interviewer has taken a seat. Let the interviewer start the discussion, and be ready to answer one or two substantial questions right away. The following are some common openers:

- Why do you want to work here?
- What do you know about us?
- Tell me a little about yourself.

The Question-and-Answer Stage

Questions and answers usually consume the bulk of the interview. Depending on the type of interview, the interviewer will likely ask about your qualifications, discuss some of the points mentioned in your resume, and ask about how you have handled particular situations in the past or would handle them in the future. You'll also be asking questions of your own.

Answer Their Questions and Ask Yours

Let the interviewer lead the conversation and never answer a question before he or she has finished asking it. Not only is this type of interruption rude, but the last few words of the question might alter how you respond. As much as possible, avoid one-word yes-or-no answers; instead, expand on a positive response or explain a negative response. If you're asked a difficult question—or the kind of offbeat questions that companies such as Zappos and Google are known to use—pause before you respond. Think through the implications of the question. The recruiter may know that you can't answer a question; instead he or she wants to see how you respond under pressure or whether you can construct a logical approach to solving a problem.

Whenever you're asked if you have any questions, or whenever doing so naturally fits the flow of the conversation, ask a question from the list you've prepared. Probe for what the company is looking for in its new employees so that you can show how you meet those needs. Also try to zero in on any reservations the interviewer might have about you so that you can address them.

Use Your Listening Skills

Paying attention when the interviewer speaks can be as important as giving good answers or asking good questions. Review the listening tips in Chapter 2. The interviewer's facial expressions, eye movements, gestures, and posture may tell you the real meaning of what is being said. Be especially aware of how your answers are received. Does the interviewer nod in agreement or smile to show approval? If so, you're making progress. If not, you might want to introduce another topic or modify your approach.

Handle Potentially Discriminatory Questions

A variety of federal, state, and local laws prohibit employment discrimination on the basis of race, ethnicity, gender, age (at least if you're between 40 and 70), marital status, religion, national origin, or disability. Interview questions designed to elicit information on these topics are potentially illegal. Table 14.6 compares some specific questions that employers are and are not allowed to ask during an employment interview.

Table 14.6 Acceptable Versus Potentially Discriminatory Interview Questions

Interviewers May Ask This . . .	But Not This
What is your name?	What was your maiden name?
Are you over 18?	When were you born?
Did you graduate from high school?	When did you graduate from high school?
Can you perform [specific tasks]?	Do you have physical or mental disabilities?
	Do you have a drug or alcohol problem?
	Are you taking any prescription drugs?
Would you be able to meet the job's requirement to frequently work weekends?	Would working on weekends conflict with your religion?
Do you have the legal right to work in the United States?	What country are you a citizen of?
Have you ever been convicted of a felony?	Have you ever been arrested?
This job requires that you speak Spanish. Do you?	What language did you speak in your home when you were growing up?

If an interviewer asks a potentially unlawful question, consider your options carefully before you respond. You can answer the question, you can ask tactfully whether the question might be prohibited, you can simply refuse to answer it, or you can try to answer "the question behind the question." For example, if an interviewer asks whether you are married or have strong family ties in the area, he or she might be trying to figure out if you're willing to travel or relocate—both of which are acceptable questions. Only you can decide which is the right choice based on the situation.

Even if you do answer the question as it was asked, think hard before accepting a job offer from this company if you have alternatives. Was the off-limits question possibly accidental and therefore not a major concern? If you think it was intentional, would you want to work for an organization that condones illegal or discriminatory questions or that doesn't train its employees to avoid them?

If you believe an interviewer's questions to be unreasonable, unrelated to the job, or an attempt to discriminate, you have the option to file a complaint with the U.S. Equal Employment Opportunity Commission or with the agency in your state that regulates fair employment practices.

The Close

Like the warm-up, the end of the interview is more important than its brief duration would indicate. These last few minutes are your final opportunity to emphasize your value to the organization and to correct any misconceptions the interviewer might have. Be aware that many interviewers will ask whether you have any more questions at this point, so save one or two from your list.

Conclude Gracefully

You can usually tell when the interviewer is trying to conclude the session. He or she may ask whether you have any more questions, check the time, summarize the discussion, or simply tell you that the allotted time for the interview is up. When you get the signal, be sure to thank the interviewer for the opportunity and express your interest in the organization. If you can do so comfortably, try to pin down what will happen next, but don't press for an immediate decision.

If this is your second or third visit to the organization, the interview may end with an offer of employment. If you have other offers or need time to think about this offer, it's perfectly acceptable to thank the interviewer for the offer and ask for some time to consider it. If no job offer is made, the interview team may not have reached a decision yet, but you may tactfully ask when you can expect to know the decision.

Discussing Salary

If you receive an offer during the interview, let the interviewer raise the subject of salary. If you're asked your salary requirements during the interview or on a job application, you can say that your requirements are open or negotiable or that you would expect a competitive compensation package.

How far you can negotiate depends on several factors, including market demand for your skills, the strength of the job market, the company's compensation policies, the company's financial health, and any other job offers you may be considering. Remember that you're negotiating a business deal, not asking for a personal favor, so focus on the unique value you can bring to the job. The more information you have, the stronger your position will be.

If salary isn't negotiable, look at the overall compensation and benefits package. You may find flexibility in a signing bonus, profit sharing, retirement benefits, health coverage, vacation time, and other valuable benefits.

Interview Notes

Maintain a notebook or simple database with information about each company, interviewers' answers to your questions, contact information for each interviewer, the status of follow-up communication, and upcoming interview appointments. Carefully organized notes will help you decide which company is the right fit for you when it comes time to choose from among the job offers you receive.

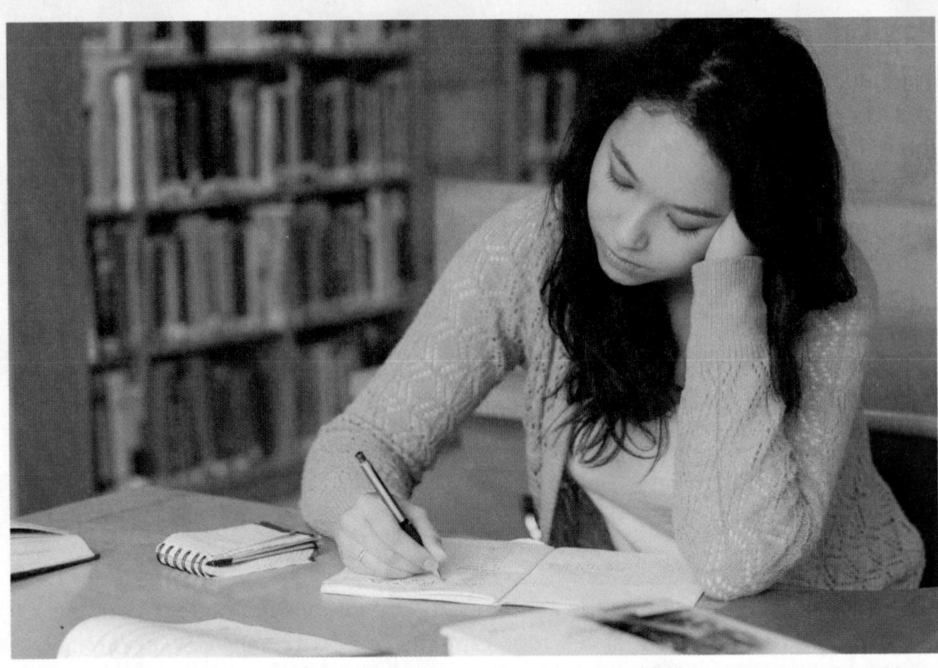

Figure 14.11
After the Interview
Make notes after each interview about who you met and what was discussed.

Following Up After an Interview

Staying in contact with a prospective employer after an interview shows that you really want the job—and are determined to get it. Doing so also gives you another chance to demonstrate your communication skills and sense of business etiquette. Following up brings your name to the interviewer's attention once again and reminds him or her that you're actively looking and waiting for the decision.

Any time you hear from a company during the application or interview process, be sure to respond quickly. Companies flooded with resumes may move on to another candidate if they don't hear back from you within 24 hours.

Follow-Up Message

Send a follow-up message within two days of the interview, even if you feel you have little chance of getting the job. These messages are often referred to as thank-you notes, but they give you an important opportunity to go beyond merely expressing your appreciation. Use the message to reinforce the reasons you are a good choice for the position, modify any answers you gave during the interview if you made a mistake or have changed your mind, or respond to any negatives that might have arisen in the interview (see Figure 14.12). Email is usually acceptable for follow-up messages, unless the interviewer has asked you to use other media.

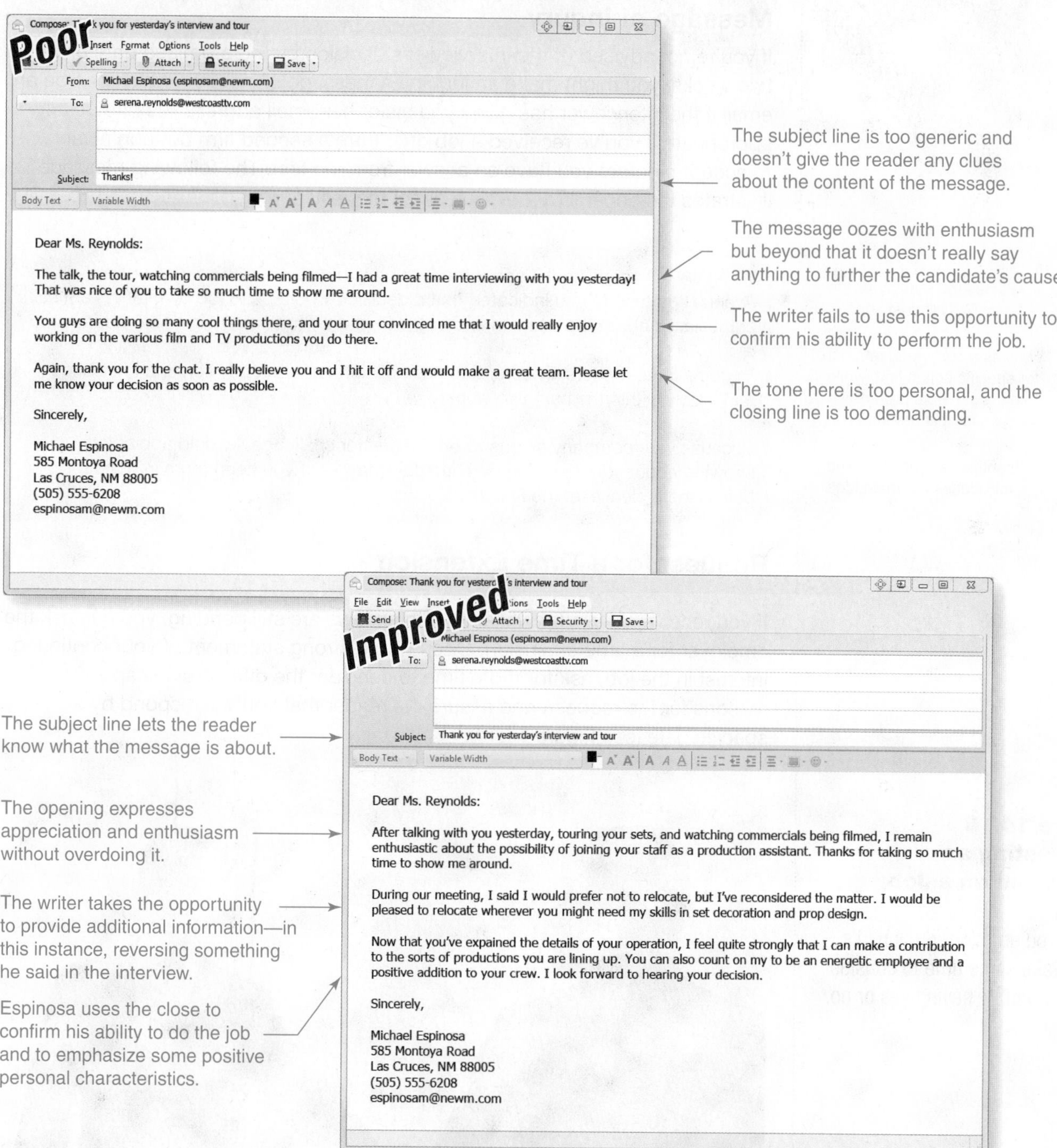

Figure 14.12
Follow-Up Message: Poor and Improved
Use the follow-up message after an interview to express continued interest in the opportunity, to correct or expand on any information you provided in the interview, and to thank the interviewer for his or her time.

Source: Microsoft Outlook 2013, Microsoft Corporation.

Message of Inqury

If you're not advised of the interviewer's decision by the promised date or within two weeks, you might make an inquiry. A message of inquiry—which can be an email if the interviewer has given you his or her email address—is particularly appropriate if you've received a job offer from a second firm but don't want to accept it before you have an answer from the first. The following message illustrates the general model for a direct request:

Places the reason for the request second →

Makes a courteous request for specific action last, while clearly stating a preference for this organization →

Identifies the position and introduces the main idea →

> When we talked on April 7 about the fashion coordinator position in your Park Avenue showroom, you indicated that a decision would be made by May 1. I am still enthusiastic about the position and eager to know what conclusion you've reached.
>
> To complicate matters, another firm has now offered me a position and has asked that I reply within the next two weeks.
>
> Because your company seems to offer a greater challenge, I would appreciate knowing about your decision by Thursday, May 12. If you need more information before then, please let me know.

Request for a Time Extension

If you receive a job offer while other interviews are still pending, you can ask the employer for a time extension. Open with a strong statement of your continued interest in the job, ask for more time to consider the offer, provide specific reasons for the request, and assure the reader that you will respond by a specific date (see Figure 14.14).

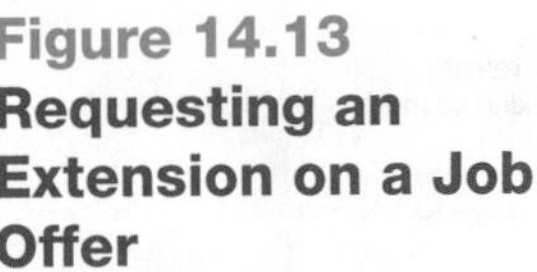

Figure 14.13 Requesting an Extension on a Job Offer
When you are offered a job, it's OK to take some time to consider the offer before saying yes or no.

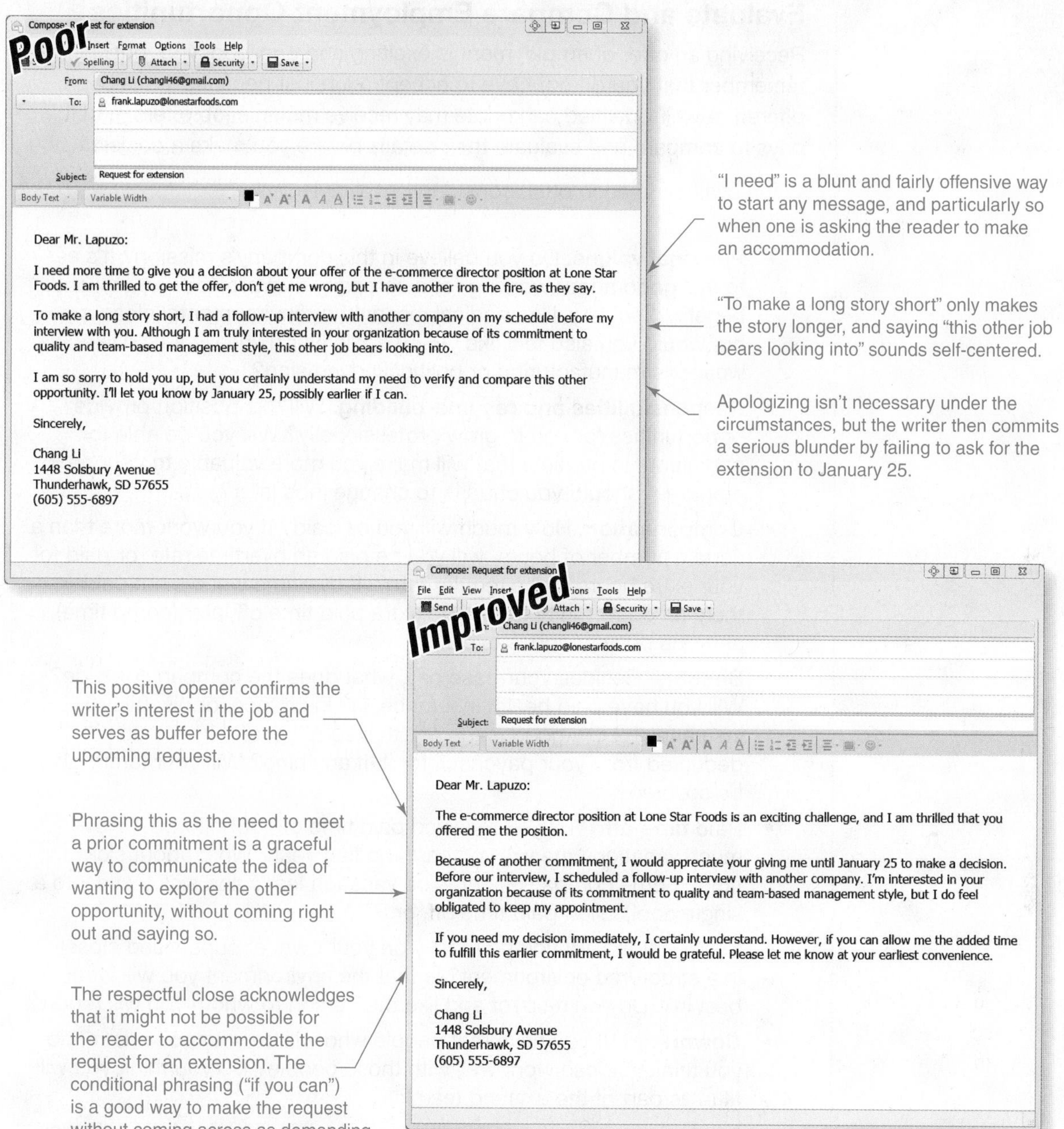

Dear Mr. Lapuzo:

I need more time to give you a decision about your offer of the e-commerce director position at Lone Star Foods. I am thrilled to get the offer, don't get me wrong, but I have another iron the fire, as they say.

To make a long story short, I had a follow-up interview with another company on my schedule before my interview with you. Although I am truly interested in your organization because of its commitment to quality and team-based management style, this other job bears looking into.

I am so sorry to hold you up, but you certainly understand my need to verify and compare this other opportunity. I'll let you know by January 25, possibly earlier if I can.

Sincerely,

Chang Li
1448 Solsbury Avenue
Thunderhawk, SD 57655
(605) 555-6897

Dear Mr. Lapuzo:

The e-commerce director position at Lone Star Foods is an exciting challenge, and I am thrilled that you offered me the position.

Because of another commitment, I would appreciate your giving me until January 25 to make a decision. Before our interview, I scheduled a follow-up interview with another company. I'm interested in your organization because of its commitment to quality and team-based management style, but I do feel obligated to keep my appointment.

If you need my decision immediately, I certainly understand. However, if you can allow me the added time to fulfill this earlier commitment, I would be grateful. Please let me know at your earliest convenience.

Sincerely,

Chang Li
1448 Solsbury Avenue
Thunderhawk, SD 57655
(605) 555-6897

Figure 14.14
Request for a Time Extension: Poor and Improved
Needing more time to decide on a job offer is not uncommon, particularly for candidates with desirable credentials. However, make the request in a respectful and subtle way. The reader understands you are comparing opportunities and looking for the best offer, so you don't need to belabor this point.

Source: Microsoft Outlook 2013, Microsoft Corporation.

Evaluate and Compare Employment Opportunities

Receiving an offer of employment is exciting and ego-boosting, but remember that you do not have to accept a job just because it has been offered. A well-qualified candidate may receive multiple job offers, and it pays to compare and evaluate their details before you make a decision.

When evaluating a job offer, consider the following:

- **Personal values.** Do you believe in this company's mission? It's easy to feel good about working for a company that provides an obvious benefit to society, like medical research or environmental cleanup, but would you also feel like your work is worthwhile in a field like weapons manufacturing or political advertising?
- **Responsibilities and resume-building.** Will this position provide opportunities for you to grow professionally? Will you be able to participate in projects that will make you more valuable to your next employer, should you choose to change jobs later?
- **Compensation.** How much will you be paid? If you work more than a certain number of hours, will you be paid an overtime rate, or paid for your extra hours at the regular rate? If overtime work is not paid, is there an opportunity to receive extra paid time off later (comp time), after the busy period is over?
- **Benefits.** Besides your base pay, what does the company provide? Will you have paid health insurance, life insurance, or disability insurance? How good is the health insurance, and how much is deducted from your paycheck for it, if anything? Will your family also be covered?
- **Paid time off.** Will you received paid time off for holidays? How much vacation time will you earn the first year? What about sick time? Some companies combine vacation leave and sick leave into a single pool called paid time off, or PTO.
- **Supervision.** Will you be mostly on your own, or supervised closely in a structured environment? Is that the environment you will work best in? Do you respect and like the person to whom you will report?
- **Coworkers.** If you have met people who will be your coworkers, do you think you can work well with those people? Do you think you will fit in as part of the existing team?
- **Work environment.** Is the environment you will be working in formal or casual? What will you be expected to wear, and how will you be expected to behave? Are you comfortable with those expectations?

Letter of Acceptance

When you receive a job offer you want to accept, reply within five days. Begin by accepting the position and expressing thanks. Identify the job you're accepting. In the next paragraph, cover any necessary details. Conclude by saying that you look forward to reporting for work. As always, a positive letter should convey your enthusiasm and eagerness to cooperate:

> I'm delighted to accept the graphic design position in your advertising department at the salary of $3,875 per month.
>
> Enclosed are the health insurance forms you asked me to complete and sign. I've already given notice to my current employer and will be able to start work on Monday, January 18.
>
> The prospect of joining your firm is exciting. Thank you for giving me this opportunity, and I look forward to making a positive contribution.

Confirms the specific terms of the offer with a good-news statement at the beginning

Covers miscellaneous details in the body

Closes with another reference to the good news and a look toward the future

Be aware that a job offer and a written acceptance of that offer can constitute a legally binding contract, for both you and the employer. Before you send an acceptance letter, be sure you really want the job.

Letter Declining a Job Offer

After all your interviews, you may find that you need to write a letter declining a job offer. Use the techniques for negative messages (see Chapter 8): Open warmly, state the reasons for refusing the offer, decline the offer explicitly, and close on a pleasant note that expresses gratitude. By taking the time to write a sincere, tactful letter, you leave the door open for future contact:

> Thank you for your hospitality during my interview at your Durham facility last month. I'm flattered that you would offer me the computer analyst position that we talked about.
>
> I was fortunate to receive two job offers during my search. Because my desire to work abroad can more readily be satisfied by another company, I have accepted that job offer.
>
> I deeply appreciate the time you spent talking with me. Thank you again for your consideration and kindness.

Closes with another reference to the good news and a look toward the future

Precedes the bad news with tactfully phrased reasons for the applicant's unfavorable decision

Lets the reader down gently with a sincere and cordial ending

Letter of Resignation

If you get a job offer while employed, you can maintain good relations with your current employer by writing a thoughtful letter of resignation to your immediate supervisor. Follow the advice for negative messages and make the letter sound positive, regardless of how you feel. Say something favorable about the organization, the people you work with, or what you've learned on the job. Then state your intention to leave and give the date of your last day on the job. Be sure you give your current employer at least two weeks' notice:

Uses an appreciative opening to serve as a buffer →

My sincere thanks to you and to all the other Emblem Corporation employees for helping me learn so much about serving the public these past two years. You have given me untold help and encouragement.

States reasons before the bad news itself, using tactful phrasing to help keep the relationship friendly, should the writer later want letters of recommendation →

You may recall that when you first interviewed me, my goal was to become a customer relations supervisor. Because that opportunity has been offered to me by another organization, I am submitting my resignation. I will miss my friends and colleagues at Emblem, but I want to take advantage of this opportunity.

Tempers any disappointment with a cordial close →

I would like to terminate my work here two weeks from today (June 13) but can arrange to work an additional week if you want me to train a replacement.

Discusses necessary details in an extra paragraph →

My sincere thanks and best wishes to all of you.

Figure 14.15
Letter of Resignation
Why do you think it's important that you maintain a professional tone when you resign from a job?

Chapter Summary

Submitting Your Resume

An application letter—also called a cover letter—introduces your resume, persuades an employer to read it, and requests an interview. Following the AIDA model, get attention in the opening paragraph. You might show how your work skills could benefit the organization, explain how your qualifications fit the job, or demonstrate an understanding of the organization's needs. To build interest and desire, show how you can meet the job requirements and refer your reader to your resume. Finally, to motivate action, ask for an interview and include your contact information.

Understanding the Interviewing Process

Most jobs require multiple interviews. These include screening interviews, which filter out unqualified applicants and identify promising candidates. Selection-stage interviews narrow the pool of applicants through a variety of structured and unstructured methods. In final-stage interviews, employers select the candidates who will receive offers and, if necessary, promote to them the benefits of joining the company.

Interviews can be structured or unstructured. They can involve one interviewer and one candidate, a panel of interviewers, or a group of interviewees. The purpose of the interview can be behavioral, situational, working, or stress-based. The most common is the behavioral interview, in which candidates are asked to illustrate their attributes using examples from past experiences. The situational interview is similar, but explores how the candidate would respond to hypothetical situations in the future.

Employers look for two things during an employment interview. First, they seek evidence that an applicant is qualified for the position. Second, they seek reassurance that an applicant will be a good fit with the "personality" of the organization and the position.

Preparing for a Job Interview

To prepare for a successful job interview, complete the research you started when planning your resume, and think ahead about questions you'll need to answer and questions you'll want to ask. Boost your confidence by focusing on your strengths and preparing thoroughly. Polish your interviewing style, present a professional image with businesslike clothing and good grooming, and arrive on time and ready to begin.

Interviewing for Success

An employment interview has three stages. The warm-up stage is the most important because first impressions greatly influence an interviewer's decision. The question-and-answer stage, during which you will answer and ask questions, is the longest. The close is your final opportunity to promote your value to the organization and counter any misconceptions the interviewer may have.

Following Up After an Interview

Following an interview, send a thank-you message to show appreciation, emphasize your strengths, and politely ask for a decision. Send an inquiry if you haven't received the interviewer's decision by the date promised or within one or two weeks of the interview—especially if you've received a job offer from another firm. You can request a time extension if you need more time to consider an offer. Send a letter of acceptance after receiving a job offer you want to take. Send a letter declining a job offer when you want to refuse an offer. Finally, if you are currently employed, send a letter of resignation after you have accepted the offer of another job.

Test Your Knowledge

1. What information or questions can you use when writing a follow-up message after submitting a resume?
2. What should your objective be for an interview during the selection stage?
3. How does a structured interview differ from an open-ended interview?
4. What are the three stages of every interview, and which is the most important?

Apply Your Knowledge

1. How can you distinguish yourself from other candidates in a screening interview and still keep your responses short and to the point? Explain.
2. How could use you the group interview format to distinguish yourself as a team player?
3. If you lack one important qualification for a job but have made it past the initial screening stage, how should you prepare to handle this issue during the next round of interviews? Explain your answer.
4. What is an interviewer likely to conclude about you if you don't have any questions to ask during the interview?
5. Why is it important to distinguish unethical or illegal interview questions from acceptable questions? Explain.

Practice Your Skills

1. **Revising Employment Messages** Revise this application letter so that it follows this chapter's guidelines.

> I'm writing to let you know about my availability for the brand manager job you advertised. As you can see from my enclosed resume, my background is perfect for the position. Even though I don't have any real job experience, my grades have been outstanding considering that I went to a top-ranked business school.
>
> I did many things during my undergraduate years to prepare me for this job.

Earned a 3.4 out of a 4.0 with a 3.8 in my business courses

Elected representative to the student governing association

Selected to receive the Lamar Franklin Award

Worked to earn a portion of my tuition

I am sending my resume to all the top firms, but I like yours better than any
of the rest. Your reputation is tops in the industry, and I want to be associated
with a business that can pridefully say it's the best.

If you wish for me to come in for an interview, I can come on a Friday afternoon
or anytime on weekends when I don't have classes. Again, thanks for considering me for your brand manager position.

2. **Revising Employment Messages** Revise this message so that it follows this chapter's guidelines.

Did you receive my resume? I sent it to you at least two months ago and haven't heard anything. I know you keep resumes on file, but I just want to be sure that you keep me in mind. I heard you are hiring health-care managers and certainly would like to be considered for one of those positions.

Since I last wrote you, I've worked in a variety of positions that have helped prepare me for management. To wit, I've become lunch manager at the restaurant where I work, which involved a raise in pay. I now manage a waitstaff of 12 girls and take the lunch receipts to the bank every day.

Of course, I'd much rather be working at a real job, and that's why I'm writing again. Is there anything else you would like to know about me or my background? I would really like to know more about your company. Is there any literature you could send me? If so, I would really appreciate it.

I think one reason I haven't been hired yet is that I don't want to leave Atlanta. So I hope when you think of me, it's for a position that wouldn't require moving. Thanks again for considering my application.

3. **Preparing for Interviews** Google yourself, Bing yourself, scour your social networking profiles, review your Twitter messages, and explore every other possible online source you can think of that might have something about you. If you find anything potentially embarrassing, remove it if possible. Write a summary of your search-and-destroy mission (you can skip any embarrassing details) in an email to your instructor.

4. **Researching Target Employers** Select a large company where you might like to work. Use online sources to gather information on the company; don't limit your search to the company's website.
   - What did you learn about this organization that would help you during an interview there?
   - What Internet sources did you use to obtain this information?
   - Armed with this information, what aspects of your background do you think might appeal to this company's recruiters?
   - If you choose to apply for a job with this company, what keywords would you include on your resume? Why?

5. **Preparing for Interview Questions** Prepare written answers to 10 of the questions listed in Table 14.3 on page 506.

6. **Assessing Your Strengths and Weaknesses** In an email to your instructor, discuss what you believe are your greatest strengths and weaknesses from an employment perspective. Next, explain how you think an employer evaluating your qualifications might view these strengths and weaknesses.

7. **Practicing Interviews (Team Project)** Divide the class into two groups. Half the class will be recruiters for a large chain of national department stores, looking to fill 15 manager-trainee positions. The other half of the class will be job candidates. The company is specifically looking for candidates who demonstrate these three qualities: initiative, dependability, and willingness to assume responsibility.
   - Have each recruiter select and interview an applicant for 10 minutes. Be creative with the questions and responses.
   - Have the recruiters discuss how they assessed the applicant in each of the three desired qualities. What questions did they ask or what did they use as an indicator to determine whether a candidate possessed the quality?
   - Have the applicants discuss what they said to convince the recruiters that they possessed each of the three desired qualities.

8. **Revising Employment Messages** Revise this message so that it follows this chapter's guidelines.

> Thank you for the really marvelous opportunity to meet you and your colleagues at Starret Engine Company. I really enjoyed touring your facilities and talking with all the people there. You have quite a crew! Some of the other companies I have visited have been so rigid and uptight that I can't imagine how I would fit in. It's a relief to run into a group of people who seem to enjoy their work as much as all of you do.

> I know that you must be looking at many other candidates for this job, and I know that some of them will probably be more experienced than I am. But I do want to emphasize that my two-year hitch in the Navy involved a good deal of engineering work. I don't think I mentioned all my shipboard responsibilities during the interview.
>
> Please give me a call within the next week to let me know your decision. You can usually find me at my dormitory in the evening after dinner
> (phone: 877-9080).

9. **Revising Employment Messages** Revise this message so that it follows this chapter's guidelines.

> I have recently received a very attractive job offer from the Warrington Company. But before I let them know one way or another, I would like to consider any offer that your firm may extend. I was quite impressed with your company during my recent interview, and I am still very interested in a career there.
>
> I don't mean to pressure you, but Warrington has asked for my decision within 10 days. Could you let me know by Tuesday whether you plan to offer me a position? That would give me enough time to compare the two offers.

10. **Revising Employment Messages** Revise this message so that it follows this chapter's guidelines.

> I'm writing to say that I must decline your job offer. Another company has made me a more generous offer, and I have decided to accept. However, if things don't work out for me there, I will let you know. I sincerely appreciate your interest in me.

11. **Assessing Ethical Dilemmas in Employment** You have decided to accept a new position with a competitor of your company and must write a letter of resignation to your supervisor. In an email message to your instructor, address the following questions:

    a. Will you notify your employer that you are joining a competing firm? Explain.
    b. Will you use the direct or indirect approach? Explain.
    c. Will you send your letter by email, send it by regular mail, or place it on your supervisor's desk?
    d. Will you notify your employer that you are joining a competing firm? Explain.
    e. Will you use the direct or indirect approach? Explain.
    f. Will you send your letter by email, send it by regular mail, or place it on your supervisor's desk?

Expand Your Skills

1. **Analyzing an Interview** Find an online video of a business professional being interviewed by a journalist.

   Your task: Using whatever medium your instructor requests, write a one-page assessment of the professional's performance and any tips that you picked up that could you use in job interviews.

2. **Writing a Solicited Application Email** Use one of the websites listed in Table 13.1 on page 455 to find a job opening in your target profession. If you haven't narrowed down to one career field yet, chose a business job for which you will have at least some qualifications at the time of your graduation.

   Your task: Write an email message that would serve as your application letter if you were to apply for this job. Base your message on your actual qualifications for the position, and be sure to echo the requirements listed in the job description. Include the job description in your email message when you submit it to your instructor.

3. **Writing an Application Email** Finding job openings that align perfectly with your professional interests is wonderful, but it doesn't always happen. Sometimes you have to widen your search and go after whatever opportunities happen to be available. Even when the opportunity is not ideal, however, you still need to approach the employer with enthusiasm and a focused, audience-centric message.

   Your task: Find a job opening for which you will be qualified when you graduate, but make it one that is outside your primary field of interest. Write an email application letter for this opening, making a compelling case that you are the right candidate for this job.

4. **Researching Target Employers** Research is a critical element of the job search process. With information in hand, you increase the chance of finding the right opportunity. You impress interviewers in multiple ways by demonstrating initiative, curiosity, research and analysis skills, an appreciation for the complex challenges of running a business, and willingness to work to achieve results.

   Your task: With a small team of classmates, use online job listings to identify an intriguing job opening that at least one member of the team would seriously consider pursuing as graduation approaches. Next, research the company, its competitors, its markets, and the specific job to identify five questions that will both help the team member decide if this is a good opportunity and show an interviewer that you've really done your homework. Go beyond basic, obvious questions to identify current, specific, and complex issues that only deep research can uncover. For example, is the company facing significant technical, financial, legal, or regulatory challenges that threaten its ability to grow or survive in the long term? Or is the market evolving in a way that positions this particular company for dramatic growth? In a post for your class blog, list your five questions, identify how you uncovered the issue, and explain why each is significant.

5. **Conducting Practice Interviews** You can improve your interviewing skills through observation and practice.

   Your task: Write a letter of application for an entry-level or management-trainee position that requires an engaging personality and intelligence but a minimum of specialized education or experience. Sign your letter with a fictitious name that conceals your identity. Next, polish (or create) a resume that accurately identifies you and your educational and professional accomplishments.

   Now, three members of the class who volunteer as interviewers divide up all the anonymous application letters. Then each interviewer selects a candidate who seems the most convincing in his or her letter. At this time, the selected candidates identify themselves and give the interviewers their resumes.

   Each interviewer then interviews his or her chosen candidate in front of the class, seeking to understand how the items on the resume qualify the candidate for the job. At the end of the interviews, the class decides who gets the job and discusses why this candidate was successful. Afterward, retrieve your letter, sign it with the right name, and submit it to your instructor.

6. **Conducting Practice Interviews** Select a company in an industry in which you might like to work and then identify an interesting position within the company. Study the company and prepare for an interview with that company.

   Your task: Working with a classmate, take turns interviewing each other for your chosen positions. Interviewers should take notes during the interview. When the interview is complete, critique each other's performance. (Interviewers should critique how well candidates prepared for the interview and answered the questions; interviewees should critique the quality of the questions asked.) Write a follow-up letter thanking your interviewer and submit the letter to your instructor.

7. **Writing a Request for a Time Extension** Because of a mix-up in your job application scheduling, you accidentally applied for your third-choice job before going after the one you really wanted. What you want to do is work in retail marketing with Neiman Marcus in Dallas; what you have been offered is a job with Longhorn Leather and Lumber, 65 miles away in the small town of Commerce, Texas.

   Your Longhorn interview was three weeks ago with the human resources manager, R. P. Bronson, who has just written to offer you the position. The store's address is 27 Sam Rayburn Drive, Commerce, TX 75428. Mr. Bronson notes that he can hold the position open for 10 days. You have an interview scheduled with Neiman Marcus next week, but it is unlikely that you will know the store's decision within this 10-day period.

   Your task: Write a letter to Mr. Bronson, requesting a reasonable delay in your consideration of his job offer.

8. **Writing a Letter of Acceptance** You have just received a job offer from your first-choice employer, Neiman Marcus, so now you must decline the other job offers you have received.

   Your task: Write a letter to R. P. Bronson at Longhorn Leather and Lumber, declining his job offer, and write an email message to Clarissa Bartle at Neiman Marcus, accepting her job offer. Make up any information you need when accepting the Neiman Marcus offer.

9. **Comparing Employment Opportunities** You have received offers of employment from two different companies. One is a small business that is directly in your field of interest. The atmosphere is informal, and you will have significant responsibilities very quickly. The other is a large company, where you would be a junior employee in a large department. There is plenty of opportunity for later advancement, although your duties will be routine and simple at first. The salaries and benefit packages are comparable, and the commuting distances are the same.

   Your task: Write a letter to someone who has been a mentor, teacher, or guide in your education. Tell him or her about the job opportunities, and explain which one you are going to take and why.

Word-Processing Basics

Appendix A

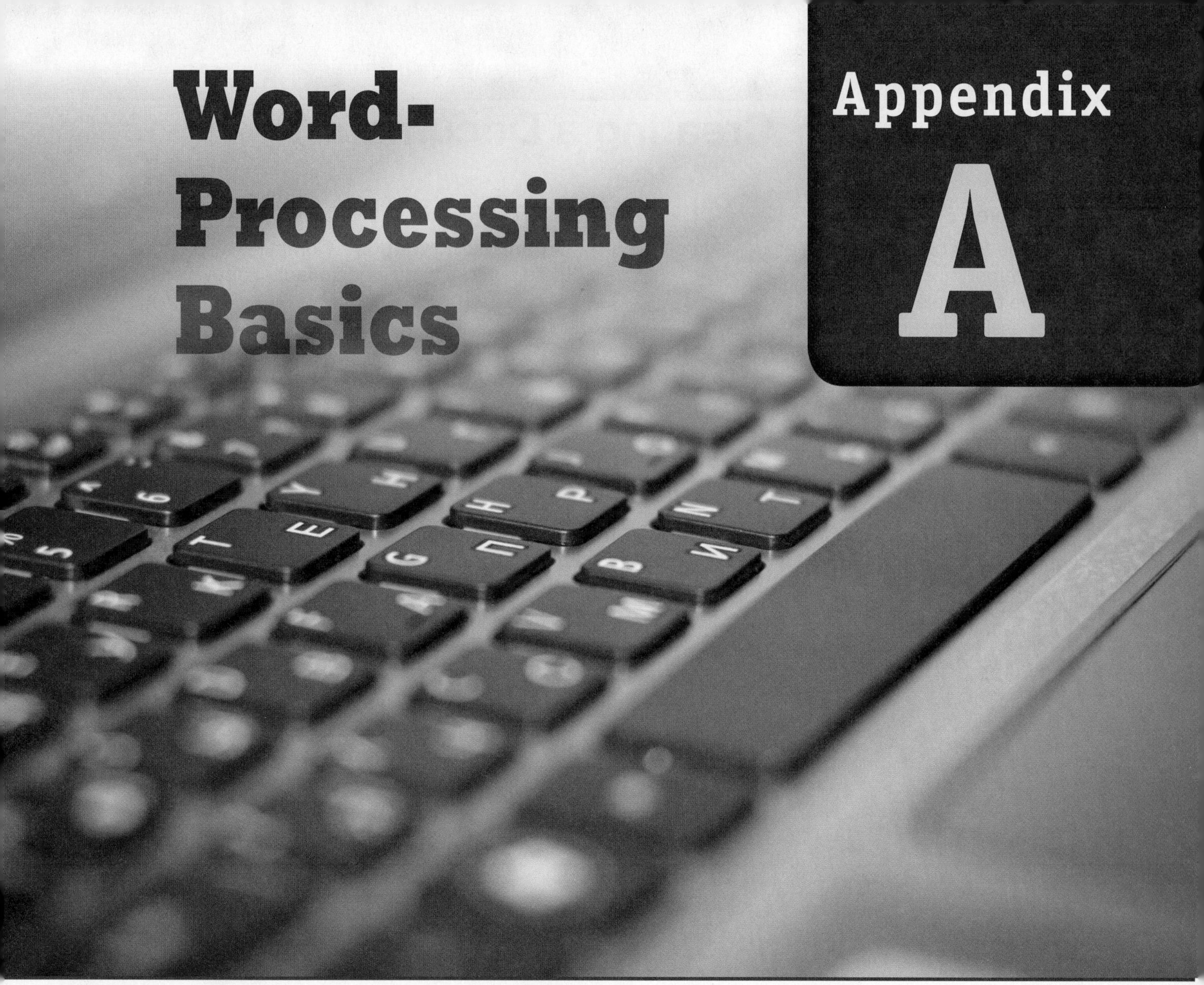

What Is Word Processing? In 1968, IBM first used the term *word processing*. The term described machines that could be used to type a document, remember the typist's keystrokes, and produce more than one copy. With this new tool, workers saved time.

That was just the beginning. Today's word-processing programs do much more. Suppose you were writing something by hand and made a mistake or changed your mind about what you wanted to say. If you were using a pen, you would probably cross out the words you wanted to change. Doing that leaves the page messy, though. With word-processing software, you can change the text and still create neat pages. You can even save what you typed and use it again a day, a week, or even a year later.

Lesson Appendix A–1

Creating a Document

Lesson Appendix A–2

Editing a Document

Lesson Appendix A–3

Formatting a Document

Lesson Appendix A–4

Basics of Desktop Publishing

Appendix A–1

Creating a Document

Objectives

- List the four basic functions of word-processing programs.
- Name two tools used to navigate a word-processing document.
- Summarize four key features of word-processing programs.
- Identify three standards for word-processing documents.

As You Read

Organize Information Complete a spider map to help you organize basic facts about word processing as you read.

Key Terms

- AutoCorrect
- autosave
- insertion point
- pagination
- word-processing program
- word wrap

Functions of Word-Processing Programs

Word-processing programs are used for creating and printing text documents. These programs have four functions:

- writing—entering text and symbols into a document
- editing—revising or reorganizing the text
- formatting—changing how the text looks on the page
- printing—producing a printed copy

These tasks do not need to be done all at once or even in the order shown here. Whatever the order, these four functions are at the heart of word processing.

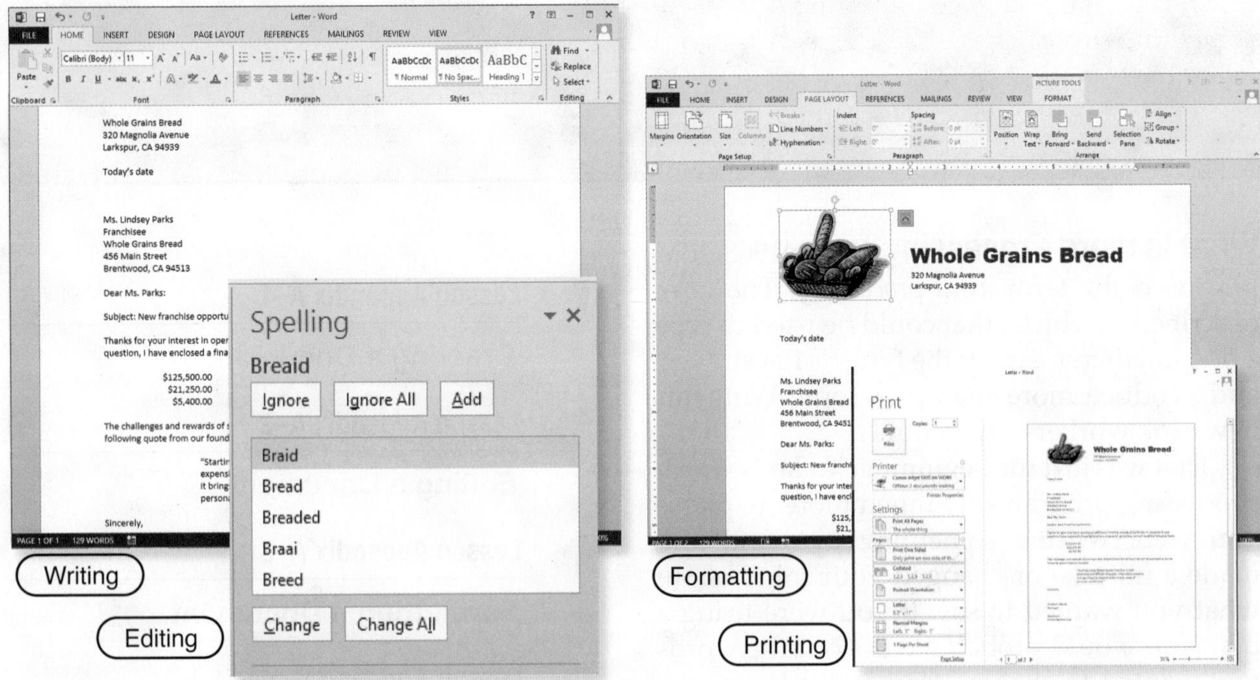

Figure A.1.1 The four main functions of a word-processing program.

Uses of Word Processing

Word-processing programs can be used to create almost any kind of printed document, such as letters, reports, and brochures. They can also be used to create calendars, return-address labels, and labels for homemade CDs. It is no surprise that word-processing software is the application that people use more than any other application.

Working with a Word-Processing Document

A new, blank word-processing document looks like a blank piece of paper on the screen. The program is ready for you to start writing. You can create another document at any time. For example, in Microsoft Word you create a new document by clicking the File tab, clicking the New command, selecting Blank Document, and clicking the Create button. Most word-processing programs allow you to create a new document using shortcut keys. For example, in a Windows-based program press Ctrl+N (hold the Ctrl key and press N). In Mac OS, press Command+N.

Click File > Save As to use the Save As command to save a new document. When the Save As dialog box opens, name your document, select a storage location, and click Save.

Insertion Point The **insertion point** shows where the text you type will appear. It moves as you type.

Scrolling As you write, you might want to reread or change something you wrote earlier. That is made easy by scrolling—using the mouse or keyboard to move through the document.

Some students sharpen their word-processing skills by writing to pen pals in other countries.

Think About It!

Before writing a letter, think about the topics you could cover. Which items listed below would you discuss in a pen-pal letter?

- your family
- your school
- your hometown
- your math class
- your favorite movie

Figure A.1.2 All word-processing programs share basic features, but commands may be located on a different toolbar or menu.

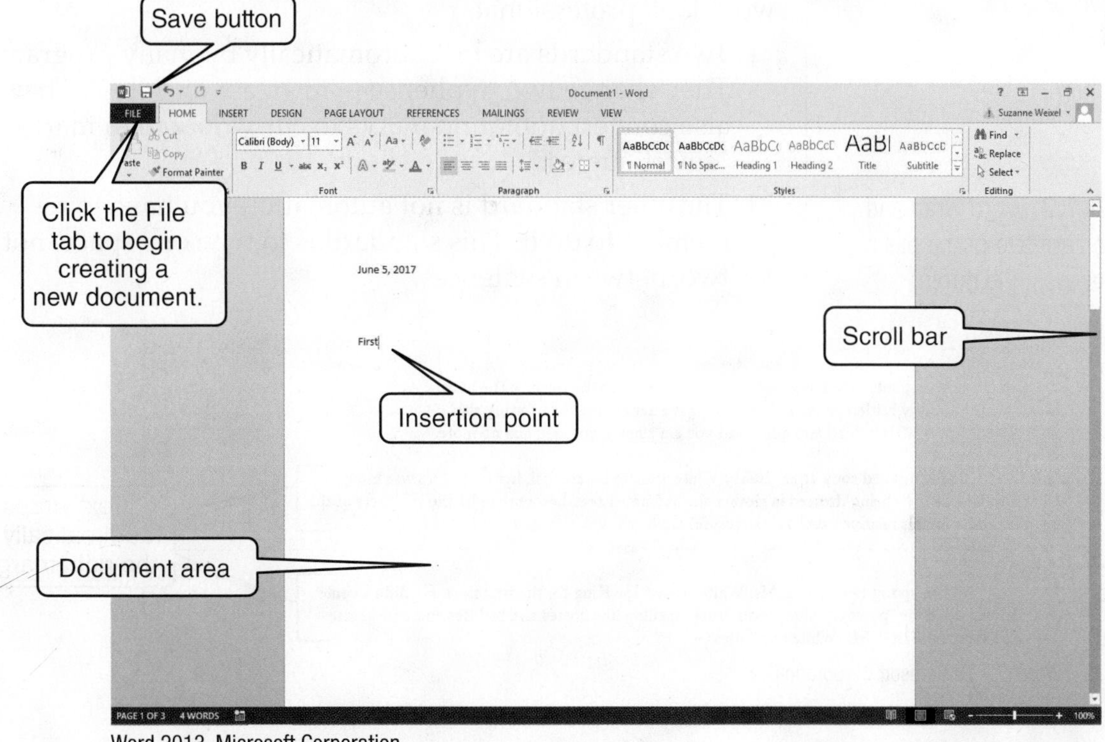

Word 2013, Microsoft Corporation.

Copy Editor Copy editors check documents for correct spelling, grammar, and consistency of style. Although some copy editors work on hard copy, or paper, many edit soft copy, or electronic files. Among the problems they look for are inconsistent or wrong formats, such as incorrect em dashes, en dashes, and spacing, or unacceptable hyphenation generated by the word processor.

You can scroll up or down by using the mouse to click the scroll bar or drag the scroll box at the right of the document window. Many mouse devices have scrolling wheels. You can also use the Up and Down arrow keys or the Page Up, Page Down, Home, and End keys to move around in the document.

Basic Features

Most word-processing programs have these features to help you write, edit, and save your work.

- With **word wrap**, the program automatically starts a new line, or "wraps" the text, when the current line is full. If you wish to force text onto a new line, press Enter or Return.
- When a page is full, the **pagination** feature automatically starts a new page. You can also force a new page by inserting a special character, called a page break.
- The **AutoCorrect** feature fixes common spelling mistakes as they are typed. You can turn off this feature or modify it to accept unusual words that you often use.
- The AutoRecover or **autosave** feature automatically saves a document as often as you want. If the computer shuts down accidentally, you can retrieve the most recently saved version.
- The spelling checker identifies spelling and grammar errors and suggests corrections. You can select a suggestion, ignore the error, or type the correction yourself.

Typing Standards for Word-Processing Documents

As you write, keep in mind three standards of style to make your work look professional.

- Two standards are met automatically by many programs. They change two hyphens (--) to an em dash (—). They also convert quotation marks to curly quotation marks, or "smart quotes."
- The other standard is not automatic—you have to remember to do it. This standard is to type one space, not two, between sentences.

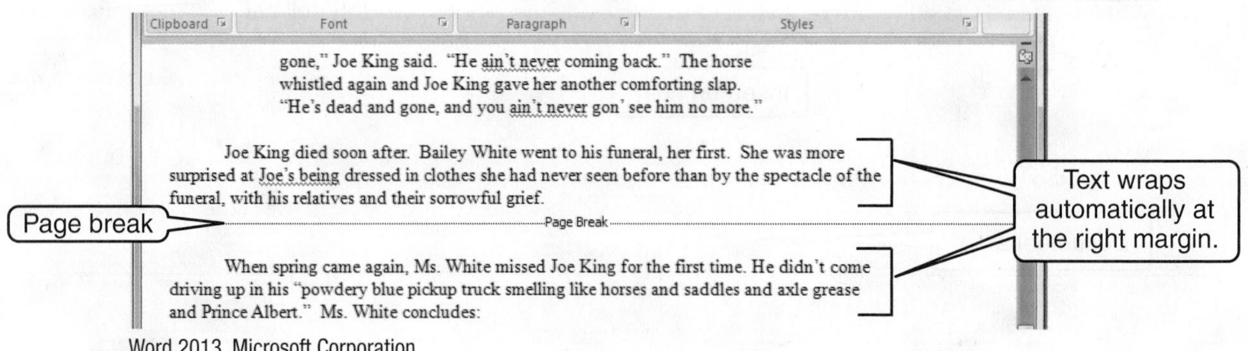

Word 2013, Microsoft Corporation.

Figure A.1.3 Word wrap and pagination are two of the basic word-processing features.

Editing a Document

Objectives

- Explain how to identify document files in a list of files.
- Describe the benefits of selecting text.
- Contrast different editing tools, such as the Cut and Copy commands, and the Undo and Redo commands.

As You Read

Identify Cause and Effect Complete a cause-and-effect chart to help you identify what happens when word-processing functions are applied as you read.

Opening a Document for Editing

Editing can take place at any time after you have created the document. You can go back and edit text you recently entered, or you can edit a document you created, saved, and closed. To do so, you open the file so you can work on it again.

You can use a word-processing program's Open command to open a file, or you can use your operating system's file management features to find files on a disk. In Windows, file names have extensions, such as .txt, .rtf, .docx, or .wpd, although these extensions may be hidden from view. On a Macintosh computer, documents are simply listed by file name.

Word-processing programs make editing easy. You can add words simply by typing them. You can delete characters by pressing the Delete or Backspace keys. Powerful features in these programs help you do even more.

Key Terms

- Clipboard
- Copy
- Cut
- data source
- mail merge
- Paste
- Redo
- select
- Undo

Selecting Text

To change text already entered in a document, you must **select** it. Then you can delete it, move it, copy it, or change its formatting.

To select text, click and drag over the text you want. Most programs also let you select text by using the keyboard. You hold down the Shift key while you use the arrow keys and other keys to select the text. Selected text is highlighted on the screen; that is, it appears with a different background color. To help you select just the text you need, use the Show/Hide command to display nonprinting characters, such as paragraph marks, tabs, and spaces.

Businesses sometimes use text called boilerplate. This is text that is used exactly the same way in many places to make certain that wording or features stay consistent in the same document or in many documents.

Think About It!

Identify which word-processing actions listed below would be best for handling boilerplate.

- Copy and Paste
- Cut and Paste
- Select and Move
- Undo and Redo

Cutting, Copying, and Pasting

Two common reasons for selecting text are cutting and copying. Both actions place the text in the Clipboard.

The Clipboard The **Clipboard** stores cut or copied text while you work. Once you close the program or shut down the computer, items on the Clipboard are no longer available. Some programs store only one item at a time, so cutting or copying new text replaces what was held before. Some programs can hold many items on the Clipboard.

- The **Cut** command removes the selected text from a document and places it on the Clipboard.
- The **Copy** command places a duplicate of the selected text on the Clipboard.

Pasting Use the **Paste** command to insert an item copied or cut to the Clipboard. Simply place the insertion point where you want the item to appear. Then, click the Paste icon on the Clipboard group of the Home tab or press Ctrl+V. The copied item or text appears where you want it.

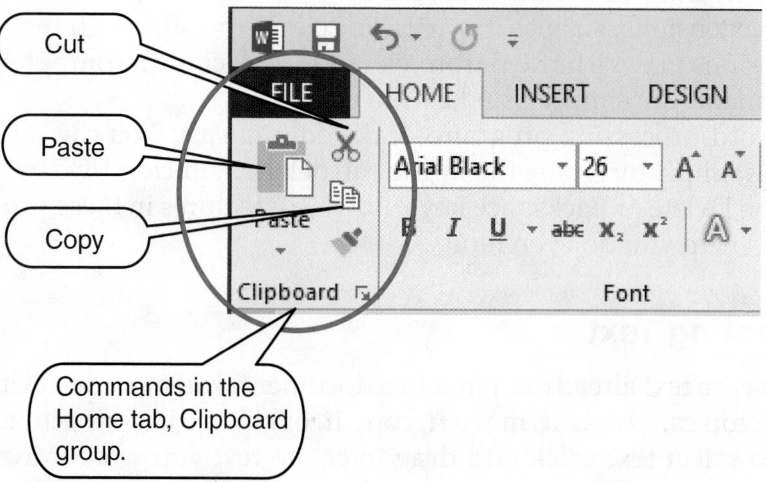

Word 2013, Microsoft Corporation.

Figure A.2.1 The Cut, Copy, and Paste buttons are located in the Clipboard group in Microsoft Word.

Moving Moving a sentence from the middle of a paragraph to the beginning can be done by selecting and dragging it. You can use Cut and Paste to move that sentence farther—for example, to another page—or to move text or a graphic from one document to another. You can even open a new window, paste the text you cut from another document, and save the pasted text as a new document.

Copying Copying and pasting saves time when you need to repeat some text. You can also copy and paste to bring a graphic from one document into another.

Undoing and Redoing

Word-processing programs have commands that can undo or cancel an edit. If you delete a word by mistake, you can use the **Undo** command to put it back. Many programs also have a **Redo** command. You can use this feature to put a change back in effect after cancelling it with Undo.

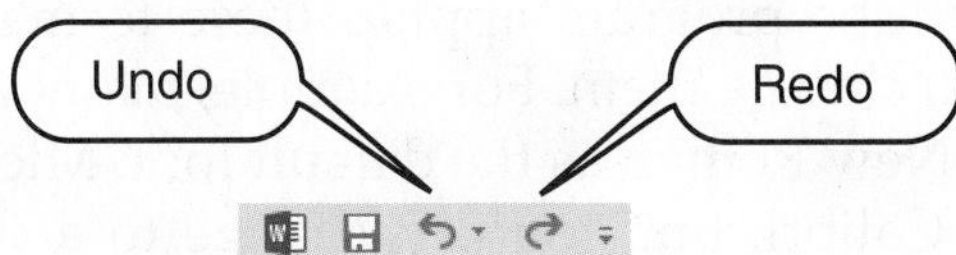

Word 2013, Microsoft Corporation.

Figure A.2.2 The Undo and Redo commands are on the Quick Access toolbar in Microsoft Office programs.

Merging

Most word-processing programs have a **mail merge** feature you can use to generate customized form letters, mailing labels, envelopes, and even e-mails. You create a word-processing document that includes the content you want everyone to receive and then merge it with a **data source** of customized information, such as names and addresses.

The Copy command isn't suitable if the copied text will change.

Think About It!

Think about what the Copy command does. For which items below would the copy command be useful? For which would it not be useful?

- the delivery address for letters to different people
- the cook's name on the top of recipe cards
- the title of a CD in a list of CDs
- a paragraph to appear in two different letters

Appendix A–3

Formatting a Document

Objectives

- Explain what default formatting is.
- Identify four parts of any document that can be formatted.
- Summarize the advantages of dividing a document into sections for formatting.
- Compare portrait and landscape orientation.

As You Read

Summarize Complete a summary chart to help you identify different features that can be formatted as you read the lesson.

Key Terms

- default
- page formatting
- sans serif font
- section
- serif font

Appearance Is Important

A document's formatting—its appearance—is sometimes as important as its contents. This is why word-processing programs have so many tools to format documents.

Word-processing programs include many preset formats, called **defaults**. The program applies these formats automatically, unless you change them. For example, many word processors use Times New Roman as the default font. Microsoft Word, however, uses Calibri, but you can change to a different font whenever you want.

You can format four distinct parts of a document: characters, paragraphs, sections, and pages.

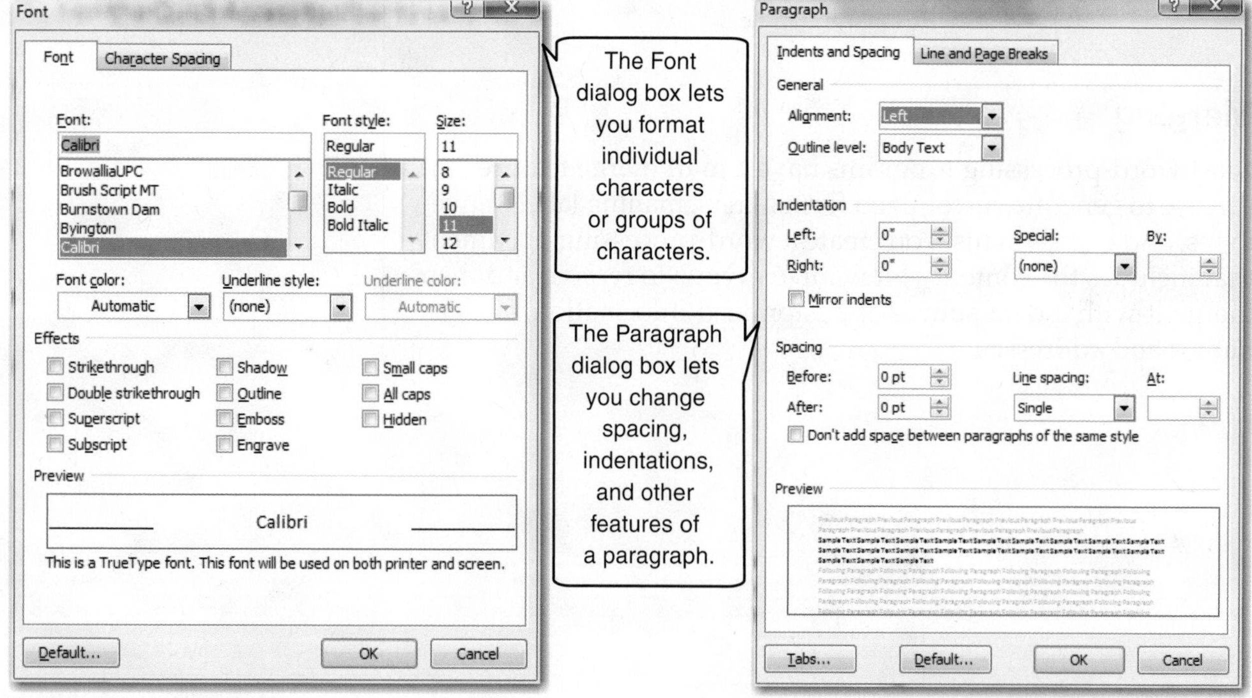

Figure A.3.1 Dialog boxes like these let you change all sorts of formatting options.

Word 2013, Microsoft Corporation.

Word 2013, Microsoft Corporation.

Formatting Characters

Character formatting lets you change the look of letters. Three primary formats are applied to characters:

- The font is the family of characters used. A font is a named set of characters that have the same appearance.
- Font size is the height of characters, measured in points. One point equals 1/72 inch.
- Font styles are characteristics such as boldface and italic.

There are four general categories of fonts. **Serif fonts**, such as Times New Roman, have serifs, or lines projecting from the ends. They are easy to read and are often used for document text. **Sans serif fonts**, such as Arial, do not have serifs, and are often used for headings. Script fonts are used to simulate handwriting. Decorative fonts have embellishments such as curlicues.

Categories of Fonts

Category	Description	Example
Serif	Serifs, or decorative flourishes, project from the ends. Easy to read in print. Often used for paragraph text.	Times New Roman Cambria
Sans Serif	No serifs. Often used for headings. Easy to read on a screen.	Arial Tahoma
Script	Simulate handwriting. Characters appear connected or almost connected. Formal script fonts usually neat and flowing. Informal script fonts usually messy and more natural.	Edwardian Script ITC Mistral
Decorative	Artistic. May have embellishments, such as curlicues. Also called ornamental or display fonts.	Jokerman Chiller

Formatting Paragraphs

A paragraph is any text that ends with the press of the Enter key. Whenever you press Enter, you create a paragraph. You can change many paragraph formats, including:

- Alignment—This is the way a paragraph lines up between the page's left and right margins.
- Line spacing—This is the amount of space between the lines of text in a paragraph.
- Indentation—This is added space between a margin and the text.
- Tabs—These are stops placed along a line. Pressing the Tab key moves the insertion point to the next stop. Tabs can be used to align text in tables or columns.

You can apply these paragraph formats through dialog boxes, but you also can apply some of them by using ruler settings. In Word, for example, you can create a tab stop by clicking the horizontal ruler at the point where the tab stop should be. You can change a paragraph's indentation by dragging indent markers, which normally are found at each end of the ruler. Ruler settings apply only to the paragraph that contains the insertion point, or to selected paragraphs.

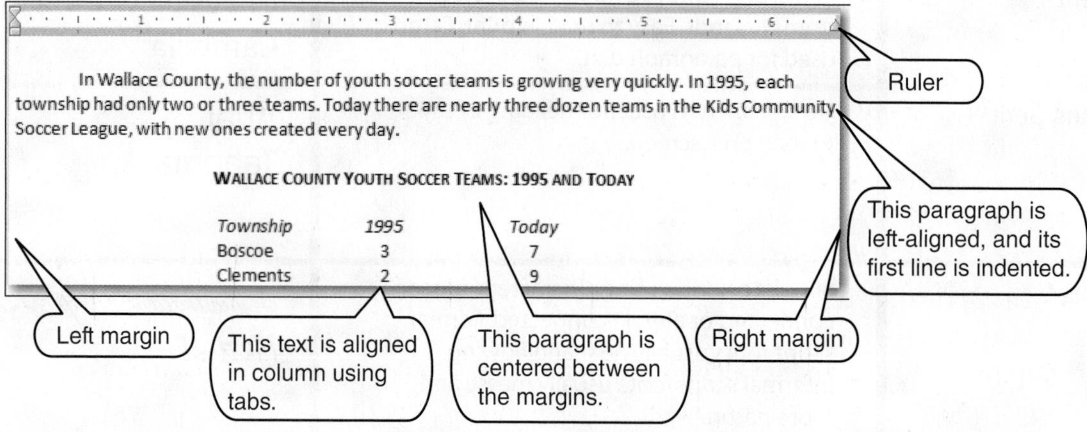

Figure A.3.2 A key feature of a word-processing program is the ability to align and position text on the page.

Formatting Sections

In some word processors, a **section** is part of a document that contains specific format settings. A document begins as one section, but you can insert section breaks to divide the document into more than one section. You can format each section in its own unique way. For example, in a most newsletters, the first section is one column, so the title spans the width of the page, but the next section is two columns, allowing more articles to fit on the page.

Formatting Pages

Page formatting affects how and where text is positioned on the page. The main features in page formatting are:

- Paper size—Various sizes of paper can be used to create documents.
- Orientation—Text can be printed in one or two directions, or orientations. In portrait orientation, text is printed down the page's long edge, creating a page that is taller than it is wide. In landscape orientation, text is printed down the page's short edge, creating a page that is wider than it is tall.
- Margins—This is the space between the four paper edges and the text. This open space frames the page and can make the text easier to read.
- Headers and footers—This is special information placed at the top of the page—headers—or at the bottom—footers. These areas can show page numbers, the date, or the document's title.
- Graphics—These include drawings, photographs, or other images. Some graphics, like charts and graphs, are informative. Others are decorative. Many word-processing programs let you create or add graphics.

Although many files are output electronically, most word-processing documents are designed for printing. Blurry or faded text, uneven margins, or incorrect paper size are just some of the printing problems that can ruin your final document.

Think About It!

How can you avoid the following printing problems before they occur?

- misaligned print heads causing uneven printing
- low ink or toner causing faded or missing text
- uneven margins causing the document to look unbalanced
- incorrect paper size causing the text to overflow the page
- incorrect paper size causing too much white space

Figure A.3.3 Word-processing programs let you print documents in portrait and landscape orientations.

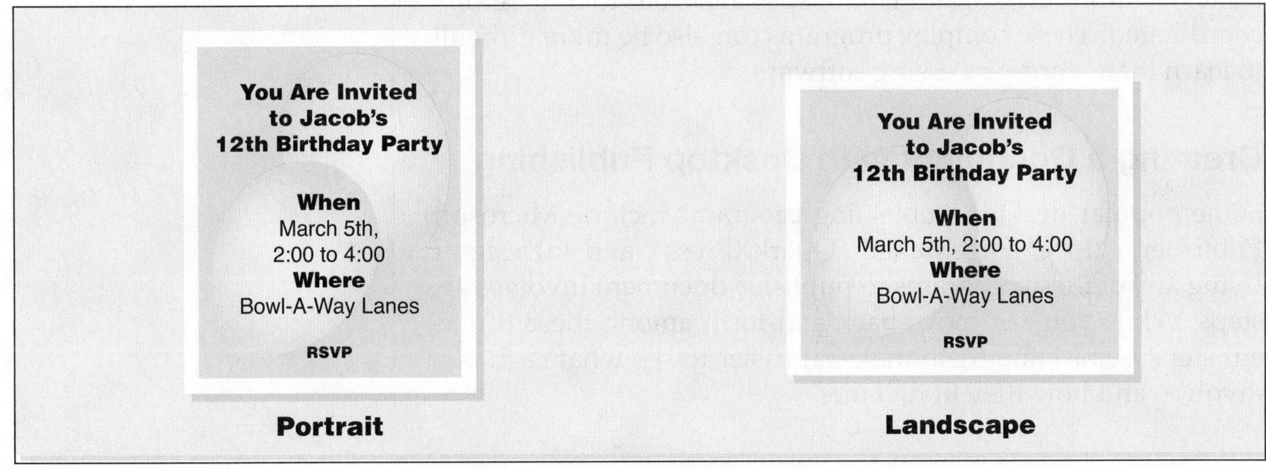

Appendix A–4

Basics of Desktop Publishing

Objectives

- Describe the benefits of creating documents in a desktop-publishing program.
- Compare word-processing and desktop-publishing programs.
- Summarize the basic steps in desktop publishing.

As You Read

Organize Information Complete a sequence chart to help you organize basic facts about desktop publishing as you read the lesson.

Key Terms

- crop
- desktop-publishing
- frame
- layout
- master page

Publishing from a Desktop

Desktop-publishing (DTP) programs are used to create high-quality publications that look as if they were produced on a printing press. They can be used to do some of the same tasks as word-processing programs, but they greatly expand design options so you can create high-quality documents.

Word-processing and DTP programs complement each other. In fact, they are often used together. Text is frequently created and edited in a word processor, and then that text is brought into a DTP program to be formatted for publishing.

Benefits of DTP Desktop-publishing software gives you tools you can use to produce the files and fonts for large projects, such as books, magazines, and other complex printed materials. DTP software also gives you more control over the final product than you would have if you hired a professional contractor or other "outside" source.

Drawbacks of DTP Desktop publishing is not without its problems. Often it is a team effort, which means that the work of writers, editors, artists, and layout specialists has to be carefully coordinated. These complex programs can also be more difficult to learn than word-processing software.

Creating a Document with Desktop Publishing

Some popular desktop-publishing programs include Microsoft Publisher, Adobe® PageMaker®, QuarkXPress®, and InDesign®. Using any of these programs to publish a document involves six steps. While you can move back and forth among these different steps, separating them makes it easier to see what each one involves and how they fit together.

Designing the Layout The most important task—and the one that is done first—is designing the document's **layout**. A designer plans how each page will look by creating a **master page**. This provides the pattern for all the pages to follow and sets the basic features of the document's look, including:

- page size and margins
- number of columns, width of columns, and space between columns
- type font, size, and treatment for all the major elements that will be repeated in the document, such as titles, headings, text, and headers and footers
- rules that will be followed in placing, sizing, and treating images

The columns on the master page create areas called **frames**. Frames are simply empty containers that will eventually hold text or graphics. They will be filled as you add text and images to the document.

Entering Text Text can be placed in the frames by typing it, but desktop-publishing software is not well suited to entering text. Therefore, text is usually created and edited in a word-processing program. Then, that text is automatically placed in the DTP frames, filling as many pages as needed.

If the writer has formatted the text by using styles in the word processor, the DTP software may be able to use those styles to identify and format different parts of the document automatically.

The Arts Desktop-publishing programs let you enhance a document in many ways. You can use color, large type, bold and italic type, drawings, and special effects to make the pages interesting. Experienced designers offer the following guidelines for using these tools:

- Use only a few fonts and choose appropriate ones for the task.
- Don't overuse color, bold, or italic type. Too much can make a document difficult to read.
- Use type size, space, and other elements to emphasize the most important parts of the document.
- Keep the reader in mind. Design a document so that it is easy to read and use.

Comparing Word-Processing and Desktop-Publishing

Word-Processing Programs	Desktop-Publishing Programs
Emphasizes content—the text	Emphasizes appearance—layout and the mix of text and graphics
Can import many kinds of graphics	Can import many kinds of graphics
Can format text in many ways	Has more tools for formatting text and for combining text and graphics
Can produce relatively simple documents, such as brochures and newsletters	Can produce very complex documents, including magazines and books
Effective at black-and white documents; not effective with full-color documents	Effective with both black-and-white and full-color documents
Prints on standard office machines such as laser and inkjet printers	Prints on high-quality printers

Workers who do desktop publishing are called graphic designers. There are about 200,000 graphic designers in the United States. Most work for companies, but about one third work for themselves.

The Bureau of Labor Statistics says that in the next few years the number of jobs for desktop publishers will grow by a huge amount—about 67 percent.

Interested students can take courses in design at some colleges and professional schools. Of course, experience in using computers is a great plus!

Importing Graphics After the text has been imported, images can be added. A location for each image is found. The text then wraps around the art.

Laying Out the Document A DTP user then formats the document by adjusting the size of art and the use of space to make the page attractive and easy to read. Program tools make it easy to change an image's size or shape or rotate it. Other tools can be used to **crop** the image, or trim it to focus only on certain parts.

Checking and Revising DTP documents are often printed several times before they are finished. Editors review these versions, called proofs, to make sure that no text has been lost and that the text reads correctly. Designers check design elements. Then DTP users make changes to the document.

Printing After the document is final, it is printed. Sometimes, DTP documents are published on the Web or are printed on powerful color laser printers. Items such as books and magazines are sent to printers who print and bind finished copies. For color documents, the DTP program can prepare color separations, which are separate versions of the document's pages. Each version contains a specific set of colors; each of which is applied in a separate pass through the printer. When the colors are combined, the full-color document is finished.

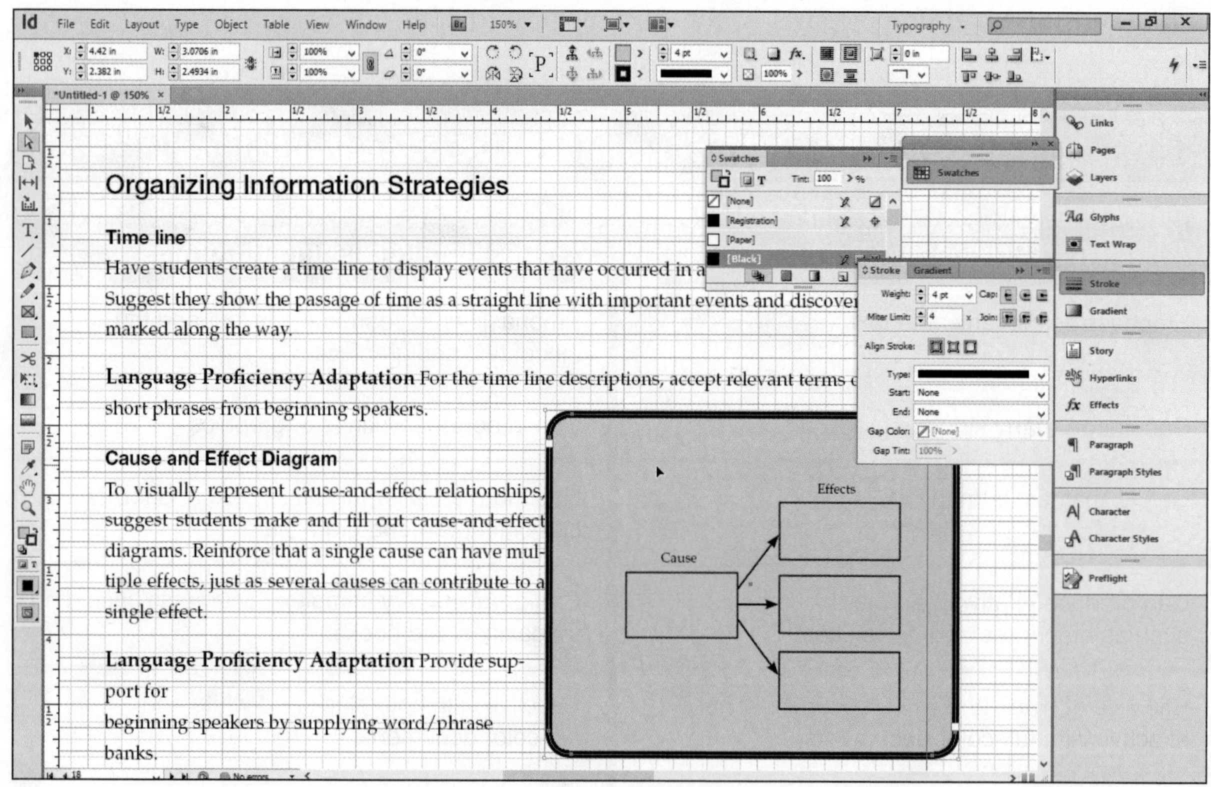

Figure A.4.1 Designing a page in a desktop-publishing program.

Using a Word-Processing Application

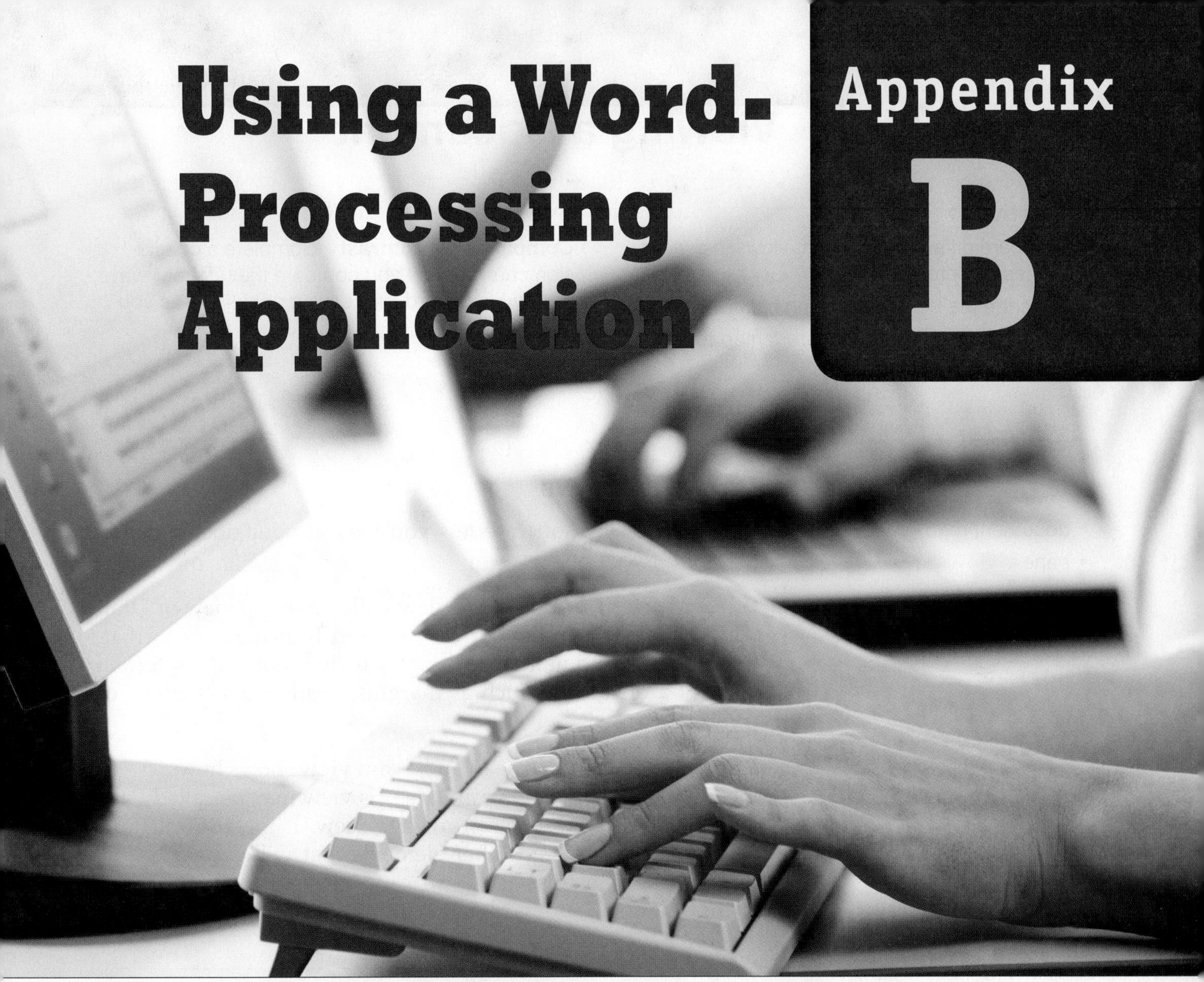

Appendix B

What Does Word Processing Do? In 1875, Mark Twain sent his publisher a historic manuscript. It was the first time that an author submitted a manuscript that had been written using a typewriter. Now, more than 125 years later, word-processing software does far more than a typewriter ever could. You can format text, add graphics, and even print documents in color.

In this appendix, you learn more about the word-processing tools you can use to create neat and professional documents. You learn how to select a view, how to insert pictures and symbols, and how to prepare a document for printing. Finally, you explore the options for collaborating with others to improve your work.

Appendix B–1 Viewing a Document

Objectives

- Compare different document views in a word-processing program.
- Describe the benefits of using split windows.
- Explain how to use a document map to move through a document.

As You Read

Compare and Contrast Complete a conclusion chart to help you compare the different ways of viewing a word-processing document as you read.

Key Terms

- document map
- pane
- Print Layout view
- Web Layout view

Changing Views

Word-processing software lets you look at your documents in several different views.

Basic View The most basic view, called Normal view or Draft view, shows text in the correct font and has character formatting like bold and italic. The basic view does not display certain parts of a document, such as margins, headers and footers, or columns.

Print Layout View The **Print Layout view** shows how a document will look when it is printed. This view may be called Page Layout view, Layout view, or Page view. It includes all text, graphics, margins, and other elements that will appear on the printed page. In this view, you can edit headers and footers, change margins, and work with columns and graphics.

Figure B.1.1 A Word document in Print Layout view.

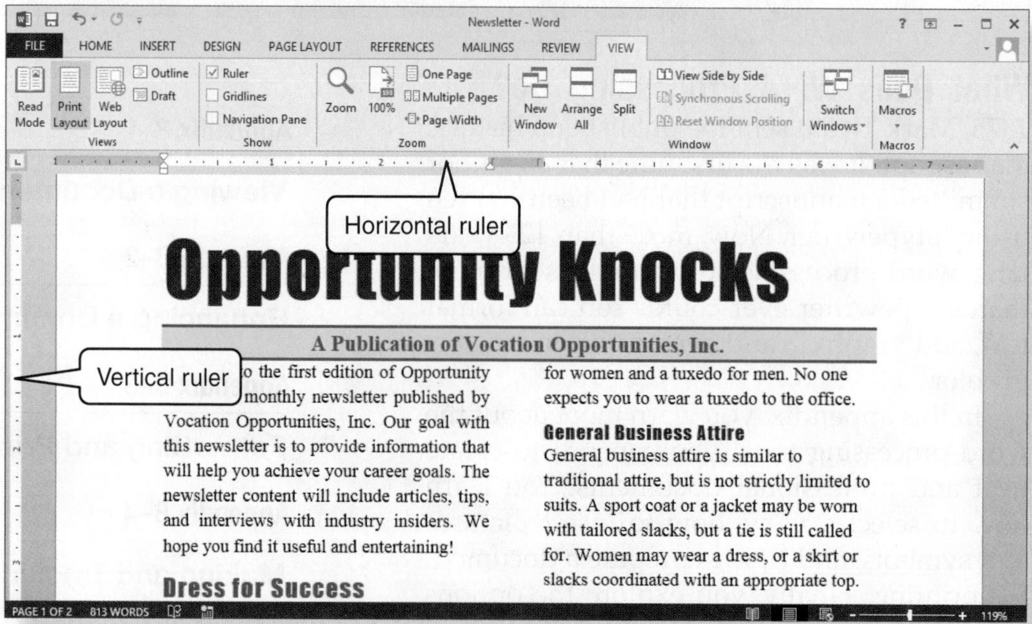

Word 2013, Microsoft Corporation.

Web Layout View Some word-processing programs have a **Web Layout view**, which shows how a document will appear when published on the World Wide Web.

Outline View An Outline view reveals the structure of a document. It breaks down the document into its major headings, subheadings, and text. You can choose to view only the main headings, both the headings and subheadings, or everything, including the entire text. This view is useful when editing a large document. Some programs let users rearrange large amounts of text simply by dragging outline headings from one place to another.

Ruler Settings Some views display a horizontal ruler—a guide at the top of the document window, showing you where each paragraph's tab stops and indents are located. In Word's Page Layout view, you also see a vertical ruler on the left side of the screen. You can use rulers to set margins, tabs, indents, and other paragraph formats.

Changing Views It's easy to change from one view to another. Just go to the View menu and select the option you want. Some programs also have small icons representing different views near the status bar. Clicking an icon changes the view.

Language Arts A writing style is a set of guidelines for the language, punctuation, and formatting of a document. There are a number of accepted styles, but many teachers prefer the *Modern Language Association* (MLA) style. Some examples of MLA style rules include double-spaced lines, 1" margins on all sides, and in-text citations of sources. Other commonly used styles include the *Chicago Manual of Style*, which does not require in-text citations, and *American Psychological Association* (APA) style, which is usually preferred for papers written about the social sciences. Before writing a research paper, ask your teacher which style you should use.

Zooming In and Out

The Zoom feature changes the size of the text displayed on the screen. While larger text is more readable, smaller text allows you to see more at once. But only at 100 percent will you have an accurate picture of the text as it will appear when it is printed. At this percentage, you get the benefit of a program's WYSIWYG (What You See Is What You Get) display, which means that the screen shows how the printed page will look.

Figure B.1.2 Use Zoom controls to change the magnification of a document display.

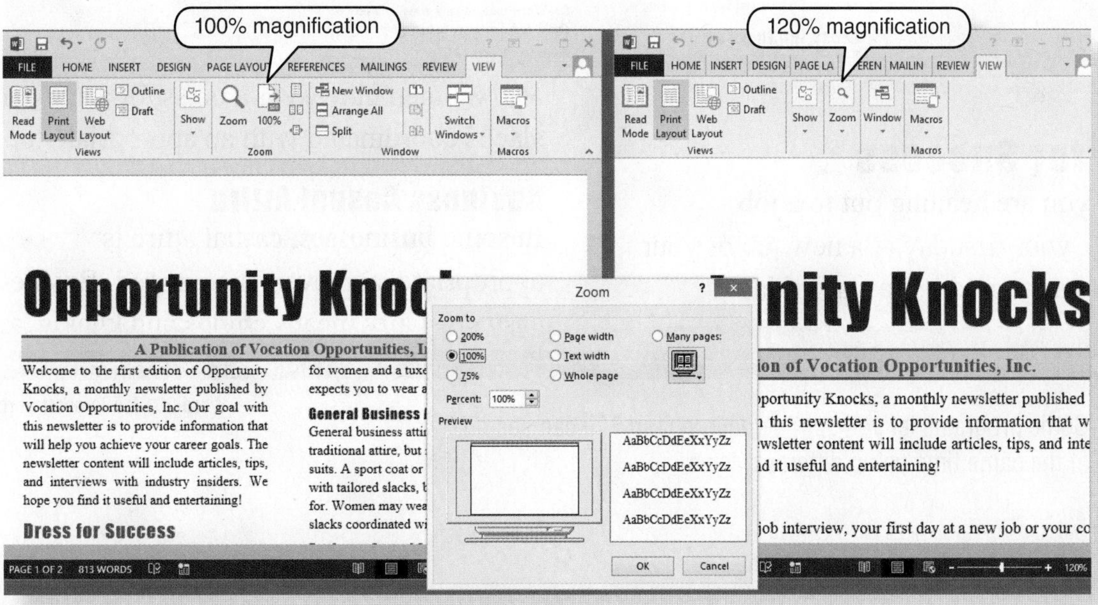

Word 2013, Microsoft Corporation.

Technical Writer A technical writer creates text-based documentation, such as user manuals for software, online help sites, guides for machinery, and design specifications for construction projects. In addition to being able to use words in a clear and concise manner to convey information, a technical writer must understand the topic about which he or she is writing.

Multiple Views of the Same Document

Some word-processing programs allow you to split the document window into two sections, or **panes**. This split screen lets you view two parts of a document at the same time. You can scroll through each pane separately to display any part of the document. This feature makes it easy to move or copy text from one part of a large document to another. You can also use this feature to compare discussions of the same topic in two different parts of a document.

Mapping the Document

Some programs also split the screen by showing text in one pane and a list of the document's headings in the other. This list is called a **document map** or navigation pane. You can use the document map to move about in the document simply by clicking a heading or by using a search feature. In some programs, you can change the display in the navigation pane to show thumbnails or icons representing each page. You can click a page to display it in the main document area.

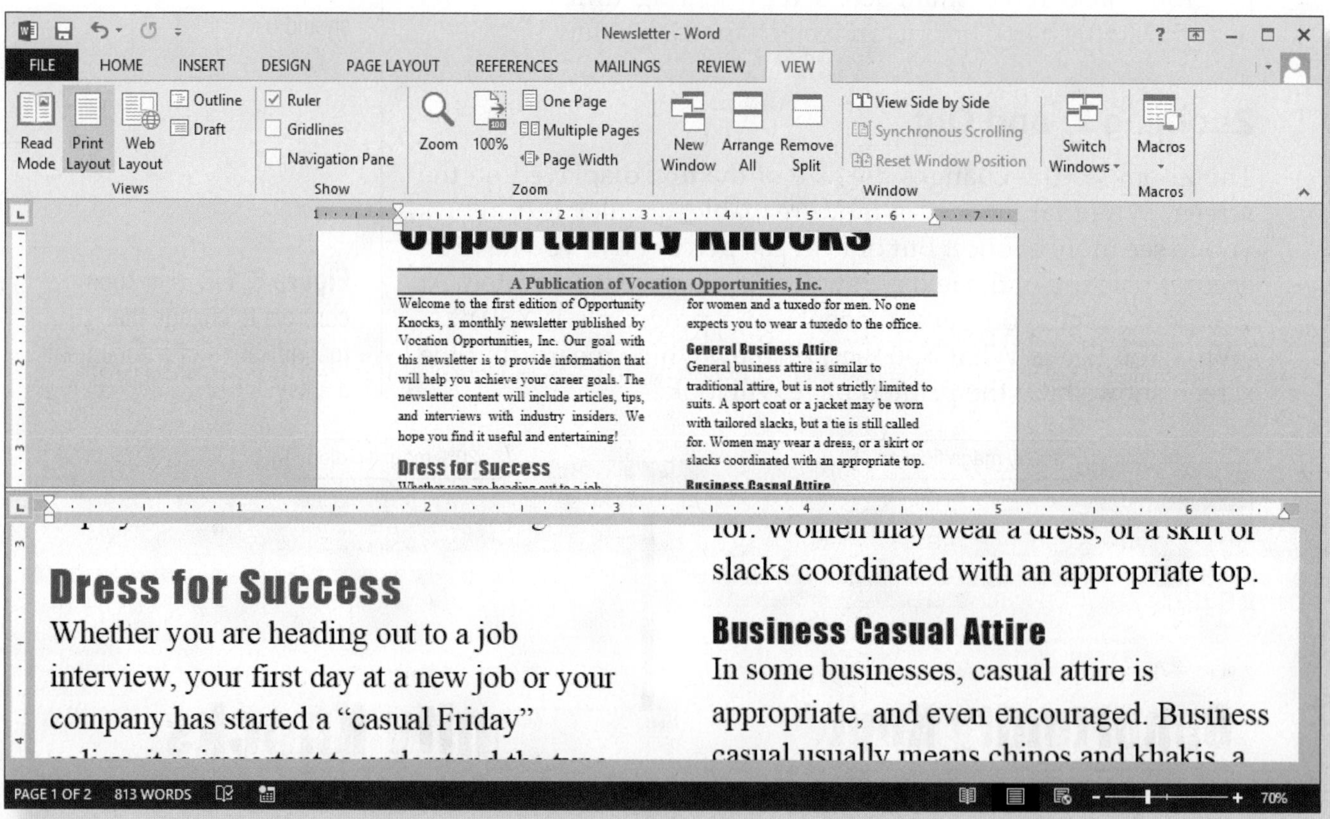

Word 2013, Microsoft Corporation.

Figure B.1.3 Some programs let you split a document so you can see different sections at the same time using different views.

Enhancing a Document

Appendix B–2

Objectives

- Identify the advantages of using keyboard shortcuts.
- Explain how to insert special characters or symbols.
- Describe the process for adding clip art.
- Describe uses for the find and replace features.

As You Read

Organize Information Complete a spider map to help you organize details about different editing features as you read.

Key Terms

- find and replace
- function key
- keyboard shortcut

Keyboard Shortcuts

Usually, you move the insertion point and select commands using the mouse. Sometimes you may find it easier and faster to keep the fingers of both hands on the keyboard. You may be able to use the keyboard to type, issue commands, and select options quicker than you can move a mouse through a series of menus.

Most programs offer **keyboard shortcuts**, combinations of keys that can carry out some actions. Usually, issuing these commands requires pressing the Control (Ctrl) key in Windows or the Command key in Macintosh in combination with some other key. Ctrl + C, for example, is a Copy shortcut on Windows computers. Some of the shortcuts use a **function key**, one from the row of keys at the top of the keyboard that are labeled F1, F2, and so on.

Common Keyboard Shortcuts

Command	Windows	Macintosh
Boldface	Ctrl + B	Command + B
Italic	Ctrl + I	Command + I
Underline	Ctrl + U	Command + U
Cut	Ctrl + X	Command + X
Copy	Ctrl + C	Command + C
Paste	Ctrl + V	Command + V
Undo	Ctrl + Z	Command + Z

Did You Know?

There are ways other than a keyboard to enter text into a document. For example, you can create digital text using speech-recognition software, a stylus pen on a tablet, or an optical scanner.

For some, these technologies provide opportunities beyond those available using a keyboard. Students with disabilities or with auditory or tactile learning styles may find these options enhance their academic skills.

Using Special Characters and Symbols

Most word-processing programs allow you to insert special characters and symbols. These are symbols and characters that cannot be created simply by pressing one key. Common symbols can be made using a combination of keys. For example, in some programs you can type (c) to make the copyright symbol ©.

There are too many special characters to have keyboard shortcuts for all of them. Many word-processing programs provide a dialog box that displays all the characters they offer. In Word, to choose a symbol, click the Insert tab and click the Symbol command in the Symbols group.

Adding Art

Suppose you are making a birthday card and want to add a piece of art to decorate it. Many word-processing programs make that easy by providing a collection of ready-to-use drawings called clip art. Most programs have an Insert command for inserting pictures and other media files from as many as three different places:

- the computer's hard drive
- a CD or DVD
- a Web site

Once you insert a picture into a document, you can resize it, move it, and even crop out parts you don't want to show. You can rotate it around an axis point. You can also add effects such as shadows or change the colors. You can also insert other types of graphics, including pictures, shapes, charts, and diagrams.

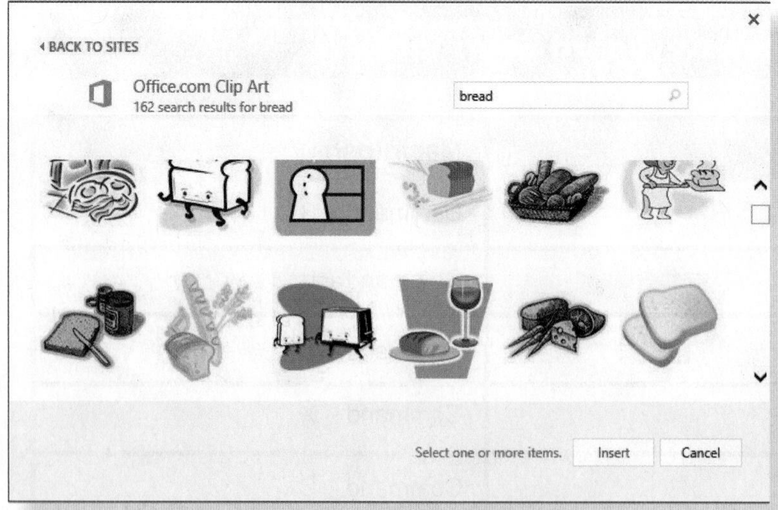

Figure B.2.1 Most word-processing progams like Microsoft Word provide access to online clip art galleries.

Finding and Replacing

Suppose you had written an essay about President George Bush. After finishing, you realized you had to make clear that you were writing about George W. Bush and not his father, George Herbert Walker Bush, who also had been president. You can use a powerful word-processing feature to search your essay for every time the name *George Bush* appears. You can even use the program to automatically replace every occurrence of *George Bush* with *George W. Bush.*

Using Find and Replace The **find and replace** (or search and replace) feature lets you:

- locate a word or combination of words
- change those words to other words
- search for text characters, including spaces, punctuation, and symbols
- search for text that is formatted a certain way

In most programs, you select the command for Find and Replace, and then use a dialog box to enter the text to find and the replacement text.

Cautions Use the search and replace feature very carefully. The feature looks for a specific set of letters, not just the word containing that set of letters. Suppose you type *his* as the search term and *hers* as its replacement. Since the program will replace every instance of *his* with *hers*, it will change *history* to *herstory* and *this* to *thers.*

You can avoid this problem by making sure you search for the word *his*, not just the letters *his*. The dialog box typically has an option for searching only for the whole word. Be sure to choose this option to avoid such errors.

Some businesses mail the same letter to many different customers. In these letters, all the text is exactly the same. Only the name and address changes.

Think About It!

Think about a word-processing feature that automatically makes the changes needed in these letters. Which features listed below would be useful for this purpose?

- changing document views
- formatting text
- inserting special characters
- find and replace
- merge

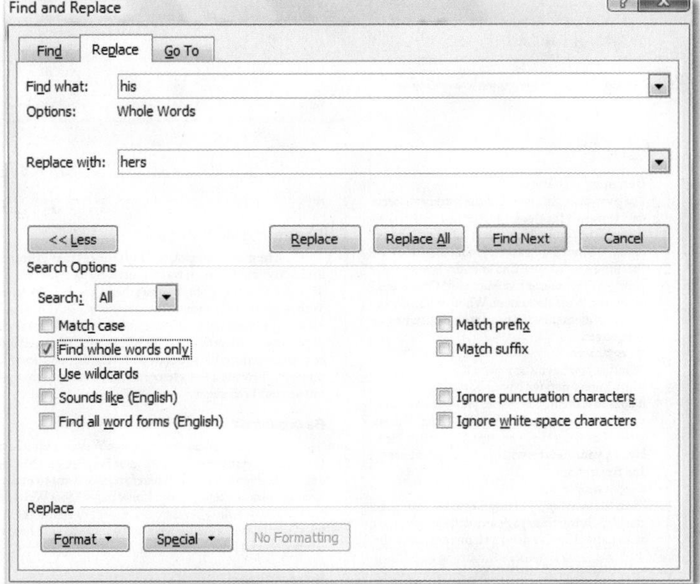

Word 2013, Microsoft Corporation.

Figure B.2.2 The Find and Replace feature can locate text anywhere in a document and replace it with different text.

Appendix B–3 Formatting and Printing

Objectives

- Explain how to use styles to format a document.
- Describe how tables can be used to display information.
- Describe the benefits of previewing a document.
- Compare print options.

As You Read

Outline Information Complete an outline to help you identify different ways of creating a professional-looking word-processing document.

Key Terms

- paragraph
- Print Preview
- style
- style sheet

Applying Styles

A **style** is a set of formats that is applied all at once. You can apply styles to text and to objects. For example, you can apply a style to a heading to quickly format the heading with a set of formats, such as bold, large font size, and an underline. You can apply a style to a picture to change the border or shape, or to add effects. Using styles to apply consistent formatting gives your document a professional look.

Using Styles Styles can be applied to selected characters or to **paragraphs**. Character styles include font formatting, such as font, font size, and font style. Paragraph styles include font formatting and paragraph formatting, such as alignment, line spacing, and tabs.

To apply a paragraph style, place the insertion point in a paragraph, and select the style.

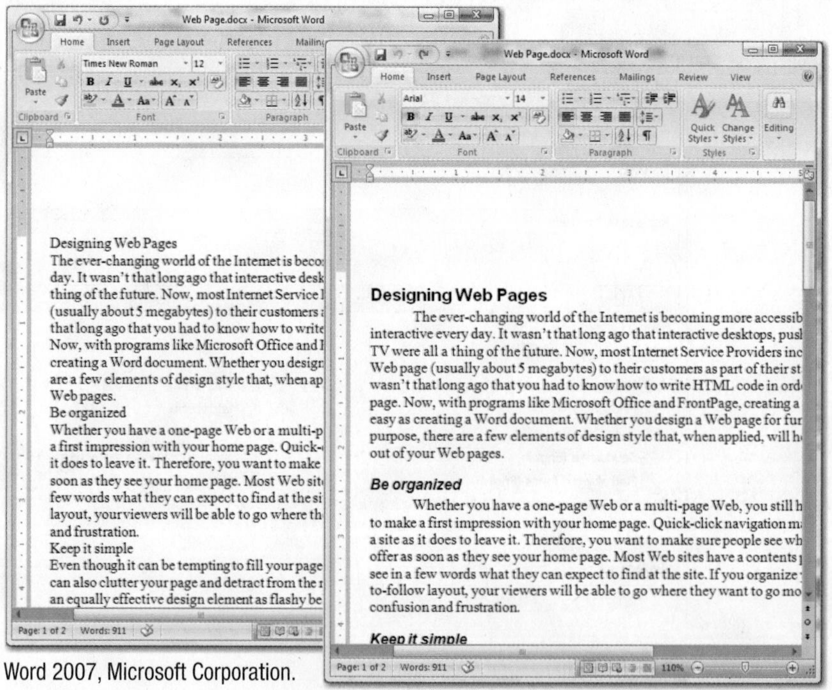

Figure B.3.1 A document before and after styles were applied.

Word 2007, Microsoft Corporation.

Some programs display each style in the correct font and type size so you can quickly see what it looks like. You simply choose the style you want for the selected paragraph. The program then assigns a set of formats to the paragraph.

Modifying Styles You can easily change the look of all paragraphs that have the same style. For example, to make all main headings larger, simply edit the *Heading 1* style and change the type size. The program automatically changes the size of all those headings.

Using Style Sheets Most programs provide a standard **style sheet**, a collection of predefined styles that go together. For instance, there are styles for text, headings, page numbers, headers, lists, and so on.

You can probably find styles you want to use in the standard set of styles. If not, you can modify existing styles or even design new ones.

Presenting Information in Tables or Lists

Suppose you wanted to show the batting averages of the players on your school's baseball team. You could do this by writing a paragraph, but tables let you compare this information more easily by placing it in columns and rows. Columns run down the table; rows go across.

In some programs, you insert tables by using the Insert menu. Others have a special Table menu. In Word, the Tables group is on the Insert tab. These methods make it easy to add a table to your document and format it. You can even add color and shading so different parts of the table stand out.

When you don't need multiple columns, you can format text as a bulleted or numbered list. Use numbers when the order matters, like for directions. Use bullets when the order does not matter. Most programs have commands that quickly apply list formatting.

Printing a Document

Although some documents are designed to be viewed on a monitor, people usually print the reports, greeting cards, letters, and posters they create.

Print Preview Before printing a document, you can see how it will look by selecting the feature called **Print Preview**. Print Preview shows everything in a document—margins, graphics, headers, page numbers, and text. If you change margins and edit text while in Print Preview, you will immediately see these changes on your document.

Tables and clip art aren't the only graphics that can be brought into documents. Word processors can bring in or create charts and graphs.

Think About It!

Think about the kinds of graphics you could use in school assignments. Which items listed below would be good ways to use charts, graphs, and tables at school?

- graph showing students' results with an experiment in science class
- chart for a book report in English class
- graph showing economic growth for social studies class
- chart of number of calories in different foods for health class
- graph of the popularity of different colors in art class

Did You Know?

In some programs, such as Microsoft Word, you can print without using the Print dialog box. Suppose you want to print just one full copy of the document on your screen without changing any printing options. Click the File tab, click Print, and click the Print button. Your document is sent to the printer immediately, and you can move on to your next task.

Print Options To print, you typically go to the File menu and then select Print. This opens a dialog box or tab that gives you several options:

- Printer—If the computer is connected to more than one printer, you can choose which one to use.
- Page range—You can choose to print every page in the document, the current page, or a group of pages.
- Number of copies—You can print one copy of the document, hundreds of copies, or any number in between.
- Print quality—You may be able to print in a faster "draft" mode or in a slower, high-quality mode.
- Orientation—You can select Portrait (the height of the page is greater than the width) or Landscape (the width of the page is greater than the height).
- Paper Size—You can select from a list of standard paper sizes, such a 8.5″ x 11″, or you can set a custom size.
- Margins—You can select from standard margin widths or set custom margins. You may also be able to select and set gutter widths. Gutters are used in bound publications. The gutter is the margin along the side of the page closest to the binding.

Depending on your printer, you might have other options. For example, if you have a color printer, you may have the option to print documents in black-and-white or grayscale modes. Most printers let you choose to print Collated which means printing multiple copies in 1, 2, 3, order; or Uncollated, which means printing all copies of one page, then all of the next, and so on. You can also usually scale pages to print multiple copies per sheet. If your printer can print in duplex (using both sides of the paper), you can set options to control this feature, too.

Figure B.3.2 Many programs let you select options for printing in a Print dialog box or on a Print tab.

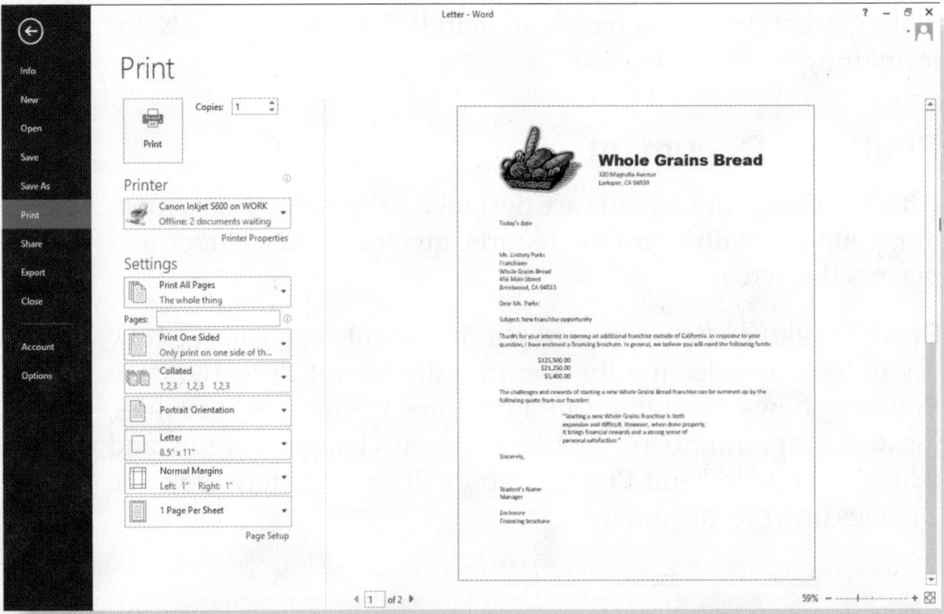

Word 2013, Microsoft Corporation.

Making and Tracking Edits

Objectives

- Explain how to check spelling, grammar, and style.
- Describe the benefits of tracking editing changes.
- Outline the steps for adding comments to a document.

As You Read

Organize Information Complete a chart to help you organize basic facts about checking tools and workgroup editing functions in word-processing programs.

Key Terms

- grammar checker
- spelling checker
- style checker
- Track Changes

Tools for Correcting Errors

Most word-processing programs offer tools to help with your writing. These tools check spelling, grammar, and writing style.

Spelling Checker The **spelling checker** matches each word in the text against a word list built into the program and gives you options for correcting a misspelling. You can accept one of the spellings or ignore the suggested change. You can also add a word to the word list so the program will accept it in the future. You can use the spelling checker in two ways:

- Check spelling as you type. The program highlights possible errors as they occur. In some programs, you can click the error to find different spellings and then quickly choose one.
- Check a word, a selection, or a whole document. As each possible spelling error is displayed, you decide whether to keep the original spelling or change it.

Spelling checkers are useful, but they accept words as long as they are spelled correctly—even if they are used incorrectly. You need to proofread your documents carefully even if you use the spelling checker.

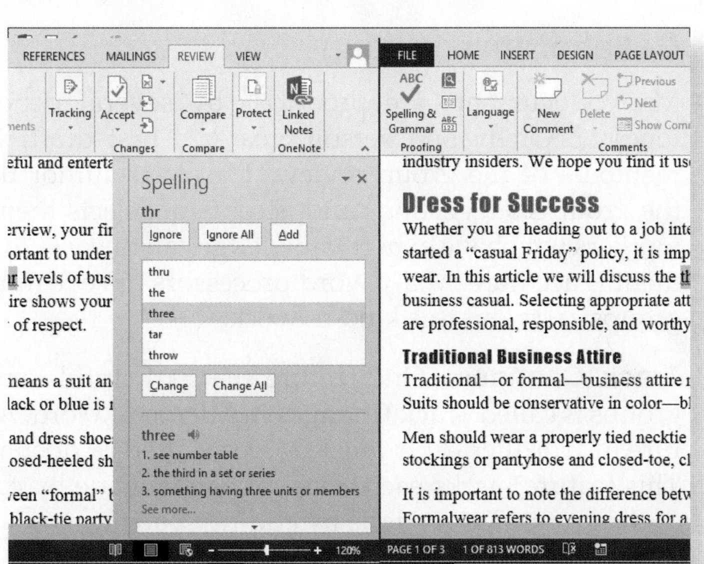

Figure B.4.1 Use the spelling checker to check spelling in a document.

Some programs can connect users to Web translation services. There, a computer program will translate text from one language into another. One word-processing program that has links to this kind of service cautions that "important or sensitive documents" should be translated by a person.

Think About It!

Think about situations in which the translation feature might be used. Which examples listed below do you think could safely be translated by computer?

- a government document
- a movie review
- a newspaper article
- a letter from a lawyer
- a person's medical records

Grammar and Style Checkers You can run grammar and style checks as you type, or you can check a selection or the entire document at once. Either way, the program highlights potential errors. You can examine each one and accept or ignore the suggested correction.

Grammar checkers look for problems such as errors in the use of verb tenses, pronouns, punctuation, and capitalization. For instance, the program would suggest fixing the sentence "He had ran yesterday." The grammar checker also finds sentence fragments (incomplete sentences) and run-on sentences (two sentences joined together incorrectly).

Style checkers suggest ways to improve the writing style in a document. They let you know whether a sentence is unclear or too wordy or long. They offer alternatives to the use of contractions or language that is too informal.

Most programs also include a Thesaurus feature that lets you look up definitions, synonyms, and antonyms for words. You can use a thesaurus to improve your writing by replacing overused or boring words.

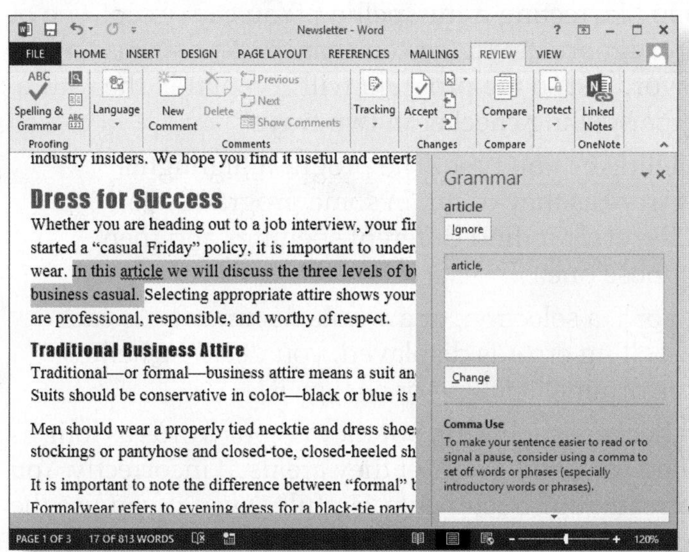

Figure B.4.2 Checking grammar in a document.

Word 2013, Microsoft Corporation.

Collaborative Writing

Many documents are produced by several people working together. Often, one person creates a first draft, which other members of the group review. The draft author then reviews the group's suggestions and accepts or rejects them. This way, workers who have expert knowledge can make sure that a document is accurate. Many word processors have features that help groups carry out this kind of work.

Track Changes One feature that is helpful for working in groups is called **Track Changes** in Microsoft Word. A similar feature in WordPerfect is the red-line method of document review. This feature marks each editing change made by each member of the group. This is done by adding specific marks to the document at the point where the changes were made.

- Inserted text is shown in a specific color assigned to each group member.
- Deleted text is not removed but appears in the assigned color with a line running through the words.
- In some programs, special boxes name the person who made the change.

When the original author reviews the document, he or she can choose to accept or reject each suggested change.

Comments Some programs let group members add notes to a document without changing the document's text. Microsoft Word does so using the Comment feature. In most programs, including Microsoft Word, to insert a comment, click Review and then click New Comment. A special pane appears at the bottom or edge of the screen, ready for you to type your comment.

Several people can add comments to a document, and the program tracks each person's comments. That way, the author can see who added what remarks to the document. Comments can be hidden or deleted, and a comment's text can be formatted and edited just like normal text.

Document Protection Most programs let you protect a document from unauthorized changes. Protection options range from allowing users to read but not edit or format a document to allowing only those with a password to open the document.

Tools that check spelling and grammar as you type are useful for correcting errors, but what if you use alternative methods to input text?

Think About It!

You can help yourself create error-free documents by practicing enunciation and reading skills for use with speech-recognition programs, and digital penmanship for use with handwriting-recognition programs. Work with your teacher to create a plan for developing these skills. It will help you improve academically in all areas.

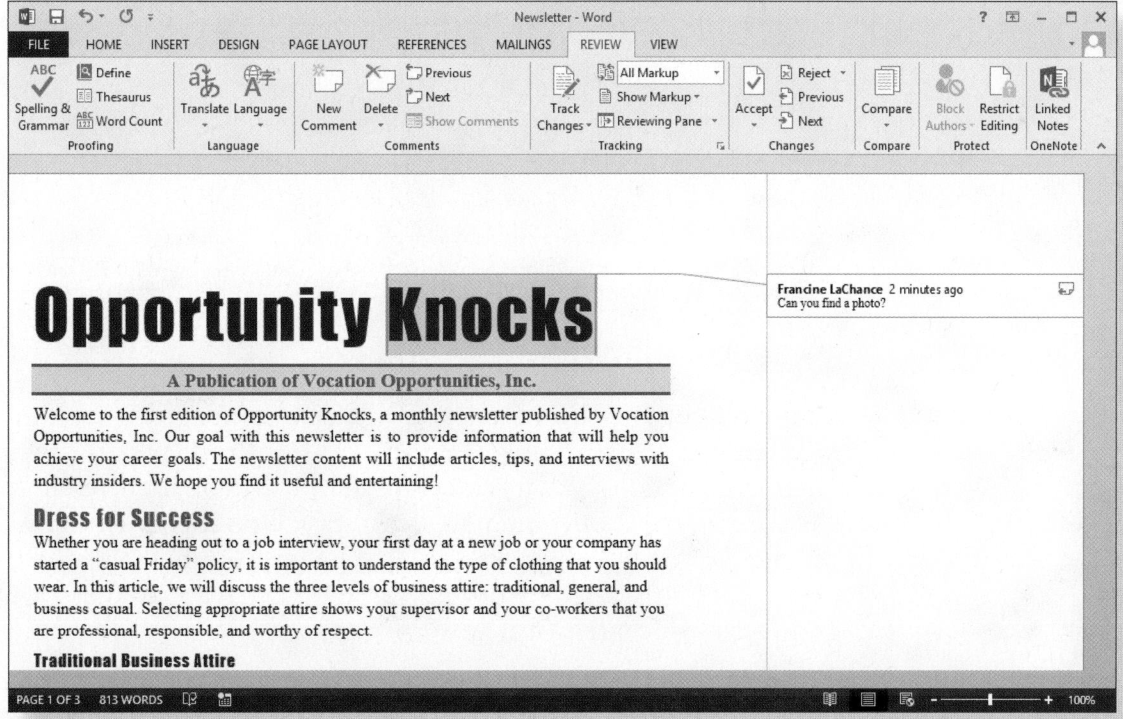

Word 2013, Microsoft Corporation.

Figure B.4.3 Comments can appear in small boxes in the document's margins.

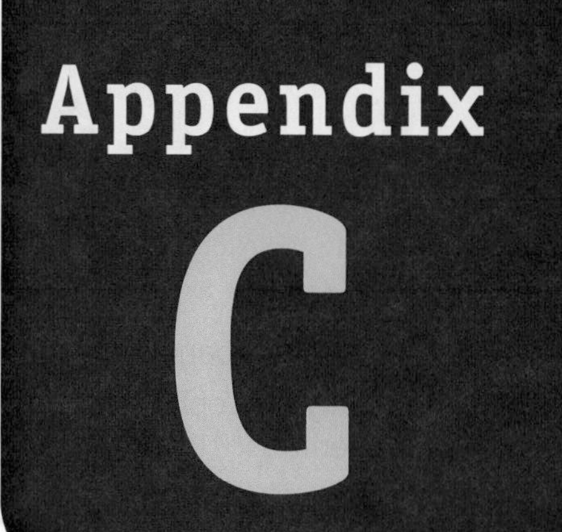

Presentation Basics

What Are Presentations? A presentation is a visual or multimedia display. Every day, presentations are shown on overhead screens in classrooms and at meetings. They help people teach ideas, sell products, and share information with others.

Before computers, creating a professional presentation took a lot of time and involved many people. First, an artist would create graphics. Next, the graphics and wording would be organized for logical flow and visual appeal. Then, this information was transferred onto transparencies or slides.

Now, thanks to presentation software, many people create presentations more quickly. Knowing how to use presentation software is an important skill in today's world.

Appendix C–1

Exploring Presentation Software

Objectives

- Identify the benefits of presentation software.
- Identify two options for creating a new presentation.
- Describe six views in PowerPoint.

As You Read

Organize Information Use a concept web to help you organize ways to create and view presentations as you read.

Key Terms

- AutoContent wizard
- Master views
- Normal view
- Notes Page view
- presentation software
- Reading view
- slide
- Slide Show view
- Slide Sorter view
- template
- thumbnails
- wizard

Introducing Presentation Software

Presentation software allows you to organize and display information visually so it can be viewed by a group of people. In most cases, this information—called a presentation—consists of both graphics and text, and may also include audio, video, and animation. Information in a presentation is organized into separate pages in an order the audience can follow easily. Each page is called a **slide**. Each slide can contain one or more main points. Information about each main point is organized into a list of short, easy-to-read key points. There are a host of good programs such as Microsoft PowerPoint, Corel Presentations and Apple's Keynote that are specifically designed for creating, saving, editing, and producing presentations.

Creating a New Presentation The most common presentation software is Microsoft PowerPoint. With PowerPoint, you have two options for creating a new presentation:

- template
- blank presentation

Template Work on a presentation may begin by selecting a **template**, or a preformatted version of a certain type of document. After choosing a template, you type in your information. You can also change the look and feel of the template by adjusting its settings.

Blank Presentation This option starts by providing a plain blank slide. While this option may require more work than using a template, it does have benefits. For instance, you can create a new presentation from scratch to make your work more original by selecting your own color scheme, art, fonts, and other design elements.

AutoContent Wizard Earlier versions of PowerPoint let you use the AutoContent Wizard to create a new presentation. A **wizard** is a series of dialog boxes that guides you through a step-by-step procedure. The **AutoContent wizard** provides the steps for creating a presentation. It asks questions about the goals and purpose of your presentation. Once its questions are answered, the wizard creates a format for the presentation. To complete the presentation, you enter the words and images into the wizard's format.

Exploring Presentation Views

While working, you can select to view a presentation in many ways, depending on the task at hand. Each view has its own strength. Depending on the program you use, you may be able to choose from these views:

- Normal view
- Slide Sorter view
- Notes Page view
- Slide Show view
- Reading view
- Master views

Screen-reading programs can make working on a computer easier for people who are blind or have poor vision.

- Job Access With Speech, or JAWS, uses your computer's sound to read aloud what is displayed on the screen.
- Hal Screen Reader also converts what is on the screen to sound. It can be used with PowerPoint and even Braille text.

Figure C.1.1 Most presentation programs let you choose a theme or template to quickly apply coordinated formatting to your slides.

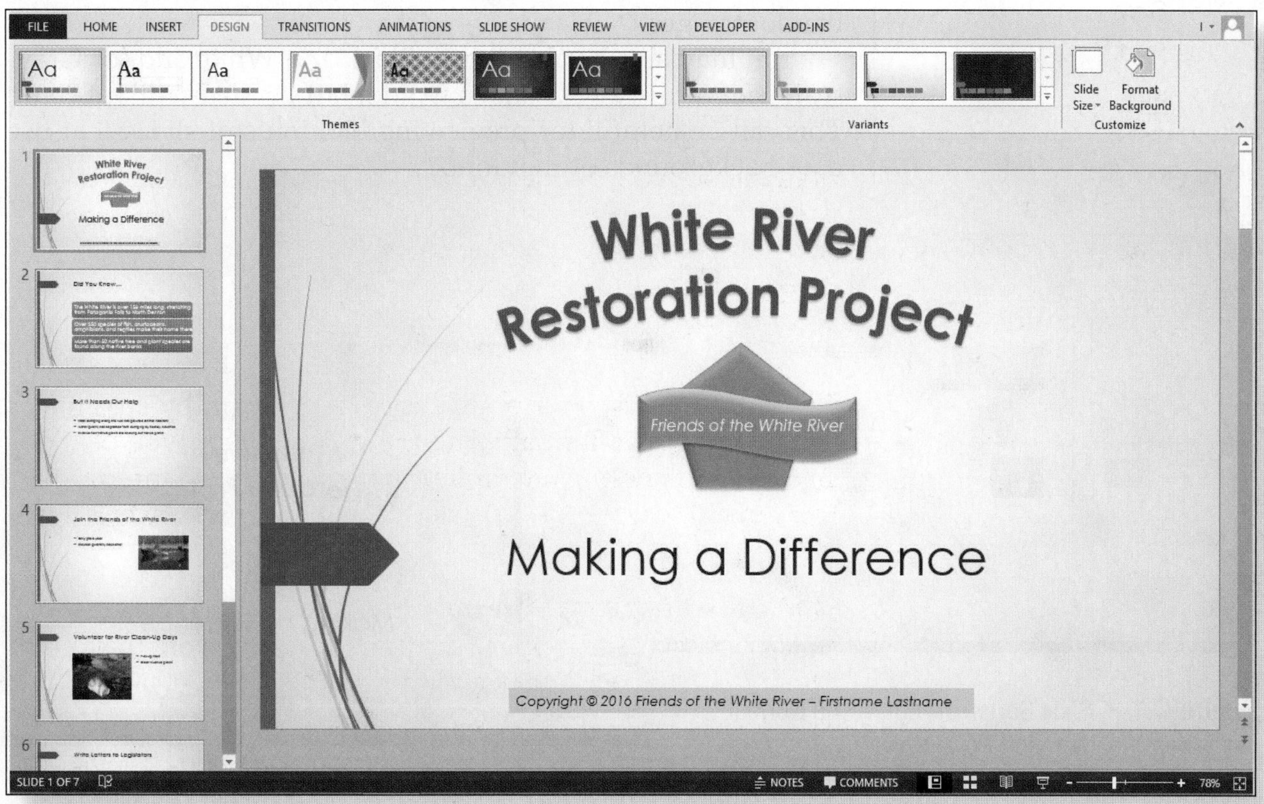

PowerPoint 2013, Microsoft Corporation.

At work, employees may be asked to make presentations to inform others about company policies, to show the results of the company's latest research, or to sell a new product.

Think About It!

Using the right view in presentation software can make creating a presentation a little bit easier. Which views listed below would help you organize your slides?

- Normal view
- Slide Sorter view
- Notes Page view
- Slide Show View
- Reading View
- Master Views

Normal View Text and graphics can be added, removed, or edited in **Normal view**. Normal view splits the screen to show a Slide view and a Navigation pane.

Slide Sorter View **Slide Sorter view** displays **thumbnails** of all of the slides in a presentation. This view allows you to change the order of the slides by dragging them to different locations.

Notes Page View In **Notes Page view**, part of the screen displays the slide and the rest of the screen shows a text box. You can type notes in the text box to use during a presentation or to print as handouts. Notes do not appear in the presentation that is shown to the audience.

Slide Show View The primary on-screen method of previewing and displaying slides during a presentation is called **Slide Show view**. Slides are displayed full-screen, one after another, in order. A slide-show presentation can be set to automatically advance slides or to wait until you—the presenter—advances the slides manually.

Reading View **Reading view** is similar to Slide Show view, except the slides are not displayed full-screen.

Master Views Many programs let you use **Master views** to make universal style changes to every slide, notes page, and/or handout pages.

You may also be able to use Black and White and/or Grayscale views to see how slides will look if printed without color. This can be helpful for previewing handouts of slides that use dark backgrounds or thin fonts.

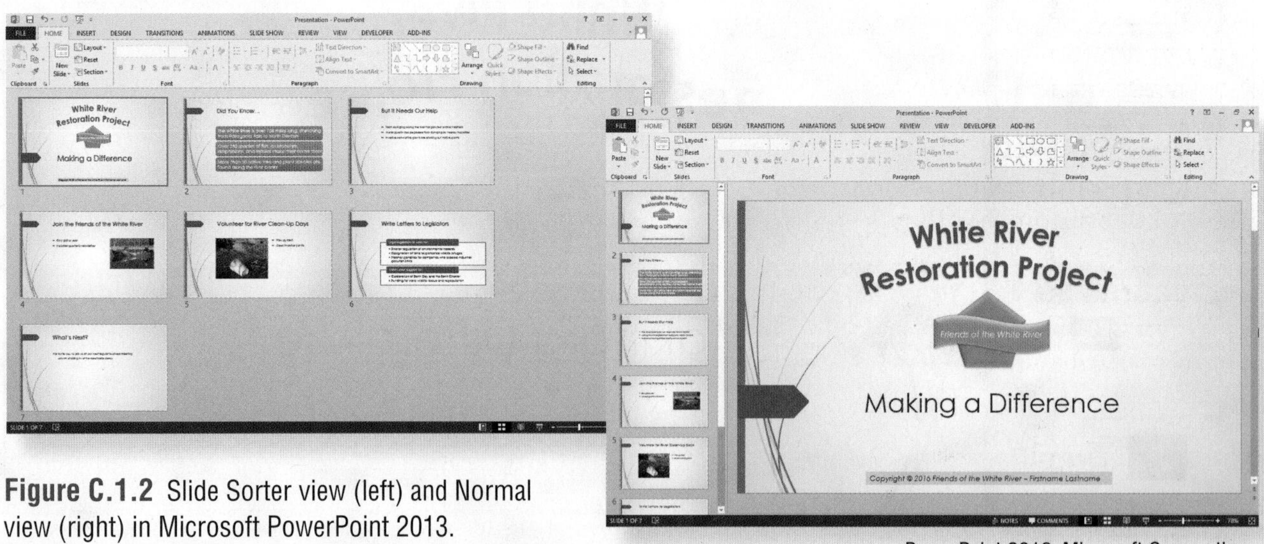

Figure C.1.2 Slide Sorter view (left) and Normal view (right) in Microsoft PowerPoint 2013.

PowerPoint 2013, Microsoft Corporation.

Creating Presentations

Objectives

- Explain how placeholders are used in presentation software.
- Identify five steps in designing presentations.
- Summarize techniques for adding content.

As You Read

Sequence Information Use a sequence chart to help you order steps for creating presentations as you read.

Key Terms

- animation
- AutoShapes
- placeholder

Designing Presentations

Following these five steps will help you plan, design, and save an effective presentation.

1. Decide How Your Slides Will Be Formatted To begin designing a presentation, choose an option for creating it. Choose either a blank presentation or a template. If none of the templates is exactly what you want, select the one that is closest. You can change much of its graphic content, format, and text. Graphics can be resized or deleted. Placeholders can be added, removed, or resized as well.

2. Choose the Slide Layout Every slide in a presentation can be formatted in a preset layout. These layouts already have placeholders in position. This allows text and graphics to be added immediately. Some examples of slide layouts include bulleted lists, tables, grids, and flowcharts. Since each slide in a presentation can have a different layout, select a layout for each new slide you add.

3. Work with Placeholders A **placeholder** is an area within a slide layout designed to hold data such as text or pictures. A placeholder automatically applies a format based on the type of content. For instance, selecting a text placeholder will change the cursor to the Text tool. Selecting a picture placeholder will bring up a prompt asking which image to insert. Placeholder prompts guide you and are overwritten, or replaced, as you enter data.

4. Insert Graphics and Sound Make your presentations come to life. Insert sound, video, clip art, drawing tools, or imported images to support or illustrate a slide's text. But, be sure that the additions don't distract from the content.

Some teachers use interactive multimedia software to help them teach. This software allows students to control the pace of the instruction.

Think About It!

Using interactive multimedia in the classroom has advantages and disadvantages. Which of those listed below could present a disadvantage for schools?

- expensive
- uses images
- uses sounds
- only some subjects available

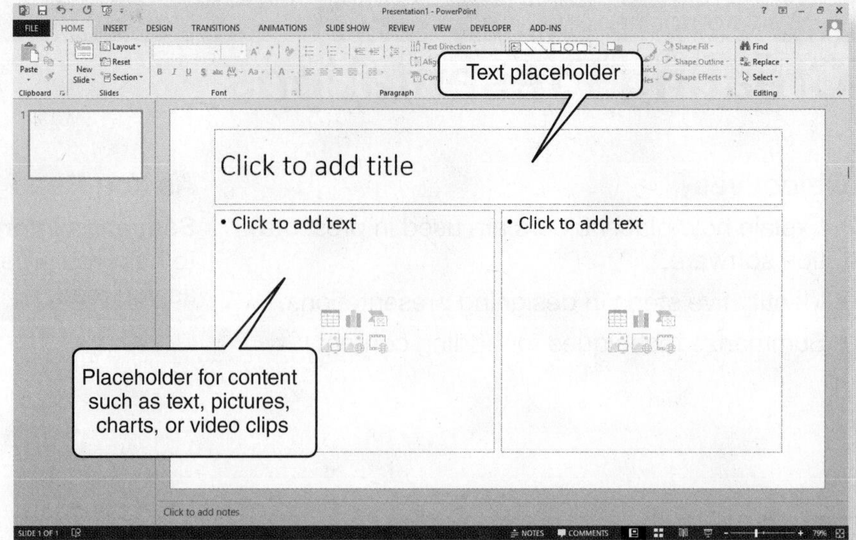

PowerPoint 2013, Microsoft Corporation.

Figure C.2.1 A Two Content slide layout in Microsoft PowerPoint 2013.

5. View and Organize the Presentation Once information has been added to the slides, save it, and then preview the entire presentation using the Slide Show view. Make any changes to the order of the slides in Slide Sorter view. Typos and text changes can be handled in Outline view or Normal view.

Adding Content to Presentations

When you create a new presentation, you must use the Insert Slide command to add the slides you need to display your content. You can also use the Delete command to remove slides you don't need.

Each new slide in a presentation has a layout with placeholders for adding content. For instance, a layout might contain a placeholder where you can add a title. Click (or, in some programs, double-click) the placeholder and begin typing. The program automatically formats the text to fit the area with a preselected font and alignment.

Adding Graphics You can insert many types of graphics including clip art, pictures, drawings, charts, diagrams, and tables. In PowerPoint, use the buttons on the Insert tab of the Ribbon, or click the appropriate icon in a Content placeholder. PowerPoint drawing tools also include ready-to-use shapes, called **AutoShapes**. The list includes banners, arrows, borders, frames, and more. Save the file after every change.

You do not need a placeholder to insert graphics. Select the desired tool and use it in a blank area of the workspace.

Adding Animation and Sound A multimedia presentation combines text and graphics with sound and **animation**. Both sound and animation, or moving images, are inserted using menu commands. For example, in PowerPoint you can choose to insert video or audio clips using buttons in the Media group on the Insert tab.

Adding Text To add text, you simply type in a placeholder or in an outline. Text on a slide is often formatted as a bulleted list, which is a neat and effective way to present information.

Software Production Manager Have you ever wondered who oversees the process of developing presentation or multimedia software? That is the job of software production managers. These are some of their job responsibilities:

- oversee people working on a project
- work with clients to develop features for the software
- oversee testing of the new software

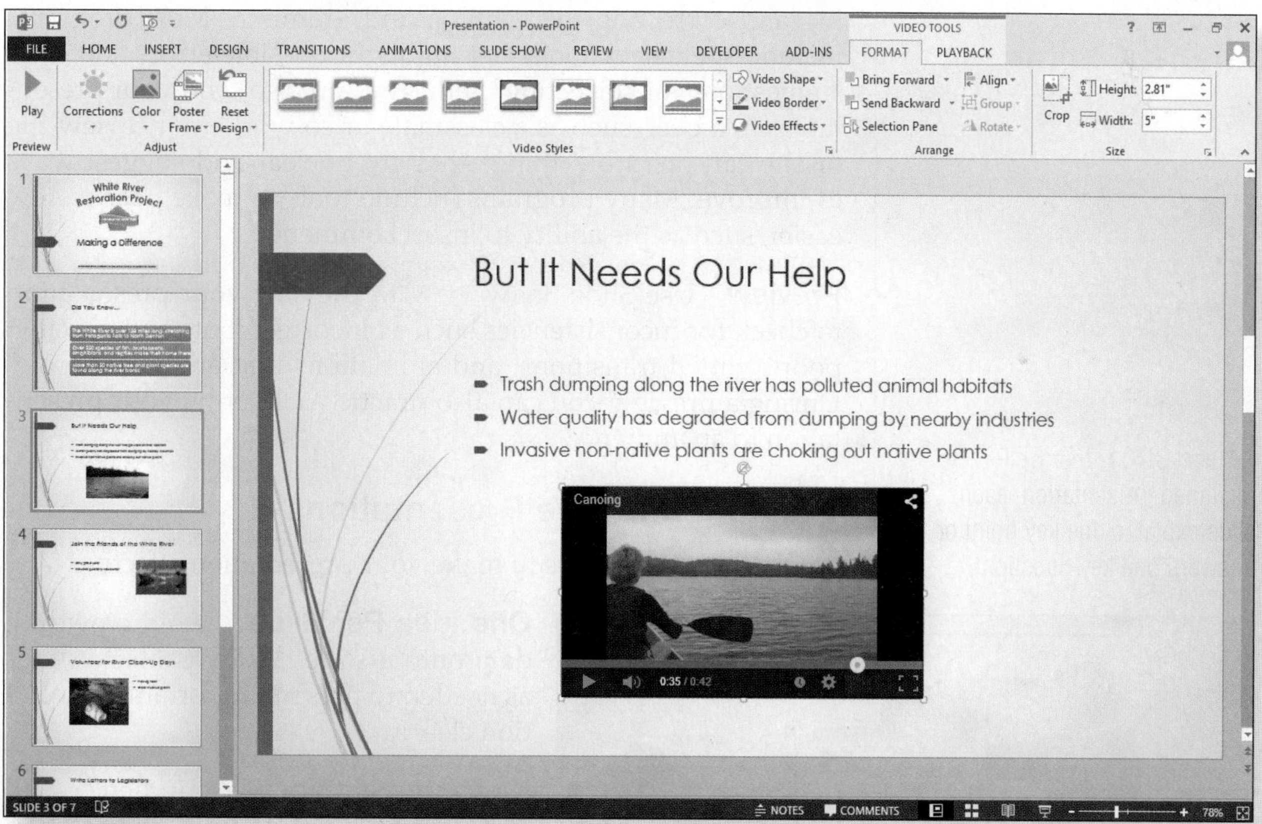

PowerPoint 2013, Microsoft Corporation.

Figure C.2.2 Previewing a video that has been inserted on a slide.

Appendix C–3

Previewing Presentations

Objectives

- Identify reasons for reviewing and previewing a presentation
- Summarize seven tips for creating effective presentations.

As You Read

Organize Information Use a main idea/detail chart to help you create useful presentations as you read.

Previewing a Presentation

Before finalizing a presentation you should review it and preview it.

Review Reviewing your presentation should include checking and correcting the spelling and grammar. Most programs include spellcheck tools that highlight possible errors and offer suggestions for correcting them. You can also send your presentation to a peer, such as a classmate or co-worker for review. He or she can point out things that are unclear and suggest ways to improve. Many programs include tools to make peer review easier, such as the ability to insert comments.

Preview Use Slide Show view to preview your presentation to check for inconsistencies such as incorrect fonts and spacing, poorly timed transitions, and animations that are out of order. During a preview you can also practice delivering your presentation to an audience.

Creating Effective Presentations

Apply these seven tips to make your presentation effective.

Figure C.3.1 In a well-designed presentation, each slide explains one key point or answers one key question.

One Idea Per Slide Avoid crowding data onto a slide. Make as many slides as needed to present important information clearly.

Keep It Simple The audience will be listening to your speech or narration while viewing your slides. Use simple words to make key points. Include clear transitions from one topic to another.

Display Key Facts Your slides should serve as an outline for the audience. Your speech will fill in the gaps in that outline. Displaying too much information can make a presentation hard to follow.

Mix It Up Vary the layouts and content of your slides to help hold the audience's attention. For instance, switch between lists that appear on the right-hand and left-hand side and break up text with illustrations.

Use Color Cautiously Select colors that are pleasing to the eye. For instance, bright pink lettering on a bright blue background will be difficult to read. Avoid using too many colors on a slide.

Watch the Fonts Do not use more than two fonts on a single slide. This helps prevent a presentation from becoming too distracting to read. Also, be sure to use fonts that fit the tone. A presentation about the Civil War, for example, would not use fonts that seem playful or humorous.

Make It Readable Choose readable font and color combinations. Check that your text and images can be seen from the back of the room so your presentation can be viewed by your entire audience.

Before giving a presentation, test it with an audience such as friends and family.

Think About It!

Ask your test audience to point out slides that were hard to see or to understand. Which items listed below are concerns for presentation slides?

- text too small
- animation
- detailed information given
- many colors used

Spotlight on...

DISTANCE LEARNING

Can you imagine creating presentations to show people who live hundreds of miles away? Distance learning teaches people at remote, or off-site, locations from the teacher. These students aren't seated together in a single classroom. Companies that develop distance-learning materials must create presentations students understand. It also means these presentations must keep students' interest.

Distance learning is offered by a large number of schools, colleges, and universities. Many people are now earning college degrees through distance learning by taking classes online. Some schools also offer classes that combine some face-to-face instruction with online presentations.

Enhancing Presentations

Appendix

D

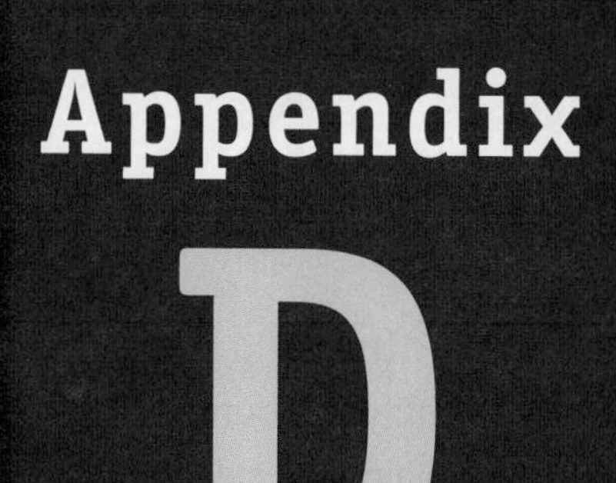

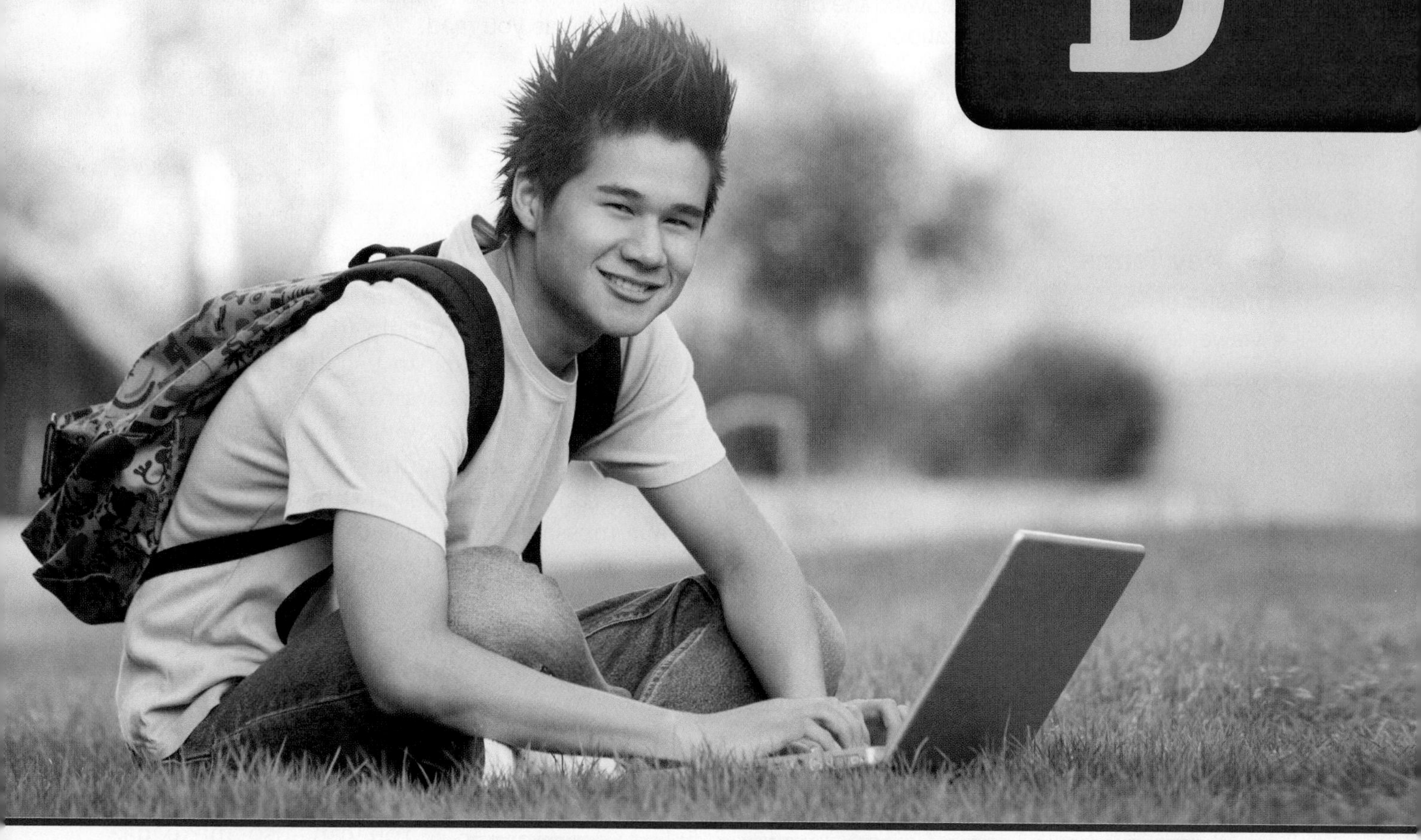

The Big Moment You have worked hard to assemble all the necessary tools and information. The stage is now properly set. The colors and lighting are perfect, and the script is well written. The show is about to begin.

Is this a Hollywood production? Is it a stage play? No, it's a computer presentation. Presentation software allows you to create a presentation with graphics, audio, text, animation, and more. Today, your computer screen is the stage. On other days, your show may be viewed on a large screen or on the Internet. The text, images, and sounds are your actors and props.

Learning to use presentation software is an important skill for school and work. Learning to use it effectively will benefit you for years to come.

Appendix D–1

Presentation Options

Objectives

- Identify the purpose of presentation software.
- Explain the importance of knowing the output before developing a presentation.

As You Read

Organize Information Use a spider map to organize tips for using presentation software effectively as you read.

 **Key Terms**

- master slide
- viewable area
- visual aid

Using Presentation Software

The main purpose of presentation software is to provide speakers with **visual aids**, or graphics that help give information to an audience. For example, a teacher can use a chalkboard, flip chart, or handouts to illustrate ideas or provide examples.

Another way to present these concepts is by using presentation software to introduce key points either as text or images or to clarify details. Users can create slides and handouts to teach a concept or convey a message. They also can deliver presentations on-screen in an office, in a conference room, and on the World Wide Web.

Most presentations use default settings suitable for creating and displaying a full color slide show to an audience on a monitor or screen, controlled by a live presenter. You can change the presentation options. For example, you can create a self-running presentation that does not require a live presenter, or that can be controlled by an individual.

Figure D.1.1 Depending on which profession you choose, you may see a lot of presentations.

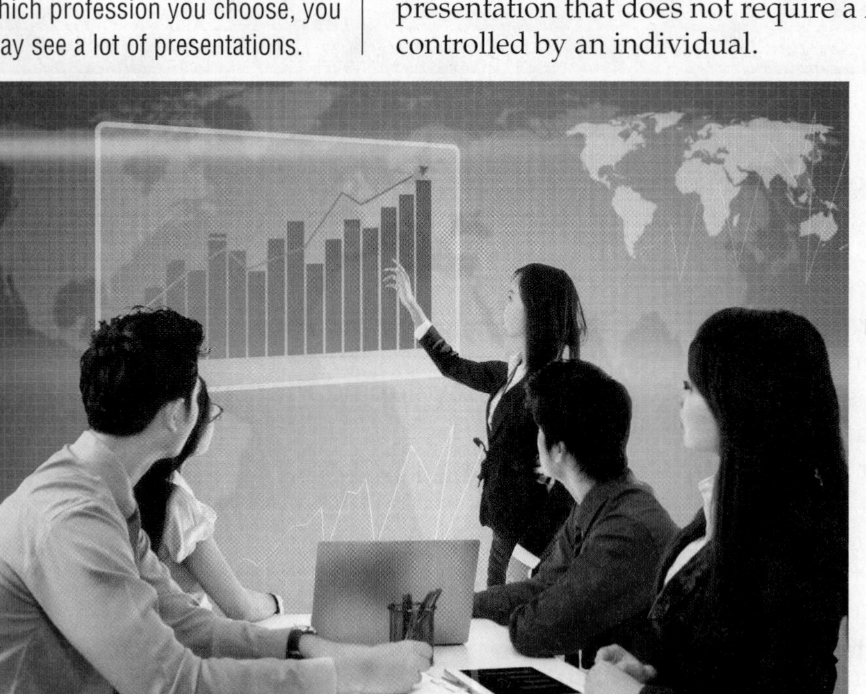

You can also make use of customization features such as designs and masters to create consistent and professional-looking presentations. For example, you can apply a design template to your presentation to give it a uniform look and color scheme.

Working with Masters

Programs such as PowerPoint let you work with Slide, Notes, and Handout masters. Masters are default templates; changes you make to a master are applied to the components based on that master.

A **master slide** is a default template that is applied to all slides of a certain type. There are two different types of master slides in a presentation program such as PowerPoint:

- Slide Master
- Title Master

By editing a master slide, you are able to change fonts, sizes, colors, and layouts for all of the slides of that type throughout a presentation. For instance, the Slide Master controls the format for the slides. A Title Master controls the appearance of the title and subtitle of a title slide.

For example, suppose you want to change the font used for the main heading at the top of each slide. You can open the master slide, select the heading placeholder, and make your change. When you close the master slide, all the slide headings in the presentation will have changed to match the new format.

When preparing a presentation for school, it may be a good idea to use Speaker Notes to help you remember what you want to say to the audience.

Think About It!

Entering notes can help remind you of details you want to share about your slides. For which of the ways listed below can Speaker Notes help you do this?

- help presenter remember dates and details
- organize layout of the slide show
- show thumbnails of the presentation
- prompt the punchline to a joke

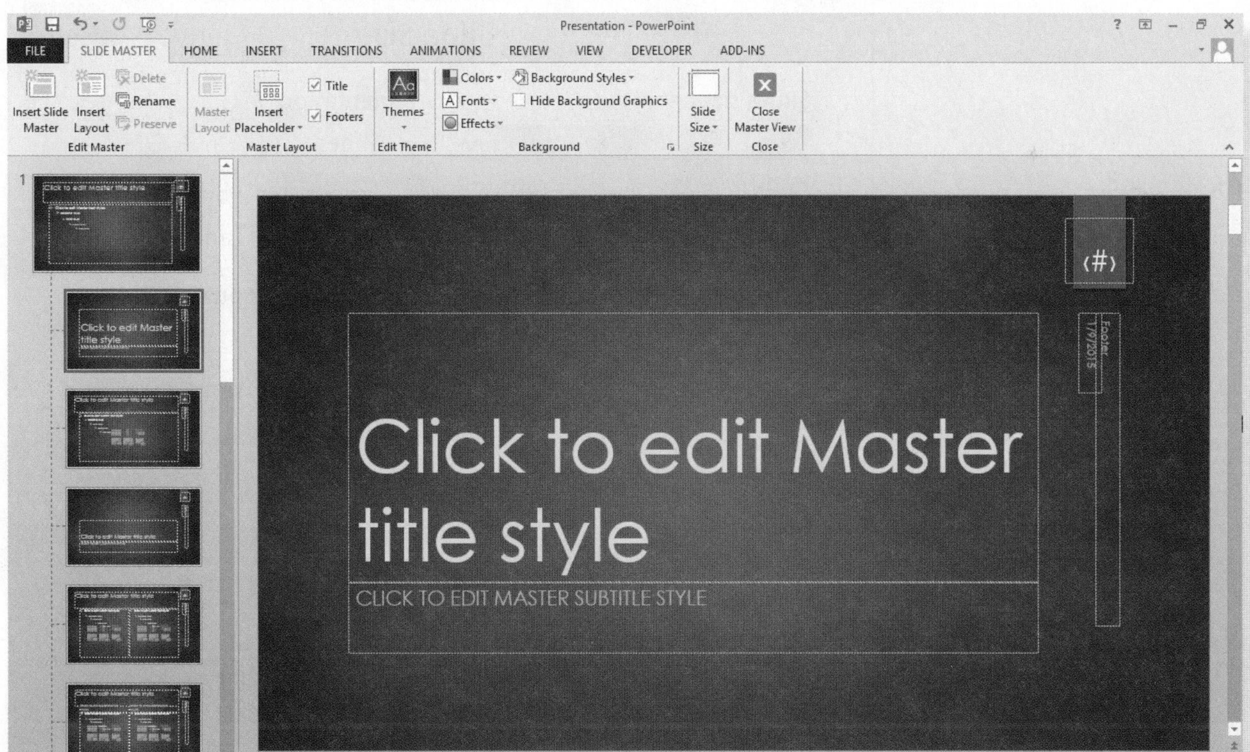

PowerPoint 2013, Microsoft Corporation.

Figure D.1.2 Like PowerPoint 2013, most presentation programs let you use a master slide to control the look of an entire presentation.

Connections

Math Consider the cost if you are thinking of printing a presentation. The more colors you use in your slides, the more it will cost to print them. For instance, a new color printing cartridge might cost about $45. It might print 100 pages using minimal color. That totals 45 cents per page. That same cartridge might only print 50 copies displaying a lot of color. That equals 90 cents per page, which can prove costly if you need several copies.

Consider the Output

Presentation software programs offer options for optimizing the settings for printing the presentation and for displaying the slides onscreen or as 35-mm slides. Other issues to consider are printer output and displays.

Printer Output If a presentation is to be printed and provided as a handout, the page setup should match the capabilities of the printer. A solid black background with green lettering might look fine on a computer screen. However, printing a colored background on every page for every person in the audience uses a lot of ink. In addition, simple color graphics lose their effect if they are printed in black. Also, dark backgrounds can make text hard to see on a printed page.

Displaying the Output For each presentation, it is important to anticipate the display's **viewable area**, or portion of the screen where an image can be shown. Different displays have different viewable areas. For instance, if the computer uses a television as an output device, some of the information may not be visible. This is also true when using an LCD (liquid crystal display) monitor to project computer-screen images for large audiences. It is important to adjust the page setup so that all of the presentation can be viewed on-screen by the audience.

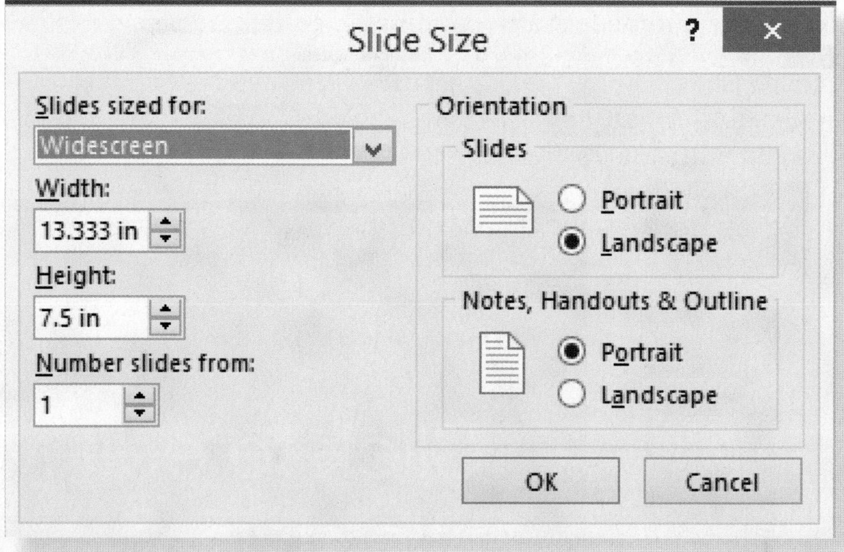

PowerPoint 2013, Microsoft Corporation.

Figure D.1.3 In Microsoft PowerPoint 2013, use the Slide Size dialog box to optimize settings for slide size and orientation. Other options may be found in the PowerPoint Options dialog box.

Developing Presentations

Objectives

- Explain the use of a presentation outline.
- Identify slide layout options.
- Explain the benefit of designing the content of a slide before choosing the layout.
- Summarize the editing process that should occur after a draft presentation is complete.

As You Read

Sequence Information Use a sequence chart to sequence the steps to organize a presentation as you read.

Using a Presentation Outline

In most presentation programs you can use an outline to develop your presentation. You can type the outline to create slide titles and bullet items, or you can import an outline from a program such as Microsoft Word.

Typing an Outline When you type a presentation outline, the first line you type displays as the slide title. From the title, you press Ctrl+Enter to start a bulleted list, or Enter to create a new slide. From the bulleted list, you press Enter to continue the bulleted list, or Ctrl+Enter to start a new slide. You can format and rearrange outline text and increase or decrease outline levels to change the way the text displays on the slide.

Importing an Outline If you have an existing outline in a file created with a program such as Microsoft Word, you can import it into your presentation program. Each heading 1 level in the outline becomes a slide title, and the subheadings become bulleted lists.

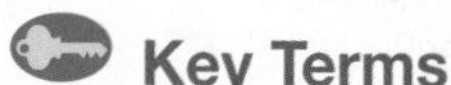

Key Terms

- transition effect
- self-running presentation
- rehearsed presentation

Figure D.2.1 PowerPoint lets you work with a presentation outline.

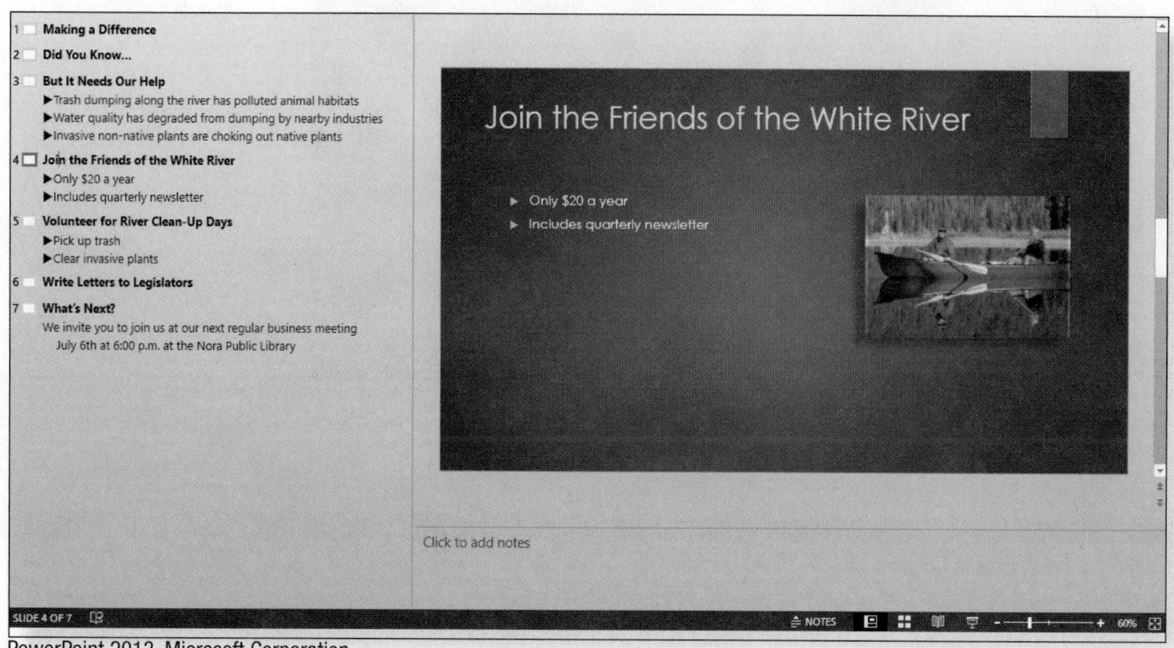

PowerPoint 2013, Microsoft Corporation.

Large companies often use organizational charts to identify the structure and responsibilities of employees. PowerPoint offers a template layout to help generate this information.

Think About It!

Which items listed below would be valuable to an organizational chart for a business?

- detailed job descriptions
- names of department heads
- telephone extensions
- work schedules

Choosing a Slide Layout

Each slide in a presentation can have its own layout. Consider the content of a slide before you choose a layout. By deciding the slide's key points first, you can then select the most appropriate layout for it.

The first slide in a new blank presentation usually has the Title Slide layout, with placeholders for entering a title and a subtitle. By default, new slides you add have the Title and Content layout, with placeholders for a title and content such as a bulleted list, clip art, picture, chart, table, or media clip. Other layout choices include Two Content, Comparison, Title Only, Blank, Content with Caption, Picture with Caption, and Section Header.

Editing Your Presentation

Good presenters edit drafts of their work. Be sure to fix the errors you find, reorganize the sequence of the slides, and improve the flow of ideas. If a slide is in the wrong location, use Slide Sorter or Outline view to move it. To revise the flow of text, use Outline view to adjust it.

Checking Errors Presentation software can check spelling as you type text in a placeholder. If a red, wavy line appears under a word, it might be spelled incorrectly. If so, in Windows, right-click the word to open the suggested-spellings list and see other spelling choices, or run a spelling checker.

Figure D.2.2 Checking the spelling in a presentation.

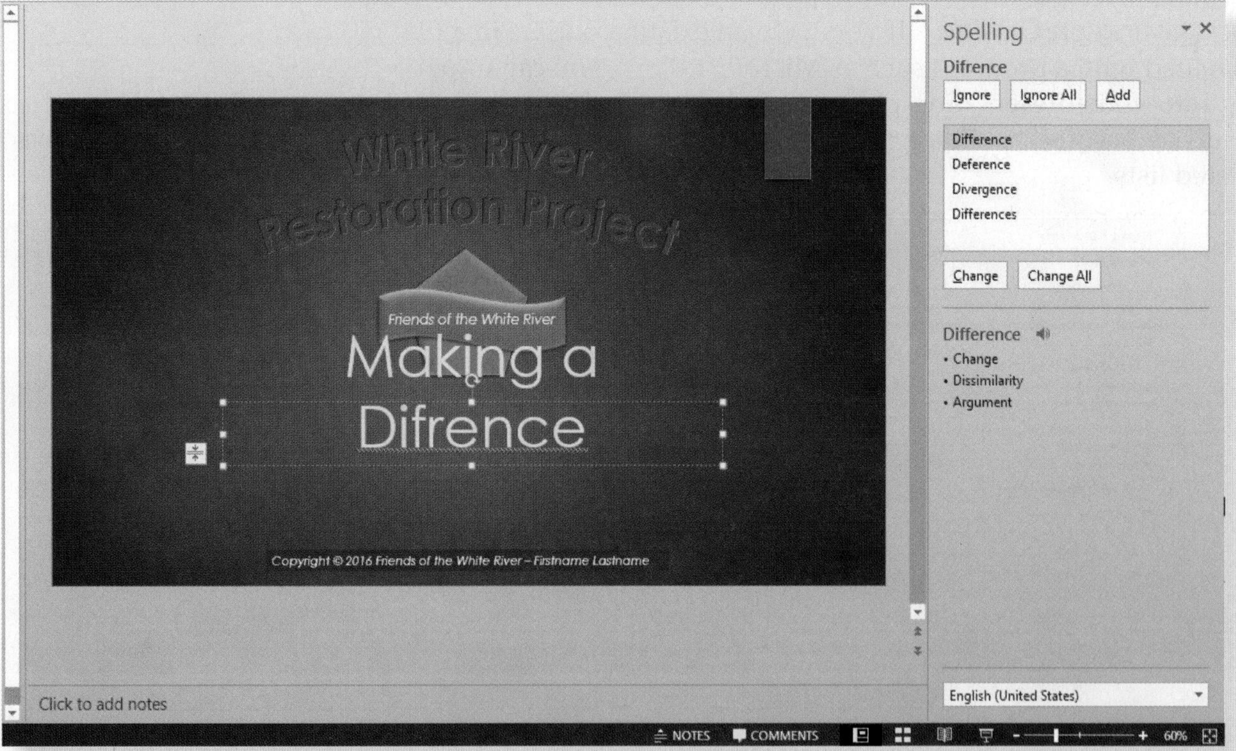

PowerPoint 2013, Microsoft Corporation.

Enhancing a Presentation

Inserting Images Text-only presentations can be dull. Insert clip art, photos, and other images to clarify and enhance key points. Use charts, shapes, and drawings to help your audience better understand the information in your slides.

Adding Animation, Video, and Sound Sound, animation, and video can make a presentation more informative and interesting. Most presentation software can import and use standard animation formats, including animated .gif clips. You can also animate objects and text on a slide. For example, you can have a title slide in from the left, or set a picture to fade out or blink.

Some presentation programs, including PowerPoint, include the ability to embed video clips or a link to a video from your presentation. You can insert sound files, such as music or recorded narration. When you insert sounds or video, an icon displays on the slide. You can hide the icon during a presentation, or set it so the clip only plays when a viewer clicks it.

Adding Transitional Effects A **transition effect** is a multimedia feature that adds visual interest as your presentation moves from one slide to the next. For example, one slide might suddenly appear to fade out as the next slide appears. A new slide can move into view from one side of the screen as the previous slide disappears from sight.

Adjusting the Timing You can adjust the timing of slide shows. In **self-running presentations**, each slide stays on the screen for a specified period of time. Timings are usually set by entering the number of seconds you want a slide to display. In a **rehearsed presentation**, you set the program to record how long you spend presenting a slide; the program automatically sets the timing based on your rehearsal.

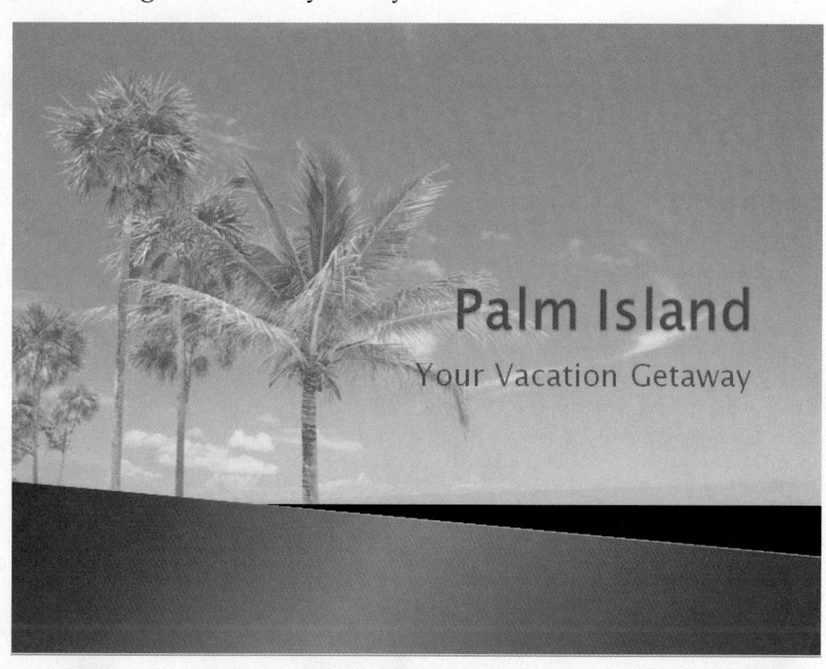

Figure D.2.3 Graphics can make slides more informative or more appealing.

Sales Representative Sales representatives often use presentation software to demonstrate or sell their company's products. Slides may show product features, compare products, explain costs, or give other information to customers or to people in the representatives' own organizations.

The ability to customize software presentations by reorganizing or replacing slides for different customers can help sales representatives better meet clients' needs.

Appendix D–3

Enhancing and Finalizing Presentations

Objectives

- Identify strategies to enhance a presentation.
- Summarize choices for presentation output.

As You Read

Draw Conclusions Use a conclusion chart to draw conclusions about finalizing a presentation as you read.

Key Terms

- digital projector
- on-screen presentation
- webcast

Making Powerful Presentations

Presentation programs are effective tools for generating high-interest, engaging presentations. Here are ten tips for finalizing presentation slides so that they are easy to understand and help you meet your presentation goals.

Remember your goal. Keep your goal, and your main message, in mind as you outline your presentation. When finalizing your presentation, review your slides and the information they convey to ensure that your goal has been met.

Support your main idea. Start by stating your main idea or topic sentence. Follow it with details that are simply presented and that clarify or support your main idea.

Know your audience. Fewer words on a slide mean fewer words your audience has to read. However, make sure that you do not oversimplify the content on your slides or you run the risk of boring your audience. Finally, rehearse in clear language and make sure your slides are also clear to others.

Preview and review. A preview slide introduces the presentation for an audience. This slide usually appears after the presentation's title slide and before the first slide that addresses a point.

A review slide usually restates the presentation's main points and may be identical to the preview slide. Used together effectively, a preview and review slide can help your audience remember the most important points of your presentation.

Figure D.3.1 The more planning you do, the better your presentations will be.

Stay on point. The purpose of slides is to highlight key facts, so it is fine to leave out supporting details. Keep your text lively but to the point.

Select and apply a consistent design. Too many different designs or too many colors and fonts can distract or confuse an audience.

Be smart with art. Use clip art, tables, charts, icons, and animations wisely to enhance a point. Don't add illustrations that do not contribute to your message.

Proofread your text. Use the spelling checker to help you eliminate typos from your work. Then, print your slides and ask someone to proofread them.

Check the output. Make sure the hardware on which you plan to display your work will be able to run your slide show. Incompatible machines can ruin your presentation.

Watch the clock. Rehearse your presentation with a timer. Make sure any timed slides are sequenced with your verbal message.

Did You Know?

Style guides are important when many people are working on the same material. They help prevent words, colors, and fonts from conflicting within a presentation, book, magazine, or newspaper. For example, one style guide might use the term *e-mail* while another might use *E-mail.* Another style guide might state that all headings must be in a specific font.

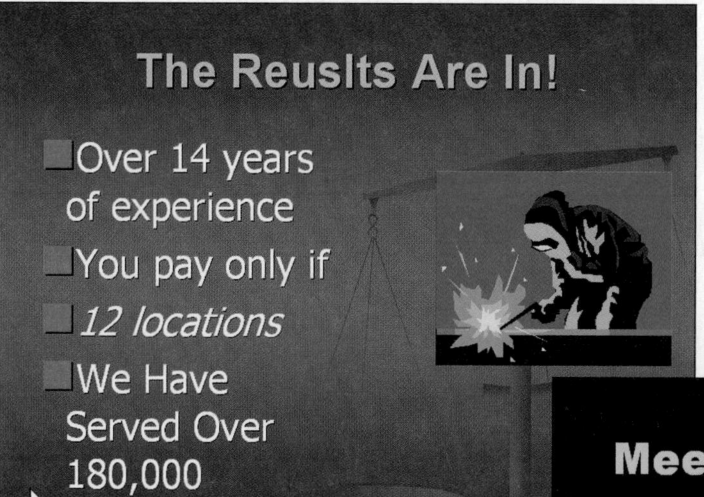

Figure D.3.2 Badly designed slides make it hard to understand your message.

Figure D.3.3 Well-designed slides make your message memorable.

Retailers use presentations in many ways. On-screen displays are often used to entice shoppers to make purchases. In home-improvement stores, presentations help customers learn how to paint a home, replace a faucet, or install blinds. Department-store monitors display the latest fashions and accessories.

Think About It!

Overhead screens are used to present information in a variety of situations. For which settings listed below would an overhead presentation be least effective?

- communicate safety information on an airplane
- play movie trailers at a theater
- teach the latest dance steps at home

Choosing a Delivery Method

There are a number of ways to deliver a presentation to an audience, including:

- on-screen delivery, with or without a speaker
- interactive presentation at a kiosk or booth
- Internet broadcast
- published in a variety of file types, such as pptx, pdf, jpg, show, or png

Choose the best delivery method to meet the needs of your audience, using the available technology.

On-screen Presentations Sometimes two or three people can comfortably gather around a single computer to view a slide-show presentation. In other cases, large groups may view a presentation on an overhead or video monitor, a presentation projector, or a "jumbo" screen. This is called an **on-screen presentation**, or a screen display of the slides.

In the past, overhead projectors were commonly used for on-screen presentations, especially in classrooms. Today, **digital projectors** are used. Overhead projectors worked by shining light through transparencies. Digital projectors project an image directly from the computer through a lens and onto the screen.

Large-format displays require special hardware, such as a digital light projector that takes the computer's output and projects it onto a wall or other large surface. Large-scale monitors are available but are expensive and difficult to move. In large settings, other equipment is often required, such as a microphone, amplifier, and speakers, which allow the audience to hear the speaker and any sound that plays during the presentation. The projector and speakers connect to your computer with cables.

Interactive Presentations PowerPoint allows users to add interactivity to a presentation. To help promote a product at a conference sales booth or a shopping mall kiosk, for example, you can set animation effects to play when a customer clicks a specific object on-screen. Depending on the object selected, the customer is routed to a specific part of the presentation and receives different information.

Internet Delivery If the audience is in a remote place, the presentation can be exported for broadcast on a Web site. The user can then view the slide show at any time through a Web browser. This method is useful for long-distance education. Group size is not an issue, and interactivity and animation are both possible presentation features. When the presentation is live and controlled by a presenter over the Internet, it is called a **webcast**.

Audience Handouts You can help your audience remember important or complex information by providing audience handouts. These handouts may be printouts of your slides or a summary of your main ideas.

Personal Communications Basics

Appendix

E

Digital Communication Email has been an important communication tool for several decades. Early in its history, email offered a huge advantage in speed and efficiency over the printed or faxed media it usually replaced. Over the years, email grew in popularity; it was widely available and relatively easy for new users to learn. Anybody with an email address can reach anybody else with an email address, no matter which systems the senders and receivers use.

Appendix E–1

Using Email

Objectives

- Describe email systems.
- Identify the purpose of a unique identifier.
- Explain the parts of an email address
- Identify the key components of an email message.
- Describe the process of creating, sending, and replying to messages.

As You Read

Sequence Information Use a sequence chart as you read to help you outline the process of receiving a message and responding to it.

Key Terms

- alias
- attachment
- distribution list
- email client
- email server
- mailbox name
- server address

Evaluating Email

Email, or electronic mail, allows people to send an unlimited number of messages quickly and easily to anyone with an email address. Messages sent through email can be a casual, like a letter to a friend, or formal, like a memo for a business. It is also less expensive than standard mail and voice, fax, and telephone messages. In fact, standard mail is sometimes called "snail mail" because it is so much slower than email. To use email, all you need is a computer, an Internet connection, email software, and an email account.

Email also lets you attach files to a message. Anything sent with an email message is called an **attachment**. Common attachments include word-processing documents, spreadsheets, photos, artwork, and movies.

Some email programs, like Outlook, include features for managing a calendar and contact list as well as taking notes and scheduling tasks.

Understanding Email Addresses

Like a computer on a network, every communication service user must have a unique identifier, usually called a username. The system uses the identifier to differentiate one user from another in order to deliver services, such as mail. For email, the identifier is the email address. All email addresses have two parts. The **mailbox name** is the part of the address before the "at" symbol (@) that identifies the user. The **server address** follows the symbol. It gives the domain name of the email server where the mailbox is stored. An **email server** is a computer, operated by your Internet service provider (ISP), that handles three key jobs:

- accepts incoming messages
- sends outgoing messages
- delivers incoming messages

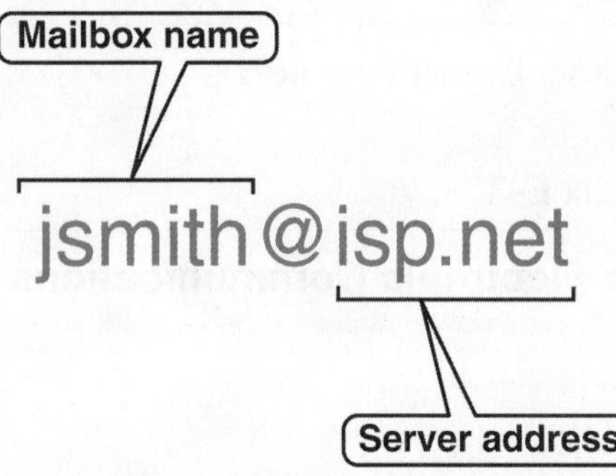

Figure E.1.1 Every email address has two basic parts—a mailbox name and a server address.

Sending, Receiving, and Forwarding Email

To send or receive email, you use an **email client**, which is a program that lets you create, send, receive, and manage email messages. You may get the program from your ISP, as part of a productivity suite, or with a Web browser. For example, Microsoft Outlook is the email client that comes with the Microsoft Office productivity suite. There are also Web-based email clients, such as Google's gmail and Microsoft's Outlook.com.

Composing Email To compose a new message, you click a button within the email client. The client displays a form for you to complete. The form includes two main parts—the header, which includes places for entering the recipient(s) and the subject, and the body, which is where you type the message.

First, you must specify the message's recipient in the To: line of the message form. Depending on your email client's features, you may select someone's name from an address book. You may also type the email address, which can be a name or a combination of letters and numbers. For example, the email address for Chris Rodriguez might be chris_rodriguez@isp.net or cjr615@isp.net. Instead of typing a complete address, you may be able to type an alias, or select it from a list. An **alias** is an easy-to-remember nickname for the recipient, such as Chris_R.

If you want to send a copy of the message to other recipients, you can add their names or addresses to the To: line or place them in the Cc: line. (The characters Cc stand for "carbon copy.") To send a copy of message without the recipient's email address appearing in the To: or Cc: line, enter it in the Bcc: line. Bcc stands for "blind carbon copy." Recipients whose addresses are in the To: or Cc: line are not able to see whose address is in the Bcc: line when they open the message.

Next, fill in the Subject line. The Subject line gives the recipient an idea of the message's content and may help the recipient decide whether to open it or delete it. Some email clients will not accept messages with blank Subject lines. When the header is complete, type the text message. You can add attachments by clicking a button and then clicking the name of the file you want to attach to the email. Finally, click Send.

Netiquette are the rules for polite online behavior.

Think About It!

Which of the following online rules help make email more useful?

- Type a lengthy description in the Subject line.
- Vary fonts and type sizes in the message.
- Edit the original message so only the part you are answering appears in your reply.
- Don't write in anger.
- Be brief, but be polite.

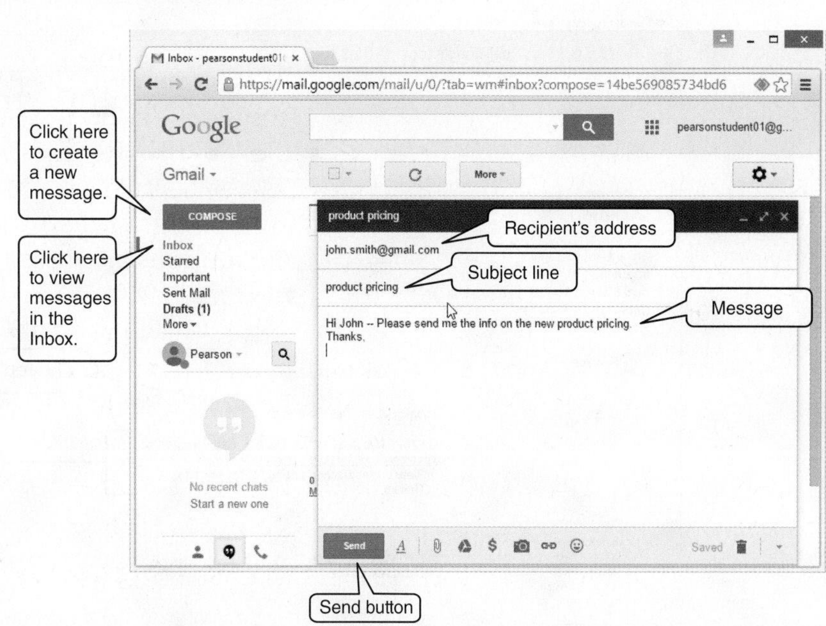

Figure E.1.2 Creating an email message with Google's gmail.

Configure Message Options Most programs let you set options such as delivery options before sending a message. You may be able to select when you want a message to send, specify the level of importance or sensitivity, set security options such as encryption, and request a confirmation that a message has been opened or read.

Replying to Email You can respond to the person who sent a message by clicking Reply. You can also click Reply All, which responds to all the people who received the original message. Several things occur when a response is prepared:

- The client displays a reply form with the original sender's address shown in the To: field.
- The subject field may show Re: in front of the subject of the original message. (*Re* stands for "regarding.")
- The original message is copied into the body of the reply. Most email programs give you the option of excluding the original text in your reply.
- You can type your reply above or below the original text, and then click Send.

Forwarding Email When you receive a message, you can pass it along to someone else. This is called forwarding a message. The Subject line of a forwarded email may include the characters *FW:* before the subject text to show that the message has been forwarded. You can add your comments before the original message's text.

Before you hit "send" on any email, it's good to remember that your email can be forwarded to other people. Don't write anything that you don't want other friends, parents, or teachers to see!

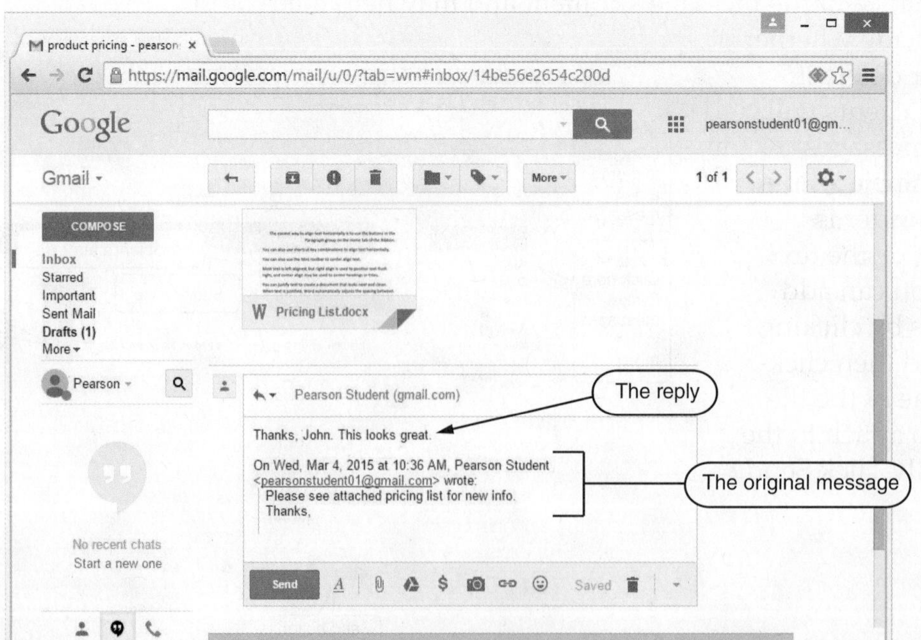

Figure E.1.3 Replying to an email message.

Avoiding Email Problems

Objectives

- Examine problems related to email.
- Define bounce messages and spam.
- Explain the use of digital signatures with email.

As You Read

Compare and Contrast Use a Venn diagram as you read to help you compare and contrast various email problems.

Key Terms

- bounce message
- digital signature
- spam

Failed Email

It is easy to send email messages, but it is also easy to make mistakes. What happens when you make a mistake?

Using the Wrong Address One of the most common email mistakes is entering an incorrect address in the To: field. When you do this, one of two things will happen:

- Your message will go to the wrong person if the incorrect address is someone else's valid address. Unless that person replies, you may never know what happened to your message.
- The email server will return the email to you with a bounce message.

A **bounce message** is a notice from the email server telling you that your message could not be delivered. Bounce messages are often a result of an incorrect email address. You sometimes see "MAILER-DAEMON@..." as the "From" address of a bounce message. Also, a message may not be delivered if the recipient's mailbox is full. This happens because many ISPs limit the amount of server space available for each user's messages. Never attempt to reply to a bounce message.

Avoiding Bounce Messages If you or your family changes ISPs, your email address will change. In that case, be sure to tell everyone in your address book about your new email address. Otherwise, people sending messages to your former address will receive a bounce message when they write to you.

Bounce messages are a part of email use. But what should you do when you get one?

Think About It!

Suppose you email the school photographer to find out whether your class pictures are ready. However, you get a bounce message. Which actions listed below might then be helpful?

- Retrieve the message from your Sent Items folder and check your typing.
- Confirm the email address of the photographer.
- Resend the message to the same address.
- Send a reply to the bounce message asking for help.

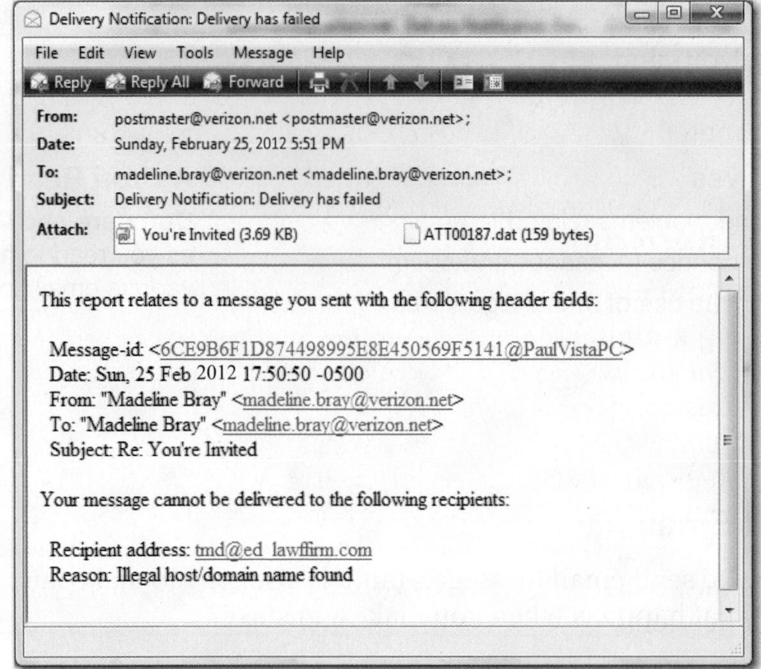

Figure E.2.1 A bounce message, due to an incorrect email address.

Junk Email, or Spam

Many email users complain about the flood of **spam**, a term used to describe unwanted, or junk, email messages and advertisements. Like physical junk mail, spam usually tries to sell something to the recipient. Spam can cause several problems:

- The recipient wastes time reviewing and deleting spam.
- Spam clogs email servers, slowing Internet traffic.
- Spam often contains incorrect or misleading information.

Sometimes you unknowingly generate the spam you get. When you make an online purchase, you might agree to get emails from the company about future sales. You might have signed up for email newsletters at many Web sites or joined a group (as in Yahoo Groups) that lets you exchange messages about a topic.

Blocking Unwanted Email You can mark unwanted messages as junk, or spam so your program automatically delivers them to the Junk or Spam folder instead of to your inbox. Most newsletters and user groups give easy directions to unsubscribe to the email. For email newsletters, you will usually find an "unsubscribe" link at the bottom of the page in tiny print. Yet, stopping spam from reaching email servers and clients is an ongoing battle. Some servers use technology to block "spammers." Some email clients provide special spam filters that users can configure to automatically delete junk mail. It is worthwhile checking your spam folder regularly, because sometimes personal or important email is mistakenly re-routed there.

Email Risks

Because you cannot see who is actually sending you a message, email is often used to commit crimes. Someone can send you a message and pretend it is from someone else. The message could contain a virus or request personal information. Because you trust the person or organization you believe sent the message, you open it or reply.

Using Digital Signatures One way to secure email messages is by using a **digital signature**—an electronic identifier which verifies that the message was created and sent by the person whose name appears in the From field.

Most current email programs support digital signatures, which you purchase from a vendor, such as Symantec's VeriSign Authentication Services. Once the certificate is installed on your computer, you can use it to "sign" any message you send by embedding the certificate in the message. The signature proves that the message comes from you.

Language Arts Did you know you can use email to improve your reading and writing? There are online magazines to which you can submit your work for publication. One of these sites, WritingDEN (www2.actden.com/writ_den), also has language-building exercises on words, sentences, and paragraphs. You complete the exercises, email your answers, and receive your scores shortly.

Real-World Tech

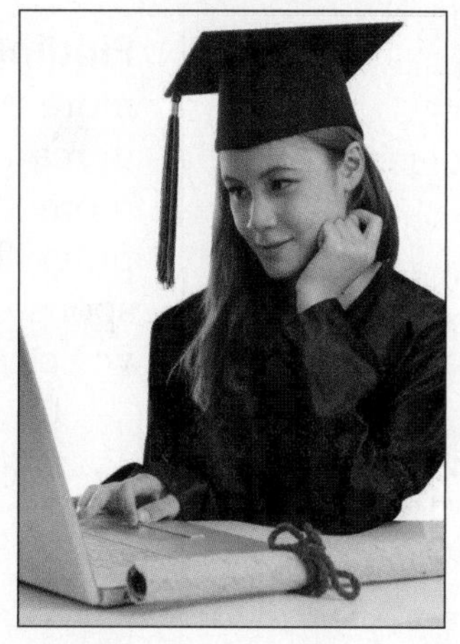

Getting Career Advice by Email What do you think you want to do when you "grow up?" It's not too early to start exploring careers and find out what conduct, dress, and behaviors are acceptable in the workplace. Career advice that appears in newspaper or magazine columns exists online as blogs. Some are geared toward specific careers and some to general career advice, like how to be a good team member, solve problems, or get organized.

Search out some career question-and-answer forums available online. Look for ones that offer general advice on how to dress and behave in the workplace. Remember, as with all online resources, be cautious about where you send email and any information you share.

Appendix E–3

Other Electronic Communications

Objectives

- Compare and contrast technology-enabled conferences.
- Describe one key advantage of teleconferencing for business.
- Examine the technical aspects of videoconferences.
- Summarize goals of Web-based training.
- Explain distance learning.

As You Read

Organize Information Use an outline as you read to help you organize information about advanced communications methods.

Key Terms

- blended learning
- flame
- Learning Management Systems (LMS)
- libel
- slander
- teleconference
- videoconference
- Web-based training

Teleconferencing

While the use of email is convenient, there are times when you need to speak with others directly. Meetings and telephone calls are ideal, but in today's world people are spread over wide areas. You may use a telephone conference to join multiple people into one telephone call, but scheduling a call or a meeting can be difficult, and expensive.

Finding a Solution A **teleconference** is an online meeting by two or more people. Many teleconferences allow participants to communicate in real time, just as they would if they were sitting together in the same room. In a typical real-time teleconference, each participant sits at a computer. They see messages typed by the other participants and type responses for the others to see immediately. Most teleconferences include voice communication as well.

Teleconferences help companies in several ways:

- They save time and money.
- They are similar to in-person meetings.
- They are convenient.
- They allow all participants to communicate in real time.

Chat Rooms Not all teleconferences are conducted for business. Informal, public real-time teleconferences in which participants discuss chosen topics are called chat rooms. Unlike business teleconferences where the participants are known to one another, chat-room participants are likely to be strangers to one another. Exercise caution and discretion when revealing personal or confidential information in a chat room. You do not know how someone might use details from your conversation without your knowledge or permission.

Videoconferencing

A **videoconference** is a teleconference that includes video as well as text or audio. Videoconferences require equipment such as cameras, a fast network connection, and video screens or computer monitors. A Web-based videoconference allows participants to connect to a Web server, identify themselves, and then join the meeting.

Types of Videoconferences Videoconferences can serve many purposes. Depending on the goal, they are set up in one of three delivery methods.

- One-to-one videoconferences allow two people to see and talk to each other on their computers. This type of conference is easy to set up through applications such as Microsoft NetMeeting or through using Voice over Internet Protocol (VoIP) with Skype, software that lets you use your computer to make voice or video phone calls.
- One-to-many videoconferences are similar to watching television programs. Many people can watch the presentation, but usually only one person speaks to the group.
- Many-to-many videoconferences are like a face-to-face meeting. Any of the participants can speak and be seen and heard at any time in the conversation.

Videoconferences are useful for collaboration on projects and training. Most Web-based videoconferences allow screen sharing, which means everyone who logs in can view the presenters' screen. In this way, the presenter can demonstrate actions instead of just talking about them. The presenter can also pass control to anyone else on the call.

Learning from a Distance

Distance learning makes use of telepresence to let you to learn anytime, anywhere—as long as you are on a computer connected to the Internet. A Learning Management System, or (LMS),

Wireless Developer How can devices like cell phones display content that you normally view on a PC? By using the wireless access protocol (WAP) and the Wireless Markup Language (WML), handheld devices can function as tiny browsers, displaying all sorts of content for their users. These protocols and languages allow devices to download content quickly and display it on a tiny screen efficiently. There is a growing demand for designers who understand WAP, WML, and other wireless solutions.

TELEMENTORING

The International Telementor Program, or ITP, matches students with workplace mentors who help them complete projects. Students and their mentors communicate online. Students at Eisenhower Middle School in Topeka, Kansas, developed their school's first Web site with help from ITP mentors. And students in Pleasant View School in Baldwin Park, California, worked with mentors to create multimedia presentations on their state's history.

Many students and teachers use distance learning.

Think About It!

Think about some of the ways schools might use distance learning. Which statement(s) listed below identify a sensible use?

- Small schools could offer a wider range of courses.
- Schools could let individuals or small groups pursue their interests.
- Schools could pair a sports team with a coach.
- A teacher in one school could share lessons with teachers on other campuses.

is an application designed for education that can manage records, report grades, and deliver subject matter content. You can complete high school courses or even earn a complete college degree online. Many schools offer classes via distance learning, and they use a variety of technologies. In many cases, the instructor provides lectures and displays slides through a one-to-many videoconference, which students can watch on their home computers. Tests and quizzes can be done via the Internet and students can work together via teleconference and email.

Web-based Training One of the newest methods of distance learning is **Web-based training**. Schools, colleges, and businesses are using the speed and technology of the Internet to deliver educational programs and activities. This method of education offers anytime, anywhere learning, as long as you have an Internet connection.

Blended Learning Some students find the best method of learning combines traditional classroom education with Web-based education. **Blended learning** offers opportunities for students to interact with others face-to-face and at a distance.

Computer-based Training Online instruction is one form of computer-based training, or CBT. But the first method for delivering computer-based training—the CD—remains popular among teachers and students. Many companies use CD tutorials to train employees on policies, products, and procedures. The advantage of this type of CBT is that the user can carry it around, and it does not require a network or Internet connection.

Text Messaging

Perhaps the most popular alternative to email is **text messaging**. Texting allows you to use a smart phone to type a brief message and transmit it to the recipient's phone. Since the text messages are brief, text messaging is also know as Short Message Service, or SMS. Text messaging is a popular way to communicate because it is fast and easy. It is important to know when it is appropriate and inappropriate to use text messaging. Because it is informal, texting is not the appropriate means of communicating sensitive or personal information.

Tweeting is a form of text messaging; you send the message to the Twitter Internet site, where any registered user can read it. Twitter allows for short messages to be read by a much larger audience. Digital messages can be sent with photos and videos, as well, using Multimedia Messaging Service (MMS).

Commenting Online

Many Web sites allow you to share and express your views on the site's content by commenting. Usually, once you register you can type a comment which is linked to the content on the site. Others can click the link to read your comment.

For example, you can comment on newspaper articles. Online stores let customers review products or share their experiences using the products or the Web site. Content sharing sites, like YouTube, allow viewers to give feedback on uploaded content and videos. You can upload your own content to these sites, or just comment on something you viewed. Social media sites allow for a great degree of freedom in posting ideas and opinions. Posts can be commented on and then those comments in turn can be commented on, creating full conversations that can include many people from many locations.

Communications Standards

Whatever type of communication you use, it is important to abide by certain standards. Personal communication may be less formal than you use for business, but you should still be polite and respectful. You never know who will read it.

- Use correct spelling. Proofread before sending to make sure there are no errors.
- Using abbreviations may be fine for personal communications with your friends and family but not for professional communications.
- Using all capital letters is considered to be shouting. Be sure to use proper capitalization.
- Don't send messages or images that may embarrass you in the future. Take a minute to think about what you are saying before you send a message.
- Don't forward or send unwanted messages like spam.
- Don't **flame**, or insult, anyone, even as a joke. Sometimes written communication is misinterpreted as being serious, even when if you said it out loud it might be considered funny.
- Don't use electronic communication to bully others.
- Don't make false statements that might hurt someone's reputation. It's called **libel** or **slander**, and it's illegal. You may be sued for damages.

Glossary

A

Abstract word: A word that expresses a concept, quality, or characteristic.

Active listening: Listening with a goal of fully understanding the message and encouraging the speaker. Active listening may involve asking questions, providing positive body language, and offering supportive feedback.

Active voice: Communication in which the object receives the action, such as "I sent the letter."

Adjustment: A settlement of a complaint.

Analogy: Reasoning from specific evidence to specific evidence.

Applicant tracking system (ATS): A software application that enables the electronic handling of recruitment needs.

Application letter: A letter accompanying a resume providing a context for sending it.

Assistive technology: Technology that helps reduce the impact of handicap on a person's ability to participate fully in an activity or conversation.

Assumptions: Things that you take for granted to be true.

Audience-centered approach: An approach that makes the audience's needs a top priority.

B

Backchannel: A line of communication in which the audience for a presentation connects with other audience members, with or without the knowledge of the speaker.

Bar chart: A chart using the height or length of rectangular bars to represent data.

Behavioral interview: An interview in which an applicant is asked to relate specific incidents and experiences from their past.

Bias-free language: A language that avoids words and phrases that unfairly or unethically categorize or stigmatize people in ways related to gender, race, ethnicity, age, disability, or other personal characteristics.

Block format: A traditional letter format in which each letter part begins at the left margin.

Boilerplate: A standard way of saying something that can be used in multiple contexts.

Boolean search: A keyword search that combines terms with operators such as AND, OR, and NOT.

Brand community: A community of people brought together by common interest in a particular product.

Brand socialization: A measure of how well a company engages its online stakeholders.

Bring Your Own Device (BYOD): The assumption that a communicator will have and prefer to use his or her own electronic device, such as a PC, tablet, or smartphone.

Buffer: A neutral, noncontroversial statement related to the point but not containing the bad news.

Buzzword: A newly coined term that is temporarily popular, but may become cliche or outdated quickly.

Caption: Text accompanying a graphic or chart that offers additional discussion of its content.

Career cluster: A grouping of careers that require similar education and training.

Chronological resume: A resume in which the work experience section dominates and appears immediately after the contact information and introductory statement.

Claim: A formal complaint.

Cliche: A term or phrase that is so commonly used that it has lost its effectiveness.

Closed question: A question that is designed to elicit a specific narrow range of answers, such as Yes or No.

Cloud computing: Computing activities that are based in an Internet environment, such as an application being run from a web browser rather than being installed on the individual computers.

Code of ethics: A policy that provides guidelines to decide what behavior is most ethical.

Collaboration: People working together to accomplish a task.

Combination resume: A resume that meshes the skills focus of the functional format with the job history focus of the chronological format.

Communication channel: A specific device or pathway used for sending a message, such as a mobile phone.

Communication medium: A means of transmitting a message, such as text message or email.

Communication studies: The academic study of how people, groups, and societies create and interpret messages.

Communication style: The choices you make to express yourself, including words, sentences, and paragraphs.

Communication: The process of transferring information and meaning using one or more media.

Community Q&A site: A site that enables visitors to answer questions posed by other visitors.

Complex sentence: A sentence that expresses one main thought and one or more subordinate thoughts related to it, often separated by a comma.

Complimentary close: The closing line of a letter, appearing below the letter body.

Compound sentence: A sentence with two main clauses that express two or more independent thoughts of equal importance.

Compound-complex sentence: A sentence with two main clauses, at least one of which contains a subordinate clause.

Conclusion: A logical interpretation of facts and other information.

Concrete word: A word that stands for something you can touch, see, or visualize.

Condolence letter: A brief personal message written to comfort someone after the death of a loved one or other significant loss.

Conflict: A disagreement between two or more people who have different ideas.

Constructive feedback: Feedback that provides helpful suggestions for improving the work and focuses on the processes and outcomes.

Content curation: The process of collecting and presenting information on a particular topic in a way that makes it convenient for target readers.

Content management system: An application that organizes, manages changes to, and controls access to a database or file storage system.

Content marketing: Providing free information that is valuable to consumers and builds ties with current and potential customers.

Contrast: The difference in color or shade between the document's background and its text.

Conversational tone: Plain language that sounds professional without being stuffy or too informal.

Copyright: A legal protection that ensures the owner of an idea or creative work will retain ownership of it.

Credibility: A measure of believability based on reliability and evoking trust in others.

Critical listening: Listening with the intent to understand and evaluate the message on several levels, including logic, evidence, validity of conclusions, implications of the conclusion, and the speaker's motivations and intentions.

Cultural competency: The ability to adjust one's communication style to ensure that messages are successfully sent across cultural boundaries.

Cultural context: The pattern of physical cues, environmental stimuli, and implicit understanding that convey meaning between two members of the same culture.

Culture: A shared system of symbols, beliefs, attitudes, values, expectations, and norms for behavior.

Data visualization: Using summary graphics to create meaning from raw data.

Decision-making meeting: A meeting that involves analysis, problem solving, and persuasive communication aimed at reaching a decision.

Decoding: The process of the message receiver extracting the idea from the received message.

Deductive reasoning: Working from a generalization to a specific conclusion.

Defamation: A false statement that damages someone's reputation.

Defensive listening: Protecting your ego while listening by tuning out anything that doesn't confirm your belief or view of yourself.

Deliberative listening: Listening with the primary goal of understanding and retaining the information in the speaker's message.

Demographics: The quantifiable characteristics of people, such as age, gender, and occupation.

Descriptive heading: A heading that identifies a topic without suggesting anything more.

Destructive feedback: Feedback that delivers criticism with no effort to stimulate improvement.

Digital citizen: A responsible member of the online community, participating in the community in knowledgeable, appropriate, and ethical ways.

Digital information fluency: Effectiveness in retrieving and understanding digital information and using it ethically.

Direct approach: A communication that starts with the main idea and follows up with supporting evidence.

Diversity: All the characteristics and experiences that define us as individuals, including physical and mental characteristics, cultural background, and personal life.

E

Economic base: The careers and industries that contribute to wealth entering the community from outside it.

Emotional appeal: An appeal that targets the audience's feelings or sympathies.

Empathetic listening: Listening to understand the speaker's feelings, wants, and needs so you can appreciate his or her point of view.

Employment interview: A meeting with a prospective employer to ask questions and exchange information.

Encoding: To express an idea as a message to share with others.

Ethical communication: Communication that includes all relevant information, is true in every sense, and is not deceptive in any way.

Ethical dilemma: A decision among alternatives that each have ethical pros and cons.

Ethical lapse: Making a clearly unethical choice or behaving dishonestly.

Ethics: Accepted principles of conduct that govern behavior within a society.

Ethnocentrism: The tendency to judge all other groups according to the standards, behaviors, and customs of one's own group.

Etiquette: Socially accepted behaviors in a specific environment or situation.

Euphemism: A synonym that conveys your meaning without negative connotations.

Executive dashboard: A customized graphical presentation of key performance parameters.

Executive summary: A fully developed mini version of a report, for readers who lack the time or motivation to read the entire document.

Fair use: An exception to copyright law that permits people to use a limited portion of a creative work for commentary, satire, parody, news reporting, teaching, or archiving.

Feedback: Information the receiver provides to the sender about the effectiveness of the communication.

Flowchart: A chart that illustrates a sequence of events from start to finish.

Font: A set of characters using a given typeface.

Forms-based search: A search performed by completing an online form.

Functional resume: A resume that emphasizes skills and capabilities, identifying employers and academic experience in subordinate sections.

G

General purpose: The broad goal of a message: to inform, persuade, collaborate, or initiate a conversation.

Group interview: An interview in which one or more interviewers meet with several candidates simultaneously.

Groupthink: A situation in which peer pressure causes individual team members to go along with decisions they don't really agree with.

Groupware: Software systems that enable people to communicate, share files, work on documents simultaneously, and connect using social networking tools.

Heading: A brief title that tells readers about the content of the section that follows.

Hidden agenda: A secret motivation that is unknown to the rest of the group, such as the desire to take control, undermine another person, or sabotage progress.

High-context culture: A culture in which nonverbal actions and environmental setting are more important than the actual words said in conveying meaning.

I

Indirect approach: A communication that starts with evidence first and follows up with a conclusion.

Inductive reasoning: Working from specific evidence to a general conclusion.

Infographics: Graphic visual representations of information or data intended to present information quickly and clearly.

Information architecture: The structure and navigational flow of all parts of a website.

Information overload: A situation in which people receive more information than they can effectively process.

Informational meeting: A meeting that involves sharing information and coordinating action to implement a plan or goals that have already been set.

Informative heading: A heading that gives the reader context and may point toward a conclusion or recommendation.

Inside address: The mailing address of the recipient of a letter, appearing near the top of the first page of the letter.

Instant messaging: Real-time text-based communication using computing devices.

Intellectual property: The ownership rights to a communicated idea such as a book, speech, or song.

Internship: A short-term educational opportunity in which the student works for a company and contributes to real-world projects.

J

Jargon: Specialized language or terminology associated with a certain profession, industry, or field of study.

Job shadowing: Following and observing someone in a particular job, to learn first-hand what that job entails.

K

Kerning: The process of adjusting the spacing between characters in a proportional font, usually to achieve a visually pleasing result.

Keyword search: A search performed by entering one or more keywords related to the subject.

Knowledge management system: A computer-based system for collecting and sharing research results.

L

Leading: The amount of space between lines of text.

Legend: A table or key that helps the reader decode a visual by explaining what various colors, symbols, or design choices mean.

Letter: A brief printed document traditionally sent to customers and other recipients outside the organization.

Letterhead: Pre-printed stationery containing the return addresses and sometimes other elements, such as a logo.

Libel: Written defamation.

Line chart: A chart that illustrates trends over time or plots the relationship of two variables using one or more lines.

Linear presentations: These are outlined like conventional messages and follow a predefined flow from start to finish.

Location-aware content: Online content that is customized depending on the reported location of the device accessing it.

Location-based service: Software that uses a reader's reported location to customize content.

Logical appeal: An appeal that is based on inductive reasoning, deductive reasoning, and/or analogy.

Low-context culture: A culture in which people rely heavily on verbal communication, rather than on circumstances and cues, to convey meaning.

M

Main idea: A specific statement about the topic.

Margins: The white space around each edge of the printed page.

Marketing message: A message that ushers potential buyers through the purchase process without asking for an immediate decision.

Memo: A brief printed document traditionally used for routine exchange of information within an organization.

Mentor: An experienced person who advises a less-experienced person in a particular area.

Mentoring: Working with someone knowledgeable and experienced in your field who is willing to teach you, advise you, and help you reach your goals.

Message: An idea expressed in words or images so another person can understand it.

Metasearch engine: A search engine that returns results from multiple databases.

Microblog: A blog variation in which character count is sharply restricted.

Minutes: A written record of the proceedings of a meeting.

Mobile-first: A design approach that plans for optimal viewing on small screens such as on smartphones or tablets.

Modified Block format: A traditional letter format in which most parts begin at the left margin, but certain parts begin at the horizontal center of the line.

Motivation: The combination of forces that drive people to satisfy their needs.

N

Natural language search: A search that accepts a question in everyday language as input.

Navigation slide: A slide that serves as a table of contents to the presentation.

Networking: The process of making informal connections with mutually beneficial business contacts.

News release: Also called a press release. A specialized document used to share relevant information with news media.

Newsletter: A document that conveys information informally in an attractive, graphical layout.

Nonlinear presentations: These do not flow in a particular direction; gives the presenter the option to move back and forth between topics.

Nonverbal communication: The process of sending and receiving information in ways other than written or spoken language.

O

Objective: Fair, without emotion, bias, or prejudice.

Online database: A database of information stored on a web server and accessed online.

Open-ended interview: An interview in which the interviewer adapts his or her line of questioning based on the answers given and the questions the applicant asks.

Open-ended question: A question that is intentionally broad or vague in scope, designed to elicit creative answers.

Organization chart: A chart that illustrates the positions, units, or functions in an organization and the ways they interrelate.

P

Panel interview: An interview in which a single applicant meets with several interviewers at once.

Paragraph alignment: The way the lines of a paragraph align with the margins: left, right, centered, or justified.

Parliamentary procedure: A formalized method of running a meeting in which a chairperson directs who may speak.

Participative management: A style of management that encourages all employees to participate in making decisions.

Passive voice: Communication in which the subject receives the action, such as "The letter was sent by me."

Performance review: An evaluation of an employee's work, providing feedback and establishing a personal plan of action for the future.

Personal information management (PIM) application: Software that enabled individuals and groups to organize, track, and share information about schedules, meetings, contacts, tasks, and activities.

Persuasion: The attempt to change an audience's attitudes, beliefs, or actions.

Plagiarism: Presenting someone else's words or ideas as your own without attributing the source.

Plagiarism: Presenting someone else's words or other creative product as your own.

Plain-text resume: An electronic version of a resume that has no formatting applied.

Podcasting channel: A set of regular recordings on a consistent theme.

Podcasting: A digital audio or video file available on blogs or websites, or downloadable to phones or computers.

Point: A measurement of type size. One point is 1/72 of an inch when printed.

Primary research: The collection of new data through surveys, interviews, and other techniques.

Problem statement: A statement of the decision you need to make or the conclusion you need to reach.

Problem: A difficulty to be resolved in order to make progress toward a goal.

Professionalism: Excellence in work performance, displaying the traits of effectiveness, accountability, teamwork, etiquette, ethics, and positivity.

Propaganda: An emotional appeal used to manipulate an audience into action.

Psychographics: The psychological characteristics of a person or group of people.

Public domain: A creative work for which the creator or owner has relinquished all rights of ownership, so that everyone may use and modify it freely without violating legal or ethical standards.

Purpose: What you want to achieve.

R

Radical connectivity: The ability to send vast amounts of data instantly, constantly, and globally.

Recommendation: A suggestion about what to do with the available information.

Reference initials: The initials of the person who produced the letter, if it is not the person signing it.

Report: A multi-page informational document, usually containing a substantial amount of technical detail and resource citation.

Representative sample: A sample that fairly represents the group you are trying to survey.

Request for proposals (RFP): A formal invitation to bid on a contract.

Rhetoric: The art of communicating to inform, persuade, and motivate audiences.

Robert's Rules of Order: A well-known set of specific rules for running a meeting in a formalized manner.

Root cause: The basic reason behind a problem.

S

Sales message: A message that encourages potential buyers to make a purchase decision immediately.

Salutation: The greeting in a letter, appearing just above the letter body.

Salutopening: An opening that omits the formal salutation but includes the recipient's name in the first paragraph.

Sampling bias: The tendency of a survey to capture only the opinions of people who are available and willing to be surveyed.

Sans serif typeface: A typeface that lacks serifs (crosslines) at the ends of each letter stroke.

Scannable resume: A resume that is formatted to be compatible with optical scanning systems that convert printed documents to electronic text.

Scope: The range of information you present, the overall length, and the level of detail.

Search engine optimization: Web development technique that increase a page's chance of being found by a search engine.

Search engine: A web content database that you access from a web browser.

Search syntax: Punctuation and codes that enable you to fine-tune a web search.

Secondary research: Research that someone else has already collected and made.

Selective listening: Listening in which your mind wanders and you do not pay careful attention to the message.

Selective perception: Hearing a message incompletely by molding it to fit your own conceptual framework.

Serif typeface: A typeface with small crosslines at the ends of each letter stroke.

Shared file storage: File storage that can be accessed by multiple users from different computing devices.

Shared workspace: An online work area in which multiple team members or coworkers can collaboratively participate in accomplishing tasks.

Signature block: The writer's name and title, appearing just below the blank area where the writer will sign.

Simple sentence: A sentence with one main clause.

Simplified format: A letter format that weaves the recipient name into the body rather than using a salutation, and does not include a complimentary close.

Situational interview: An interview in which questions focus on how the applicant would handle various hypothetical situations on the job.

Slander: Spoken defamation.

Slide build: Animation within a single slide that controls the gradual appearance of text, graphics, and other elements.

Slide transition: A movement from one slide to the next slide using an animated effect.

Social communication model: A communication model in which everyone may participate freely, such as using online social media tools like Facebook or Twitter.

Social Media: Digital communication systems that empower individual users to participate by sharing content and responding to others.

Social network: A specific company or site that hosts a social media community.

Specific purpose: The specific thing you hope to accomplish with a message, such as a certain person agreeing to a request.

Spokesperson: The person who speaks or writes as a representative of a group.

Stakeholders: People or groups affected by a business decision.

Statement of purpose: A statement of why you are preparing the report and what you plan to deliver.

Stealth marketing: The practice of secretly embedding marketing content into non-marketing communications.

Stereotyping: Assigning a wide range of generalized and often inaccurate attributes to an individual on the basis of membership in a particular group.

Stress interview: An interview in which questions are asked designed to unsettle the applicant to see how they will react to stress.

Structured interview: An interview in which the applicant is asked a series of questions in a predetermined order.

Subheading: A subordinate heading indicating a subsection within a major section.

Subjective: Affected by existing opinions, feelings, and belief.

Surface chart (area chart): A variant of the line chart that shows a cumulative effort.

Synopsis (abstract): A brief overview of a report's most important points.

T

Table: A systematic arrangement of data in columns and rows.

Tag: To mark a passage of text with descriptive words for ease of later lookup.

Team: A unit of two or more people who share a mission and the responsibility for working together to achieve a goal.

Text messaging: An instant message delivered via SMS, usually to a mobile device such as a smartphone.

Title: A short description that identifies the content and purpose of the item.

Tone: The overall impression in your messages.

Topic sentence: A sentence that introduces the topic of the paragraph.

Topic: The overall subject of a message.

Topical organization: A direct type of organization that arranges material into logical topics or groupings.

Transition: A word or phrase that connects ideas by showing how one idea is related to another.

Transparency: Openness with the information needed to accurately process received messages.

Typeface: The physical design of letters, numbers, and other text characters.

Type style: Any modification that lends contrast or emphasis to type, such as boldface, italics, underlining, and color.

U

Unified communication: A communication system that integrates multiple communication methods, such as voice and video conferencing, instant messaging, and real-time collaboration on electronic.

User-generated content (UGC) site: A site or service in which users contribute most or all of the content.

V

Virtual meeting: A meeting that uses technology to connect people in different physical locations.

Virtual whiteboard: A whiteboard that people can access remotely to work collaboratively.

Visual literacy: The ability to create effective images and correctly interpret visual messages.

W

Wearable technology: A computing device that the user can wear, such as a watch, wristband, or eyeglasses.

Web browser: Software that displays web pages.

Web directory: A searchable website database generated by human editors.

Webinar: A web-based seminar.

White space: An unused area that provides visual contrast and resting points for the reader.

Wiki: A web-based collaborative database of information.

Work plan: A plan that describes the scope and tasks involved in a project.

Working interview: An interview in which the applicant performs a job-related activity.

"You" attitude: Speaking and writing in terms of your audience's wishes, interests, hopes, and preferences.

Index

A

D

E

F

G

H

I

J

K

L

M

N

Q

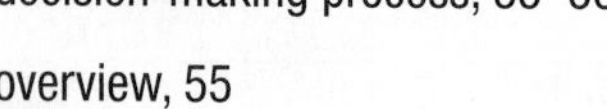

R

S

T

U

V

W

Y

Z

Photo Credits

p. 2 Pearson Education, Inc. **p. 3** Goodluz/Shutterstock. **p. 4** Pressmaster/Shutterstock. **p. 8** Pressmaster/Shutterstock. **p. 10** Blend Images/Shutterstock. **p. 10** Monkey Business Images/Shutterstock. **p. 10** Stuart Jenner/Shutterstock. **p. 11** Wavebreakmedia/Shutterstock. **p. 12** Pearson Education, Inc. **p. 14** Pearson Education, Inc. **p. 15** Tyler Olson/Shutterstock. **p. 16** Dolgachov/123RF. **p. 17** Stuart Jenner/Shutterstock. **p. 18** Kostenko Maxim/Shutterstock. **p. 19** Muemoon/Shutterstock. **p. 20** G-stockstudio/Shutterstock. **p. 24** ARENA Creative/Shutterstock. **p. 25** Merzzie/Shutterstock. **p. 26** Monkey Business Images/Shutterstock. **p. 28** Wavebreakmedia/Shutterstock. **p. 28** Auremar/123RF. **p. 31** Pearson Education, Inc. **p. 32** Lichtmeister/Shutterstock. **p. 34** Goodluz/Shutterstock. **p. 37** Redav/Shutterstock. **p. 37** Oliver Sved/Shutterstock. **p. 38** StockLite/Shutterstock. **p. 50** Dmitry Kalinovsky/Shutterstock. **p. 51** Wavebreakmedia/Shutterstock. **p. 52** Edhar/Shutterstock. **p. 53** Pressmaster/Shutterstock. **p. 54** Monkey Business Images/Shutterstock. **p. 57** Philip Date/Shutterstock. **p. 60** Monkey Business Images/Shutterstock. **p. 61** Andresr/Shutterstock. **p. 61** Pearson Education, Inc. **p. 62** Dotshock/123RF. **p. 63** Pearson Education, Inc. **p. 64** Milan Zokic/Shutterstock. **p. 65** Pearson Education, Inc. **p. 66** Blend Images/Shutterstock. **p. 67** Pressmaster/Shutterstock. **p. 70** 101imges/Shutterstock. **p. 71** Junial Enterprises/Shutterstock. **p. 72** Racorn/Shutterstock. **p. 73** Wavebreakmedia/Shutterstock. **p. 75** Rido/Shutterstock. **p. 76** Shyshak roman/Shutterstock. **p. 78** Pressmaster/Shutterstock. **p. 86** Pearson Education, Inc. **p. 89** Outlook 2016, Windows 10, Microsoft Corporation. **p. 90** Stephen Coburn/Shutterstock. **p. 92** Dmitriy Shironosov/123RF. **p. 93** Studio 8/Pearson Education Ltd. **p. 105** Outlook 2016, Windows 10, Microsoft Corporation. **p. 106** Nyul/123RF. **p. 115** Khakimullin Aleksandr/Shutterstock. **p. 119** Monkey Business Images/Shutterstock. **p. 122** Viorel Sima/Shutterstock. **p. 150** Ronstik/Shutterstock. **p. 175** Wavebreakmedia/Shutterstock. **p. 187** Vitchanan Photography/Shutterstock. **p. 190** StockLite/Shutterstock. **p. 191** Artur Marciniec/Fotolia. **p. 197** Wavebreak Media Ltd/123RF. **p. 210** Junjie/Shutterstock. **p. 224** Outlook 2016, Windows 10, Microsoft Corporation. **p. 224** Outlook 2016, Windows 10, Microsoft Corporation. **p. 226** Photographee.eu/Fotolia. **p. 227** Outlook 2016, Windows 10, Microsoft Corporation. **p. 231** Outlook 2016, Windows 10, Microsoft Corporation. **p. 235** Outlook 2016, Windows 10, Microsoft Corporation. **p. 236** vgstudio/Shutterstock. **p. 258** wavebreakmedia/Shutterstock. **p. 263** Viktor Gladkov/Shutterstock. **p. 288** Outlook 2016, Windows 10, Microsoft Corporation. **p. 296** Outlook 2016, Windows 10, Microsoft Corporation. **p. 298** Dusit/Shutterstock. **p. 316** Pearson Education, Inc. **p. 325** jaboo2foto/Shutterstock. **p. 326** Kheng Guan Toh/Shutterstock. **p. 330** wavebreakmedia/Shutterstock. **p. 348** wavebreakmedia/Shutterstock. **p. 360** Andrey Popov/Shutterstock. **p. 361** U.S. Department of Agriculture. **p. 365** Google Inc. **p. 367** igorkol ter/Fotolia. **p. 421** dotshock/Shutterstock. **p. 423** Monkey Business Images/Shutterstock. **p. 425** tmcphotos/Shutterstock. **p. 427** Yanugkelid/Shutterstock. **p. 427** Andresr/Shutterstock. **p. 437** Monkey Business/Fotolia. **p. 439** wavebreakmedia/Shutterstock. **p. 450** Elena Elisseeva/Shutterstock. **p. 452** Auremar/Shutterstock. **p. 454** Mert Toker/Shutterstock. **p. 455** grafvision/Shutterstock. **p. 458** Jules Selmes/Pearson Education Inc. **p. 458** Africa Studio/Shutterstock. **p. 478** Gozaik.com. **p. 480** Alexander Raths/Shutterstock. **p. 495** oneword/Shutterstock. **p. 496** Rob Marmion/Shutterstock. **p. 497** StockLite/Shutterstock. **p. 499** Andrey Popov/Shutterstock. **p. 500** Robert Kneschke/Shutterstock. **p. 506** InnervisionArt/Shutterstock. **p. 508** vgstudio/Shutterstock. **p. 508** Maridav/Shutterstock. **p. 510** wavebreakmedia/Shutterstock. **p. 514** wavebreakmedia/Shutterstock. **p. 515** Outlook 2016, Windows 10, Microsoft Corporation. **p. 516** Stephen Coburn/Shutterstock. **p. 517** Outlook 2016, Windows 10, Microsoft Corporation. **p. 520** alexskopje/Shutterstock. **p. 530** Outlook 2016, Windows 10, Microsoft Corporation. **p. 531** Outlook 2016, Windows 10, Microsoft Corporation. **p. 532** Outlook 2016, Windows 10, Microsoft Corporation. **p. 533** Outlook 2016, Windows 10, Microsoft Corporation. **p. 535** Outlook 2016, Windows 10, Microsoft Corporation. **p. 536** Outlook 2016, Windows 10, Microsoft Corporation. **p. 546** Outlook 2016, Windows 10, Microsoft Corporation. **p. 549** Outlook 2016, Windows 10, Microsoft Corporation. **p. 550** Outlook 2016, Windows 10, Microsoft Corporation. **p. 552** Outlook 2016, Windows 10, Microsoft Corporation. **p. 553** Outlook 2016, Windows 10, Microsoft Corporation. **p. 554** Outlook 2016, Windows 10, Microsoft Corporation. **p. 555** Outlook 2016, Windows 10, Microsoft Corporation. **p. 559** Outlook 2016, Windows 10, Microsoft Corporation. **p. 562** Outlook 2016, Windows 10, Microsoft Corporation. **p. 563** Outlook 2016, Windows 10, Microsoft Corporation. **p. 569** Outlook 2016, Windows 10, Microsoft Corporation. **p. 570** Outlook 2016, Windows 10, Microsoft Corporation. **p. 571** Outlook 2016, Windows 10, Microsoft Corporation. **p. 572** Outlook 2016, Windows 10, Microsoft Corporation.